This is another volume in the new Cambridge series of companions to major philosophers. Each volume will contain specially commissioned essays by an international team of scholars, together with a substantial bibliography, and will serve as a reference work for students and nonspecialists. One aim of the series is to dispel the intimidation such readers often feel when faced with the work of a difficult and challenging thinker.

Plato stands at the head of our philosophical tradition, being the first Western thinker to produce a body of writing that touches upon a wide range of topics still discussed by philosophers today. In a sense he invented philosophy as a distinct subject, for although many of these topics were discussed by his intellectual predecessors and contemporaries, he was the first to bring them together by giving them a unitary treatment. He conceives of philosophy as a discipline with a distinctive intellectual method, and he makes radical claims for its position in human life and the political community. This volume contains fifteen new essays discussing Plato's views about knowledge, reality, mathematics, politics, ethics, love, poetry, and religion. There are also analyses of the intellectual and social background of his thought, the development of his philosophy throughout his career, the range of alternative approaches to his work, and the stylometry of his writing.

New readers and nonspecialists will find this the most convenient, accessible guide to Plato currently available. Advanced students and specialists will find a conspectus of recent developments in the interpretation of Plato.

THE CAMBRIDGE COMPANION TO

PLATO

OTHER VOLUMES IN THIS SERIES OF CAMBRIDGE COMPANIONS:

AQUINAS *Edited by* NORMAN KRETZMAN *and* ELEONORE STUMP
ARISTOTLE *Edited by* JONATHAN BARNES
DESCARTES *Edited by* JOHN COTTINGHAM
FOUCAULT *Edited by* GARY GUTTING
FREUD *Edited by* JEROME NEU
HEGEL *Edited by* FREDERICK BEISER
HEIDEGGER *Edited by* CHARLES GUIGNON
HOBBES *Edited by* TOM SORRELL
HUME *Edited by* DAVID FATE NORTON
HUSSERL *Edited by* BARRY SMITH *and* DAVID WOODRUFF SMITH
KANT *Edited by* PAUL GUYER
LEIBNIZ *Edited by* NICHOLAS JOLLEY
LOCKE *Edited by* VERE CHAPPELL
MARX *Edited by* TERRELL CARVER
MILL *Edited by* JOHN SKORUPSKI
NIETZSCHE *Edited by* BERND MAGNUS
SARTRE *Edited by* CHRISTINA HOWELLS
SPINOZA *Edited by* DON GARRETT

The Cambridge Companion to

PLATO

Edited by Richard Kraut
University of Illinois at Chicago

PUBLISHED BY THE PRESS SYNDICATE OF THE UNIVERSITY OF CAMBRIDGE
The Pitt Building, Trumpington Street, Cambridge, United Kingdom

CAMBRIDGE UNIVERSITY PRESS
The Edinburgh Building, Cambridge CB2 2RU, UK http://www.cup.cam.ac.uk
40 West 20th Street, New York, NY 10011-4211, USA http://www.cup.org
10 Stamford Road, Oakleigh, Melbourne 3166, Australia
Ruiz de Alarcón 13, 28014 Madrid, Spain

First published 1992
Reprinted 1993 (twice), 1995, 1996 (twice), 1997, 1999 (twice)

Printed in the United States of America

Typeset in Trump Mediaeval

A catalog record for this book is available from the British Library

Library of Congress Cataloging in Publication Data is available

ISBN 0 521 43018 6 hardback
ISBN 0 521 43610 9 paperback

FOR GREGORY VLASTOS
1907–1991

CONTENTS

CONTRIBUTORS

ELIZABETH ASMIS is Associate Professor of Classics at the University of Chicago. The author of *Epicurus' Scientific Method* (Cornell University Press, 1984) and numerous articles on Hellenistic philosophy, she is currently working on Greek views of poetry from Plato to the Neoplatonists.

LEONARD BRANDWOOD is Lecturer in the Department of Greek and Latin at Manchester University. He is the author of *A Word Index to Plato* (W. S. Maney & Son, 1976) and *The Chronology of Plato's Dialogues* (Cambridge University Press, 1990).

G. R. F. FERRARI is Associate Professor of Classics at the University of California, Berkeley. He is the author of *Listening to the Cicadas: A Study of Plato's Phaedrus* (Cambridge University Press, 1987) and of articles on Plato, the pre-Socratics, and archaic Greek culture.

GAIL FINE is Professor of Philosophy at Cornell University. She is the author of numerous articles on the metaphysics and epistemology of Plato and Aristotle. Her book *On Ideas: Aristotle's Criticism of Plato's Theory of Forms* is to be published by Oxford University Press.

DOROTHEA FREDE is Professor of Philosophy at the University of Hamburg. She is the author of *Aristoteles und die Seeschlacht* (Vandenhoeck & Ruprecht, 1970) and has written numerous articles on Plato, Aristotle, later Greek philosophy, and the philosophy of Martin Heidegger. Her translation of Plato's *Philebus* is forthcoming (Hackett Publishing Company).

MICHAEL FREDE is Professor of the History of Philosophy at Oxford University and Fellow of Keble College. He is the author of *Prädika-*

tion und Existenzaussage (Vandenhoeck & Ruprecht, 1967), *Die stoische Logik* (Vandenhoeck & Ruprecht, 1974), and (with Günther Patzig) a translation of and commentary on Aristotle's *Metaphysics Z* (C.H. Beck, 1988). Some of his many papers on Plato, Aristotle, Stoicism, Skepticism, ancient medicine, and ancient grammatical theories have been collected in *Essays in Ancient Philosophy* (University of Minnesota Press and Oxford University Press, 1987).

T. H. IRWIN is Professor of Philosophy at Cornell University. He is the author of *Plato's Moral Theory* (Clarendon Press, 1977), *Aristotle's First Principles* (Clarendon Press, 1988), *Classical Thought* (Oxford University Press, 1989), and translations of and commentaries on Plato's *Gorgias* (Clarendon Press, 1979) and Aristotle's *Nicomachean Ethics* (Hackett Publishing Company, 1985), as well as numerous articles on Greek philosophy.

RICHARD KRAUT is Professor of Philosophy at the University of Illinois at Chicago. He is the author of *Socrates and the State* (Princeton University Press, 1984) and *Aristotle on the Human Good* (Princeton University Press, 1989) and is currently writing a translation of and commentary on Aristotle's *Politics: Books VII and VIII.*

CONSTANCE C. MEINWALD is Assistant Professor of Philosophy at the University of Illinois at Chicago. The author of *Plato's Parmenides* (Oxford University Press, 1991), she is currently working on Plato's late metaphysics.

MICHAEL L. MORGAN is Professor of Philosophy at Indiana University, Bloomington. He is the author of *Platonic Piety: Philosophy and Ritual in Fourth-Century Athens* (Yale University Press, 1990) and has written numerous articles on Plato as well as on Jewish thought.

IAN MUELLER is Professor of Philosophy at the University of Chicago. He is the author of *Philosophy of Mathematics and Deductive Structure in Euclid's Elements* (MIT Press, 1981), as well as numerous articles on ancient Greek philosophy, science, and mathematics. He is currently preparing a translation of Alexander of Aphrodisias's commentary on Aristotle's *Prior Analytics.*

TERRY PENNER is Professor of Philosophy at the University of Wisconsin, Madison. He is the author of *The Ascent from Nominalism:*

Some Existence Arguments in Plato's Middle Dialogues (D. Reidel Publishing Company, 1987) and is currently at work on a sequel to that volume, *Plato and the Philosophers of Language*. He is also preparing a study of the philosophy of Socrates.

TREVOR J. SAUNDERS is Professor of Greek at the University of Newcastle upon Tyne. He has produced three volumes in the Penguin Classics series: a translation of Plato's *Laws* (1970), a revision of T. A. Sinclair's translation of Aristotle's *Politics* (1981), and (as contributing editor) *Plato, Early Socratic Dialogues* (1987). He has written numerous articles on the political philosophy of Plato and Aristotle, and his latest book is *Plato's Penal Code* (Clarendon Press, 1991).

NICHOLAS P. WHITE is Professor of Philosophy at the University of Michigan. He is the author of *Plato on Knowledge and Reality* (Hackett Publishing Company, 1976), *A Companion to Plato's Republic* (Hackett Publishing Company, 1979), and numerous articles on Plato, Aristotle, and Stoicism. He is also the translator of Epictetus's *Handbook* (Hackett Publishing Company, 1983), and his translation of Plato's *Sophist* is forthcoming (Hackett Publishing Company).

CHRONOLOGY

Plato's life[*]	*Plato's writings*[†]	*Other events*
427: born		431–404: Peloponnesian War
	c. 399–c. 387: composes early dialogues: *Ap., Chrm., Cri., Euphr., H. Mi., Ion, La., Prt.; Euthd, Grg., H. Ma., Lys., Menex., Rep.* I.	399: death of Socrates
387: first visit to Sicily; makes contact with Pythagorean philosophers; founds Academy upon his return to Athens	c. 387–c. 367: composes middle dialogues: *Meno, Cra., Phd., Smp., Rep.* II–X, *Phdr., Prm., Tht.*	384: birth of Aristotle
367–365: second visit to Sicily, upon death of Dionysius I of Syracuse; involvement in Syracusan politics, described in *Seventh Letter*	c. 365–347: composes late dialogues: *Ti., Criti., Sph., Pol., Phil., Laws*	367: Aristotle joins Academy
361: third visit to Sicily, described in *Seventh Letter*		
347: dies		

[*]For further information, see Chapter 1, notes 1, 3, 24, and 25.
[†]For further information, see Chapter 1, notes 16–18, 20, 21, 25, 39, 57, and 61.

ABBREVIATIONS

I. ANCIENT AUTHORS

ARISTOPHANES

Acharn.	*Acharnians*

ARISTOTLE

Ath. Pol.	*Constitution of the Athenians*
De An.	*De Anima*
Met.	*Metaphysics*
N.E.	*Nicomachean Ethics*
Poet.	*Poetics*
Soph. El.	*De Sophisticis Elenchis*
Top.	*Topics*

ISOCRATES

Antid.	*Antidosis*
Panath.	*Panathenaicus*

OLYMPIODORUS

Prol.	*Anonymous Prolegomena to the Philosophy of Plato*

PLATO

Alc.	*Alcibiades*
Ap.	*Apology*
Chrm.	*Charmides*
Cleit.	*Cleitophon*
Cra.	*Cratylus*
Cri.	*Crito*
Criti.	*Critias*

Epin.	*Epinomis*
Epist.	*Epistles (Letters)*
Euphr.	*Euthyphro*
Euthd.	*Euthydemus*
Grg.	*Gorgias*
H. Ma.	*Hippias Major*
H. Mi.	*Hippias Minor*
La.	*Laches*
Lys.	*Lysis*
Menex.	*Menexenus*
Phd.	*Phaedo*
Phdr.	*Phaedrus*
Phil.	*Philebus*
Pol.	*Politicus (Statesman)*
Prm.	*Parmenides*
Prt.	*Protagoras*
Rep.	*Republic*
Smp.	*Symposium*
Sph.	*Sophist*
Theag.	*Theages*
Tht.	*Theaetetus*
Ti.	*Timaeus*

SEXTUS EMPIRICUS

A.M.	*Adversus Mathematicos*

II. MODERN TEXTS

D.K.	H. Diels and W. Kranz, *Die Fragmente der Vorsokratiker,* Seventh edition, 1954
O.C.T.	Oxford Classical Texts

RICHARD KRAUT

1 Introduction to the study of Plato

I

Plato (427–347 B.C.)[1] stands at the head of our philosophical tradition, being the first Western thinker to produce a body of writing that touches upon the wide range of topics that are still discussed by philosophers today under such headings as metaphysics, epistemology, ethics, political theory, language, art, love, mathematics, science, and religion. He may in this sense be said to have invented philosophy as a distinct subject, for although all of these topics were, of course, discussed by his intellectual predecessors and contemporaries, he was the first to bring them together by giving them a unitary treatment. He conceives of philosophy as a discipline with a distinctive intellectual method, and he makes radical claims for its position in human life and the political community. Because philosophy scrutinizes assumptions that other studies merely take for granted, it alone can give us genuine understanding; since it discovers a realm of objects inaccessible to the senses and yields an organized system of truths that go far beyond and in some cases undermine common sense, it should lead to a transformation in the way we live our lives and arrange our political affairs. It is an autonomous subject and not the instrument of any other discipline, power, or creed; on the contrary, because it alone can grasp what is most important in human life, all other human endeavors should be subordinate to it.[2]

This conception of philosophy and the substantive philosophical theories that support it were controversial from the very start; al-

I am most grateful to Terence Irwin, Constance Meinwald, and Ian Mueller for their helpful comments on an earlier draft of this essay.

though there have been long periods during which some form of Platonism flourished,[3] there have always been at the same time various forms of opposition to Plato's astonishingly ambitious conception of the subject.[4] For this reason he can be considered not only the originator of philosophy but the most controversial figure in its historical development. For one cannot argue that philosophy must limit its ambitions without understanding the almost limitless hopes that gave birth to the subject and explaining why these – all of them or some – are misguided or unachievable. If we are forced to retreat from his ideal of a comprehensive and unitary understanding that transforms our lives and society, we must decide what alternative intellectual goal to put in its place. For this reason, Plato provides us with an invaluable test case and standard of comparison: Our conception of what philosophy should be (and whether there should be any such thing) must be developed in agreement with or opposition to alternatives provided by the history of the subject, and so inevitably we must ask whether the ambitions of the subject's inventor are worthy and capable of fulfillment.

Although Plato invented philosophy as a unified and comprehensive discipline, he of course could not have created it from nothing, and so to understand how he arrived at his views we must take account of the currents of his time. His attitudes toward political developments in Athens and Sparta and his reaction to the intellectual issues raised by the science, speculation, and poetry of the fifth and fourth centuries decisively shaped his philosophical development. The sophistic movement, the mathematical work of the Pythagoreans, the theory of flux advocated by Heraclitus and Cratylus, the unchanging and unitary being postulated by Parmenides – all of these played an important role in his thinking.[5] But the intellectual influence that was paramount was Socrates, a man who wrote nothing but whose personality and ideas were so powerful that no one who came into contact with him could react to him with indifference. For Socrates, to philosophize was to engage in adversarial conversation about how one's life should be lived; because the ideas he expressed and the questions he raised were perceived as threatening, he was tried and convicted on the charge of refusing to recognize the gods of the city, introducing other new divinities, and corrupting the young.[6] While Socrates was alive, Plato was one of many young people who fell under his spell, and so great was his influence that

Plato made him the central figure in many of his works, most or all of which were composed after the death of Socrates in 399 B.C.[7] Plato's writings are almost without exception in dialogue form,[8] and frequently the figure who takes the leading role in these conversations is Socrates.[9] Plato did not write a part for himself in these dialogues; rather, when they advance philosophical positions, it is often the character named "Socrates" who expounds them.[10] And so newcomers to these works naturally raise the question how any distinction can be made between the philosophy of Socrates and that of Plato. How can we distinguish them, since in many dialogues they have the same lines, the former doing all the talking, the latter all the writing? Could we not say with equal justice that it was Socrates (and not just Plato) who invented philosophy?

We could not, for Plato's works themselves provide us with good evidence that Socrates focused his investigative skills on one question only – How should one live one's life? – and was not similarly preoccupied with the broader range of issues that absorbed their author. We have in Plato's *Apology* an account of the speech Socrates gave in his defense, and he says here that although his whole life has been devoted to the discussion of virtue, he has, despite his best efforts, not been able to acquire any wisdom about it – except for the wisdom that consists in knowing that he does not know. Knowledge of such matters, Socrates thinks, is possessed by the gods alone; the best we humans can do is to imitate his own example and recognize the severe limitations in our moral understanding. This profession of ignorance is a feature of several other Platonic dialogues: In the *Laches*, the *Charmides*, the *Hippias Major*, and the *Euthyphro*, for example, Socrates searches for an understanding of virtue and morality, but each dialogue ends with a confession that such understanding still eludes him. By contrast, when we turn to the *Republic*, we find the interlocutor called "Socrates" giving definitions of justice, courage, temperance, and wisdom; and in addition he puts forward an ambitious program of study, ranging over arithmetic, geometry, harmonics, and astronomy, that will take us away from the unreal world of sensible objects and eventually culminate in understanding the Form of the Good and the unification of all branches of knowledge.

How can Socrates be so opposed to himself: a seeker who professes ignorance about the one subject that absorbs him – the human good – and yet (in the *Republic* and elsewhere) a confident theoretician who speculates at length not only about morality but also about knowledge, reality, politics, and the human soul? The most plausible answer, one that is now widely accepted by many scholars, is this: In the *Apology* and in several other works that search for ethical definitions but show no deep interest in mathematics and make no inquiry into metaphysics, we have a portrait of the historical Socrates;[11] but then, as Plato continued to develop in his thinking, he retained Socrates as the main interlocutor of his dialogues, even though the doctrines of this more ambitious "Socrates" go well beyond anything dreamt of by that philosopher.[12] And this interpretation of Plato's development accords with the distinction Aristotle makes between the real Socrates and the Socrates who is a mouthpiece for Plato: the former, he says, professed ignorance and inquired about ethical matters but not "the whole of nature";[13] to the latter he attributes no such limitations, but instead regards him as a thinker who speculated about a wide range of issues and fell into utter confusion when he posited a realm of separately existing Forms and made the Form of the Good central to ethical theory.[14] Evidently, Aristotle reads the *Republic* as a presentation of the philosophy of Plato and not of Socrates.[15] We can assume, then, that for some time Plato continued to use "Socrates" as the name of his principal interlocutor because he wanted to emphasize the continuity between himself and his teacher. Socrates gave to Plato the fundamental idea that it is vital to our well-being to discover the single uniting factor in our diverse use of moral terms; and Plato also inherited from Socrates the method of seeking the truth by exposing our beliefs to the systematic cross-examination of interlocutors. When Plato used that method to make the discoveries that Socrates also sought to make, he paid tribute to his teacher by letting him continue in his role as the main interlocutor.

This way of distinguishing between the philosophies of Socrates and Plato has been given further support by studies of Plato's style of composition that have been undertaken since the nineteenth century.[16] There has now emerged a broad consensus that we can say, at least in many cases, which of Plato's works were written during which periods of his life; for it is widely accepted that he wrote the *Laws* in his later years,[17] and we can determine which dialogues are stylistically closest and which farthest from this late work. And so, partly because of these stylistic studies, and partly because of Aristotle's distinction between Socrates and Plato, it has now become common to divide Plato's writings into three periods: early, middle, and late.[18]

The early dialogues are the ones in which he is most fully under the influence of Socrates (hence these are often called Socratic dialogues), and among them are the works which unsuccessfully seek definitions of moral properties. During this period, Plato wrote the *Apology, Charmides, Crito, Euthyphro, Gorgias, Hippias Minor, Ion, Laches,* and *Protagoras.*[19] These have been listed in alphabetical order, for although there may be good reason for saying of some of them that they were written later than others in this group, scholars are very far from a consensus about such issues. It would be safe to say, however, that the *Gorgias* is one of the latest in this group – and probably *the* latest – for it contains a number of features that link it with dialogues that do not belong to this early period.[20] Other works besides those just mentioned are widely accepted as early, but since they have a greater stylistic similarity to the middle dialogues than do the ones listed above, there is some basis for thinking that, like the *Gorgias,* they were composed after the earliest of the early dialogues, but prior to the middle dialogues. These are (in alphabetical order) the *Euthydemus, Hippias Major, Lysis, Menexenus,* and *Republic* Book I.[21]

Although many of these works portray Socrates as someone who raises questions that neither he nor his interlocutors are able to answer, it would be a serious mistake to regard him as a purely negative thinker who had no convictions of his own. On the contrary, he passionately defends a number of theses that are radically at odds with the common sense of his time (and ours). For example, he holds that human well-being does not consist in wealth, power, or fame, but in virtue; that so long as one remains a good person one is immune to misfortune; that to possess the virtues is to have intellectual mastery over a distinct subject matter; that this mastery can be acquired only by means of a successful investigation of what the virtues are; and that if one leaves these questions unexamined, one's life is not worth living.[22] Although Plato no doubt accepted these doctrines when he was under the spell of Socrates and wrote his earliest dialogues, he was eventually to modify them in important ways. For example, one of his most significant departures is his belief that Socrates had overlooked a nonrational aspect of human motivation; as he argues in the *Republic,* a training in virtue involves both an appeal to reason and an education of the emotions and appetites, and is not a purely intellectual matter, as Socrates had thought.

But although Plato was eventually to disagree with some of the views of his teacher, the greatest contrast between them, as I have been emphasizing, lies in the different scope of their intellectual interests: Socrates does not conduct investigations into matters outside of ethics, whereas Plato explores in detail a much wider range of issues. We can see this broadening of intellectual interests when we turn to the *Meno,* for here for the first time the interlocutor named "Socrates" devotes considerable attention to an issue outside the realm of moral philosophy; although he begins with a typically Socratic question – What is virtue? – and finds no adequate answer, he soon faces an unprecedented question about the legitimacy of his method of inquiry, a question that challenges our ability to move from a state of ignorance and acquire knowledge. "Socrates" responds to this challenge by proposing a radical theory of knowledge according to which the human soul is born with the ability to recollect what it once learned in a previous existence; and he defends this theory by conducting an experiment in which it is shown that a slave can make significant progress toward an understanding of geometry, if he is asked the right sorts of questions.[23] It is widely believed that when this doctrine of recollection is introduced, Socrates the interlocutor is entering a terrain that had not been investigated by the historical Socrates, a terrain that was explored by Plato for the first time in his middle period. This shift is signaled by the fact that an experiment about the learning of a geometrical theorem is chosen to support the doctrine of recollection, for Plato's deep interest in mathematics is evident throughout the middle and late dialogues, but is not yet present in his early works.[24] The *Meno* is therefore commonly regarded as a "transitional" dialogue, one that comes between Plato's early and middle periods, and contains elements of both. It is here that we can most clearly see the transformation of "Socrates" into Plato. It is thought to have been written at some point between 386 and 382, when Plato was in his early or middle forties and Socrates had been dead for at least thirteen years.[25]

The separation of body and soul is a theme more fully investigated in the *Phaedo*, and although this dialogue portrays the last conversation and death of Socrates – and therefore forms a dramatic unity with the *Euthyphro* (Socrates on his way to court), *Apology* (Socrates on trial), and *Crito* (Socrates refusing to escape from prison) – it is widely agreed that unlike these works it belongs to Plato's middle period. It refers (72e–73a) to the conversation held in the *Meno* and therefore can safely be assumed to have been written after it; and in the *Phaedo* we see how Plato's interest in questions Socrates had left unexplored or undeveloped continues to grow. Here for the first time in Plato's writings we find a decisive declaration and argument[26] that there exists a realm of objects utterly different from the ones with which we are familiar: These objects are changeless (78d),[27] revealed to us by thought rather than sensation (79a), different from both body and soul (79b–c), and everlasting (79d).[28] Equality[29] is one of Plato's foremost examples of such an object; and his attention to this mathematical property, like his discussion of geometrical learning in the *Meno*, reflects the fact that he is moving beyond the exclusively ethical explorations of Socrates. He argues (74b–d) that Equality itself cannot be identical to equal sticks or any other observably equal objects; for it is possible to make a mistake about two equal objects and to believe them unequal, but no one can make a comparable mistake about Equality itself, and take it to be unequal. The equal sticks are in some way inferior to Equality, though when Plato makes this assertion (74d–e) he does not say explicitly what it is about them that is defective, and why Equality does not share this deficiency.[30] The defectively equal sticks "participate in" Equality and are therefore "called after" that Form, but they are not Equality itself.[31]

The singular Greek terms Plato often uses to designate the new kind of object he discovered – *eidos* and *idea* – are conventionally translated "Form" and "Idea," though the latter term must be used with caution, for he clearly thinks that these entities are not thoughts or any other creations of a mind;[32] they are by nature uncreated, and their existence is not dependent on being known or thought. He takes these to be the objects that we are trying to understand when we ask the sorts of questions Socrates asked, and in this way he sees his own philosophy as continuous with that of Socrates. Although Socrates asked such questions as What is virtue? – and, according to Aristotle, was the first to engage in this sort of inquiry[33] – he showed no interest in a further series of second-order questions that can be asked about the objects of the very question he was asking: Is what we are looking for something that exists independently of human beings? Is it something that can be detected by means of the senses? Can it change or perish? How is it possible for us to learn about it? What is its relationship with people and acts that are rightly considered virtuous but are not identical to what virtue is? How are these objects of thought related to each other?

Plato's attempt to answer these questions by positing the existence of a separate realm of abstract objects[34] called "Forms" and exploring their special properties is often called his theory of Forms, but this phrase should not mislead us into assuming that after writing the early dialogues he quickly developed a dogmatic system that gave decisive and unambiguous answers to all of the important questions that can be asked about the Forms. On the contrary, it is more reasonable to take him to be developing and perhaps even revising the theory as he continues to explore the nature of these objects.[35] For example, Plato makes no attempt in the *Phaedo* to say which Forms there are; he clearly believes that there are Forms of Equality, Beauty, Goodness, Justice, and Piety; but we are not told how to decide what else is on this list.[36] By the time he writes the *Republic* (a middle dialogue), he gives a general, but imprecise, answer: Whenever a name is applied to many different things, there is a Form corresponding to the name (596a).[37] And he posits the existence of Forms corresponding to commonplace artifacts (beds, for example), no less than Forms for moral and mathematical properties. Does this mean that whenever we invent a word and apply it to a plurality of objects, we must posit a corresponding Form, even when we have no justification for introducing the new word and the objects to which it applies ought not to be classifed together? In the *Statesman* (a dialogue belonging to the late period) Plato makes it clear that in his opinion there are no Forms corresponding to names that are not supported by a justified classification of reality into groups. For example, he says, it is arbitrary to divide the peoples of the world into two groups – Greeks and non-Greeks – because there is nothing that unifies the latter group into a genuine whole (262c–e). And so there is no Form corresponding to "barbarian," even though the Greek term – which simply designated anyone other than a Greek – was a name of long standing and familiarity. And so we can see some progression or development in Plato's articulation of the theory of Forms: At first he does not try to delimit their range; then he gives their range in a general way; and finally he refines or modifies his criterion.[38]

II

In the *Meno* and *Phaedo* Plato's thought had not yet fully matured into a comprehensive philosophy, and had he died at this early stage in his development he would have been recognized as a thinker who had to some degree broken away from Socrates, but he would merely be a minor star in the philosophical firmament. His claim to greatness rests principally on later works of the middle period – the *Symposium, Republic, Parmenides, Theaetetus,* and *Phaedrus* (to list them in one plausible chronological order);[39] and on the late dialogues – the *Timaeus* (to which the *Critias* is a brief sequel), *Sophist, Statesman* (*Politicus*), *Philebus,* and *Laws.*[40] And although the *Phaedo* is continuous with the later works of Plato's middle period in its decisive positing of a realm of Forms, there are also important ways in which Plato's later work in the middle period moves away from his initial formulations in the *Phaedo.* In this dialogue, all of the impediments to philosophical progress are located in the body's incessant demands; and because the body blocks any attempts we make to achieve a pure understanding of the Forms, the strongest wish of the true philosopher is to die and be freed from corporeal imprisonment (65e–67b). By contrast, in the *Republic* Plato argues that the soul is divided into three components, and this allows him to locate the impediments to philosophical progress in the soul itself, rather than the body. More important, the longing for death and the pessimism about our prospects for understanding that pervade the *Phaedo* give way in the *Republic* to a confidence that if one pursues the right course of study one can, while one is still alive, achieve a full understanding of the realm of the Forms, including the Good, the Form that Plato declares to be of greatest importance.[41] Those who grasp this Form will not only attain supreme happiness for themselves, but their contact with an otherwordly realm, so far from making them unfit for political life, will enable them to be of immense value to other members of the community.[42] Perhaps the most important difference between the *Phaedo* and the *Republic* is that although in the later dialogue Plato once again argues (in Book X) for the immortality of the soul, it is principally devoted to the project of demonstrating the great advantage of leading a philosophical and fully virtuous life quite apart from the posthumous rewards that those who lead such a life will eventually receive in another world. Even though the soul is immortal, we can dispense with this thesis and still show that for the sake of one's own happiness there is overwhelming reason to lead a virtuous and philosophical life.

In the *Republic* we see how Plato intends to solve the problems that had preoccupied Socrates. In Book I, we have a typically Socratic attempt to define a central moral property – justice – and here too it ends in failure. Although Socrates argues that justice and self-interest coincide, his interlocutors ask him to make a fresh attempt to defend this thesis in Book II; and this reflects the fact that Plato is about to use new materials to defend one of the principal ethical beliefs of his teacher. What follows is a unified metaphysical, epistemological, ethical, political, and psychological theory that goes far beyond the doctrines of the early dialogues.[43] The *Republic* is in one sense the centerpiece of Plato's philosophy, for no other single work of his attempts to treat all of these topics so fully; but at the same time it gives us only a small glimpse of his mature thought, because nearly all of the dialogue's components are developed further and in many cases treated more fully in works that he wrote afterward. Metaphysics is more thoroughly explored in the *Parmenides* and *Sophist*;[44] epistemological issues are treated with greater profundity and thoroughness in the *Theaetetus*; our prospects for understanding the sensible world through the Forms are most fully explored in the *Timaeus*; the question of how best to lead one's life is reopened in the *Philebus*;[45] feasible institutions for a good political community are most fully described in the *Laws*; and his thoughts about human psychology continue to be developed in the *Phaedrus*, *Philebus*, and *Laws*. So the *Republic* gives us only a partial, though an indispensable, picture of Plato's philosophy.

It is in Book VII of the *Republic* that we find Plato's well-known and powerful image of the human condition: Ordinary human beings, untouched by philosophical education, are likened to prisoners in a cave who are forced to gaze on shadows created by artificial light and cast by artifacts paraded by unseen manipulators (514a–519a). Their conception of what exists and of what is worth having is so severely limited and the deception by which they are victimized is so systematic that they cannot even recognize that they are confined, and would not immediately regard an interruption in their routine ways of thought as a liberation. Here Plato is of course thinking of the psychological resistance Socrates encountered to his questioning (517a); but he is also making a far more audacious claim, because he means somehow to downgrade the reality of the ordinary world of sensible objects. The shadows cast on the wall of the cave are less real than the objects of which they are images (515a–e); and in the same way, when the prisoners make progress, leave the cave, and learn to understand the Forms, they recognize the existence of a realm of objects that are more real than anything they saw in the cave (518c). Similarly, in Book X of the *Republic,* Plato distinguishes three types of thing to which the word "bed" can be given – a painting of a bed, a bed created by a carpenter, and the Form – and he holds that they constitute a series of increasing reality. The painter does not make a real bed, but only an image of a bed, and the product of the carpenter is not completely real either. It is only the Form that is really real (596e–597a).[46]

It would be a mistake to think that in these passages Plato is trying to cast doubt on the *existence* of the sensible world. After all, in saying that the painter's image of a bed is not a true bed, he is not expressing doubts about the existence of the painting; rather, he is trying to express the point that the painter's image is in some way derivative from or dependent on the functional object he is representing. It is this same relationship of dependency that he thinks exists between the visible bed of the carpenter and the Form. When we point to an image in a painting and call it a bed, what we say is in a way correct, if our claim is taken in the right way. What makes it something that is properly called a bed is its having the right relationship to the functional bed, even though it has radically different properties from the latter. In this case, the right relationship consists in visual similarity. In the same way, Plato is suggesting, there is a dependency of ordinary sensible objects like beds upon the Forms after which they are named. When we point to the carpenter's creation and call it a bed, our assertion is acceptable only if it is construed in the right way. That physical object is not precisely what it is to be a bed – and if this is what we mean when we call it a bed then we are confused and not simply mistaken. Rather, what we say when we call it a bed is acceptable only if the sensible object has the right relationship to the Form, even though the Form has radically different properties from physical beds. In this case, of course, the relationship is not one of visual resemblance, since nothing can be an image of a Form in that way. Instead, the point is that whether an observable object can properly be called a bed depends on what it is for something to be a bed; it depends, in other words, on the Form, since this is the object one succeeds in understanding when one has a proper conception of what a bed is. So, when Plato says that Forms are completely real, he means that they are at the top of a scale that ranks objects according to their degree of ontological dependency: Just as images of sensible objects receive their names because of their relationship with something with radically different properties, so the sensible objects also receive their names because of the kind of relationship they have to Forms; but the Forms are not in turn dependent for their names on anything else.[47]

The analogy of the cave also brings out a pervasive feature of Plato's political philosophy: Those who are limited in their conception of what exists and what is worthwhile are not the best judges of their own interests, and they can be expected to resist initial efforts to improve their lives. What makes a political system a good one is not the consent of the governed, for if false values are prevalent people may willingly accept only those political systems that perpetuate their confinement. A good political community, Plato assumes, must be one that promotes the well-being of all the citizens; and if the citizens fail to understand where their own good lies, then it is the proper task of political leaders to educate them. Although Plato is therefore in favor of giving extraordinary powers to rulers who themselves have a philosophical understanding of the human good, he is not unconcerned about the possibility that such power might be misused or arouse resentment. It is partly for this reason that private wealth and the family are abolished in the ruling class: These powerful sources of political corruption and favoritism must be eliminated in order to give reasonable assurances to those who are ruled that they will not be exploited by those who are more powerful. One of the driving forces behind Plato's depiction of an ideal society is that in such a society there must be a deep feeling of community among all the citizens, in spite of the fact that they cannot all share an equal understanding of the human good. No one individual or group is to be favored at the expense of any other. The ideal city is not one designed for the maximal happiness of the philosophers or any other group; instead, institutions must be designed so that there is a fair pattern of benefits for all (419a–421a). Although there is a great deal in the political philosophy of the *Republic* that we rightly reject,[48] it also contains elements that many still find appealing. Plato has an attractive vision of a certain kind of community: one in which no one is favored by traditional privileges of wealth, birth, or gender;[49] one in which no one's well-being is ignored and no one is allowed to be indifferent to others; one in which every member of the community leads a life that is to some degree objectively worthwhile.[50]

Another remarkable feature of the *Republic* is that Plato takes there to be a kinship between the kind of community that human beings are capable of forming and the more rarified community he thinks exists among the Forms. The Forms are not a mere aggregate of abstract objects, but are in some way connected to each other: They form an ordered *kosmos* (500c) and therefore each must be studied not in isolation from others but as a member of a unified whole. What we must strive for in our souls and as members of a political order – the unification of diverse elements into a harmonious whole – is something that the Forms already possess by their very nature. But Plato devotes very little attention in the *Republic* to the articulation of the structure possessed by the Forms; what he insists upon is that there is one Form that is central to the being and knowability of all the others: the Form of the Good (505a–509c). The project of studying the relationships that exist among the Forms is taken up by a number of dialogues written after the *Republic.* In the *Phaedrus* he assigns to the dialectician the tasks of finding unity in a diversity of Forms and diversity in a unity, and uses his conception of love as one kind of divine madness as an illustration of such a structure. In the *Parmenides,* there is a complex treatment of the relationship between Unity and such other Forms as Sameness and Difference, Motion and Rest, Limited and Unlimited. And the exploration of such relationships is a recurring feature of much of Plato's late work, playing an especially important role in the *Statesman, Sophist,* and *Philebus.* If Plato equates Goodness and Unity – and there are some reasons to believe that he does[51] – then the elaborate treatment of Unity found in the *Parmenides* might be read as a continuation of Plato's preoccupation with the Good. And in the *Timaeus* the entire sensible world is viewed as an expression of the goodness of a divine craftsman who looks to the pattern of the Forms and shapes the recalcitrant and disorderly material at his disposal into a good (29a–30b) though far from perfect (46d–e) series of structures. So some of the metaphysical ideas briefly suggested in the *Republic* – that the Forms constitute a structured whole, that the Good is foremost among them, that the goodness of a complex group of objects consists in their unification – continue to guide Plato's development in his later works.

III

Thus far, we have seen how Plato's thought underwent a transition in the *Meno*, and, beginning with the *Phaedo*, developed into a comprehensive philosophy based on the theory of Forms. And I have just been discussing some themes that connect the *Republic* and dialogues that postdate it. But it should not be thought that the course of Plato's development after the *Republic* is a matter about which scholars have achieved consensus. On the contrary, even among scholars who believe that Plato continued to develop throughout his life, there are deep divisions about the overall shape of the changes he made. At one extreme, some hold that he entirely abandoned the theory of Forms, having seen that it is not necessary to posit such objects.[52] A somewhat less radical proposal is that Plato faced an emergency as he became increasingly aware of deficiencies in the theory of Forms, but that he did not alter the theory because he could not locate the source of his difficulties.[53] Others believe that while he did retain his belief in the existence of these abstract objects, he recognized that his conception of them during his middle period went badly astray, and he therefore developed a new understanding of their nature.[54] Still another view is that Plato changed the theory of Forms not so much by rejecting certain components of it as by adding new elements that make his conception of Forms more suble and less vulnerable to misunderstandings and objections.[55] In addition to these disagreements about whether Plato changed, and how, there are related disagreements about the chronological sequence of his works.

To understand these controversies, it is best to look more carefully at the division of Plato's works into three phases – early, middle, and late – and to be more specific about which works are generally thought to belong to the latter two groups. As I said earlier, studies of Plato's style initiated in the nineteenth century and continuing to the present have begun with the point, about which there is universal consensus, that the *Laws* is a late work. A good deal of cumulative evidence has pointed to the conclusion that there are five other works that are closely related to the *Laws* as measured by a variety of stylistic features. These are (to list them alphabetically) the *Critias, Philebus, Sophist, Statesman,* and *Timaeus.* Within this group, we can confidently say that the *Statesman* was written after the *Sophist,* since it refers back to it several times,[56] and that the *Timaeus* precedes the *Critias,* since the latter's depiction of the lost island of Atlantis is obviously a sequel to the account of this subject initiated in the former work. Any further attempt to order their composition is more conjectural; for example, though Diogenes Laertius says that the *Laws* is Plato's last work, the *Critias* is obviously incomplete and is therefore a competing candidate for this position. But stylistic studies suggest that they were composed in the following order: *Timaeus, Critias, Sophist, Statesman, Philebus, Laws.*[57]

The greatest source of contention regarding the late dialogues is the *Timaeus,* for it is not universally agreed that it does belong to his late period. It was argued by G. E. L. Owen some forty years ago that the stylometric studies that placed this dialogue in the late period were mistaken; furthermore, Owen argued, the philosophical content of the dialogue and any coherent account of Plato's development requires us to place the *Timaeus* in the middle period, after the composition of the *Republic,* and prior to the major shift in Plato's thought that Owen sought to locate in the *Parmenides* and *Theaetetus.*[58] It might be thought that Owen's thesis is confirmed by the opening page of the *Timaeus,* for it refers to a conversation, held on the previous day, in which Socrates was describing the institutions of the best city, and those institutions are the very ones we find in the *Republic.* From this it might be inferred that the *Timaeus* was the dialogue Plato composed immediately after completing the *Republic,* but such an inference would be unsound, since Plato may have had literary or dramatic reasons for drawing a close connection between these two dialogues. Their dramatic proximity is not a reliable guide to the closeness of their dates of composition.

Before giving further consideration to the place of the *Timaeus,* it will be helpful to call attention to a conspicuous and puzzling feature of five of the six dialogues that are often classified as late – the *Timaeus, Critias, Sophist, Statesman, Philebus,* and *Laws:* With the exception of the *Philebus,* Socrates either plays a minor role (in the *Timaeus, Critias, Sophist,* and *Statesman*) or is completely absent (in the *Laws*). Now, it might be thought that this feature can be of no significance precisely because Socrates is restored to a major role in the *Philebus.* But there is an explanation for Plato's deviation in this one case from a general rule he had decided to adopt: The *Philebus* is devoted to an examination of the place of pleasure in the best human life, and so it is understandable that Plato should bring back his teacher as the dialogue's main interlocutor. It is unlikely, then, that Plato's decision about whether to let Socrates be the chief interlocutor is unmotivated and arbitrary; he has a special reason for giving him the leading role in the *Philebus.* And so it is plausible to assume that he also has a good reason for giving Socrates a small role or none at all in these other late dialogues. But what is his reason? One hypothesis that leaps to mind is that Plato is consciously rejecting at least some of the major tenets of his middle period, and that he therefore signals this divergence by giving Socrates a smaller role to play.[59] But of course this explanation is merely an initial hypothesis and must be substantiated by a careful examination of the content of these later works.

It is important to be aware of the fact that there are two other dialogues outside this group of six that also give Socrates an unusual role to play: the *Parmenides* and *Theaetetus.* It is widely agreed that these belong to the middle period, but it is extremely likely that they were written after the *Republic,* because each subjects to critical scrutiny a doctrine that is regarded in the *Republic* as unproblematic: In the first part of the *Parmenides* (126a–135d) the theory of Forms is exposed to criticism, and in the *Theaetetus* we find an unsuccessful search for an adequate definition of knowledge and a critical discussion of the conception of knowledge taken for granted in the *Republic* and earlier works.[60] In the *Parmenides,* the difficulties in the theory of Forms are pressed by Parmenides, and Socrates is too young to have developed successful answers (135d); in the *Theaetetus*, Socrates takes a leading role in asking questions and raising difficulties, but, like a barren midwife who can only help others give birth, he says he cannot produce positive views on his own (148e–151d). Both of these roles – the object of unanswered criticism, the intellectual midwife – are new departures in the dramatic structure of the middle dialogues.[61]

Now, the fact that these two critical works give an unusual role to Socrates is easily explained: If, for the first time since he began to develop the metaphysics and epistemology associated with Forms, Plato is subjecting that theory to hard questioning, then he would naturally assign a more passive role to the chief expounder of that theory. And if we accept this hypothesis, then we can also propose a conservative explanation of why Socrates continues to play so small a role throughout the remainder of Plato's work, with the exception of the *Philebus:* having become accustomed in the *Parmenides* to writing a large part for someone other than Socrates, and having continued in the *Theaetetus* to use Socrates in a role other than that of a mouthpiece for positive doctrine, perhaps Plato sees no reason to revert to his earlier habit of making his teacher the main expounder of doctrine, except when the subject matter specifically calls for such a change. In other words, there may be no more involved in Plato's frequent practice of minimizing the role of Socrates in the late dialogues than a certain kind of conservatism. Having good reason for altering the role of Socrates in the *Parmenides* and *Theaetetus*, Plato simply saw no reason (except in the *Philebus*) to make yet another change.

If we find that the late dialogues contain nothing that rejects positions adopted in the middle works, and that Plato has survived the self-criticism of the *Parmenides* and the *Theaetetus* without altering what he had earlier believed, then we can account for the smaller role of Socrates in this way. But it is also open to us to combine several ways of accounting for this change in the conversational roles of the later works. If we find that Plato altered his views in moderate rather than radical ways after writing the *Parmenides* and *Theaetetus*, then, although these moderate changes might not on their own have been a sufficient reason for demoting Socrates as a speaker, they may have been large enough to discourage him from reverting to the earlier pattern of Socratic leadership in conversation. So the change Plato makes in the role assigned to Socrates by itself tells us nothing about the pattern of his own intellectual development. To see whether Plato's later works are continuous with his middle dialogues or whether there are mild or sharp breaks, there is no substitute for looking at the actual content of these late dialogues; our interpretation of that content will tell us what to make of the smaller role assigned to Socrates, and not vice versa.

And when we look at the content of the late dialogues (*Timaeus, Critias, Sophist, Statesman, Philebus,* and *Laws*) and the two middle dialogues that assign Socrates an unusual role (*Parmenides* and *Theaetetus*), what do we find? A radical break, smooth continuity, or something in between? There are really many questions here, for it is possible that on some issues Plato saw no need for modifications whereas on others he made significant revisions. On such questions, scholars have been deeply divided. One of the crucial issues in this debate concerns a series of objections presented in the opening pages of the *Parmenides* against the theory of Forms. These objections receive no explicit answer in this or any other dialogue. Aristotle thought that one of them was fatal to some ways of arguing for the existence of Forms, and sought to avoid a similar problem for his conception of universals.[62] As expressed in the *Parmenides,* this objection holds that if there is a reason for positing a single Form of Largeness then there is equally a reason for positing an unlimited number of Forms of this same kind. The reason for positing the "first" Form of Largeness is that whenever a number of things are large, there must be a single Form by virtue of which they are large; but now when we consider that Form of Largeness together with those large things, there must be a further Form of Largeness, by virtue of which the large things and Largeness Itself are large; the process by which we recognize "new" Forms of Largeness can be repeated indefinitely, and so there is no one Form of Largeness, contrary to our initial hypothesis. It has seemed to many scholars that this argument depends crucially on the highly questionable assumption that a Form of Largeness is itself a large thing. But does Plato's theory of Forms, as developed in such middle dialogues as the *Phaedo, Symposium, Republic,* and *Phaedrus,* commit him to such an assumption? Is this the assumption that he meant to single out for further examination in the *Parmenides*? Did he modify his theory of Forms, or did he perhaps entirely abandon his belief in the existence of these objects, in the light of the objections recorded in the *Parmenides*? These are among the main questions scholars have raised in their debates about the pattern of Plato's later development.[63]

The evidence of stylometric studies plays an especially important role in this debate, because if their results are accepted they place the *Timaeus* among the late dialogues and therefore assign it a position after the writing of the *Parmenides*. In the *Timaeus*, Plato clearly continues to uphold some of the views about the Forms that play a large role in the middle dialogues. He holds that these objects alone are changeless, and contrasts their invulnerability to alteration with the constant fluctuation that characterizes objects in the world of sensation; because of these radical differences, the Forms are capable of being known, whereas objects of sensation are not.[64] Furthermore, the Forms are described in the *Timaeus* as paradigms[65] – objects to which the divine craftsman looks in creating the sensible world, and to which we must look in order to acquire knowledge – and this too is a doctrine that is central to Plato's philosophy in the middle dialogues.[66] So, if we give serious consideration to stylometric studies and accept the finding of so many of them that the *Timaeus* is among Plato's latest works, then we must conclude that nothing in the *Parmenides* or *Theaetetus* led him to abandon some of the central doctrines of his middle period. Of course, this does not mean that there are no new developments in the late dialogues; obviously there are. And it may also be that Plato modified his conception of abstract objects in significant ways. But if the *Timaeus* is late, then there is also a good deal of continuity in Plato's thought.

Any consideration of Plato's development beyond his middle period must also pay careful attention to the further work he did in political and moral theory after writing the *Republic*. It is remarkable that after giving, in this dialogue, a rather elaborate blueprint for an ideal society, he took up a similar project near the end of his life and devoted his longest work – the *Laws* – to the development of a complex political system and legal code. Some of the main doctrines of the *Republic* are preserved intact here: Moral education is the principal business of the political community, and there is no toleration for those who put forward doctrines that would undermine the virtue of the citizens. But there are also striking differences between the ideal community of the *Republic* and the new utopia depicted in the *Laws:* No specialized training in mathematics or dialectic is prescribed for an elite group of citizens, and instead of assigning total responsibility and power to one small group of decision makers, Plato widely distributes the functions of government and establishes an elaborate system of safeguards against the abuse of power. Although power is unevenly divided, no citizen is completely deprived of a legislative or judicial role. Does this mean that in his later period Plato came to be less opposed to democratic ideas than he once had been? Perhaps. But it may also be that in the *Laws* he accepts limited democratic features and envisages a smaller role for philosophers because in this work he is merely describing a second-best political community (739a–740a); if that is the proper explanation, then he might have continued to believe that ideally philosophers should have absolute control over political matters.[67]

IV

Thus far, we have been focusing our attention exclusively on what we can learn about Plato from his own writings, but something should be added now about whether there are any other important sources for our understanding of his philosophy. Of course, we are remarkably fortunate to have so much from Plato's own hand; in fact, we possess every philosophical work he ever composed, in the form of copies made during the medieval period, which derive ultimately from the original sheets of papyrus on which Plato wrote.[68] (By contrast, most of Greek tragedy and comedy, and a good deal of early Greek and Hellenistic philosophy, are lost to us.) But in addition to the abundance of material we have from Plato himself, we also have reports from Aristotle and later philosophers of antiquity about Plato's teaching in the Academy. The value of these reports for our understanding of Plato is, however, a matter of considerable debate among scholars.

Before turning to these reports, we should take note of Plato's recognition, at *Phaedrus* 274b–278b, of the limitations of the written word and his insistence upon the superiority of speech as an instrument of teaching and learning. For some scholars believe that, in view of Plato's low opinion of writing, it is a matter of urgency that we try to interpret the reports we have about his oral teaching.[69] He points out in this dialogue that when one discusses philosophy with another person, one has an opportunity to respond to questions and defend one's assertions. In addition, what one says to one person may be different from what one says to another; and to some one should say nothing at all – presumably because some listeners will be less sympathetic or prepared than others, and will therefore raise different challenges or obstacles. Written philosophy lacks this flexibility; it says the same thing to everyone, and leaves the questions of its audience unanswered (275c–276a). Furthermore, the existence of philosophical books can lead to a deterioration of memory, if they are used as a substitute for understanding; and they entice students into thinking that reading by itself creates wisdom (275a–b). They are no substitute for the give-and-take of dialogue, for this alone, and not the mere spouting of doctrine, can give rise to understanding and wisdom.

Of course, these assertions of the supremacy of speech and reservations about the value of philosophical writing do not lead Plato to reject the written word completely. As we have seen, he did a great deal of writing after the *Phaedrus,* and so we cannot take this dialogue as a farewell to the written word or a repudiationn of the value of writing philosophy. After all, Plato does say in the *Phaedrus* that writing, when properly used, can come to the aid of a memory weakening with age, and can also be helpful to the students with whom one discusses philosophy (276d). The point then, is that written works can serve a purpose, but only so long as they are accompanied by philosophical dialogue. It is no mystery, then, that Plato wrote voluminously, and continued to do so even after expressing his reservations about the written word. So the *Phaedrus* gives us no good reason to think that Plato decided not to put into writing his sincere views about philosophical matters; nor does it give us evidence that he deliberately refrained from putting some of his convictions into writing. This is a significant and controversial point, because some scholars do believe that Plato refused to write down the most important points of his philosophy, and that we can recover these ideas only through reports of his oral teaching.

Strong misgivings about the writing of philosophy are also expressed briefly in the second (314b–c) and more fully in the seventh (341b–345a) of Plato's *Letters* – though the authenticity of these works, it should be recalled, is a matter of controversy. In the *Seventh Letter,* the author writes that he, Plato, is greatly annoyed because he has heard that Dionysius, the tyrant of Syracuse, recently composed a work based on philosophical discussions they had had. Plato is eager to dissociate himself from anything Dionysius may have written, and to do so he announces his objections to putting the most serious matters into writing. The matters he discussed with Dionysius are ones he never has and never will commit to writing (341b). Why not? One reason is that this written work will be of no help to the many, and will be used by some as a substitute for wisdom; on the other hand, the few who are capable of understanding his views will be able to discover the truth without relying on a written exposition (341d–e). Some of these misgivings about writing correspond to those expressed in the *Phaedrus,* but Plato's repudiation of expressing certain matters in written form seems to go beyond anything said in the *Phaedrus.* The *Seventh Letter* tells us that there are certain thoughts that Plato refuses to put into writing, whereas the *Phaedrus* expresses no such self-imposed limitation. In fact, certain portions of the *Seventh Letter* appear to say that certain thoughts are not to be expressed either orally or in written form, because words themselves are matters of convention and this makes them ill-suited instruments for grasping true being (341c, 342e–343c). If Plato is saying that certain truths cannot or should not be captured in language, he is again going far beyond the reservations expressed in the *Phaedrus* about writing. And he is saying that we should not look to either his oral or his written teachings for an expression of the deepest truths.

However, if we take the *Seventh Letter* to be saying that Plato will orally divulge his most important thoughts to his students, but will not put them in writing, and if we take this work to be authentic, then it becomes a matter of urgency to see whether we can discover what it is that he said but refused to write. Now, it is a certainty that Plato expressed some philosophical views that he did not put into writing; not only is that a natural assumption to make about any philosopher, especially one who sees so much value in dialogue, but in addition we have a passage from Aristotle's *Physics* in which a distinction is made between what Plato says about place in the *Timaeus* and what he says in "so-called unwritten opinions" (IV.2 209b14–15). But significantly, Aristotle gives no special weight to the latter; that is, he does not suggest that we should downgrade Plato's views in the *Timaeus* because this is merely a written composition or that we should attach priority to the unwritten opinion of

Plato precisely because it was unwritten. In fact, Aristotle frequently looks to Plato's dialogues for his information about what Plato thought; he never suggests that because of Plato's views about the defects of writing he communicated his deepest philosophical thoughts only in speech and that it is therefore to the "so-called unwritten opinions" that we must turn whenever we can. So Aristotle's way of treating the written works and the unwritten opinions counts heavily against the suggestion we might have drawn from the *Seventh Letter* that to understand Plato we must give greatest weight to what he said but did not write.

Elsewhere, Aristotle attributes to Plato certain views without assigning them to any particular dialogue, but also without saying explicitly that these opinions were unwritten. For example, in the *Metaphysics* he says that according to Plato there are, in some way between sensible objects and Forms, mathematical objects which differ from sensible objects in that they are eternal and unchangeable and from Forms in that they are many and alike (I.6 987b14–18). In addition, he attributes to Plato the doctrine that the elements of the Forms are the great and the small – which constitute the material element – and unity – which is substance (987b18–21). This latter passage is especially significant, for it indicates that in Plato's opinion the Forms are not the most basic entities, but are in some way derived from something else. Here we have a view that might be called Plato's deepest thought about reality, since it posits something more basic than even the Forms.

But on what basis does Aristotle attribute this view to Plato? And at what point in Plato's career does he think this view was adopted? He does not answer either of these questions. And so a number of different options are open to us:

1. We might think that Aristotle attributes this view to Plato (whether justifiably or not) on the basis of what he reads in some dialogue or group of dialogues. In this case, Aristotle is not providing us with information about Plato's philosophy that is not already available in the dialogues.[70]
2. We might think that Plato did not express this view in writing, and that it was a fresh idea that did not occur to him until very late in his philosophical career. In this case, it could be a mistake to take anything in the dialogues to have

been shaped by unspoken assumptions revealed to us only by later reports of his oral teaching. Alternatively, even if Plato's unwritten opinions occurred to him at the same time that he was writing some of his latest work, it is possible that he did not develop these opinions about the generation of the Forms into a dialogue because he thought that these new ideas were too tentative and undeveloped to merit their preservation for future generations.[71] In this case, any reports we have of opinions that do not find expression in the dialogues should be given less emphasis in our attempt to understand the dialogues than the evidence of the dialogues themselves.

3. We might think that Plato held this view about the generation of the Forms at an earlier point in his philosophical career, and that he refused to write it down for reasons given in the *Seventh Letter.* This third option, of course, is open to us only if the latter work was written by Plato, and only if it is taken to mean that he reveals his deepest convictions in conversations with a few students and refuses to divulge them in written form.

Which of these options is most credible is a matter of ongoing debate among scholars. The central question in the debate is whether reports of Plato's teaching give us greater insight into what we find in the dialogues. If his works can be understood well enough without recourse to these later reports about his philosophy, then the later material may supplement our knowledge of Plato, but they should not play a controlling role in our interpretation of the dialogues. On the other hand, if we find that the only way we can make sense of Plato is by letting the later reports guide our reading of the dialogues, then of course those reports will have proven to be of great worth. At present, it is fair to say that only a small number of scholars believe that Plato's written works are a mystery that can be solved only by recovering oral doctrines that he refused to commit to writing because of their great importance. But it should not be concluded that the reports of Plato's unwritten opinions deserve no attention whatsoever. They may give us helpful clues about the tendency of Plato's latest thoughts, and perhaps they can help us solve some interpretive difficulties about his last dialogues.

v

There is another kind of disagreement among scholars about how Plato's dialogues are to be read, in addition to the question of the relationship between his writing and his oral opinions. This second controversy stems from the fact that so much of his writing (almost all of it, if we exclude the *Letters*) takes the form of a dialogue between several interlocutors, and that Plato never gives a speaking part to himself. A question can therefore be raised about how we can tell, on the basis of what the interlocutors of the dialogues say, what Plato himself believes. After all, when we read a play of Sophocles or Euripides, we all recognize that what the characters say need not represent the beliefs of the author. And so it is reasonable to ask why we should make a different assumption when we read a Platonic dialogue. Why assume that some one figure in these works presents the convictions of Plato himself? Some scholars, using this analogy between a dramatic work and a Platonic dialogue, hold that Plato's thought is no more contained in the words of any one interlocutor than the beliefs of dramatists are revealed by the words of any of their characters.[72]

But the comparison between Plato's dialogues and dramatic works is misleading in a number of ways, in spite of the fact that in each genre there is dialogue among two or more characters. To begin with what is most obvious: Plato's works were not written to be entered into competition and performed at civic religious festivals, as were the plays of the Greek tragedians and comedians. Plato is not assigning lines to his speakers in order to win a competition or to compose a work that will be considered beautiful or emotionally satisfying by official judges or an immense audience. The dramatist does have this aim, and if it suits his purpose to have his main characters express views that differ from his own, he will do so. But if Plato's aim in writing is to create an instrument that can, if properly used, guide others to the truth and the improvement of their souls, then it may serve his purpose to create a leading speaker who represents the sincere convictions of Plato himself. The point is that, if Plato's aims differ from those of a dramatist, then he will have a reason that the dramatist lacks for using his main speakers as a mouthpiece for his own convictions.

Furthermore, many of Plato's dialogues in his middle and later periods exhibit a high degree of collaboration among the interlocutors: Although they involve questions and answers among several speakers, these characters cooperate in developing and refuting philosophical theories. In the *Phaedo,* Socrates listens to the attempts of his interlocutors to undermine his conception of the soul, but he argues against them and has little trouble in securing their agreement. Similarly, in the *Republic* Socrates accepts questions and challenges from Glaucon and Adeimantus, but soon persuades them to accept his answers. In the *Theaetetus* Socrates and the dialogue's eponymous interlocutor cooperate in undermining the various conceptions of knowledge that are discussed. In the *Philebus* Socrates completely wins over an initially recalcitrant Protarchus, and the latter becomes a docile yes-man whose role is primarily to seek clarification. So, Plato's dialogues cannot have been intended merely to dramatize conflict between opposing characters and to give expression to competing philosophical ideas. Nor can they have been designed merely to give mental exercise to the reader, for that purpose would have been much better served by simply recording as many arguments as possible on opposite sides of a question.

When the dialogues are read in their entirety, they take on the shape that we would expect of works that record the intellectual development of a single individual who is struggling to express and argue for the truth as he best understands it. There is development and perhaps there are even reversals, but there is at the same time the kind of continuity that indicates that Plato is using his main speaker to express his own views. And so although the dialogue form might be used by a philosopher in order to reveal the deficiencies of the views expressed by all of the interlocutors, we have strong reason for thinking that this is not in fact what Plato is doing. The dialogue form of his works should not keep us from saying that they are vehicles for the articulation and defense of certain theses and the defeat of others. Though they are not philosophical treatises, many of them share these purposes with philosophical treatises.

But why, then, did he not simply write philosophical treatises, rather than dialogues?[73] Relying on some points that were made earlier, we can answer as follows:[74] Plato begins his career as a writer in order to give expression to the philosophy and way of life of Socrates. His purpose in doing so is not purely historical; rather, he regards Socrates as a model of wisdom and insight, and he sets down his portrait of Socrates so that he and others will have an enduring reminder of this remarkable man. Since Socrates is above all someone who enters into dialogue with others, and not a propounder of systematic doctrine, the dialogue form is the perfect medium for the expression of his life and thought. But Plato is himself a philosopher and not merely a follower of Socrates, and when he develops views that go beyond those of his teacher, he continues to use the dialogue form for their expression. His decision to do so need not be regarded as a mystery. The dialogue form provides a natural way to air challenges the reader might be expected to make to the theories under discussion; assigning an objection to a speaker is a vivid way of clarifying and defending the views being presented. Furthermore, the misgivings expressed in the *Phaedrus* about writing may have added to Plato's reasons for retaining the dialogue form. Oral exchange is the essential tool of philosophy, yet reading books can entice one into thinking that this encounter with the written word is by itself sufficient for wisdom. Therefore, it is entirely appropriate to put into one's writing something that reminds the reader that insight comes through discussion with others and not through mere reading. What better way to give expression to this warning against the misuse of books than to make each of one's works a dialogue? Even when the dialogue conveys no drama and no real opposition of viewpoints – as in such earlier works as the *Protagoras* and *Gorgias* – it continues to serve this further purpose.

But my answer to the question Why did Plato write dialogues? would not be accepted by all scholars. Some students of Plato take him to be less than fully forthcoming and straightforward in the expression of his philosophical views, and they take the dialogue form as a device by which he avoids telling us everything he believes. According to this interpretation, one of Plato's aims in writing is to get his readers to think for themselves; and to accomplish this goal, he deliberately inserts fallacies, ambiguities, and other deficiencies into his works. He of course does have his own convictions, but he has reasons for making his readers do a considerable amount of work before they discover his true views. And so, in order to see what Plato is driving at, we must go beyond what any of the dialogues actually says, using the speeches of the interlocutors as signs of a concealed message. This way of approaching Plato need not regard his unwritten opinions as the truths to which he is trying to point in the dialogues. Rather, the idea is that each dialogue contains within itself all the materials we need for its understanding, but that these materials are like an anagram that must be unscrambled before its meaning can be revealed. The explicit statements of the interlocutors are the materials from which we must construct Plato's hidden message.[75]

But this is a hazardous way of approaching Plato. First, even if one locates what one takes to be a deficiency in the reasoning of an interlocutor, it is a further matter to say that Plato himself regarded it as a deficiency and meant it to be recognized as such by the reader. To show that Plato is engaged in this kind of project one must uncover a pattern of egregious error in the dialogues, for only in this case could we legitimately infer that these deficiencies are meant to convey something to us. And it is difficult to establish that such a pattern exists.

Second, to defend this approach, we would have to suggest a motive for Plato's deceptive practices as a writer, and, unless we wish to appeal to the *Seventh Letter*, it is not easy to find such a motive. Might Plato have feared political persecution, had he said what he really believed? Plato's objections to Athenian democracy are declared openly in the *Republic* (555b–565e); he obviously is not writing in order to curry favor with the masses.[76] Did he want to conceal his message because he thought his readers should be forced to think for themselves rather than take him as an authority? That is unlikely, because we can see from reports by Aristotle and other ancient writers about the Platonists that they were internally divided, and Aristotle provides in his own person evidence that at the Academy there were many opponents of the theory of Forms.[77] In the midst of all this controversy, Plato could hardly have believed that his writings would be treated by many as authoritative pronouncements to be accepted without question.

Third, if we think that the manifest meaning of a dialogue must be set aside and its hidden message revealed, we leave ourselves little or nothing to serve as evidence. For example, suppose we think that Plato has deliberately given bad arguments in the *Republic* for the thesis that justice is more advantageous than injustice. Even if we are convinced that the deficiencies of the argument can only have been deliberate, and even if we can plausibly arrive at Plato's motive for this deception, we are still left with the problem of what hidden message we should bring away from this dialogue. Is Plato trying to show that in fact justice is *less* advantageous than injustice? Is he trying to show that although justice is *more* advantageous, we must not try to establish this thesis by means of the arguments used in the *Republic*, but must seek new arguments of our own? Or is he trying to show that when we try to present arguments about what is advantageous, we inevitably fall into error, and that therefore this is an area of human life inaccessible to human reason? And of course there are many other possibilities. None of them can be discounted on the grounds that it cannot be found in any text of Plato, because the whole point of this approach to reading Plato is that we cannot expect to find what *he* believes (as opposed to what his interlocutors say) in the text. But, having abandoned the text on the grounds that it does not contain what Plato believes, we have no way of supporting one suggestion as opposed to another regarding what he does believe.

Our best chance of understanding Plato is therefore to begin with the assumption that in each dialogue he uses his principal interlocutor to support or oppose certain conclusions by means of certain arguments because he, Plato, supports or opposes those conclusions for those reasons. In reading him this way, we need make no hazardous assumptions about why he wrote, and why he wrote in dialogue form. And of course we are always free to question our working hypothesis when certain passages or even whole dialogues resist this approach, and plausible motives for deception are suggested by the text itself. It is fair to say that this is the approach adopted by a great many scholars, and that it has considerably enhanced our understanding of the dialogues. This methodological principle is not an a priori assumption about how Plato must be read, but is rather a successful working hypothesis suggested by an intelligent reading of the text and confirmed by its fruitfulness.

Reading Plato in this way allows us to make use of whatever material we have in the dialogues to contribute to our understanding of them: If the scene-setting that occurs at various points of the dialogue helps us understand the argument, or if the characterization of the interlocutors gives us clues as to why the argument takes the course it does, so much the better for our interpretation.[78] The fundamental idea is that unless we have good evidence to the contrary, we should take Plato to be using the content of his interlocutors' speeches, the circumstances of their meeting, and whatever other material he has at his disposal, to state conclusions he believes for reasons he accepts.

NOTES

1 Modern accounts of Plato's life and thought give different dates for his birth, reflecting a discrepancy among the ancient sources. I have followed W. K. C. Guthrie, *A History of Greek Philosophy,* vol. 4 (Cambridge: Cambridge University Press, 1975), 10. R. Robinson and J. D. Denniston, in their entry on Plato in N. G. L. Hammond and H. H. Scullard, *The Oxford Classical Dictionary,* 2d ed. (Oxford: Clarendon Press, 1970), give 429. W. D. Ross, *Plato's Theory of Ideas* (Oxford: Clarendon Press, 1951), 10, gives 429–7. For references to further discussion, see Guthrie, *History of Greek Philosophy,* 4: 10 n. 2. For methods used in the ancient world for keeping track of the year, see Alan E. Samuel, "Calendars and Time-Telling," in *Civilization of the Ancient Mediterranean,* vol. 1, ed. Michael Grant and Rachel Kitzinger (New York: Scribner's, 1988), 389–95.

2 Plato's name for the discipline described in this paragraph is *dialektikē* ("dialectic"), and he conceives of the philosopher as someone who is studying or has mastered this subject. The principal texts I have used in my account of dialectic are *Republic* 509d–511d and 531d–534e. The Greek noun *dialektikē* is derived from a verb, *dialegesthai,* which means "to engage in conversation" (cf. "dialogue"); accordingly, a dialectician is, among other things, someone who is trained at asking and answering questions and in this way defending a position against criticism (534b–d). Other characterizations of dialectic, which add considerably to the *Republic,* are found at *Phaedrus* 265d–266b and *Philebus* 16–17a, 57c–59c. The equation of philosophy and dialectic is not accepted by Aristotle (see for example *Metaphysics* 1004b25–6), though it is not immediately clear whether this merely reflects a verbal difference from Plato or whether Aristotle, in making philosophy superior to dialectic, intends to find fault with dialectic as Plato conceives it. For the latter interpretation, see T. H. Irwin, *Aristotle's First Principles* (Oxford: Clarendon Press, 1988), 137–8.

The references made in this note, and throughout this volume, to passages in Plato's works cite "Stephanus pages," and the reader might like a brief explanation of this common practice. To maintain a uniform system of reference, the outer margins of modern editions and translations of Plato's works supply the pagination of the edition of Plato published in 1578 by Henri Estienne (c.1528/31–1598). These are called

Stephanus pages after the Latinized form of "Estienne." A brief account of his contributions to scholarship can be found in John Edwin Sandys, *A History of Classical Scholarship,* vol. 2 (New York: Hafner, 1958), 175–7. His edition of Plato was standard for over two centuries. Unless otherwise indicated, it should be assumed that the Greek text of Plato used in this volume is that of John Burnet, *Platonis Opera,* 5 vols. (Oxford: Clarendon Press, 1900–7) (often referred to as the Oxford Classical Text or O.C.T.). Similarly, all modern editions and translations of the works of Aristotle supply the pagination of the edition of the Greek text produced in 1831 by Immanuel Bekker.

3 The school Plato founded (c. 387 B.C.), called the Academy after a park located on the outskirts of Athens and sacred to the hero Academus, was in continuous existence for many centuries, but those who in turn succeeded Plato as leaders of the Academy – Speusippus, Xenocrates, Polemon, and Crates – deviated from his philosophy in important ways. When Crates died in c. 276 B.C., his successor, Arcesilaus, heavily influenced by certain Platonic dialogues that seem to show that philosophy can achieve no positive results, made the Academy a center of skepticism; but a watered-down, Stoic version of Platonism was revived when Antiochus of Ascalon abandoned skepticism and founded the Old Academy (c. 87 B.C.). At this time, and continuing for two centuries, there begins a Platonist movement in Athens and Alexandria, called Middle Platonism by some scholars, to distinguish it from both Plato himself and the Neo-Platonist school later founded by Plotinus; the representative of Middle Platonism best known today is Plutarch (c. A.D. 45–125). For a valuable treatment of this movement, see John Dillon, *The Middle Platonists* (Ithaca, N.Y.: Cornell University Press, 1977). Plotinus (c. A.D. 205–70) founded his own school at Rome in 244, and although he is heavily influenced by Middle Platonism as well as other philosophical currents, he places greatest weight on Plato's dialogues. His writings have as much influence as do Plato's on the development of later forms of Platonism. A revived and syncretic form of Platonism was the ascendant philosophical trend in the pagan world from the time of Plotinus until the closing of the pagan schools by Justinian in 529. Other Neo-Platonic thinkers of this period who had a decisive influence on medieval thought were Plotinus's student, Porphyry (232–c. 305), Iamblichus (c. 250–c. 325), and Proclus (410/412?–485). On the influence of Platonism, see Raymond Klibansky, *The Continuity of the Platonic Tradition during the Middle Ages* (London: Warburg Institute, 1939); Ernst Cassirer, *The Platonic Renaissance in England* (Edinburgh: Nelson, 1953). Plato's influence on Renaissance thought is discussed in many of the contributions to Charles B. Schmitt, ed., *The Cambridge History of Renaissance Philoso-*

phy (Cambridge: Cambridge University Press, 1988). A brief overview of Platonism from antiquity to the twentieth century is presented by D. A. Rees, "Platonism and the Platonic Tradition," in *The Encyclopedia of Philosophy,* ed. Paul Edwards (New York: Macmillan and Free Press, 1967), 6:33–341. On the influence of Plato in Victorian Britain, see Frank M. Turner, *The Greek Heritage in Victorian Britain* (New Haven: Yale University Press, 1980), chap. 8. Other works on later Platonism are listed in the bibliography to this volume under the heading Platonism after Plato.

4 This feature of Plato's relation to the philosophical tradition is distorted by the widely known tribute paid to him by Alfred North Whitehead: "The safest general characterization of the European philosophical tradition is that it consists of a series of footnotes to Plato." See *Process and Reality: An Essay in Cosmology,* corrected ed., ed. D. R. Griffin and D. W. Sherburne (New York: Free Press, 1978), 39. Since footnotes are mere supplements and are not intended to contradict the body of the text, Whitehead's statement misleadingly suggests not only that subsequent philosophers were less significant than Plato but also that Plato's work was the universally accepted starting point for all later philosophy. In fact, the context of Whitehead's remark shows that he did not mean to say that Plato's thought was uncontroversial; rather, he was alluding to "the wealth of general ideas scattered throughout" Plato's writings (ibid). This is certainly a remarkable feature of the Platonic corpus, but it is also a fair characterization of other major figures in the history of philosophy.

5 The essay of T. H. Irwin in this volume (Chapter 2) discusses these historical influences, as well as the political and moral climate of Plato's time, and tries to show how these materials are transformed by Plato as he develops his principal positions in metaphysics, epistemology, and political philosophy. Irwin also addresses the question of why Plato's writings take the form of dialogues – an issue I briefly consider later in this essay. Plato's relationship to the religous currents of the fifth and fourth centuries, briefly treated by Irwin, are more fully discussed by Michael L. Morgan in his contribution to this volume (Chapter 7). He focuses on the influence of mystery religions on Plato's thought, with their emphasis on an ecstatic experience in which one achieves a kind of union with what is divine.

6 For two excellent accounts of the trial of Socrates, see Thomas C. Brickhouse and Nicholas D. Smith, *Socrates on Trial* (Princeton: Princeton University Press, 1989); and C. D. C. Reeve, *Socrates in the Apology* (Indianapolis: Hackett, 1989). A more controversial account, and one more hostile to Socrates, can be found in I. F. Stone, *The Trial of Socrates* (Boston: Little, Brown, 1988). For detailed criticism of Stone's interpreta-

tion, see T. H. Irwin, "Socrates and Athenian Democracy," *Philosophy and Public Affairs* 18 (1989): 184–205.

7 Diogenes Laertius, *Lives of Eminent Philosophers,* 3.35, reports that Socrates heard Plato give a reading of the *Lysis,* and German scholars of the nineteenth century, relying on this testimony, assumed that some of Plato's writings were written before the death of Socrates. This assumption was attacked by George Grote in *Plato and the Other Companions of Socrates,* and later scholars have generally accepted his arguments. For a brief account of this debate and a survey of scholarly opinion, see Guthrie, *History of Greek Philosophy,* 4: 54–6. Some of those who believe that Plato did not begin to write until after the death of Socrates also conjecture that the *Apology* was his first work, since he would have wished to preserve the memory of his teacher while the trial was still fresh in his memory. See ibid., 4: 71–2.

8 The exceptions are the *Apology* and the *Letters,* but there is considerable disagreement among scholars about whether the latter were actually written by Plato. (Conflicting views about the authenticity of the *Seventh Letter* are found in this volume: contrast the essays of T. H. Irwin and Terry Penner.) The *Apology* consists almost entirely of a courtroom speech and is not happily classified as a dialogue, although there is some interchange when Socrates examines one of his accusers. Conversely, in a number of the works that begin with an interchange between characters, and that are therefore classified as dialogues, there is little or no alteration of speakers after the introductory section. These are the *Menexenus, Timaeus,* and *Critias.*

9 We will later return to the question of what significance should be attributed to the fact that Socrates plays a much smaller role in some dialogues than in others, and is entirely absent from some of them.

10 Some scholars question the assumption I make in this sentence that Plato endorses the views expounded by the main interlocutor (often Socrates). Instead, they would say that Plato refuses to insert himself in the dialogue and address the reader directly precisely because he does not endorse the views of any one interlocutor – even Socrates – and wants to leave the truth unstated. I will discuss this approach more fully and express my doubts about it later in this essay.

11 This does not mean that for a certain portion of his life Plato was merely trying to write an accurate historical account of what Socrates said, and that he decided to postpone the project of expressing his own philosophical ideas. It is more plausible to assume that for a period of time Plato accepted the philosophy of Socrates and therefore did not distinguish the historical and the philosophical aspect of his works: To write a historically faithful account of a conversation between Socrates and other inter-

locutors was to write a philosophical work that expresses the truth as he, Plato, saw it.

12 For a fuller presentation of this general line of interpretation, see the essay by Terry Penner in this volume (Chapter 4), as well as Gregory Vlastos, *Socrates: Ironist and Moral Philosopher* (Cambridge: Cambridge University Press, 1991), Chaps. 2–4. The thesis that we can and should distinguish the philosophies of Socrates and Plato is widely accepted, but the further claim of Vlastos that they are "so diverse in content and method that they contrast as sharply with one another as with any third philosophy you care to mention" (p. 46) is more controversial. Vlastos holds that Socrates' ontological beliefs do not advance beyond common sense (pp. 53–66) and that his ethical inquiries produce "no spill-over into epistemology" (p. 67). To this it can be objected that Socrates did take a step beyond common sense by explicitly assuming that a single factor unites whatever is virtuous and by requiring a wise person to know this single factor.

13 See *De Sophisticis Elenchis* 183b7–8: "Socrates asked questions but did not answer them; for he agreed that he did not know"; *Metaphysics* I.6 987b1–4: "Socrates was concerned with ethical matters and not with the whole of nature, and in ethical matters he sought the universal and fixed thought for the first time on definitions."

14 For Aristotle's view that Plato arrived at the theory of Forms by "separating" the universal, which Socrates had not separated, see *Metaphysics* I.6 987b1–10, XIII.9 1086b2–5. Some of Aristotle's main objections to the Forms are presented in *Metaphysics* I.9 and XIII.4–5. His complaints about the Form of the Good are presented in *Nicomachean Ethics* I.6.

15 A further indication of this is the statement in *Magna Moralia* I.1 1182a15–28 (written either by Aristotle or one of his followers) that Socrates neglects the irrational part of the soul, and that Plato corrects this error. Here the *Republic* is taken to present the thought of Plato rather than that of Socrates. For a fuller presentation of the way in which Aristotle distinguishes between the historical Socrates and the character who presents Platonic doctrine, see W. D. Ross, *Aristotle's Metaphysics* vol. 1 (Oxford: Clarendon Press, 1924), xxxiii–xlv.

16 For a critical and historical review of the widely varying measures used to study Plato's stylistic development, see Leonard Brandwood's essay in this volume (Chapter 3). For a more detailed historical survey of stylometric studies, see, by the same author, *The Chronology of Plato's Dialogues* (Cambridge: Cambridge University Press, 1990). A brief and accessible introduction to stylometry can be found in Ian Mueller, "Joan Kung's Reading of Plato's *Timaeus*," in *Nature, Knowledge and Virtue: Essays in Memory of Joan Kung*, ed. Terry Penner and Richard Kraut

(Edmonton, Alberta: Academic Printing and Publishing, 1989), 1–27. Prior to the stylistic studies initiated in the nineteenth century, the dialogues were arranged in groups according to their content. For example, Diogenes Laertius, *Lives of Eminent Philosophers*, 3.57–61, records the arrangement into tetralogies made by Thrasyllus (d. A.D. 36). For a comprehensive list of chronological studies and their results, ranging from 1792 through 1981, see Holger Thesleff, "Studies in Platonic Chronology," in *Commentationes Humanarum Litterarum* (Helsinki: Scientarum Fennica) 70 (1982): 8–17.

17 Some of the evidence for the lateness of the *Laws:* Aristotle says in the *Politics* (1264b26) that it was written after the *Republic;* Plutarch (*De Iside et Osiride* 370*ff.*) says that Plato wrote it when he was an old man; a battle referred to at *Laws* 638b is often identified as one that took place in 356 B.C. (nine years before Plato died). Diogenes Laertius, *Lives of Eminent Philosophers*, 3.37, implies that work on the *Laws* was not entirely finished when Plato died, but in the same paragraph he reports a story that the *Phaedrus* was Plato's first dialogue, so his chronological information does not inspire confidence. For further references, see Guthrie, *History of Greek Philosophy*, 5:322.

18 In addition to the works widely accepted as Plato's there are several others attributed to him in antiquity by Diogenes Laertius and included among his works in medieval manuscripts, but whose Platonic authorship is either a matter of current controversy or widely rejected. Some of the *Letters* (there are thirteen of them) are widely assumed to be spurious, and some scholars take all of them to be unauthentic; but in most cases there is no consensus about whether Plato was their author. If they are genuine, they were written during his later period. References to scholarly treatments of their authenticity can be found in Guthrie, *History of Greek Philosophy*, 5:399–401. Other works that were attributed to Plato in antiquity, but whose authenticity is now a matter of debate, include: *Alcibiades I, Alcibiades II, Cleitophon, Epinomis, Hipparchus, Minos, Rivals* (sometimes the alternative title *Lovers* is used), and *Theages*. The *Epinomis* is late, and is thought by some to be the work of Plato's student, Philip of Opus; this attribution is also reported by Diogenes Laertius, *Lives of Eminent Philosophers*, 3.37. The other dialogues just listed have affinities to Plato's early works. In addition, a brief list of succinct *Definitions* is included in the medieval manuscripts of Plato's works, but it is universally considered spurious. Two of the doubtful or spurious works – the *Letters* and *Epinomis* – are widely available in English, but translations of all those mentioned above except the *Definitions* can be found in the Loeb Classical Library. See IA and IB of the bibliography to this volume for further information on

texts and translations. For doubts about the authenticity of the *Hippias Major* – now widely accepted as genuine – see Charles Kahn, "The Beautiful and the Genuine," *Oxford Studies in Ancient Philosophy* 3 (1985): 261–87. This is a review of a work that defends the authenticity of the dialogue: Paul Woodruff, *Plato: Hippias Major,* trans. with commentary and essay (Indianapolis: Hackett, 1982).

19 The essay of Terry Penner in this volume (Chapter 4) discusses some of the main elements of the moral philosophy contained in these dialogues, emphasizing their mutual dependence and coherence, and stressing the egoism of Socrates, his rejection of relativism, his profession of ignorance, and his method of education. Penner does not share the view I just expressed in the text that in these early works Socrates is unsuccessful, and takes himself to be unsuccessful, in his search for definitions. I defend this interpretation in *Socrates and the State* (Princeton: Princeton University Press, 1984), chap. VIII.

20 See E. R. Dodds, *Plato: Gorgias, A Revised Text with Introduction and Commentary* (Oxford: Clarendon Press, 1959), 18–24; Terence Irwin, *Plato: Gorgias,* translated with notes (Oxford: Clarendon Press, 1979), 5–8. For an alternative proposal about the place of the *Gorgias* within the early dialogues, see Charles H. Kahn, "Did Plato Write Socratic Dialogues?" *Classical Quarterly* 31 (1981):305–20, esp. 308–11. He argues that the early dialogues in which Socrates seeks definitions (e.g., *Laches, Charmides, Euthyphro*) are designed to orient the reader toward the doctrines of the middle period, and he therefore places them later than the *Gorgias.* Kahn holds (pp. 307–8) that although the *Apology* might give us a reliable historical portrait of Socrates, all of the other early works of Plato involve significant departures from Socrates. He therefore doubts (p. 310 n. 13) the value of Aristotle's testimony regarding the differences between Socrates and Plato.

21 There are reasons other than those having to do with style for assuming that *Euthydemus, Lysis,* and *Hippias Major* were written at the end of the early period. See Vlastos, "The Socratic Elenchus," *Oxford Studies in Ancient Philosophy* 1 (1983):57–8; and Vlastos, *Socrates,* chap. 4. It should also be noted that if one pays no attention whatsoever to philosophical content and looks only for stylistic similarities, then one would place the *Cratylus, Meno, Phaedo,* and *Symposium* among the later dialogues of the early period. See Leonard Brandwood, *A Word Index to Plato* (Leeds: Maney & Son, 1976), xvii. But there are sound reasons based on philosophical content to place three of these – the *Cratylus, Phaedo,* and *Symposium* – in the middle period, and that is a widely held opinion (though the position of the *Cratylus* is disputed; see n. 39). Similarly, because of its philosophical content, the *Meno* is often labeled

a "transitional" dialogue that cannot be happily classified as early or middle.

22 The first two claims are made at *Gorgias* 470e and *Apology* 30c–d respectively; the last at *Apology* 38a. However, it is not always clear whether Socrates means to identify virtue and happiness, or whether he thinks there is a weaker relation between them. For discussion, see Vlastos, *Socrates*, chap. 8. The *Apology* makes it clear that according to Socrates a virtuous person must be able to pass intellectual tests, and many of the early dialogues take it for granted that since being virtuous is a matter of being an expert on a certain subject, one who has developed this expertise is able to explain the subject to others.

23 On the way in which this geometrical experiment provides an answer to the methodological challenge of the dialogue, see the essay by Gail Fine in this volume (Chapter 6). She argues that it is the distinction between knowledge and true belief, rather than the theory of recollection, that plays the crucial role in Plato's attempt to show that lacking knowledge is not a bar to acquiring it.

24 For this contrast, see Vlastos, *Socrates*, chap. 4. Plato's developing interest in mathematics can also be found in the *Gorgias*, a dialogue often thought to be somewhat earlier than the *Meno*. See Vlastos, *Socrates*, 128–9; Irwin, *Plato: Gorgias*, 7–8. Plato's association with such leading mathematicians of his time as Archytas and Timaeus is cited in the *Seventh Letter* (350a–b) and Cicero's *Academica* I.10.16. For Plato's high degree of involvement in the mathematical research of his time, see the essay by Ian Mueller in this volume (Chapter 5). He discusses Plato's fundamental idea, pursued in the *Meno*, *Phaedo*, and *Republic* Books VI–VII, that progress can be made in philosophy if it adopts the "method of hypothesis" that had been working so smoothly in mathematics. This aspect of Plato's methodology is central to his philosophy, since he regards the existence of Forms as a "hypothesis" (see *Phd.* 99d–105b).

25 See R. S. Bluck, *Plato's Meno* (Cambridge: Cambridge University Press, 1961), 108–20, for a discussion of the dialogue's date; he locates it in the vicinity of 386/5. Platonic scholarship would have a much easier task if each dialogue had made reference to some historical event to which we could confidently assign a precise date. Unfortunately, there is at best meager evidence of this sort, and assigning dates to the dialogues is a highly conjectural matter. Because of its reference to historical events, we know that the *Menexenus* – a work likely to have been written around the same time as the *Gorgias* – was composed after 386; see Dodds, *Plato: Gorgias*, 24. The *Theaetetus* (142a–b) refers to the fatal wounds of its eponymous interlocutor after a battle at Corinth, and this is generally assumed to have taken place in 369. Book I of the *Laws*

(638b) refers to the defeat of the Locrians by the Syracusans, and this has been taken as a reference to events of 356. One other method of finding approximate dates for the dialogues involves using historical sources other than the dialogues to determine dates for certain events in Plato's life. (These sources include the *Letters,* which may give us accurate information about Plato's life even if they were not composed by Plato himself.) The *Seventh Letter* says that Plato was forty when he made his first visit to Sicily (324a, 326b); later writers say that the motive of the trip was to enter discussions with Pythagoreans living there. Pythagorean influences can be seen in the *Gorgias* and *Meno,* and so assigning these works a date not far from 387 is plausible. He returned within the year and is said to have established the Academy, a center for philosophical study, soon afterward. He made a second visit to Syracuse after the death of its tyrant, Dionysius I, in 367, and returned to Athens in 365; a third and final visit occurred in 361. The purpose of these two further visits, according to the *Seventh Letter,* was political: At the urging of his friend, Dion, Plato was attempting to mold the politics of Syracuse by giving a philosophical education to its new tyrant, Dionysius II. These later dates, of course, give us an earliest time of composition for the *Seventh Letter,* whether it is by Plato or not. And they are sometimes used as a general framework for speculating about the dates of composition of the dialogues.

26 There is, however, disagreement among scholars about whether Plato gives arguments for the existence of Forms, or whether he merely takes their existence for granted. The latter view can be found in R. Hackforth, *Plato's Phaedo* (Indianapolis: Bobbs-Merrill, 1955), 50; David Gallop, *Plato's Phaedo* (Oxford: Clarendon Press, 1975), 95; William J. Prior, *Unity and Development of Plato's Metaphysics* (London: Croom Helm, 1985), 10. But it may be that this interpretation is based on too narrow a conception of what constitutes a proof of or an argument for their existence. If positing the existence of the Forms provides solutions to problems not otherwise solvable, or explains phenomena not otherwise explainable, then that would constitute an argument on their behalf. This latter approach to the theory of Forms is defended by H. F. Cherniss, "The Philosophical Economy of the Theory of Ideas," in *Studies in Plato's Metaphysics,* ed. R. E. Allen (London: Routledge & Kegan Paul, 1965), 1–12. Aristotle (see note 14 above) takes the Platonists to have arguments (bad ones, of course) for the existence of Forms. For a recent account of what those arguments are, with special attention to the argument of *Phaedo* 74b–e that Equality is not identical to any observable equal objects, see Terry Penner, *The Ascent from Nominalism: Some Existence Arguments in Plato's Middle Dialogues* (Dordrecht: D. Reidel, 1987).

27 It is a frequent refrain of Plato's thought that by contrast with the Forms the objects we can sense are always becoming and never remain the same. See *Phd.* 78e; *Cra.* 439b–d; *Smp.* 211a–b; *Rep.* 479a–e; *Ti.* 27e–28a, 37e–38b, 49d–50d, 52a. But the proper interpretation of this thought is a difficult matter. For discussion, see Nicholas White's contribution to this volume (Chapter 9). He argues that for Plato the flux of sensible objects is part of their general predicament, namely that they do not have their properties in a way that is independent of their circumstances or the viewpoints from which they are perceived. Aristotle tells us that because Plato came under the influence of Heraclitus and Cratylus, he took all sensible objects to be in constant flux and therefore unsuitable as objects of knowledge. See *Metaphysics* I.6 987a32–b7, XIII.4 1078b12–17, XIII.9 1086a32–b13. It is a controversial matter whether the flux attributed to all things by Heraclitus and all sensible objects by Plato is a matter of change as we normally understand that notion; instead, they may have a broader notion of flux that includes not only alteration of quality over time but the presence of opposite qualities at the same time. For discussion, see Charles H. Kahn, *The Art and Thought of Heraclitus* (Cambridge: Cambridge University Press, 1979); Jonathan Barnes, *The Presocratic Philosophers,* vol. 1 (London: Routledge & Kegan Paul, 1979), chap. 4; G. S. Kirk, J. E. Raven, and M. Schofield, *The Presocratic Philosophers,* 2d ed. (Cambridge: Cambridge University Press, 1983), chap. 6.

28 Some scholars believe that in the *Timaeus* Plato distinguishes between mere everlastingness and eternity, and attributes the latter property to the Forms. What is everlasting (the term "sempiternal" is sometimes used) endures as long as time itself: There is no time at which it fails to exist. What is eternal is not in time at all, and so it does not undergo the passage of time. The body and soul of the created universe are eternal and indestructible, having come into existence with the creation of time, whereas the Forms are not in time. The crucial statement in which this distinction may be found is the one in which Plato calls time a "moving image of eternity" (*Ti.* 37d). See too *Parmenides* 140e–142a for the claim that the One is not in time and has no share of time. For discussion and reference to scholarly literature, see Richard Sorabji, *Time, Creation and the Continuum* (Ithaca, N.Y.: Cornell University Press, 1983), 108–12; and Richard Patterson, "The Eternality of Platonic Forms," *Archiv für Geschichte der Philosophie* 67 (1985):27–46. In any case, whether or not Plato made this distinction, it is present in Plotinus at (among other places) *Enneads* 3.7.2. See Sorabji, *Time, Creation and the Continuum,* 112–14.

29 It has become a widespread practice to use uppercase initial letters (as in

Form, Idea, Equality, The Good, The Large) to designate either the eternal and changeless objects posited by Plato or some member of this class, but it is important to realize that this is our own convention and not Plato's. The ancient Greeks wrote only in uppercase letters; the lowercase was introduced much later as a cursive device. See Rachel Kitzinger, "Alphabets and Writing," in Grant and Kitzinger, *Civilization of the Ancient Mediterranean*, vol. 1, esp. 412; Herbert Weir Smyth, *Greek Grammar* (Cambridge, Mass.: Harvard University Press, 1963), 8. Though capitalizing words that refer to Forms is a helpful and widely used convention, it unfortunately forces one to use the lowercase for two different types of occurrence, namely: those in which one is sure that Plato is not referring to a Form, and those in which one wants to leave it open whether or not he is referring to a Form.

30 A reasonable conjecture is that Equality cannot fail to be Equality, whereas the sticks that are in fact equal can fail to be equal sticks. The deficiency of the equal sticks is that they derive their equality from their meeting the definition of Equality itself; whereas the latter entity does not derive its nature from anything else: It *is* Equality. It is this ontological difference that underlies the fact that we can make mistakes about equal sticks (misperceiving them as unequal) but cannot make an analogous mistake about Equality (judging that it fails to measure up to Equality itself). This passage in the *Phaedo* (74d–e) has been taken by some scholars to depend on the assumption that no two physical objects can be *exactly* equal, but this interpretation is not widely accepted. An influential attack on it was made by Alexander Nehamas, "Plato on the Imperfection of the Sensible World," *American Philosophical Quarterly* 12 (1975):105–17. For further discussion, see Richard Patterson, *Image and Reality in Plato's Metaphysics* (Indianapolis: Hackett, 1985), chap. 5. Nicholas White's contribution to this volume (Chapter 9) also discusses this passage.

31 See *Phd.* 100c, 101c, 102b; *Smp.* 211b; *Rep.* 476d; *Prm.* 130b, 130e–131a.

32 It should not be assumed that the mere presence of these words in Plato indicates that he is referring to the abstract objects posited by his theory of Forms. *Eidos* and *idea* in their ordinary usage can designate any class or kind of object, without committing the speaker to the eternity of the class or any of the other special characteristics Plato attributes to the Forms. Plato frequently uses these terms in this ordinary way. See e.g. *Ti.* 35a4 and *Sph.* 219c2. Occurrences of *eidos* and *idea* at *Euphr.* 5d4, 6d11, and 6e3 are a matter of debate; they are taken by R. E. Allen to indicate that a theory of Forms is present even in the early dialogues. See *Plato's "Euthyphro" and the Earlier Theory of Forms* (London: Routledge & Kegan Paul, 1970), 28–9. Against this, see Vlastos, *Socrates*, 56–66.

33 See *Metaphysics* I.6 987b2–4, XIII.4 1078b17–19, XIII.9 1086b2–5.

34 These terms – "separate," "realm," "abstract" – call for comment: (A) At *Prm.* 130b it is agreed that the Forms exist separately, and although this separate existence is not treated as one of their problematic features, neither is it explained. Aristotle says that Plato, unlike Socrates, separated universals and thereby went astray (*Metaphysics* XIII.4 1078b30, XIII.9 1086b4–7), but he too does not explain what is involved in separation. A likely conjecture is that the separation of the Forms from sensibles consists in their ontological independence: They exist whether or not sensible objects participate in them. For discussion, see Gail Fine, "Separation," *Oxford Studies in Ancient Philosophy* 2 (1984):31–87; Vlastos, *Socrates*, 256–65. (B) By the term "realm" I mean to convey the idea that according to Plato the Forms are united together in a systematic arrangement. See e.g. *Rep.* 500c; I will briefly comment on this aspect of the Forms later in this essay. (C) To call the Forms "abstract objects" is to use a contemporary philosophical phrase that does not correspond to any equivalent term in Plato's Greek. An abstract object is not merely one that cannot be detected by means of the senses – otherwise the soul as Plato conceives it would count as an abstract object, and so would atoms as we conceive them. In addition to being unobservable, abstract objects lack spatial location and are incapable of change.

35 This is now a common view, but it has had its detractors. For an opposing interpretation, see Paul Shorey, *The Unity of Plato's Thought* (Chicago: University of Chicago Press, 1960). He says (p. 88), "Plato on the whole belongs to the type of thinkers [*sic*] whose philosophy is fixed in early maturity (Schopenhauer, Herbert Spencer), rather than to the class of those who receive a new revelation every decade (Schelling)." But the two extremes Shorey mentions here are not the only possibilities.

36 See *Phd.* 75c–d, where Plato connects the existence of Forms with the question "What is . . . ?" that typically arises in a Socratic interchange. In the *Parmenides* (130b–e), Socrates is portrayed as someone who is not yet sufficiently practiced in the theory of Forms, and although he is confident that there are Forms of Justice, Beauty, and Goodness, he is less confident about Human, Fire, and Water; then, when he is asked about such alleged Forms as Hair, Mud, and Dirt, he expresses confidence that they do not exist, but is immediately criticized by Parmenides for shying away from such objects. This suggests that in Plato's development there was, at least initially, some uncertainty about which Forms to posit.

37 An alternative reading was proposed many years ago according to which Plato is merely saying that if there is a Form of *X* then it is one Form. See J. A. Smith, "General Relative Clauses in Greek," *Classical Review* 31

(1917):69–71. Recent discussion of this alternative can be found in Gail Fine, "The One Over Many," *Philosophical Review* 89 (1980):213 n. 25; and Patterson, *Image and Reality in Plato's Metaphysics,* 203 n. 8.

38 It is not easy to decide whether in the *Statesman* Plato has *modified* his position in the *Republic,* or whether he is making explicit a point he had been assuming earlier. If he is taking it for granted in the earlier dialogue that any word commonly applied to a plurality is a genuine name, then he has changed his mind by the time he wrote the later dialogue. But if he is assuming in the *Republic* that there are narrow restrictions on what counts as a true name, then there need have been no change of mind. The *Cratylus,* which is often thought to be chronologically closer to the *Republic* than to the *Statesman* (though see n. 39), discusses the idea that name-giving is a skill, and that names in use can fall short of ideal names. See, e.g., 389d–390e. But this allows that a bad name is a name nonetheless – just as a badly crafted bed is still a bed. If "barbarian" is a name, but a bad one, then the criterion given in the *Republic* needs modification, and Plato has come to recognize this in his later period. On the other hand, if "barbarian" is not a true name – that is, if it is not really a name at all – then Plato has merely become more explicit in his later work. For futher discussion, see Patterson, *Image and Reality in Plato's Metaphysics,* 123–8; and Fine, "The One Over Many," 197–240.

39 I have listed these works in the order presented in Brandwood, *Word Index,* xvii. It is tempting, however, to think that the *Phaedrus* should be placed after the *Republic* and prior to the *Parmenides* and *Theaetetus,* because of philosophical resemblances between the *Symposium, Republic,* and *Phaedrus.* On the other hand, the method of division and collection advocated by the *Phaedrus* (265d–266b) connects it with a great deal of material in the later period. To see the diversity of opinion about where the *Phaedrus* should be placed, see Ross, *Plato's Theory of Ideas,* 2. Another dialogue commonly assigned to Plato's middle period is the *Cratylus,* but there is some difference of opinion about this. Stylometric tests suggest that it is earlier than the *Republic,* but some scholars argue that its philosophical content requires a later date. For a brief account of the dispute, see Guthrie, *History of Greek Philosophy,* 5:1–2. Vlastos proposes the following ordering of the middle dialogues: *Cratylus, Phaedo, Symposium, Republic* II–X, *Phaedrus, Parmenides, Theaetetus.* See Vlastos, *Socrates,* 47. On the position of the *Symposium,* see K. J. Dover, "The Date of Plato's *Symposium,*" *Phronesis* 10 (1965):2–20.

40 Again, I follow the order presented in Brandwood, *Word Index,* xvii. However, the position of the *Timaeus* is controversial; some locate it

among the middle rather than the late dialogues. I will return to this issue.

41 There is an obvious similarity between the lover's ascent to the Form of Beauty, as described in the *Symposium* (210a–212b), and the philosopher's ascent to the Form of the Good in the *Republic.* These two Forms need not be identical, but it is plausible to think that according to Plato one cannot have knowledge of either one without the other. (At *Philebus* 64d–65a, Plato says that the good consists, at least partially, in beauty; and it is arguable that this is meant as an account of the Form of the Good.) Just as it is said in the *Symposium* that one must not confine one's affection to some one individual, but must love what all objects of beauty have in common (210b–d), so in the *Republic* the family is abolished among the guardians so that no single individual will be favored in a way that detracts from the well-being of all (457d–466b). The essay by G. R. F. Ferrari in this volume (Chapter 8) discusses the way in which Plato moves in the *Symposium* from the familiar topic of falling in love with other people to the love of the good that motivates all human action. He also explores the connections among the several speeches of the *Symposium,* and the relationship between Plato's treatment of love in this dialogue and in the *Phaedrus.*

42 This paradoxical idea is anticipated in the *Gorgias:* Although Socrates may seem to be the antithesis of a politician because of his indifference to worldly goods (485a–486d), it is really conventional politicians who have the least power (466a–e) and it is Socrates who alone practices the true art of politics (521d).

43 In my contribution to this volume, "The Defense of Justice in Plato's *Republic*" (Chapter 10), I try to show how Plato's metaphysics plays a central role in his attempt to defend the Socratic thesis that justice coincides with self-interest.

44 In the *Sophist* Plato finally comes to terms with a problem that had puzzled him throughout his career: A true statement says what is and a false statement says what is not; but since all statements must say something, and that something must be, it is unclear how false statements are possible. See *Euthd.* 283e–286d and *Tht.* 187c–200c. To solve the difficulty in the *Sophist,* Plato conducts a complex discussion of the nature of being and not-being. Michael Frede's contribution to this volume (Chapter 13) offers an interpretation of Plato's solution.

45 This dialogue contains Plato's fullest discussion of pleasure and its role in the good life – a topic that he had explored earlier in the *Gorgias* and *Republic* Book IX. As in the *Republic,* he uses metaphysics to solve the problem of how we should lead our lives, and he makes important distinctions among the different kinds of pleasures there are. For an over-

view of the dialogue's complex structure and its relation to Plato's earlier treatments of pleasure, see Dorothea Frede's contribution to this volume (Chapter 14).

46 Plato's insistence upon the artist's remoteness from true reality in Book X of the *Republic* is the central element in his radical critique of the role of the poet in the political community, but his attitude toward poetry is far more complex than is often realized, as other dialogues besides the *Republic* reveal. See the essay of Elizabeth Asmis in this volume (Chapter 11) for a comprehensive overview of Plato's lifelong quarrel with poetry.

47 For further discussion of degrees of reality in Plato, see Gregory Vlastos, *Platonic Studies* (Princeton: Princeton University Press, 1981), essays 2 and 3.

48 The most obvious objections are directed against Plato's exclusion of nearly all citizens from political participation and his eagerness to suppress unorthodox ideas. In K. R. Popper's phrase, Plato is an enemy of "the open society." See *The Open Society and its Enemies,* vol. 1, 4th ed. (New York: Harper & Row, 1963). Popper attributes to Plato the view that "the criterion of morality is the interest of the state" (p. 107), but it is more plausible to take the *Republic* to contain a theory of what is good for any individual and to presuppose that an ideal state is one that best promotes the good of its individual citizens. For a full reply to Popper, see R. B. Levinson, *In Defense of Plato* (Cambridge, Mass.: Harvard University Press, 1953); also see Renford Bambrough, ed., *Plato, Popper, and Politics* (Cambridge: Cambridge University Press, 1967). For a recent overview of Plato's political theory, see George Klosko, *The Development of Plato's Political Theory* (New York: Methuen, 1986). Two older treatments of this topic that are still worth consulting are E. Barker, *Greek Political Theory: Plato and His Predecessors* (London: Methuen, 1918); and the chapter on Plato in George Sabine, *A History of Political Theory,* 4th ed. (Hinsdale, Ill.: Dryden Press, 1973). Plato's proposal for controlling poetry is discussed by Iris Murdoch, *The Fire and the Sun: Why Plato Banished the Artists* (Oxford: Clarendon Press, 1977).

49 One feature of Plato's political philosophy that has received considerable attention recently is his thesis that qualified women of the ideal city ought to hold high political office. Trevor Saunder's contribution to this volume (Chapter 15) emphasizes Plato's eagerness, even in a nonutopian work like the *Laws,* to enlarge the political role played by women. For recent discussion, see Julia Annas, "Plato's *Republic* and Feminism," *Philosophy* 51 (1976):307–21; Susan Moller Okin, "Philosopher Queens and Private Wives: Plato on Women and the Family," *Phi-*

losopher and Public Affairs 6 (1977):345–69; Nicholas D. Smith, "Plato and Aristotle on the Nature of Women," *Journal of the History of Philosophy* 21 (1983):467–78; Gregory Vlastos, "Was Plato a Feminist?" *Times Literary Supplement*, March 17–23, 1989, pp. 276, 288–9; Dorothea Wender, "Plato: Misogynist, Paedophile and Feminist," *Arethusa* 6 (1973):75–80.

50 However, even if Plato is right in thinking that the state should favor a definite conception of the good (and many philosophers in the liberal tradition would dispute this claim), he can still be criticized for proposing too narrow a conception as the one that should be officially endorsed.

51 The closest he comes to such an identification is at *Philebus* 65a, where Socrates says that even if the good cannot be captured by means of one characteristic, it can be understood in terms of beauty, measure, and truth. The first two members of this triad are tied by Plato to some notion of unity. Beauty and measure result when a limit is placed on what is unlimited and excessive (*Phil.* 24a–26b), and so goodness (insofar as it involves beauty and measure) is conceptually connected with unity (insofar as what is limited in thereby unified). Note that at *Rep.* 462a–b the unification of the city is called its greatest good; certainly Plato would add that the unification of the soul is also its greatest good. For further discussion, see my essay on the *Republic* in this volume (Chapter 10). Aristotle was aware of the view that the one itself is the good itself: See *Metaphysics* XIV.4 1091b13–15, and compare *Eudemian Ethics* I.8 1218a15–28. But he does not in these passages attribute this view to Plato. A student of Aristotle's, Aristoxenus, reported in his work, *Elementa Harmonica* II.30–31, that Plato gave a public lecture on the good, and it is possible to interpret his report to mean that this lecture maintained that the Good is Unity – although the statement may instead mean that there is one Good. Contrast the Revised Oxford Translation in Jonathan Barnes, ed., *The Complete Works of Aristotle* (Princeton: Princeton University Press, 1984), 2397, and that of Hans Joachim Krämer, *Plato and the Foundations of Metaphysics* (Albany: State University of New York Press, 1990), 203.

52 This is the view advocated by Gilbert Ryle in several publications. See "Plato's *Parmenides*," in *Studies in Plato's Metaphysics*, ed. R. E. Allen (London: Routledge & Kegan Paul, 1965), 97–147; *Plato's Progress* (Cambridge: Cambridge University Press, 1966); "Plato," in *The Encyclopedia of Philosophy*, ed. Paul Edwards, 6:314–33, esp. 324–5. Ryle's view has won few supporters, for even after the theory of Forms is severely criticized in the early pages of the *Parmenides*, Parmenides maintains that if one refuses to posit the existence of these objects one destroys the power of discourse (135b–c). For discussion of his interpretation, see G.

E. L. Owen, "Notes on Ryle's Plato," in *Ryle*, ed. O. P. Wood and G. Pitcher (Garden City, N.Y.: Doubleday, 1970), 341–72.

53 This view, forcefully presented by Gregory Vlastos in "The Third Man Argument in the *Parmenides*," in Allen, *Studies in Plato's Metaphysics*, 231–63, has been at the center of scholarly controversy ever since its initial publication in 1954.

54 For a highly influential interpretation of this sort see G. E. L. Owen, "The Place of the *Timaeus* in Plato's Dialogues," in Allen, *Studies in Plato's Metaphysics*, 293–338. Owen holds that Plato gives up the view that Forms are paradigms to which sensible objects have a resemblance, as well as the view that being and becoming are mutually exhaustive categories. It is quite possible to accept Owen's general thesis – that Plato changed his conception of the nature of the Forms – while differing with him about the nature of that change. For a recent interpretation of this type, see Kenneth M. Sayre, *Plato's Late Ontology: A Riddle Resolved* (Princeton: Princeton University Press, 1983). He holds that Plato gave up the view that the existence of Forms is independent of the existence of sensible objects.

55 This is the approach defended by Prior, *Unity and Development in Plato's Metaphysics*: "Without altering . . . the Theory of Forms . . . he augments and clarifies his metaphysics" (p. 2). Similarly, Constance C. Meinwald, *Plato's Parmenides* (New York: Oxford University Press, 1991), 171: "Instead of seeing the middle dialogues as a perfected edifice that the late works then tear down, we can think of the masterpieces of the middle period as showing the need for work that the difficult final dialogues in fact take on."

56 *Statesman* 257a, 258b, 266d, 284b, 286b.

57 The reader may find it helpful to have an integrated list of the various chronologies suggested at various points in this essay: (A) early dialogues: (1) first group (in alphabetical order): *Apology, Charmides, Crito, Euthyphro, Hippias Minor, Ion, Laches, Protagoras*; (2) second group (in alphabetical order): *Euthydemus, Gorgias, Hippias Major, Lysis, Menexenus, Republic* I; (B) middle dialogues (in chronological order): *Meno, Cratylus, Phaedo, Symposium, Republic* II–X, *Phaedrus, Parmenides, Theaetetus*; (C) late dialogues (in chronological order): *Timaeus, Critias, Sophist, Statesman, Philebus, Laws*. This order differs from the one found in Vlastos, *Socrates*, 46–7, in only three minor respects: He puts the *Gorgias* and *Republic* I in A1 and the *Meno* in A2.

58 See "The Place of the *Timaeus* in Plato's Dialogues," in Allen, *Studies in Plato's Metaphysics*, 313–38. This volume contains an influential reply to Owen by Cherniss, "The Relation of the *Timaeus* to Plato's Later Dialogues," 339–78. For further discussion, see Prior, *Unity and*

Development in Plato's Metaphysics, 168–93; Sayre, *Plato's Late Ontology*, 256–67; Mueller, "Joan Kung's Reading of Plato's *Timaeus*." Mueller says (p. 20): "The stylistic arguments advanced by Owen show at most that the *Timaeus* may be the first of the late dialogues. . . . There are . . . no stylistic grounds for treating the *Timaeus* as part of an intellectual project abandoned by Plato."

59 This is not intended as a hypothesis that Owen would embrace, since he takes the *Timaeus* to be an expression of the theory of Forms of the middle period, in spite of the fact that Socrates has so small a role to play in it. It may be that the *Timaeus* rejects some of the doctrines of the middle period; if so, this escaped Owen's notice.

60 For the view that possessing knowledge of something involves having the ability to reason about it or to give an account of it, whereas merely having a belief is compatible with lacking this ability, see *Gorgias* 465a, 500e–501a; *Meno* 98a; *Phaedo* 76b; *Republic* 531e, 534b, (cf. 475c, 493c, 497c, 510c, 533c); *Timaeus* 51d–e. For Plato's puzzles about what an account (*logos*) is, see *Theaetetus* 201c–210a. An extensive discussion of these puzzles can be found in Myles Burnyeat, *The Theaetetus of Plato* (Indianapolis: Hackett, 1990), 128–241.

61 A stylistic feature of the *Parmenides* and *Theaetetus* also indicates that these come after some of the other dialogues of the middle period: At *Tht.* 143c, it is announced that the interlocutors will talk directly to each other, and thus the use of "he said" and the like is avoided. Such streamlining is also adopted in the *Parmenides* (starting at 137c). This suggests that these works were written after such dialogues as the *Republic*, which makes frequent use of phrases reporting dialogue. See Brandwood, *Chronology of Plato's Dialogues*, 1, 251. One other chronological signal deserves mention: At *Tht.* 183e, Socrates says that he met Parmenides when he was young. We have no evidence about the birth or death of Parmenides that would make such a meeting an impossibility, but since we are taking the theory of Forms to be a product of Plato's middle age, the conversation depicted in the *Parmenides* between its eponymous speaker and Socrates is of course a fiction cast back in time for dramatic purposes. The reference at *Tht.* 183e to a meeting between Parmenides and Socrates is therefore plausibly treated as an indication that this dialogue was composed after the *Parmenides*.

62 See *De Sophisticis Elenchis* 179a3, *Metaphysics* I.9 990b17, VII.13 1039a2. For discussion, see Joan Kung, "Aristotle on Thises, Suches, and the Third Man Argument," *Phronesis* 26 (1981):207–47.

63 A crucial issue in the debate is whether the *Parmenides* itself provides a way of answering the objections raised against the theory of Forms – even though the dialogue does not make this answer explicit. In her

contribution to this volume (Chapter 12), Constance Meinwald argues that in the remainder of the dialogue Plato makes and exploits a distinction between two different kinds of predication, and that this distinction provides him with solutions to the problems presented in the first part of the dialogue.

64 See *Ti.* 27e–28a, 37e–38b, 49b–50d, 51e–52b.

65 See *Ti.* 29b, 48e–49a, 50d, 52a, 53c.

66 See e.g. *Rep.* 500e, 540a; *Prm.* 132d.

67 For a comprehensive discussion of the major institutions of the *Laws,* and its relationship to the political philosophy of the *Republic,* see the contribution of Trevor Saunders to this volume (Chapter 15).

68 On the process by which Greek texts were produced and preserved from antiquity through the Renaissance, see L. D. Reynolds and N. G. Wilson, *Scribes and Scholars: A Guide to the Transmission of Greek and Latin Literature,* 3d ed. (Oxford: Clarendon Press, 1991). For a brief account of methods of preserving written works in the classical world, and a full bibliography, see Susan A. Stephens, "Book Production," in Grant and Kitzinger, *Civilization of the Ancient Mediterranean,* 1:421–36.

69 For an introduction to the problem and a guide to some of the literature, see Guthrie, *History of Greek Philosophy,* 5: chap. 8. For a full defense of approaching Plato's philosophy via the testimony about his unwritten doctrines, see Hans Joachim Krämer, *Plato and the Foundations of Metaphysics,* ed. and trans. John R. Caton (Albany: State University of New York Press, 1990). This is the interpretive method used by Giovanni Reale in *A History of Ancient Philosophy,* vol. 2, ed. and trans. John R. Caton (Albany: State University of New York Press, 1990). For criticism of this approach, see Harold Cherniss, *The Riddle of the Early Academy* (Berkeley: University of California Press, 1945); Gregory Vlastos, "On Plato's Oral Doctrine," in Vlastos, *Platonic Studies,* 379–403.

70 This is the view of Cherniss, *The Riddle of the Early Academy.* He takes Aristotle to be giving questionable interpretations of what he reads in the dialogues rather than accurate reports of what he heard. By contrast, Sayre, in *Plato's Late Ontology,* argues that the doctrines Aristotle attributes to Plato are accurate reports of doctrines Plato puts forward in the *Philebus,* although Aristotle's reports use a different terminology.

71 This is the suggestion of Vlastos, "On Plato's Oral Doctrine," 397–8.

72 "In none of his dialogues does Plato ever say anything. Hence we cannot know from them what Plato thought. If someone quotes a passage from the dialogues in order to prove that Plato held such and such a view, he acts about as reasonably as if he were to assert that according to Shakespeare life is a tale told by an idiot, full of sound and fury, signifying nothing." Thus Leo Strauss, *The City and Man* (Chicago: University of

Chicago Press, 1964), 50. Citing Plato's attitude toward writing in the *Phaedrus* and Xenophon's account of Socrates in the *Memorabilia,* Strauss goes on (pp. 53–5) to suggest that a Platonic dialogue is contrived to lead the ordinary reader to "salutary opinions" while revealing the truth to "men possessing the best natures." Plato's own convictions, therefore, may be quite different from the ones for which Socrates argues. For example, Strauss takes Plato to be saying in the *Republic* that "the just city is against nature because the equality of the sexes and absolute communism are against nature" (p. 127). See too Rudolf H. Weingartner, *The Unity of the Platonic Dialogue* (Indianapolis: Bobbs-Merrill, 1973), 1–7, for the view that Plato's purpose in composing his dialogues is not to endorse the view of any one of his speakers.

73 For a treatment of this issue that differs from the one I put forward here, see the essays collected by Charles L. Griswold, Jr., in *Platonic Writings, Platonic Readings* (New York: Routledge, 1988). Many of the papers are guided by the premise that (as Griswold puts it) "deficiencies, paradoxes, tensions, and even fallacies in a Platonic dialogue ought to be taken not as signaling Plato's inability to reason well but as intentionally designed invitations to the reader to sort through the topic at hand himself" (p. 5). Note the assumption implicit in this sentence that Plato's reasoning is defective in all of these ways, and so we must choose between accusing him of being a bad philosopher and taking the text not as containing an argument for a thesis Plato himself held but merely as an invitation to think for oneself. A survey of different methodologies for reading Plato, with special emphasis paid to the nineteenth and twentieth centuries, can be found in E. N. Tigerstedt, *Interpreting Plato* (Uppsala: Almquist & Wiksell International, 1977). His overview is marred, in my opinion, by his assumption that because of internal conflicts in every dialogue we cannot take Socrates to be a mouthpiece for Plato's views. See esp. pp. 98–9. No doubt there are difficulties of interpretation in every dialogue and on nearly every page of Plato, but our own difficulties in understanding the text should not lead us to believe that it is filled with contradictions.

74 For treatments of this issue that are consonant with my own, see the essay of Terence Irwin in this volume (Chapter 2) and Vlastos, *Socrates,* 51–3.

75 This way of reading Plato is suggested by Leo Strauss in *Persecution and the Art of Writing* (Glencoe, Ill.: Free Press, 1952), 22–37. For criticism of Strauss's methodology, see Myles Burnyeat, "Sphinx Without a Secret," *New York Review of Books* 32 (May 30, 1985), 30–6; later issues contain replies.

76 To support his view that Plato, like many other thinkers, concealed his views for fear of persecution, Strauss says: "A glance at the biographies of

Anaxagoras, Protagoras, Socrates, Plato, Xenophon, Aristotle . . . [there follows a long list of medieval and modern philosophers] is sufficient to show that they witnessed or suffered, during at least part of their lifetimes, a kind of persecution which was more tangible than social ostracism." See *Persecution and the Art of Writing,* 33. Strauss is certainly right that Plato witnessed persecution in the form of the trial of Socrates. But this does not show that he himself concealed his true views in order to avoid the same fate. One could by the same method of argument show that all contemporary writers who have witnessed persecution must be writing in an esoteric manner.

77 Aristotle's *Metaphysics,* Books XIII and XIV, are filled with accounts of the differing opinions about mathematical objects in Plato's Academy. Plato's first and second successors as head of the Academy, Speusippus and Xenocrates, departed from Plato's views in significant ways. For an account of their views, see Guthrie, *History of Greek Philosophy,* 5:457–83.

78 That these features of the dialogues can help us understand their content has been argued by many scholars. For references, see Charles L. Griswold, Jr., *Self-Knowledge in Plato's Phaedrus* (New Haven: Yale University Press, 1986), 244–6 nn. 7–8. See too Michael C. Stokes, *Plato's Socratic Conversations: Drama and Dialectic in Three Dialogues* (Baltimore: Johns Hopkins University Press, 1986), 1–36. Paying attention to scene-setting and characterization is by no means incompatible with holding that Socrates or some other interlocutor is a mouthpiece for Plato's philosophy; but if one denies the latter, then these dramatic features of the dialogues take on all the more significance, for they may provide clues to the hidden message of the dialogue. Needless to say, just as it is possible to misconstrue the content of an interlocutor's speech or its connection with other speeches, so it is possible to misunderstand the significance of the dramatic features of a dialogue; and either kind of mistake may lead to the other.

T. H. IRWIN

2 Plato: The intellectual background

I. INFLUENCES ON PLATO

We lack the materials for a proper biography of Plato.[1] He hardly refers to himself at all in the dialogues.[2] The ancient "Lives" are infected by gossip, legend, and fiction;[3] and the ostensibly autobiographical *Seventh Letter* is probably spurious.[4] Fortunately, however, Aristotle provides us with important evidence on Plato's intellectual development. He says that Plato was first influenced by Cratylus the Heraclitean, and later by Socrates (*Met.* 987a32–b10). It is unlikely that Aristotle derived his claim about Craytlus from reading Plato's dialogues;[5] he probably had some independent source. And since he was probably well informed about Socrates and Plato, his statement deserves to be taken seriously.

Aristotle implies that Plato is influenced both by the older, "pre-Socratic"[6] tradition of the "naturalists" (*phusiologoi;* cf. Aristotle, *De Caelo* 289b25–9) and by the more recent application of philosophy to moral and political questions. What, then, did Plato find when he looked at these two movements in Greek philosophy?

II. NATURAL PHILOSOPHY AND RELIGION

The dialogues reveal Plato's interest in many aspects of Greek naturalist thinking. He mentions Pythagorean mathematical speculation,[7] Heraclitus,[8] Anaxagoras,[9] Zeno and Parmenides,[10] and Empedocles.[11] Though he never mentions Democritus by name, he probably sometimes refers to him.[12] He also refers to the medical theories that are

I have benefited from helpful criticisms and suggestions by Gail Fine, Richard Kraut, and Susan Sauvé.

often closely related to pre-Socratic speculations.[13] What does he accept or reject from the naturalists?

Naturalists give arguments (*logoi*), in contrast to the traditional stories (*muthoi*) told about the gods by the poets (Aristotle, *Met.* 1000a9–20). Instead of appealing simply to authority and tradition, they claim to explain natural processes by some rationally convincing principle or argument. In Aristotle's view, they appeal to a material cause, arguing that if these material elements are combined in the right way, a given result necessarily follows. The appeal to necessity and natural law leaves no room for the traditional Homeric view that natural processes are basically irregular and unpredictable, and that gods can interfere with them or manipulate them as they please.[14]

On this basic issue both Socrates and Plato agree with the pre-Socratics; in doing so they challenge widespread and deep-seated religious assumptions of their contemporaries. For in rejecting the Homeric picture of the irregular universe the naturalists also reject the view that we sometimes incur divine punishment by failing to sacrifice the right number of oxen or by fighting on an ill-omened day, and that we can sometimes placate the gods by offering the right sacrifices. Traditional and civic religion – from a farmer's sacrifices to the local nymphs and heroes to the Panathenaic civic procession bringing a new robe to Athena in the Parthenon[15] – was understood as a means of securing a god's favor by offering gifts; and people regularly assumed that a natural disaster or a defeat in a war must result from some ritual offense.[16]

Naturalism does not imply atheism. Anaximander and Heraclitus (among others) regard the world order as a manifestation of divine justice; they see divine action in the order itself, not (as the Homeric view suggests) in capricious interference by the gods. But some pre-Socratic systems, especially the Atomism of Leucippus and Democritus, clearly tend to eliminate any role for a designing or controlling intelligence; given the motions of the atoms in the void for infinite past time, and given the laws of their combination, nothing else is needed (in the Atomist view) to explain the existence, maintenance, and eventual dissolution of the world order.[17]

According to Plato, Socrates was interested in naturalism early in his career, but was disappointed, because naturalists did not try to explain how the natural order is ordered for the best by an intelligent designer (*Phd.* 96a–99d).[18] Plato accepts the belief in an intellectual designer; he criticizes the pre-Socratics for regarding the natural order as merely the product of "chance" and "necessity" without any design or purpose (*Laws* 889a–890a; cf. *Phil.* 28c–30e). When he presents his own cosmology in the *Timaeus,* he recognizes two causes – intelligent design aiming at the best and the nonteleological necessity of the "wandering" cause (47e–48e).[19] The wandering cause marks Plato's agreement with nontheistic naturalism, since he allows that some tendencies of matter are simply brute facts, with no explanation showing why it is best for them to be as they are. But in recognizing intelligence as the cause partly controlling the matter, Plato affirms a theistic view.

In Plato's view, the gods are entirely just and good, with no anger, jealousy, spite, or lust (*Ti.* 29e). They lack the desires, aims, and caprices that might well seem to be essential to the gods who are the traditional objects of propitiatory cult and sacrifice.[20] Plato recognizes this conflict with the tradition; for in his ideal state he advocates a thorough censorship of the Homeric poems and other sources of the traditional views (*Rep.* 377b–392a).

Plato's attitude is not completely alien to Greek tradition. From Homer onward Zeus leads a double life. He is sometimes a god with ordinary passions and caprices who just happens to be more powerful than the rest; but sometimes he is the controller of the universe, and his designs are above the normal anthropomorphic level of the Homeric gods.[21] Greeks were familiar with the view that the gods demand justice and punish injustice (in later generations or in an afterlife); but they had not succeeded in reconciling this view with the presuppositions of propitiatory sacrifice, which sought to placate the gods by material transactions independent of the moral character of the sacrificer.[22]

Some of the tensions between different elements of the traditional views can be seen in Euthyphro, a self-styled expert in piety. In prosecuting his father for causing the death of a slave, he violates a traditional bond of filial loyalty (whose influence is strong in, e.g., the Aeschylean Orestes).[23] On the other hand, failure to act might be taken to show indifference to the pollution resulting from unpunished homicide; and Euthyphro himself argues that if an injustice has been committed, the gods demand punishment for it (*Euphr.* 4b7–c3, 5d8–6a5, 7b7–9). He tries to reconcile his view of the gods' demands with his other moral convictions; but he has not worked out a satisfactory connection between his religious and his moral views. At first, he claims that the approval of the gods by itself determines what is pious (9e1–3). He is shown that this claim makes the gods' moral outlook, and therefore the requirements of piety, the mere product of their arbitrary will; and then he agrees that the gods demand piety and justice because of the nature of these virtues themselves, not simply because the gods happen to approve of justice and piety (10d–11b). Euthyphro is by no means a thoughtless or unenlightened representative of traditional views; and Socrates' interrogation of him shows that when the moral component of traditional views receives its proper emphasis and articulation, it undermines other elements of traditional views.[24]

People were wrong, but not completely wrong, to suppose that Socrates and Plato were abandoning belief in the gods of Athens and the gods of the Greeks, and thereby shattering people's conception of what it meant to be Athenians and Greeks.[25] In the *Clouds* Aristophanes presents Socrates as a believer in nonpersonal cosmic forces, rather than the gods who support morality;[26] his charge is false and probably malicious, but not entirely baseless.

III. NATURALISM, METAPHYSICS, AND EPISTEMOLOGY

Naturalism could never have been taken seriously if naturalists had claimed to rely exclusively on the evidence of naive observation and appearance; from this point of view it does not seem that natural processes are as regular as the naturalists claim they are. The naturalist must claim to describe some reality that underlies and explains the appearances, and so must claim to have some cognitive access to this reality, beyond what is immediately accessible to the senses; this cognitive access must come through reason, argument, and theory.

By relying on reason against the senses, we discover the nonapparent facts underlying the apparent, and in doing so we discover (according to the naturalists) "nature" (*phusis*) as opposed to mere "convention" (*nomos*).[27] "Convention" consists of the beliefs that rest on mere appearances and that have no basis in "nature," which is the reality discovered by reason. Democritus states the contrast sharply. He argues that all the properties recognized by the senses are mere matters of convention, and have no basis in reality: "By convention there is sweet, bitter, hot, cold, color, but in reality atoms and void" (Sextus Empiricus, *A.M.* VII 135).

While naturalists agree in drawing this contrast between nature and convention, they do not agree about the character of the reality that reason discovers. Plato explores some of the questions raised by two accounts of reality: Heraclitus's claim that there is far more change and instability than the senses reveal to us, and Parmenides' claim that there is no change at all.

Aristotle testifies to Plato's early interest in the Heraclitean doctrine of flux. According to Plato himself, "Heraclitus says somewhere that everything passes away and nothing remains, and in likening beings to the flow of a river says that you could not step into the same river twice" (*Cra.* 402a).[28] Elsewhere he ascribes to Heraclitus the view that everything "is always being drawn together in being drawn apart" (*Sph.* 242e2–3). Plato thereby implies that the doctrine of flux includes two claims.[29]

The first claim is about succession of properties in the same subject over time. Heraclitus argues that there is more change over time than we suppose there is. The river has been replaced by a different one when we step into "it" for the second time; for, since it has different waters, it violates our assumption[30] that X is the same from time t_1 to time t_2 if and only if X has the same components at t_2 that X had at t_1. The same assumption implies that trees, rocks, and other apparently stable things go out of existence during the time when we suppose they are stable (since everything is always having some of its matter replaced).

The second claim about flux is about compresence of opposite properties in the same subject at the same time. We suppose that things have stable, fixed, and unqualified properties; for we suppose that some things are straight and other things are crooked, some good and others bad, some just and others unjust. In fact, however, things lack this sort of stability; they are both "drawn together" and "drawn apart" at the same time (not just at different times, as in the first kind of flux), and in general opposites are compresent in them. One and the same letter at the same time is both straight (if it has a straight stroke) and crooked (if it has a crooked stroke), sea water is good (for fish) and bad (for human beings), and striking a blow is just (if done by an official exacting a punishment) and unjust (if done by an individual in a private feud).

For these reasons Heraclitus believes in universal flux and instability. His claims provoke an extreme reaction in Parmenides, who rejects the possibility of change altogether (D.K., 28 B 5.7–9). Parmenides affirms that we cannot speak of, think of, or know, what is not; but any true cosmology requires the existence of change and requires us to be able to speak and think of what is not (since change requires something to become what it previously was not); hence no cosmology is true.[31]

Parmenides draws these startling conclusions from premises that seem self-evident, even trivial. He argues:

1. We cannot think (say, know) and think nothing (since thinking nothing is not thinking at all).
2. But what is not (or "not being") is nothing.
3. Hence we cannot think (say, know) what is not.

Parmenides assumes that thinking, saying, and knowing are analogous to other activities referred to by transitive verbs. For to kick or grasp what is not is to kick or grasp nothing, and so is not to kick or grasp at all; similarly, it seems obvious that to think or say what is not is to think or say nothing, and so not to think or say at all; and to know what is not would be to know what is false, and so not to know anything at all. To Parmenides' naturalist successors, his argument seemed largely convincing; and they tried to show in various ways that their cosmological principles did not require the sort of reference to "what is not" that Parmenides had challenged.[32]

Heraclitus and Parmenides reach their conclusions because they reject the senses in favor of reason. Parmenides goes further than Heraclitus; he rejects the evidence of the senses altogether, since they seem to present a world that includes change. The belief in change is simply a result of human convention (D.K., 28 B 8.38–9). Parmenides, however, does not try to abolish cosmology; instead he confines it to "belief" or "seeming" (*doxa*); he seeks to give the best account he can of how things appear, while denying that this appearance corresponds to any reality. Parmenides, like Heraclitus, evidently does not intend this skepticism about the senses to extend to reason as well.

Democritus follows Heraclitus and Parmenides in relying on reason against the senses; but he develops a skeptical argument, from conflicting and equipollent sensory appearances. If the same water appears cold to you and warm to me, there is no reason (Democritus claims) to prefer either your appearance or mine (the two appearances are equipollent); but they cannot both be true (since they are contradictory), and so they must both be false (Aristotle, *Met.* 1009a38–b12; cf. Plato, *Tht.* 152b–c). The same form of argument applies to all colors, sounds, smells, tastes, temperatures; and so things cannot really have any of these properties.

In contrast to ordinary sensible things, the atoms that constitute reality have, in Democritus's view, only weight, shape, size, and motion. But this restriction on their properties does not seem to protect them against skeptical argument. For Democritus claims that the characteristics of the atoms explain the appearances of sensible things, because, for instance, sharp atoms produce bitter tastes; but if sensory evidence is totally unreliable, the sensory evidence and analogies that support the claim about sharp atoms are apparently worthless. And so Democritus's skeptical argument seems to undermine his own theory. As he makes the senses say in a conversation with reason, "Wretched mind, do you take your proofs from us and then overthrow us? Our overthrow is your downfall" (D.K., 68 B 125; cf. Aristotle, *Met.* 1009b11–12).

The sophist Protagoras reacts to the skeptical argument not by supposing (as Democritus does) that there is some objective, mind-independent world that we cannot claim to know, but by rejecting the basic naturalist contrast between reality and appearance. He claims that "a man is the measure of all things, of those that are, of how they are, and of those that are not, of how they are not," and that "as things appear to each of us, so they are" (Plato, *Tht.* 152a). According to Protagoras we should not argue that if the wind appears warm to you and cold to me, then at least one of us must be wrong; instead we should conclude that the wind is both warm and cold, and that there is no objective, mind-independent world. He rejects a presupposition of Democritus's naturalist argument – the existence of some objective "nature" that can be contrasted with "convention."

In considering Protagoras we have passed beyond the succession of naturalists. For Protagoras raises the questions about skepticism not because he is interested in cosmological speculation, but because he is concerned with the epistemological issues that affect his views of morality and moral education. To understand these views and their effect on Plato we must turn to the influence of Socrates.

IV. POLITICAL DEVELOPMENTS AND MORAL QUESTIONS

In Aristotle's view, Socrates turned philosophy away from the study of nature as a whole to the study of moral and political questions (*Parts of Animals* 642a25–31). Greek philosophy began with the application of rational, critical, argumentative, nonmythical thinking to cosmology and to nature as a whole. In the lifetime of Socrates reflection on morality and human society ceased to be the monopoly of Homer and the poets; it became another area for critical thinking.[33] Critical thinkers began to recognize a potential conflict that had long been present in traditional Greek thinking about ethics. To see the sources of the conflict we must review some earlier developments.

The moral outlook of the Homeric poems permanently influenced Greek thought.[34] Homer expresses the highest admiration for a hero such as Achilles – well-born, rich, powerful, fiercely jealous of his own honor, concerned to display his power and status, and comparatively indifferent to the interests of other members of his community.[35] Throughout Greek history the self-absorbed, jealous hero remains an object of fear, resentment, suspicion, and admiration all at the same time. He appears in Plato's dialogues in the figures of Callicles and Alcibiades;[36] and he appears again later on a larger scale in Alexander the Great, who modeled himself on Achilles.

Admiration for this sort of Homeric character fits badly with the attitudes that tended to favor Greek democracy – or indeed any sort of constitutional system concerned with the interests and rights of the governed. The first moves of Athens toward democracy involved equal treatment for rich and poor under written laws; the constitution of Solon removed politics and law from the whims of aristocratic families. The strengthening of democratic institutions deprived aristocrats of a traditional field for the expression of their competitive impulses. Moreover, the growth of attitudes favorable to democracy illustrates the remark of the historian Herodotus that different societies encourage different outlooks and different patterns of education and upbringing (e.g. Herodotus, II 35.2, VII 102.1).[37] Herodotus has Athens especially in mind, for he remarks on how the introduction of democracy in Athens increased the Athenians' enthusiasm for their city (V 78). If it had this effect, it must correspondingly have tended to create conflicts with some aspects of the Homeric outlook.

On the other hand, democracy did not require completely uncompensated sacrifice from the upper classes. Between the end of the Persian Wars in 478 and the outbreak of the Peloponnesian War in 431, Athens reached the peak of its power and prosperity in the Greek world. It kept a stable democratic constitution (without interruption from 506 to 411) and established an empire among Greek states (in the Aegean islands and in Asia Minor) that had been its allies against the Persians. The stability of the democracy and the extension of the Athenian Empire were probably not unconnected. Athens was governed by an assembly in which all citizens (adult, male, free) were eligible to attend, speak, and vote; but the richer and nobler families still tended to take a leading role as speakers, as generals (elected officials with both military and political roles), and as govenors of the dependent states in the Empire. Contributions from the dependent states were used not only for their original purpose of defense against the Persians, but also to build temples in Athens and to pay Athenians for sitting on juries (large courts, chosen by lot from the citizens). In this way the Empire both paid for some aspects of Athenian democracy and offered the upper classes a constructive way to display their Homeric ambitions and competitive spirit. Aristocrats like Cimon, Aristeides, and Pericles could compete for leadership in a great city with extensive military and political responsibilities overseas; and less preeminent members of the upper classes could hope to govern a subject city in the Empire.

In 431 the Peloponnesian War broke out between Athens and Sparta. It lasted for twenty-seven years (with interruptions), including the first twenty-four years of Plato's life.[38] Athens was eventually defeated, partly as a result of treachery by an oligarchic fifth column. After a long war, Athenian resources of money and manpower were severely strained. The strains encouraged opponents of democracy to plot, with Spartan help, to set up an oligarchic regime and to abolish the democratic assembly and jury-courts. The first result of these plots was the short-lived regime of the Four Hundred in 411–10; the second result was the regime of the Thirty, which came to power (with Spartan help) after the end of the war in 404 and was defeated by the supporters of democracy (with Spartan help, after a change of kings in Sparta) in 403. This was the oligarchical junta that included two of Plato's relatives, Critias and Charmides (who appear in the *Charmides*).[39] These two were also associates of Socrates; and Socrates' connections with such dubious characters probably help to explain why he was tried and convicted, under the restored democracy, of not recognizing the gods of the city and of corrupting the young men.[40]

Thucydides' history suggests how the Peloponnesian War may have affected moral and political attitudes. Thucydides interprets the war as a manifestation of the conflicts resulting from antagonisms between the perceived interests of different classes and groups in a state. He suggests that a relatively stable state is the product of some force strong enough to keep the peace and to assure some protection for the different groups; but when one or another group sees a chance to take the dominant place, it takes the chance (III 82.2; V 89, 105.2). Since war involves an external power willing to support a revolution, it tends to increase political instability within a state. Thucydides describes the civil conflict in Corcyra (esp. III 82–5) that resulted from Athenian support for the democrats and Spartan support for the oligarchs. He intends this to indicate the pattern followed by civil wars all over the Greek world – and eventually Athens itself. In these circumstances, according to Thucydides, the basic tendencies of human nature – the desire for security for oneself and domination over others – inevitably come to the surface.

The Peloponnesian War created the sorts of tensions in Athens that would appear to support Thucydides' analysis. Obligations to the community required greater sacrifice and presented a clearer conflict with the self-seeking "Homeric" pursuit of one's status, power, and pleasure. In political terms people had to decide whether or not to plot against the democracy to bring off an oligarchic coup. In moral terms they had to decide whether or not to ignore the demands of the community, summed up in the requirements of "justice," in favor of their own honor, status, power, and in general their perceived interest. Plato was familiar with people who preferred self-interest over other-regarding obligation; his own relatives, Critias and Charmides, made these choices when they joined the Thirty Tyrants.

Arguments from natural philosophy did not restrain people like

Critias and Charmides. Democritus argues unconvincingly that the requirements of justice and the demands of nature, as understood by Atomism, can be expected to coincide.[41] Protagoras rejects the view that moral beliefs are true and well grounded only if they correspond to some reality independent of believers; admittedly they are matters of convention, but so are all other beliefs about the world. This line of argument removes any ground for preferring nature over convention, but at the same time seems to remove any rational ground for preferring one convention over another. Matters of convention are the product of human agreements and cannot be taken to rest on any basis independent of these agreements. Now it seems obvious that some provisions of law and other moral and social norms are matters of convention, for they are established by human enactment, differ from one society to another, and can be changed by new legislation. It is easy to infer that they have no standing in any independent reality, and that if the requirements of other-regarding morality conflict with the demands of self-interest, there is no reason to pay attention to other-regarding morality. Self-interest might appear to be nonconventional, determined by human nature, and therefore entitled to override the purely conventional demands of morality.

This challenge to other-regarding morality and justice is most easily seen in some passages in Thucydides, in Antiphon the sophist, and in Plato's characters Callicles (in the *Gorgias*) and Thrasymachus (in *Republic* Book I); and it is presented in comically exaggerated form by the "Unjust Argument" in Aristophanes' *Clouds* (1075–82).[42] Plato might reasonably conclude that none of the philosophical outlooks of his naturalist contemporaries and predecessors promised any convincing defense of other-regarding morality.

V. POLITICAL ISSUES

The second half of the fifth century provides the dramatic setting of the dialogues, and it is the appropriate background for understanding many of Plato's moral and political reflections. But he wrote the dialogues during the rather different circumstances of the fourth century. The democratic regime that was restored in 403 lasted through the rest of Plato's lifetime, past his death in 347, and even beyond the conquest of Greece by Alexander (who died in 323). Plato did not know, as we do, that he was living in the last years of Athenian power and independence. On the contrary, he is likely to have been impressed – and quite rightly – by the stability of democracy in Athens. In the fourth century the essential institutions of democracy remained, even without an empire to pay for them, and the burden of paying for them must have fallen more heavily on the richer citizens; still, there were no further attempts at an oligarchic revolution.[43]

These features of fourth-century Athens perhaps help to explain Plato's attitude to existing political systems. He does not offer proposals for the reform of democracy;[44] nor does he advocate a violent antidemocratic revolution of the sort that his relatives had attempted at the end of the Peloponnesian War. However much he objects to democracy, he assumes that, practically speaking, the Athenian democracy is stable, and that no feasible alternative is likely to be superior.

In dismissing practical alternatives to democracy, Plato refuses to advocate oligarchy on the Spartan model; and on this point he stands apart from the oligarchs of the fifth century. The main rival to democratic Athens, with its relatively free, unregulated, tolerant, and open-minded social and cultural atmosphere,[45] was the rigidly controlled, militaristic, and oligarchic society that developed in Sparta.[46] Plato certainly admires some aspects of Sparta – in particular its systematic and rigorous policy of state-supervised upbringing, education, and indoctrination that regulated every aspect of life for the ruling class; but this admiration does not lead him to admire the moral and political outlook that underlay the Spartan way of life, or to suppose that it would be better to replace the Athenian democracy with a constitution modeled on Sparta. While he argues that the "timocratic" type of constitution found in Sparta (*Rep.* 547b–548d) is, as such, superior to democracy as such, this does not lead him to advocate an attempt to imitate Sparta. His admiration for Sparta is excessive and misguided, but still highly selective and critical.[47] The disastrous experiments of two pro-Spartan regimes – first the Four Hundred and then the Thirty – had shown that oligarchy did not arouse broad enough support in Athens to be maintained without force, intimidation, and foreign military aid. Plato might fairly conclude that critics of democracy needed to reject the crude, brutal, and ultimately self-defeating tactics that had given oligarchy a bad name in Athens.[48]

Plato's doubts about the prospects of gradual reform or a purely political revolution rest partly on his views about the sources of political conflict. For existing cities he agrees with part of Thucydides' analysis. In Plato's view, every city contains the sources of the instability that sometimes breaks out in open struggle; for each of them is really not just one city, but two – the city of the rich and the city of the poor (*Rep.* 421d–422a, 422e–423b). Here Plato recognizes the conflict of perceived interests that results in class conflict and, in the appropriate circumstances, in civil war and revolution. He even agrees with Thucydides' view that people's perceived interests will conflict as long as the dominant class consists of either the rich or the poor. He argues, however, that class conflict is not inevitable; to avoid it, the ruling class must be removed from the conflicts that result from private property, and must educate the other citizens in a true conception of their interest.[49] Though Plato's proposals for resolving class conflict are certainly open to objection, his diagnosis of the conditions that need to be removed is defensible in the light of Greek, and especially Athenian, historical experience.

These political problems lead Plato back to ethical problems. The conflict between justice and self-interest for the individual, and the conflicts between the interests of different groups and classes within a state, both result from a particular conception of the interests of individuals and groups. Plato seeks to show that a correct understanding of human interests and welfare will show why neither conflict needs to arise.

VI. THE SOPHISTS

Socrates and Plato could not take it for granted that moral and political questions were appropriately treated by philosophers – by those who recognized some allegiance to the forms of inquiry begun by the naturalists. They had to define the subject matter and methods of philosophy in contrast to the claims of other outlooks and approaches. The two main rival approaches that Plato confronts are those of the sophist and the rhetorician. We must see why he regards them as serious rivals whose claims need to be disputed.

Once democracy was firmly established in Athens, the popular assembly became used to exercising its power to make the vital decisions and to scrutinize the conduct of political leaders. A successful politician had to be a good speaker who could present a convincing case to a critical audience.[50] Since the Athenians had no newspapers, radio, or television, they relied on political speakers for information as well as for advice about what to do. A speaker who was ill-informed or incapable of using his information to reason cogently could expect to be beaten by someone who could show himself to be a better-informed and more reliable adviser. Gradually the role of "politician" (*politeuomenos*) became more professional, and the trained and well-informed speakers tended to dominate debate in the assembly.[51] Systematic instruction that would help in these areas would be useful to the aspiring political leader. This instruction was provided by sophists.

"Sophist" (*sophistēs,* derived from *sophos,* "wise") occurs in fifth-century Greek as a nonpejorative term applied to experts in different areas.[52] In the second half of the century the term is applied especially to teachers offering higher education for fees. The education varied in content from sophist to sophist, but its main goal was to equip someone to take an active part in public life (*Prt.* 318d–319a). The leading sophists traveled from city to city and gained an international reputation as "stars" in Greek cultural life. The *Protagoras* (309a–314e) describes the excitement aroused in upper-class Athenian circles by the visit of the eminent sophist Protagoras, and the sense of anticipation among his potential students.

Sophistic also aroused suspicion, especially among people who thought that someone's birth, family, and gentlemanly upbringing gave him a right to be listened to. From this conservative point of view, sophistic training might seem to make people too clever by half, and the sophists might be accused of teaching unscrupulous people the skills they needed to achieve undeserved success. This is the attitude of Anytus in the *Meno* (91a–92e); and it helps to explain why Socrates at his trial suggest that his accusers want to arouse prejudice against him by accusing him of being a sophist (*Ap.* 19d–e).

Many modern readers have supposed that Plato blames the sophists as a group for defending a specific theoretical position that he takes to be responsible for some decay in moral standards that he sets out to correct.[53] In particular, it is sometimes supposed that the rejection of conventional morality by such speakers as Callicles in the *Gorgias* and Thrasymachus in *Republic* Book I is a typical result of sophistic teaching.[54]

There is no foundation, however, for this view of the sophists, or for this view of Plato's objections to them. Certainly some sophists hold the position of Callicles and Thrasymachus; Antiphon seems to have held such a position.[55] Other sophists, however, held quite a different position. Protagoras was a firm defender of conventional justice and morality; Plato never denies that this is Protagoras's view, and never suggests that Protagoras's teaching tends to turn people against conventional morality. In the *Meno* Socrates pointedly dissociates himself from Anytus's indiscriminate hostility to the sophists. In the *Protagoras* Plato's portrait of leading sophists is sometimes humorous (*Prt.* 315c–d; cf. *H. Ma.* 281a–283b), but never hostile. Both in the *Protagoras* and in the *Theaetetus* Protagoras is taken seriously; indeed Plato defends his views against premature dismissal and points out that Protagoras can be defended against Socratic objections that might satisfy us too easily (*Prt.* 350c–351b, *Tht.* 165e–168c).

Plato criticizes the sophists not primarily for their conclusions, but for the arguments they rely on. He denies that the sophists are the main influence on moral and political education; on the contrary, he argues, the prejudices of the masses determine the range of acceptable views, and the sophists simply repeat these prejudcies (*Rep.* 493a). This description most obviously fits Protagoras, whose whole epistemological position is designed to show that the views that appear true to the many are true (cf. *Tht.* 167c). But Plato thinks it also fits the sophists in general; they do not attempt to found their views on any rational basis that goes beyond the unexamined beliefs and prejudices of the majority. This is why he connects sophistic with "appearances" and "images" (*Rep.* 515a5–6; *Sph.* 232a–236d).

By criticizing sophists Plato sets standards for his own philosophical inquiries. At first sight it is not easy to distinguish Socrates and Plato from sophists. For Socrates' characteristic method of inquiry is a systematic cross-examination of an interlocutor, seeking to expose conflicts in the interlocutor's views and to reconstruct his beliefs as a result of reflection on the conflicts and on possible resolutions of them. This sort of inquiry clearly begins from commonsense beliefs and seems to rely on them at each stage; for Socrates often insists that the interlocutor must state his own view (instead of maintaining something for the sake of argument to avoid refutation; *Prt.* 331c). Why is this not the uncritical appeal to popular views that Plato criticizes in the sophists?

The use of cross-examination and refutation does not distinguish Socrates and Plato from the sophists. Though Protagoras is represented as being unfamiliar with Socratic conversation (*Prt.* 334c–335c), he was familiar with techniques of destructive argument.[56] The *Euthydemus* is an exhibition of the techniques of eristic (*eristikos*, "contentious") argument, a technique practiced by some sophists.[57] Techniques of cross-examination and refutation are obviously useful in debate and argument; and the young men who learned them from Socrates enjoyed practicing them on others.[58] But they do not distinguish Socrates from an eristic. In the dialogues his interlocutors sometimes accuse him of using eristic techniques;[59] and Plato's opponents describe him as an eristic.[60] If Plato tries to go beyond eristic to constructive argument, he needs to show how he has something more to offer than the conventional beliefs that are the sophist's stock-in-trade. In trying to distinguish Socratic and Platonic method from sophistic, we raise some far-reaching questions about Plato's epistemology.

VII. RHETORIC

Sophistic was closely connected with another development in higher education: the growth of rhetorical theory and teaching.[61] Many sophists probably included some rhetorical training in their courses of study; but there still seems to have been a distinction between a rhetorician and a sophist. Rhetoricians concerned themselves primarily with techniques of persuasion, and not with the general moral and political education promised by the sophists.[62] This does not mean that they were wholly concerned with rhetorical "form" rather than "content"; they advised their students that this opinion rather than that one was likely to be well received. But they did not engage professionally in the concerns of the sophist and the philosopher.

One of the most influential rhetoricians among Plato's contemporaries was Isocrates, whose speeches contain many implicit and explicit attacks on Plato. Isocrates regards training in rhetoric as "philosophy" in the truest sense (*Antid.* 50, 270, 285). It differs, however, from the studies practiced by naturalists, mathematicians, and eristics, because it is practically relevant and applicable. Isocrates accuses Plato of formulating absurd paradoxes about morality (*Helen* 1). In general, "plausible belief about useful things is far superior to exact knowledge about useless things" (*Helen* 5). It is pointless, in Isocrates' view, to examine the foundations of moral and political theory; one should stick to the recognized virtues (*Antid.* 84–5) and present conventional views about these in a persuasive and attractive form.

Plato's remarks about Isocrates are not completely hostile. He regards him as something between a philosopher and a politician, intellectually promising but unable to distinguish genuine dialectic from eristic (*Euthd.* 305b–306c).[63] He suggests that Isocrates has some philosophical ability (*Phdr.* 279a); but Isocrates' account of his version of "philosophy" exposes clearly the ways in which Plato thinks Isocrates misses the point.

The political role of rhetoric arouses Plato's suspicion and criticism. He asks why the Athenian democracy should regard rhetorical ability as a sufficient qualification for giving political advice, and he presents two objections against rhetoric: (1) If, as Isocrates admits, the orator does not try to reach independent rational convictions of his own on moral and political questions, he will simply repeat popular prejudices. If he simply follows the ignorant and prejudiced moral and political assumptions of the majority, his advice will not promote the common good. (2) If the orator persuades people, not because he convinces them that the course of action he advises will really benefit them, but because he arouses their feelings and prejudices, even against their better judgment, what he persuades people to do will not even be what they want to do.

In his first charge against rhetoric Plato argues that the method of democratic government undermines its stated goal – to govern in the interest of all the citizens. In his second charge he argues that government by rhetorical persuasion does not even execute the will of the majority. The rhetorician would be bad enough if he simply expressed the views that people, after reflection, actually hold; but he is even worse if in fact he does not simply express public opinion, but molds and manipulates it for his own purposes.

In attacking rhetoric, Plato also attacks a much older Athenian institution, tragic drama (*Grg.* 502b, *Rep.* 602c–606d).[64] His objections are easier to understand if we remember that the Athenian dramatic festivals took the place of some of the mass media familiar to us. Plato recognizes the cultural influence of tragedy, and assumes that people are influenced by the moral views expressed in and through the plays. He criticizes tragedy as a form of rhetoric; it makes particular moral views appear attractive to the ignorant and irrational audience, and it is written by writers who do not understand the moral questions any better than the audiences do. Euripides arouses our sympathy for Medea not because he can rationally convince us to see on reflection that Medea deserves our sympathy, but because he presents some features of her situation in ways that appeal to our prejudices. The tragedians do not know what sort of person in what sort of situation ought to arouse admiration, sympathy, or revulsion.[65]

Plato's criticisms do not show that there could be no legitimate use for rhetoric, or that everyone who practices it is morally misguided.[66] But they raise some legitimate questions about the particular social, educational, and political role of rhetoric in contemporary Athens. Some of Plato's opponents, and most notably Isocrates, presented rhetoric as a sufficient moral education for a good citizen aspiring to a leading role in public life. Plato points out that the student of rhetoric learns the moral and political assumptions that will seem plausible and attractive, but learns to scorn any systematic thinking about whether these are the right assumptions or not. Ancient Athens is not the only society that has allowed skill in nonrational manipulation to be a dominant influence in democratic debate; and for that reason the force of Plato's criticisms is not confined to his own historical situation.

VIII. SOCRATIC INQUIRY

Plato's earlier dialogues present Socrates' attempts to answer the moral questions that arose from the conflicting views of his contemporaries. Socrates relies on philosophical argument, and in particular on the sort of systematic questioning and refutation that had been begun by Zeno.[67] But in contrast to Zeno and the eristics, his aim is not purely negative. He argues constructively, in support of his own paradoxically uncompromising defense of the moral virtues. His argument is philosophical but he distinguishes himself sharply from naturalists. He does not rely on premises derived from natural philosophy, which (as the example of Democritus might easily suggest) might appear both dubious in themselves and unlikely to answer the most important questions about morality.

Socrates argues that we can be rationally convinced that there is really no conflict between justice and self-interest; the whole "Homeric" conception of self-interest, and therefore the assumption that self-interest must conflict with morality, can be shown (in his view) to rest on assumptions that we find, on reflection, we reject.

Socrates seems to Plato to promise a method and a line of argument that might explain and justify morality. But Plato sees that Socrates' promises are not completely fulfilled. Socrates wants to distinguish Socratic method from the methods of sophistic, eristic, and rhetoric; and in some transitional dialogues Plato examines these claims and tries to develop a theory of Socratic argument that will justify its claims to arrive at objective truth.

More generally, Plato's early association with Cratylus suggests to him that he must go beyond Socrates and take up the wider philosophical questions that Socrates had set aside in order to concentrate on ethics. Socrates' efforts to define the virtues assume that objectively correct answers can be found, and that they must correspond to some objective realities independent of our beliefs and inquiries. But what sorts of objective realities could correspond to our moral beliefs? And even if we can conceive what the relevant realities might be like, how can we reasonably suppose that we know anything about them?

For these reasons Plato finds himself returning to some of the metaphysical and epistemological preoccupations of the Pre-Socratics; but whereas the Pre-Socratics are forced into them by questions arising in the study of nature, he is forced into them by questions about morality.

IX. BEYOND SOCRATES

A full account of Plato's treatment of the metaphysical and epistemological questions that he derives from naturalism would be a full account of most of his middle and later dialogues. I will confine myself here to a few remarks on his treatment of the questions in Heraclitus, Parmenides, and Protagoras that I discussed earlier. In each case Plato's treatment shows his developing recognition of the interest and depth of the questions raised by his predecessors.

Plato's reflections on Socrates' search for definitions make him aware of the second type of Heraclitean flux, involving the compresence of opposites (the writing that is straight and crooked, the water that is good and bad, and so on). Plato points out that ordinary observable examples of just or good actions or people turn out to suffer compresence of opposites; bright color, for instance, is both beautiful (in some contexts) and ugly (in others), and giving back what you have borrowed is both just (in normal circumstances) and unjust (if a suicidal person asks you to return his sword).[68]

Plato, however, rejects the Heraclitean conclusion that justice itself suffers from the same sort of flux and instability. The examples just given are the sort that induce Heraclitus to infer that justice is both paying your debts and not paying them. Plato, on the other hand, infers that a different sort of account of justice is needed. Though observable types of just actions are in flux from just to unjust, it does not follow, he argues, that justice itself is in flux. Reflection on Heraclitus's problems and examples leads Plato to the sharply non-Heraclitean conclusion that justice itself must be exempt from the compresence of opposites. An adequate definition of the Forms (of Justice, Bravery, etc.) that Socrates was trying to define must, in Plato's view, show that the Forms display Parmenidean stability rather than Heraclitean flux.

In a later dialogue, the *Theaetetus,* Plato examines the first kind of Heraclitean flux, involving change over time in (what we naively take to be) one and the same object. He argues that if the doctrine of total flux is accepted without qualification, so that we deny the existence of persisting subjects altogether, it actually refutes itself; for we cannot say what is in flux, and since we cannot speak of flux without saying that something is in flux, the extreme doctrine of flux cannot be true unless it is false.[69] Once again Plato finds Heraclitus's doctrine of flux a stimulating point of departure toward a strongly non-Heraclitean conclusion.

In the *Republic* Book V Plato presents his first reaction to Parmenides. He agrees (in a sense) with Parmenides' claim that we cannot know what is not, but he disagrees (in a sense) with his claim that we cannot speak or think of what is not. His disagreement with

Parmenides rests on implicit distinction between different ways in which Parmenides speaks of "what is not." It is plausible to claim:

1. We cannot hit or kick what is not (= the nonexistent).
2. We cannot think or say what is not (= something that has no content at all); all saying or thinking must be saying or thinking something.
3. We cannot know what is not (= what is not true).

Now Parmenides' argument rules out change only if "what is not" is taken in the existential sense, as in (1); but since the crucial premises (2) and (3) seem to involve only the predicative sense, as in (2), or the veridical[70] sense, as in (3), his argument seems to be invalid. In the *Republic* Book V Plato claims that while we cannot know what is not (in sense [3]; knowledge that p implies that p is true), we can believe what is or what is not (since beliefs include true and false beliefs); and believing what is not does not constitute believing nothing (having no belief).[71] But though Plato implicitly rejects Parmenides' account of being, and hence his views about the objects of knowledge and the possibility of change, the *Republic* does not explain where Parmenides has gone wrong.

Some explanation is needed, however; for Parmenides is not refuted by a simple appeal to different senses of the verb "to be." He can remove any damaging appearance of equivocation on senses of "to be" if he can argue for a particular account of what is involved in thinking or speaking or knowing. If he can show that they are sufficiently similar to grasping and kicking and other interactions with external objects, then he can argue that speaking or thinking of what does not exist is really speaking or thinking of nothing, and therefore is not really speaking or thinking at all. And some arguments for such a conclusion seem quite plausible. We might suppose that if thinking gives us genuine knowledege of external reality, it must make some real contact with this external reality, in the way the senses make contact with it; and for the senses something like Parmenides' conclusion is true, since we cannot see or hear or touch the nonexistent. Something similar seems to be true if we try to understand speaking of something. We can use words as we can use gestures to point out and identify something; and just as I cannot point out something that is not true, I apparently cannot name what is not there. And so if we look at certain aspects of thinking, saying, and knowing, it seems natural to agree with Parmenides' assumption that they consist in some direct causal interaction with some external object, and therefore require an existing object.

If a particular conception of thinking, saying, and knowing tempts us to accept the premises that imply Parmenides' startling conclusions, then a proper reply to Parmenides should present a conception of thinking, saying, and knowing that removes any temptation to make the fatal concessions to Parmenides. Once we have the right conception, then we should be able to see that "You cannot think (say, know) what is not" is true only in a sense that does not lead to Parmenides' conclusions.

Plato's claims about knowledge and belief in the *Republic* Book V show that he thinks the appropriate alternative to Parmenides' position can be worked out. But he does not work it out in the *Republic*. In the *Theaetetus* he reexamines the Parmenidean view that since belief is like seeing or grasping, we cannot have beliefs about the nonexistent (*Tht.* 188a–189b). Here he explains why false belief will be impossible if we accept a Parmenidean view of belief; and so he asserts that we must be able, in one sense, to speak of what is not. In the *Sophist* the "Eleatic stranger" remarks that the question of how things can appear, but not be, and how one can speak of something but speak falsely "has always been full of puzzlement, in previous times and up to the present"; and then he introduces Parmenides' rejection of not-being (*Sph.* 236e–237a). The rest of the dialogue seeks to explain how, and in what sense, it is possible to speak and think of what is not. The main speaker is a visitor from Elea, the home of Parmenides and Zeno; his presence indicates the importance that Plato attaches to Parmenides' views. On the other hand, the visitor sharply emphasizes the basic disagreement with Parmenides that must result from a full inquiry into not-being.

The challenge of skepticism is important for Plato, since, following Socrates, he believes in the possibility of knowledge, which the skeptic denies. It is equally important for him to reject Protagoras's solution to the question raised by skepticism. For Plato believes in the existence of a knowable mind-independent reality, whereas Protagoras believes that we can refute skepticism only if we agree with the skeptic that there is no knowable mind-independent reality. In developing his theory of Forms, Plato makes it clear that he rejects both skepticism and Protagoras's solution; but in the early and middle dialogues Plato simply assumes the falsity of Protagoras's position and discusses it only briefly.[72]

In the *Theaetetus*, however, Plato discusses both Protagoras and Heraclitus at some length. He argues that Protagorean epistemology rests on an indefensible metaphysics; for it leads to the self-refuting extreme Heraclitean doctrine about change. To this extent his attitude to Protagoras is similar to his attitude to Heraclitus and Parmenides; Plato realizes fairly late in his career that the questions raised by his predecessors require a direct and fundamental examination.

The dialogues bear out Aristotle's claim that reflection on Socratic inquiry about ethics leads Plato back to the study of questions derived from the naturalists; throughout his career Plato remains a careful and appreciative critic of his predecessors. But while he faces some of the same questions, Plato thinks he can avoid the skeptical conclusions that seem to threaten the foundations of Presocratic naturalism. For he thinks we have enough firm and reliable convictions about some moral questions to justify us in arguing from these convictions to whatever conditions are required for their truth.

X. THE PLATONIC DIALOGUE

In his reflections on his predecessors and his contemporaries Plato not only had to decide what to say in defense and explanation of Socrates; he also had to decide how to say it. In distinguishing himself from naturalists, sophists, and rhetoricians, he also chose a literary form that sets his work apart from theirs.

The modern reader, used to the surviving Aristotelian corpus[73] and to the literary form of later philosophical works, naturally wonders why Plato chose to write dialogues rather than treatises. This question may rest on the false presupposition that it would have been more natural for him to choose to write continuous treatises. Since Plato was a pioneer in writing moral philosophy (as opposed to including some remarks on morality within a treatise on natural philosophy), there was no established literary form for the sort of thing he was trying to write.[74] Even natural philosophy had no fixed literary form.[75] Among the earlier Pre-Socratics, Parmenides and Empedocles wrote in epic verse, while Heraclitus apparently expressed his views (at least sometimes) in aphorisms, maxims, riddles, and paradoxes. The Pre-Socratics offered a wide choice of literary forms; and in any case Plato had no special reason to believe that any of these literary forms used for natural philosophy was the right way to develop arguments in moral philosophy.

Herodotus and Thucydides (and no doubt other historians whose works have not survived) may have suggested to Plato some aspects of the literary form of the dialogues. Both historians insert speeches ostensibly delivered on particular occasions to advocate a particular decision by a king, or generals, or an assembly, or to encourage troops before a battle. They also use fictitious speeches and debates to explore the moral and political issues involved in a particular incident or situation. Herodotus inserts a debate on different Greek political systems during an episode in Persian history (Herodotus, III 80–2); and Thucydides inserts an elaborate dialogue between Athenians and Melians about whether the Athenians ought to massacre all the Melians for their support of Sparta (Thucydides, V 84–113). The historian probably does not intend to tell us what was said on that occasion by that particular speaker; he wants to draw our attention to the moral and political issues raised by situations of that kind.

The same use of debates to present the different sides of moral and political questions is an obvious feature of Athenian tragedy.[76] Tragic characters often face difficult decisions and debate their rights and wrongs; and especially in the plays of Euripides and the later plays of Sophocles,[77] the debates are quite elaborate, theoretical, and sometimes rhetorical. Plato's audience was used to dialogue as a medium for exploring moral questions.

Athenian comedy is equally relevant. The interlocutors in Plato's dialogues are not the heroic figures from the distant and legendary past who appear in tragedies. They are Socrates' upper-class contemporaries, in conversation with Socrates, who is himself in many ways an ordinary (even exaggeratedly ordinary) plain-spoken person. For the dramatic presentation of such characters Plato might reasonably turn to comedy.

A comic hero in Aristophanes – Dikaiopolis in the *Acharnians* provides a good example – is usually unheroic, outside the circle of Athenians who distinguished themselves by their wealth, breeding, and military and political careers. Though he appears to be an ignorant and vulgar peasant, Dikaiopolis in fact understands (according to the play) why the Peloponnesian War broke out, while his "betters" do not; and he stands alone against them in concluding his own peace treaty with the Peloponnesian enemy. The "establishment" figures mentioned in the play – including the "Olympian" Pericles who started a war for the sake of a few prostitutes and the boastful, empty-headed general Lamachus – are shown to be pretentious and foolish. Dikaiopolis outwits his "betters" by his clever tongue and his understanding of the situation.

After he makes his private peace with the Peloponnesians, Dikaiopolis begins his own idyllic peacetime existence, fulfilling the dreams of Athenians who were suffering from the rigors of war. This fantastic element is developed further in the utopian Cloudcuckooland of the *Birds.* This use of utopia and fantasy to make a serious moral and political point may well have helped to suggest to Plato that the description of a utopia (not without some humorous elements; cf. *Rep.* 372c–d) would be an effective way to present some of his own moral and political views.[78]

While details cannot be pressed, these features of comic heroes suggest that Athenians who had laughed at the foolishness of Aristophanes' Athenian generals and cheered for Dikaiopolis or Lysistrata would be able to appreciate the comic aspects of Socrates and the other characters in the dialogues. Many of the interlocutors are quite strongly characterized in ways that make them suitable for deflation. Often they are Socrates' social superiors – the aristocrats in the *Laches* and *Charmides,* the leading intellectuals and experts in the *Protagoras, Gorgias, Ion,* and *Hippias Minor* and *Major.* Often they begin with a rather complacent, even patronizing, attitude to Socrates; but it eventually turns out that he understands more than they do. Socrates says that while he cannot claim to know that his views are true, he has found that anyone who rejects them has turned out to be "laughable" (*Grg.* 509a; cf. *Prt.* 355a6); Plato underlines the comic side of his dialogues, the unlikely hero deflating the pretensions of people whose reputation exceeds their understanding. Aristophanes enables us to understand the comic aspects of the dialogues better, not merely because the dialogues are sometimes funny, but because a particular type of comic situation that occurs in Aristophanes provides one of the most important elements – comic and serious at the same time – of the dialogues.[79]

These precedents from historical and dramatic works may help to explain why Plato decided that fictional debates and conversations were the best way to explore the moral and political issues that concerned him. But they do not explain the distinctive character of the Platonic dialogues. As we have seen, Plato regards dramatic presentation, in itself, as nothing better than a form of rhetoric, tending to move and persuade hearers or readers, regardless of the merits of the case. Mere conversational interrogations may seem to be displays of bullying eristic. The sort of argument that Socrates thought he had discovered required some different medium.

Plato chose the dialogue because he thought it stuck most closely to the essential features of Socratic argument. Socrates claims that the systematic, rule-governed form of interrogation that he practices allows him to secure his interlocutors' agreement to moral positions that they would have firmly, often indignantly, rejected before they faced Socrates' questions. The interrogation is not simply the way Socrates happens to reach his conclusion on this occasion; the fact that the conclusion is reached through this sort of interrogation of this sort of interlocutor is part of the reason Socrates offers us for believing his conclusion. He claims that the arguments are not simply those that strike him, but arguments that actually convince a normal interlocutor who approaches the questions in the right way.[80] The interlocutor (Socrates claims) is not dazzled by rhetoric, or bullied by eristic, or overawed by elaborate disquisitions on natural philosophy; he is rationally convinced. A Platonic dialogue is meant to show how such conviction is possible.

Now if Socrates makes these claims about the epistemological role of the dialogue, and if Plato agrees with Socrates about them, he might reasonably find it difficult to present the essential elements of Socratic philosophy in any other form than the one he chooses. He might have been able to explain in his own voice what Socrates was trying to do and why Socrates thought he could do it; and such an explanation would have been useful to us. But it would scarcely have been an effective or economical method for capturing our attention and forcing us to take Socrates seriously. Since Plato takes Socratic philosophy seriously, he writes Socratic dialogues. We need not suppose that the dialogues are, or were taken to be, transcripts of actual conversations; but they are intended to communicate a central element in Socrates' defense of his moral position.

The epistemological claims implied in Socrates' use of the dialogue are themselves controversial; and once Plato reflects on these claims, he decides that they need to be modified. Modifications in the epistemological claims also require modification in the sort of dialogue that Plato regards as the best medium for his philosophical views; and so he writes different sorts of dialogues, following different rules, to achieve different ends. In some of the late dialogues, the conversational and adversarial character of some Socratic dialogues is drastically modified; the *Timaeus* and *Laws*, for instance, contain long stretches of continuous exposition. But Plato does not simply drop the Socratic dialogue characteristic of his early period. The *Theaetetus* and *Philebus* are late dialogues sharing many important characteristics with the dramatic and conversational early dialogues. Plato's choice of the dialogue form, and of a particular variety of dialogue, is determined by his philosophical aims.

It is legitimate to point out that Plato never speaks in his own person in the dialogues, and legitimate to wonder whether this is a device for dissociating or detaching himself from the arguments or conclusions attributed to the main speaker (usually Socrates).[81] The ancient evidence, however, offers no sound basis for doubting that Plato is presenting his own philosophical views.[82]

In deciding how to take the dialogues, our most important external witness is Aristotle. He has sources of information about Plato's life and philosophy that are independent of the dialogues. He mentions Plato's early association with Cratylus, and he refers to Plato's unwritten teachings. And yet he shows no hesitation in attributing the views of the Platonic Socrates[83] to Plato; his procedure would be totally unfair if Plato were known to be putting forward these views without endorsing them, and if this had been Plato's clear intention, many in the Academy would know that, and would immediately denounce Aristotle's unfairness. But while a number of ancient Platonists defend Plato against Aristotle, none of them argues that Plato does not accept the views he attributes to Socrates. Since Aristotle was in a position to know much more than we can ever know about Plato's life, we ought to accept his estimate of Plato's intentions unless we find strong reasons in the dialogues themselves for believing that Aristotle must be wrong. Until we find such reasons we should follow Aristotle in believing that the arguments and conclusions of the Platonic Socrates (and other main speakers) generally represent the views of Plato.[84]

We would have good reasons for disagreeing with Aristotle, and detaching Plato from the views expressed by the leading speakers in the dialogues, if we found that the views did not display enough unity, consistency, and coherence to be the views of one philosopher. A reasonable case can be made for the view that there are inconsistencies between different dialogues and that Plato probably recognized the inconsistencies; but we can still reasonably claim that he endorses the inconsistent views if we can attach them to different stages of his philosophical development. Aristotle again helps us here, since he gives us reason to believe that some dialogues maintain the views of the historical Socrates and others maintain non-Socratic views.[85] When we try to assess different attempts to see a plausible line of development in the Platonic dialogues, we pass from questions about Plato's intellectual background to questions about the interpretation of the dialogues themselves and about the philosophical questions they raise.

NOTES

1 A helpful book on the general topic of this chapter is G. C. Field, *Plato and his Contemporaries* (London, 1930). See the review by Harold Cherniss in *Selected Papers* (Leiden, 1977), chap. 11, from *American Journal of Philology* 54 (1933):79–83. I have given a short account of Greek thought before Plato in *Classical Thought* (Oxford, 1989), chaps. 2–4.

2 Plato's only references to himself are at *Ap.* 38b6 and *Phd.* 59b10.

3 The best of the ancient lives is Diogenes Laertius, III 1–47. We cannot trust Diogenes even when he cites an early and well-informed source; for he cites Plato's own nephew Speusippus, who succeeded Plato as head of the Academy, as a source for the story (which Speusippus is not said to endorse) that Plato was the son of Apollo (III 2). For accounts of the life of Plato see I. M. Crombie, *An Examination of Plato's Doctrines*, vol. 1 (London, 1962), chap. 1; W. K. C. Guthrie, *A History of Greek Philosophy*, vol. 4 (Cambridge, 1975), chap. 2.

4 The long controversy about the authenticity of the Platonic *Letters* is still not settled. I am inclined to agree with those who reject all of them. See Ludwig Edelstein, *Plato's Seventh Letter* (Leiden, 1966); Norman Gulley, "The Authenticity of Plato's Epistles," in *Pseudepigrapha I* (Geneva, 1972), chap. 5. For a defense of the authenticity of some of the *Letters*, including the seventh, see, e.g., G. R. Morrow, *Plato's Epistles*, 2d ed.

(Indianapolis, 1962); K. von Fritz, "The Philosophical Passage in the Seventh Platonic Letter," in *Essays on Ancient Greek Philosophy,* ed. J. P. Anton and G. L. Kustas (Albany, 1971), 408–47. The incongruity of several claims in the *Seventh Letter* (about philosophy, politics, and history) with the dialogues constitutes a strong (though not conclusive) case for rejecting the letter. But even if it is spurious, it was probably written by someone who knew Plato well and who wanted his forgery to be undetected; hence many of the more straightforward and (for contemporaries) easily verifiable historical claims may be accurate. But we should not assume that the author must be telling the truth about Plato's motives, attitudes, or aims on political or philosophical questions.

5 See W. D. Ross, "The Problem of Socrates," *Proceedings of the Classical Association* 30 (1933):7–24, esp. 16–19 (reprinted in *Der historische Sokrates,* ed. A. Patzer [Darmstadt, 1987]). Cratylus is the eponymous interlocutor in a Platonic dialogue, but Plato's unflattering treatment of him could hardly by itself have led Aristotle to believe that he must have been an early influence on Plato. As Crombie remarks: "It is incidentally interesting, in view of the fact that Aristotle tells us that it was Cratylus who persuaded Plato of Heracliteanism, that he is treated in this dialogue as a noodle" (*An Examination of Plato's Doctrines,* vol. 2. [London, 1963], 476).

6 In using this conventional label one should not forget that the later "pre-Socratics" were in fact contemporaries of Socrates and Plato. Democritus, indeed, is alleged to have lived to the age of 109 (and so to have died around 350, only a few years before Plato); Diogenes Laertius, IX 43.

7 On Pythagorean mathematics and metaphysics, see D. J. Furley, *The Greek Cosmologists,* vol. 1 (Cambridge, 1987), 57–60; C. H. Kahn, "Pythagorean Philosophy Before Plato," in *The Presocratics,* ed. Alexander P. D. Mourelatos (Garden City, N.Y., 1974), chap. 6. On the importance of mathematics see *Grg.* 507e6–508a8; *Rep.* 522c–525c. On astronomy and cosmology see esp. G. Vlastos, *Plato's Universe* (Seattle, 1975).

8 See *H. Ma.* 289a; *Cra.* 402d, 440c; *Phd.* 78d–e; *Smp.* 187a–b, 207d; *Rep.* 485b; *Tht.* 152e, 179d–e; *Sph.* 242e.

9 See *Ap.* 26d6–e4; *Cra.* 400a9, 409a7; *Phd.* 72c, 97b–98c.

10 See *Smp.* 178b–c; *Prm.* 127a–128e; *Tht.* 183e; *Sph.* 217c.

11 See *Meno* 76c; *Tht.* 152e; *Sph.* 242d–e; *Ti.* 73d7, 77c6, 78e. On the *Timaeus* see F. M. Cornford, *Plato's Cosmology* (London, 1937), 334; A. E. Taylor, *A Commentary on Plato's Timaeus* (Oxford, 1928), 650–4.

12 Democritus called his atoms *ideai* ("shapes"), using the word that Plato uses for his "Forms" or "Ideas"; see D.K. 68 A 57, B 141. Different views of the relevance of Democritus to the *Timaeus* and *Laws* are taken by Taylor, *Commentary on Timaeus,* 83–5, 355; Cornford, *Cosmology,*

210; Vlastos, *Plato's Universe,* 67. Plato's failure to name Democritus is not by itself surprising if Democritus was still alive at the time these dialogues were written (see note 6). Plato characteristically refrains from discussing the views of his contemporaries by name. He normally uses descriptions; see, e.g., *Sph.* 251b6; *Phil.* 44b–c.

13 See *Chrm.* 156d–e; *Smp.* 186b–e; *Phdr.* 270c–e; *Laws* 719e–720e. On the *Timaeus,* see note 11 on Empedocles.

14 On natural law, see Irwin, *Classical Thought,* chap. 3; Vlastos, *Plato's Universe,* chap. 1.

15 This is the subject of the Elgin Marbles, the sculptures taken from the Parthenon to the British Museum. The Panathenaic festival is mentioned as evidence of traditional beliefs at *Euphr.* 6b7–c4.

16 On popular religion, see E. R. Dodds, "The Religion of the Ordinary Man in Classical Greece," in *The Ancient Concept of Progress,* ed. E. R. Dodds (Oxford, 1973), chap. 9, esp. p. 148.

17 On Democritus's view of the gods, see Guthrie, *History of Greek Philosophy,* 2:478–83.

18 This passage may accurately describe both Socrates' and Plato's views; they may have agreed with the limitations of naturalist speculation. See R. Hackforth, *Plato's Phaedo* (Indianapolis, 1955), 127–31.

19 On the importance of the contrast between teleological reason and nonteleological necessity in Plato, see Gregory Vlastos, "Slavery in Plato's Thought," in *Platonic Studies,* 2d ed. (Princeton, 1981), chap. 7; G. R. Morrow, "The Demiurge in Politics," *Proceedings of the American Philosophical Association* 27 (1954):5–23, at 7–9.

20 In the *Apology* (26a4–5) Socrates mentions the charge against him of not believing in the gods of the city, but in "other newfangled supernatural beings" (*hetera de daimonia kaina*). We have no way of telling whether Socrates' accusers really knew anything about his religious views or (as Socrates suggests at 19c) they were simply trying to exploit the religious charges made in Aristophanes' *Clouds.*

21 For a protest against the view that gods are to be blamed for causing harm to human beings, see Zeus's remarks in *Odyssey* I 32–43. Cf. Aeschylus, *Agamemnon* 1481–8. Protests against stories of immorality among the gods appear in Xenophanes (D.K. 21 B 11) and Euripides (*Hercules Furens* 1340–6). On Xenophanes' influence on Euripides, see G. W. Bond, ed., *Euripides: Heracles* (Oxford, 1981) *ad loc.*

22 Contrast Aeschylus, *Agamemnon* 67–71 with the commonsense attitude expressed by Cephalus at *Republic* 330d–e. Plato comments on Cephalus's attitude at *Laws* 905d–907b.

23 See Aeschylus, *Choephori* 924–5. On the religious and legal issues raised by Euthyphro's action, see R. Parker, *Miasma* (Oxford, 1983), 366–

8. For related issues about pollution, see chap. 4 and pp. 196–8. See also W. A. Heidel, ed., *Plato's Euthyphro* (New York, 1902), on 4b; I. G. Kidd, "The Case of Homicide in Plato's *Euthyphro*," in *Owls to Athens*, ed. E. M. Craik (Oxford, 1990), chap. 25.

24 Plato agrees with some of the spirit of Heraclitus's remark that "the only wise thing is willing and unwilling to be called by the name of Zeus" (D.K., 22 B 32). In Plato's view, the god Euthyphro believes in is the Zeus of traditional religion (and so he "is willing" to be called Zeus), purified of the elements of traditional cult and myth (and so he "is unwilling" to be called Zeus) that conflict with his role as cosmic designer and upholder of morality.

25 The Greeks' sense of their identity as a people depended partly on their shared cults and shrines of the Greek gods, according to Herodotus, VIII 144. On the role of religion and kinship (themselves closely connected) in Greek "national" consciousness, see F. W. Walbank, "The problem of Greek nationality," in *Selected Papers* (Cambridge, 1985), chap. 1 (from *Phoenix* 5 [1951]: 41–60), esp. pp. 10–13.

26 See *Clouds* 367–381, 423–4. A naturalistic explanation of traditionally recognized divine signs is provided at 368–411.

27 On the translation of *nomos* ("convention," "custom," "law," "rule," "norm" are appropriate on different occasions), see Irwin, *Plato: Gorgias* (Oxford, 1979), 171*f.*

28 The accuracy of Plato's report is denied, on insufficient grounds, by Kirk, Raven, and Schofield, *The Presocratic Philosophers*, 2d ed. (Cambridge, 1983), 194–7. It is defended by G. Vlastos, "On Heracleitus," *American Journal of Philology* 76 (1955): 337–68, at 338–44. See also Guthrie, *History of Greek Philosophy*, 1:488–92.

29 The claim that Heraclitus's doctrine of flux covers both types of instability is supported by Plutarch, *De Exilio* 392b–c (= D.K., 22 B 91); Plutarch introduces compresence in his explanation of the river fragment. This account of Plato's interpretation of Heraclitus and Aristotle's interpretation of Plato is defended in Irwin, *Plato's Moral Theory* (Oxford, 1977), 148–53.

30 Heraclitus takes this to be assumed by common sense; it is not clear (as Plato and Aristotle point out) that he is right either about common sense or about the truth of the assumption.

31 Parmenides states his main thesis in D.K., 28 B 2.7–8; 3.1; 6.1–2, and he develops its consequences for time and change in B 8. On the interpretation of his main thesis, see G. E. L. Owen, "Eleatic Questions," in *Logic, Science and Dialectic* (Ithaca, N.Y., 1986), chap.1; M. Furth, "Elements of Eleatic Ontology," in *The Presocratics*, ed. A. P. D. Mourelatos (Garden City, N.Y., 1974), chap. 11.

32 Replies to Parmenides are discussed briefly by David J. Furley, *The Greek Cosmologists* (Cambridge, 1987), 1:42–8, and more fully by J. Barnes, *The Presocratic Philosophers* (London, 1979), vol. 2, chap. 6.

33 Hume comments on this interval between the development of natural philosophy and the development of moral philosophy (in terms favorable to himself), in the Introduction to the *Treatise.*

34 Irwin, *Classical Thought,* chap. 2, is a brief introduction to the Homeric outlook. It is discussed further by A. W. H. Adkins, *Merit and Responsibility,* (Oxford, 1960); Adkins, "Homeric Values and Homeric Society," *Journal of Hellenic Studies* 91 (1971): 1–14; A. A. Long, "Morals and Values in Homer," *Journal of Hellenic Studies* 90 (1970): 121–39; H. Lloyd-Jones, *The Justice of Zeus,* 2d ed. (Berkeley, 1983). Some relevant issues about the fifth century are discussed by J. L. Creed, "Moral Values in the Age of Thucydides," *Classical Quarterly* 23 (1973): 213–31. Adkins replies in "Merit, Responsibility, and Thucydides," *Classical Quarterly* 25 (1975): 209–20. A useful general book is K. J. Dover, *Greek Popular Morality in the Time of Plato and Aristotle* (Oxford, 1974), well discussed and criticized by Adkins, "Problems in Greek Popular Morality," *Classical Philology* 73 (1978):143–58; and C. C. W. Taylor, "Popular Morality and Unpopular Philosophy," in Craik, *Owls to Athens,* 233–43.

35 The hero's indifference to other people is only comparative; he is expected to fulfill certain obligations to others and is criticized for failing in them, as Achilles is criticized. Still, when there is a sharp conflict between these obligations to others and the hero's own power and status, he is expected to choose for himself and against others, as both Achilles and Hector do.

36 A good summary of attitudes to someone like Alcibiades is given in the speeches of Euripides and Aeschylus in Aristophanes, *Frogs* 1422–32. Significantly, it is the old-fashioned Aeschylus who turns out to be more sympathetic to Alcibiades.

37 For possible references in Plato to Herodotus, see *Rep.* 566c; *Ti.* 25c; *Laws* 609a–d, 692e (cf. Herodotus, VII 139), 805a (cf. IV 116–7), 947a6 (cf. II 37). All except the first passage are discussed by G. R. Morrow, *Plato's Cretan City* (Princeton, 1960), 91, 330, 417. P. Shorey, *What Plato Said* (Chicago, 1933), asserts confidently that Plato "had certainly read" Herodotus and Thucydides (p. 8), and that "the influence of Herodotus would be the theme for a dissertation, but is too obvious to need illustration here" (p. 447); and so he does not trouble to mention any of the evidence underlying his conviction. Nor have I been able to find any convincing evidence of clear allusions anywhere else. For a brief introduction to Herodotus and Thucydides see Irwin, *Classical Thought,* chaps. 4–5.

38 The major source for the history of the Peloponnesian War is the history of Thucydides. A good introductory modern account is V. Ehrenberg, *From Solon to Socrates*, 2d ed. (London, 1973). A useful introductory book on Athens is J. W. Roberts, *City of Sokrates* (London, 1984).

39 Both Socrates and Plato, however, also had friends and connections on the democratic side (Chaerephon the disciple of Socrates; Pyrilampes the great-uncle and stepfather of Plato). It should not be assumed that Plato's aristocratic background must have turned him against democracy. Many upper-class Athenians must have supported the democracy.

40 I have discussed some questions about Socrates' trial and its background in "Socrates and Athenian democracy," *Philosophy and Public Affairs* 18 (1989):184–205. The *Seventh Letter* purports to describe Plato's attitude to the democracy, the Thirty, and the trial of Socrates (324c–325c). But if the letter is spurious, the author's political aims may well have colored the views he attributes to Plato, and it is unwise to treat them (as most accounts of Plato's life do) as historical.

41 On Democritus's ethics, see G. Vlastos, "Ethics and Physics in Democritus," in *Studies in Presocratic Philosophy*, vol. 2, ed. D. J. Furley and R. E Allen (London, 1975), 381–408; C. C. W. Taylor, "Pleasure, Knowledge, and Sensation in Democritus," *Phronesis* 12 (1967):6–27. The writer known as Anonymus Iamblichi (in D.K. 89 #6) presents a defense of conventional morality. On this writer and Democritus, see E. L. Hussey, "Thucydidean History and Democritean Theory," in *Crux* (*Essays Presented to G. E. M. de Ste Croix*), ed. P. Cartledge and F. D. Harvey (London, 1985), 118–38. An intriguing point about Democritus's familiarity with some features of political life in his native Abdera is made by D. Lewis, "The Political Background of Democritus," in Craik, *Owls to Athens*, chap. 18.

42 The Unjust and Just Arguments are characters in the school ("reflectory") of Socrates, who does not take responsibility for what either of them says. The stupidity of the Just Argument, ostensibly representing conventional morality, suggests that Aristophanes' view of conventional morality may not have been wholly uncritical; see K. J. Dover, ed., *Aristophanes' Clouds* (Oxford, 1968), lvii–lxvi.

43 On fourth-century history see C. Mossé, *Athens in Decline* (London, 1973), chaps. 1–2; S. Hornblower, *The Greek World 479–322 BC* (London, 1983), chaps. 13–15.

44 This claim needs to be qualified, though not abandoned, in the light of the *Laws*.

45 See Thucydides, VII 69.2; Plato, *Grg.* 461e1–3, *Rep.* 557b–c. On Athenian democracy see A. H. M. Jones, *Athenian Democracy* (Oxford, 1957), chaps. 3, 5.

46 It is oversimplified, but not too misleading, to describe the Spartan constitution as oligarchical, in comparison with Athens.

47 On Sparta see, e.g., *Cri.* 52e5; *Smp.* 209d; *Rep.* 544c, 545a, 547d–e; *Laws* 631a; Morrow, *Plato's Cretan City,* chap. 2.

48 If the *Seventh Letter* is genuine, it provides important evidence of Plato's attitude to practical politics. In fact, it probably provides nothing more than evidence of how the author wanted Plato to be regarded.

49 This is the solution offered in the *Republic.* In the *Laws* Plato does not advocate the abolition of private property as a practical proposal; but he advocates other measures for the distribution and restriction of property with the same aim of preventing the sorts of inequalities between rulers and ruled that provoke civil war.

50 On the sophistication of Athenian audiences, see Thucydides, III 38.7. Cleon denounces the use of sophisticated techniques in debate; his denunciation of them is itself a standard rhetorical ploy.

51 On *hoi politeuomenoi,* see Demosthenes, 3.30–1; cf. Plato, *Grg.* 473e6. On political speakers see J. Ober, *Mass and Elite in Democratic Athens* (Princeton, 1989), chap. 3.

52 See G. B. Kerferd, *The Sophistic Movement* (Cambridge, 1981), 24. A striking fourth-century example is Isocrates, *Antid.* 235 (which, however, may involve some straining in order to suit Isocrates' argument). At 268 Isocrates refers to the Presocratic naturalists as "the old sophists." The sense and force of the term in Aeschylus (?), *Prometheus Vinctus* 62, 944, raises special problems. The passage might indicate that the term could be used in an unfavorable sense, or that it normally had a favorable sense and it is being used ironically here. The issue is complicated by questions about the date and authorship of the play. On line 62, see M. Griffith, ed., *Aeschylus: Prometheus Bound* (Cambridge, 1983).

53 Some of the main contributions to discussion about the sophists and Plato's attitude to them are: G. Grote, *A History of Greece,* 6th ed., 10 vols. (London, 1888), chap. 67; E. M. Cope, "The Sophists," *Journal of Philology* 1 (1854):145–88; H. Sidgwick, "The Sophists," in *Lectures on the Philosophy of Kant and Other Philosophical Lectures and Essays* (London, 1905); Guthrie, *History of Greek Philosophy,* vol. 3, chaps. 1, 3; Kerferd, *Sophistic Movement,* chap. 2. Sidgwick's discussion remains the best one.

54 The attack on atheism and immorality in *Laws* X is directed against naturalists rather than sophists.

55 The main evidence on Antiphon is found in D.K. 87 B 44. The interpretation of the fragment is disputed. I see no sufficient reason for denying the identity of this Antiphon with the oligarchic politician mentioned

in Thucydides, VIII 68.1. See further J. S. Morrison, "Antiphon," in *The Older Sophists*, ed. R. K. Sprague (Columbia, S.C., 1972).

56 On Protagoras, see D.K., 80 A 1 (= Diogenes Laertius, IX 55), B 1 (where "Destructive Arguments" is an alternative title for his work "On Truth"), 6.

57 The rules of the eristic game require the interlocutor to answer yes or no; he is not allowed to qualify his reply or to point out that he did not mean it in this sense (e.g., *Euthd.* 287c–d, 295b–c, 296a–b). See also *Meno* 75c–d; E. S. Thompson, *The Meno of Plato* (London, 1901), 272–85; A. E. Taylor, *Varia Socratica* (Oxford, 1911), 91–8; Kerferd, *Sophistic Movement*, 62–6. I discuss Plato's attempt to distinguish himself from eristic in "Coercion and Objectivity in Plato's Dialectic," *Revue Internationale de Philosophie* 40 (1986), pp. 49–74.

58 See *Ap.* 23c–d, *Rep.* 537d–539a. An amusing example of this kind of thing is Xenophon, *Memorabilia* I 2.39–46.

59 See *Grg.* 482d, 489b–c; *Rep.* 338d. In each case Plato goes to some lengths to make it clear that this charge against Socratic method is false.

60 See Isocrates, *Panath.* 26; *Antid.* 265–6 (cf. Plato, *Grg.* 484c).

61 Pericles is supposed to have spoken in public from a written text instead of improvising ("Pericles," in the medieval lexicon *Suda*; see R. C. Jebb, *The Attic Orators from Antiphon to Isaeos*, 2 vols. [London, 1893], 1:cxxviii); and the popular leader Cleon is supposed to have begun the use of ostentatious techniques of intonation and gesture (Aristotle, *Ath. Pol.* 28.3).

62 This distinction, suggested by *Grg.* 464b–465c, seems to me (though not to everyone) to be broadly supported by the other evidence.

63 It is widely and reasonably assumed that Plato alludes to Isocrates without naming him. For a defense of this view, see *The Phaedrus of Plato*, ed. W. H. Thompson (London, 1868), 170–83; *The Euthydemus of Plato*, ed. E. H. Gifford (Oxford, 1905), 17–20. On Isocrates and the *Gorgias*, see Guthrie, *History of Greek Philosophy*, 4:308–11; T. Irwin, *Plato: Gorgias* (Oxford, 1979), index *s.v.* Isocrates. On the *Phaedrus* see R. L. Howland, "The attack on Isocrates in the *Phaedrus*," *Classical Quarterly* 31 (1937):151–9 (speculative but interesting).

64 For further discussion, see Irwin, *Gorgias*, 211–13.

65 Indeed, tragedies mistakenly induce us to suppose that people's external fortunes and situation are the most important elements of their welfare; for they do not see that, as Socrates argues, their moral character is far more important. When Socrates claims that nothing can harm a good person (*Ap.* 41c–d), he upsets the scale of values that causes his audience to be moved in the way they are moved by tragedies. Socrates thereby rejects for himself any of the pity that would normally be excited by a

person in his situation. For further discussion, see Irwin, "Socrates and the Tragic Hero," in *Language and the Tragic Hero*, ed. P. Pucci (Atlanta, 1988).

66 Plato himself takes a different view of rhetoric in the *Phaedrus* from the one he takes in the *Gorgias* (partly because of developments in his moral psychology).

67 Aristotle's remarks about the early history of dialectical reasoning seem to suggest some role for Zeno, but insist that Socrates marks a new development; cf. *Met.* 1078b23–30 with *Sophist* fr. 1 (see W. D. Ross, *Aristotelis Fragmenta Selecta* [Oxford, 1955], 15).

68 See *H. Ma.* 293a–b; *Phd.* 74a–c, 78c–e; *Smp.* 211a–b; *Rep.* 331c–332a, 479a–c, 485b, 495a–b.

69 Plato introduces Heracliteanism (embracing both types of flux, 152d2–3) to explain the consequences that he takes to follow from the acceptance of a Protagorean position. There is no basis for supposing that he himself agrees with Heraclitus about the extent of flux (of the first type) in the sensible world. See T. Irwin, *Plato's Moral Theory* (Oxford, 1977), 318 n. 27; G. Fine, "Plato on Perception," *Oxford Studies in Ancient Philosophy,* supp. vol. (1988):15–28; M. F. Burnyeat, ed., *The Theaetetus of Plato* (Indianapolis, 1990), 7–10.

70 In Greek "what is" and "what is not" are idiomatically used interchangeably with "true" and "false."

71 On the argument of *Rep.* 475–9, see G. Fine, "Knowledge and belief in *Republic* V–VII," in *Companions to Ancient Thought: Epistemology,* ed. S. Everson (Cambridge, 1990), chap. 5.

72 *Prt.* 356d4 might be an allusion to Protagoras's characteristic doctrine, which, however, is not the focus of discussion in this dialogue. *Cra.* 384c–391c contains a discussion of Protagoras's position, and 439b–440e contains a discussion of Heraclitean flux. In these ways the *Cratylus* (which I take to be a middle dialogue, earlier than the *Phaedo*) anticipates the *Theaetetus* and shows that the *Theaetetus* indicates Plato's return to questions that had occupied him earlier (just as the *Sophist* returns to some questions raised in the *Euthydemus,* which I take to be an early dialogue).

73 In fact, Aristotle also wrote dialogues, though they survive only in fragments.

74 There are some references to "Socratic discourses"; see Aristotle, *Poet.* 1447a28–b20, *De Poetis* fr. 4 (in Ross, *Aristotelis Fragmenta Selecta);* Field, *Plato and His Contemporaries,* chap. 11. But we do not know their historical relation to Plato's dialogues.

75 The fragmentary character of our surviving evidence on Anaxagoras and Democritus, for instance, makes the exact literary form of their works

obscure, though some of their works must presumably have been continuous treatises. Kirk, Raven, and Schofield, *Presocratic Philosophers*, 356, suggest that in fact Anaxagoras wrote only one book. Democritus wrote a large number of works, perhaps including a body of brief ethical aphorisms (though many of the extant ethical aphorisms are post-Democritean). It is interesting, though we cannot tell how significant it is, that one fragment of Democritus presents a conversation between the intellect and the senses (D.K., 68 B 125, quoted in section 3).

76 The story that Plato wrote tragedies but burned his compositions after hearing Socrates (Diogenes Laertius, III 5) is as worthless as most stories about Plato's life are; it might well be the invention of someone who was struck by the dramatic qualities of the dialogues and their criticism of tragedy.

77 These features are especially clear in (e.g.) the *Hecuba* and *Troades* of Euripides and in the *Philoctetes* and *Oedipus Coloneus* of Sophocles. See further F. Solmsen, *Intellectual Experiments of the Greek Enlightenment* (Princeton, 1975), chap. 2.

78 It has sometimes been suggested that there is some connection between the views on marriage and property in the *Republic* and the views parodied in Aristophanes' *Ecclesiazusae;* but there is insufficient reason to believe that the similarities between the two works indicate any knowledge by either writer of the work of the other. The vexed questions arising here are discussed by J. Adam, *The Republic of Plato,* 2 vols. (Cambridge, 1902), 1:345–55.

79 Aristophanes' speech is a comic suggestion of some aspects of Diotima's speech; see *Smp.* 191c–d, 205d–206a. On Socrates see also 215a–217a. On the *Smp.* see D. Clay, "The Tragic and Comic Poet of the Symposium," in *Essays in Ancient Greek Philosophy,* vol. 2, ed. J. P. Anton and A. Preus (Albany, 1983), 186–202, at 198; K. J. Dover, ed., *Plato's Symposium* (Cambridge, 1980), 104, 113 (who misunderstands the relation of Aristophanes' speech to Diotima's). For Plato and comedy in general some useful material is collected by R. Brock, "Plato and Comedy," in Craik, *Owls to Athens,* chap. 5. W. C. Greene, "The Spirit of Comedy in Plato," *Harvard Studies in Classical Philology* 31 (1920), 63–123, is suggestive though diffuse.

80 The importance of the interlocutor and the contrast with eristic and rhetoric are well emphasized by L. Coventry, "The Role of the Interlocutor in Plato's Dialogues," in *Characterization and Individuality in Greek Literature,* ed. C. B. R. Pelling (Oxford, 1990), chap. 8, at 174–84.

81 In this essay I am not discussing the Socratic problem. I believe that Plato's early dialogues in fact give a substantially accurate account of the views of the historical Socrates, and I believe that Aristotle's testi-

mony supports this view. See Irwin, *Plato's Moral Theory,* 291f (a brief statement), and for a fuller discussion see G. Vlastos, "Socrates," *Proceedings of the British Academy* 74 (1988), 89–111.

82 I will comment very briefly on some alleged evidence that has wrongly led some readers to discount the dialogues as sources of Plato's philosophical views. (1) The comment on written philosophical treatises at *Phdr.* 274b–278b insists that simply reading a treatise is neither the same as nor a substitute for actual philosophical reasoning. It does not say that the content of such a treatise should not be taken seriously. (And obviously it should be noted that the Platonic dialogues come closest, because of their conversational form, to overcoming the limitations of written works.) (2) The *Seventh Letter* (341b–342a) claims that philosophical truths are inexpressible (not only incapable of being put into writing). This claim goes far beyond the *Phaedrus,* and we should note that (i) the exaggerated claim suits the writer's immediate apologetic and polemical purpose (since he wants to cast doubt on the accuracy of all written accounts of Plato's philosophy); and (ii) the letter is probably spurious. (3) The *Second Letter* (314c) claims that there is no treatise by Plato and that the so-called writings of Plato really belong to "Socrates become handsome and young" (or "Socrates become handsome and up-to-date"). The same exaggeration is detectable here as in the *Seventh Letter* and the same apologetic motive is evident. (4) Some modern writers have claimed that Plato's real views are contained in his oral teaching (the "unwritten doctrines" referred to by Aristotle at *Physics* 209b11–17). For an introduction to the many, and mostly unrewarding, discussions of this question see Guthrie, *History of Greek Philosophy,* vol. 5, ch. 8. Some of the issues are set out clearly and with devastating effect by G. Vlastos, "On Plato's Oral Doctrine," in *Platonic Studies,* 2d ed. (Princeton, 1981), 379–403. It should be noticed: (i) There is no evidence to suggest that there was a large body of oral doctrine constituting a complete system that would underlie, explain, or undermine the dialogues. (ii) There is no evidence to suggest that Plato's oral teachings were esoteric; one of the firmest pieces of evidence refers to a lecture on the Good that was delivered to a general audience (Aristotle, *On the Good,* fr. 1 [in Ross, *Aristotelis Fragmenta Selecta*]). (iii) There is no evidence to suggest that Plato or anyone else took his oral teaching any more seriously than he took the dialogues. Some points may have been "unwritten" simply because Plato regarded them as tentative.

In summary, no internal or external evidence gives us any good reason whatever for denying that the dialogues express Plato's own philosophical views.

83 The treatment of the *Republic* and *Laws* in *Politics* II provides a striking

example. After speaking of the Socrates in the *Republic,* Aristotle goes on to speak of the *Laws* as another "Socratic discourse" (1265a10–13), even though (in the surviving version of the *Laws*) "Socrates" is not a speaker in the *Laws.* He then goes on to treat the *Laws* and the *Republic* as evidence of Plato's views (*Politics* 1266b5, 1271b1, 1274b9).

84 It does not follow that these main speakers represent the whole of Plato's philosophical position at the time he wrote a given dialogue.

85 On Aristotle's devices for referring to the historical and the Platonic Socrates see W. D. Ross, *Aristotle's Metaphysics,* vol. 1 (Oxford, 1924), xxxiii–xli.

3 Stylometry and chronology

For a correct understanding of Plato, account needs to be taken of the fact that his philosophical activity spanned some fifty years, during which time certain doctrines underwent considerable changes. To trace this development and so be able to identify the final expression of his thought, it is essential to know in what order the dialogues were written, but there is little help in this quest either from external sources or from the dialogues themselves.[1] Regarding the former, the only information likely to be reliable is Aristotle's statement that the *Laws* was written after the *Republic*.[2] This is repeated by Diogenes Laertius (III 37) and Olympiodorus (*Prol.* VI 24), who add that the *Laws* was still in an unrevised state on wax tablets when Plato died and was published posthumously by one of his students, Philip of Opus. As for internal evidence, cross references in the *Sophist* (217a) and *Politicus* (257a, 258b) indicate the prior composition of the former, while the *Timaeus* (27a) mentions the *Critias* as its sequel. Rather less definite is the apparent reference in the *Timaeus* (17b–19b) to the *Republic*, in the *Sophist* to the *Parmenides* (217c)[3] and *Theaetetus* (216a), and in the *Theaetetus* to the *Parmenides* (183e). There is one other important piece of evidence: In the introduction to the *Theaetetus* (143c), Plato renounces the reported dialogue form with a clear indication that the use of introductory formulae, such as καὶ ἐγὼ εἶπον ("I myself said"), and of interlocutors' replies, was becoming a nuisance. It seems unlikely, therefore, that any of his works written in this form are later than the *Theaetetus*.

In the eighteenth century and the first half of the nineteenth attempts to establish the chronological sequence were based on an assessment of each dialogue's argument, followed by the formulation of a line of development for the philosopher's ideas. Not surprisingly the subjective nature of this approach led to a considerable discrepancy among the conclusions of the various scholars,[4] so that by the 1860s hope was beginning to fade, and G. Grote, for example, was to be found declaring that the problem was incapable of solution.[5]

Two years later, however, hope was revived with the introduction of the stylistic method by L. Campbell.[6] Observing an increased use of technical terminology in what were then taken to be Plato's latest works, the *Timaeus, Critias,* and *Laws,* he calculated from Ast's *Lexicon* the number of words that each of twenty-four dialogues[7] had in common exclusively with these three. Then dividing this figure by the number of pages in each dialogue, he arrived at the average occurrence per page and arranged the dialogues in a series according to their relative degree of affinity to the three latest works in respect of vocabulary. The series was headed by the *Politicus, Phaedrus,* and *Sophist,* each showing an average occurrence of more than one word per page. Mindful of the influence of subject matter on the choice of words, Campbell did not follow his figures slavishly in drawing conclusions about chronological order, but remarked that, combined with some further observations on rhythm and word order,[8] they did at least support his view of the close temporal affinity of the *Sophist* and *Politicus* to the *Timaeus, Critias,* and *Laws.*

The usefulness of this method for determining the chronological order of works was discovered independently by W. Dittenberger,[9] who investigated two aspects of Plato's vocabulary, the first being the use of μήν ("indeed") with certain other particles. The distribution of three of these (see Table 1) enabled him to divide the dialogues into two groups according to their occurrence or nonoccurrence,[10] the later group being indicated by the presence in it of the *Laws.* The fact that all three expressions were found together in each work except for the *Symposium* and *Lysis* led him to conclude that these two works were the earliest of the second group. Since the date of the *Symposium*'s composition was fixed as shortly after 385 B.C. by what is clearly a topical allusion in it to the dispersal of Mantinea, which took place in that year,[11] he believed that τί μήν was a conversational idiom of the Dorians in Sicily, which Plato had visited a few years before. In support of this view he noted that the expression was not to be found either in earlier Attic prose or in Aristophanes, though significantly the equivalent Doric σὰ μάν did occur in the latter.[12]

Table 1. *Frequency of occurrence of certain expressions in the dialogues, used by Dittenberger as a means of ordering them chronologically*

	Pages (Didot)	τί μήν;	ἀλλὰ . . . μήν;	γε μήν	ὥσπερ	καθάπερ	ἕως(περ)	μέχριπερ	τάχα ἴσως
I									
Ap.	19.7				31		3		(1)
Cri.	9.5				8				
Euphr.	11.7				7				
Prt.	39.5				68		6		
Chrm.	18.1				9		3		
La.	17.8				12	1	2		
H. Mi.	10.1				8				
Euthd.	27.9				30	1	2		
Meno	23.3				21	1	4		
Grg.	61.6				69	1	3		
Cra.	42.3				80	2	8		
Phd.	49.2				80		16		

IIa									
Smp.	39.3		2	1	55	2	8		
Lys.	14.9	1	4		17		(2)		
Phdr.	39.0	11	1	1	27	4	5		
Rep.	194.0	34	11	2	212	5	23		
Tht.	53.0	13	1	1	47	2	10		
IIb									
Prm.	31.2	6	2	5	9		(5)		
Phil.	43.2	26	2	7	9	27	3	1	3
Sph.	39.6	12	2	5	9	14	3	1	2
Pol.	43.2	20	3	8	16	34	5	3	3
Ti.	53.0			6	10	18	3	4	1
Criti.	11.2			1	2	5	1	1	
Laws	236.8	48	2	24	24	148	16	16	11

Notes: Different texts can produce different occurrences of a given word. The figures in the tables are those provided by the scholar concerned except for large errors, when the original figure is replaced by one in parenthesis; this always refers to the Oxford Classical Text. Further details are supplied in the tables of L. Brandwood, *The Chronology of Plato's Dialogues.*

The ἕως(περ) figures for groups I and IIa, apart from those in parenthesis, were provided later by Ritter.

ἴσως τάχ᾽ ἄν at Ap. 31a3 was ignored by Dittenberger, though he included the similarly inverted form at *Ti.* 38e2.

Observing the difference in frequency of γε μήν between the *Republic* with four instances and the *Laws* with twenty-five, and recalling Aristotle's testimony about their relative dates, Dittenberger concluded that the works of group IIa in the table, where the occurrence of this expression is sparse, were earlier than those of IIb.

As the subject of his second investigation he took two pairs of synonyms, ὥσπερ–καθάπερ ("like") and ἕως(περ)–μέχριπερ ("until"), together with the pleonastic combination τάχα ἴσως ("maybe perhaps"). Although these criteria did not distinguish works of the first group from those of the second, they did reinforce the evidence of γε μήν for a division of the second group, since all the IIb dialogues with the exception of the *Parmenides* show a preference for καθάπερ over ὥσπερ and the exclusive (apart from a solitary instance in the *Apology*) use of μέχριπερ and τάχα ἴσως. As for the *Parmenides,* he was so puzzled by its inconsistencies that he was inclined to doubt its authenticity.

Dittenberger, like Campbell, considered his main achievement to be the demonstration of the lateness of the *Sophist* and *Politicus,* works that previously had been thought to be much earlier. He had also provided evidence for a later dating of the *Philebus, Phaedrus,* and *Theaetetus,* the former after the *Republic,* the latter two close to it, the position for the *Phaedrus* being especially significant in that it had frequently been regarded in the past as one of Plato's earliest compositions.

The next worthwhile contribution came from M. Schanz,[13] whose research resembled Dittenberger's second investigation in that it compared pairs of synonyms, in this case three in number, all denoting "in reality" or "in truth" (Table 2). On the basis of his figures he too divided the dialogues into three chronological groups. The last, comprising the *Philebus, Politicus, Timaeus,* and *Laws,* was characterized both by the complete absence of two of the synonyms, τῷ ὄντι and ὡς ἀληθῶς, and by the occurrence in it alone of a third, ἀληθεία,[14] while the middle group, consisting of the *Cratylus, Euthydemus, Phaedrus, Theaetetus, Republic,* and *Sophist,* was distinguished from the earlier by the presence in it of ὄντως.

Comparison of his results with those of Dittenberger reveal only slight differences; indeed his allocation of the *Sophist* to the middle group on the basis of a single occurrence of τῷ ὄντι and three of ὡς ἀληθῶς is hardly justified, considering that their frequency in rela-

Table 2. *Frequency of occurrence of three pairs of synonyms in the dialogues, used by Schanz as a means of ordering them chronologically*

	Pages (Didot)	τῷ ὄντι	ὄντως	ὡς ἀληθῶς	ἀληθῶς	τῇ ἀληθείᾳ	ἀληθείᾳ
Ap.	19.7	5		2	1	3	
Euphr.	11.7	1		1	1		
Grg.	61.6	9		7		6	
La.	17.8	2		7			
Lys.	14.9	6		2			
Prt.	39.5	2		2	1	1	3[a]
Smp.	39.3	5		3			
Phd.	49.2	14		11	2		
Cra.	42.3	1	1	3		4	
Euthd.	27.9	4	1	2	1	2	
Tht.	53.0	6	1	8	1	2	
Phdr.	39.0	8	6	7	1	2	
Rep. I–IV	80.5	13		19	2	3	
V–VIII	60.5	18	5	6	3	3	
VIII–X	53.0	10	4	3	3	9	
Sph.	39.6	1	21	3	6		
Phil.	43.2		15		7		1
Pol.	43.2		11		4	1	
Ti.	53.0		8		3	1	1
Laws	236.8		50		6	3	3
Chrm.	18.1			5			
Cri.	9.5			2		2	
H. Ma.	19.0	5				3	
Menex.	11.6	6			1	1	
Meno	23.3				2		
Prm.	31.2			1	1	1	
Epin.	14.1	1	16				1

Note: The last seven works were not included in his table by Schanz, some because, like *H. Mi.* and *Criti.*, they contained examples neither of τῷ ὄντι nor of ὄντως, others because they were considered unauthentic. The figures for these relate to the O.C.T.
[a]See note 14.

tion to the respective synonyms is the reverse of that found in the other works of this group. As for the *Cratylus* and *Euthydemus*, the argument for placing them in the middle group is weak, consisting of a solitary instance of ὄντως; in each case furthermore this is the reading of inferior manuscripts. In this connection it is also worth noting that ὄντως does not appear in the first four books of the *Republic,* casting further doubt on the reading of this form in the text of the *Cratylus* and *Euthydemus.* Unlike Dittenberger he found no evidence to suggest that the *Symposium* and *Lysis* belonged in the middle rather than the early group.

The next feature of Plato's style to be recognized[15] as useful for chronological purposes, his varying use of reply formulae, was to form the subject of several investigations during the following three decades.[16] Since these cannot all be treated here, that of Ritter, which was by far the most extensive, may be taken as representative. Convinced by the work of Dittenberger and Schanz that the *Sophist, Politicus, Philebus, Timaeus, Critias,* and *Laws* formed a discrete chronological group, he compiled a list of forty-three linguistic features, both reply formulae and others, which supported the view that these six dialogues marked the culmination of Plato's literary activity. A sample of these is reproduced in Table 3. By counting how many were present in each diaglogue he was able to determine its degree of linguistic resemblance to the *Laws,* which he regarded as the last to be written. The result was as follows: *Laws* 40, *Phil.* 37, *Pol.* 37, *Sph.* 35, *Rep.* 28, *Tht.* 25, *Phdr.* 21, *Prm.* 17, *Epin.* 12, *Cra.* 8, *Lys.* 8, *Phd.* 7, *La.* 5, *Euthd.* 4, *Prt.* 4, *Menex,* 4, *Smp.* 3, *Chrm.* 3, *Gg.* 3, *H.Ma.* 3, *Ion* 3, *Ap.* 2, *Meno* 2, *Cri.* 2, *Euphr.* 1. This seemed to confirm the view of his predecessors, that between the late works and the mass of early dialogues there was a middle group consisting of the *Republic, Theaetetus,* and *Phaedrus.*[17]

To determine whether the *Timaeus* and *Critias* belonged to the last or middle group, it was necessary to exclude from consideration those of the forty-three linguistic features, such as reply formulae, which were connected with dialogue, these two works being almost wholly narrative in form. Of the nineteen features remaining, the middle and late works possessed the following share: *Laws* 18, *Ti.* 17, *Phil.* 16, *Pol.* 16, *Sph.* 14, *Criti.* 11, *Rep.* 9, *Phdr.* 8, *Tht.* 6, *Prm.* 1 – indicating a position for the *Timaeus* and by implication its sequel the *Critias* in the last rather than the middle group.

Turning next to the question of the order of composition within each of these groups, Ritter first had to consider the possibility that an extensive work such as the *Republic* did not all appear at one time, but that the other dialogues were composed either contemporaneously with or in between parts of it. When to this end he produced statistics of his forty-three criteria for each of the ten books, it became apparent to him that, while Books II–X had a fairly uniform style, Book I exhibited a number of features that were typical of the early rather than the middle chronological group.[18] This seemed to justify the assumption that Book I was written separately some time before the rest, and the sporadic occurrence in it of expressions characteristic of the middle group[19] could be explained by the assumption that it underwent some revision before being incorporated into the larger work.

Of the dialogues in the final group Ritter considered the *Sophist* to be the earliest, since certain expressions characteristic of Plato's earlier style were still to be found in it before disappearing entirely, for example, τῷ ὄντι and ὡς ἀληθῶς (cf. Table 2). On the evidence of other features that he considered particularly significant, he antedated the *Politicus*, to the whole of the *Laws*, which he took to be the last work of all, and assigned to the *Philebus* a position contemporary with the first half of the *Laws*, and to the *Timaeus* and *Critias* one contemporary with the second half.[20]

Regarding the middle group, he refused to draw any conclusion from the fact that out of the forty-three expressions used as criteria for lateness of composition the *Republic* contained twenty-eight, the *Theaetetus* twenty-five, and the *Phaedrus* twenty-one, since the difference in the size of the figures corresponded to that of the works. A direct comparison of the *Theaetetus* and *Phaedrus* revealed that seven of the expressions favored a later date for the *Phaedrus*, only four the reverse order. Where the *Republic* stood in relation to the other two dialogues he could not say; on account of the time that the composition of such a lengthy work must have taken he was inclined to believe that the *Theaetetus*, and perhaps even the *Phaedrus* too, might have been written contemporaneously with it.[21]

About the chronological relationship of the rest of the works, which he assigned to the earliest group, he was not prepared to hazard any conjecture, since their style was generally uniform and such differences as were apparent were insignificant.

Toward the end of the last century the separate threads of research were pulled together by W. Lutoslawski.[22] His method was similar to that of Ritter, being an enumeration of the "late" linguistic features in each work, but whereas Ritter used only about 40 criteria, he amassed 500. This was made possible by the fact that for him a

Table 3. *Frequency of occurrence of selected linguistic features in the dialogues, used by Ritter as a means of ordering them chronologically*

	La.	*Chrm.*	*Prt.*	*Euthd.*	*Cra.*	*Ap.*	*Cri.*	*Euphr.*	*Grg.*	*Phd.*	*Meno*	*Smp.*	*Tht.*	*Phdr.*	*Rep.*	*Sph.*	*Pol.*	*Phil.*	*Ti.*	*Criti.*	*Laws*	*Ion*	*H. Ma.*	*H. Mi.*	*Menex.*	*Lys.*	*Prm.*	*Epin.*
Total of reply formulae	77	110	50	107	203	10	22	64	336	176	182	36	285	69	1260	315	251	314	13		568	43	95	71	5	120	486	9
1. αληθῆ λέγεις	5	2	6	3	9		2	4	5	6	4	5	2	1	9	3	1	2			7	3	5	1		3	4	
2. ἀληθῆ	1	3	1							1			9		29	7	5	2			4		(1)			6	18	
3. ἀληθῆ (λέγεις), ὀρθῶς λέγεις	6	6	6	3	10		2	5	5	8	5	5	14	2	48	10	8	6			22	(3)	(5)	(1)		10	24	
4. αληθέστατα (λέγεις), ὀρθότατα λέγεις	1				1					4		1	8	3	40	8	15	22			36						7	
5. πάνυ γε	10	16	3	20	38	3		12	48	23	27	6	5	1	40	10	7	9			4	4	12	3	1	18	28	
6. πάνυ μὲν οὖν	5		3	3	13		1	3	7	17	5		16	2	64	14	18	21	2		49		6			1	15	
7. παντάπασι μὲν οὖν	1												9	3	38	10	4	4	1		13						7	
8. καὶ μάλα				1				1		1			4	3	47	4	2	7			6					1	2	
9. πῶς;				1	1					1			4	2	32	20	17	18	1		14	1					10	
10. πῇ;															4	7	6	3			3						3	
11. (τὸ) ποῖον (δή);	1				2					1			13	4	48	32	36	33			47						3	

Pages (ed. Didot)	18	18	40	28	42	20	10	12	62	49	23	39	53	39	194	40	43	43	53	11	237	9	19	10	12	15	31	14
12. δῆλον ὅτι	7	2	15	11	17	7	3	5	15	6	12	6	1	8	47	10	10	8	1		16	5	7	3	1	5	(3)	1
13. δῆλον ὡς														3	2	8	2	5	4	1	14							
14. σχεδόν τι	7	3	3	2	2		2	1	2	6	1	3	1		12				1		2	2	5			1	1	
15. σχεδόν		1				2	1		3	2				4	7	26	13	14	9	4	122	1						20
16. ἕνεκα	8	6	14	5	9	5	2	4	31	13	2	16	12	9	69	6	22	19	13	2	111		4	(1)	1	25	(1)	3
17. χάριν			1		(1)				3			1	4	8	12	1	3	3	7	2	33				1			4
18. τὸ/τὰ νῦν		1	1							1			1		1	5	5	9	7	3	79	1	(1)					
19. χρεών (ἐστι)																1	1		3	2	57							4
20. Ionic dative form														3	6		4		2		85							2
21. πέρι (%)[a]	13	0	2	10	3	11	0	8	10	4	10	8	12	23	23	22	26	34	16	10	31	3	0	4	20	6	7	19

Note: 1. "You speak truly." 2. "Truly." 3. "(You speak) truly/rightly." 4. Superlatives of no. 3. 5 and 6. "Certainly." 7. "Most certainly." 8. "Very much so." 9. "How?" 10. "In what way?" 11. "What sort (indeed)?" 12 and 13. "It is obvious that." 14 and 15. "Just about." 16 and 17. "For the sake of." 18. "At the present." 19. "It is necessary." 20. Attic form with iota suffix. 21. "About."

The dialogues in the right-hand columns (*Ion*, etc.) were not included by Ritter in his main investigation on the grounds of unauthenticity.

[a]Numbers in this line indicate the anastrophic use of πέρι, expressed as a percentage of the total occurrence of the preposition.

characteristic of Plato's later style did not necessarily mean an expression occurring in the *Laws,* as it did for Ritter still trying to prove the lateness of the *Sophist, Politicus, Philebus, Timaeus,* and *Critias,* but one occurring in any of these six dialogues. To produce this larger total he selected what he considered to be the most important of the statistics published by earlier investigators of Plato's style, both chronologists and philologists, in the case of the latter determining himself which features were meaningful. To each he allocated a value of one, two, three, or four units, according to the degree of importance that it seemed to him to have, then after counting how many of the 500 features occurred in each dialogue, evaluated in terms of units of affinity its approximation to the final group or, in the case of the works in this group, to the *Laws.* Like Ritter he concluded that the last chronological group was preceded by one consisting of the *Republic* II–X, *Phaedrus, Theaetetus,* and also the *Parmenides.* His results, however, were vitiated by several flaws in his method, the most serious being the arbitrary nature of his evaluation of the importance of the various features and the use of some that were unsuitable, such as those which instead of being characteristic primarily of the last group were characteristic of another or of none.[23]

Contemporaneously with Lutoslawski's work, C. Baron published the results of research into Plato's use of the anastrophe of περί ("about"), that is, its occurrence after instead of before the substantive.[24] He discovered that its incidence was noticeably higher in works generally thought to be late (cf. Table 3, where it is expressed as a percentage of the total occurrence of the preposition),[25] though the behavior of the *Parmenides* was conspicuously deviant from this trend, as it had been in Ritter's investigation.[26] There appears to have been no one reason for the increasing use of anastrophe by Plato, but at least in works of the final group the avoidance of hiatus may plausibly be surmised.[27]

By the turn of the century, then, research into Plato's style had succeeded in separating the dialogues into three chronological groups, but had failed to determine the sequence within any of these, apart from some evidence to suggest that the *Sophist* was the earliest work of the last group. Shortly afterward new ground was broken, when G. Janell,[28] following comments made much earlier by F. Blass,[29] investigated the frequency of hiatus.[30] He began by

Table 4. *Frequency of "objectionable" hiatus in the dialogues, as calculated by Janell*

	Instances of hiatus	Pages (Didot)	Average per page		Instances of hiatus	Pages (Didot)	Average per page
Lys.	685	14.9	46.0	*Rep.* II	607	18.8	32.3
Euthd.	1258	27.9	45.1	*Rep.* III	706	22.0	32.1
Prm.	1376	31.2	44.1	*Rep.* V	695	22.2	31.3
Chrm.	797	18.1	44.0	*Cra.*	1319	42.3	31.2
Rep. I	901	20.5	44.0	*Menex.*	327	11.6	28.2
H. Ma.	779	19.0	41.0	*Phdr.*	932	39.0	23.9
Phd.	2017	49.2	41.0	*Laws* V	126	15.9	6.7 (7.9)
Prt.	1591	39.5	40.3	*Laws* III	121	19.4	6.2
Rep. IX	601	15.1	39.8	*Laws* XII	152	21.1	5.7 (7.2)
Rep. IV	757	19.1	39.6	*Laws* X	108	19.5	5.6
Ap.	764	19.7	38.8	*Laws* II	89	16.3	5.5
Meno	892	23.3	38.3	*Laws* XI	172	19.4	5.4 (8.9)
H. Mi.	378	10.1	37.4	*Laws* I	95	18.6	5.1
Cri.	342	9.5	36.0	*Laws* IX	189	22.2	5.1 (8.5)
Smp.	1414	39.3	36.0	*Laws* IV	77	14.7	4.8 (5.2)
Grg.	2182	61.6	35.4	*Laws* I–XII	1389	236.8	4.7 (5.9)
Euphr.	413	11.7	35.3	*Phil.*	160	43.2	3.7
Rep. I–X	6833	193.7	35.3	*Laws* VIII	94	16.9	3.7 (5.6)
Rep. VII	661	18.8	35.2	*Epin.*	40	14.1	2.8
Rep. X	664	19.3	34.4	*Laws* VII	71	27.6	2.5
Ion	312	9.1	34.3	*Laws* VI	95	25.2	2.4 (3.8)
La.	598	17.8	33.6	*Ti.*	62	53.0	1.2
Rep. VIII	615	18.6	33.1	*Criti.*	9	11.2	0.8
Tht.	1733	53.0	32.7	*Sph.*	24	39.6	0.6
Rep. VI	626	19.3	32.4	*Pol.*	19	43.2	0.4

Notes: For the figures in parenthesis, see *CPD,* 155 n.3.

The figures for *H. Ma., Ion,* and *Epin.*, which Janell omitted from his investigation, are the author's.

distinguishing two types, permissible and objectionable. In the former he included two broad classes of hiatus: those which Plato could have avoided, if he had wished, by some simple means such as elision, crasis, or the choice of an alternative form, and those involving words of common occurrence, such as the definite article and καί ("and"), where avoidance seemed to be scarcely practicable.[31] The incidence of the rest, which he classed as objectionable, is shown in Table 4.

The conclusion that Janell drew from these figures was that

Plato's treatment of hiatus differed considerably in two separate periods. In the first, comprising all the works down to the *Phaedrus*, Plato was not troubled by hiatus of any kind, but in the second, he carefully avoided those types of hiatus identified as objectionable. He made no attempt to deduce anything about chronology from the figures for the dialogues of the first period, and clearly there would be little point in it, since, if Plato's avoidance of hiatus was an abrupt, not a gradual development in his style, as the statistics would seem to indicate, then any variation in its frequency here would probably be accidental. With the last group of dialogues, however, one might well expect to find some development, either an increasing or a decreasing avoidance, or a third possibility, an avoidance that increased up to a certain point, then decreased. Janell himself, however, was not greatly concerned with chronology, his sole contribution in respect of the order of the last group of works being that "obviously Plato was prevented by death from applying the last touches to the *Phil.* and *Laws*. This seems to be the explanation of the difference in frequency of hiatus between these two and *Sph., Pol., Ti., Criti.*"

Lastly he remarked on the frequency of hiatus in the *Phaedrus* being somewhat lower than in the rest of the earlier dialogues. To explain this he accepted Blass's view, that Plato later revised it, and in support of this thesis cited several passages where hiatus appears to be avoided more carefully than usual, such as (1) 250c ταῦτα μὲν οὖν–251a τοῖς παιδικοῖς, (2) 259b οὐ μὲν δὴ–259e μέλλῃ, (3) 265a ᾤμην σε–265d ἄχαρι, and (4) 265e τὸ πάλιν–267d τίθενται ὄνομα, with two, two, one, and ten instances of objectionable hiatus respectively.[32] It could be argued that similar passages may occur in other dialogues outside the last group. Without examining the whole Platonic corpus in detail it is impossible to refute this hypothesis absolutely, but one may at least cast some doubt on it. On the basis of the figures in Table 4, *Menexenus* and *Cratylus* are the works in which there would be an expectation of finding passages with a scarcity of hiatus similar to that in the *Phaedrus*; yet in reading them one is not consciously aware, as with the *Phaedrus*, that some parts of the text contain fewer instances of hiatus than the rest.

This subjective impression can be given a numerical expression; if, for instance, with the first passage above one counts the number of words between the hiatus immediately preceding ταῦτα μὲν οὖν and that immediately succeeding τοῖς παιδικοῖς, the result is 210 (O.C.T.). For purposes of comparison, therefore, it may be described as 2 instances of hiatus in 210 words. Similarly the second passage will be 2 in 211 words, the third 1 in 196 words, and the fourth 10 in 600 words. By contrast, in the *Cratylus* (a work of roughly equal length), there are only two passages of note: 400c7–401b7 with 5 in 217 words and 404e7–405c5 with 3 in 183 words. In the *Menexenus* there are three passages: 234c6–235b8 with 2 in 124 words, 242d8–243b4 with 3 in 151 words, and 240e3–242a7 with 10 in 285 words. Since neither can be said to match the *Phaedrus*, there is some evidence to support Janell's view of an apparent tendency on Plato's part to avoid hiatus more carefully in some parts of the *Phaedrus* than in others.

Janell's inquiry confirmed the unity of the final chronological group established by earlier research. Regarding a possible development of hiatus avoidance within this group, if one assumes that it was not haphazard and that the *Laws*, at least in part, was probably the last to be written, it would appear that toward the end of his life Plato was less strict in his approach. This would be psychologically plausible in that, having demonstrated his ability to match his rival Isocrates in this aspect of prose style, he could afford to adopt a more relaxed attitude. As the incidence of hiatus in the *Philebus* is similar to that in the *Laws*, one might argue that it is the closest to it of the other five or that it represents the first serious attempt to put Isocrates' principles into practice before achieving greater success in the *Timaeus, Critias, Sophist*, and *Politicus*.

Yet another aspect of Plato's style was revealed by W. Kaluscha, who examined the rhythm of his prose.[33] Since prior to the advent of computers it was impracticable to analyze the whole text in this respect, he confined his investigation to the part of the sentence considered in antiquity to be the most important rhythmically, namely the clausula, which he interpreted as the end of a period or colon. This, for the same reason of economy, was regarded as consisting of only five syllables, either long (–) or short (⏑) metrically, yielding thirty-two different combinations.

He first looked at the clausulae of the *Laws* in order either to corroborate or to contradict Blass's belief that in the latter part of his life Plato began, under Isocrates' influence, to prefer certain rhythms to others. He then compared with them the clausulae of the *Sophist*,

Politicus, Philebus, Timaeus, and *Critias,* supposedly late works on the one hand, and those of the *Protagoras, Crito,* and *Apology,* supposedly early works on the other, to see which showed the greater similarity. Since his initial survey of the *Laws* indicated that the four most frequent combinations in every book were types ending in a long vowel and only in a few books did the fifth most frequent end in a short vowel, he decided that it was possible to regard the ambiguous quantity of the final syllable[34] as long in every case and reduced his statistics accordingly to cover sixteen combinations (Table 5).[35]

He observed a preference for five clausulae in the *Laws:* II 4, III 9, and IV 4, each of which represented one of the five highest figures in all twelve books; II 10 likewise with the exception of Books III and VIII; V, which had one of the five highest figures in half of the books. These five formed the following percentage of the total number of clausulae in each book:

I	46.9	IV	54.4	VII	54.4	X	60.1
II	55.3	V	53.1	VIII	51.2	XI	52.4
III	51.7	VI	55.9	IX	56.8	XII	54.6

That is to say, in all except Books I they were more frequent than the other eleven taken together. Conversely, there appeared to be a particular aversion to four clausulae: II 7, III 3, III 6, and III 8.

On comparing the *Protagoras, Crito,* and *Apology* with the *Laws,* Kaluscha noted the following differences: First, only two of the clausulae favored in the latter work (III 9 and IV 4) occurred frequently, but then they did so in every period of Plato's literary activity;[36] secondly, the clausulae to which there was an aversion in the *Laws* were not avoided – on the contrary, they were common, thus lending support to the view that their later avoidance was deliberate.

By contrast he found that the prose rhythm of the *Sophist, Politicus, Philebus, Timaeus,* and *Critias* was similar to that of the *Laws.* In the case of the *Philebus* it was practically identical, since its five most frequent clausulae were the same, and it avoided the four unpopular clausulae to an equal degree. In both the *Sophist* and *Politicus,* three of the five most common *Laws* clausulae also showed the highest frequencies, and the unpopular ones were avoided, though II 7 and III 6 not so carefully in the *Sophist* as in the *Politicus* and *Philebus.* In the *Timaeus* also, three of the five highest frequencies coincided with those of the *Laws,* but with a difference; whereas in

Table 5. *Prose rhythm in the dialogues: relative frequency by percentage of different types of clausula, as calculated by Kaluscha*

											Laws										
			Prt.	*Cri.*	*Ap.*	I	II	III	IV	V	VI	VII	VIII	IX	X	XI	XII	*Phil.*	*Pol.*	*Sph.*	*Criti.*	*Ti.*
I	5	⏑⏑⏑⏑–	4.2	2.6	3.4	5.6	6.4	**8.5**	6.4	9.1	7.9	6.7	5.6	5.1	3.6	5.2	4.9	7.3	4.5	5.3	**7.3**	5.9
II	4	–⏑⏑⏑–	3.8	1.9	3.6	**8.8**	**9.0**	**16.6**	**11.7**	**12.3**	**14.2**	**12.4**	**12.3**	**14.4**	**14.8**	**10.1**	**13.2**	**9.3**	6.5	5.9	**8.0**	**7.2**
	7	⏑–⏑⏑–	5.2	3.1	6.1	4.1	3.0	4.1	2.1	3.7	1.4	2.2	1.6	2.7	3.9	2.6	4.3	2.8	4.2	6.4	4.0	**8.6**
	9	⏑⏑–⏑–	4.0	3.8	4.2	4.4	3.8	6.0	6.8	7.8	5.2	4.7	6.3	5.4	6.4	5.2	6.6	4.5	5.6	5.7	4.7	4.1
	10	⏑⏑⏑––	4.2	6.3	6.6	**10.0**	**11.3**	6.6	**10.3**	**9.9**	**12.0**	**8.2**	**7.9**	**7.5**	**8.4**	6.0	6.6	**9.4**	7.5	**7.5**	**13.3**	**7.3**
III	3	––⏑⏑–	6.3	5.1	6.1	5.6	2.6	2.2	4.6	4.1	5.2	2.7	2.4	2.7	3.1	6.0	3.6	4.7	3.9	5.5	6.0	6.7
	5	–⏑–⏑–	**8.0**	**7.6**	**7.5**	3.8	4.5	2.8	5.3	5.8	2.5	5.6	3.6	4.8	4.2	3.4	3.6	4.3	4.2	6.1	3.3	6.4
	6	–⏑⏑––	**7.3**	**7.0**	**8.6**	1.8	1.1	1.6	1.8	0.8	0.8	1.3	0.8	1.2	1.4	0.4	1.0	1.5	1.2	5.1	6.0	4.5
	7	⏑⏑–––	6.9	6.3	6.4	6.2	3.0	4.7	2.8	2.5	6.3	6.0	5.6	3.0	3.4	3.7	4.6	5.7	**7.7**	6.4	4.0	6.0
	8	⏑–⏑––	6.3	**9.5**	6.6	2.3	1.5	1.9	2.8	0.8	1.1	2.9	2.0	2.7	1.4	2.2	3.3	1.9	1.9	2.9	5.3	5.5
	9	⏑––⏑–	6.9	**9.5**	5.5	**11.1**	**10.2**	**11.0**	**10.3**	**9.5**	**12.0**	**12.9**	**9.5**	**15.3**	**10.9**	**11.2**	**13.5**	**12.0**	**9.7**	**7.8**	**8.0**	6.4
IV	1	⏑––––	7.1	**7.0**	**7.7**	5.9	7.5	6.6	4.6	3.3	5.4	5.8	**9.1**	7.2	3.4	**9.7**	5.3	6.7	6.2	5.4	5.3	4.6
	2	–⏑–––	**8.1**	**7.0**	**8.5**	**7.6**	5.3	**6.9**	5.7	5.3	6.3	4.2	6.7	5.4	5.0	6.7	**6.9**	4.5	**8.3**	**7.2**	4.7	6.3
	3	––⏑––	**7.6**	6.3	**7.4**	5.9	6.0	3.1	2.5	3.7	2.2	3.6	4.8	3.0	4.2	2.2	1.3	3.1	4.8	**6.7**	**8.0**	**9.7**
	4	–––⏑–	**7.7**	**10.1**	5.6	**11.7**	**13.9**	**11.6**	**11.4**	**11.5**	**9.3**	**11.8**	**15.5**	**10.8**	**18.2**	**17.6**	**13.5**	**14.5**	**13.6**	**9.9**	4.7	**6.8**
V		–––––	6.3	6.9	6.6	5.3	**10.9**	6.0	**10.7**	**9.9**	**8.4**	**9.1**	6.3	**8.7**	**7.8**	**7.5**	**7.9**	**7.8**	**10.1**	6.0	**7.3**	4.0

Note: The figures of the five most frequent types of clausula in each work are in bold type.

the *Sophist, Politicus,* and *Philebus* the three highest-frequency positions were occupied by members of this favored group, here the top two positions were claimed by other clausulae, leaving only the third, fourth, and fifth places for the *Laws* forms. Moreover, the unpopular clausulae of the *Laws* were avoided less scrupulously than in the other three works.[37]

Kaluscha concluded that these works belonged together chronologically and that in accordance with the degree of similarity of their prose rhythm to that of the *Laws* the probable order of composition was *Timaeus, Critias, Sophist, Politicus, Philebus,* and *Laws.* In support of this sequence he referred to the following: The *Politicus, Philebus,* and *Laws* were connected by their stricter avoidance of the four clausulae mentioned previously (II 7, III 3, III 6, and III 8), their combined occurrence as a percentage of the total number of clausulae being *Ti.* 25.3, *Criti.* 21.3, *Sph.* 19.9, *Pol.* 11.2, *Phil.* 10.9, *Laws* 10.0. On the other hand the *Timaeus, Critias,* and *Sophist* were connected by the small variation in frequency of their various clausulae, neither a strong preference for nor prejudice against particular forms being observable. This can be shown numerically by a calculation based on Table 5; taking 6.3 as the mean percentage frequency for the sixteen clausulae and observing the difference from this of the actual percentage of each, the average deviation is *Ti.* 1.3, *Criti.* 1.8, *Sph.* 1.0, *Pol.* 2.5, *Phil.* 2.9, *Laws* 3.1.

Turning to the remaining dialogues, Kaluscha discovered that they resembled the *Protagoras, Crito,* and *Apology* in lacking any consistent tendency to prefer certain clausulae and therefore concluded that together they belonged to an earlier period, in which Plato showed little or no conscious interest in prose rhythm.

This same subject was investigated again some years later by L. Billig,[38] who condemned Kaluscha's treatment of it as "unsatisfactory in many ways." Although he did not say what these were, they may have included the failure to mention the edition used, to specify the minimum length of sentence, and to define certain principles of scansion, all of which made it difficult to verify the accuracy of Kaluscha's statistics. He attempted to forestall similar criticism of his own inquiry by providing information about his procedure in these respects.

His primary reason for a reinvestigation, however, came from observing in the *Laws* the frequent occurrence of the fourth paeon

(⏑⏑⏑⏓) as a clausula, the rhythm recommended by Aristotle (*Rhetoric* III 8) for this position. Unlike Kaluscha he did not restrict the clausula to the last five syllables of the sentence, but permitted such variation between four and six syllables as seemed appropriate, the basic fourth paeon, for instance, being extendable by one or two extra syllables (Table 6).

In the *Laws* Billig noted the high incidence not only of the fourth paeon and its variants but also of two other clausulae (– – ⏑⏓ and – – – ⏓). If there were an even distribution of the fifteen clausulae, these six forms would constitute 40 percent. Perceiving that their actual occurrence in the *Timaeus* barely exceeded this, but was almost double in the *Laws,* and assuming an increasing expertise on Plato's part in achieving these preferred forms, he reached the conclusion that the chronological sequence corresponded roughly with their increasing occurrence: *Ti.* 45.6 percent, *Criti.* 52.2 percent, *Sph.* 55.8 percent, *Pol.* 70.7 percent, *Phil.* 78.2 percent, *Laws* 77.9 percent.

More recently, the use of statistical techniques to evaluate the significance first of Kaluscha's figures, then of data from a fresh examination of the clausulae has confirmed the results obtained by the two earlier investigations.[39]

The by this time somewhat hackneyed subject of reply formulae enjoyed a late revival through a second article by H. von Arnim, which reached book proportions.[40] The aim he set himself was to make the results of his new inquiry conclusive. Previous investigations had failed to achieve this because, while they showed that certain dialogues belonged together by reason of a common possession of particular stylistic features, they did not prove that an alternative arrangement according to others was impossible. Although it had been discovered, for instance, that a large number of such features connected the *Sophist* and *Politicus* to the *Philebus, Timaeus,* and *Laws,* no one had thought of finding out how many connected these same two dialogues to, say, the *Symposium, Phaedo,* and *Critias.* Yet it was theoretically possible that such an investigation would reveal a greater number than in the former case, necessitating a complete revision of the "established" chronology.

In order to eliminate any doubt in this respect, each work needed to be compared with every other, a task of several lifetimes if the material were to be all the possible features of style. However, an

Table 6. *Prose rhythm in the dialogues: relative frequency by percentage of different types of clausula (broadly defined), as calculated by Billig*

<table>
<tr><th></th><th></th><th></th><th></th><th></th><th></th><th colspan="12">Laws</th></tr>
<tr><th></th><th>Ti.</th><th>Sph.</th><th>Criti.</th><th>Pol.</th><th>Phil.</th><th>I</th><th>II</th><th>III</th><th>IV</th><th>V</th><th>VI</th><th>VII</th><th>VIII</th><th>IX</th><th>X</th><th>XI</th><th>XII</th></tr>
<tr><td>(I) ⏑⏑⏑⏓</td><td>12.0</td><td>11.5</td><td>16.2</td><td>14.2</td><td>17.1</td><td>16.2</td><td>14.0</td><td>22.8</td><td>18.8</td><td>23.5</td><td>21.8</td><td>19.7</td><td>17.4</td><td>22.4</td><td>17.5</td><td>15.5</td><td>18.6</td></tr>
<tr><td>⏑⏑⏑–|⏓</td><td>6.4</td><td>7.3</td><td>14.4</td><td>8.7</td><td>11.0</td><td>9.3</td><td>11.5</td><td>8.8</td><td>9.1</td><td>10.8</td><td>12.4</td><td>8.4</td><td>10.7</td><td>9.6</td><td>10.4</td><td>6.3</td><td>7.7</td></tr>
<tr><td>⏑⏑⏑–|⏑⏓</td><td>2.9</td><td>3.9</td><td>1.8</td><td>3.7</td><td>4.4</td><td>3.8</td><td>2.0</td><td>8.0</td><td>6.6</td><td>8.3</td><td>4.9</td><td>5.5</td><td>6.2</td><td>6.9</td><td>6.3</td><td>6.3</td><td>7.7</td></tr>
<tr><td>⏑⏑⏑–|–⏓</td><td>3.1</td><td>4.8</td><td>–</td><td>6.6</td><td>6.2</td><td>4.1</td><td>3.0</td><td>4.4</td><td>4.6</td><td>0.6</td><td>5.3</td><td>5.5</td><td>5.0</td><td>4.1</td><td>4.9</td><td>1.2</td><td>5.0</td></tr>
<tr><td>Total of (I)</td><td>24.4</td><td>27.5</td><td>32.4</td><td>33.2</td><td>38.7</td><td>33.4</td><td>30.5</td><td>44.0</td><td>39.1</td><td>43.2</td><td>44.4</td><td>39.1</td><td>39.3</td><td>43.0</td><td>39.1</td><td>29.3</td><td>39.0</td></tr>
<tr><td>(II) ––⏑⏓</td><td>12.6</td><td>17.8</td><td>13.5</td><td>21.2</td><td>23.5</td><td>21.3</td><td>20.1</td><td>21.7</td><td>27.4</td><td>22.3</td><td>22.3</td><td>23.4</td><td>23.6</td><td>25.0</td><td>30.5</td><td>37.4</td><td>24.9</td></tr>
<tr><td>(III) –––⏓</td><td>8.6</td><td>10.5</td><td>6.3</td><td>16.3</td><td>16.0</td><td>14.2</td><td>23.2</td><td>11.6</td><td>12.2</td><td>10.8</td><td>13.6</td><td>13.9</td><td>18.6</td><td>16.8</td><td>11.1</td><td>11.5</td><td>13.6</td></tr>
<tr><td>Total of (I), (II) & (III)</td><td>45.6</td><td>55.8</td><td>52.2</td><td>70.7</td><td>78.2</td><td>68.9</td><td>73.8</td><td>77.3</td><td>78.7</td><td>76.3</td><td>80.3</td><td>76.4</td><td>81.5</td><td>84.8</td><td>80.7</td><td>78.2</td><td>77.5</td></tr>
<tr><td>–⏑––⏓</td><td>5.5</td><td>7.0</td><td>5.4</td><td>8.1</td><td>4.4</td><td>7.9</td><td>8.5</td><td>5.2</td><td>5.6</td><td>5.1</td><td>5.3</td><td>6.5</td><td>5.6</td><td>5.0</td><td>3.7</td><td>7.5</td><td>6.8</td></tr>
<tr><td>––⏑–⏓</td><td>10.1</td><td>7.3</td><td>9.9</td><td>4.1</td><td>2.9</td><td>5.2</td><td>4.5</td><td>2.8</td><td>2.0</td><td>0.6</td><td>1.5</td><td>2.5</td><td>4.5</td><td>2.7</td><td>3.0</td><td>2.9</td><td>2.7</td></tr>
<tr><td>⏓–⏑⏑⏓</td><td>16.1</td><td>11.5</td><td>9.9</td><td>6.8</td><td>5.9</td><td>7.9</td><td>6.5</td><td>6.4</td><td>5.6</td><td>5.1</td><td>4.5</td><td>4.4</td><td>3.4</td><td>2.3</td><td>4.9</td><td>5.2</td><td>5.9</td></tr>
<tr><td>–⏑⏑–⏑⏓</td><td>3.1</td><td>2.3</td><td>2.7</td><td>2.4</td><td>1.0</td><td>1.1</td><td>2.0</td><td>2.0</td><td>2.0</td><td>0.6</td><td>1.5</td><td>1.9</td><td>–</td><td>0.9</td><td>0.8</td><td>1.7</td><td>1.4</td></tr>
<tr><td>–⏑⏑––⏓</td><td>1.8</td><td>3.2</td><td>2.7</td><td>1.3</td><td>1.4</td><td>1.9</td><td>1.0</td><td>1.6</td><td>–</td><td>1.3</td><td>1.5</td><td>1.5</td><td>1.1</td><td>0.5</td><td>0.8</td><td>1.2</td><td>0.9</td></tr>
<tr><td>⏑–⏑–⏓
–⏑–⏑⏓ }</td><td>12.4</td><td>8.4</td><td>11.7</td><td>5.8</td><td>5.3</td><td>6.0</td><td>2.0</td><td>3.2</td><td>5.6</td><td>8.3</td><td>4.1</td><td>6.1</td><td>2.8</td><td>3.2</td><td>4.2</td><td>3.5</td><td>5.0</td></tr>
<tr><td>–⏑⏑–⏓</td><td>5.2</td><td>4.7</td><td>5.4</td><td>1.1</td><td>0.8</td><td>1.1</td><td>1.5</td><td>1.2</td><td>0.5</td><td>2.6</td><td>1.1</td><td>0.9</td><td>1.1</td><td>0.9</td><td>2.2</td><td>–</td><td>–</td></tr>
<tr><td>Total of remainder</td><td>54.2</td><td>44.4</td><td>47.7</td><td>29.6</td><td>21.7</td><td>31.1</td><td>26.0</td><td>22.4</td><td>21.3</td><td>23.6</td><td>19.5</td><td>23.8</td><td>18.5</td><td>15.5</td><td>19.6</td><td>22.0</td><td>22.7</td></tr>
</table>

Notes: The figures for the *Criti.*, which Billig did not include in his investigation, were calculated by the author in accordance with his principles; likewise those for the *Sph.*, since a check failed to substantiate Billig's own figures.

The total occurrence for each work is not always exactly 100 % owing to rounding up or down of decimals.

alternative was available in the smaller, yet self-contained material of affirmative reply formulae, which Arnim reexamined in order to acquire as accurate data as possible, even though the ground had been partially covered before by Ritter and himself. He then compared each pair of works in respect of both types of reply formulae employed and their relative frequency.[41] In this way he identified the following groups, arranged in chronological sequence:

1. *Ion, Prt.*
2. *La., Rep.* I, *Lys., Chrm., Euphr.*
3. *Euthd., Grg., Meno, H. Mi., Cra.*
4. *Cri., H. Ma., Smp., Phd.*
5. *Rep.* II–X, *Tht., Prm., Phdr.*
6. *Sph., Pol., Phil., Laws.*

Despite the extensive nature of Arnim's material, which comprehended a much larger number of reply formulae than any previous investigation, the reliability of his results was diminished by methodological faults.[42] Nevertheless, it may be noted that the chronological sequence that he arrived at corresponded broadly with that obtained by his predecessors.

In his later years C. Ritter returned to the subject of research into Plato's style, which he had done so much to promote, for the specific purpose of determining the order of composition of the early dialogues.[43] By looking at the occurrence in them of five features[44] he was able to subdivide this group into an earlier and later set, the former comprising the *Hippias Minor, Charmides, Laches, Protagoras, Euthyphro, Apology, Crito,* with the *Gorgias* and *Meno* at the end, the latter the *Hippias Major, Euthydemus, Menexenus, Cratylus, Lysis, Symposium, Phaedo,* and *Republic* I. It must be said, however, that this conclusion, based as it was on low frequency figures in every case, should be regarded as no more than a probability.

Nearly a century after its inception through Campbell the stylistic method came full circle with an examination of Plato's vocabulary by A. Díaz Tejera.[45] His approach, however, was different; whereas Campbell's standard of reference was internal, in that he measured the degree of affinity of the other dialogues to the *Laws,* Díaz Tejera's was external. Assuming that the development of the various Greek dialects into the *Koine* should be traceable, he collected together what he called "the non-Attic vocabulary,[46] which is well-documented in the *Koine*," then examined its occurrence in Plato's works.

Leaving aside the *Laws*, which he took for granted as the final work, he found the highest incidence in the *Timaeus* and *Critias*, followed by the *Politicus*, then the *Sophist* and finally the *Philebus*. In a "later middle group," which showed a considerably lower incidence, he placed the *Theaetetus*, *Phaedrus*, and *Parmenides*,[47] preceded in turn by an "earlier middle group" consisting of *Republic* II–X, *Phaedo*, *Symposium*, and *Cratylus*. Observing that the incidence in the latter three was roughly comparable with that in the early books of the *Republic* (as far as VI 502e), he inferred that the first part of the *Republic* was written between 388/7 B.C. (Plato's return from Sicily) and 384 B.C. (*terminus post quem* of the *Symposium*)[48] and was followed by the *Cratylus*, *Symposium*, and *Phaedo* before the *Republic* was resumed.

The main differences between Díaz Tejera's chronological order and that arrived at by his predecessors were the separation of the *Republic* by other works and the reversal of the positions in the final group of *Timaeus/Critias* and *Philebus*. If the investigation that produced these results had been sound, they would have required serious consideration, but it was seriously flawed in both concept and procedure. Starting, as it did, from the chronological divisions established by earlier research and accepting as evidence of late composition words common to the *Koine* and the final group of dialogues, its argument tended to be circular, and this basic fault was aggravated by various procedural errors, such as incorrect or inconsistent classification of words, incomplete statistics, and faulty calculations.[49]

The rhythm of Plato's prose was once more examined for chronological purposes by D. Wishart and S. V. Leach,[50] who analyzed in this respect not merely the clausula, as Kaluscha and Billig had, but the whole sentence. Owing to the exhaustive nature of the investigation, samples rather than whole works were looked at, and both the initial categorization of the text into long or short syllables and the subsequent assessment of the statistics were carried out by computer.

The authors took as their unit of measurement a group of five syllables, yielding thirty-two permutations. Every sentence was analyzed into such groups sequentially, that is, first syllables 1–5, then 2–6, then 3–7, and so on, after which the occurrence of each of the thirty-two types was expressed as a percentage of the total number of syllable groups in the sample. The works that they considered were as follows: *Sym.* (4), *Phdr.* (5), *Rep.* (3), *Sph.* (1), *Pol.* (1), *Phil.* (1), *Epist.* VII (1), *Ti.* (9), *Criti.* (3), *Laws* (5). The figures in parenthesis indicate the number of samples taken from the work in question, each sample comprising between two and three thousand groups of five syllables.

To determine the interrelationships of the various samples and works, five different statistical techniques were used: three of cluster analysis, one of principal components analysis, and one of multidimensional scaling. The purpose of cluster analysis was to identify groups of works or samples exhibiting a uniform use of prose rhythm. If it resulted in the clustering of separate samples from the same work, it would confirm that the work in question displayed consistent rhythms and so could be regarded as homogeneous; if, on the other hand, any sample could not be clustered with the rest, it would suggest either a difference of genre or a chronological separation or unauthenticity. The same would be true of whole works.[51]

It turned out that the thirty-three samples were grouped together according to their origin with the exception of those from the *Republic* and *Phaedrus.* In the former the sample from Book II appeared to be widely separated from those from Book X, which the authors were at a loss to explain, though they suggested as possible causes the shortness of the Book II sample and the fact that it came from a speech, whereas the other two were from a narrative. Another reason might be that the Book II sample contained several quotations in verse which clearly should not have been included in an analysis of prose rhythm (cf. *CPD,* 240). In the *Phaedrus,* while the four samples from Socrates' two speeches were grouped together, that from Lysias's speech was quite different. They considered that in view of the uniformity of rhythm in the four *Symposium* samples, despite their being parodies, imitation of Lysias's style would not account for its deviation and so concluded that it was probably Lysias's own composition.[52]

Regarding the ten works the authors decided that the chronological sequence was *Phdr.,* (*Smp.* and *Rep.*), *Ti., Sph., Criti.,* (*Epist.* VII and *Pol.*), *Phil., Laws,*[53] thus confirming the order arrived at by earlier investigators of Plato's prose rhythm, at least from the *Timaeus* onward.[54]

The most recent attempt to solve the chronological problem[55] was based on a computer analysis of the occurrence in words of certain letters, the occurrence being classified according to whether it was (a) anywhere in the word, (b) at the end,[56] or (c) in the penultimate position. The incidence of the significant letters, or variables, which were found to be thirty-seven in number,[57] was determined for sequential samples of 1,000 words from both Plato and other contemporary prose authors. The statistical profiles of the samples formed by these thirty-seven variables were then compared with one another by various techniques, such as cluster analysis and discriminant analysis, in the expectation of finding insignificant differences indicative of homogeneity between samples from the same author, but significant ones between those from different authors. While this expectation was for the most part fulfilled, there was a disturbing number of instances where statistical analysis failed to distinguish the works of two authors.[58] Nevertheless Ledger concluded that the results of comparisons with genuine works suggested the authenticity of *Alcibiades* I, *Theages, Epistles* VII, *Hippias Major, Epinomis,* and possibly also of *Alcibiades* II and *Hippias Minor.*

A comparison of the Platonic works using canonical correlation analysis to establish the chronological order indicated the existence of a sharply defined final group consisting of *Phil., Cleit., Epist.* III, VII, and VIII, *Sph., Pol., Laws, Epin., Ti.,* and *Criti.,* written in that order between 355 B.C. and 347 B.C.[59] Prior to these came the *Phaedrus* and *Menexenus.* While accepting this fairly late position for the *Phaedrus* in compliance with his statistics, Ledger rejected it for the *Menexenus* in deference to the traditional view of an earlier date, based in part on a supposedly topical reference (245e) to the Peace of Antalcidas of 386 B.C. Immediately before these was a "middle group" of works written probably between 380 B.C. and 366 B.C. in the order *Euthd., Smp., Cra., Rep., Prm., Tht., Epist.* XIII,[60] preceded in turn by an "early middle group" consisting of *Grg., Menex., Meno, Chrm., Ap., Phd., La., Prt.,* written in this order probably between 387 B.C. and 380 B.C. Finally the earliest group comprised *Lys., Euphr., Minos, H. Mi., Ion, H. Ma., Alc.* I, *Theag.,* and *Cri.,* the *Lysis* being dated to 400 B.C. before the death of Socrates on the basis of the anecdote in Diogenes Laertius (II 35).

The study of Plato's literary style has revealed two broad developments, an earlier one which was slow and gradual, and a later one, starting when he was about sixty, which was sudden and rapid. Regarding the former, where the changes concerned his vocabulary and were for the most part probably unconscious, one would expect the trend to be uneven and at times haphazard;[61] in the latter, which concerned the euphony of his prose and involved a deliberate choice in respect of hiatus avoidance and rhythm, a more rational and systematic evolution might be anticipated, with any aberrations in it explicable by known or deducible factors.

The early research on Plato's vocabulary by Campbell, Dittenberger, and Schanz, culminating in Ritter's book on the subject, identified in the *Sophist, Politicus, Philebus, Timaeus, Critias,* and *Laws* a group of dialogues distinguished from the rest by an exclusive or increased occurrence in them of certain words and phrases. Subsequent investigations into this aspect of style arrived at the same conclusion, and the dichotomy was confirmed by two further criteria with the discovery that only in these works, together with the *Epinomis* and *Epistle VII,* did Plato make a consistent attempt to avoid certain types of hiatus and achieve a different kind of prose rhythm.

It has been argued that Plato avoided hiatus changeably rather than consistently after a certain date.[62] This is to attribute to an elderly philosopher a fickle attitude, which is hardly compatible with the character of one who in his works emphasizes the importance of rational, consistent behavior. Of course Plato could change his style within a single dialogue, as in the *Symposium* and *Phaedrus,* but these changes were made for a specific purpose that is immediately apparent. No reason has so far been adduced why he should have employed the principle of hiatus avoidance intermittently, and in the absence of such a reason it is unsatisfactory to resort to the use of analogy, especially of Isocrates' forensic speeches, where the greater or lesser avoidance of hiatus is explicable on various grounds, not least temporal and commercial, considerations that hardly applied to Plato.

Regarding the question of sequence within the final chronological group, in comparing the various kinds of evidence particular weight should perhaps be attached to prose rhythm and the avoidance of hiatus, because unlike vocabulary they appear to be independent both of a work's form and of its content. Although the testimony of the data for hiatus avoidance was ambiguous, three independent investigations of clausula rhythm and one of sentence rhythm agreed in concluding that the order of composition was *Ti., Criti., Sph., Pol., Phil., Laws.* In the light of this the ambiguity of the hiatus evidence regarding the place of the *Philebus* may be resolved in favor of its proximity to the *Laws,* a position supported by particular aspects of hiatus[63] and by other features, such as the reversion to longer forms of reply formulae after a predominance of abbreviated versions in the preceding works,[64] the culmination of a trend toward the more frequent use of superlative expressions,[65] the high proportion of πέρι,[66] and an increased preference compared with the *Timaeus, Critias,* and *Sophist* for a long final syllable in clausulae (*CPD,* 188–90).

The final position allocated by Ledger to the *Timaeus* and *Critias* would indicate a fluctuating level of hiatus avoidance in the final group: less strict in the *Philebus,* strict in the *Sophist* and *Politicus,* less strict in the *Laws,* strict in the *Timaeus* and *Critias.* Likewise with clausula rhythm: The forms preferred by Plato in the *Laws* would appear with similarly high frequency right at the start in the *Philebus,* with much lower frequency in the *Sophist,* increasing in the *Politicus* toward that of the *Laws,* but falling away again in the *Timaeus* and *Critias,* to the level of the *Sophist.* As both these linguistic features were adopted consciously by Plato, such indecisiveness would be remarkable. Since the *Timaeus* and *Critias* are for the most part continuous narrative compared with the dialogue form of the *Sophist, Politicus,* and *Philebus,* the difference in Ledger's statistics might be attributable to the same cause that he adduced[67] for the odd results obtained for the *Apology* and *Menexenus,* works of a rhetorical character, namely a difference of genre.

By comparison with the differences that distinguish the final group, those which separate the dialogues of Plato's middle period from all preceding it are not as sharp, connected as they are with the earlier, gradual development of his style. Ritter, incorporating the results of his predecessors' research with his own, found that many of the criteria used to identify the final group also served to separate the *Parmenides, Phaedrus,* and *Theaetetus* from the remaining dialogues,[68] and the same division was made by later investigators.[69] On the question of the unity of the *Republic,* Siebeck,[70] Ritter, and Arnim arrived independently at the view that Book I, which contains several features characteristic of the early dialogues, was originally a separate work written some time before the rest, but possibly revised at the time of its incorporation.

Despite the fact that there cannot be the same certainty about the sequence within this group as about that in the last, examination of Ritter's criteria (cf. *CPD*, 79*ff*) suggests that the order of composition was *Republic, Theaetetus, Phaedrus,* which agrees with his own conclusion (cf. *CPD*, 77).[71] While the *Parmenides* unquestionably belongs in the same group (cf. *CPD*, 66), its peculiar character makes it difficult to determine its relationship to the above three works (cf. *CPD*, 84). On the other hand, if one also takes into account the apparent reference in the *Theaetetus* to the *Parmenides* and the fact that in the *Theaetetus* Plato renounces the use of the reported dialogue form, which seems to be merely an explicit declaration of a practice already implicity adopted early in the *Parmenides* (137c), presumably induced by recollection of the wearisome repetition of ἔφη ("he said"), and so on, in the *Republic* and the prospect of its still greater occurrence in a dialogue with such frequent changes of speaker, then the correct place for the *Parmenides* would appear to be between the *Republic* and *Theaetetus.*

On the sequence of dialogues in the early group little can be said. Division into subgroups also seems out of the question. The difficulty is that the statistics produced by past research usually relate to linguistic features that are primarily characteristic of works belonging to Plato's middle and late periods; consequently, their occurrence in the early period tends to be slight and spasmodic.

The problem is compounded by two other factors: first, many investigations concerned the use of reply formulae, which was prejudicial to works containing little dialogue (e.g., *Menex., Ap., Cri.*); second, most scholars of the last century omitted certain works altogether from their inquiries, especially those suspected at that time of being unauthentic, making a general comparison impracticable. Nevertheless, if the frequency with which features characteristic of the middle and late works occur in the early dialogues is accepted as an indication of their chronological proximity, then the *Phaedo, Cratylus, Symposium, Republic* I, *Lysis, Menexenus, Euthydemus,* and *Hippias Major* would certainly have to be regarded as among the last of this group. Their relative order, however, cannot be determined on the basis of the stylistic evidence that has so far come to light.

NOTES

1 For a full discussion of the evidence, see H. Thesleff, *Studies in Platonic Chronology* (Helsinki, 1982), 7–66.
2 *Pol.* II 6, 1264b24–27.
3 Cf. *Prm.* 127b2, c4–5.
4 See the tables in C. Ritter, *Platon* (Munich, 1910), 230–1, and Thesleff, *Studies in Platonic Chronology, 8ff.*
5 G. Grote, *Plato and the Other Companions of Socrates,* 2d ed., 3 vols. (London, 1867), 1:185–6, 278–9.
6 L. Campbell, *The Sophistes and Politicus of Plato* (Oxford, 1967), introduction.
7 In the last century many dialogues now accepted as genuine were considered unauthentic. As scholars' views in this respect varied, so too did the number of works forming the subject of any investigation.
8 See L. Brandwood, *The Chronology of Plato's Dialogues* (Cambridge, 1990) 5–7 (hereafter referred to as *CPD*).
9 W. Dittenberger, "Sprachliche Kriterien für die Chronologie der platonischen *Dialoge,*" *Hermes* 16 (1881): 321–45.
10 τί μήν; ("What else indeed?") and ἀλλὰ . . . μήν; ("But what else indeed?"), the intermediate word normally being τί, are strong affirmative replies, while γε μήν ("but indeed") is usually adversative. The absence of the first two from *Ti.* and *Criti.* results from their lack of dialogue.
11 K. J. Dover, "The Date of Plato's *Symposium,*" *Phronesis* 10 (1965): 2–20.
12 *Acharn.* 757, 784.
13 M. Schanz, "Zur Entwicklung des platonischen Stils," *Hermes* 21 (1886): 439–59.
14 The three examples in *Prt.* occur in the analysis of a poem by Simonides and, being quotations, ought to be discounted.
15 Simultaneously and independently, it seems, by H. Siebeck, *Untersuchungen zur Philosophie der Griechen* (Halle, 1888), 253*ff,* and C. Ritter, *Untersuchungen über Platon* (Stuttgart, 1888).
16 *CPD,* chaps. 10, 11, 13, and 19.
17 At this time the *Prm.* was held by Ritter to be unauthentic. Otherwise his statistics would have required it to be placed in this group.
18 E.g., (1) the complete absence of καὶ μάλα ("very much so"), τί μήν; and ὀρθῶς ("rightly") together with its superlative, though they occur in all the other books; (2) six of the eleven instances in the *Rep.* of δῆτα ("indeed") with a reply occur in this book, as do eight of the twenty instances of φαίνεται ("apparently"); (3) the preponderance of πάνυ γε over πάνυ μὲν οὖν (16 : 5) is the reverse of that in every other book (total 24 : 59).

19 E.g., one instance each of ἄριστα εἴρηκας ("Well said!"), καὶ πῶς ἄν; ("How might that be?"), Ionic dative (the Attic form with an iota suffix), γε μήν, παντάπασι μὲν οὖν ("Most certainly"), together with a preponderance of ἀληθῆ over ἀληθῆ λέγεις (5 : 2).
20 His argument for these dispositions, however, is not convincing (*CPD*, 74–6).
21 A reassessment of Ritter's data (*CPD*, 77, 82) shows that there are reasonable grounds for concluding that the *Phdr.* was written after both the *Tht.* and *Rep.*
22 W. Lutoslawski, *The Origin and Growth of Plato's Logic* (London, 1897), chap. 3, "The Style of Plato."
23 For a more detailed criticism see *CPD*, 130–5.
24 C. Baron, "Contributions à la chronologie des dialogues de Platon," *Revue des Etudes grecques* 10 (1897): 264–78.
25 Instances of περί in the various forms of the phrase περί πολλοῦ ποιεῖσθαι ("to rate highly"), which never appears to admit of anastrophe, were excluded from the calculation. The figures are the author's and relate to the O.C.T. Baron's, referring to another text, sometimes differ, but only slightly.
26 The high percentage for the *Menex.* and *La.* may be explained by the low overall occurrence of the preposition in the former, and by special factors such as repetition in the latter (cf. *CPD*, 119).
27 See below and *CPD*, 120.
28 G. Janell, "Quaestiones Platonicae," *Jahrbücher für classische Philologie*, Supp. 26 (1901): 263–336.
29 F. Blass, *Die attische Beredsamkeit* (Leipzig 1874), 2: 426.
30 I.e., a word beginning with a vowel following one ending in a vowel. In the fourth century with the advance of rhetorical technique such a clash of vowels came to be regarded as detracting from the euphony of prose.
31 Reinvestigation showed that in his later works Plato did try to avoid hiatus with these too (*CPD*, 162).
32 Janell used Schanz's text. In Burnet's there are even fewer instances: only one in the second passage, none in the third.
33 W. Kaluscha, "Zur Chronologie der platonischen Dialoge," *Weiner Studien* 26 (1904): 190–204.
34 In the sense that even a short syllable would be lengthened by the pause in speech between the end of one sentence and the beginning of the next.
35 The true situation is a little more complex. Clausulae in works of the middle period show a preponderance of long final syllables; e.g., in *Rep.* VIII–X, 478 end in a long, 251 in a short syllable, an excess of long over short of 90%. Although in the *Ti.* the position is reversed, with a 2% excess of short over long, the preponderance of the long syllable re-

appears in the *Criti.* with a 20% excess (though in this case the low number of clausulae makes the calculation less reliable), and gradually increases through the *Sph.* (7%), *Pol.* (20%), and *Phil.* (34%) to the *Laws* (66%).

36 Cf. *CPD*, table 18.4.

37 About the *Criti.* he drew no conclusions owing to the limitations of its size and the resulting statistics, but contented himself with attaching it to the *Ti.*

38 L. Billig, "Clausulae and Platonic Chronology," *Journal of Philology* 35 (1920): 225–56.

39 Cf. *CPD*, 198*ff.*

40 H. von Arnim, "Sprachliche Forschungen zur Chronologie der platonischen Dialogue," *Sitzungsberichte der Kaiserlichen Akademie der Wissenschaften in Wien: Philos. Hist. Klasse* 169.1 (1912): 1–210.

41 Counting the books of the *Rep.* and *Laws* separately there were forty-two works to be compared, the *Ap., Menex., Ti., Criti.,* and *Laws* V and XI being excluded owing to their lack of dialogue.

42 Cf. *CPD*, 215*ff.*

43 C. Ritter, "Unterabteilungen innerhalb der zeitlich ersten Gruppe platonischer Schriften," *Hermes* 70 (1935): 1–30.

44 E.g., (a) the particle μήν ("indeed"), (b) ὡς with a superlative adjective or adverb in the sense "as (e.g., great) as possible," (c) the change in use of ἕτερος ("other of two") to that of ἄλλος ("other"), (d) the interchange in function of ὥσπερ ("like") and οἷον ("like for example").

45 A. Díaz Tejera, "Ensayo de un metodo lingüístico para cronología de Platón," *Emerita* 29 (1961): 241–86.

46 By this he meant neologisms, Ionicisms, and poeticisms.

47 The incidence in the *Prm.* was less than half that in the other two, but he attributed this to the monotonous nature of its subject matter, especially in the ontological section.

48 See note 11.

49 Cf. *CPD*, esp. 233–4.

50 D. Wishart and S. V. Leach, "A Multivariate Analysis of Platonic Prose Rhythm," *Computer Studies in the Humanities and Verbal Behavior* 3 (1970): 90–9.

51 For an explanation of these techniques and their respective results see *CPD*, 238–46.

52 The absurdity of their further conclusion, that it was later than the other samples from the *Phdr.*, appears not to have struck them (cf. *CPD*, 247).

53 The relative order of works in parenthesis could not be determined.

54 Concerning the position allocated to the *Phdr.*, serious doubts arise from the choice of samples; all were taken from speeches rather than the

dialogue section, and Socrates' two speeches, which provided four samples, are specifically denoted by Plato himself as poetical in character (241e1 and 257a4), a fact borne out by observation (cf. *CPD*, 57–8).

55 G. R. Ledger, *Re-counting Plato* (Oxford, 1989).

56 Iota subscript was ignored, perhaps putting these statistics in some doubt.

57 Listed at ibid, 9.

58 Cf. ibid., 66–8 and 93*ff.* Discriminant analysis, for instance, attributed three of the eight samples from *Rep.* I to Xenophon (p. 103), while in a comparison of Xenophon's *Oeconomicus* and *Memorabilia* with several dialogues the *Phdr.* proved to be closer than the *Oeconomicus* in style to the *Memorabilia,* and the *Prt.* closer than the *Memorabilia* to the *Oeconomicus* (p. 160).

59 In this scheme the unfinished state of the *Criti.* was ascribed to Plato's death. However, one may also conjecture that the *Tht.* with its apparent reference to the Isthmian war of 369/8 B.C., was the last work to be written before Plato's departure for Syracuse in 367; that the exuberant expression of delight in the attractions of the countryside near Athens, which has induced some to regard the *Phdr.* as a youthful work, may instead be attributed to Plato's relief on returning home a year later after being subjected to a period of virtual imprisonment; and that the reason for the interruption to the composition of the *Criti.* was his sudden departure for Syracuse again in 361.

60 Like several earlier investigators Ledger found the *Prm.* awkward to place, differing so much in style from the other dialogues that "most tests of authorship would lead us to conclude that it was not written by Plato" (*Re-counting Plato,* 213).

61 Nevertheless, in the case of individual linguistic features it is necessary to assume initially that the trend is, if not even, at least unilinear. Comparison of several such criteria provides the necessary correction.

62 E.g., G. Ryle, *Plato's Progress* (Cambridge, 1966), 297; R. A. H. Waterfield, "The Place of the *Philebus* in Plato's Dialogues," *Phronesis* 25 (1980): 274–6.

63 E.g., the frequency in both works of addresses like ὦ ἑταῖρε ("my friend") and ὦ ἄριστε ("my good man"), six times in the *Phil.* and seventeen in the *Laws,* whereas in the other works of this group they are not found at all. If the *Phil.* had represented Plato's first serious attempt at reducing the occurrence of hiatus, he would hardly have failed to eliminate such eminently avoidable instances. Moreover, in the *Ti.* and *Criti.* there is a temporary increase in "permissible" hiatus to a level exceeding even that in works where hiatus was not avoided (cf. *CPD,* 162–3), indicative perhaps of Plato's first serious attempt to avoid the "objection-

able" kind, which at this transitional stage succeeded only at the expense of a rise in the former.

64 E.g., ἀληθῆ λέγεις and ἀληθέστατα/ὀρθότατα λέγεις instead of ἀληθῆ and αληθεστατα/ὀρθότατα (cf. *CPD*, 88 and 99*ff.*).

65 Only in the *Phil.* and *Laws* do the superlative reply formulae equal or surpass the positive forms (cf. *CPD*, 87–9).

66 See Table 3. Note also that its occurrence in *Ti.* and *Criti.* is much lower than in the other works of the late group.

67 E.g., *Re-counting Plato*, 127, 145, 163.

68 *CPD*, 57–66.

69 E.g., Arnim (*CPD*, 97*ff.*) and Baron (*CPD*, 116*ff.*).

70 *Untersuchungen zur Philosophie der Griechen.*

71 The late position of the *Phdr.* is further supported by its higher proportion of ὄντως to τῷ ὄντι (cf. *CPD*, 81), a percentage of rhetorical questions as reply formulae equaling that found in works of the last group (cf. *CPD*, 103), the frequency of πέρι (cf. *CPD*, 121) and passages in which there appears to be a conscious effort to avoid hiatus (cf. *CPD*, 155), leading to its lowest incidence outside works of the final group (cf. *CPD*, 156). In addition, the evidence of an interest in prose rhythm (cf. *CPD*, 158) together with mention of Isocrates (cf. *CPD*, 160) perhaps presages the development of this in subsequent works.

TERRY PENNER

4 Socrates and the early dialogues

Can the philosophical views of the historical Socrates be distinguished from those of his pupil Plato? And if so, how do the master's views differ from the pupil's? And do these Socratic views add up to a coherent philosophical position?

In Section I of this chapter, I explain the basis on which, following most modern interpreters, I feel able to divide Plato's dialogues into a group of (earlier) "Socratic" dialogues, where the character Socrates speaks more or less for the historical Socrates; and a group of (middle and later) dialogues in which the main character (now not always Socrates) speaks rather for Plato. I argue that the Plato of the middle and later dialogues, though some of his views remain the same, and though he attacks some of the same enemies and for some of the same reasons, has nevertheless in some ways gone well beyond the master. On some points, I suggest, he even contradicts him. In Section II, I contrast these Socratic dialogues with the other dialogues – first, in their form, method, tone, and subject matter; second, in their attitude to the sciences (arts, crafts, expertises), education, rhetoric, and mathematics; and third, in their theories of virtue, desire, and "weakness of will." In Section III, I address myself to the question with what right I attribute any views at all to a philosopher who claimed that he knew only that he knew nothing –

I would like to thank Antonio Chu, Paula Gottlieb, and Ruth Saunders for reading an earlier draft, saving me from many errors, inaccuracies, and infelicities. My greatest debt, in this article as in several other recent articles of mine on Socrates, is to Richard Kraut, who gave me a superb and testing set of comments on, and objections to, my penultimate draft. To persuade him on some of these matters would be to achieve something in Socratic studies. I fear I may still be some distance from that goal.

especially when the Socratic dialogues virtually all end negatively. I then make a suggestion as to the sort of thing I think Socrates is doing in these dialogues, with an illustration from the *Hippias Minor.* And then I draw a moral from the illustration: *Never consider any one expression of Socrates' views in isolation from other expressions of Socrates' views.* In Section IV, I explore the central Socratic concern with care for the soul, showing its connection with (what I shall, for convenience, call) Socrates' ethical egoism. In Section V, I consider Socrates' response to those he thinks of as his principal adversaries in his drive to get people to care for their souls: the sophists and rhetoricians, as well as the politicians and the poets. And I conclude, in Section VI, by addressing myself to various questions about Socratic method and Socratic ignorance. Sections III–VI, taken together, are also meant to exemplify, if somewhat sketchily (given the scope of the essay), ways in which one may come to see the overall coherence of Socrates' doctrines.

I have tried to keep the exposition of my picture of Socrates in the main text fairly uncluttered with objections and responses, so that it can be read on its own without the footnotes. At the same time, I should alert the reader to the fact that many of my interpretations of Socratic passages in Sections II–VI will be controversial. I have therefore tried to provide some objections and replies in the footnotes, along with some indications of where at least some opposing viewpoints can be found.[1]

I. CAN WE MAKE A DISTINCTION WITHIN PLATO'S DIALOGUES BETWEEN THOSE IN WHICH THE CHARACTER SOCRATES EXPRESSES VIEWS AND CONCERNS OF THE HISTORICAL SOCRATES AND THOSE IN WHICH HE EXPRESSES INSTEAD DISTINCTIVE VIEWS OF PLATO HIMSELF?

There is a tradition within recent philosophy and scholarship that says we can. This tradition has two principal sources: testimony from Aristotle that contrasts Socrates and Plato; and stylometric evidence on the dating of Plato's dialogues.

Aristotle tells us that (i) Socrates asked only, and did not reply; for he confessed that he knew nothing. He also tells us that (ii) Socrates concerned himself with ethical matters only, being not at all concerned with nature as a whole; that (iii) he was the first to argue "inductively"; that (iv) he was the first to search (systematically) for the universal, and for definitions – that is, to ask What-is-it? questions: questions of the sort, What is justice?, What is courage?, What is piety?, and so forth; but that, on the other hand, (v) he did not "separate" these universals, as Plato did: for Plato supposed that, since perceptibles are constantly changing, there could be no knowledge of the perceptibles, but only of some *other* things, the Ideas (or Forms).[2]

Now it is far from clear what "separation" (*chōrismos*) is.[3] But at least it *is* clear from the above testimony that where in the Platonic dialogues we see the character Socrates characterizing entities like *justice itself* and *the good itself* as changeless, and contrasting them with the ever-changing perceptibles, we should suppose that the character Socrates speaks not for the historical Socrates but for Plato. This becomes even clearer when we notice Aristotle's testimony that Plato, while young, studied with Cratylus, "becoming familiar first with Cratylus and Heraclitean opinions" (to the effect that all perceptibles are always in flux, and that there is no knowledge of them); and that Plato held these Heraclitean views even later. This Heracliteanism of Plato's is plainly a second source of Plato's views – a source that is relatively independent of Socrates' views.[4]

There is a third possible, relatively independent, source of Plato's views that Aristotle tells us of: the views of the Pythagoreans whom Plato "follows in many things" (*Met.* I.6.987a30). Aristotle tells us that the Pythagoreans, noting such phenomena as the mathematical ratios involved in musical intervals, thought the elements of all things were the elements of numbers. He also tells us that in at least a few cases, for example, justice, soul and reason, opportunity, and marriage, they tried, in a rather rudimentary way, to give answers to the Socratic What-is-it? question in terms of numbers.[5] The suggestion seems to be that as the Pythagoreans thought perceptibles had to be understood by reference to abstract structures (numbers), so Plato thought perceptibles had to be understood by reference to other abstract entities – the Forms. The Pythagoreans say perceptibles "imitate" the numbers, Plato says that the perceptibles "partake in" the Forms; only the name is different, Aristotle says.[6]

Thus Aristotle's testimony gives us a leg up on distinguishing dialogues where the character Socrates speaks for the historical Socrates and dialogues where the character Socrates speaks rather for Plato. Wherever there is talk of flux, or of perceptibles partaking or participating in Forms, and wherever there is substantive argument about cosmological matters (such as teleology in nature or the immortality of the soul), we are hearing Plato rather than the historical Socrates.

The distinction between Socratic and more distinctively Platonic dialogues has been made more secure by the stylometric investigations of the past hundred and more years.[7] This study has enabled scholars to reach some considerable degree of consensus about the placing of Plato's dialogues into three broad chronological groups: early, middle, and late. Scholars then note that a satisfying historical picture of the relations between Socrates and Plato can be built up if (i) we identify (most of) the stylometrically early dialogues as "Socratic" – that is, as dialogues in which the main character, Socrates, can be taken to express views of the historical Socrates; and (ii) we treat the remaining dialogues as ones in which the main character (often, but now not always, Socrates) speaks for the views of Plato – views that are sometimes, though very far from always, distinct from, and even conflicting with, the views of Socrates. This division – with a few dialogues considered transitional – pretty well preserves, it can be argued, the distinction between Socrates and Plato demanded by Aristotle's testimony.

By these criteria, then, I take the following as Socratic: *Hippias Minor, Charmides, Laches, Protagoras, Euthyphro, Apology, Crito, Ion; Gorgias, Meno; Lysis, Euthydemus, Menexenus, Hippias Major, Republic* Book I, with only the barest probability on stylistic grounds that there are breaks at the semicolons,[8] but with no further orderings within these subgroups. This list includes all of the stylometrically early group, except for the *Cratylus, Symposium,* and *Phaedo,* since, by the Aristotelian criteria above, they are clearly more Platonic than Socratic.[9] Following Dodds, I single out the *Gorgias* and *Meno,* with their Pythagorean elements, as being transitional to Platonic doctrine. Indeed, parts of those dialogues may be taken to be Platonic rather than Socratic, showing as they arguably do the effects of Plato's encounters with Pythagoreanism during his first visit to Sicily in 387 B.C. (I am thinking here principally of the myth in the *Gorgias* and a few other oblique references in that dialogue to Sicily and Pythagoreanism; and of the theory of recollection, and perhaps also the introduction of the method of hypothesis, in the *Meno.* As we have already seen, Aristotle seems to believe in a connection between the [non-Socratic] Platonic theory of Forms and Pythagorean attitudes to mathematics.)[10]

II. SOME CONTRASTS BETWEEN THE SOCRATIC DIALOGUES AND THE OTHERS

On the above account, we can now advance the following generalizations, some of them rough in themselves, but cumulatively worth attending to. First, on form, method, tone, and subject matter:

1. The Socratic dialogues tend to be short (notable exceptions: *Grg.* and *Prt.*); the other dialogues tend to be much longer.

2. The Socratic dialogues tend to be aporetic and without positive results, as befits a principal investigator who confesses his own ignorance; the other dialogues often have positive results, the main character often laying out much positive doctrine (notable exceptions: *Tht.* and the *Prm.*).

3. The Socratic dialogues are amusing, bantering, extroverted, optimistic, and mischievous in tone; the other dialogues are most often more inspirational or scientific in tone, but also more introverted, pessimistic, and brooding.[11]

4. The Socratic dialogues are almost exclusively ethical in content, concerned with individual ethics and individual education – "care for the soul" both for oneself and for the young; other dialogues are interested in many other topics besides ethics.[12]

5. On the question of the immortality of the soul, there is little interest in the Socratic dialogues. The *Apology* seems almost agnostic about it (40–41), though it is affirmed in the horrific myth at the end of the *Gorgias* (which I have suggested is Pythagorean) and (in the mouth of the Laws) at the end of the *Crito* (53b–c). But there are certainly no arguments for it. Elsewhere, beginning with the *Phaedo,* the immortality of the soul is passionately embraced, and argued for with intensity.[13]

Now for some considerations relating to Socrates' attitude to the sciences:

6. The Socratic dialogues treat of virtue as an expertise (science, art, craft) like any other expertise (such as medicine, navigation,

cobblery, boxing, horse training, arithmetic, geometry).[14] This expertise is evidently thought of by Socrates as intellectual, and as involving the ability to "give an account," to explain to others, and to teach them; it is not just a matter of "knowing how."[15] It does not involve any (propaedeutic) training of the emotions *independent of* the understanding to be reached by discussion. Socrates is unlikely to have granted that there could be any education that is not routed via the intellect. (Even of little children, there is no reason to believe that Socrates would think any kind of training worthwhile that doesn't proceed by way of getting the child to understand things for himself or herself.) By contrast, in middle and later dialogues, virtue is no longer merely an intellectual expertise, but involves, at least as a precondition, a degree of training of emotions and attitudes in ways that do not involve very substantially the intellect of the trainee. The right stories must be told, the right music listened to – never mind any discussion – before Socratic dialogue can do the slightest good (*Rep.* II 376e*ff*).[16]

7. There is a similar contrast in attitudes to rhetoric. While the denial that rhetoric is a science remains common to Socratic and Platonic dialogues,[17] it is evidently Socrates' view that the only science there could be of persuading someone that *p*, is the the science of *teaching* them that *p*. Extrapolating from the whole of the Socratic dialogues, we may reasonably identify this "teaching" with bringing people to understand – for themselves, and, indispensably, by way of Socratic cross-questioning – how it can be the case that *p*. By contrast, though Plato agreed that there can only be a science of persuading someone that *p* in people who themselves have knowledge of *p*, he did not doubt that this science could proceed by way of appeals to emotion and without what Socrates called teaching. (Cf. the entire scheme for nursery and elementary education at *Rep.* II 366c–III 412b, including the "noble falsehood" of 414b–415d with 416e–417a; cf. 382c–d, 378a, 389b–c.)[18]

8. Returning to expertises and sciences proper, the Socratic dialogues treat arithmetic and geometry as just ordinary expertises like any other, such as cobblery and boxing; they are not marked off as bringing us special knowledge, or as bringing us objects of some special epistemological status. By contrast, in some of the other dialogues, especially the *Republic* (Books V–VII), it is clear that the sciences of arithmetic and geometry are being taken to be a cut

above such sciences as medicine, navigation, cobblery, and boxing. It is also clear that the objects of the mathematical sciences are being singled out as akin to such objects as *the good, justice itself, the beautiful itself,* and so on, which emerge, in the Platonic dialogues, as the objects of the inquiries into the "What is it?" of things that first Socrates and then Plato undertook.[19]

The remaining differences between Socratic and other dialogues all turn on the difference already noted in (6) and (7) above, between *Socrates'* intellectual attitude to virtue, where virtuous activity will result when and only when the agent is possessed of intellectual understanding of what is good and bad for us as humans; and *Plato's* attitude to virtue, where the training of the emotional and irrational more or less independently of the intellectual is a necessary precondition to virtue.[20]

9. In the Socratic dialogues, we have a doctrine that, depending upon how one interprets it, may be called either the Unity of Virtue (UV) or the Unity of the Virtues (UVV). On either interpretation, the doctrine requires at least this: that a person will be brave if and only if temperate, wise, just, and pious; temperate if and only if brave, wise, just, and pious; and so forth. By contrast, in the *Republic* (especially Book IV) it is possible for the military class to have courage and the lower class to have temperance, without either of them having wisdom – that being a virtue confined to the intellectual class. What the military class has instead of wisdom is true belief. Furthermore, in the *Statesman* (306a–311c), temperance and courage are actually treated as opposite virtues: if one has the one, one is unlikely to have the other. (Once one gives up the idea that virtue is an intellectual expertise, it becomes a lot easier for the emotional sides of different virtues to assert themselves in opposite ways.)[21]

There may be some temptation to soften the contrast between the Socratic dialogues and the *Republic* by invoking the (strongly puritanical) distinction between "philosophic" and "demotic" virtues at *Phaedo* 68c–69d, 82a–84b, and suggesting that the virtues as we see them in the *Republic* Book IV are merely demotic virtues. It could then be argued (as I did in my "The Unity of Virtue") that Plato might still hold to something like a unity of the *philosophic* virtues. This temptation may be reinforced by *Republic* 435c–d and 504a–b, which suggest that the account of the virtues in the *Republic* Book IV is lacking because it fails to show how the Form of the Good enters into the account of the virtues. But even if we succumb to this temptation – and I am not sure we should – it cannot be denied that any interest at all in demotic virtue represents a slide away from the Socratic position. And in the *Statesman,* the abandoning of any unity between temperance and courage represents a complete repudiation of the Socratic position.

10. In the Socratic dialogues we find an intellectualist theory of desire, according to which all desires, and not only the desires of the virtuous, are desires for the good[22] – that is, for whatever is best for me[23] in the circumstances I am in. The result is that the virtuous differ from the vicious not in their motivations but in their intellects. (All persons desire the same end – whatever is really best for them in the circumstances they are in. Where they differ is in their beliefs about what courses of action and styles of life will be the best means to that end.)[24]

The point that everyone desires the same end is a little tricky. If a good person equates his or her good with virtue, and a bad person equates his or her good with pleasure, it might seem Socrates must think that only the good person desires his or her real good. But I am denying this. What Socrates is saying, I claim, is that in these circumstances, the good person correctly chooses virtuous activity as a means to his or her real good, and the bad person mistakenly chooses pleasurable activity as a means to his or her real good. Each person chooses his or her *real* good as an end. (More on this point in note 42.)

I return now to the intellectualist theory of desire. According to this theory, all desires to do something are rational desires, in that they always automatically adjust to the agent's beliefs about what is the best means to their ultimate end. If in particular circumstances I come to believe that eating this pastry is the best means to my happiness in the circumstances, then in plugging this belief into the desire for *whatever is best in these circumstances,* my (rational) desire for whatever is best becomes the desire to eat this pastry.[25] On the other hand, if I come to believe that it would be better to abstain, then once again my desire for whatever is best will become the desire to abstain.[26] Rational desires adjust to the agent's beliefs. In fact, on this view the *only* way to influence my conduct is to change my opinion as to what is best. Hence the intellectualism of Socrates' theories of education and persuasion noted under (6) and (7), and the effective identifying of any virtue whatever with wisdom under (9).

The basis of this adjustability of desire to belief is desire's being for the good – for *whatever is best.* The "what is best" provides a kind of substitution device for plugging in one's beliefs about particular actions that are in fact best in the circumstances. Different beliefs, different actions.

Plato, on the other hand, in the parts of the soul doctrine of *Republic* IV 436–440, explicitly *attacks* the doctrine that all desire is for the good.[27] In Plato we find desire for good only in the rational part of the soul. (What Plato speaks of as the rational part of the soul is the entire soul by Socrates' lights.) Desires of the appetitive part of the soul, on the other hand, are brutely irrational, or, as we might say, blind. That is, they are blind to such changes of belief as the example above envisages. If my desire to eat the pastry is an irrational desire, then even if you convince me that it would be better for me not to eat it, the desire does not go away and I may in fact act on that desire. Furthermore, my behavior can be changed without any change in my beliefs – simply by acting on or awakening my irrational desires.

The (alleged) phenomenon of *acting contrary to what I think is best* – called, at least since Aristotle, *akrasia* (weakness of will) – gives us a way of restating the difference between Socrates and Plato. Socrates denies there is such a phenomenon, while Plato affirms there is. Indeed, the pessimism of the Platonic dialogues about human nature in politics[28] is largely the product of Plato's coming to believe in brutely irrational desires.[29]

11. Corresponding to the preceding distinction is a distinction between two different ways of interpreting the famous dictum "No one errs willingly." In the Socratic dialogues, the point is precisely that if anyone errs, it is due to ignorance. By contrast, when this dictum is echoed in later dialogues, error is not restricted to ignorance (which in Plato would be a defect in the operations of the rational part of the soul), but can be due also to the action of the two lower parts of the soul, or to a madness that is due either to a bad state of the body or to a bad upbringing.[30]

12. Finally, though we find both in Socratic and more properly Platonic dialogues the view that knowledge is something strong that cannot be overcome by pleasure or passion (*Prt.* 352b–d, 357c), what lies behind the doctrine is quite different in the two cases. In Socrates, knowledge alone – sheer understanding – enables one to avoid

the kind of wavering (shifting up and down) that a person without knowledge[31] is subject to (*Prt.* 365d5–7, *Euph.* 11b–e, *Meno* 97d–98a).[32] It is true that in later dialogues, Plato also implies that those who know won't go wrong, and won't be overcome by pleasure or passion. But a great deal more is involved in the explanation of the Platonic claim than just understanding. In the *Republic,* the reason the guardians won't be overcome once they have knowledge is that they can only get to *acquire* the knowledge of a guardian if they have been so trained and conditioned in their early life by the songs they have had sung to them, the stories they have been told, the gymastic and military exercises they have gone through, and fifty years of education, that one might almost be tempted to say understanding is hardly necessary any longer to their avoidance of dangerous pleasures or passions.[33] It is an accidental fact, I suggest, that in Plato knowledge is strong. One who knows is strong against temptation because one cannot get around to *acquiring* knowledge till true belief has been so pounded into one, and emotions and desires so checked and trained out of one, that one would have been strong against temptation even if one were failing solid geometry. (And it is arguable that Aristotle's account of the relation between practical wisdom and moral virtue is in this respect closer to Plato's than Socrates' view.)

* * * * *

Here then are some of the contrasts that can be made between the Socratic and the Platonic dialogues. Some of these contrasts are quite extraordinary, and their very extraordinariness helps make them more believable. Why? Consider Plato's *Seventh Letter,* dating from late in his life, the sheer power and brooding, pessimistic tone of which[34] almost by itself recommends the letter as genuine, as written by the same Plato we have got to know in the *Republic* and the *Laws.* We ask: How could a man like this have produced the sunny, mischievous intellectual adventures in the early, Socratic dialogues? Only one answer readily suggests itself: that there lies behind the character Socrates in those early dialogues an extraordinary personality, whose sheer intellect and character virtually swamped the personality of the young Plato, literary and philosophical genius though he was. Not till he was around forty was Plato's own almost entirely opposite personality, with some intellectual help from the Pythagorean mathematician-philosophers, able to begin asserting itself in his writings.

III. A PRIOR QUESTION, A TYPICAL SCENARIO, AN ILLUSTRATION, AND A USEFUL GENERAL STRATEGY

So far I have been saying how some of Socrates' views differ from those of Plato. It may have occurred to some to wonder whether *any* views can be attributed to Socrates if he is described as someone who always questions and never asserts anything because he confesses he knows nothing, and if the dialogues from which these views are to be drawn are aporetic and without positive results. (Those who are, in addition, appalled by what they see as distressingly many silly views and fallacious arguments in the Socratic dialogues may even suggest that Socrates is not trying to convey *any* views to us. He is simply educating us by the deliberate production of bad arguments and fallacies; and that is *all* he is doing.)

My reply is that the claim to know nothing in no way implies that Socrates does not hold strong convictions about a great many ethical matters. And the fact that Socrates' ethical method is to refute people rather than tell them what he thinks is no argument against what I now wish to suggest. This is that the whole point of the Socratic dialectic is to get people to see things for themselves, as a result of his refutations – and without their understanding being short-circuited by the device of giving them a formula.

Now there *are* quite a few passages where Socrates lets us know fairly directly what he thinks, though it is true that none of them are at the conclusions of dialogues.[35] What I want to maintain here, however, is that there are also many *negative* passages in which it is nevertheless clear what Socrates is trying to get us to see. One typical scenario is (a) to present us with a view we have reason to think Socrates holds – perhaps even having his interlocutor anxious to defend this Socratic view; then (b) to put it together with another view that Socrates and his interlocutor will both have some reason to want to defend, but which, when put together with yet other obvious considerations, conflicts with the original view; then, (c) when the interlocutor cannot see how to resolve the conflict, leave the interlocutor to stew over the difficulty; but (d) leave enough hints in the course of the dialectic that, even though the interlocutor can't figure it out, a perceptive and persistent reader or hearer can.

Let me give just one, rather powerful, example of this scenario. It is in the *Hippias Minor,* where the claim that justice is a science or power (cf.: virtue is knowledge) is subjected to the difficulty of the "Ambivalence of the Arts (or Sciences)" – the claim that

given two people who err at ϕ-ing, one who errs willingly and one who errs unwillingly, it is the one who errs willingly who is the better ϕ-er.[36]

These two claims together get us the outrageous conclusion that the more just person (the better person)[37] is the one who does unjust deeds willingly rather than the one who does unjust deeds unwillingly – contrary to what the law and our general ethical consciousness seem to suggest.

Now Socrates really sticks it to Hippias over this difficulty, and suggests that he himself is in difficulty over this conclusion (372c–373a). But, as most interpreters agree, even though Hippias cannot see his way out of it, Socrates' final setting up of the difficulty dangles the solution before Hippias's eyes (376b4–6):

Therefore the person who errs willingly in doing disgraceful and unjust things, Hippias, *if there is such a person,* will be no other than the good person.

That is, if there were anyone who *did* err willingly at doing just (or virtuous)[38] things, they *would* be more virtuous than those who err unwillingly. But – the reader or hearer is invited to conclude – *there isn't any such person,* since "no one errs willingly" at being just (or virtuous) – that is, at getting what is best for him- or herself. (For "no one errs willingly," see [11] in section II; and for the connection of being just or virtuous with being good at getting what is best for one, see the discussion of Socrates' ethical egoism in section IV.) So the teeth of the outrageous conclusion are drawn; and though Hippias does not see this, the perceptive and persistent reader or hearer can.

Socrates drops hints of this solution along the way. He goes out of his way to establish that with other sciences, such as arithmetic, there are such people as err willingly (367a8–b3). That is, with these other sciences there can always be a motive for the relevant expert to err willingly at that science, namely, whenever erring willingly will enable one to achieve whatever is best for one overall. (Theodorus the arithmetician has a motive for giving a wrong answer because doing so will help encourage his child, and Theodorus thinks encouraging his child best for himself overall. Or perhaps Theodorus has a motive for giving a wrong answer because giving the wrong answer will give Theodorus a way of testing how well his student has understood what he was saying earlier.) But with the one science of achieving what is best for one overall, one can't have *that* motive: to err willingly at that science in order to help one achieve what is best over all(!).[39]

We see then what Socrates is doing in the *Hippias Minor:* He is forcing those who are both willing and able to work things out for themselves to see how we can perfectly easily reconcile justice's being a science (or virtue's being knowledge) with the Ambivalence Principle for the sciences – by pointing out that with this science alone one cannot have a motive for erring in order to achieve what is best for one overall. Socrates is showing us how, in spite of ambivalence, it can still be the case that virtue is knowledge.[40] At least one difficulty in the way of a full answer to the question, What is virtue? has been gotten rid of.

It is true that in the *Hippias Minor* we have a particularly clear case of this scenario. There is hardly anywhere else where this sort of argument can be made with such confidence as it can in this humanly delicious, highly philosophical, and really superbly constructed little masterpiece. All the same, if we work with due caution, we can, I think, find the same or similar scenarios elsewhere.[41]

The *Hippias Minor* argument also illustrates what I think is a useful general strategy for responding to charges that particular Socratic views are silly and indefensible – that they are material for the diagnosis of philosophical error more than anything else. The strategy is this: Refuse to consider suggested expressions of Socrates' views in isolation from other expressions of Socratic views. Yes, it sounds strange to say "Virtue is a science," since it seems to ignore the ethical neutrality of the sciences. It seems to make it possible for the virtuous person to show his or her virtue by doing unjust deeds more successfully than anyone else. It seems to show Socrates ignoring the Kantian point that science is compatible with a bad or evil will. Reply: What for Kantians and many moderns would be an unacceptable ethical slack in the idea of virtue being a science is taken care of by something Socrates says in another expression of his views – about motivation: that we all seek what is best for us. So while for Kant and most moderns, good people differ from bad in their *wills*, for Socrates we are all the same with respect to our wills (cf. *Meno* 78b4–8). We all seek what is best for us. Where good people differ from bad is in their *knowledge* – their knowledge of what is best for themselves.[42]

It is true that this last defense prompts a further objection: Why wouldn't people who know what is best for themselves use that knowledge to seek their own benefit at the price of harming, or doing injustice to, others? But that difficulty in turn can be met by looking to yet other expressions of Socrates' views. For, as we shall see in the second half of the next section, Socrates also holds that it is never in one's interest to harm, or do injustice, others.

IV. CARE FOR THE SOUL AND ETHICAL EGOISM

So far, I have said next to nothing about what was certainly the central concern of Socrates' life – as it was the central theme of the *Apology* – namely, "care for the soul." About this care for the soul, Socrates thought it was a science in just the way horse training is a science.[43] For Socrates this concern was both for his own soul and for the souls of others – especially in the education of the young.[44] Indeed in expressing the centrality of Socrates' concern for the education of the young in virtue, Plato the author even receives some unconscious help from Socrates' accusers in the *Apology.* For their charge of corrupting the young brings up for Socrates the very point on which he would most like to be examined: Who cares for the young, and who makes them better human beings? (If the charge had not existed, Plato would have had to invent it.)

But before looking at the question why Socrates was especially concerned with the education of the young, let us ask first a more general question: Why should we care for our souls at all? Socrates' answer is this: because the soul is the human being's *instrument*,[45] that by which the person lives – and, if it be so, lives well. Like the horse, the pruning knife, the eye, the bow, the archer, and the doctor, the soul has an *ergon* (function); and the *virtue* (or goodness) of each of these is the fulfilling of that function. The goodness of a knife is cutting; of an eye, seeing; and of a doctor, healing. What then of the soul? The soul's function is to care for, rule, and deliberate, and so lead to the person's doing well and being happy (*Rep.* I 353d–354a). We must care for the soul, then, because what will enable us to be happiest is the best possible soul. And we all wish to be happy (*Euthd.* 278e; cf. *Meno* 77b–78b).[46]

But what does Socrates suppose doing well, or being happy, is? Is it to have good things, such as health, wealth, power, honor, or even temperance, justice, and bravery? Only if we use them, and use them well.[47] To have these so-called good things and use them badly would actually be worse for us than if we didn't have them. But that means that the only thing good in itself is wisdom, that is, the knowledge of how to use, for one's own happiness, the so-called good things (*Euthd.* 278d–282e). This wisdom is the knowledge or science that Socrates elsewhere (*La.* 195c–d, 196a2–3; cf. 199c6–7; also *Chrm.* 172c–174d, esp. 174b–d, e3) calls the science of goods and bads.[48] This is the science of caring for the soul that, we have seen, Socrates holds to be analogous to horse training.

Now it is amazing for a modern to be told that there is one thing that is unconditionally good, namely wisdom, when Kant told us so clearly – in unwitting parody of the *Euthydemus* – that there is only one thing in the world, or out of the world, that is unconditionally good, namely, a good *will*. It is also amazing for a modern to be told that the goodness of a good human being is goodness *at* something, namely, getting happiness. A philosopher like Kant might agree that *some* good is goodness *at* performing a function – the goodness of knives to cut well, the goodness of architects to build well, and even the goodness of parents to nurture well and the goodness of friends to care for their friend and look out for their friend's interest. But Kant and others are likely to draw the line with good *person*. Here, they will say, we are speaking of *moral* good, not functional good.[49] How can you call people good, or just, they will ask, merely on the grounds that they are good at doing what they need to do in order to be happy? Surely that would make it possible to call people good or just who get their happiness by harming others! And that surely cannot be deemed the part of an ethical person.

This damaging implication of virtue as knowledge, of course, bids fair to render Socrates' ethical egoism a nonstarter as an ethical theory. And it certainly does make *some* versions of ethical egoism nonstarters. But not Socrates' ethical egoism. To see why, we must look at a doctrine of Socrates' that I have only just mentioned so far: the doctrine that it is never in one's interest to harm, or do injustice to, others.

Socrates' position here is *not,* I maintain, that it is *immoral* ever to harm others. Rather, like Gandhi and at least some other proponents of nonviolence – who argue that violence is, as a sheer matter of fact, *not* in your political interest – Socrates grabs the bull by the horns and argues that harming others is, as a sheer matter of fact, not in your interest.[50] The argument in its simplest form shows up in Socrates' response, in the *Apology,* to the charge of corrupting the young. Do I do so willingly or unwillingly? he asks Meletus. If willingly, do I not know that bad people have a bad effect on those around them, so that by willingly corrupting the young I am doing myself harm (*Ap.* 25c–26a, esp. 25d–e)? But then what I deserve is not punishment but instruction.[51] Elsewhere, at *Gorgias* 472c–481b with 482c*ff,* Socrates argues, at greater length – though unfortunately at a fairly high level of generality, and with some complexity of structure – the comparable thesis that doing injustice to others is always worse than having others do injustice to oneself.

Now it must be admitted that many moderns will find these arguments unconvincing.[52] Certainly making out that harming others can never be in one's interest will involve as risky and chancy an argument for Socrates in the ethical sphere as the corresponding argument is for Gandhi and others in the political sphere.

Some modern philosophers will in any case be uncomfortable with having their ethical theory be a hostage to such a controversial hypothesis as that it is never in one's interest to harm others. They will prefer to think, like Kant, that ethical theory needs to be independent of the actual details of human psychology.[53] ("What if some Hitler says he is happier harming others?" we will hear. To which Socrates may reply: Saying it doesn't make it so, and neither does sincerely believing it. We should distinguish between a bully's having rhetorically effective words to hit us with and the bully's saying something that is true.)[54] On the other hand, if ethics is to be *for us humans,* then it is arguable we must take the kind of risk involved in having our ethical theory raise such questions as the bearing on our happiness of doing harm to others. Few think that in educating their children they can insulate themselves from such questions. Why should ethical theory be any better off?[55]

At any rate, whatever the risks Socrates incurs by having his ethics depend upon considerations of human psychology,[56] what cannot be denied is that he does argue that harming others is never in one's best interest. The risks that philosophers like Kant will point out to Socrates' notion of care for the soul, and to the ethical egoism that goes along with it, are to be met by appealing to yet another expression of Socrates' views: that it is never in one's interest to harm others.[57]

V. SOCRATES' MAIN ENEMY

If virtue is the knowledge of how best to care for one's soul in order to be happy; and Socrates, the wisest human in Greece, knows only that he knows nothing; then, of course, no one has the knowledge of how best to care for one's soul – and indeed no one has virtue.[58] Why, then, is Socrates so passionate about this knowledge, forever asking what it is (under its various different names: courage, wisdom, justice, piety, temperance[59]); whether it is teachable; whether it is strong; whether it can be used for bad purposes; whether one is happier with this knowledge than if one is unjust; whether politicians, poets, artisans, rhetoricians, or sophists have it; and so forth?[60]

To answer this question, we must look at the alternatives open to one who does not have knowledge. They must be: either (a) continually strive to get closer and closer to this knowledge, even if one is virtually guaranteed never to gain it totally; or (b) try some other method for being happy and getting on in life – in particular the methods of rhetoricians and sophists. The Socratic dialogues are clear testimony to the fact that Socrates cleaves to (a). To see why, let us look briefly at Socrates' rejection of (b).

For Socrates, as for Plato, there is no doubt that the main philosophical enemy is the sophists and rhetoricians whose form of education is one that offers neutral techniques for "getting on" in private and political life – neutral in that they are indifferent to any *good* in human life other than what the individual *chooses to think* is good – the individual's "values" (as we say).[61] The sophists and rhetoricians purport to put persuasive *means* in their students' hands to achieve whatever goals "seem best" to them (*Grg.* 466b*ff,* esp. b11–e2, 467a8–468e5; and cf. 464d–465c), without raising any questions about what people take to be their ends. For Protagoras in the *Theaetetus,* it is all but explicit that there *are no further questions about ends:* What the individual *thinks* good is what *is* good "for" that individual.[62]

When the sophists say they can impart to their students a science of the best means to whatever the students' ends may be (the end being whatever the students *value* most, à la note 61 – whatever "seems best" to them à la *Grg.* 466–469), Socrates attacks the supposed science, and contrasts with it sciences like medicine, carpentry, cobblery, and navigation. The latter sciences are no more neutral about the end than they are about the means. As medicine looks to what is objectively best for health (and not just to what *seems* best to the patients for their health), so the science of virtue looks to what is objectively best for humans (not just to what humans *think* best for themselves). Thus Socrates urges against relativism the objectivity of the *sciences,* and suggests that the knowledge that is virtue is just one more objective science.

Another form of Socrates' attack on alternatives to the Socratic "examined life" is the characterizing of the minds of rhetoricians, sophists, politicians, and poets as working more by divine inspiration than by any understanding of what they are doing. When poets say true things, that is purely a product of divine inspiration (*phusei tini kai enthousiazontes*), and not at all a product of any kind of wisdom or understanding of what they have said (*Ap.* 21c*ff,* esp. 22c3). So too, interpreters of Homer like Ion say what they say not out of knowledge but by "divine dispensation" (see *Ion* 534c, 535a, 536c–d). For this "divine dispensation" as the source of *politicians'* uncomprehending activities, see *Meno* 99e.[63] Similarly, in the *Euthydemus* 289c–290a, the art of speech-making is said to be "lofty" and "divine" (*thespesia*) – like the art that charms snakes, tarantulas, and scorpions! And at *Apology* 20d–e, Socrates speaks of sophists like Gorgias, Prodicus, Hippias, and Euenos as having a wisdom "beyond that of humans." Consider now all of those pursuits of the good for humans – the pursuits of poets, exegetes, politicians, rhetoricians, and sophists – that Socrates sees as rivals to the pursuit *he* thinks humans should take up. To each of these, Socrates will say what he says of rhetoric: that it is *not a science* (*Grg.* 463a*ff* with 454d–457c). What the references to divinity betoken is the suggestion that the activities of poetry, politics (as practiced by Pericles et al.), and the interpretation of Homer (as practiced by Ion) are, like rhetoric, *not sciences.* Unlike the expertises of artisans (when they stay within the boundaries of their own expertise), these activities do not involve knowledge. How do rhetoricians, politicians, poets, and so forth achieve as much as they evidently do if they have no science, no expertise? It's by divine intervention – a gosh-darned miracle!

This, then, is Socrates' response to relativism: to deny that the states of mind of such alleged experts as rhetoricians, sophists, politicians, poets, and the like are those of legitimate scientists.

Of course I have only hinted here at *why* Socrates thinks none of these disciplines is a science. The answer has to do with the lack of coherence involved in the ends of these would-be sciences. Since rhetoric promises to get for you whatever *seems* best to you *whether or not it is in fact best,* the possibility of a serious incoherence results. (I want to be happy, and think I'll be happiest if I have a political rival exiled; so I hire an orator to find and employ the best persuasive means to my end. In fact I'm wrong that I'll be happiest that way. The result is that there is an incoherence in my desire to be happy. What I want is *that exile of my political rival which will in fact make me happiest;* but given that any exile available to me in these circumstances will *not* make me happy, there can be no science of the sort rhetoric claims to be, that can secure me that end.)[64]

In the next section, I offer another explanation of why Socrates will say that poets, rhetoricians, and the like have no knowledge of "anything they say."

VI. SOCRATIC METHOD AND SOCRATIC IGNORANCE

I conclude with some remarks on the (often doubted) sincerity of Socrates' claim to know only that he knows nothing. We can defend this sincerity, I suggest, if we attend to the strategy announced in Section III – if we notice how, for Socrates, discussing any one ethical question seems inevitably to involve one in discussing (what one might at first have thought to be) quite different ethical questions.

Consider first how Socrates argues that he knows nothing (*Ap.* 19b*ff,* esp. 20c–d). Those whom one might think wiser than Socrates, because they know something substantive about how a person should live – poets like Aeschylus, say–turn out upon Socratic examination to "know nothing of what they are saying" (*Ap.* 22c3). The difference with Socrates is that Socrates *knows* that he "knows nothing of what he is saying," while Aeschylus and others do not realize this fact. (In spite of his *concern* for care of souls, Socrates actually *knows* nothing about improving humans in the way horse trainers know about improving horses; *Ap.* 19d–20c.)

Now there are various problems with the claim to know only that one knows nothing which I haven't space to deal with here.[65] But the crucial question here is: Why does Socrates maintain that *no one at all*, himself included, knows anything substantive about the matters he is inquiring into? Let us engage in a thought experiment here. Imagine the poet Aeschylus believing that it is good to know oneself (cf. *Prometheus Bound*, 309) and Socrates affirming in his own person that it is good to know oneself (cf. *Alc.* I 127e–135e), thus apparently granting that Aeschylus's belief is true. Finally, imagine that Aeschylus believes this because he has been told so by the Oracle; that the Oracle is reliable in never saying anything untrue; and that neither Socrates nor Aeschylus has any reason to doubt what the Oracle says on this occasion. On such grounds, should we not infer that Aeschylus *knows* that it is good to know oneself? Certainly we should by the rather nonintellectual standards that modern philosophers tend to be contented with for knowledge.

Socrates, we know, will not allow that Aeschylus knows any such thing. Faced with such a claim, Socrates will ask Aeschylus a whole bunch of questions – not just narrowly homing in on the truth of the sentence "It is good to know oneself," but questioning the *reasons* why Aeschylus thinks this true, and indeed all sorts of other matters connected with knowledge generally: whether such knowledge is the whole of virtue or only a part, whether this knowledge is teachable, whether this knowledge by itself is enough to make one happy, whether passions and pleasures can overcome this knowledge, and so forth – hardly stopping short of an examination of Aeschylus's whole life (*La.* 187e–188c). If Aeschylus trips up over *any* such questions in traversing this Socratic minefield, Socrates will say Aeschylus doesn't know *even that it is good to know oneself* (*Ap.* 22c3).

A modern would be likely to defend Aeschylus by saying, "Look, it's true enough that Aeschylus doesn't know about these *other* things; but he does know that self-knowledge is good." (Just so, a modern might have defended Oedipus when he said, "I don't know what else may be true about Jocasta; but I do know I am married to her and that she is Laius's widow." Surely Socrates couldn't deny that?)

But Socrates' view was that unless Aeschylus can sustain a typical Socratic cross-examination in the vicinity – near or more remote – of the claim that it is good to know oneself, he doesn't know that it is good to know oneself.

Now why should this be? Why should knowing that self-knowledge is good require one also to know that virtue is not teachable? The hypothesis I wish to suggest here is one about the *identity of the thing known*. For Socrates, it is not enough for purposes of knowing that it is good to know oneself, that one know (as we put it nowadays) the *proposition* that it is good to know oneself.[66] Or to make a closely related point,[67] it is not enough to know that a sentence with the same meaning and grammar as "It is good to know oneself" is true. We do not know that little, I suggest, if, by Socrates' lights, we know that it is good to know oneself. For Socrates, the thing known when one knows that it is good to know oneself includes not just what the words mean, or what words are used for expressing the opinion, but also what the words refer to. Is the knowledge that one has of oneself knowledge of what is good for oneself? And is that a knowledge that cannot be overcome by pleasure? If it is, then Socrates will suppose that to know that it is good to know oneself must also involve knowing that knowledge cannot be overcome by pleasure. Now, *that knowledge cannot be overcome by pleasure* is hardly included in the *proposition* that it is good to know oneself; and it could hardly be learned from the dictionary meaning of the words "it is good to know oneself." So, for Socrates, knowing that it is good to know oneself involves a good deal more than just knowing the proposition that it is good to know oneself.

Another example may make this clearer. Take Nicias's offering of "courage is the knowledge of the fearful and the hopeful" as an account of what courage is. Nicias claims that this is a Socratic account (*La.* 194c8–d2), and Socrates acknowledges that it is (*La.* 194d3; cf. *Prt.* 358d5–7, 360c6–d5). Yet at 197e–199e, Socrates reduces this account to absurdity as follows:

> The fearful = future bads, and the hopeful = future goods;
>
> So, courage = the knowledge of future bads and goods.

> But the science of future *K*'s = the science of all *K*'s, past, present, and future;
>
> Therefore, courage is the knowledge of all bads and goods, past, present, and future.
>
> But the knowledge of all goods and bads = virtue;
>
> And, at that rate, courage, which was supposed to be only a part of virtue, would have to be the whole of virtue;
>
> So, courage can't after all be the knowledge of the fearful and the hopeful.

What has happened here? Socrates has apparently refuted his own account of what courage is. Or has he? In my "Unity of Virtue," I suggest that Nicias gets refuted because he thinks courage is only a part of virtue. Once we see, what Nicias does not see, that Socrates is here arguing for (UV), the difficulty disappears.

Now, evidently Socrates is not here in the business of refuting the *proposition* that courage is the knowledge of the fearful and the hopeful. If he were, he would be refuting a proposition he himself accepts. No, it is not propositions that he is concerned with. It is the nature of courage that he is concerned with. The courage that Nicias believes to be the knowledge of the fearful and the hopeful is a courage that is only a part of virtue. The courage that Socrates believes to be the knowledge of the fearful and the hopeful is the whole of virtue – as in the *Protagoras* (see [e] in note 21). For Socrates, to know that courage is the knowledge of the fearful and the hopeful *is* (or at least *requires*) the knowledge that courage is not merely a part of virtue.[68] Similar arguments could be developed to show that knowing that courage is the knowledge of the fearful and the hopeful also requires one to know that knowledge is strong, that no one errs willingly, that virtue is not teachable, and so forth. To know anything at all about human goodness, one will have to know everything about it.[69]

It is a mistake, then, to look at the Socratic elenchus as a process of trying to establish certain propositions on the basis of certain deductive arguments.[70] The issue is one of the *identity conditions* for *things known*. Where many moderns think that its being good to know oneself is one fact to be known, while knowledge's being strong is another fact to be known, and virtue's being knowledge another, virtue's being unteachable another, Socrates does not see the truths about good and bad as breaking up into these and so many other atoms clearly marked off from each other. For Socrates, a lack of understanding about how it is that virtue can be unteachable and yet be knowledge will show a defect in one's knowledge that it is good to know oneself.

Now, it is true that something like the point I am making here can be translated into a point using propositions. The fact that Socrates will not allow something to be knowledge that involves affirmation of one expression of Socratic belief but denial of another can be accounted for by saying what I am saying – that the thing to be known is broader than a proposition. But it can also be accounted for by saying that knowledge of one proposition is not possible in isolation from knowledge of all sorts of other propositions.[71] It is because interpreters often seem implicitly to grasp this interconnection of the propositions they find in Socrates, that they for the most part stay so well in touch with Socrates' views – in spite of their being wedded to propositions.[72] The danger for such interpreters comes when, for example, they start thinking of Socratic "definitions" as giving necessary and sufficient conditions for the application of a virtue-word to an action. For then they are tending to think of such "propositions" as intelligible in isolation from other propositions. (Cf. note 60.)

So much, then, in explanation of Socrates' claim that poets don't know anything of what they are saying. Their supposed knowledge of some one proposition, in isolation from others, won't count as knowledge of anything. This explanation of why Socrates says that poets (and indeed politicians, interpreters of Homer, rhetoricians, and – outside of their specific expertise – artisans) know nothing of anything they say, thus supplements the explanation sketched briefly at the end of Section V.[73]

Besides helping us to understand why Socrates appears to attack views he himself accepts, these remarks may also help us to understand the role of the so-called Socratic paradoxes. A paradoxical remark – Socrates sometimes speaks of "riddles" – is just the sort of thing to force one to see the surprising interweavings of (what moderns tend to think of as) quite different Socratic claims – an interweaving that is central to Socrates' whole approach to ethics. (Socratic paradoxes are in this respect just like contradictions or absurd conclusions reached after some Socratic dialectic.)

Again, my explanation helps us to see that when Socrates reduces his interlocutors to absurdity by his elenchus, he is not turning his back on them in a failure of love.[74] For Socrates does not think giving someone a formula, such as "Courage is the knowledge of the fearful and the hopeful," will be any help at all to them if they don't understand – and understand *for themselves* – what that broad *thing to be known* is that that sentence makes reference to. (Compare "Oedipus is married to Jocasta" not being of any help to the Department of Public Health in Thebes, when, in tracking down the sources of the plague, it asks, "Whom is Oedipus married to?" The verbal formula, without the whole truth about the person asked about, will be no help at all.) Only someone in possession of the whole truth about courage and knowledge will for Socrates *know* that courage is the knowledge of the fearful and the hopeful. Only such a person will have the knowledge that is virtue. Love for one's interlocutors involves *precisely* trying to bring them to such knowledge in probably the only way it can be done – by Socratic elenchus – and without the corrupting influence of Socratic (or any other) authority.

My explanation also handles two other explananda. First, why does Socrates insist on examining only people's actual beliefs?[75] Because he is not interested in having them hand *him* a mere formula for examination – any more than he thinks they will be helped by being handed a mere formula.[76] Particular expressions of belief on a person's part are also to cover parts of the interlocutor's belief not given merely by the words in that expression or by their (dictionary) meanings. As we have seen, Nicias's belief that courage is the knowledge of the fearful and the hopeful is a belief about *a (supposed) courage which is only part of virtue. That* is the belief of Nicias's which is to be examined – not a belief that the *proposition*

> Courage is the knowledge of the fearful and the hopeful (whether courage is a part of virtue or the whole of it)

is true.

Second, what is the connection between the Socratic questioning of beliefs and the "existential dimension" of the elenchus – the examining of people's whole lives (*La.* 187e–188a)? It is not a case of a "double objective" for the elenchus: examining the truth of a proposition and examining the whole life of a person.[77] No, since (a) to examine a person's belief about courage will be to examine that person's total body of belief about virtue, knowledge, and the good life; and (b) desires always automatically adjust to one's beliefs (see [10] in section II); it will follow that to examine a person's belief about courage will be to examine that person's whole life.

As to Socrates' own knowledge, Socrates is not saying he has no grip whatever on any part of the whole, or indeed on the whole. He is just claiming that what is known when one knows any part of the whole adequately will in fact include knowledge of the whole. It follows, as a consequence, that the only way to set people on the path of virtue will be to begin that process of self-examination that alone will make sure that, little by little, they come to see (all together) that virtue is knowledge, that virtue is one, that knowledge is strong against pleasure and passion, that virtue is not teachable (at least in the ordinary way), and that desire is for good. Or, lest the last sentence seem to speak of five different propositions,[78] that the virtue which is knowledge, strong against pleasure and passion (cooperating always with desire which is always for the good), and unteachable in the ordinary way, is one. We may suspect, though Socrates never tells us so, that Socrates thinks himself rather farther along than anyone else in this attempt to grasp the whole. But unless he thinks there is nothing left for him to figure out and fit together, he may still fairly claim to know only that he knows nothing.

One final objection. Does Socrates really think there are still things for him to figure out? Richard Kraut asks, appropriately enough, what evidence I have, on my interpretation of Socrates, that Socrates thought there were still problems left for him to solve.[79] He points out that I should feel this difficulty particularly acutely because I hold (in Section III and note 41) that Socrates often seems to know just what he is trying to get us to understand, and even dangles before our noses solutions to puzzles he has propounded. Where then are there examples of unsolved problems, if the solutions are always being dangled before us? Why would Plato represent Socrates as a searcher who lacks answers and not give us any examples of Socrates lacking answers? (On Kraut's own approach to Socrates, we are supposed to find examples of unsolved problems in Socrates' really not knowing what to suggest to us at the end of the *H. Mi.* or at the end of the refutation of Nicias's [Socratic] account of courage as the knowledge of the fearful and the hopeful. See notes 40, 41.)

My response is this: First, wherever a dialogue leaves us in *aporia*, experience has suggested to me that the strategy of Section III – assuming that there is something Socrates wants us to see and trying to track it down – almost always pays dividends. I am willing for this principle to stand or fall by the accounts it yields of passages like those just cited from the *Hippias Minor* and the *Laches,* as well as others cited in note 41. Does this suggest that Socrates has all the answers? I don't see why it should. The whole point of the present section of the paper – as of Section III and of note 41 – is that to get anything right about the human good, you have to get everything right about it. Socrates still had lots of things to say more about, and to get right.

But what specific things did Socrates still have to figure out? Some examples that spring to mind right away are (a) the nature of happiness (about which Socrates, unlike Aristotle, says very little that is useful); (b) the nature of pleasure (again the contrast with Aristotle is striking); (c) the defects of radical Protagoreanism (here it is the contrast with Plato's *Theaetetus* that is striking) – though Socrates is less likely to have reflected on the possibility of any anti-Protagorean strategy other than the appeal to the sciences; (d) a more articulated and more convincing set of arguments that it always harms you to harm others; (e) more convincing accounts of the *function* of humans and of the art of ruling; and so forth. I feel all of these as unsolved problems in Socrates. It is true that none of them gets mentioned as such by Socrates. But it is hard to believe he didn't actually feel at least the problems in (a), (b), (d), and (e). And the fact that they don't get mentioned as unsolved problems is perhaps well enough explained merely by the fact that Socrates is busy enough trying to get his interlocutors to think their way through some of the problems Socrates *has* more or less seen his way through.

The crux of the issue is this. Kraut sees knowing what courage is as knowing the definition of courage; and this he sees as knowing some one particular proposition about courage (see the references in note 72). This proposition, Kraut maintains, Socrates doesn't know to be true. So he can't mean us, in the *Laches,* to see that courage, the knowledge of the fearful and the hopeful, is identical with the knowledge of goods and bads which is virtue.

As against this, I say this propositional view of what courage is is too dangerously like the view that "What is courage?" asks for the *meaning* of "courage," rather than the reference. (Propositions are meanings of sentences.) There is no reason why Socrates should not have wanted us to see – as a *partial* account of what courage is, and as providing the solution to a problem Nicias can't see his way through – that courage is the whole of virtue. But to have such a partial account is not yet to know what the reference of "courage" is. To know what courage is, it is not enough to offer some one proposition (the meaning, or sense, of some sentence) as a definition. One needs to know what the *reference* of courage is. Frege says about reference: "Comprehensive knowledge of the reference would require us to be able to say immediately whether any given sense belongs to it. To such knowledge we never attain."[80] That is the kind of knowledge of virtue, knowledge, power, desire, good, and so forth that I see Socrates striving for.[81]

NOTES

1 The most considerable alternative interpretations of Socrates overall that I know of, and the ones I most admire, are those of Terence Irwin, *Plato's Moral Theory* (Oxford, 1977); Richard Kraut, *Socrates and the State* (Princeton, 1984); G. X. Santas, *Socrates: Philosophy in Plato's Early Dialogues*, (London, 1979); and Gregory Vlastos, *Platonic Studies*, 2d ed. (Princeton, 1981), and a plethora of earlier articles by Vlastos. Though on a number of points Irwin's views are close to mine (in, for example, my "The Unity of Virtue," *Philosophical Review* 82 [1973]: 35–68), he also seems to me rather to straitjacket Socrates for purposes of getting a neat exegetical opposition with Plato. (See, as an indication, note 14 below.) In Kraut I find both more to agree with (notes 72, 14, 16 below) and more to disagree with (notes 12, 16, 40, 51, 54, 60, 63) than in any of the others. Vlastos was of course the greatest Socrates scholar of the century, and his *Socrates: Ironist and Moral Philosopher* (Cambridge, 1991) adds to the many important Socratic studies he had already published. Like most people's in the field, my views about Socrates have been formed in great part by thinking about what Vlastos says about Socrates. My own differences with Vlastos, which are many, flow mainly, I think, from philosophical differences between us.

2 For (i), see *Soph. El.* 183b6–8; for (ii)–(v), see esp. *Met.* I.6.987a29–b14 (with 6.987b22–24, 27–33, and 5.987a20–25) and XIII.4.1078b12–34, as well as the discussion in W. D. Ross, *Aristotle's Metaphysics* (Oxford 1924), 1:xxxiii–xlv, xlvii, 158–161; 2: 420–3. It has been plausibly suggested that the term "induction" (*epagōgē*) refers to the wide use of analogy in Plato's early dialogues, especially the Analogy of the Arts: If,

in medicine, the doctor looks to the health of his or her patients; and, in navigation, the pilot looks to the safe passage of his or her passengers; then surely in ruling, the ruler will look to the interests of those over whom he or she rules. As the horse trainer stands to horses, so those who would teach virtue stand to humans. And so forth. See Vlastos, ed., *Plato: Protagoras* (Indianapolis, 1956), xxix n. 18, with n. 49; Richard Robinson, *Plato's Earlier Dialectic* (Oxford, 1953), 41*ff.*

3 The question has become controversial in recent years. Though I disagree strongly with recent accounts, adequate treatment of the notion is beyond the scope of the present paper.

4 There is reason to believe Aristotle's testimony is based on more than just Plato's dialogues. For example, Aristotle could not have learned from the dialogues that Cratylus was an early teacher of Plato. (Vlastos, "Socrates," *Proceedings of the British Academy* 74 [1988]: 104–5, citing a 1934 remark of Ross's quoted in Andreas Patzer, ed., *Der Historische Sokrates* [Darmstadt, 1987].)

5 For example, the what-is-it of justice is the square, or the number 4: As the factors of 4 (2 × 2) behave to each other in exactly the same way, so it is with the citizens of a just state. See Ross's commentary in *Aristotle's Metaphysics* on 985b29, 987a22, 30, 1078b23; see also *Grg.* 507e6*ff*, esp. 508a6.

6 The point of Aristotle's remark is presumably that both notions are problematic in the same way. (Aristotle seems content to leave the relation between particulars and his own universals unexplained and primitive.)

7 For an explanation of stylometry and its coordination with our meager knowledge of the chronology of Plato's dialogues, along with a sketch of the history of stylometric scholarship, see Leonard Brandwood's authoritative essay that is Chapter 3 of this volume and his *The Chronology of Plato's Dialogues* (Cambridge, 1990). The latter volume describes in some detail, and for the first time in print, the results of Brandwood's important doctoral dissertation (1958). All Plato scholars will applaud its appearance at long last. Unfortunately, this volume appeared too late to be considered in my article. I was able, however, thanks to Brandwood's kindness, to see a draft of his contribution to this volume while preparing my own.

8 See Brandwood's guarded remarks in Chapter 3 ("no more than a probability") on Ritter's 1935 examination of the early dialogues, as well as his remarks at the end of the essay. In Brandwood's *A Word Index to Plato* (Leeds, 1976), xvii, the *Grg.* and *Meno* are not distinguished from the dialogues of the third subgroup. I see no difficulty in the possibility that the *Lys.*, *Menex.*, and *Euthd.* may be later than the *Grg.* and *Meno*. *Rep.* I may be a second edition, stylistically revised for inclusion in the

Rep. as a whole. As Brandwood stresses, the great triumphs of stylometry reside in the treatment of later dialogues. A general grouping of early dialogues separate from middle and late is assured, but not much is certain about the ordering within the early dialogues.

9 This is true of the *Phd.* more or less throughout, of the upward path of the *Smp.* (210–212), and of the discussion of flux and the Forms in the *Cra.*, especially at the end of the dialogue. The placing of these three dialogues as closer to middle dialogues like the *Rep.* (Books II–X), *Prm.*, *Tht.*, and *Phdr.* coheres with Brandwood's cautious stylometric judgment. Cf. also his *Word Index*, xviii.

10 See E. R. Dodds, *Plato: Gorgias* (Oxford, 1959), 18–30; also W. K. C. Guthrie, *A History of Greek Philosophy* (Cambridge, 1969, 1975), 3:29–39; 4: 39–56. Very little can be said about exact dates. See, for example, K. J. Dover, "The Date of Plato's Symposium," *Phronesis* 10 (1965): 2–20.

11 On optimism vs. pessimism, I have this sort of thing in mind: Socrates thought he could make a difference (at any rate some small difference) in improving himself and those around him – especially the young – by engaging in what he enjoyed most: rational discussion of questions as to how to live. The attitudes to the masses and to the military in Plato's totalitarian political theory reflects Plato's despair about reaching any but a few via rational discussion – and then only after long training.

12 For the small interest even in political theory in the Socratic dialogues – in sharp contrast to the later dialogues – see Vlastos, "Socrates," 97–8. For a remarkable and instructive discussion of the *Crito*, which sometimes (esp. in chap. 8) differs sharply from my own views, see Kraut, *Socrates*.

13 See Vlastos, "Socrates," 94–5.

14 Socrates uses *technē* ("art" or "craft") and *epistēmē* ("knowledge" or "science") interchangeably. "Expertise" seems to me the best word for the single conception Socrates has in mind here, and "science" next best (for the continuity it keeps with Plato's *epistēmē*).

One needs to be careful with "craft" if that word is taken as suggesting a *dis*continuity with "science" – and even more if it is taken as suggesting that Socrates has a "craft-knowledge" conception of ethics (Irwin, *Plato's Moral Theory*, 71–101, thence structuring the discussions in chaps. 4, 5). On this supposed "craft-knowledge" conception, ethics is a science studying only objectionably narrow *instrumental* means to some further (independently identifiable) end. Here Irwin contrasts Socrates unfavorably with Aristotle and Plato, in whom the virtuous activity that ethics studies is itself an *ingredient* means to happiness – not a mere instrument for gaining some further goal of happiness, but itself *part* of the activity in which happiness consists. (To use J. L. Ackrill's examples from lectures in the 1960s, a bathing suit, or taking the train to Eastbourne, are instrumental means to having a good holiday, while going swimming is an ingredient of having a good holiday: cf. Ackrill, "Aristotle on *Eudaimonia*," *Proceedings of the British Academy* [1974]: 339–59.)

Now I am not at all convinced that Socrates thinks virtue a mere instrumental means to happiness. For Socrates surely thinks that, other circumstances being favorable, the life of wisdom *is* the happy life (*Euthd.* 281d–e: cf. Kraut, *Socrates*, 211 n. 41); and he surely thinks that care for the soul and care for the souls of the young – the unremitting and lifelong inquiry into how to live (*Rep.* I 352d and *Grg.* 500c, 487e–488a, 472c–d), the constant and thorough testing and examining of others and oneself – is a principal *ingredient* of happiness. Cf. also *Ap.* 41c, where Socrates tells us that if, after his execution, there happens to be an afterlife, what an incredible happiness it will be to be with, discuss with, and examine the heroes of the Trojan War. Why need Socrates have thought happiness to be recognizable independently of the sort of hard ethical thinking and discrimination that he so evidently spent his whole life engaging in and getting others to engage in?

15 See Vlastos, "Socratic Knowledge and Platonic 'Pessimism,'" *Philosophical Review* 66 (1957): 226–38.

16 Cf. the modern either-or question, Do we let our younger children watch such and such programs on TV or not? For Plato, as for Aristotle, that would be exactly the right question. For Socrates, this would be sidestepping the central issue, which is: Do we, or do we not, discuss with our children the content of what they are watching?

If I am right, Socrates would have thought of Platonic or Freudian attitudes to childhood training, or Aristotelian or Skinnerian conditioning – all of them emphasizing an early more or less reason-independent training – as exceedingly blunt instruments for childhood nurture. He would have resisted the (Protagorean!) suggestion in Kraut, *Socrates*, 219–25, 296, that the laws of Athens by themselves provide (something of a) training in virtue – leading to the additions of some true propositions to one's beliefs. (On propositions, cf. note 72 below, with notes 68, 78.) On the other hand, I have no problem with the quite different suggestion in *Socrates*, 226–8, that Socrates would have approved of the laws of Athens for their facilitating of free inquiry.

17 *Grg.* 463a (cf. 454c–456c); *Rep.* VI 493a–c; *Phdr.* 259e*ff*, esp. 261e–262c, 272d–274a. For parallel attitudes to poetry, see *Ion* 536c, 541e–542b; *Rep.* X 598b–d. Cf. also my "Socrates on the Impossibility of Belief-Relative Sciences," in *Proceedings of the Boston Area Colloquium in*

Ancient Philosophy, ed. John J. Cleary, 3:263–325, as well as section V of this chapter.

18 Some may wonder, How exactly are Socrates and Plato supposed to differ here? (a) It is true that Socrates will say that when we persuade via the emotions we are not teaching. But couldn't Plato grant that point? On the other hand, (b) surely Socrates will have to grant that when we persuade via the emotions – and indeed even when Gorgias persuades – we are just as much getting people to hold the beliefs we want them to hold as we do when we teach them? (I am grateful to Richard Kraut for pointing out that what I have said so far leaves me open to objections of this general sort.)

As to (a), Plato will still need a distinction between teaching and correct indoctrination (knowledge and correct, or true, belief). But the distinction between knowledge and true belief is virtually absent from the Socratic dialogues. It is true that to say this is not to say much, since this absence is itself an urgent explanandum (see further note 31). But the difference between Socrates and Plato remains.

On (b), see my discussion of why rhetoric is not a science in my "Power and Desire in Socrates: The Argument of *Gorgias* 466a–468e that Orators and Tyrants Have no Power in the City," *Apeiron* 24 (1991): 147–202; also my "Belief-Relative Sciences." I argue in the former paper that Socrates held that without the science of goods and bads, one can never do the very thing one wants to do. (For a little on his reasoning here, see note 25 below, as well as section V, next-to-last paragraph.) It will be a corollary of this claim that without getting the persons to be persuaded to *understand for themselves* just what is good or bad about what is to be done, one will not be able to persuade them of the very thing one wants to persuade them of. This has Socrates placing limitations on persuasion via appeals to the emotions that Plato simply ignores.

19 I have suggested in my *The Ascent from Nominalism: Some Existence Arguments in Plato's Middle Dialogues* (Dordrecht, 1987), xi–xii, 12–16, 26–33, 40–3, that Plato, for as long as he is obsessed with the theory of recollection, tends to suppose that our knowledge of the Forms, once attained, can have the kind of self-evidence that knowledge of the axioms of geometry seemed to many Greeks to have. This tempts Plato to give mathematical sciences a special status, higher than that belonging to, say, carpentry; and to think of *the square, the odd, equality,* and *the number one* (*one itself*) as special objects to which he may liken *the just itself, the good itself,* and so forth.

Against this more Pythagorean attitude to mathematics, Plato is elsewhere more evenhanded about the sciences, showing himself willing to grant to the shuttle itself and the bed itself, along with Forms of the elements Earth, Air, Fire, and Water, quite as much right to exist as Forms as do the Good Itself or the Square Itself. If the tendency to give greater weight to mathematics is more Pythagorean, the evenhandedness about Forms for the shuttle, the bed, and so forth, is more heir to a Socratic strain about the sciences.

20 Why might not persons act virtuously by acting as virtuous persons would – though by good fortune, since they do not understand why they should act that way? I have tried to respond to this question in a number of places elsewhere. See "Belief-Relative Sciences," Appendix II, 316–20, where I ask what the chances are that someone entirely ignorant of the science of engineering should by good fortune hit on just the right specifications for building the Golden Gate Bridge. (Living a good life, I suggest, is not fundamentally easier than building complicated bridges.)

21 A word on the differences between (UV) and (UVV). According to (UV) – for which, see my 1973 paper "The Unity of Virtue" – there is really just one virtue, with five different names. (Cf. *Prt.* 329c6–d1, 349b2–3, and compare "The Morning Star" and "The Evening Star": though these two expressions have different meanings, they refer to the same object, the planet Venus. They have the same reference.) According to (UVV) – for which see Vlastos, "The Unity of the Virtues in the *Protagoras*," in *Platonic Studies*, 221*ff*, with 410*ff*, 418*ff* – Socrates believes there are five different virtues, and whoever has any one of them has all the others.

(UV) is naturally put together with the well-known Socratic doctrine that virtue is knowledge, and the specification of the knowledge in question as *the knowledge of goods and bads*, to yield

> that one and the same thing that is named by these various virtue-names is the knowledge of goods and bads.

Thus (UV) + "Virtue is knowledge" says that the one thing whose presence explains not only courageous deeds (in situations of danger), but also temperate deeds (in situations of temptations of desire and pleasure), and wise, just, and pious deeds in other sorts of situations, is – and is no more than – the knowledge of goods and bads.

Those interpreters who claim that Socrates holds only (UVV) must obviously give a somewhat different account of the relation the knowledge of goods and bads has to the five supposedly different virtues. They must also offer a somewhat more complex explanation of Socrates' suggesting in some places that (a) *wisdom* is identical with virtue (*Euthd.* 281e, *Meno* 88b–89a), and in others that (b) *justice* is the whole of virtue (asserted in *Rep.* I 335c, cf. 350b–d, 351a–c, 353e–354b; implied by *H. Mi.* 375d–376b); perhaps also implying in others that (c) courage is the whole of virtue (*La.* 197e–199e) and in others that (d) temperance, as the knowledge of good and bad (*Chrm.* 174b–d), is the whole of virtue (*La.* 199d–e). Cf. also the suggestion (implication?) that (e) the temperance at *Prt.* 356c8–e4, 357a5–b6, is identical with the courage at 360c6–d5, both being sciences for measuring goods and bads, the pleasant and the painful (360a8; so also C. C. W. Taylor, *Plato's Protagoras* [Oxford, 1976], 162–3, 209, 213–14, and J. C. B. Gosling and C. C. W. Taylor, *The Greeks on Pleasure* [Oxford, 1982], 55).

One other important difference between (UV) and (UVV) is in their reading of answers to the "What is it?" question. For (UVV), "Courage is the knowledge of the fearful and the hopeful" gives the *meaning* (Fregean sense) of "courage," while for (UV) it gives the *reference* – in exact parallel with "The knowledge of future *K*'s is the knowledge of all *K*'s past, present, and future" (an obvious identity of reference rather than meaning; cf. *La.* 194e–195a1 with 198d1–199a4, as well as the brief discussion of this account of courage in section VI).

The real issue between (UV) and (UVV) lies in the question whether Socrates sought the *meaning* of "courage" or the *reference.* (Or, put in another way, whether the unity Socrates speaks of is a matter of *equivalence of meanings* or of *identity of reference:* see my "Unity of Virtue.") That the issue is one of meaning vs. reference may be obscured if too much attention is paid to my speaking of the virtues as causal entities in my "Unity of Virtue." In fact I only introduced this expression under pressure from the editors of the *Philosophical Review* (whose concern for the welfare of the paper I, as a young philosopher, much appreciated, in spite of my feeling that they were wrong on this point). I had wished to keep the discussion on the level of virtues being *references* rather than *meaning* (or things with the identity conditions of meanings). On the other hand, the talk of causal entities will do no harm, provided one realizes that virtues are causal entities *not* because all abstract nouns stand for causal entities rather than meanings, but because all abstract nouns stand for their references rather than their meanings. In the case of virtue-words, the references just *happen* to be causal entities. Vlastos, in "What Did Socrates Understand by His 'What Is *F*' Question?" *Platonic Studies,* 410–17, misses this last point. He takes it to be a refutation of (UV) that "shape" in the *Meno* does not refer to a causal entity. But it is no refutation at all, but rather an *ignoratio elenchi,* since the reference of "shape" is not a causal entity. The *Meno* passages are in fact inconclusive as between the meaning and the reference of "shape." (One might note in this connection, however, that the two possible accounts of shape that are offered are very far from synonymous. But shouldn't they look something like synonymous if both are supposed to be good candidates for the meaning?) Vlastos also argues that "quickness" at *La.* 192a1–b4 can't be a state of soul, so must be a meaning. But (a) that doesn't show that "quickness" isn't the reference rather than the meaning; and, in any case, (b) on Vlastos's reading of "quickness" here, he should say that the "quietness" or "slowness" that is contrasted with "quickness" at *Chrm.* 159b3*ff,* esp. c4, 6–9, d5, 10–11, e3–10, 160a1–d3, also can't be a state of soul. But plainly it is: The contrast being debated in the *Chrm.* passage is precisely that between people in whose souls there is quietness and those in whose souls there is energy. Other arguments of Vlastos on this point will have to be postponed to another time.

Again, (UV) has the advantage of giving a far simpler and cleaner reading of *La.* 197e–199e. As the identity of

the science of future goods and bads

with

the science of all goods and bads, past, present, and future

is an identity of references and not of meanings, so for the identity of the science of the fearful and the hopeful with the science of all goods and bads which is identical with virtue. (Again, see the brief discussion in Section VI.) Contrast the complicated reading Vlastos must give to this argument in *Platonic Studies,* 266–9 – with Socrates making gratuitous meaning-reference confusions.

Finally, on the other side, I should note that (UV) lies best open to attack in passages about justice, courage, and so forth being "parts" of virtue in the way that odd is a part of number (cf. *Grg.* 462e*ff*): as at *Euphr.* 11e–12e (though piety's being a part of justice is not followed up here; and cf. *Grg.* 507a7–b4) and *Meno* 73d–75a.

(Something should be said about the last passage, since Vlastos makes so much of it in "Socrates on 'The Parts of Virtue,' " *Platonic Studies,* 418–23. The force of the crucial passage 73d7–e2 – about justice just being *a* virtue – is considerably lessened when we notice the same theme reappearing later at 78d3–79c10. The latter passage in turn leads us on toward the discussion of whether virtue as a whole is knowledge at 87b*ff.* As already noted in [a] above, Socrates in 87b*ff* in effect argues that wisdom is *identical* with virtue as a whole – which can only happen if courage, etc., are identical with wisdom. See esp. 88b1–d3. More precisely, what Socrates is saying here is that virtue *is* wisdom, or a part of wisdom. [Cf, "a kind of wisdom" at 88d3, cf. *La.* 194d10, and compare 89a1 with 88d2.] Note that, like other recent commentators, including Bluck, I here depart from Guthrie, who translates that wisdom is virtue or a part of virtue, rather than virtue being wisdom or a part of wisdom. Aside from the parallels I have just cited against this, there is the point that if Socrates were saying here that wisdom might be only a *part* of virtue, then 89c2–3 would be a nonsequitur: if wisdom might be only a part of virtue, we could not infer that virtue is teachable.)

I should record here that it was Vlastos who, some twenty-five years ago, brought home to me the importance of the point that the military class in *Rep.* IV can have (at least demotic) courage without having wisdom, just by having true belief – thus contradicting anything that could have been said in the Socratic dialogues, whether we interpret them in terms of (UV) or in terms of (UVV). Also that the credit for using *Meno* 87b*ff* against the earlier part of the *Meno* belongs to Irwin, *Plato's Moral Theory,* 301 n. 57 and 305–6 n. 3.

22 Cf. *Meno* 77b*ff,* esp. 78b, with passages cited in note 24.

23 "best for *me*": I here assume what I shall argue briefly in Section IV, that Socrates is an ethical egoist. For the move from "good" to "good for *me,*" see *Meno* 77c8, as noted by R. S. Bluck, *Plato's Meno* (Cambridge, 1961), 71, as well as *Grg.* 468b6. For the move from "good" to "best," see *Grg.* 466a–468e.

24 On the importance of the means–end distinction to the Socratic theory of desire, see esp. *Grg.* 466a–468e, *Lys.* 219b–220b, *La.* 185c–e, as well as *Euthd.* 281d–282a, and possibly *Meno* 77e5–78a8. Usually, the Socratic theory that all desire is for the good is interpreted without reference to the means–end distinction – as saying that all desire is for the *apparent* good. (*Apparent* good because of the following sort of case: I desire to do this action, thinking it good, though in fact it is a bad action – a mistake. So how is my desire for the good? It's for what I *think* good – the apparent good.)

But once one notices the centrality of the means–end distinction to Socrates' account of desire, it becomes clear that the usual interpretation cannot be right – especially when we are speaking of ends. (On means, see also notes 42, 64.) On the usual interpretation, to desire something as a means to an end can only be to desire what one *thinks* the best means to what one *thinks* is the best end. But then on that interpretation, one will desire the *apparently* best end, not the really best end.

As against this, careful study of the passage cited above will make it clear that Socrates held that one desires the really best end. (For Plato's grasp on this point, and Aristotle's apparent missing of it, see *Rep.* VI 505e–506a, *Top.* VI 146b36–147a11. See also my "Power and Desire," esp. Section 12. The latter paper is the first in a series of discussions in which I shall be opposing the view that Socrates thinks we desire the *apparently* best end, not the really best end, and examining the Socratic theory of desire that results from paying due attention to the means–end distinction.)

25 "Desire to eat this pastry": Strictly, this should be: desire to eat *this pastry which will lead to the end which is in fact best for me in the circumstances.* (The latter is in fact the "very thing one wants to do" of note 18; cf. also note 24.) When the pastry is in fact bad for me, there results a certain incoherence in the desire for the means, in the way in which when we apply beliefs we suppose to be about the real world *to* the real world, we get an incoherence in our beliefs. (Compare: "I believe of Jocasta – *whoever* she is [you plug it in – that's whom my belief is about] – that she is not my mother.") I discuss this incoherence briefly in Section 12 of "Power and Desire"; and in a little more detail in two hitherto unpublished manuscripts: "Plato and Frege" and "Plato and Protagoras." Cf. also the next-to-last paragraph of Section V of this chapter, with note 64.

26 Strictly: the desire to do that abstaining which will lead to . . . (as in note 25).

27 So N. R. Murphy, *The Interpretation of Plato's Republic* (Oxford, 1951), 28–9, and Penner, "Thought and Desire in Plato," in *Plato,* vol. 2., ed. Gregory Vlastos, 96–118. Cf. also *Phdr.* 237d–238c.

28 See note 11.

29 The simpler picture Plato gives us of irrational and weak human behavior has been widely believed to be correct, more or less from the time of Plato's parts of the soul doctrine; and Socrates' account has been thought to be incorrect. See, for example, the impressive attacks on Socratic intellectualism in Gregory Vlastos, *Plato: Protagoras,* xxxix–xl, xlii–xliii, and Vlastos, "Introduction: The Paradox of Socrates," in *The Philosophy of Socrates,* ed. G. Vlastos (Garden City, N.Y., 1971), 15–16, and the endorsement of the parts of the soul doctrine in Vlastos, "Socrates," 99, with n. 63. See also my exposition of that doctrine in "Thought and Desire" and my attack on it in "Plato and Davidson: Parts of the Soul and Weakness of Will," in *Canadian Journal of Philosophy,* supp. vol. 16 (1990): 35–74.

30 Cf. *Laws* 860d–863e, *Sph.* 227e–230e; *Ti.* 86c–e, *Laws* 731c and 734b.

31 Even a person with true opinion, be it noted (though true opinion is not mentioned in the *Prt.* – or indeed anywhere in the Socratic dialogues, save only the transitional *Meno* and *Grg.*). This absence of true opinion is a key explanandum for interpreters of the Socratic dialogues.

32 The question of the instability of opinion is omitted in almost all accounts of the actual *argument* for the strength of knowledge in the *Prt.* These accounts of the strength of knowledge simply follow from "No

one errs willingly" together with "Whoever knows that *p* also believes (or truly believes) that *p*." So, for example, the fine pieces by G. X. Santas, *Socrates: Philosophy in Plato's Early Dialogues* (London, 1979), chap. 7, and by James J. Walsh, *Aristotle's Conception of Moral Weakness* (New York, 1963), chap. 1. Such accounts have the consequence that Socrates should hold that knowledge is strong because *belief* is strong (or – if erring is a form of weakness – because *true belief* is strong). For a sketch of the view presented in the text (and to be elaborated elsewhere) see my "Plato and Davidson."

33 I am not here denying that knowledge is necessary to the rational part. What I am questioning is whether that knowledge is the real source of the strength that the rational part has in holding out against appetite. And I am suggesting that the source of the strength resides in the training of emotions and desires to follow whatever reason says. (If one's reason perchance came to a false conclusion, reason would still be strong. This is at the furthest remove from Socrates' conception of the strength of knowledge.) Richard Kraut has suggested to me that Plato would have said that understanding of the Forms would intensify one's desire to be virtuous. This can be granted, I think, without entirely removing the suspicions about the source of the strength of reason that I have been raising here.

34 Again, see note 11.

35 Just a few examples: *La.* 194d1–9; *Euthd.* 278d–e; *Rep.* I 339b with 354a; *Euphr.* 14b–c. (Euthyphro turns away [14a11] just when he is on the verge of an answer [13e10–11]. If justice is the service [*therapeia*] of humans and piety the service of gods [11e*ff*, esp. 12e6–8], what is the work [*ergon*] the gods undertake when our service helps them? *Euphr.* 14c*ff* simply shows the bad effects of this turning aside.)

In addition, *Meno* 77b–78c; *Lys.* 207d–210d with 211a4–5; *Ap.* 24c–26a, 26b–27a; *Chrm.* 172b–174b7 (Socrates' dream); *Grg.* 453b7–455a6; are just a few examples of actual bits of dialectic where Socrates lets us know what positive result he seeks, and indeed that he has gained it. Cf. also *La.* 192b–193d where Nicias at 195c5–d10 sees what Socrates wanted Laches to see.

36 *H. Mi.* 375d*ff*; cf. *Rep.* I 335c, cf. 350b–d, 351a–c, 353e–354b.

37 Socrates evidently uses justice and virtue in the passage interchangeably: cf. also *Rep.* I 350d, 351a–c, 353e, and (b) in note 21.

38 See preceding note.

39 In my "Socrates on Virtue and Motivation," in *Exegesis and Argument*, ed. E. N. Lee, A. P. D Mourelatos, and R. M. Rorty (Assem, 1973), 133–51, I use the following analogy: Economic man never errs willingly at maximizing his own profit. For he can never have an economic motive

to fail to maximize his own profit. But any other expert *can* have an economic motive for erring willingly at their particular science. For example, it may be more economically profitable for a doctor to subtly kill off a patient in order to gain earlier and more profitable access to the patient's legacy. Cf. also *Grg.* 502c2–d7, as well as the similar argument I make at note 49. Cf. also *Rep.* 505d–e for a close relative of this point in Plato.

40 As against the interpretation of the *H. Mi.* offered here, Kraut, *Socrates,* 311–16, argues that Socrates is honestly perplexed by the conflict between virtue's being a science and the sciences being ambivalent, appealing in particular to the sincerity of 372d7–e1. I would argue that the immediate context (b4–d7, e3–d6) suggests irony rather than sincerity. Mainly, however, I just don't see the dictum "No one errs willingly" not occurring to Socrates as relevant to resolving the announced conflict as he wrote the last lines of this dialogue. Kraut and I are agreed, however, on the seriousness of the issue raised by ambivalence for Socrates' ethical egoism. See also notes 51 and 54.

41 Here are some (sketchily indicated) examples:

a. *Lys.* 216d–217a plus 217a–218c – in spite of 218c*ff,* esp. 220c1–e6 with escape clause at 220e6*ff,* esp. 221a5–c1 (with more puzzles for the interlocutors to follow).
b. *La.* 197e–199e, esp. 198c6–7 (cf. 194d1–9 with 194e11–195a1) plus 198a4–5 – and cf. the dropped hint at 195a4–5 of what Nicias is missing at the end. (This passage is discussed briefly in Section 6.)
c. *Meno* 78c–79e, esp. 78c4–5 (Socrates' own answer to the question what virtue is!) plus c5–d3 (Meno's disastrous view of what things are good) plus 79a3–5.
d. *Chrm.* 172c–174d. Here Socrates reduces to absurdity Critias's view that temperance is the supposed knowledge (science) of the things one knows and doesn't know, by showing that the knowledge that makes medicine, house building, and all the other sciences beneficial is the knowledge (science) of good and bad (174b10–c4, d5–6, e2). It is the knowledge of good and bad, and not temperance – i.e., not the supposed knowledge (science) of the things one knows and doesn't know (174b12–c2 with 174d3–6). And though the hint is plainly dropped that Critias should identify temperance with the knowledge (science) of good and bad, Critias is too anxious of victory (cf. earlier 162c–e, 169c–d) and hangs on tenaciously to the supposed knowledge (science) of what one knows and doesn't know (174d–175a8). It is also noteworthy that Critias's main account of temperance (to which Socrates steers him at 164a–c), as knowing what one

knows and doesn't know, is plainly intended by Critias to be (what *Critias* thinks of as) *the* Socratic virtue, the human wisdom of *Ap.* 22e–23b: being able to examine oneself and others to see whether they *think they know* (when they don't) or whether they *know they don't know* (167a1–7, 170d5). (Critias, like Nicias on courage, seems in general to put forward accounts of temperance that aim at being Socratic.) But Socrates doesn't let Critias get away with *this* apparently Socratic position, since Critias doesn't see the whole picture – and in particular doesn't see that true virtue is the substantive knowledge of good and bad that Socrates acknowledges he doesn't have.

e. *Meno* 89d–96d (virtue is teachable if and only if there are teachers – leading briefly to the doubt that there may not even be any good men) plus 96d–100c (supposedly virtuous politicians, not being able to impart their virtue, have virtue by "divine dispensation" and without intelligence [*nous:* 99e6], but no politician has the kind of virtue that can be taught to others). See further notes 58 and 63.

For opposing readings of the above passages, and of other similar passages, see the powerful and all-but-persuasive Kraut, *Socrates,* chap. 8.

42 I first suggested this general strategy, as well as the claim that the good differ from the bad not in their wills but in their intellects, in my "Socrates on Virtue and Motivation." On the latter claim, we can make this much accommodation to the usual view, in the light of note 24: People don't differ in the ultimate end they desire, merely in the means they choose to that end. So if we distinguish the will's desire for means from the will's desire for the ultimate end, we *can* say good people differ from bad in their wills. But it has to be clear that it is the will's desire for *means* that is in question. And the fact is that the will's desire for means derives immediately from (a) desire for the ultimate end (the same in everyone), together with (b) the agent's beliefs as to the best means for achieving that end in the circumstances the agent is in. So, once more, the good differ from the bad solely in their *beliefs* (as to what is a means to what). (Compare and contrast Aristotle on "ignorance in the choice" vs. ignorance of circumstances at *N.E.* III.1.) See also notes 24–26 and 64.

Notice that in saying people all desire the same ultimate end, I am implicitly rejecting the view that good people differ from bad people by good people desiring virtue for its own sake and bad people desiring such things as pleasure for its own sake. This peculiar Aristotelian use of "for its own sake" – where one can both desire sight for its own sake and for the sake of happiness – only invites confusion, I think. On the view I attribute to Socrates, bad people only seem to desire pleasure above everything else because they think falsely that getting pleasure is the best means to their real good. That is, they *don't* desire pleasure for its own sake. What they desire for its own sake is their own real happiness – even if what that consists in is different from what they think it is. (See note 24, 25, 66, esp. the remarks about incoherence in the desire in note 25; also my "Power and Desire," Section 12.)

43 See *Ap.* 20a–b, 24c–25c, with *Cri.* 46c–47d; *Euphr.* 13b–c, *Grg.* 520a4 with c4–5; and on care for the soul generally, cf. also *Ap.* 29d–30a, 31b, 32d, 36c, 39d.

44 *La.* 180c, cf. 180e–181a, 185a1; *Lys.* 203a–204b; *Chrm.* 153d–154e.

45 For "instrument," see *H. Mi.* 374e3. Cf. also the souls of horses, dogs, and other animals; archers, doctors, and lute players; slaves; and our own souls at 375a4, 6–7, 8, b5, 7–8, c4, and 6–7. Notice also the comparison of the soul with such instruments as eyes, ears, and pruning knives at *Rep.* I 352e–354a, esp. 353a9–11 with d3–e11.

46 Thus Socrates takes it here that the good person is the person good at getting happiness – an outrageous conclusion by modern lights. See the discussion in the paragraph after next, as well as in note 49.

47 Socrates here implies – inconsistently with either (UV) or (UVV) – that it is possible to have courage and justice without having wisdom – when one uses one's courage or justice not well. Cf. note 21.

48 In the first protreptic of the *Euthd.* (278c–282e), as at *Chrm.* 173a–174d, Socrates all but speaks of a science of happiness. There is of course much more that needs to be said about the first protreptic. For example, there is the paradox Socrates propounds here that wisdom *is* happiness, on which see my "Belief-Relative Sciences." There is also the second protreptic in the *Euthd.* at 288c–292e, where Socrates raises difficulties about identifying this science he calls wisdom, and of which we must give an account that will cohere with our account of the first protreptic.

49 To think that the mere making of the distinction between moral and functional good is, by itself, enough to defeat the Socratic argument is to underestimate the resources of the Socratic position. Socrates can ask: *Why* isn't moral good (or, better, ethical good, given that "moral" suggests a rule-based ethics as opposed to a happiness-based ethics) functional? *Must* the difference between a good *parent* or a good *friend* (which are functional) and a good *person* be all that great? *Must* there be a difference of *kind* here? (This line of thought is familiar in modern times from P. T. Geach, "Good and Evil," *Analysis* 17(1956): 33–42, and Stuart Hampshire, *Thought and Action* (London, 1959), 227*ff*, esp. 229, 231–2, 236.

It might be thought that the following sort of argument could be made against Socrates' use of "function":

> The function of a hammer is to fulfill the standard expectations for a hammer – certain purposes of other beings (humans). But what is the function of the human being? Not now the purposes of others, but of the self: doing well, happiness! So the function argument breaks down for *good human being.*

(For an argument of this sort, see Irwin, *Plato's Moral Theory,* 14–15.) But the function argument no more breaks down, I think, than the following argument:

> The function of expertises like medicine and cobblery is not the maximizing of the experts' own economic good; but it is the function of economic experts to maximize their own economic good. Therefore, the function argument breaks down for economic experts.

The objection that follows in the main text – about the permissibility of harming others on the ethical egoist view – is of course quite another matter.

50 My analogy between Socrates and harm on the one hand, and Gandhi and violence on the other, may tempt some – impressed by Socrates' apparently willing military service – first, to object that there is no evidence that Socrates was nonviolent, and, second, to suggest that by "harm" Socrates simply meant psychic harm in the form of "making people more unjust." These reactions seem to me to go too far. I would grant only that he thought psychic harm a greater harm than physical harm. I myself find it hard to dissociate physical harm from psychic harm.

What of self-defense and punishment? Would Socrates not have thought violence in the pursuit of these goals acceptable? It might be thought that Socrates could have no (political) objections to pre-announced postures of self-defense designed to avoid violence on the part of bullies. But then Socrates was not a very political person. Still, it is not clear that he has ruled out individual, unpremeditated acts of self-defense. In any case, I suggest in the next note that Socrates might well have had doubts about punishment. (I am grateful to Richard Kraut for pressing me on the question of harm.)

51 There is an interesting corollary to this argument: Since no one errs willingly, the only "punishment" that is ever appropriate is instruction (Socratic questioning)! Merely another instance of Socrates' political innocence (or insouciance)? Or is he serious about the point? I believe he

is. Certainly he would not have supposed that legal punishment has, by itself, much to do with care for anyone's soul. See the interesting discussion of this issue at Kraut, *Socrates,* 313 – which cites passages both for and against the possibility that we should take Socrates as expressing serious doubts about the institution of legal punishment. But of the passages Kraut cites against, only *Cri.* 49a is at all troubling. And an explanation of it too is possible. (For example, along the lines of *Ap.* 25e on willingly harming those around one: Try to avoid willing injustice = try to be clear that nothing you willingly do is in fact unjust. Cf. Kraut's own remarks at *Socrates,* 213 n. 46.)

52 Socrates also maintains that it is bad to harm others at *Cri.* 49a–e and *Rep.* I 335b–e, though we do not have in these passages a clear intimation that the argument is made on the basis of self-interest. Socrates simply assumes that what is best for us will be best for others at, for example, *Grg.* 520a*ff,* esp. 520e, 521b–c.

53 In my "Belief-Relative Sciences," I try to explain why Socrates would reject the possibility of such sciences as the psychology-free moral science that Kant envisages. For Kant, most of the brilliant argumentation that Aristotle gives us on pleasure and happiness in Books I, VII, and X of the *Nicomachean Ethics* is entirely irrelevant to moral philosophy.

54 We confront here the claim that ethics must deal with moral "evil geniuses," which I deny in my "Virtue and Motivation." Kraut, *Socrates,* 314–15, thinks Socrates *would* have worried about this question.

55 Of course many modern philosophers will *agree* with Socrates (as with Plato and Aristotle) that ethics should not be insulated, in the Kantian manner, from facts about human nature. Their quarrel with ethical egoism will not be for bringing psychology into ethics; it will reside in the charge that egoism cannot provide a complex enough psychology on which to base ethics. (I am indebted here to Richard Kraut.) Can ethical egoists love their children, for example? This is not the place to defend egoism on such points.

56 Another controversial psychological hypothesis to which Socratic ethical theory is committed if its ethical egoism is to be defensible has to do with the fear of death. Ethical egoists, it is alleged – at least those who don't believe in immortality – must always in the end go to any lengths (including immorality) to avoid death. So, once again, it might be thought, ethical egoism is a nonstarter. But it is clear, especially in the *Ap.,* that Socrates rejects the claim that one must go to any lengths to avoid death. What Socrates will refuse to give up, even under the threat of death, is caring for wisdom and truth and that one's soul be the best it can be (29a–30e, 32a–e, 35a, 36c, 38e–39b; cf. *Grg.* 522d–e). In such care, indeed, lies one's happiness. Socrates is well aware that the medi-

cal question, Can I keep this patient alive? is a quite different question from Is it better for this patient to live or die? (*La.* 195c–d). And he would have agreed with John Stuart Mill that "the conscious ability to do without happiness gives the best prospect for realizing such happiness as is attainable" (*Utilitarianism,* chap. 2). It is *not* in our interest to do just anything to escape death. That is no recipe for happiness.

57 Thus I meet the objection in the last paragraph of Section III by yet another use of the general strategy in the next-to-last paragraph of Section III.

58 I have suggested in Appendix II of my "Belief-Relative Sciences," as well as in "Virtue and Motivation," n. 32, that the fact that no one has virtue is the resolution of the apparent conflict – central to both the *Protagoras* and *Meno* – between Socrates' claims that (a) virtue is knowledge, yet (b) virtue is not teachable. If we add to (a) and (b) that something is knowledge if and only if it is teachable, we get a contradiction. The *Meno* makes it clear that Socrates' claim that virtue isn't teachable is based upon the claim that *there are no teachers,* since the politicians who are supposed to be the teachers of virtue evidently don't have the knowledge in question. And, sure enough, there can't be any teachers of virtue if even the wisest of mortals has no substantive knowledge of goods and bads. (See further [e] in note 41; also note 63.)

59 *Prt.* 329c6–d1, 349b2–3.

60 This is a representative list of central Socratic questions. Many interpreters claim that a subclass of these – the What-is-it? questions, asked of the virtues – are the central philosophical questions for Socrates. Properly understood, this is not far wrong. But if it is supposed that the correct answers to these questions will give us in each case one true proposition as the "definition"; and that the point of the definition is to give us "standards" – necessary and sufficient conditions – for judging whether particular actions qualify as just, brave, temperate, and so forth; then I have some difficulties with the claim. Since I speak of my difficulties with propositions below (Section VI, with note 66, 72, and 78), I will say nothing more on that point here. I note only that several important What-is-it? questions have no very strong connections with standards. Take, for example, What is friendship? (or, perhaps, What is desire for good?, since the *Lys.* is really a dialogue about *desire for good* rather than friendship), What is the experience of being overcome by pleasure? (*Prt.* 352e7–353a6, 353c1–2, 354e6–7, 357c7–d1, e2, cf. 355e2–3), and What is rhetoric? (*Grg.* 447c with 448e–449a; 451a–b; 453a4–5 with 6–7; 462b, 463c). (The latter two are hardly ever listed as amongst the What-is-it? questions.)

For two of the best of these authors who see the What-is-it? questions as directed at standards, see Kraut, *Socrates*, 209, 213–14, 233–4, 247, 251–2, 300, 309, and esp. 254–8; Irwin, *Plato's Moral Theory*, 42–4, 61–2, 65, 68, 72. As against this view, I don't myself think Socrates was particularly interested in casuistry, except where, as at *Euphr.* 4e–9e (the principal evidence to which these interpretations appeal), it gives him a way into the examination of those characteristics of *people* (as opposed to actions) that will lead to their good. *Euphr.* 9e–11b is profoundly irrelevant to the "standards" Socrates is supposed to be especially interested in; and the end of the dialogue (13a*ff*) seems to concern itself entirely with *sciences* – which are characteristics of people: cf. 13a–b. Indeed, it seems likely Socrates thinks the answer to the question What is piety? lies here – in some sort of science. (See esp. 14b8–c1, which locates Euthyphro's turning away at 14a11 from deciding [a] what the science the gods have is to accomplish, in order to see [b] what the science of serving the gods [13e10–11] is to accomplish.)

Kraut thinks Socrates is interested in standards for actions, in part because of (political) passages that seem to him to imply that an expert in virtue should command others and others should obey. But most of the passages Kraut cites in support of this claim seem to me have to do less with politics, ruling, and casuistry than with one-on-one education of the *individual* (*Socrates*, 196–9, 257). (That is, once more, the concern is with characteristics of *people*, not of *actions*.) That Socrates should, even in these passages, be more concerned with individual acquisition of virtue rather than moral judgments on actions is what one would expect, I think, given how little a practical proposition political life seemed to Socrates for a person bent upon acquiring human goodness. (Cf. *Socrates*, 208–15.)

61 An individual's "values" are what the individual "thinks-good," where the hyphen indicates we have one inseparable word. Though what somebody *thinks red* can be contrasted with what *is red*, "thinks-good" does not contrast with "is good" because of the hyphen. (Cf. the modern notion of a "value judgment" as opposed to judgments on scientific matters or matters of fact.) That is the notion of values that Socrates and Plato were fighting. It is still around today.

62 The phrase "for that individual" of course takes some unraveling. All I am saying here is that the upshot of "What appears good to *A is* good for *A*" is that on that view, one's final end is whatever it appears to one to be. For Protagoras in the *Tht.* see 152a–b, 166d4–8 ("is and appears") 172a1–5, b2–6.

The argument of the present paragraph in the main text of course presupposes that there *is* a distinction between getting what is best and getting what *seems* best to you. And, as I remarked three paragraphs ago,

Protagoras would deny this. Though Socrates' argument here will work against positions like those of Gorgias and Polus, it will not work against any position so radical as that of Protagoras. The radical Protagorean position is not argued against head-on until the *Tht.* Even *Cra.* 385e–386d is simply a replay of Socratic appeals to the sciences.

63 Obviously I am taking the *Meno* to be ironic in its suggestion that there could be virtue based on true belief rather than knowledge. In other words, I have this part of the *Meno* looking backward to the *Ion* on "divine dispensation." (How is it that politicians attain virtue, given that they don't have knowledge? It's a gosh-darned miracle! Socrates says.)

Other interpreters take the *Meno* rather to be looking forward to the virtues of the military class in the *Republic.* That is, they take the *Meno*'s broaching of true belief without knowledge as a form of virtue to be making a serious suggestion about virtue – opening the way to the *Rep.*'s virtue of courage in a military class that *does not itself possess knowledge, but merely true belief* (cf. point 9 in Section II). I was myself a little soft on this interpretation in my "Unity of Virtue," n. 32.

Against such interpreters, it may be urged that Socrates' rough treatment of Anytus in this context in the *Meno* counts strongly against the view that Socrates is seriously suggesting politicians have a pretty adequate sort of virtue. For it is the dangerously angry Anytus – most formidable of the eventual accusers of Socrates – whom Socrates chooses as the representative and defender of politicians; see esp. 95e with 100b, and notice Burnet's reasonable conjecture that it is Anytus who is referred to at *Ap.* 21c. Cf. also the rough treatment of Pericles and Themistocles (*Meno* 93b–94e, taken very ill by Anytus at 95a; and *Grg.* 515c–519d). I treat of this point in a little more detail in "Belief-Relative Sciences," Appendix II. For an opposing view, see Kraut, *Socrates,* 278, 285*ff,* esp. n. 81; and see further notes 41 and 58 above.

64 For my insistence on "wanting that exile of my rival *which will in fact make me happiest*" as opposed to simply ("simply": *Grg.* 468c3) "wanting the exile of my rival," see notes 25 and 26, with note 24. There is a rather fuller discussion of the entire issue here in my "Power and Desire."

65 For example, the alleged contradiction in *knowing only that one doesn't know;* the apparent contradiction of this last claim by claims at *Ap.* 29a6–b9 and 37b5–9; and Socrates' alleged claims of moral superiority at *Ap.* 34e–35a which have suggested to some a claim to moral knowledge.

66 It is axiomatic within modern philosophy that (a) *things known,* (b) *things truly believed,* and even (c) *things falsely believed* are all the same kind of things: *propositions.* (So that if any one of these kinds of things exists independently of our thought and language [as one might

hope facts and things known would], so do the others; and if any one of these is a mere convenient artifact of theory [as one might suspect false beliefs and even some true beliefs would be], they all are.) Though I understand the convenience to philosophers of regimenting the objects of knowledge and belief in this way, I have some doubts about the underlying assumptions – reinforced by other doubts about propositions made familiar by Quine, Davidson, and others. (Cf. also my "Belief-Relative Sciences.") But this is not the place to discuss these doubts.

67 Due to Kent Anderson.

68 This example of course depends upon the correctness of my interpretation of *La.* 197e–199e. Both Vlastos, *Platonic Studies,* 422–3, and Kraut, *Socrates,* 260, argue that Socrates cannot be attacking the claim that courage is only a part of virtue since *he himself introduces it* at 190c8–d8. The whole first pass with Laches at 190c8*ff* needs discussion. I shall be offering such a discussion, with a response to the Vlastos-Kraut objection, elsewhere.

69 Arguments parallel to those just given about Nicias in the *La.* can be made about Critias's obvious attempts to give Socratic accounts of temperance in the *Chrm.,* and about Meno's giving of a Socratic account of what virtue is in the *Meno.* See examples (c) and (d) in note 41.

70 As in accounts of the elenchus, like Vlastos, "The Socratic Elenchus," *Oxford Studies in Ancient Philosophy* 1 (1983): 39–42, 47–9, which work with a sharp deductive–inductive distinction and the narrowest possible criteria of propositional identity.

71 I owe this point to Ruth Saunders. Those who believe in propositions have merely to attribute the view to Socrates that you can't know the proposition that self-knowledge is good if you don't know the (quite different) proposition that knowledge is strong. (Some defeasibility theorists might find a way for knowledge of the one proposition to be defeated by defects in one's knowledge of the other.)

72 The position of Kraut, *Socrates,* 280–5, is interesting in this connection. For it comes *very* close to the position I am maintaining here, as earlier in my "Virtue and Motivation" – in spite of a very strong commitment on Kraut's part to propositions of neo-Fregean ilk. (For Kraut's commitment to propositions, see *Socrates,* 197 n. 8, 211, 220–2, 225, 231, 241, 246, 260, 264, 269, 272, 278–9, 283–4; in many of these passages Kraut is actually *counting* propositions ["some true beliefs, some false beliefs"].) Kraut shows this same closeness to my position in his review of Irwin's *Plato's Moral Theory, Philosophical Review* 88 (1979): 633–9. Curiously, we can also find in Irwin (*Plato's Moral Theory,* 63–4, 69–70) passages reminiscent of the similar positions in Kraut and myself. Thus it is both the case that Kraut rightly criticizes Irwin in places for too

little attention to the broader picture (too narrow an interest in individual propositions, as I would put it) and that Irwin too sometimes *does* quite adequately have his eye on the broader picture.

73 On the connection between the two explanations: In the preceding section, one fairly trivial false belief ("For want of a nail . . .") can throw off an entire means–end structure, just as in the present section, one's knowledge that virtue is knowledge may be thrown off by not knowing why there are no teachers of it. In both cases, one is failing to see the whole picture.

74 See Vlastos, "Introduction: The Paradox of Socrates," 16–17. Here Vlastos claims that behind (what Vlastos sees as) Socrates' failure to see that knowledge by itself cannot be the way to the saving of human souls, lies "a failure of love."

> In saying this, I am not taking over-seriously the prickly exterior and the pugilist's postures. I have already argued that he does care for the souls of his fellows. But the care is limited and conditional. If men's souls are to be saved, they must be saved this way. And when he sees they cannot, he watches them go down the road to perdition with regret, but without anguish. Jesus wept for Jerusalem. Socrates warns Athens, scolds, exhorts it, condemns it. But he has no tears for it. One wonders if Plato, who raged against Athens, did not love it more in his rage and hate than ever did Socrates in his sad and good-tempered rebukes. One feels there is a last zone of frigidity in the soul of the great erotic; had he loved his fellows more, he could hardly have laid on them the burdens of his (as Nietzsche has it) "despotic logic," impossible to be borne.

75 Vlastos, "The Socratic Elenchus," 35.

76 See the preceding paragraph.

77 Ibid., 37.

78 No doubt most of Socrates' interlocutors would have considered them to be five different beliefs, since they will have thought that any one of them could be true while any other one is false. Such is the standard Fregean and neo-Fregean criterion of identity for propositions: if Oedipus thinks that (a) he is married to Jocasta, but that it is false that (b) he is married to his mother, then *even for Tiresias,* who knows the truth, (a) and (b) express different beliefs, and (a) and (b) are therefore different facts. (Cf. note 66.) But is it clear this is right? If we want Oedipus's beliefs to be beliefs *about Jocasta,* is it clear we can leave out of the fact (a) just *everything* about her except perhaps her being named "Jocasta"?

In any case, my suggestion about Socrates here is this: To know that virtue is one, we shall have to know of this virtue that it is the virtue which is knowledge – as in knowing that 11 + 1 = 12, we had better know that 12 is the successor of 11, and maybe even that 11 is the successor of 10. The idea is that knowing that virtue is such and such will, for Socrates, be knowledge *about virtue;* so the question will arise: Which virtue? A virtue which is the mere genus of five different virtues, wisdom, temperance, and so forth? Or a virtue which is *identical with* wisdom, which is identical with temperance, and so forth? We must know the reference of "virtue," not just the meaning. (On orthodox Fregean propositional analyses of belief and knowledge contexts, the belief that virtue is knowledge is not about the reference of "virtue" so much as the meaning of virtue.) I discuss these topics further in the unpublished manuscripts cited in note 25.

It will be obvious that the remarks of the previous paragraph also speak directly to the alleged "Socratic fallacy" which has long puzzled and annoyed modern readers. (See P. T. Geach, "Plato's *Euthyphro:* An Analysis and Commentary," *Monist* 50 (1966): 369–82; also Taylor, *Plato's Protagoras,* 212–13, on *Prt.* 360e6–361a3.) The "Socratic fallacy" is found in Socrates' claim that we can't know whether *x* is *F* until we know what *x* is. Moderns deny this claim. They say that we *can* know that *x* is *F* without (exhaustive or essential) knowledge about what *x* is. What is more, we only get to know what the reference of "*x*" is (= what *x* is) by knowing first lots of "facts" like *that x if F.* (Facts being true propositions, and propositions being meanings, all we need access to, on this view, in order to know that *x* is *F,* is the meaning of "*x*." We don't need to know the reference of "*x*.") It is this picture I am denying when I say that for Socrates knowledge that *x* is *F* is knowledge of the *reference* of "*x*."

79 Cf. also Kraut, *Socrates,* 245*ff.*

80 Frege, "On Sense and Reference," in *Translations from the Philosophical Writings of Gottlob Frege,* ed. Peter Geach and Max Black, 2d ed. (Oxford, 1960), 58.

81 By the same token, what is important in an *interpretation* of Socrates is that (as one might say) the different pieces – about virtue being knowledge; about desire being for the good; about ambivalence, advantage, rhetoric, power, and poetry; about harming others; about being overcome by pleasure; and so forth – all hang together as a single whole. Though I have not been able to *show* this in the space available, but merely to hint at it, I hope this is true of my interpretation, as it is (in fact) of the quite different interpretations of Vlastos, Santas, Irwin, Kraut, and others. There is no substitute for working out a whole view of all these matters simultaneously. This means, of course, that the risk of error in interpretation is correspondingly greater. As will become clear, I believe this has something to do with explaining the fact that though Socrates appears to hold a great many beliefs very seriously, he never

claims to know *anything substantive.* Knowledge of anything substantive could only come if one could be sure of every part of the picture. By the same token, though I believe my interpretation is better than its rivals, I would not claim to *know* it is correct.

IAN MUELLER

5 Mathematical method and philosophical truth

I. PLATO'S ACADEMY AND THE SCIENCES

At some time between the early 380s and the middle 360s Plato founded what came to be known as the Academy.[1] Our information about the early Academy is very scant. We know that Plato was the leader (scholarch) of the Academy until his death and that his nephew Speusippus succeeded him in this position. We know that young people came from around the Greek world to be at the Academy and that the most famous of such people, Aristotle, stayed there for approximately twenty years. However, it appears that, at least in Plato's time, there were no fees attached to being at the Academy.[2] Thus it does not seem likely that it had any official "professorial staff" or that "students" took a set of courses to qualify them to fill certain positions in life. The Academy was more likely a community of self-supporting intellectuals gathered around Plato and pursuing a variety of interests ranging from the abstractions of metaphysics to more concrete issues of politics and ethics.

In Book VII of the *Republic* Socrates describes a plan of higher education designed to turn the most promising young people of a utopian city-state into ideal rulers. It is frequently assumed (and quite naturally) that this curriculum bears a significant relation to Plato's plans for the Academy; sometimes it has even been described as essentially the plans themselves.[3] It is important to see that this assumption is subject to major qualifications. For, first of all, fourth-century Athens is not even an approximation to Plato's utopia; Plato could

I would like to thank Richard Kraut for his comments on an earlier version of this paper.

not expect entrants in the Academy to have been honed in the way the utopian citizens are supposed to be. Secondly, the educational timetable of the *Republic* seems totally impracticable for a privately organized institution in a free city: ten years of mathematics – that is, of numbers, geometry, stereometry, mathematical astronomy, and harmonics;[4] five years of dialectic; fifteen years of practical experience; and then, for a few select fifty-year-olds, ascent to the Good, followed by alternating periods of ruling and philosophizing. We do not know whether the Academy had any curricular requirements at all, but it seems to me highly likely that the Academy would have been stillborn if Plato had announced to new enrollees that they would begin their most important studies thirty years later.

We must, I think, assume that Academic "education" was more compressed than this, that mathematics, dialectic, and discussion of goodness were carried on simultaneously. But how were they carried on? Again, I think one should stress informality. Groups of people gathered together to discuss subjects of common interest. In these discussions there would obviously be leaders, teachers. We know that Plato gave at least one public lecture on the Good, and several references in Aristotle give us grounds for thinking that Plato put forward some ideas in discussion that he did not express in the dialogues.[5] Presumably, mathematics, too, would involve some lecturing, but there is reason to think that forms of Socratic discussion were also common.

As for subjects of scientific discussion, it is important to be aware that our evidence suggests that more disciplines than those mentioned in the *Republic* were treated in the Academy. The most general kind of evidence is just the interests of various people closely associated with the Academy.[6] But we have valuable more specific indicators as well. One comes from a conversation between unnamed speakers in a fragment (Theodorus Kock, ed., *Comicorum Atticorum Fragmenta,* 3 vols. [Leipzig, 1880–8], 2: 287–8) of a comedy by Plato's contemporary Epicrates:

> What about Plato, Speusippus, and Menedemus?[7] What subjects are they dealing with now? What thought, what argument are they investigating? If you've come knowing anything please tell these things to me with discretion.
>
> I can talk about these things clearly. At the Panathenaic festival I saw a band of gay youths in the gymnasium of the Academy[8] and heard them say

unutterably weird things. They were making distinctions concerning nature, the life of animals, the nature of trees, and the genera of vegetables. Among other things they were studying the genus of the pumpkin.

How did they define it? What is the genus of the plant? Reveal this to me if you know.

Well, first they all stood silently, bent over, and they thought for a considerable time. Suddenly, while the young men were still bending over and reflecting, one of them pronounced it a round vegetable, another a grass, a third a tree. A Sicilian doctor who heard these things blew a fart at the fools.

That must have made the students very angry. I suppose they shouted out against the man's derision. For it is out of place to do such things during a discussion.

It didn't bother them. Plato was there, and he enjoined them, very gently and without agitation, to try again from the beginning to distinguish the genus of the pumpkin. They proceeded to do so.

The reliability of a comic representation is always subject to the skepticism of scholars who hold theories incompatible with the representation. This representation of Plato overseeing a biological classification in the Academy does not fit well with the educational scheme of the *Republic*. But, as I have already indicated, that scheme is an ideal one for an ideal state. And it is also pitched to the specific philosophical purpose of showing how certain studies turn the soul from the sensible world to the intelligible one. (Note especially 521c–d.) This philosophical purpose very much colors Socrates' description of the course of higher education; although it would be wrong to downplay things he says to the extent of denying that Plato thinks them true, one should not suppose that what he says exhausts Plato's position on science or is free of rhetorical exaggeration.

The other piece of evidence I wish to consider brings us directly into the domain of mathematics. It is an account of Plato's activities found in Philodemus's history of the Platonic school, written in the first century B.C.[9] Unfortunately, it is preserved in a papyrus roll in tenuous condition, and requires supplementation of varying degrees of certainty. In my translation I indicate some of the major problematic places.[10]

At that time great progress was seen in mathematics, with Plato serving as general director (*architektonountos*) and setting out problems, and the mathematicians investigating them earnestly. In this way the subject of metrology (*metrologia*) and the problems concerning ⟨. . .⟩[11] then reached their high point for the first time, as E⟨udo⟩[x]us[12] and his followers transformed the old-fashioned work (*a[rch]aismon*) o⟨f Hip⟩po⟨cra⟩tes.[13] Geometry, too, made great progress; for analysis and the [lemma] concerning *diorismoi* were created, and in general the subject of geometry was advanced greatly. And ⟨op⟩t⟨ic⟩s and mechanics were not at all ignored.

There is much to say about this passage, but for the moment I wish only to consider the subjects that it associates with Plato. The term *metrologia* occurs nowhere else in surviving Greek literature. Its best translation is "theory of measurement," but it is not clear what such a theory might be.[14] Eudoxus's best-known work in pure mathematics concerns the theory of ratios and the measurement of areas and volumes by indirect procedures (Euclid, *Elements*, books V and XII); it is particularly characterized by the logical scrupulousness of its methods. If readers of the *Republic* are not surprised to be told that geometry advanced under Plato's direction, they may be by the reference to optics (conjectural) and mechanics (unquestionable). Some may wish to resort to conjectures of their own to explain away this reference, but, as I have indicated, it seems more reasonable to accept as a fact that Plato's Academy was not nearly as "Platonic" as the institution of higher education of the *Republic*.

The Philodemus passage speaks of Plato's directorship of mathematics, of his setting out problems that the mathematicians eagerly investigated with great success. There are two well-known anecdotes relating to this aspect of Plato's activity. The first concerns the so-called duplication of the cube, the construction of a cube twice the volume of a given one.[15] According to ancient stories interest in this problem was stimulated by a Delian appeal to Plato to help them to appease the god Apollo who had commanded them to double the size of an altar. According to another story Plato reproached Eudoxus, Archytas, and Menaechmus for reducing the duplication problem to mechanical constructions, thereby destroying the goodness of geometry, "turning it back to sensible things instead of rising upwards to grasp eternal and incorporeal images" (Plutarch, *Quaestiones Convivales* ["Table-Talk"], 718e–f). This is good "Platonism," quite in keeping with the *Republic*. Unfortunately the solution of the duplication problem ascribed to Plato is more mechanical than the ones he is said to have censured, in the sense that it involves the construction of an instrument. Of course, we have the option of rejecting the ascription to Plato, but that ascription is harder to explain than the story of his reproach of the other solutions.

The second example of Plato's setting out problems relates to the anomalous motions of the planets by comparison with the sun or moon.[16] The sun and moon appear to make a uniform daily trip through the heavens from east to west and a uniform yearly or monthly trip from west to east. The planets make the same uniform daily east–west trip, but their west–east trips involve striking anomalies including periods of apparent motion from east to west. In his commentary on Aristotle's *On the Heavens* Simplicius (sixth century A.D.) remarks on the problem of "saving" these anomalous motions, that is, producing an explanation of them:

> In order to save these many motions in each case, some assume eccentrics [circular orbits with centers other than the earth] and epicycles [circles with centers on the circumference of revolving circles], while others hypothesize so-called counteractive homocentrics.[17] In the true account the planets do not stop or retrogress nor is there any increase or decrease in their speeds, even if they appear to move in such ways; nor are hypotheses that they are this way introduced, but the heavenly motions are shown to be simple and circular and uniform and ordered from the evidence of their own substance. For since it is not possible for a faculty restricted to appearances (*phantasia*) to grasp accurately how the planets are disposed and since the consequences drawn by such a faculty are not the truth, it was asked that one try to discover how the apparent motions of the planets could be saved by uniform, ordered, and circular motions. And, as Eudemus [an associate of Aristotle] reports in the second book of his history of astronomy – and so does Sosigenes [second century A.D.], who is relying on Eudemus – , Eudoxus of Cnidus is said to be the first Greek to have concerned himself with such hypotheses; according to Sosigenes, this problem was made up by Plato for those who concerned themselves with these subjects: by hypothesizing what uniform and ordered motions is it possible to save the appearances relating to planetary motions.
>
> (Simplicius, *Commentary on Aristotle's "On the Heavens,"* 488.7–24)

Astronomy is included in the *Republic* curriculum, but, as we will see, Socrates' description of it is not at first sight reconcilable with Plato's reported interest in "saving the phenomena." Again there is an apparent contrast between the practice of a science and Plato's attempt in the *Republic* to incorporate the science into the education of rulers in an ideal state.

However, the point I wish to emphasize now is the evidence that Plato did play some kind of role as general mathematical director, posing problems to the mathematicians of his time, sometimes with striking results. We need not suppose that the work associated with Plato's inspiration was all done at the Academy, and, in the case of Eudoxus, there is good reason to suppose it was not. Nor need we think that Plato's role as director precluded his applying his own talents to the solution of scientific problems. However, there is no compelling evidence that Plato showed any great success in this arena, and many of the mathematical and scientific passages in his writing are fraught with impenetrable obscurity. It is best, then, to think of Plato as a source of challenge and inspiration to mathematicians and not as a mathematician of real significance.[18]

II. MATHEMATICAL METHOD: ANALYSIS, SYNTHESIS, *DIORISMOI,* AND LEMMAS

In addition to referring to branches of mathematics, the Philodemus passage mentions "analysis and the lemma concerning *diorismoi.*" The notions of analysis and of a *diorismos* are treated in a somewhat confusing way in Greek discussions,[19] although the fundamental ideas are not difficult. My treatment will be somewhat simplified. Analysis can be thought of as the process of looking for the proof of an assertion P by searching for propositions that imply P, propositions that imply those, and so on until one reaches propositions already established; in synthesis one simply writes down the proof discovered by analysis, that is, one goes through the steps of analysis in reverse order. In the most common case one focuses on a single established proposition Q which (conjoined with propositions $Q_1, \ldots Q_n$ taken as given) implies P, that is, is a sufficient condition for the truth of P; it might happen that P also implies Q in which case Q will also be a necessary condition for the truth of P.

A *diorismos* is usually explained as the determination of the necessary and sufficient conditions for the solution of a problem or the truth of a proposition. The standard example is provided by proposition 22 of Book I of Euclid's *Elements:*

> I.22 Out of three straight lines which are equal to three given ones to construct a triangle; thus it is necessary that two of the straight lines taken together in any manner should be greater than the third.

Here the second sentence, the *diorismos*, states the necessary and sufficient condition that a triangle be constructible out of three given lines. Euclid, however, formulates it as a necessary condition and shows (by carrying out the construction) that it is sufficient.[20] He has already proved that the condition is necessary in proposition I.20:

> I.20 In any triangle two sides taken together in any manner are greater than the remaining one.

In his *Commentary on the First Book of Euclid's Elements*, Proclus explains what a lemma is:

> The term "lemma" is frequently predicated of any premiss assumed in establishing something else, as when people say they have made a proof from so and so many lemmas. But in geometry a lemma is specifically a premiss which needs verification (*pistis*). Whenever in a construction or proof we assume something which has not been shown but needs an account (*logos*), we call the assumption a lemma because we consider it worth investigating although doubtful in itself; we distinguish it from a postulate or axiom because it is provable whereas we assume them directly without proof to verify other things. The best thing for finding lemmas is mental address. . . . Nevertheless, methods have been transmitted. The best is reduction of what is sought to an agreed-upon principle by analysis, a method they say Plato transmitted to Leodamas; from it Leodamas is said to have become the discoverer of much in geometry.
>
> (*Commentary on Euclid*, 211.1–23)

Proclus mentions Leodamas[21] in an account of the history of mathematics before Euclid, particularly the history of geometry:

> Plato made geometry and the rest of mathematics undergo great progress because of his earnestness concerning them, which is evident from the density of mathematical considerations (*logoi*) in his writings[22] and from his everywhere awakening in adherents of philosophy an admiration for mathematics. Also alive at this time were Leodamas of Thasos, Archytas of Tarentum, and Theaetetus of Athens. . . . Neoclides and his pupil Leon were younger than Leodamas, and they added discoveries to those of their predecessors, so that Leon both composed an *Elements* which was superior in the

number and the usefulness of its results and discovered *diorismoi,* [which indicate] when a problem under consideration can be solved and when it cannot. (*Commentary on Euclid,* 66.8–67.1)[23]

Although Philodemus's phrase "lemma concerning *diorismoi*" is hardly transparent, it seems to me quite likely that it has no more specific meaning than the term "analysis," and that the Philodemus passage ascribes to the time of Plato a concern with the search for lemmas and *diorismoi,* that is, for propositions sufficient (and perhaps necessary) for the proof of other theorems and for conditions under which a problem can be solved (or a theorem proved). Clearly, despite the variety of terms, we are dealing with one central piece of methodology. The search for premises (analysis) needed to establish a proposition or solve a construction problem may lead back to established propositions or constructions (successful analysis), or to a lemma in need of proof, or to a restriction on the proposition or construction to conditions under which it can be proved or carried out (*diorismos*). Plato himself is credited with transmitting this methodology to others.[24] I shall not be further concerned with this aspect of Plato's activity, but rather with certain crucial passages that show the influence of these mathematical methods and concepts on Plato's own methodological thinking.

III. INVESTIGATION FROM A HYPOTHESIS IN THE *MENO*

Plato does not use the words "lemma," "*diorismos,*" "analysis," or "synthesis" in their technical sense, but in the *Meno,* he invokes as a procedural precedent a mathematical practice of setting out the conditions under which a problem can be solved. Meno asks Socrates to tell him whether virtue can be taught, and Socrates asks to be able to consider the question "from a hypothesis."

What I mean by "from a hypothesis" is like the way in which the geometers often consider some question someone asks them, for example, whether it is possible for this area to be inscribed in this circle as a triangle. Someone might say, "I don't yet know whether this is such that it can be inscribed, but I think I have a certain hypothesis, as it were, which is useful for the question, as follows: if this area is such that, when one places it alongside its given line, it falls short by a figure similar to the one that was placed alongside, I think one result will follow, and another, on the other hand, if this cannot happen to it. Making a hypothesis, then, I am willing to tell you the result concerning the inscribing of it in a circle, whether it is possible or not." (*Meno* 86e–87b)[25]

Socrates here seems to be describing a situation in which a geometer is considering the problem that Euclid would formulate as

> Problem. To inscribe a triangle of a given area in a given circle.

Socrates' geometer "solves" this problem by giving a condition that the area must satisfy. Euclid would add this condition to his statement of the problem as a *diorismos:*

> *Diorismos.* Thus it is necessary that, "if one places the area alongside its given line, it falls short by a figure similar to the one that was placed alongside."

Clearly for this *diorismos* to be effective one will need to know (or assume) a theorem to the effect that

> Theorem. If the area of a triangle inscribed in a circle is "placed alongside its given line, it falls short by a figure similar to the one that was placed alongside."

Socrates' presentation of the geometric example does not make clear whether he takes the *diorismos* or the theorem to be the hypothesis on which the problem depends. In fact, of course, it depends on both: To solve the problem one needs to impose the condition given by the *diorismos* and rely on the theorem. When Socrates returns to the topic of virtue, he says.

Similarly then concerning virtue, since we don't know either what it is or what sort of thing it is, let's make a hypothesis and consider whether it is teachable or not, as follows: what sort of thing among those connected with the soul would virtue be to make it teachable or not teachable? First, if it is different from or like knowledge, is it teachable or not? . . . Or is this at least clear to everyone, that a person isn't taught anything other than knowledge?

But if virtue is some sort of knowledge, it's clear that it will be teachable.

Then we've quickly finished with this point: if virtue is of one sort it's teachable, and, if of another, not. (*Meno* 87b–87c)

In this application of the hypothetical method Socrates does not describe a *diorismos,* but performs what I have called an analysis, that is, he reduces the question of establishing that virtue is teachable to the claim that virtue is knowledge if and only if it is teachable, or at least:

> Hypothesis-theorem. If virtue is knowledge, then it is teachable.

But corresponding to the need for a *diorismos* in the case of the geometric example, the hypothesis-theorem is of use only if one can establish

> Hypothesis-lemma. Virtue is knowledge.

There has been scholarly disagreement as to which of these two hypotheses Socrates considers to be the hypothesis to which he has reduced the question of teachability. The most explicit texts (89c–d) suggest the hypothesis-theorem, and this is what one would expect in terms of the model of geometric analysis. But, of course, the hypothesis-lemma is also an assumption, and needs to be established in order to show (using the hypothesis-theorem) that virtue is teachable. And Socrates proceeds to establish it by using the further hypothesis that virtue is good (87c–89a; Socrates refers to "virtue is good" as a hypothesis at 87d). It is not clear whether this new hypothesis is conceived as a "theorem" or as a "lemma" still needing justification. Socrates speaks of it as holding (*menein,* 89d) and it is maintained to the end of the *Meno,* as is the hypothesis-theorem. To this extent the *Meno* involves an adaptation of the method of analysis to reduce the teachability of virtue to two hypotheses-theorems. However, there can be no question of a perfect fit with successful mathematical analysis since the dialogue ends with Socrates arguing against both the hypothesis-lemma and the teachability of virtue (89c*ff*).

The absence of a perfect fit is, I think, a reflection of a practical difference between mathematics and philosophy. When one looks at mathematics one cannot help but be impressed by its success, at the apparently definitive way in which it solves open questions and resolves disputes. This perspective on mathematics is reflected in a Greek tendency to think of geometric analysis as successful analysis, as a method of finding rather than a method of searching. It may also explain why, in the *Meno,* no attempt is made to relate the subsequent refutation of the claim that virtue is knowledge to the mathematician's investigation from a hypothesis. However, in philosophy, "analysis" and the discovery of lemmas is much less likely to produce a definitive answer to a question; for, as in the *Meno*, a lemma will frequently be found questionable. If it is relatively clear that in the *Meno* a philosophical hypothesis is a "theorem," it will become clear that Plato comes to apply the word "hypothesis" to lemmas that are thought of as tentative and subject to investigation. Indeed, one might say that Plato's development of the hypothetical method involves an attempt to unite the generally smooth working of mathematics with the rough-and-tumble of the Socratic examination of doctrines.

The absence of a perfect fit between mathematical method and Plato's adaptation of it might not present serious obstacles to interpretation if Plato himself were clear about the discrepancies. But the *Meno* is a good example of Plato's tendency to ignore differences. This tendency and the looseness of fit has led some interpreters to downplay the connection between Platonic methodology and mathematics. But the historical evidence of a connection is too strong to make this approach viable. Our task should be to make as much of the connection as we can without losing sight of the imperfect fit. This task is not made easier by Plato's general unwillingness to use precise vocabulary. Where Plato uses one word, "hypothesis," we find it advisable to distinguish among theorems, lemmas, and *diorismoi.* As I proceed in this chapter I will point to further examples of problematic vocabulary and looseness of fit. I do not intend thereby to disparage Plato's accomplishments, but simply to improve our understanding of Plato's adaptation of mathematical method.

IV. THE METHOD OF HYPOTHESIS IN THE *PHAEDO*

In the *Phaedo,* starting at 95e7,[26] Socrates gives a general description of a philosophical method that seems to be based on mathematical analysis and synthesis, but goes well beyond them in important ways. In the passage, Socrates describes, as a preliminary to an argument for the immortality of the soul, a method he has worked out for determining "the explanation (*aitia*) of each thing, why it comes-to-be, why it ceases-to-be, why it is" (96a9–10):

On each occasion I hypothesize the thing (*logos*) which I judge to be strongest, and I lay down as true whatever seems to me to agree (*sumphōnein*) with it, whether the subject is cause or anything else, and I lay down as false whatever does not seem to me to agree with it. (*Phd.* 100a3–7)

Socrates' recommendation here should be understood to be relativized to a subject of inquiry. He suggests that on any subject of inquiry one should take as hypothesis the relevant belief in which one has most confidence, add further relevant ideas that (in some sense) agree with the hypothesis and reject relevant ideas that do not agree.[27] He illustrates what he has in mind in the case of the question of immortality (or the explanation of each thing) by hypothesizing that each Form is something (apparently the assumption that the Forms exist) and adding the belief that each thing is or comes to be (what it is) by participating in the appropriate Form. The example (and also the later example at 105b–c) indicates that the method espoused is to answer a given question by building up a consistent theory applicable to an issue through the addition of compatible beliefs. In later ancient logical texts, the word "agreement" used by Socrates can mean simple logical consistency. Here it includes the notion of logical consistency but is presumably stronger; many explanations of being and coming to be are consistent with the existence of Forms, but explanation by participation is, in some reasonably clear but not easily explicable sense, suitable for the believer in Forms.

At 101c Socrates says that, confronted by alternative explanations of coming to be, the person following his method should leave them for others and "hang on to the safety of the hypothesis." Prior to this Socrates has only referred to the original assumption as a hypothesis, but what he is referring to now must include the additional explanation of being and coming to be. I suspect he means the whole theory that has been built up by accreting harmonious assumptions.[28] Socrates now turns to the status of the "hypothesis":

But if anyone were to grab on to the hypothesis itself, you would say goodbye to him and not answer until you had investigated whether [it seemed] to you that the things which came from it (*ta hormēthenta*) agreed or disagreed with one another. And when it was necessary for you to give an account of the hypothesis itself, you would give it in the same way, hypothesizing another hypothesis, whichever among higher hypotheses seemed best, until you came to something sufficient. (*Phd.* 101d3–e1)

It is easy enough to see how the method of analysis can be related to this last sentence. Forced to justify an assumption one has made, one finds an assumption that would justify it, and, if demands for justification continue, one proceeds in the same way until one finds an assumption not needing justification. Socrates does not indicate what conditions a hypothesis would have to fulfill to be "sufficient," but obviously mathematics itself would provide examples of successful analysis in which sufficiency was attained, or was at least thought to be. However, even at this point it is clear that Plato's philosophical interest is widening the gap between his hypothetical method and geometrical analysis. For, although the ideal of an ultimately satisfactory justification remains in play, the earlier hypotheses, however strong or good they may be, are not established "theorems," but provisional lemmas subject to test and possibly still needing justification.

Moreover, in successful analysis the hypothesis-theorem becomes a starting point from which the proposition under consideration is deduced in the synthesis. However, we have already seen that in his initial description Socrates treats the original hypothesis as a basis for the acceptance of additional ideas judged harmonious with it and the rejection of those judged inharmonious. Socrates' only illustration of the rejection of beliefs is the rejection of explanations of being and coming to be other than participation in the appropriate Form (100c–101d), that is to say, the rejection of beliefs blatantly incompatible with beliefs already accepted as harmonious with the original hypothesis. In the second passage Socrates speaks of checking whether the things that come after the hypothesis are harmonious with one another.[29] He seems to have in mind the sort of testing of people's views that he practices in other dialogues such as the *Euthyphro.* This procedure does not seem to be important in mathematics, and it is not easy to see how it can be fit into the method Socrates is introducing. Perhaps what he has in mind can be understood in terms of his example. The problem Socrates confronts is the explanation of things in our world, why they come to be, cease to be, and are. To attain such an explanation Socrates posits that there are Forms and adds the apparently harmonious assumption that things come to be and are what they are by participating in the Forms. (We are not told how Socrates would use his theory to explain the ceasing to be of things.) To investigate fully the adequacy of this theory one would investigate the "things which come from it," not only consequences but also other assumptions apparently harmonious with it, for example, about the character and relation of Forms, the nature of coming to be, and so on. Ultimately this investigation will involve tests for consistency, but the tests will be applied to a rich set of apparently harmonious beliefs about the world. Given the apparent harmoniousness of this rich set, one may still find it insufficient for some reason – for example, one may doubt that there are Forms. The task of the defender of Forms is to search for a "higher" hypothesis harmonious with the developed set. Socrates says nothing about what such a higher hypothesis might be, but the present passage and others in the *Phaedo* (e.g., 107b) suggest at the very least that he does not consider the demand for a hypothesis higher than that of the Forms inappropriate.

In analysis the attack on a problem is the search among propositions until one finds a hypothesis-theorem from which a solution to the problem can be deduced (synthesis). In the method of the *Phaedo* the attack on a problem involves making a hypothesis judged to be the strongest available and building up through the addition of harmonious ideas a theory adequate to solve the problem. The closest one gets to a hypothesis-theorem is a satisfactory hypothesis. And the closest one gets to a deduction is the harmonious expansion of a hypothesis. From our point of view there is a considerable difference between deduction and harmonious expansion, between a consequence of and a plausible addition to a theory. I suspect that Plato did not assign this difference fundamental importance. By this I do not mean that Plato would have been willing to overlook the substitution of plausibility considerations for proof in mathematics. I only mean that for philosophical purposes he was willing to class together deduction and less formal methods of serious argumentation. The model of mathematical method remains, but it has been expanded in its adaptation to philosophy. This expansion of the notion of synthesis to include harmonious elaboration will be important in the next section.

V. MATHEMATICS AND DIALECTIC IN *REPUBLIC* VI AND VII

Mathematics comes to the fore in the *Republic* in the famous divided-line passage at the end of Book VI. I shall pass over many of the interpretive issues associated with this passage to discuss a few of concern to me.[30] The divisions of the line apparently include all things, the sensible world consisting of objects and their images and presided over by the sun, and the intelligible world presided over by the idea of the Good. Socrates is not clear about the relationship between these two worlds. The line and the comparison between the sun and the Good suggest a strong division, but the cave allegory and the mathematical curriculum suggest a considerable continuity which is likely to have been an important feature of Plato's general outlook. Socrates divides the intelligible world by reference to two mental conditions (*pathēmata*) or what we might call modes of cognition.[31] He identifies one of these (*noēsis*)[32] with the use of dialectic and illustrates the other (*dianoia*) by reference to mathematics, "geometry and its sister arts" (511b1–2). There is some question about whether the illustration exhausts the content of the relevant section or whether there are nonmathematical instances of *dianoia*. For my purposes it is sufficient that the section includes mathematics, which totally dominates Socrates' discussion.

Socrates makes two contrasts between *dianoia* and *noēsis:*

1. *Dianoia* is compelled to study its objects by proceeding from a hypothesis toward an ending, but *noēsis* studies its objects by proceeding from a hypothesis to an unhypothetical beginning (principle).
2. *Dianoia* uses sensible things as images, but *noēsis* uses no images and proceeds through Forms in a systematic way.

There is little doubt that Socrates has in mind here two features of mathematics that we associate particularly with geometry: the use of diagrams in arguments and the derivation of conclusions from initial assumptions (synthesis). The first point to notice about Socrates' explication of the mathematicians' use of diagrams is that, according to him, although mathematicians make their arguments (*logoi*) about images,

> they are not thinking (*dianoein*) about them, but about the things which resemble them; they make their arguments for the sake of (*heneka*) the square itself and the diagonal itself [i.e., the Forms of square and diagonal] and not for the sake of the one they draw. . . .[33] The things which they mold and draw . . . they use as images seeking to apprehend things which cannot be apprehended except by *dianoia*. (510d6–511a1)

A modern philosopher of mathematics might say that although geometers use drawn figures in their arguments, they are not arguing about figures (since figures satisfy their hypotheses only approximately) but about something else (which does satisfy the hypotheses exactly). Socrates says instead that geometers argue about visible figures, but do so for the sake of, that is, in order to apprehend, something else, namely (intelligible but not perceptible) mathematical Forms. It is difficult to be certain how far to press Socrates' vocabulary here ("arguing about," "thinking about," "arguing for the sake of"), but it certainly looks as though he thinks of mathematics as an attempt to understand the intelligible world by reasoning about sensible things rather than (as we might suppose) as an attempt to reason about the intelligible world using sensible things.

The importance of this contrast may be made clearer by reference to the fact that Socrates twice speaks of the mathematicians being compelled (*anangkadzomai*) to use hypotheses, but he never speaks of them as being compelled to use images. Moreover, what he says at 510b may mean that the use of images compels the soul to inquire hypothetically. Thus Socrates may mean that the mathematician is forced to use hypotheses because he is reasoning about sensible things in an attempt to understand intelligible ones. In another passage Socrates speaks similarly of geometers being forced to use the language of action, although this language is misleading with respect to the intelligible objects for the sake of which they are pursuing geometry:

> They speak in a way which is ridiculous and compulsory (*anangkaiōs*); for they are always talking about squaring and applying and adding as if they were doing things and were developing all their propositions for the sake of action; but, in fact, the whole subject is pursued for the sake of understanding. (*Rep.* 527a6–b1)

The general picture then is that the mathematician is in the position of trying to apprehend an intelligible, static world of Forms, but attempting to do so by arguing about visible things. This mode of arguing forces the mathematician to speak about acting on the things and to argue from hypotheses.

It is presumably clear enough why argument about diagrams necessitates talk about activities or operations, but not immediately clear why the use of diagrams necessitates the making of hypotheses.

This is made somewhat clearer by looking at what Socrates has to say about the hypotheses of the mathematicians, who, according to him,

> hypothesize the odd and the even and the figures and the three kinds of angles [acute, right, obtuse] and related things in the case of each science (*methodos*); they hypothesize these things as known, and do not think it worthwhile to give any account of them to themselves or others, as being clear to all; beginning from these, they proceed through the remainder and finish consistently with that for which the investigation was undertaken. (*Rep.* 510c3–d3)

Here the parallel with Socrates' hypothesizing in the *Phaedo* is striking. There the discussion shows that Socrates' initial hypothesis is a rather elaborate one about Forms, but he formulates the hypothesis simply as "that a beautiful itself by itself is something, and a good, and a large, and the rest." Similarly whereas we think of the mathematician as making rather elaborate assumptions about parallel lines, equality, and the meaning of certain terms, Socrates in the *Republic* mentions only "the odd and the even and the figures and the three kinds of angles and related things in the case of each science." We do not know enough about the way mathematics was presented in the early fourth century to judge the accuracy of Socrates' characterization, but we can see that he is not worried about details. Nothing he says implies that the mathematician deduces consequences from assumed propositions as opposed to making arguments on the basis of some assumed background knowledge about various concepts.[34] It may be exactly this latter sort of knowledge that Socrates thinks must be presupposed if one "argues about" figures.

The situation becomes more opaque when we turn to dialectic. Socrates tells us that, whereas the mathematician inquires from hypotheses and proceeds to a finishing point rather than to a starting point, the dialectician proceeds from a hypothesis to an "unhypothetical starting point," and proceeds "by means of Forms and through Forms," not using images. The directional contrast is presumably related to the analysis–synthesis contrast, but here the upward movement is assigned to the philosopher and distinguished from the mathematical procedure by more than its direction. Socrates goes on to assign a downward method to the dialectician as well:

> [Dialectical argument] does not make hypotheses starting points but genuine things laid down[35] like footholds and sources of impetus (*hormai*) in order to proceed to the unhypothetical, the starting point of everything: having grasped that and again the things right after it, it moves down to a finish, using nothing sensible at all, but only Ideas, moving through Ideas and into Ideas and finishing in them. (*Rep.* 511b5–c2)

The differences between this passage and the methodological description of the *Phaedo* need not be as significant as they are sometimes suggested to be. Some of them, notably, the insistence on the use of images, seem to stem from the fact that Socrates is concerned specifically with mathematics in the *Republic,* whereas in the *Phaedo* he is making a general methodological point, albeit one based on mathematical method. In the *Republic* there is no clear difference between the upward and downward movements of dialectic except for their direction. It is natural for us to assume that the downward method of dialectic is the same as the downward method of mathematics and to assimilate the former to what we know of the latter, namely that it is propositional deduction (synthesis). It is then natural to suppose as well that the upward method is propositional deduction or something reasonably like it. But in the *Phaedo* the upward "method" is simply a matter of making "higher" hypotheses, and the downward method seems to include the making of additional hypotheses harmonious with a given one. I see no good reason to think Plato is being more restrictive in the *Republic.* For Socrates' examples of the mathematicians' hypotheses in the *Republic* are of a piece with his taking the Forms as his sample hypothesis in the *Phaedo.* The most striking difference between the two passages is perhaps the contrast between Socrates' invocation of the unhypothetical principle of all things in the *Republic* and his rather bland reference to something satisfactory in the *Phaedo.* However, the latter reference is sufficiently bland to accommodate what is said in the *Republic.*[36]

We have seen that in the *Phaedo* and the *Meno* the presentation of hypothetical reasoning gets connected with ideas of refutation which seem to have less of a role to play in mathematics than in philosophy. In the divided-line passage of the *Republic* there is no sense that either the mathematician or the dialectician ever finds a hypothesis unsatisfactory. Mathematicians end up consistently with their hypotheses, and dialecticians move up from their hypotheses and back down, presumably to the same "hypotheses." Later, in Book VII, Socrates indicates that dialectic does involve refuting arguments, but he makes clear that successful dialecticians will be able to defend their position against all attempts at refutation (534b–d). However, just before this passage Socrates describes dialectic as "doing away with or destroying (*anairein*) hypotheses" (533c8), and he speaks rather denigratingly about mathematics:

> Geometry and the studies associated with it . . . do apprehend something of being, but . . . they are dreaming about it. They cannot have a waking vision of it as long as they use hypotheses and keep them fixed, unable to give an account of them. For when the starting point is not known and the finishing point and what comes in between are woven together out of what is not known, there is no way that such a consistency will ever become knowledge. (*Rep.* 533b–c)

Some later Platonists used this passage to belittle mathematics,[37] and modern scholars have debated what Socrates could have in mind by destroying the hypotheses of mathematics. I think it is fair to say that there is now consensus that the only destruction Socrates has in mind is the destruction of the hypothetical character of mathematical hypotheses through subsumption under an unhypothetical starting point. Equally when he denies that ordinary mathematics is knowledge he does not mean that it is false, but only that it lacks the requisite foundation to count as known. Insofar as mathematics provides dialectic with its hypotheses, dialectic starts with truths that it will test but not refute.

The divided-line passage, then, emphasizes the following features of mathematics:

1. Reasoning about sensible objects, figures, for the sake of, that is, in order to understand, intelligible ones.
2. The laying down of hypotheses, presented as the assumption of certain objects (the odd and even, the figures, the kinds of angle), but in fact involving assumptions about the nature of these objects and the ways they can be manipulated.
3. The downward development of these hypotheses, including, but not necessarily restricted to, deduction.

Plato sees the first of these as the cause of the second and, presumably, of the third: Because mathematicians reason about sensible things, they must make hypotheses and they must move downward from them, as they must speak about acting on sensibles. It is reasonable to suppose that Plato's description of mathematics as depending on hypotheses that the mathematician never attempts to justify is an accurate description of the mathematics of his time. But why does Plato think of the downward direction as a necessary feature of mathematics? After all, mathematicians do perform analyses on propositions below the level of their ultimate hypotheses. Why couldn't they attempt to do the same thing on those hypotheses?

The answer here may be a simple matter of definition: For Plato such an upward movement would take one outside the domain of mathematics. But there may be more involved. For Plato, to justify the hypotheses of mathematics will be to answer questions like What is a figure? and What is an angle? Answering this kind of question satisfactorily requires one to move from arguing about sensibles to arguing about Forms. Obviously the same person can switch from mathematically developing hypotheses to asking Platonic/Socratic questions about the hypotheses, but this change is a change from arguing about sensibles to arguing about intelligibles, that is, a change from mathematics to dialectic. Socrates makes something like this point at 523*aff* when he is describing the mathematical curriculum. There Socrates is no longer interested in the downward aspects of mathematics, but in its power to turn the soul's attention upward from sensibles to intelligibles. To argue that arithmetic, properly pursued, has this power, he distinguishes between aspects of things that seem contradictory to the senses and those that do not. Supposedly, seeing a finger does not lead or compel (*anagkadzein*)[38] an ordinary person to ask what a finger is, but seeing that one finger is larger than a second but smaller than a third does lead or compel a person to ask what largeness is, that is, to ask a question about Forms. Glaucon volunteers that unity falls in the second category because we see the same thing simultaneously as one and infinitely many.[39] Socrates adds that the same will be true of all number.

Socrates' way of speaking about the abandonment of sensibles in dialectical argument was taken by the Neoplatonists to involve reference to a mysterious "nondiscursive" thought, which, among other things, violates Aristotle's dictum (*On the Soul* III.7.431a16–17) that "the soul never thinks (*noein*) without an image (*phantasma*)."[40] Nothing in the *Republic* seems to me to justify this Neo-Platonist reading, although one cannot preclude the possibility that Plato had something of the sort in mind. However, I am inclined to think that when Socrates describes dialectic as restricted to Forms, he is not talking about what goes on in the consciousness of a dialectician at work, but is simply developing the contrast between dialecticians and mathematicians. Mathematicians reason about sensibles for the sake of intelligibles; they use sensibles. Dialecticians reason about intelligibles for the sake of intelligibles; whether or not images occur in their minds or they refer to sensible things, they do not reason about sensible things, they do not use them.

It becomes clear from Book VII of the *Republic* that the unhypothetical first principle of all things is the Idea of the Good (532a*ff*). It also becomes reasonably clear (534b–d) that its unhypothetical character depends upon the fact that people who apprehend it fully can defend themselves when someone tries to "grab onto" their hypothesis. That is to say, for a principle to be unhypothetical is for it to require no higher hypothesis for justification, that is, to be capable of withstanding argumentative assault on its own. The notion of being the first principle of all things seems to me impossible to construe sensibly in terms of a strictly deductive model of the downward path. The Good becomes such a hypothesis only by the addition of other hypotheses harmonious with it. From a modern logical point of view additional hypotheses are additional hypotheses, but for Plato the hypothesis of the Good is the condition that restricts these further hypotheses and so is higher than they. I do not believe that one can make ultimately satisfactory logical sense of Plato's position here,[41] but appreciating it seems to me a precondition of understanding the implication of the *Republic* that mathematical hypotheses are subsidiary to the Idea of the Good. Plato is not suggesting that mathematical hypotheses can be deduced from assumptions about the Good,[42] but "only" that they will fit harmoniously into a fully developed theory anchored in the Good. For Plato it is good that a sum of even numbers is even and that the planets move uniformly in circular orbits. We may try to explain the latter of these beliefs by reference to a teleological conception of the world and the former by reference to the beauty and goodness of mathematical truth. But Plato is unlikely to have distinguished the two features clearly; for him, as far as we can tell, it is for the best that even numbers add up to an even number and it is true that the world system is a beautiful thing.

I have already mentioned that when Socrates expounds his mathematical curriculum, he is interested almost exclusively in the power of mathematics to draw the soul away from the sensible to the intelligible. After his argument that arithmetic has this power, he adds a second consideration to show that the arithmetician really is concerned with intelligibles:

> For I imagine that you know that those who are formidable in these matters, if someone tries to divide the one itself by argument, laugh and will not accept it, but if you chop it up, they multiply, taking care that the one will never appear not one but many parts.[43] . . . Glaucon, what do you think would happen if someone were to ask them, "What kind of numbers are you discussing in which the one is the sort you deem it to be: each equal to every other, not differing even slightly, and containing no part?" What do you think they would answer?
>
> I suppose they would say that they are talking about things which can only be thought and cannot be treated in any other way.
>
> (*Rep.* 525d8–526a7)

Here Socrates indicates that the way arithmeticians talk commits them to an intelligible world. He does not draw the distinction made in the divided-line passage between what the arithmetician reasons about and what he reasons for the sake of. Indeed, he says explicitly that the arithmetician discusses intelligible units rather than saying (as I think he should for consistency) that the arithmetician discusses sensibles for the sake of intelligibles. The reason for this discrepancy is that Plato wants to use the way arithmeticians talk as an indication that their concern is with the intelligible. In his immediately succeeding treatment of geometry and his subsequent treatment of astronomy and harmonics, he wants to stress that mathematical practice is misleading. Geometers, he says, speak as if they were doing something, but their knowledge does not concern changing things but what always is. Socrates does not argue for this conclusion;[44] it is volunteered by Glaucon, who, we may suppose, has been carried along by Socrates' treatment of mathematics since the divided-line passage. But even Glaucon does not seem totally prepared for Socrates' discussion of astronomy,[45] a discussion that must be interpreted in the light of the specific role of drawing upward that Socrates assigns to mathematics.

Geometers reason about sensible figures for the sake of intelligible things, the square itself, the diagonal itself, and so forth. In astronomy what is observed in the heavens takes the place of sensible figures. What corresponds to the mathematical Forms is, in one of Plato's more opaque phrases, "the true things, the movements by which are moved real speed and real slowness in true number both by all true figure and in relation to one another, and by which they move the things in them" (529d1–5). Socrates goes on to say that no one should expect to find the truth about ratios in the visible heavens or think that the periods of the various heavenly bodies will remain constant through time; that is to say, as sensible objects the heavens cannot perfectly embody scientific laws. Socrates concludes,

> We will pursue astronomy as we also pursue geometry, using problems, but we will leave things in heaven alone, if, sharing in genuine astronomy, we are going to change what is naturally intelligent in the soul from uselessness to use. (*Rep.* 530b6–c1)

Socrates' treatment of astronomy has caused Plato's admirers a good deal of discomfort. Various expedients have been proposed, but none can eliminate the fact that "true" astronomy does not concern the visible heavens any more than arithmetic and geometry concern sensible objects. Our custom is to distinguish applied and pure sciences. Even if some of us do not accept Plato's position on the pure sciences, most of us will at least acknowledge the force of the idea that arithmetic and geometry, for example, deal with imperceptible realities. But the suggestion that true astronomy deals with such realities seems bizarre. Can anything be said to ameliorate the difficulty?

First of all, we can be reasonably certain that Plato did not himself ignore the importance of giving some account of the apparent motions of the heavenly bodies. For, if we can believe Simplicius, he set astronomers the task of accounting for these apparent motions through a hypothesis of uniform circular motions. Plato himself sketches the beginnings of such an account in the *Timaeus* (36b–d), and he reaffirms the importance of understanding planetary motion at 822a of the *Laws*.[46] Simplicius refers to the task as a problem, and in the Philodemus passage Plato is also described as setting problems. It would seem likely, then, that in the *Republic* Socrates has in mind for astronomy the attempt to resolve outstanding questions by reduction to better-understood things. But whereas in geometry Plato can cite the (true) hypotheses that the geometer does not question, he has no analogue in astronomy. In other words in geometry successful reductions or analyses of problems move to hypotheses-theorems, but in astronomy there are no such theorems; the task of analysis is to move to hypotheses-lemmas – in the case of Plato's astronomical problem, uniform circular motions. Plato does not address the question of the status of these lemmas when they are hypothesized, but I think we can reasonably say that in the downward movement of dialectic they will be established as "theorems" harmonious with the Idea of the Good.

There remains the question of how Plato understood the relationship between astronomical phenomena and the true astronomer's hypotheses. If we follow the *Republic* those hypotheses cannot be about the phenomena any more than what the geometer apprehends is truths about sensible things. And when Socrates says that in true astronomy one should leave things in heaven alone, it is perhaps natural to take him to be implying that astronomy might be developed without anyone ever looking at the heavens. But such a view is so implausible that one is reluctant to ascribe it to anyone. We may prefer to rely on Socrates' comparison between astronomy and geometry. Geometers reason about sensible things for the sake of intelligibles; this means that their truths, like the truths of arithmeticians, are not truths about sensible things. However, geometers know this last fact, so there is no reason to tell them to leave sensible things alone in the sense of attending to intelligibles. However, we need not suppose that Plato would urge geometers to stop using diagrams in their reasoning.[47] By analogy we can say that Plato is urging astronomers to stop thinking that their subject is sensibles, but he is not urging them to stop using astronomical appearances as astronomical appearances. Astronomers can attend to appearances, argue about them, but they must do so for the sake of, that is, in order to understand, an intelligible world containing "the true things, the movements by which are moved real speed and real slowness in true number both by all true figure and in relation to one another, and by which they move the things in them."

We find this position hard to accept because for us astronomy is about the phenomena, not about an intelligible world. But Socrates, in the *Republic*, holds that scientific knowledge is of eternal unchanging truths, and he does not think that the heavens or anything sensible is unchanging in a way that permits such knowledge. However, this does not mean that astronomical truth makes no contribution to our understanding of the sensible world any more than the fact that arithmetic and geometry are about the intelligible world means that they make no contribution to our understanding of the sensible world.[48] The crucial point is that for Plato such understanding depends upon understanding another, ideal world over which the Good reigns.

NOTES

1 There is a useful discussion of Plato's Academy in chap. 2 of John Patrick Lynch, *Aristotle's School* (Berkeley, 1972). The evidence for most assertions about Plato and the Academy is very complicated. I try to indicate clearly when what I say is generally accepted and when it is more controversial.

2 See Diogenes Laertius, *Lives of the Philosophers,* IV.2; Olympiodorus, *Commentary on the First Alcibiades,* 140. 16–17 Creutzer; and Olympiodorus, *Anonymous Prolegomena to the Philosophy of Plato,* 5.24–27 Westerink.

3 For two influential examples see Paul Shorey, *What Plato Said* (Chicago, 1933), 30; and F. M. Cornford, "Mathematics and Dialectic in the *Republic* VI–VII," *Mind* 41 (1932): 173–4 (reprinted in *Studies in Plato's Metaphysics,* ed. R. E. Allen [London, 1965], 77–8). For criticism see Harold Cherniss, *The Riddle of the Early Academy* (Berkeley, 1945), 66–82.

4 Socrates calls these subjects *mathēmata,* a general term for things to be learned. Because of the influence of the *Republic* the word came to be applied to these subjects specifically, and so *mathēmata* became a technical term that it is customary to translate "mathematics." I shall use this translation, but it is important to realize that for Plato and other ancient writers "mathematics" includes subjects we associate with physics as well as some we associate with pure mathematics.

5 For an introduction to this very complex topic see Konrad Gaiser, "Plato's Enigmatic Lecture *On the Good,*" *Phronesis* 25 (1980): 5–37.

6 See G. C. Field, *Plato and his Contemporaries,* 3d ed. (London, 1967), 40–5.

7 Menedemus, a pupil of Plato, was almost elected scholarch of the Academy after the death of Speusippus in 339. See François Lasserre, *De*

Léodamas de Thasos à Philippe d'Oponte, vol. 2: *La scuola di Platone* (Naples, 1987), 93–6 with commentary.

8 Here the Academy is the public area in the outskirts of Athens from which Plato's Academy took its name. Plato taught in the public area and established a residence nearby. The two uses of the term "Academy" give rise to some confusion in our sources.

9 The so-called *Academicorum Philosophorum Index Herculanensis*. Philodemus preserves excerpts from earlier authors, but the question of what author he is quoting in our passage is disputed. For discussion see Konrad Gaiser, *Philodemus: Academica* (Supplementum Platonicum 1) (Stuttgart–Bad Cannstatt, 1988), 76–7, 88–91, whose reconstruction (pp. 152–3) I have largely followed.

10 Letters enclosed in angle brackets (⟨⟩) correspond to gaps in the papyrus, and letters within square brackets ([]) to letters that cannot be read with certainty. I have introduced these niceties only in cases of significance for my topic.

11 The gap here is about seven letters long, followed by the legible letters ΣΜΟΥΣ. Conjectures: definitions, numbers, ratios, *diorismoi*, altars, astronomy, atoms. Gaiser mentions as other possibilities rhythms and sections.

12 Perhaps the greatest mathematician and astronomer of the fourth century, Eudoxus probably spent some time at the Academy, although he also spent considerable time elsewhere and led a school in Cnidus. Materials relating to him can be found in François Lasserre, *Die Fragmente des Eudoxos von Knidos* (Texte und Kommentare IV) (Berlin, 1966). There is a brief summary of his accomplishments in Charles C. Gillispie, ed., *Dictionary of Scientific Biography* (New York, 1970–80). The *Dictionary* is a generally reliable source of information on the scientific achievements of most of the Greek mathematicians mentioned in this paper and in other works on Greek science.

13 If the restoration is correct, the reference is to Hippocrates of Chios, the earliest person (late fifth century) to whom we can ascribe specific mathematical accomplishments with confidence. According to Proclus (*A Commentary on the First Book of Euclid's Elements*, 66.7–8), Hippocrates was the first person known to have written a book of *Elements* (more than a century before Euclid).

14 Like Gaiser I am inclined to think that it has something to do with the treatment of common measures and their absence (i.e., incommensurability). However, it might also concern the determination of areas and volumes.

15 The problem must have been considered before Plato's time since Hippocrates of Chios is said to have been the first person to realize that

the problem of constructing a cube that is double the volume of one with side of length l was solvable by finding x and y such that $l : x :: x : y :: y : 2l$. For detailed information about the Greek treatment of this problem see Thomas Heath, *A History of Greek Mathematics,* vol. 1 (Oxford, 1921), 244–70. Heath describes Plato's alleged solution on pp. 255–8. Another mathematical accomplishment ascribed to Plato in antiquity was a procedure for finding square integers equal to the sum of two square integers; see ibid., 79–82.

16 The description that follows is simplified. The Greeks classed sun and moon as planets because, unlike the fixed stars, they had an apparent west–east motion. Among the many sources one may consult on ancient Greek astronomy I mention D. R. Dicks, *Early Greek Astronomy to Aristotle* (Ithaca, N.Y., 1970).

17 Simplicius here refers to theories of the kind put forward by Eudoxus. They involve the view that the sun, moon, and planets are attached to spheres rotating about the earth as center. To explain the anomalous motions, Eudoxus postulated additional spheres rotating in other directions and counteracting the motion of the primary sphere of a heavenly body.

18 See on this topic the fundamental paper of Harold Cherniss, "Plato as Mathematician," *Review of Metaphysics* 4 (1951): 395–426, reprinted in his *Selected Papers,* ed. Leonardo Tarán (Leiden, 1977).

19 The major source of perplexity (and controversy) stems from descriptions of analysis that represent it as a matter of deducing conclusions rather than of searching for presuppositions. For discussion see Norman Gulley, "Greek Geometrical Analysis," *Phronesis* 3 (1958): 1–14.

20 Clearly there might be situations in which one had to settle for sufficient but not necessary conditions or know that certain conditions were necessary but not be able to prove them sufficient, but the Greeks do not mention this point in discussing *diorismoi.*

21 Leodamas is also the addressee of Plato's *Eleventh Letter,* the contents of which concern politics. Otherwise we know nothing about him except what Proclus tells us.

22 There is a quite good list of mathematical passages in Plato with discussion in Attilio Frajese, *Platone e la matematica nel mondo antico* (Rome, 1963).

23 The whole of this passage (which extends to 68.6 and can be read in an English translation by Glenn R. Morrow in *Proclus: A Commentary on the First Book of Euclid's Elements* [Princeton, 1970]) is a fundamental document for interpreting Plato's relationship to the mathematics of his time. The clear implication of the passage (which probably derives ultimately from Eudemus) is that all mathematical work done in the fourth

century was done under the influence of Plato and probably at the Academy. But Plato himself is described only in the passage quoted, where he is treated as an enthusiast able to inspire others.

24 Clearly the task of "saving the apparent motions of the planets" is also a demand for the analysis of the apparent motions and a reduction of them to uniform circular motions.

25 My translations from the *Meno* are very slight revisions of those of R. W. Sharples, *Plato, Meno* (Warminster, 1985). Sharples briefly discusses the obscurities of the mathematical example on pp. 158–61. I shall write as if the meaning of the example is transparent, that is, I simply reproduce the example without explanation. My interpretation of the whole passage is indebted to Ernst Heitsch, "Platons hypothetisches Verfahren im *Menon*," *Hermes* 105 (1977): 257–68.

26 I do not undertake to give a full treatment of the issues raised by this passage. For thorough discussion see the notes in *Plato, Phaedo*, translated with notes by David Gallop (Oxford, 1975).

27 The parallel between Socrates' methodological proposal and Plato's challenge to the astronomers is suggestive: To save the phenomena the astronomer is urged to hypothesize uniform ciruclar motions and refine their description until they characterize the phenomena.

28 The phrase used by Socrates is more literally translated "that [part?] of the hypothesis which is safe," and hence *may* refer to the explanation by participation as a "safe" addition to the original hypothesis of Forms. See Paul Plass, "Socrates' Method of Hypothesis in the *Phaedo*," *Phronesis* 5 (1960): 111–12.

29 At 101e Socrates insists that the hypothesis should not be questioned until one has tested the things that come from it for agreement. His separation of the question of the possibility of justifying a hypothetical theory by reference to a higher one and checking the internal soundness of a theory is no doubt methodologically sound, but in practice it seems highly unlikely that people could be restrained from asking about the doctrine of Forms and participation until the doctrine had been fully tested for harmoniousness. Moreover (at least from a contemporary point of view), if the hypothesis were shown to be harmonious and to give a reasonable account of the coming to be, ceasing to be, and being of each thing, one might find the question of satisfactoriness relatively insignificant.

30 The reader may wish to consult chaps. 10 and 11 of Julia Annas, *An Introduction to Plato's Republic* (Oxford, 1981).

31 The term "mode of cognition" is intended to indicate rather than explain what Socrates is talking about. As examples of different modes of cognition one might consider the difference between knowledge and

belief or between a person who has witnessed an event and one who has heard about it or inferred that it must have happened.

32 Socrates' terms for the two modes of cognition are of no real help in understanding the distinction he intends. I prefer to leave them untranslated to avoid importing misleading connotations.

33 Here and elsewhere I have transformed a Socratic rhetorical question into an assertion.

34 For further discussion of the mathematical hypotheses mentioned by Socrates and of mathematical principles in early Greek mathematics and philosophy see my paper "On the Notion of a Mathematical Starting Point in Plato, Aristotle, and Euclid," in *Science and Philosophy in Classical Greece,* ed. Alan Bowen (London and New York, 1991), 59–97.

35 Socrates here relies on the etymology of the Greek *hupothesis.*

36 For arguments that the unhypothetical principle of the *Republic* is an instance of something satisfactory in the sense of the *Phaedo,* see Harold Cherniss, "Some War-Time Publications concerning Plato. I," *American Journal of Philology* 68 (1947): 141 (reprinted in his *Selected Papers*).

37 See Proclus, *Commentary on Euclid,* 29.14–24.

38 Socrates mentions that mathematics compels one to move upward to the intelligible world already in the Divided Line passage at 511c7.

39 It seems that Plato is here taking for granted Zeno's argument that an extended thing can be divided into indefinitely many parts and his own conviction (cf. *Prm.* 127d–130a) that Zeno's arguments apply to visible rather than intelligible things. This conviction is perhaps justified by the belief that all and only visible things are extended, but the claim that we actually see things as one and many (rather than argue that extended things are one and many) would seem to need more justification than Socrates provides.

40 For discussion of nondiscursive thought see A. C. Lloyd, "Non-Discursive Thought – An Enigma of Greek Philosophy," *Proceedings of the Aristotelian Society* 70 (1969–70), 261–74.

41 There seems to be something reasonable about the idea that the hypothesis of Forms is "higher than" the hypothesis that things are what they are by participation in the Forms. But if the second is really a *further* hypothesis not implicit in the first one, it is hard to see how the first can be thought to rule out alternatives to the second in any strictly logical sense of "rule out."

42 Contrast, for example, F. M. Cornford's position in "Mathematics and Dialectic," esp. 178–81, 187–90 (*Studies in Plato's Metaphysics,* ed. Allen, 82–5, 91–5).

43 It is not clear what, if anything, Socrates has in mind by this attempt to divide up the one or the actual division and multiplication of the one. For

one attempt to relate what Socrates says to Greek mathematical practice see B. L. van der Waerden, *Science Awakening* (New York, 1963), 115–16. For a different and more plausible reading see M. F. Burnyeat, "Platonism and Mathematics: A Prelude to Discussion," in *Mathematics and Metaphysics in Aristotle*, ed. Andreas Graeser (Bern and Stuttgart, 1987), 226.

44 Later philosophers, including ancient ones, argue that sensibles do not satisfy the conditions laid down by geometers, e.g., that widthless lines cannot be perceived. Such arguments are grist to Plato's mill, but, if he was aware of them, he never invokes them explicitly. For an attempt to assign some such argument to the *Republic* see Burnyeat, "Platonism and Mathematics," 221–5.

45 I here pass over Socrates' remarks about stereometry. His claims about the backward state of stereometry have been taken to reflect Plato's conception of the situation in mathematics in the fourth century. It is hard to resist the suggestion that Socrates' call for a director of stereometrical studies has some connection with Plato's role in the Academy. I shall also pass over Socrates' treatment of harmonics, which seems to me quite of a piece with his description of astronomy. For some discussion of both astronomy and harmonics see my paper "Ascending to Problems: Astronomy and Harmonics in *Republic* VII," in *Science and the Sciences in Plato*, ed. John P. Anton (Albany, 1980), 103–21. The papers by Mourelatos and Vlastos in the same volume are very useful treatments of the same material, focusing on astronomy.

46 See Gregory Vlastos, *Plato's Universe* (Seattle, 1975), 49–61 with the relevant appendices.

47 I here take a position on a very difficult issue. In the Divided Line passage Socrates describes the mathematician as using figures and hypotheses. The dialectician destroys the hypothetical character of those hypotheses, but there is no reason why the mathematician might not still continue to draw conclusions from them. What about the use of figures? Does the dialectician somehow make possible a geometry in which figures are no longer used in argumentation? One can see how one might infer such a possibility from what Socrates says. But he doesn't say it, and customary ways of trying to make sense of the possibility are anachronistic. (For an extreme example of such anachronism see A. E. Taylor, *Plato the Man and his Works*, 5th ed. [London, 1948], 289–95.) I doubt very much that Plato envisaged the possibility, but I am uncertain what Plato took the connection between the use of diagrams and the apprehension of truth about the intelligible world to be. His lack of explicitness on this question is paralleled by his lack of explicitness on the relation between astronomical phenomena and astronomical knowledge.

48 On the importance of applied mathematics see the *Phil.* 55d*ff.*

GAIL FINE

6 Inquiry in the *Meno*

In most of the Socratic dialogues, Socrates professes to inquire into some virtue.[1] At the same time, he professes not to know what the virtue in question is. How, then, can he inquire into it? Doesn't he need some knowledge to guide his inquiry? Socrates' disclaimer of knowledge seems to preclude Socratic inquiry.[2] This difficulty must confront any reader of the Socratic dialogues; but one searches them in vain for any explicit statement of the problem or for any explicit solution to it. The *Meno*, by contrast, both raises it explicitly and proposes a solution.

I. THE PRIORITY OF KNOWLEDGE WHAT (PKW)

Meno begins the dialogue by asking whether virtue is teachable (70a1–2). Socrates replies that he doesn't know the answer to Meno's question; nor does he at all (*to parapan*, 71a7) know what virtue is. The latter failure of knowledge explains the former; for "if I do not know what a thing is, how could I know what it is like?" (*ho de mē oida ti estin, pōs an hopoion ge ti eideiēn*; 71b3–4). Nonetheless, he proposes to inquire with Meno into what virtue is. Here, as in the Socratic dialogues, Socrates both disclaims knowledge and proposes to inquire. Socrates' disclaimer rests on his belief that he satisfies the antecedent of the following conditional, when "virtue" is substituted for *x*:

The first version of this paper was written while I was on leave in Oxford in the spring of 1987. Since then, various versions have received helpful comments. I am especially indebted to Jyl Gentzler, both to discussions with her and to her writings, and also to Lesley Brown, David Brink, Terry Irwin, and Richard Kraut.

> (PKW) If one doesn't at all know what *x* is, one can't know anything about *x*.

I shall call this claim the Principle of the Priority of Knowledge What (PKW). There is considerable dispute about how to interpret PKW. One suggestion is that it means:[3]

> (A) If one has no idea what *x* is – has no beliefs at all about *x* – then one can't (intend to) say anything about *x*.

(A) is independently plausible; but it is difficult to believe it is what Socrates intends. For the self-confident way in which he examines Meno about virtue suggests he satisfies neither the antecendent nor the consequent of (A): He appears to have some ideas, some beliefs, about virtue; and he proceeds to say various things about it. Moreover (focusing for the moment on the antecedent of PKW), Socrates doesn't say he has no ideas or beliefs about virtue; he says he doesn't *know (oida) what virtue is.*[4] Here there are two points: first, he claims to lack *knowledge,* not all beliefs or ideas; second, he claims to lack knowledge about *what virtue is.* This second claim, taken in context, suggests that the knowledge he (believes he) lacks is knowledge of the definition of virtue, of its nature or essence; he doesn't know the answer to the Socratic What is *F*? question, where *F* is virtue. We might then try altering the antecedent of (A) so as to yield (B):[5]

> (B) If one doesn't at all know the definition of *x*, one can't (intend to) say anything about *x*.

In contrast to (A), (B)'s antecedent is one Socrates seems to satisfy (believe he satisfies). However, unlike (A), (B) seems self-defeatingly strong. For if it is a precondition of saying anything (intending to say anything) about *x* that one know what *x* is, and one does not know what *x* is, then it is difficult to see how one can inquire into *x*. How can one inquire into something if one can't even (intend to) say anything about it? Moreover, we have seen that Socrates acts as though he doesn't satisfy the consequent of (B), for he says quite a lot about virtue. If he is committed to (B), and (believes he) doesn't know what virtue is, yet continues to talk about virtue, then his theory and practice conflict.

There is an alternative to (B) that is worth considering. Just as

Socrates says, not that he lacks *beliefs* about what virtue is, but that he lacks *knowledge* of what virtue is, so he says that such knowledge is necessary, not for *saying* (intending to say) anything about virtue, but for *knowing* anything about virtue:[6]

> (C) If one doesn't at all know the definition of *x*, one can't know anything about *x*.

In contrast to (B), (C) uses "know" in both clauses; so too does Socrates. What he *says* is that one needs to *know* what virtue is, not in order to say anything about virtue, or in order to have any beliefs about virtue, but in order to *know* anything about virtue. This claim leaves open the possibility that one could have beliefs about virtue, and (intend to) say various things about virtue, without knowing what it is; and, if beliefs that fall short of knowledge are adequate to guide inquiry, then even if Socrates lacks all knowledge about virtue, he can still inquire if he has and relies on suitable beliefs.

Although (B) and (C) can thus be read so as to be quite different, it does not follow that Plato is alive to, or exploits, their difference. For him to do so, he must be clear, among other things, about the difference between knowledge and belief. Yet it has been argued that he is unclear about their difference, at least in the Socratic dialogues.[7] We shall need to see, then, whether Plato is able to exploit the difference between (B) and (C) that their phrasing leaves open.

Whether we read PKW as (B) or (C), Socrates claims not to know what virtue is, in the sense of not knowing the definition of virtue.[8] One might wonder why he does so. Does not his ability to pick out examples of virtuous actions, to use virtue terms coherently, and the like, show that he knows the definition of virtue? If to know the definition of virtue were simply to know the meaning of the term "virtue," in the sense of knowing something like a dictionary or lexical definition of it, then it would indeed be odd for Socrates to claim not to know the definition of virtue.[9] But for Socrates, to know the definition of virtue is not simply to know the ordinary meaning of the term "virtue"; it is to know what the thing, virtue, really is, its explanatory properties. Knowing what virtue is, for Socrates, is more like knowing a Lockean real than nominal essence – more like knowing, say, the inner constitution, the atomic number, of gold, than like knowing, or having some idea of, the surface, observable features of gold, such as that it is yellow and shiny.[10] If this is right, then Socrates' claim not to know what virtue is is reasonable; for as the progress of science reveals, real essences are difficult to discover.

Even if it's reasonable for Socrates to disclaim knowledge of the real essence of virtue, one might wonder whether it's reasonable for him to claim that such knowledge has the sort of priority he accords it. Here (B) and (C) demand different verdicts.[11] It certainly doesn't seem reasonable to say, as (B) does, that such knowledge is necessary for *saying* (intending to say) anything about virtue. Surely most of us lack knowledge of the real essence of virtue, but have some reliable beliefs about virtue. Socrates seems to agree; at least, in the Socratic dialogues, certain beliefs about virtue – for example, that it is admirable (*kalon*), good (*agathon*), and beneficial (*ōphelimon*) – are regularly relied on.[12] But (C) seems more reasonable; it says that knowledge of the real essence of virtue is necessary for *knowing* anything else about virtue. If we place strong conditions on knowledge, and clearly distinguish knowledge from belief, then it is reasonable if controversial to claim that knowledge of the nonessential properties of a thing must be suitably rooted in knowledge of its nature.[13]

PKW raises a prima facie problem. For it says that if one doesn't know what x is, one can't know anything about x. Socrates claims not to know what virtue is, yet he proposes to inquire into what virtue is. How can he inquire, or be justified in inquiring, given his disclaimer of knowledge? Doesn't inquiry demand some initial knowledge?

On some conceptions of his disclaimer and his project, there is no difficulty. One conception, for example, is that (a) Socrates is not really inquiring into virtue, at least, not in the sense of seeking knowledge of what virtue is; he seeks only to expose the ignorance of others, and this less demanding aim does not require moral knowledge. Hence, his disclaimer does not conflict with his project after all.[14] Another conception is that (b) although Socrates wants to know what virtue is, he is hypocritical or ironical in disclaiming moral knowledge or, more charitably, he disclaims knowledge only in an effort to force interlocutors to think for themselves. If Socrates does not intend the disclaimer seriously, then, again, there is no difficulty in squaring his project with his disclaimer.[15]

Yet a third conception is that (c) both the disclaimer of knowledge and the desire to know what virtue is are genuine – but the disclaimer is less sweeping than it is sometimes thought to be. On one version of this view (c1), Socrates disclaims knowledge in the sense of "certainty," but not in the different sense of "justified true belief"; and knowledge in this latter sense can guide inquiry. On another version of this view (c2), Socrates disclaims knowledge of *what virtue is* – of its essence or nature – but not of *what virtue is like;* he does not, for example, disclaim knowledge of instances of virtuous action, and his knowledge of them can guide inquiry.[16]

If any of these conceptions is correct, then the problem disappears. Unfortunately, however, none of them works for the *Meno.*[17] Plato claims in what follows that inquiry can achieve knowledge (85c9–d1). It would be perverse to suggest that although he believes it *can* achieve knowledge, its true goal is only to perplex interlocutors; rather, as we shall see, he elicits perplexity only as an interim stage in a journey whose ultimate destination is the acquisition of moral knowledge. Conception (a) is thus inadequate.

Conception (b) is also inadequate. As Irwin argues, Socrates' "repeated disclaimers of knowledge are too frequent and emphatic to be dismissed as ironical without strong reason; Aristotle takes them seriously (*Soph. El.* 183b6–8), and so should we."[18]

Nor is (c1) adequate. At *Meno* 98a, Plato offers just one definition of knowledge – as justified true belief (true belief coupled with an *aitias logismos*) – and it is presumably knowledge of this sort that he disclaims. Yet it is just this sort of knowledge that, according to (c1), Socrates (believes he) possesses.[19]

Nor is (c2) adequate. For Socrates claims not to know what virtue is; given PKW, it follows that he knows nothing at all about virtue. He can't then, as (c2) proposes, know some things about virtue.

Our problem remains, then. On the one hand, Socrates professes not to know what virtue is; given his affirmation of PKW, it follows that (he believes) he knows nothing at all about virtue. How, then, can he inquire into virtue? As we shall see, this is just the question Meno asks him.

II. MENO'S PARADOX

Although Socrates claims not to know what virtue is, and so not to know anything about virtue, he proposes to inquire into what virtue is. Meno valiantly offers several suggestions; but Socrates rebuts him at every turn, using his familiar elenctic method. He asks an interlocutor a What-is-*F*? question – What is courage (*Laches*), or friendship (*Lysis*), or piety (*Euthyphro*). He cross-examines the interlocutor, appealing to various agreed examples and principles. Eventually the interlocutor discovers that, contrary to his initial beliefs, he does not know the answer to Socrates' question. For it emerges that he has contradictory beliefs about the matter at hand and so lacks knowledge about it; if I have contradictory beliefs about *x*, then I lack knowledge about *x*.[20] The Socratic dialogues typically end at this stage, with the interlocutor at a loss (in a state of *aporia*). In the *Meno*, however, matters are carried further. Meno turns to the offensive, challenging Socrates' right to question him when Socrates himself lacks knowledge. He poses a paradox, generally known as the eristic paradox or as Meno's paradox:

> How will you inquire into something, Socrates, when you don't at all know what it is? Which of the things that you don't know will you suppose it is, when you are inquiring into it? And even if you happen upon it, how will you know it is the thing you didn't know? (80d5–8)

Socrates reformulates the paradox as follows:

> I understand what you mean, Meno. Do you see what an eristic argument you're introducing, that it isn't possible for one to inquire either into what one knows, or into what one doesn't know? For one wouldn't inquire into what one knows – for one knows it, and there's no need to inquire into such a thing; nor into what one doesn't know – for one doesn't know what one is inquiring into. (80e1–6)

Meno poses three questions:

a. How can one inquire into something if one doesn't at all know what it is?
b. Which of the things one doesn't know is one inquiring into?
c. How will one recognize the object of one's inquiry, even if one finds it?

Socrates recasts Meno's paradox into the form of a constructive dilemma:[21]

1. For any *x*, one either knows, or does not know, *x*.
2. If one knows *x*, one cannot inquire into *x*.
3. If one does not know *x*, one cannot inquire into *x*.

4. Therefore, whether or not one knows *x*, one cannot inquire into *x*.

The argument seems valid. (1) is a harmless instantiation of the law of the excluded middle – either one does, or does not, know *p*; *tertium non datur.* (2) and (3) tell us that whichever of these exclusive and exhaustive options obtains, inquiry is impossible. (4) then validly concludes that inquiry is impossible.

Although the argument seems valid, one might question its soundness.[22] (1) is harmless; but what about (2) and (3)?

In defense of (2), Socrates says only that if one already knows, there is no need to inquire. This is not a very good defense of (2); I don't need another meal at Lutece but, for all that, I might still go there. Nor is it clear why, if one knows *x*, one cannot inquire into it. I might know who Meno is, but seek to know where he is; I might know something about physics, but seek to know more about it. Of course, if I know *everything* there is to know about Meno, or physics, *then* there is no need – or possibility – of inquiring about them. But surely not all knowledge of a thing is tantamount to complete or total knowledge of it; generally, one has only partial knowledge. (2) thus seems false.[23]

(3) also seems false. To be sure, if I do not know *x* in the sense that my mind is a complete blank about it, if I am totally ignorant about it, have no ideas whatsoever about it, then I cannot inquire into it. But being totally ignorant about *x* does not seem to be the only way to lack knowledge about it. I might lack all knowledge about *x*, but have some (true) beliefs about it; and perhaps they are adequate for inquiry. Having (true) beliefs that fall short of knowledge is one way of lacking knowledge; but it is not a way of lacking knowledge that seems to preclude inquiry. (3) thus also seems false.[24]

Notice that in arguing that (3) is false, I appealed to the sort of distinction I mentioned above, in distinguishing between two readings, (B) and (C), of PKW. I suggested earlier that PKW (if it is read as [C], and [C] is carefully distinguished from [B]) is controversial but not outrageous. It is not outrageous, I suggested, because, although one might need to *know* what *x* is to *know* what *x* is like, one need not *know* what *x* is to have *beliefs* about what *x* is like, and perhaps beliefs can guide inquiry. If, however, one speaks of a lack of knowledge without differentiating between total ignorance (being a blank) and having beliefs that fall short of knowledge, then this way of distinguishing between (B) and (C) will not be available. One might expect, then, that if Plato is aware of the falsity of (3), he can also distinguish between (B) and (C); if, however, he is not aware of the falsity of (3), then perhaps, equally, he will not be able to distinguish between (B) and (C).

I have argued so far that the eristic paradox is unsound, since both (2) and (3) are false. But how does Plato view the matter?

We might expect him to be especially troubled by (3). At least, we should expect him to be especially troubled by (3) if he takes Socrates' disclaimer of knowledge seriously, thinks Socrates was genuinely inquiring, through the elenchus, in an effort to find moral knowledge, and also wants to defend Socrates. For if (3) is true, Socrates cannot, as he claims to, inquire in the absence of knowledge. (3) thus threatens the core of Socratic inquiry. However, the *Meno* is a transitional dialogue – transitional between the thought of the Socratic dialogues, on the one hand, and that of the middle dialogues, on the other – and one might think that it is transitional in part because it finds fault with Socrates' claim to be able to inquire in the absence of knowledge.[25] Let us see, then, whether Plato attempts to dislodge (3), and so to vindicate Socrates; or, alternatively, whether he abandons the Socratic procedure – a procedure that requires the falsity of (3) – in favor of some other epistemological program.

III. THE ELENCTIC REPLY TO THE PARADOX

In reply to Meno's paradox, Socrates initially describes a priests' and priestesses' story, according to which:

> Since the soul is immortal and has been born many times, and has seen (*heōrakuia*) all the things both here and in Hades, there is nothing it has not learned. Hence it is no wonder if it can recall virtue and other things which it previously knew. For since all nature is akin, and since the soul has learned all things, there is nothing to prevent it, when it has recollected one thing – which men call learning – from discovering all the other things, if he is brave and does not tire of inquiring. For inquiring and learning are just recollection. (81c5–d5)

This is Plato's famous theory of recollection, according to which the soul is immortal and, in a prior life, knew "virtue and other things," so that what is called learning is really just recollection of things previously known.[26] Meno professes not to understand what it means to say that learning is just recollection, and so he asks Socrates to teach him that it is (81e3–5). Socrates points out that, since learning is just recollection, there is no such thing as teaching, and so he cannot teach him that learning is just recollection; but, he says, he will show (*epideixomai,* 82b2) Meno that it is. He then embarks on a standard Socratic-style elenchus, along with a running commentary, with one of Meno's slaves (82b–85d). He then reverts to the theory of recollection (85d–86c). There are, then, two accounts of the theory of recollection; sandwiched in between, there is a sample elenchus.[27]

How do the elenchus and the theory of recollection fit together? How does either reply to the paradox? I begin by considering the elenctic reply.

Socrates draws a square with sides two feet long, and asks the slave how long a side is needed for a square with double the area of the original square (82c–e). The slave replies that we need a side with double the length of the original side (82e). Like most of Socrates' interlocutors in the earlier dialogues, and like Meno at the beginning of this one, the slave thinks he knows the answer to Socrates' questions, though he does not. Socrates then questions him further, until the slave realizes that he doesn't know what he thought he did; he is then puzzled and confused (84a–b). This aporetic result is often reached in the Socratic dialogues too, as it was earlier in the *Meno.* The Socratic dialogues typically end at this point, which is one reason Socrates is often thought to be purely negative and destructive in his use of the elenchus. Here, however, Plato defends him against that charge. Initially the slave thought he knew the answer to Socrates' geometrical question, but he didn't; he then realizes that he doesn't know the answer. But realizing this is not merely destructive; it makes (or ought to make) him more willing and able to inquire (84b–c). The exposure of ignorance is thus of positive value.

Plato also points out that although the Socratic dialogues typically end aporetically, elenchus need not end in *aporia;* the elenctic method can take one all the way to knowledge. To show this, Socrates questions the slave further, until the slave eventually states the right answer (84d–85b); this further stage of questioning involves the elenctic method no less than does the initial stage, and so Plato shows that the elenchus can go beyond the exposure of ignorance to the articulation of true beliefs.[28] For although the slave still lacks knowledge, he "has in himself true beliefs about the things he does not know" (85c2–8). Not only that, but "if someone asks him the very same [sorts of] questions [alternative translation: "asks him questions about the very same things"] often and in different ways, you can see that in the end he will know these things as accurately as anybody" (85c10–d1).

Now if the slave can inquire about geometry in the absence of knowledge then so too, Socrates assumes, can we all. Nor is there anything special about geometry; inquiry in the absence of knowledge is likewise possible for "every other subject" (85e2–3), including virtue, and so, Socrates concludes, they ought to resume their inquiry into virtue, even though they don't know what it is (86c).

Plato has just rejected (3) of the paradox. Contrary to (3), one can inquire even if one lacks all knowledge of the subject, for the slave has just done so. The slave can inquire, although he entirely lacks knowledge, because he has both true beliefs, and also the capacity for rational reflection and revision of his beliefs, and these are adequate for inquiry.[29] Similarly, Socrates was justified, in the Socratic dialogues and earlier in the *Meno,* in claiming to be able to inquire into virtue in the absence of knowledge. For although he disavows all moral knowledge, he never claims to lack true moral beliefs; and, indeed, he seems to believe he has them.[30] Moreover, in clearly distinguishing between knowledge and (true) belief, and in insisting that inquiry requires only the latter, Plato shows that PKW is not self-defeatingly strong, that he can distinguish between (B) and (C), and accepts only (C).[31]

Various objections to Plato's claims about the powers of the elenchus might be raised, however; let us consider some of them, along with some possible replies.

Objection 1: I am overly optimistic about the force of 85c6–7, where Plato distinguishes between knowledge and true belief. Alexander Nehamas, for example, argues that the passage is merely an intermediate step in Plato's resolution of the paradox, not his final conclusion.[32] Even if it is true that using the elenchus can take us all the way to knowledge, and that knowledge and true belief differ, surely 85c6–7 is not the core of Plato's reply to the paradox?

Reply: It is true that there is more to come: We have not yet looked at the theory of recollection. But there is reason to believe that, whatever the importance of the theory of recollection, the distinction Plato draws between knowledge and true belief is of vital importance, not only to Plato's epistemology generally, but also to his resolution of the paradox. For at the close of the dialogue, he recurs to, and elaborates on, the distinction between knowledge and true belief (97a–98c). He argues first that true belief is as good a guide for right action as knowledge is. This reemphasizes the present point that one can inquire on the basis of true belief; knowledge is not necessary for inquiry. Nonetheless, he insists, knowledge is more valuable. For although both knowledge and true belief are truth-entailing, knowledge is true belief tethered with an *aitias logismos*, an explanatory account. He also insists that the process by which one works out an explanatory account is recollection. Hence the difference between knowledge and true belief is not a mere aside; Plato returns to it later, and connects it to the present context.[33]

Objection 2: Socrates has not shown that inquiry is possible in the absence of knowledge. For even if the slave lacks knowledge, Socrates, in this case if not in the moral case, has the relevant knowledge, and that is what makes progress possible.

Reply: Socrates does not claim that he *knows* the answers to the questions he asks, and it is not clear that (he believes) he does; perhaps he only has a correct belief about the answers. In just the same way, Socrates can guide elenchi in the Socratic dialogues, not because he knows the answers, but because he has true beliefs.[34]

But even if Socrates knows, or believes he knows, the answers, the point of the elenctic demonstration is not undermined. For although Socrates asks the slave leading questions, he does not feed him the answers. On the contrary, Socrates emphasizes that the slave should not rely on Socrates' authority, but should say what he believes (83d); this point is brought home by the fact that the slave twice offers wrong answers by relying uncritically on what Socrates says. The slave's progress – from initial misguided confidence, to a realization of his ignorance, to the discovery of the right answer – ultimately comes from his own independent reflection. At each stage he decides to resolve a conflict in his beliefs by discarding those beliefs that seem less reasonable, or less well entrenched – just as other interlocutors do in moral inquiry. Socrates' geometrical knowledge (or true belief) makes the elenchus proceed more quickly and smoothly; but it is not what makes it possible. What makes it possible is the slave's own true beliefs and his capacity for reflection and revision.[35]

Objection 3: The slave can make progress in the geometrical case because geometry is a deductively closed system, consisting of necessary, a priori truths; since morality is not like this, progress cannot be achieved in the same way in its case.

Reply: If the objector concedes that one can inquire in the absence of knowledge in the geometrical case, then he concedes that the paradox has been disarmed; for that concession involves abandoning (3). Still, the objector has a point; for we want to be able to vindicate Socratic moral inquiry in the absence of moral knowledge. But are the geometrical and moral cases so different? To be sure, geometry (unlike morality) may well be a deductively closed system, consisting of necessary, a priori truths. But these are not the facts about it that Socrates emphasizes. He describes the mathematical inquiry in much the same way that we would describe scientific inquiry. We begin with a variety of beliefs about, say, gold. Some of these are true, others false; we gradually refine our beliefs – discovering, for example, that fool's gold is not gold – until we arrive at knowledge of the real essence of gold, its atomic constitution. We have moved from belief about gold to knowledge of its real essence, not by rigorous deduction, but by trial and error; in just the same way, we can make progress in the moral sphere.

Objection 4: The scientific analogy is unhelpful. After all, one thing that enables us to make progress in the scientific case is the availability of samples or examples of gold; but what samples or examples are available in the moral case?

Reply: The answer is: examples of virtuous behavior. Although Socrates denies that we know what virtue is, he never denies, but in fact assumes, that we have fairly reliable beliefs about virtue.[36] To be sure, sometimes we make mistakes – we falsely believe, for example, that lions are courageous (*La.* 196e1–197c4). But then, people once believed that fool's gold was gold. We also correctly believe that returning a sword to a madman is not just (*Rep.* 331).

But doesn't Socrates insist, contrary to my suggestion, that there are irresoluble disputes in the moral cases? Well, he does believe there is great dispute about the correct definition of virtue terms, and of course there is *some* dispute about particular moral cases. But there is also considerable agreement, enough agreement to secure the reference of the terms and so to ground inquiry.

Objection 5: How can we know which of our beliefs are true, which false? Beliefs don't come neatly labeled "true" and "false"; what's to stop us from relying on the false ones instead? The mere fact that I have true beliefs is not sufficient to ground inquiry.[37]

Reply: Plato's claim is that one can inquire, even if one lacks knowledge, so long as one *in fact* relies on one's true beliefs; he does not claim that one can inquire, even if one lacks knowledge, only if one *knows* that one is relying on true beliefs. Of course, from a first-person perspective, I will be subjectively justified in inquiring only if I believe that I am relying on true beliefs. But I do not need to be able to identify my true beliefs as such in order to be able to inquire. We need to distinguish the question of what makes inquiry possible from the question of what subjectively justifies one in thinking one is in a position to inquire. In neither case, however, do I need to know (or even have true beliefs about) which of my beliefs are true, which are false. In the first case, I need to rely on some beliefs that are in fact true; in the second case, I need to believe I have some true beliefs. Neither of these ways of appealing to true beliefs requires one to know (or have true beliefs about) which of one's beliefs are in fact true.[38]

Of course, someone might rely on false, rather than on true, beliefs. As in science, one can follow a false track; progress requires luck. Socrates seems to assume, however, that everyone, or at least everyone rational, will, if they inquire systematically, progress in the same direction. That's because he also seems to assume that some important true beliefs are better entrenched than are various false beliefs (or will seem more reasonable to us when we first consider them) so that, in cases of conflict, we tend, upon reflection, to reject the false beliefs.[39] This is a substantial, and optimistic, claim about human nature – one that requires and, as we shall see, receives, further explanation.

IV. THE THEORY OF RECOLLECTION

The elenctic reply disarms the paradox by arguing that, contrary to (3), inquiry is possible in the absence of knowledge. It seems to be a good, and complete, reply. Why, then, does Plato supplement the elenctic reply with the theory of recollection? What role does it play in replying to the paradox?

I suggest that the theory of recollection is introduced, not as a direct reply to the paradox (the elenctic reply plays that role),[40] but to explain certain facts assumed in the elenctic reply. For example, the elenctic reply assumes that in inquiring, we tend to favor true over false beliefs. Plato believes that this remarkable tendency cannot be a brute fact, but requires further explanation; the best such explanation, in his view, is the theory of recollection. We can all inquire, and tend toward the truth in doing so, because, although we now lack the relevant knowledge, we once had it, in a prior life. Like advocates of innate knowledge, Plato believes that certain remarkable features of human beings require explanation in terms of prior knowledge – though for Plato, in contrast to the innatists, the knowledge is had not from birth, but only in a previous existence.

Even though the theory of recollection is thus not a theory of innate knowledge,[41] its motivation is similar to the motivation for innatist theories of knowledge. As such, it is vulnerable to similar objections. Many would prefer to say that even if a given tendency is remarkable, still, it is just a brute fact that we have it; there is no further explanation. Or, if there is a further explanation, it consists not in immortal souls that had knowledge in some previous life, nor in innate knowledge, but in, for example, evolution.

In claiming that we once had the relevant knowledge, Plato inevitably invites the question of how we acquired it. If the answer is "through inquiry," then we can raise Meno's paradox again, and we might then seem to be launched on a vicious infinite regress. But there is no regress, vicious or otherwise; for Plato does not commit himself to the claim that we *acquired* the previous knowledge at all. He seems to think we simply had it at some previous stage, without having gone through any process of acquiring it.[42]

Notice that whatever account one favors of how the soul once knew, the theory of recollection (in contrast to the elenctic reply) does not by itself provide a sufficient answer to the paradox – for if one once knew, but now lacks the ability to inquire, the prior knowledge is idle. We should therefore be reluctant to put the whole weight of Plato's reply to the paradox on the theory of recollection; and on my account of its role, we need not do so. It is also important to be clear that, no matter what account one favors of how the soul once knew, Plato's introduction of the theory of recollection does not show that he has abandoned the elenchus as the sole method of inquiry (in this life). The demonstration with the slave is just a standard elenchus; and in it, Socrates claims that if one follows it long enough one will achieve knowledge. The theory of recollection goes beyond Socrates, not by replacing the elenchus with an alternative route to knowledge, but by explaining how something he took for granted (the possibility of inquiry in the absense of knowledge, and the remarkable fact that in so inquiring we tend toward the truth) is possible. To say that *p* is best explained by *q*, or is possible because of *q*, is not to abandon *p*. The theory of recollection is introduced to vindicate, not to vitiate, Socrates' claims about the powers of the elenchus.

However one spells out the details of the theory of recollection, few nowadays are likely to believe it. The elenctic reply, however, remains convincing, and it can be accepted even by one who rejects the theory of recollection; one can accept Plato's claim that one can inquire in the absence of knowledge, because of one's capacity for reflection and because of one's true beliefs, without accepting his account of what explains the capacity and the beliefs. It is thus pleasing to see that Plato himself seems to place less weight on the theory of recollection than on the elenchus. He introduces the theory as something said by priests and priestesses and by Pindar and other poets (81a5–6, a10–b2); later he makes it plain that he thinks such people lack knowledge (99c). Socrates says he would not like to take an oath on all that he has said (86b); but later he says that if he were to claim to know anything, one of the few things he would claim to know is that knowledge differs from true belief (98b1–5).[43] And it is of course the difference between knowledge and true belief that is crucial to the elenctic reply.

At least in the *Meno*, then, Plato replies to the eristic paradox by reaffirming the powers of the elenchus and by vindicating Socrates' claim to be able to inquire, through the elenchus, in the absence of knowledge. At least in this respect, the *Meno* does not depart from, but is continuous with, the project begun in the Socratic dialogues.

NOTES

1 The Platonic dialogues are often divided into four groups: (i) early Socratic dialogues; (ii) transitional dialogues: (iii) middle dialogues; and (iv) late dialogues. Group (i) includes *Ap., Cri., Euphr., Chrm., La., Lys., H. Mi., Euthd., Ion,* and *Prt.* (ii) includes *Grg., Meno, H. Ma.,* and *Cra.* (iii) includes *Phd., Smp., Rep.,* and *Phdr.* (iv) includes *Prm., Tht., Ti., Criti., Sph., Pol., Phil.,* and *Laws.* Some scholars favor a tripartite division instead, into early, middle, and late. The dates of some of these dialogues are disputed, but it is generally agreed that the *Meno* belongs after the dialogues I have included in (i), and before the dialogues I have included in (iii). For some discussion of the dating of the dialogues, see Leonard Brandwood, "The Dating of Plato's Works by the Stylistic Method: A Historical and Critical Survey," Ph.D. thesis (University of London, 1958) (available from University Microfilms); see also Brandwood's "Stylometry and Chronology," Chapter 3 of this volume. The *Meno* is often taken to be transitional on the grounds that (a) it is more self-conscious about methodology and epistemology than are the dialogues in group (i); on the other hand, (b) the theory of Forms that is prominent in group (iii) is muted in the *Meno.*

2 There are actually two questions here: (a) Does Socrates need to have some knowledge in order to inquire? (b) Does he need to believe he has some knowledge in order to be subjectively justified in inquiring? If Socrates believes he lacks knowledge but in fact has knowledge, then (b) but not (a) arises. If he believes he has knowledge but does not in fact have any knowledge, then (a) but not (b) arises. I shall generally ignore the difference between (a) and (b), though see my reply to Objection 5 in section III.

I take inquiry to be a directed, intentional search for knowledge one lacks. Hence, perceiving, happening upon an object one is looking for, and being told are not forms of inquiry. Ordinary scientific research, on the other hand, is an example of inquiry. Inquiry can take various forms. In the Socratic dialogues (and, I shall suggest, in the *Meno*), it takes the form of elenchus, on which see further below.

3 See Alexander Nehamas, "Meno's Paradox and Socrates as a Teacher," *Oxford Studies in Ancient Philosophy* 3 (1985): 5–6.

4 Unfortunately, many translations obscure this crucial point. For example, although W. K. C. Guthrie (*Plato: Protagoras and Meno* [Harmondsworth: Penguin Classics, 1956]) translates 71b3–4 accurately enough, he mistranslates similar passages in the surrounding context. He translates 71a5–7 as: "The fact is that far from knowing whether it can be taught, I have no idea what virtue itself is." Here "I have no idea" should be rendered as "I do not know (*eidōs*)." He translates 71b4–6 as: "Do you suppose that somebody entirely ignorant who Meno is could say whether . . . ," when he should have: "Do you suppose that someone who does not at all know (*gignōskei*) who Meno is could know (*eidenai*) whether . . . ." Nehamas ("Meno's Paradox," 8) translates 80d5–6 as "in what way can you search for something when you are altogether ignorant of what it is?"; but the last clause is better rendered by "when you don't at all know what it is."

5 See P. T. Geach, in "Plato's *Euthyphro:* An Analysis and Commentary," *Monist* 50 (1966): 369–82.

6 What he literally says is that one needs to know what *x* is (*ti*) to know what *x* is like (*poion*). But I take the present contrast between *ti* and *poion* to be exhaustive. (In the case of things like virtue, this will be the exhaustive contrast between the essence of *x* [*ti*] and its nonessential properties [*poion*]; cf. the contrast at *Euphr.* 11a–b between *ti* and *pathos.*) Hence, if one needs to know what *x* is to know what *x* is like, then one needs to know what *x* is to know anything at all about *x*.

Strictly speaking, I would prefer to say that (C) is an instance of, rather than a version of, PKW. That is, PKW claims quite generally that in order to know anything about *x*, one must know what *x* is. But I think Plato believes that the relevant knowlege-what differs from case to case: To know anything about virtue, one must know its definition; but to know, e.g., who Meno is, one need not know his definition – here, the relevant knowledge-what consists in something other than knowing a definition. Hence, even if Meno cannot be defined, it does not follow that he cannot be known. I focus on definitions in this chapter, since I shall not be discussing Plato's views about knowledge of such things as Meno; but see notes 19, 21, and 26.

7 See, e.g., John Beversluis, "Socratic Definition," *American Philosophical Quarterly* 11 (1974): 331–6.

8 I assume PKW is not to be read as (A), and so I shall not consider it further here.

9 This might be disputed. David Bostock, e.g., in *Plato's Phaedo* (Oxford: Clarendon Press, 1986), 69–72, argues that knowing the meanings of terms is actually quite difficult. That is no doubt true on some views about meanings; but if we take meanings simply to articulate ordinary usage, then even if not everyone can readily state them, it would be odd for Socrates to believe that knowledge is as difficult to come by as he seems to assume it is. In other respects too, it is unlikely that Socrates is searching for knowledge of the meanings of terms. For some brief considerations against the meaning view, see my "The One over Many," *Philosophical Review* 89 (1980): 197–240; see also note 10.

10 For Locke on real vs. nominal essences, see John Locke, *An Essay Concerning Human Understanding,* ed. P. Nidditch (Oxford: Clarendon Press, 1975) (originally published in 1690), III. iii; III. vi; III. x; IV. vi.4–9; IV. xii.9. For a defense of the claim that Socrates is more interested in something like the real essence of virtue than in the meaning of virtue terms, see Terry Penner, "The Unity of Virtue," *Philosophical Review* 82 (1973): 35–68; and Terence Irwin, *Plato's Moral Theory* (Oxford: Clarendon Press, 1977), esp. chap. 3.

11 At least, this is so if (B) and (C) are taken to differ in the way described above.

12 See, e.g., *Chrm.* 159c1, 160e6; *La.* 192c5–7; *Prt.* 349e3–5, 359e4–7. See also *Meno* 87e1–3. Socrates also seems to believe that his, and his interlocutors', beliefs about examples of virtuous actions are generally reliable.

13 In *Posterior Analytics,* i 1–10, Aristotle defends a version of (C), claiming that one can know the nonessential properties of a thing only by deducing certain propositions about them from its real definition.

14 For conception (a), see Gregory Vlastos, "Introduction," in *Plato: Protagoras* (New York: Bobbs-Merrill, 1956), esp. xxvi–xxxi; contrast Vlastos, "The Socratic Elenchus," *Oxford Studies in Ancient Philosophy* 1 (1983): 27–58, esp. 45*ff.* In "Elenchus and Mathematics," *American Journal of Philology* 109 (1988): 362–96, Vlastos rejects (a) for the Socratic dialogues; but he argues that in the *Meno* Plato believes that elenchus (the form of inquiry favored in the Socratic dialogues) can do no more than detect contradictions.

15 For conception (b), see, e.g., Richard Robinson, *Plato's Earlier Dialectic* (Oxford: Clarendon Press, 1953), chap. 2.

16 Conception (c1) distinguishes between two types or kinds of knowledge (certainty and justified true belief); (c2) distinguishes between different ranges of things known or not known (what virtue is, what it is like). For

(c1), see Gregory Vlastos, "Socrates' Disavowal of Knowledge," *Philosophical Quarterly* 35 (1985): 1–31. For (c2), see Richard Kraut, *Socrates and the State* (Princeton: Princeton University Press, 1984), chap. 8. There are traces of (c2) in Vlastos's article, though he focuses on (c1). Alexander Nehamas, in "Socratic Intellectualism," in *Proceedings of the Boston Area Colloquium in Ancient Philosophy*, vol. 2, ed. John J. Cleary (Lanham, Md.: University Press of America, 1987), esp. 284–93, also seems to endorse a version of (c2). One might try to defend (c1) by appealing to two types of knowledge other than those Vlastos appeals to; for such an attempt, see Paul Woodruff, "Plato's Early Theory of Knowledge," in *Companions to Ancient Thought 1: Epistemology*, ed. Stephen Everson (Cambridge: Cambridge University Press, 1990), 60–84. The consideration I adduce below against Vlastos's version of (c1) applies to other versions of it as well.

17 It is of course possible that one or more of them is adequate for one or more of the Socratic dialogues. Kraut, e.g., explicitly defends (c2) only for some of the Socratic dialogues; he agrees that it is inadequate for the *Meno*.

18 Irwin, *Plato's Moral Theory*, 39–40.

19 Even if one denies that 98a defines knowledge as justified true belief, the fact remains that Plato offers only one definition of knowledge, and that would be odd if he intended his disclaimer to apply only to some other sort of knowledge. Hence we should be reluctant to endorse any version of (c1).

It is sometimes denied that 98a defines knowledge as justified true belief. For example, it is sometimes said that (i) what Plato believes must be added to true belief to get *epistēmē* is not justification but explanation, so that (ii) *epistēmē* is not knowledge but understanding. (Further arguments have also been offered in support of [ii]. For various versions of this view, see, e.g., Nehamas, "Meno's Paradox," esp. 24–30; M. F. Burnyeat, "Socrates and the Jury," *Proceedings of the Aristotelian Society*, supp. vol. 54 [1980]: 173–92, esp. 186–8; and Burnyeat, "Wittgenstein and *De Magistro*," *Proceedings of the Aristotelian Society*, supp. vol. 61 [1988]: 1–24, esp. 17–24.) However, (i) does not imply (ii); for Plato might believe that knowledge requires explanation. I also doubt that (i) is true. Plato of course believes that in many cases, adequate justification consists in explaining the natures of the entities one claims to know; but he doesn't believe that it always does – one can adequately justify one's claim to know, e.g., who Meno is, or the road to Larissa, without explaining their essences; here some less demanding sort of justification will do. (Hence, contrary to Nehamas, if we take *epistēmē* to be knowledge, Plato does not have an impossibly demanding conception of knowledge; this removes one reason for wanting to believe [ii].) Plato focuses on explanation, not because he thinks it is necessary for *epistēmē* as such, but because he thinks it is necessary for knowledge of things like virtue, which are his primary concern here. See also notes 6, 21, and 26.

Gregory Vlastos, "*Anamnesis* in the *Meno*," *Dialogue* 4 (1965): 154–5, believes that Plato's definition of knowledge as true belief "bound" by an *aitias logismos* is meant to restrict knowledge to necessary truths. But this is too narrow, nor are Vlastos's arguments convincing. He appeals, e.g., to pre-Socratic usage of *anangkē*, a word the *Meno* does not at this stage even use. He himself notes that *logismos* is often used for rational thought in general, and it is of course well known that *aitia* can be used quite broadly.

20 It might be argued that having contradictory beliefs does not automatically debar one from having any knowledge about the subject matter; for this argument, see, e.g., Alvin Goldman, *Epistemology and Cognition* (Cambridge, Mass: Harvard University Press, 1987); and Gilbert Harman, *Change in View* (Cambridge, Mass.: Bradford Books, 1986). However, the contradictions Socrates uncovers are so blatant that it seems reasonable to conclude that his interlocutors lack knowledge.

21 For this point, see Nicholas P. White, "Inquiry," *Review of Metaphysics* 28 (1974): 290 n. 4.

Some differences between Meno's and Socrates' formulations are worth noting: (a) (2) has no analogue in Meno's formulation. (b) Conversely, Socrates' formulation ignores Meno's third question. (c) Meno asks how one can inquire into what one does not know *at all* (*to parapan*, 80d6; cf. 71a7, 71b3, 5); Socrates asks only how one can inquire into what one does not know. (For further discussion of [c], see note 29.)

Some details about the scope of the paradox are also worth noting. The paradox does not ask whether, in general, one can acquire knowledge; it asks only whether one can come to know things like virtue through inquiry. Hence Meno's paradox does not question one's ability to come to know things quite unlike virtue (e.g., the road to Larissa); nor does it question one's ability to come to know things in some way other than through inquiry (e.g., through perception, or by being told). Correspondingly, Plato's reply does not address the question of whether it is possible to know things unlike virtue; nor does it say whether it is possible to know things in some way other than through inquiry. It does not follow that Plato restricts knowledge to things like virtue, or restricts the method of achieving knowledge to inquiry. For what it is worth, I think the *Meno* leaves open the possibility of knowing, e.g., who Meno is and the road to Larissa; I also think it leaves open the possibility of achieving knowledge by means other than inquiry. I shall not defend these claims in any detail here, but see notes 6, 19, and 26.

22 The argument can be read so as to be invalid, through equivocation on "know." But since Socrates' reply seems to attack only its soundness, I shall assume it is valid.

23 (2) can be read so as to be more plausible than I have made it seem. It is more plausible, e.g., if it is read to say that if I know that *p*, then there is no need to inquire whether *p*. One reason to favor a plausible reading of (2) is that although Socrates (I shall argue) goes on to argue that (3) is false, he does not explicitly reject (2). Though rejecting (3) is sufficient for showing that the paradox is unsound, one might expect him to reject (2) as well, if it is indeed false. Perhaps the fact that he does not do so suggests (2) should be read so as to be true. On the other hand, there are good reasons for him to be especially troubled about (3), and so it is not surprising that he focuses on it. Moreover, if (2) is read so as to be plausible in the way just suggested, it does not fit as well into the overall argument as it does if it is read in the way suggested in the text; see note 24.

24 Although (2) and (3) seem false, they would seem true to anyone who believed that there was an exclusive and exhaustive dichotomy between complete knowledge and total ignorance, such that if one has any knowledge at all about a thing one has complete knowledge of it, and such that if one lacks any knowledge at all about a thing one is totally ignorant of it. And someone who accepts a certain sort of acquaintance model of knowledge would believe just this. (This perhaps provides some reason to read [2] as I read it in the text, rather than in the more plausible way suggested in the previous note.) For a lucid account of how one might be seduced by the paradox in virtue of accepting such a model, see John McDowell, *Plato: Theaetetus* (Oxford: Clarendon Press, 1973), 194–7. He is explaining a puzzle about false belief raised in *Tht.* 188a–c which, like the eristic paradox, begins from the assumption that for all *x*, one either knows, or does not know, *x*. However, McDowell believes Plato *accepts* the underlying acquaintance model. If he were right, then Plato might well be seduced by the eristic paradox. In "False Belief in the *Theaetetus*," *Phronesis* 24 (1979): 70–80, however, I argue that Plato does not accept the underlying acquaintance model in the *Theaetetus*. The account I go on to give here suggests he does not accept it in the *Meno* either, but I cannot defend this view in detail here. The similarity between the eristic paradox and the puzzle at *Tht.* 188a–c, and the possible connection to some sort of acquaintance, are also noted by Irwin, *Plato's Moral Theory*, 315 n. 12.

25 For the dating of the dialogues, see note 1.

26 At 81c6–7 (cf. d1), Socrates says that (a) the soul has been "all things," which might suggest omniscience. However, at 81c8, he talks instead of (b) "virtue and other things"; and at 81d4–5 he talks about (c) all *zētein kai manthanein* ("inquiry and learning"). I assume that (b) and (c) restrict the scope of (a), which makes it reasonable to assume that recollection is restricted to general truths about such things as virtue and geometry. Hence there is no implication that our discarnate souls knew truths falling outside the scope of such disciplines, or even particular (as opposed to general) truths within such disciplines. One might argue that if such truths are not recollected, then they cannot be known. For at *Meno* 98a Plato says that *this* – working out a suitable *aitias logismos* – is recollection, and having a suitable *aitias logismos* is necessary for knowledge. However, Plato means only that working out a suitable *aitias logismos* is, in certain cases, a case of recollection. He does not mean that every case of working out an *aitias logismos* involves recollection, or that working out an *aitias logismos* is all there is to recollection. Hence he leaves open the possibility that one can have a knowledge-constituting *aitias logismos* of, e.g., the way to Larissa, but one that does not involve recollection. See Irwin, *Plato's Moral Theory*, 316–17 n. 17; contrast Nehamas, "Meno's Paradox," 10–11.

27 See Irwin, *Plato's Moral Theory*, 139, 315–16, for a lucid and detailed defense of the claim that the whole of the demonstration with the slave is a standard Socratic elenchus. For a different view, see Vlastos, "Elenchus and Mathematics," esp. 375. See also note 28.

28 Vlastos, in "Elenchus and Mathematics," 375, agrees that the negative stage of the inquiry involves the elenchus, but he argues that the positive stage does not: "[e]lenchus is good for this, and only this [i.e., only for "convicting him of error"]. It does not begin to bring him to the truth he seeks." However, his reasons for this claim are weak. They seem to be that (a) in the positive stage of inquiry, Socrates sheds his adversarial role; and that (b) the inquiry concerns geometry rather than morality. But as against (a), elenchus does not require anyone to play an adversarial role in the sense Vlastos seems to intend. As to (b), the initial stage of inquiry equally involves geometry, yet Vlastos allows that it involves elenchus. See also the replies to objections at the end of this section for a defense of the claim that geometrical and moral inquiries are (for Socrates) quite similar. For cogent criticism of Vlastos's view, see Jyl Gentzler, "Knowledge and Method in Plato's Early through Middle Dialogues," Ph.D. thesis (Cornell University, 1991).

29 I pointed out above (note 21, difference [c]) that one difference between Meno's and Socrates' formulations of the paradox is that Meno asks whether one can inquire into what one doesn't *at all* know, whereas

Socrates asks only whether one can inquire into what one doesn't know. This difference is sometimes thought to suggest that Plato believes that one can't inquire into what one doesn't *at all* know, but can inquire into what one doesn't know *in a way* (so long as one knows it in some different way); see, e.g., Julius M. E. Moravcsik, "Learning as Recollection," in *Plato,* vol. 1: *Metaphysics and Epistemology,* ed. Gregory Vlastos (Garden City, N.Y.: Anchor Books, Doubleday, 1970), 57. On my account, however, Plato allows that one can inquire into what one doesn't at all know, in any way, and so his omission of "at all" is not significant, at least, not in the suggested way. Plato is cavalier in his use of *to parapan* elsewhere too: Despite its occurrence in 71a7 and b3, 5, it is omitted in the statement of PKW at 71b3–4.

30 For a justification of this claim, see Irwin, *Plato's Moral Theory,* chap. 3. The frequency with which Socrates relies on various claims in the dialogues (see note 12) also supports this view. It is sometimes wrongly thought that Irwin's view is that Socrates identifies knowledge and true belief; see, e.g., Woodruff, "Plato's Early Theory of Knowledge," 64. Vlastos, in "Socrates' Disavowal of Knowledge," 6 n. 12, on the other hand, wrongly suggests that Irwin's view involves conflating knowledge and certainty. Irwin's view is that for Socrates, knowledge is justified true belief (which does not involve certainty); Socrates disavows all moral knowledge, but he thinks he has (not moral knowledge but) true beliefs about virtue.

31 Further, in noting that knowledge and total ignorance are not exhaustive options, that (true) belief is a *tertium quid,* Plato says something that is incompatible with the acquaintance model on which the paradox arguably rests; see note 24. This suggests that, at least in the *Meno,* he does not accept that sort of acquaintance model of knowledge.

32 Nehamas, "Meno's Paradox," 29.

33 On Plato's account of knowledge as true belief coupled with an *aitias logismos,* see note 19. For his claim that working out an account is recollection, see note 26.

34 Socrates (believes he) has, not just true beliefs, but also true beliefs that are better justified than are those of his interlocutors (though not well enough justified to count as knowledge – justification comes in degrees). Hence, Socrates belongs at the second stage of the Line; he has *pistis,* whereas his interlocutors have only *eikasia,* about morality. See my "Knowledge and Belief in *Republic* V–VII," in *Companions to Ancient Thought 1: Epistemology,* ed. Stephen Everson (Cambridge: Cambridge University Press, 1990), esp. 101–4.

35 See Vlastos, "*Anamnesis* in the *Meno,*" esp. 158–9, and "Elenchus and Mathematics," 374 n. 42.

36 See notes 12 and 30. One might argue that although we have fairly reliable beliefs about the nature of virtue and about what sort of behavior and what sort of person would count as virtuous, there are no actual examples of virtuous actions or of virtuous people available for us to rely on. For Socrates thinks that knowledge of what virtue is is necessary for being a virtuous person; since no one knows what virtue is, no one is virtuous, and so, one might also think, neither are there any virtuous actions, although, of course, some people and actions might nonetheless be better than others. (*A* can be better than *B* even if neither is good.) If this is so, then we could not say, in reply to Objection 4, that examples of virtuous behavior play the role in moral inquiry that examples of gold, e.g., play in scientific inquiry into the nature of gold. However, reliable moral intuitions and beliefs could still guide inquiry.

37 For something like this objection, see Nehamas, "Meno's Paradox," 16–17.

38 Cf. note 2. One might argue that it is not necessary to have true beliefs in order to inquire; all that is necessary is that one's use of a term be on a suitable causal chain; see Saul Kripke, *Naming and Necessity* (Cambridge, Mass: Harvard University Press, 1980) (originally published in 1972); and Hilary Putnam, "The Meaning of 'Meaning,' " in *Philosophical Papers* (Cambridge: Cambridge University Press, 1975), 2: 215–71.

39 See Irwin, *Plato's Moral Theory*, 41–2, 66–70.

40 It is sometimes thought that the theory of recollection is the direct reply, and that it replies by denying (2): The slave can inquire because he has knowledge; more generally, everyone can inquire, because everyone has some relevant knowledge. If Plato does claim that everyone now knows, then he contradicts his claim at 85b–d, that the slave does *not* now know. But Plato does not claim that everyone (or the slave) now knows; all of his references to knowledge are either forward-referring (to the time when, by further questioning, the slave will acquire knowledge) or backward-referring (to our previous lives, when we did know). The passage that seems most difficult to square with this claim is 86a8; but it too can be accommodated, for all it says is that the slave's soul "has for all time been in the state of having once been [in a] learned [condition]" – that is, it is always true of him (and so it is now true of him) that he was once in a learned condition, i.e., once had knowledge. To claim that it is always (and so is now) true of him that he once had knowledge is not to claim or imply that it is now true of him that he now knows. (For a similar suggestion, see Vlastos, "*Anamnesis* in the *Meno*," 153 n. 14.) I count 85d1, 3–4 (*epistēsetai*), d6, 9 as forward-referring; 81c9 as backward-referring. 86b1 says that the truth about the things that are is always in the soul, but that is not

to say that *knowledge* is; perhaps we always have the truth in our souls in that we once knew, can come to know again, and indeed are predisposed to the truth though we do not now know it. Similarly, Leibniz says that innate ideas are in us in something like the way in which Hercules is in rough marble before it has been carved, because its veins make it easier to carve a Hercules shape than various other shapes; the use of "in" is very weak. See G. W. Leibniz, "Meditations on Knowledge, Truth, and Ideas," in *Philosophical Essays,* trans. R. Ariew and D. Garber (Indianapolis: Hackett, 1989), 27.

Nicholas P. White, *Plato on Knowledge and Reality* (Indianapolis: Hackett, 1976), 47*ff,* attempts to disarm the seeming contradiction by claiming that in those passages where Plato says that the slave has belief but not knowledge, he is speaking with the vulgar. Given the importance the *Meno* attaches to the difference between knowledge and (true) belief, this seems unlikely.

If Plato nowhere claims that anyone now knows, then he nowhere replies to the paradox by denying (2). I do not think he believes (2) any more than he believes (3) – at least, that is so if (2) is construed as I construed it in the text above, rather than as it is construed in note 23. But he focuses only on (3), and does not address (2) – because, I take it, he wants to vindicate Socrates' claim to be able to inquire in the absence of knowledge, and to encourage us (who, in his view, lack knowledge) to inquire. Aristotle, by contrast, disarms the paradox by denying (2): We can inquire into what we know in one way, so long as we do not know it in some other way; indeed, Aristotle suggests that inquiry requires some prior knowledge. See *Posterior Analytics,* i 1.

41 Contrast Leibniz, *New Essays on Human Understanding,* tr. and ed. Peter Remnant and Jonathan Bennett (Cambridge: Cambridge University Press, 1981), book I, chap. 1; and Dominic Scott, "Platonic Anamnesis Revisited," *Classical Quarterly* 37 (1987): 346–66, esp. 351–3. Nor, contrary to Moravcsik, "Learning as Recollection," 59, 61–2, is the theory of recollection a theory of innate beliefs or concepts. The theory of recollection does accord us innate abilities, and it is sometimes suggested that concepts or beliefs are abilities. But as Aristotle points out (*De An.* ii 1), there are two different ways of construing abilities. A child is able to be a general in that she might become one under certain circumstances when she grows up (this is what Aristotle calls a first potentiality); and I am able to study Greek, even though I am not doing so now, because I can do so immediately if I choose (a second potentiality). If one construes abilities as first potentialities, then concepts and beliefs are not abilities; but that is the only way in which the theory of recollection postulates innate abilities.

Nor is the theory of recollection a theory of concept acquisition. It explains, not how one acquires concepts, but how one can move from concepts and beliefs to knowledge, how, given our various beliefs (however they are acquired in the first place, a question Plato does not address), we tend to favor the true ones over the false ones. For this point, see further my "The Object of Thought Argument," *Apeiron* 21 (1988): esp. 137–42; and Scott, "Platonic Anamnesis Revisited."

For some discussion of innatist theories, see Stephen Stich, ed., *Innate Ideas* (Berkeley: University of California Press, 1975).

42 As I noted (in note 40), 86a8 says that the soul is always in a state of once having been in a learned condition; the perfect tense leaves open the possibility that there was no process of learning (contrast Vlastos's translation of the passage, "*Anamnesis* in the *Meno*," 153 n. 14). The claim that it is *always* true of the soul that it earlier knew also suggests that there was no initial stage in which it lacked, and then acquired, knowledge. Even if (contrary to my suggestion) the soul did go through an initial process of learning, a vicious regress can be avoided – even if the process was simply (elenctic) inquiry all over again. Plato might argue, e.g., that when the soul was discarnate, it was not hampered by perception and bodily desires; without such distractions, it could acquire knowledge through inquiry even if it did not know in some still earlier life. On this account, the theory of recollection would be introduced to explain not how inquiry is in general possible, but how inquiry is possible in this life, or when incarnate.

Plato's claim that the soul "saw" various things is sometimes thought to suggest that the soul acquired its previous knowledge through some sort of acquaintance; see, e.g., R. S. Bluck, ed., *Plato's Meno* (Cambridge: Cambridge University Press, 1961), 286–7; Vlastos, "Anamnesis in the *Meno*," 164–5; Harold Cherniss, "The Philosophical Economy of the Theory of Ideas," *American Journal of Philology* 57 (1936): 445–56. However, I take it that we saw all things in that we saw their point, i.e., understood them; for this sort of interpretation of Plato's visual vocabulary, see J. C. B. Gosling, *Plato* (London: Routledge & Kegan Paul, 1973), chap. 8; Burnyeat, "Wittgenstein and *De Magistro*," esp. 19–21.

Other attempts to argue that in the *Meno* Plato accepts some sort of acquaintance model of knowledge are similarly weak. For example, at 71b4–7, Plato illustrates PKW by saying: "Does it seem to you possible for one who does not at all know who Meno is (*Menona mē gignōskei to parapan hostis estin*) to know whether he is fine or wealthy or well-born or the opposites of these?" It is sometimes inferred that for Plato, all knowledge is like knowledge of persons which, it is assumed, consists in or involves acquaintance; see, e.g., Bluck, *Plato's Meno*, 213–14. But

Plato speaks here, not of knowing Meno, but of knowing who Meno is; and it is not at all clear that I need to be acquainted with Meno to know who he is – I know who he is from having read Plato's dialogues. (The syntax is "know Meno who he is"; but the natural sense of the phrase is "know who Meno is." White seems to agree, though he also argues that for Plato, one can know who Meno is only if one knows Meno, by being acquainted with him; see *Plato on Knowledge and Reality*, 36–7, 54 n. 8.) Or again, at 97a9–b3, Plato seems to suggest that someone can know the road to Larissa only if she travels along it (although he does not actually quite say so); this too is sometimes thought to suggest that all knowledge involves some sort of acquaintance. But even if one in some sense needs to be acquainted with a route to know it, it does not follow that knowledge in general requires acquaintance. Plato's point is that in order to know something, one must have some sort of first-hand understanding or experience. In the case of a route, this first-hand understanding may require traveling along it (a not implausible claim in Plato's day, when there were no detailed road maps), and so in some sense it may require being acquainted with it; but in other cases, understanding will be gained by independent thought and reflection, which does not involve acquaintance in any interesting sense. For this point, see Burnyeat, "Socrates and the Jury" and "Wittgenstein and *De Magistro*." Further, if, as I suggested, Plato's reply to the eristic paradox presupposes a rejection of an acquaintance model of knowledge (see notes 24 and 31), then we should be reluctant to saddle him with it elsewhere in the dialogue; and there is no need to do so.

43 The passage can be read to say that one of the few things Socrates actually claims to know is that knowledge and true belief differ, in which case it provides even stronger support for my view. But if the passage is taken that way, then Socrates would be claiming, contrary to PKW, that he knows something about knowledge and true belief (that they differ) without knowing what they are. Although, on my view, Socrates does not flatly claim to know that knowledge and true belief differ, he expresses considerable confidence in that claim, saying that he does not issue it on the basis of *eikasia*. Perhaps he thinks he has *pistis* about it. (On the differences between *eikasia* and *pistis*, see *Rep.* VI–VII and my "Knowledge and Belief in *Republic* V–VII.") I am indebted to Hannes Jarka for discussion of this passage.

MICHAEL L. MORGAN

7 Plato and Greek Religion

Religion permeated life in classical Athens and in classical Greece generally.[1] It is hardly surprising, then, that religious vocabulary – mention of gods, festivals, beliefs, and rites – also pervades Plato's dialogues. These dialogues reveal a man struggling to understand human life and how it ought to be lived, a man engaged in deep reflection about rational inquiry, the human roles in society and in the cosmos, and man's relationship to the divine. Religion, as rite, conception, motif, and vocabulary, is integral to his thinking. By showing how this is so we can illuminate Plato's thinking from the religious side, as it were, and thereby exhibit Plato's relationship to Greek religion and piety.

It is hard to exaggerate the prominence of religion in Greek life. Greek religion was pluralistic and heterogeneous; there was a host of divinities with overlapping roles and features. A dozen gods formed the conventional core of this pantheon (Zeus, Hera, Poseidon, Athena, Apollo, Artemis, Aphrodite, Hermes, Demeter, Dionysos, Hephaistos, Ares); broadly conceived as Zeus's family, these, and lesser divinities such as the goat-god Pan, are the Olympians, so called after Mount Olympus, site of Zeus's palace. They and other gods, such as Hades and Persephone, were themselves varied and multiple, each present at dozens of places in various guises, serving a variety of purposes and roles. Zeus, for example, manifest as a thunderbolt, was the strongest of the gods and the father of gods and men.[2] But in fact there were many Zeuses present in many places and with many specifications – for example, "Zeus of the city," "Zeus of the stranger," "Zeus of boundaries," and "Zeus of the mountain tops."[3] Greek polytheism, then, incorporated a plurality of gods, each with many domains and roles. At the local level, there was centralization and continuity, for the family, the phratry (a subdivision of a tribe, of which there were originally four in Athens), the deme (the local community of which each Athenian was a citizen), and the polis. And there was some weak unity at the international level, through the celebration of certain Panhellenic festivals like the Great Panathenaea, held every four years, and the Olympic games, and through the international use of oracles, primarily at the sanctuary of Apollo at Delphi and the sanctuaries of Zeus at Dodona and Ammon. Moreover, Homer and Hesiod were universally honored to some degree by all Greeks.[4] Nonetheless, Greek religion was disparate and diverse. The unifying factors of Greek religion notwithstanding, not all gods were worshiped everywhere and where they were, their character and status differed. This tremendous plurality and variety in part enabled Greek religiosity to be so pervasive and so complexly interconnected. In classical Greece everything – politics, ethics, science, painting, music, dance, drama, agriculture – had a religious character.[5]

Each of the twelve months was filled with festivals of varying degrees of significance,[6] from the monthly festival celebrating the new month to deme or phratry festivals and general Athenian festivals. Perhaps as many as half of the days of the Athenian year involved festivals and their processions, sacrifices, dancing, hymns, and competitions. It is clear that festivals and new moons shaped the calendar and that the Greeks lived from festival to festival. Each month was named after a festival, some minor and some major. The month of Thargelion, for example, was named after the Thargelia, a celebration of Apollo that included the creation of a scapegoat (*pharmakos*) and the offering of a pot of boiled grain and vegetables to the god. But the months contained many other festivals as well; another one that took place in Thargelion was introduced into Athens in 429 B.C. It was a celebration of Bendis, a Thracian goddess, akin to Artemis, the huntress, and held in the Peiraeus, the Athenian port; it involved a procession and a torch race on horseback, a novelty, so we are told.[7] Indeed, it is on the occasion of the inaugural Bendidia that Plato sets the *Republic,* when Socrates, after worshiping and seeing the sights, meets Cephalus and his son Polemarchus on the way back to Athens and is invited to their home.

Sacrifice was the central feature of Greek religious life. Oxen, sheep, goats, and pigs were the most common victims of such acts of ritual slaughter and communal consumption, acts that were conducted constantly, some for the polis as a whole, some for the deme or the phratry, and some for the family.[8] Gifts were continually being offered to the gods; solidarity of the community was thereby secured and the proper relationship between gods and humans was established.[9] Oracles too were consulted for advice and counsel, and acts of divination were performed by priests, local diviners, and less dignified peddlers of prophecy.[10] Temples, with their sacred trees and boundary stones, sacrificial altars, statues, and cult images, were numerous; herms (small stone representations of Hermes placed outside Athenian homes) were everywhere. In any given year the average Athenian would participate in hundreds of religious acts and inhabit thousands of regions of religious space. In a sense, his entire world of time and space was a religious one, a complex, variegated symbiosis of land and architecture in which divinity was pervasive.[11] His life and the writings of his literary tradition expressed this sense of divine presence, of divinity that was both ubiquitously intimate and yet awesome and separate.

Let me focus on two features of the religious life of Plato's time: the prominence of new cults and the existence of a common theology underlying the traditional pluralistic religion. Many new cults, rites, and practices flourished in Athens in the late fifth century B.C., during and after the Peloponnesian War (431–404), that traumatic struggle between Athens and Sparta that culminated in Athens's defeat and the ruin of Athenian hegemony and the Athenian Empire. To be sure, Greek religion was always changing and especially in Athens. Throughout the fifth century, Athens was a major importer and exporter of forms of religiosity. The spiritual movement of Orphism, with its mythic poetry of the origins and fate of humankind, its emphasis on mystery rites of initiation and purification, and its associations with Pythagoreanism, came early in the century. The cult of Pan arrived following the battle of Marathon (490). The Eleusinian Mysteries, with their own Orphic elements and their associations with Dionysos and Bacchic rites of purification, became an Athenian festival in the first half of the fifth century.[12] All of this is true. But still it is clear that the plague, isolation, and self-doubts of the war years, the fears and anxieties of the lingering siege and ultimately of the premonition and reality of defeat, led to a proliferation of novel religious forms.

We have already mentioned the celebration of Bendis, imported when the war had just begun. There was also the worship of Asclepius, son of Apollo and god of healing, imported from Epidaurus during the war and temporarily housed in Sophocles' residence. There is also evidence of increased interest in various forms of ecstatic rituals and personally oriented salvation rites, Bacchic (associated with Dionysos) and corybantic rites among them.[13] The central feature of these practices was an aspiration to purification and catharsis from earthly ills, to transcend the physical world, to achieve an ecstatic kinship with the divine, to become in some sense divine, what Plato in the *Theaetetus* calls *homoiōsis theō* (176b1). These rites often involved the use of wine and erotic stimulation to bring the celebrant to a state of raving or frenzy. Their goal was to gain release from distress and the pressures of physical life and to achieve a postcarnate blessedness. This aspiration was specifically associated with the immortality of the soul, metempsychosis, and the achievement of divinity, as we find, for example, in Pindar's second *Olympian Ode*. Walter Burkert compares Pindar's poetic paean to a blessed afterlife with similar thoughts in Herodotus, Empedocles, and Plato, thus showing how pervasive these ideas were in the late fifth century.[14]

This concern with the state of divinity as a real human possibility was exemplified in other developments, such as the prominence of charismatic, almost shamanistic religious figures like Empedocles and Pythagoras, and the deification of heroes, an old tradition now newly revived in important ways.[15] These developments, of course, did not all involve the human aspiration to divinity in the same way. But they did contribute to the existence of a context in which the gap between gods and humankind was conceived as frequently traversable. One key to this set of changes, which Burkert calls a revolution, was the belief in the immortality of the *human* soul.[16]

In Athens, then, there was, at least during the fifth century, a dominant religious attitude and a variety of alternative religious styles, such as mystery cults, ecstatic rites, and salvific societies organized around charismatic leaders. This dominant religiosity is what Burkert has called the "polis tradition."[17] It was a conglomerate of traditional religious practice – sacrifices, festivals, oracles, divination, and more – that hardly had a single, uniform theology. Religious belief and mythology in classical Greece were as complex and pluralistic as was religious practice. Even amid this pluralism, however, with its world of separated, powerful, and immortal deities, we can distinguish a common theological posture, one succinctly framed by the slogans associated with the Pythia, the oracle at Delphi: nothing too much, and know thyself. What these maxims meant was that human beings should recognize their limitations with respect to the gods: The gods are immortal, perfect in knowledge, and exceedingly powerful; human beings are mortal and limited in power and knowledge. Human beings should not want more than they as humans should; they should not overestimate their knowledge or capabilities, nor should they confuse who they are and who the gods are. Underlying the world of polis religion, then, was this theological attitude of separation between the divine and the human, of discontinuity, of human limits and hence of the temptation to illicit self-esteem and pride (*hubris*). I call it the Delphic theology.[18]

Contrasted with this posture was the attitude of those committed to the alternative religious styles that involved ecstatic rites and salvation-oriented cults. Unlike traditional Athenian piety, this attitude assumed that there was continuity between the human and the divine – for example, that both were immortal, and that the gap between them could be bridged by the divine possession of human beings (as in shamanism) or by human attainment of the status of divinity or by both.[19] In short, the Orphic-Bacchic-Pythagorean-Eleusinian world assumes that relief from our physical world and its distress could be achieved by human beings becoming as completely divine as they could possibly be. There is an element in human life, the soul or *psyche,* that has a quasi-divine nature; it is immortal. And that element, through ecstatic ritual performance or perhaps through a life of ecstatic practice, could grow stronger and aid in the attainment of salvation.

Let us locate Plato in this religious setting and in this historical context. We find someone trying to conceptualize and articulate an understanding of the good life and its relation to the philosophical life. In so doing Plato appropriates the two religious tendencies to which we have called attention, but in both cases his appropriation is qualified. At certain points he accepts but also criticizes the polis tradition of festivals, sacrifices, oracles, and so forth. At other times, however, Plato adopts the alternative mode of piety, the mode that includes mystery cults and ecstatic rites of initiation, purification, and salvation. In adopting this latter mode, moreover, Plato modifies it significantly. The model is ecstatic insofar as it involves a kind of transformation whereby the soul of the human initiate steps out of its physical environment and becomes purified of worldly distress; it thereby gains a kind of divine blessedness and becomes as divine as it can be. The soul, in a sense, crosses the divide that separates the human from the divine; already divine to a degree, it seeks to perfect its divinity. In the Orphic-Bacchic rites, this transformation is achieved through a process of emotional excitement, induced by music, dance, and other means. Plato accepts the ecstatic model, that human beings can, by bringing their souls to a certain state, achieve divine or nearly divine status. But he replaces the emotional character of the ritual process with cognitive content. For Plato, that is, a life aimed at salvation takes the form of a life of rational inquiry, a philosophical life.

Once he realizes this, Plato then develops an epistemological and metaphysical view of what such inquiry requires in order for it to occur; this is Plato's attempt to understand what philosophy is. It involves in part showing that inquiry aims at knowledge of divine objects, the Forms, and that the gaining of such knowledge makes the soul more and more like these objects. Platonic learning, then, is an ecstatic ritual process because it is precisely organized, religiously motivated by the desire to become divine, and facilitated by the assumption that the human soul, which is immortal, can become divine or nearly divine. The result of this Platonic appropriation of the ecstatic model, then, is a conception of philosophy as a lifelong quest for salvation.

What I have just said, of course, is only a proposal, but it is one that gains support when we look at the dialogues for confirmation. Here I will only be able to make some modest steps in that direction.

To begin, what features of *Socratic piety* does Plato choose to emphasize? Socrates is Plato's model of the philosopher and the philosophical life. In his early dialogues Plato portrays him as a tenacious elenctic interrogator, a moral philosopher, and a devoted Athenian citizen. In later dialogues, when Socrates also appears as a dramatic participant, Plato's portrait changes. Often Socrates is no longer engaged in elenchus, and his interests and views become much broader, including mathematics and metaphysics, politics and psychology. It is possible, then, that there is a shift in the dialogues. That shift may be either from a historically attentive portrait to one that employs Socrates as a Platonic mouthpiece or from an earlier to a later Platonic perception of Socrates. For now, we do not have to decide which is the case. By the time we reach a middle dialogue such as the *Symposium,* on either reading, we clearly have Plato's perception of Socrates as he thinks Socrates suits Plato's own views and interests. Hence, in the *Symposium* Plato can be taken to have portrayed Socrates religiously in a way that he finds congenial to his own thinking. How does Plato draw this portrait of Socratic piety?

In the *Symposium* we should notice two features of Plato's Socrates. First, the dialogue, like the *Phaedo,* is a eulogy to Socrates and the Socratic life. But in the central passage, Socrates does not engage in his characteristic elenctic interrogation; rather he reports a conversation between himself and Diotima, a female diviner from Mantinea, in Arkadia.[20] In the first part of their conversation Diotima plays the role of a Socratic interrogator in a dialectical exchange about the nature and effects of Love (Eros). Then, at a crucial juncture, when Socrates expresses his bewilderment about the implications of their results, Diotima jettisons dialectic in favor of soliloquy and presentation, indeed revelation. Moreover, what the prophetess reveals in her speech to Socrates is an account of the ascent of desire and love that culminates in the grasping of the Form of Beauty and then spills over into virtuous conduct, what she had earlier called "procreation in beauty" (*tokos en kalō,* 206b7–8).

Diotima's description of the ascent of philosophical desire uses vocabulary from the mystery rites – *myēsis, epopteia,* and *orgiazein* – and it is widely agreed that Plato's model for this account was the Eleusinian Mysteries. These famous rites were celebrated in the month of Boedromion by large numbers of Athenian and non-Athenian initiates (*mystai*) and included a spectacular procession (*pompē*) from Athens to Eleusis, fourteen miles along the Sacred Way. The parade passed through several stages, culminating in an initial entrance of the *mystai* into the temple, the Telesterion. Later, the initiates reentered the temple and received, in the deepest recesses of the sanctuary, a final, secret revelation (in the words of *Symposium* 210a1, *ta telea kai epoptika*); the Hiera (sacred things) included things enacted (*dromena,* possibly the sacred marriage), objects shown (*deiknymena*, possibly an ear of grain), and words spoken (*legomena*).

In the central passage of the *Symposium*, then, Plato, using terminology reminiscent of the Eleusinian Mysteries, depicts Socrates simultaneously as the interlocutor in a preliminary elenchus, as the recipient of a religio-philosophical teaching, and as an initiate in a mystery rite. Moreover, the content of Diotima's teaching shows that Socrates is being initiated not into an episode of emotional frenzy and psychological disorder, but into the practice of philosophy and the philosophical ascent to a kind of knowledge that will result in cognitive contact with the Forms.

This picture of Socrates as a philosophical initiate is complemented by Alcibiades' remarkable, inebriated reminiscence of Socrates (*Smp.* 215b–216e). Alcibiades, a pupil and associate of Socrates, had been a brilliant but unscrupulous Athenian general and statesman. Notoriously, he was implicated in profanations of the Eleusinian Mysteries that supposedly took place in his home in the summer of 415, events alleged to have enraged the gods and thereby led to the failure of the Sicilian expedition and Athens' demise.[21] Here, in the *Symposium*, set dramatically at the party celebrating Agathon's victory at the dramatic competition at the festival of the Lenaia in 416, Alcibiades enters drunk and proceeds to portray Socrates as a Bacchic satyr whose ugly exterior hides a divine core. According to Alcibiades, Socrates throws people into a trance by use of words alone and turns them into corybantic celebrants. Once, moreover, while on a military campaign, Socrates himself remained in a daylong trance, engaged in silent inquiry, immune to cold and ice, showing his true character and his intense devotion to wisdom and truth. Plato, in short, has Alcibiades exhibit a Socrates very much like a Bacchic celebrant. Like them, Socrates prepares for a postcarnate journey, seeks a final blessed state, and experiences a trancelike detachment. Unlike them, he eschews wine and drunkenness (the counterpoint with Alcibiades' own drunkenness is clear), music, and frenzied dance; instead he engages in intense rational thought. He is, therefore, an ecstatic of a unique sort, indeed of just the sort that I earlier described.

The ascent passage in the *Symposium* does not of course give a complete account of philosophical inquiry. It is primarily about the desire for knowledge and beauty and does not deal with the cognitive stages of inquiry that begin with belief and culminate in knowledge. Plato attends to these matters in the *Meno, Phaedo,* and *Republic.* I have suggested that Plato's conception of this process, and indeed of the philosophical life, is religious and particularly ecstatic. This means that not only does he characterize it in terms drawn from mystery rites and ecstatic practices; he also develops his account of inquiry and education in part *from* these traditions and in the end takes philosophy to be a form of such initiation rites. If this is so, the dialogues should show that the philosopher moves through systematically related steps in order to gain divine wisdom, thereby becoming virtually divine himself. The soul, that is, which is immortal by nature, becomes intelligent and as much like the divine, which is eternal, stable, and pure, as human beings can be.

We have already sketched some features of the alternative, ecstatic type of piety that Plato is adopting. From many sources, including Plato himself in dialogues such as the *Euthydemus, Ion, Phaedo, Republic,* and *Phaedrus,* we gain a rich understanding of the practices, cults, and theoretical foundations of the ecstatic tradition in classical Greece. What we learn is this. The central divinity associated with the Orphic writings and mystery rites was Dionysos, the god of wine and ecstasy. As one of the twelve central Olympian deities, Dionysos was widely worshiped and in Athens was the object of several festivals: the Anthesteria, the Lenaia, the rustic Dionysia, and the Great Dionysia.[22] The dark side of Dionysos involved worship of a heterodox kind; this worship first developed in Italy and became widespread on the Greek peninsula as the mysteries of Dionysos. Sometimes the frenzied worshiper went mad for Dionysos alone and in private, but more frequently there was a group or religious community (*thiasos*), especially of maenads (female celebrants) and male satyrs, who danced to wild music and used other means to achieve a delirious state (*baccheia*). The goal of all this was a "change effected in the soul (*psyche*)" in which the soul was purified and gained new powers appropriate to its blessed state.[23] Plato, in the *Phaedrus* (249d–256e, esp. 254b–c), portrays this state as a kind of amazement or stunned recoil in which the celebrant becomes immobilized and also as a kind of madness (*mania*) by means of which misery is cured (244d5–245a1). At its most extreme – one recalls the fate of Pentheus in Euripides' *Bacchae* – Bacchic worship resulted in omophagy, the eating of raw flesh as an act of ingesting the god.[24]

A central feature of these mystery rites and the Orphic-Pythagorean conglomerate associated with them was the belief in the soul's immortality. In the Homeric poems and elsewhere, until the fifth century, the dominant view of soul (*psyche*) was that of a complex of features and functions associated with different parts of the body, with dreams, trances, and such phenomena, and with death. Although it is clear that Greeks of the Archaic period could say "I," it is doubtful that they had the notion of a unitary soul that was the locus of conscious events.[25] Nonetheless, even in Homer, there is the view that some kind of soul, a shadow or vaporous image of the body, continues to exist after death. But reincarnation only seems to have become prominent through the teachings of Pythagoras of Samos in the late sixth century and then in the Orphic texts of the fifth century. It was in this Orphic-Pythagorean context, moreover, that the soul was taken to be immortal and divine. Whether the Homeric poems entertain the possibility of the soul's immortality is doubtful, but by the fifth century the idea was available, if not yet widely accepted.[26]

Plato clearly did accept it. In the *Meno* Plato shows that his understanding of inquiry or learning was closely tied to the belief in the soul's immortality. At *Meno* 80d, frustrated by the *aporiai* ("perplexities") that have arisen out of Socrates' interrogation about the nature of *aretē* ("excellence"), Meno puts forth a puzzle about inquiry. Socrates rephrases the puzzle into a dilemma: If one knows what one is seeking, there is no point in searching for it, and if one does not know it, search cannot be directed to it; therefore inquiry is impossible, for it cannot be initiated. Socrates then replies to this paradox by offering a teaching that he claims to have learned from "priests and priestesses who make it their business to be able to give an account concerning what they do"; Pindar and other poets who are *theoi* ("divine") also hold the view.

The teaching is presented in two parts, a poetic quotation and Plato's account of what the quotation implies to him about inquiry or learning. For our purposes we shall forgo detailed discussion of the meaning of the paradox, the doctrine of learning as recollection, and the questioning of the slave that follows.[27] Two points are important. First, Plato is decisive about the connection between the doctrine that he finds in the quoted text, that learning is really recollection of truths that are always present in the soul but not in one's mental grasp, and the soul's immortality. He believes that the former position entails the latter; the desirability of accepting the account of learning as recollection counts in favor of accepting the immortality of the soul. Moreover, this text is not the last in which Plato advocates and argues for the soul's immortality. The *Phaedo* of course contains a series of such arguments, and there are further examples in *Republic* X and the *Phaedrus.* In at least one argument in the *Phaedo* and again in the *Phaedrus,* the soul's immortality is explicitly tied to Plato's understanding of inquiry and learning. Here in the *Meno* the tie is secured by Socrates' affirmation, as this stretch of dialogue concludes, that "if the truth of things that are is always in the soul, then the soul must be immortal" (86b1–2). Learning as recollection solves the paradox of inquiry, and it does so only if its objects are in the soul always. But this permanence requires, Plato thinks, the soul's immortality, which means that Plato can only save the possibility of inquiry if the soul is immortal. Hence, there are good philosophical reasons for him to adhere to the Orphic-Pythagorean doctrine.

The second important point is that Plato tells us that he is drawing on Orphic-Pythagorean sources for these twin doctrines. He cites a fragment from Pindar, the fifth-century poet influenced by Orphic teachings and mystery rites:

> [Those from whom] Persephone receives requital for ancient grief,
> In the ninth year she restores again
> Their suns to the sun above,
> From whom arise noble kings,
> And men mighty in strength and greatest in wisdom,
> And for the rest of time
> They are called heroes and sanctified by men.
> (81b7–c4; trans. W. K. C. Guthrie)

Here Pindar alludes to the Orphic myth recounting Dionysos's birth. Burkert tells it this way:

> Zeus raped his mother Rhea-Demeter and sired Persephone; he raped Persephone in the form of a snake and sired Dionysos. To the child Dionysos he hands over the rule of the world, places him on a throne, and has him guarded by Korybantes. But Hera sends the Titans who distract the child with toys, and while the child is looking into a mirror he is dragged from the throne, killed, and torn to pieces, then boiled, roasted, and eaten. Zeus thereupon

hurls his thunderbolt to burn the Titans, and from the rising soot there spring men, rebels against the gods who nevertheless participate in the divine. From the remains that were rescued and collected, Dionysos rises again.[28]

It is a well-known myth – Plato alludes to it again in the *Cratylus* (400c) – and one that clarifies "the ancient grief" for which Persephone receives requital; that is, when people die, their souls are held by Persephone beneath the earth, as compensation for the crime of their Titanic ancestors. Then, however, she allows these human souls to become reincarnate, and from them come heroes, kings, and "men of wisdom." Plato latches onto this last phrase. The soul is immortal and undergoes reincarnation; from this experience it has learned all that is; hence, when it engages in inquiry and learns, what is really occurring is a process of recollection. The men of wisdom and indeed wisdom itself – knowledge – depend upon the soul's immortality and the conception of learning as recollection. But immortality is a credential of divinity, as is perfect wisdom. By becoming heroes and men of wisdom, those who inquire – later in the *Phaedo* and *Republic* Plato will call them "lovers of wisdom (*philosophoi*)" – enhance their divinity.

At *Meno* 86b, near the conclusion of his response to the paradox, Socrates says, "I shouldn't like to take an oath on the whole story," and it is a crux how much of the previous account Plato would disavow. My sense is that he would have held to his understanding of inquiry and the belief in the soul's immortality; the myth of the Titans and its details are another matter. This is after all myth, and it includes some horrifying acts, just the type that later, in the *Republic,* Plato will criticize. In the *Meno,* then, Plato's resources are Orphic-Pythagorean; he both appropriates and rejects features of that inheritance.

In the *Phaedo, Republic,* and *Phaedrus,* Plato elaborates his account of rational inquiry and learning, his understanding of the soul's nature and its immortality, the religious character of the philosophical life, and the ways in which the polis tradition of Greek religion can be adapted to his purposes. The *Phaedo* contains several arguments for the soul's immortality and employs a variety of expressions from Orphic and Bacchic rites to characterize the philosopher. Early in the dialogue, for example, Plato compares philosophical thinking to purification and philosophers to Bacchic initiates (*bacchoi,* 69c8–12). His religious terminology in the *Phaedo* is Bacchic, Orphic, and Pythagorean all at once. In addition, Plato here first introduces the Forms as unchanging, pure, eternal objects of knowledge; some of their features arise from his critique of physical items and characteristics as proper objects of knowledge and from his critique of sensory experience as a vehicle for genuine inquiry, but some derive from the need for such objects to be of divine status.[29]

The *Republic* does not use the vocabulary of ecstatic ritual as explicitly as the *Phaedo,* but the general framework is still present in Plato's mind. One might interpret his conception of philosophical education in Books VI and VII, a conversion (*periagogē*) of the soul as it passes through the stages of the mathematical curriculum on its way to a dialectical understanding of the Forms, as Plato's Pythagorean revision of the stages of the Eleusinian Mysteries. Moreover, in the *Republic,* Plato addresses the role of religion in the polis in a number of ways. In Books II and III, for example, he inveighs against bogus healers and charlatans who peddle Orphic placebos to the superstitious; he also offers his famous critique of Homeric religion and the Olympian pantheon, charging that the disgusting and immoral acts in which the gods are depicted are poor models for the young and hence inappropriate models for public education. In Book X, finally, Plato argues for the soul's immortality and then presents a myth of transition, in which he shows how the conduct of one's life influences subsequent incarnations and hence how worldly virtue has its importance, even within the context of the philosopher's ultimate otherworldly goal.

The *Phaedrus* culminates this set of dialogues. Within the framework of an account of interpersonal love, Plato argues for the soul's immortality once again and then constructs an extraordinary myth of the soul and its experiences and aspirations, of personal psychology, cognitive resources, and philosophical method. It is a portrait of philosophy as a special kind of *mania,* akin to but distinct from the madness of poets, oracles, mantics, and cathartic initiates. Here again, as in the *Phaedo* and *Symposium,* Plato uses the vocabulary of ecstatic ritual to characterize the soul's vision of the Forms. Moreover, with more detail than elsewhere, Plato describes phenomenologically the soul's experience of rationally grasping the Forms.

There is a further aspect of Plato's appropriation of Greek religiosity that takes us beyond the *Phaedrus.* Plato's thinking about the nature of divinity takes two paths. On the one hand, he identifies as divine the highest objects of knowledge and rational aspiration, the Forms, and he comes to associate one kind of divinity with such generic features of the Forms as changelessness, purity, and simplicity. On the other hand, Plato figures in a tradition that criticizes the Olympian gods and seeks to rethink the notion of divinity in terms of our understanding of the cosmos and especially of soul, life, and motion. In *Laws* X, Plato pursues this second line of inquiry as he tries to say something about impiety and religious ritual in the ideal polis.

This is what we might call Plato's natural theology. Natural theology involves arguing for the nature and existence of the divine from the understanding of nature. It is an attempt to show that nature, and especially change or order, requires the divine as an ultimate causal explanation, and hence natural theology seeks to show the continuity between science and religion. The early Greek natural philosophers, the first figures in this tradition, explored the nature of divinity, *ho theos,* by associating it with a variety of attributes (control, power, indestructibility) and identifying the ways in which divinity occurred as natural substances, like air and fire.[30] Such natural divinities function in a variety of ways in relation to the cosmos and to human aspiration. Heraclitus, for example, says that thunderbolt (fire) steers all things, Xenophanes says that the one god moves all things with the effortlessness of its mind. Plato, in many ways, figures in the tradition that includes such thinkers, together with Parmenides, Anaxagoras, and Empedocles. In the *Republic* (II 380c–383c and Book X) and *Phaedrus* (245c5–246a2), for example, he reflects on the causal and hence providential dimensions of divinity, how divinity is responsible for motion, life, and goodness in the natural world.[31] But these developments, which later are manifest in Aristotle's accounts of the unmoved movers in the *Metaphysics* and *Physics,* reach new heights in the *Timaeus* and the *Laws* as Plato ties together divinity, motion, and soul. Here I restrict myself to some comments on the *Laws.*

The argument that Plato offers in the *Laws* for the existence of the gods, reminiscent of the *Phaedrus* (the argument for the soul's immortality at 245c5–246a2) and an anticipation of Aristotle's argument in the *Physics,* associates divinity with priority, self-sufficiency, motion, and life.[32] Plato's reasoning is of course focused on soul as self-generating motion, but he is explicit that soul is a divinity (897b2; cf. 899a7–c1). Indeed, Plato goes further: Heavenly motions, like rotary motion, reflect the order of rationality;[33] hence it must be "the best kind of soul [i.e., rational and supremely virtuous] that cares for the entire universe and directs it along the best path" (897c7–9). Each rational soul that guides a heavenly body in its orbit, moreover, is a god. As Burkert puts it, "astronomy becomes the foundation of religion."[34] Plato then concludes that in order to cope with his argument, one must either deny the motive priority of soul, reject his reasoning, or agree to believe in the existence of gods.

Even in the face of such reasoning, there is contrary evidence. The apparent "good fortune of scoundrels and criminals in private and public life" (899d8–e1) compels many to doubt divine providence and to contend that the gods are indifferent to human affairs.[35] To show that this result is false Plato draws on a feature of the previous argument, a feature that recalls a famous caveat in *Republic* II, that the gods are good, for they possess moderation, rationality, and order and in no way their opposites.[36] Being good, fully capable, and attendant to details (*Laws* 900c–903b), then, the gods must be thought to care for each individual through "the control of ruling powers that have perfected the minutest constituents of the universe" (903b7–9). We need not attempt a detailed discussion of Plato's psychological description of how this process works. Suffice it to say that he believes it does: Individuals act according to psychological laws and their actions contribute to the cosmic order and suit the laws of destiny (904a–b). Eventually appropriate reward and punishment come to all.

Finally, since the gods do indeed care for individuals and since destiny is fixed by laws, one should not believe that sinners can buy off the gods with gifts (905d). Those who believe this demean the gods' affinity with justice and commit the most impious of acts. Reasoning, then, should persuade citizens of the worth of genuine piety, that is, of as much piety as a normal citizen is capable of. In the polis only a small number of citizens will be competent to attain the richest level of ecstatic transcendence and philosophical piety portrayed in the *Phaedo, Republic,* and *Phaedrus.* Others, however, can at least achieve an understanding of what the *Laws* teaches about the divine and about how to live in terms of such an account of the gods. Many others can be made to conduct their lives in harmony with divine providence, even if they have no clear understanding of it.

In the *Republic* Plato had vilified Bacchic-Orphic charlatans who proliferated in the late fifth and early fourth centuries and who sold ritual panaceas like the phony medicines of itinerant quacks.[37] He also presented a revised and refined picture of education, music, art, and dramatic poetry. In the *Laws* he levels his criticisms at those who believe that the gods can be bought off and who become themselves "sub-human" who "take everybody for fools and delude many a man during his life. . . . by promising to influence the gods through the alleged magic powers of sacrifices and prayers and charms, they try to wreck completely whole homes and states for filthy lucre" (909b; trans. Trevor Saunders). This is a group of fakes similar to those attacked in the *Republic,* religious entrepreneurs who, in the service of *hubris* and self-aggrandizement, capitalize on the remoteness of divinity.

What, however, is the political and cultural impact of this opposition between philosophical and nonphilosophical piety? Should a polis abolish and prohibit shrines, altars, sacrifices, and so forth? Burkert raises this question and gives Plato's response: "the religion of the Platonic polis appears altogether familiar," with sanctuaries, temples, altars, images, priests, seers, exegetes, sacrifices, prayers, processions, and festivals.[38]

Burkert of course is right. Plato's polis must be constructed in strict accord with the oracular directives of Delphi, Dodona, or Ammon about the gods that ought to be worshiped and the temples that ought to be founded (738b). A sacred acropolis is to be set aside as a central precinct for worship of Hestia, Zeus, and Athena (745d), and each of the city's twelve tribes, with its own festivals and temples, will occupy a plot dedicated to its particular god (738d; cf. 771c–d). The law courts, marriage, childrearing, and much else are to be conducted under divine auspices, and the polis has a full sacred calendar, filled with festivals, competitions, processions, and all their accoutrements. Much of this and more is certainly familiar and normal for a fourth-century Greek polis.

But, we might ask, how can this be? And if it is, what is the relation between the philosophical ecstasy that is the goal and orienting experience of only a few and this traditional, widely accessible religion of the polis? To answer these questions, Plato must first explain why polis religion of the traditional kind is necessary at all. Then he must show how both philosophical and nonphilosophical piety are related to the state.

In the *Laws* Plato makes it clear that not all citizens are equally equipped to become philosophers and members of the Nocturnal Council, the supreme governmental institution in his polis. This Council combines a variety of functions, among which is the articulation of the state's moral aims based on philosophical inquiry into human excellence (*aretē*). Not all are capable of such inquiry and hence of the moral knowledge to which philosophy aspires. Members of the Council must be "particularly well qualified by natural abilities and education" (961a–b) and able to gain an "adequate understanding of virtue (*aretē*)," the goal of each person's soul. They must also be articulate, open-minded, and committed to the truth.

Furthermore, this same distinction, between those who are and those who are not suited to philosophy, applies to theological knowledge. "The man in the street may be forgiven if he simply follows the letter of the law, but if any intended guardian fails to work hard to master every theological proof there is, we must certainly not grant *him* the same indulgence" (966c; trans. Trevor Saunders). Plato fixes precisely the content of what the philosopher must grasp, that the soul is immortal and controls the material world and that "reason is the supreme power among the heavenly bodies" (967d–e). To orient their attention and practice to the gods in appropriate ways, on the other hand, most people require a regimen of rituals and celebrations. Plato is keenly aware of the needs of the masses and of the excesses to which they are prone. This is especially clear in his prohibition against private shrines or altars (909d3–910e4). One must do what is necessary to prevent ordinary citizens from responding to anxiety and distress by seeking the gods' help through sacrifice and prayer.

Familiar Greek religious practices, then, are required for those incapable of an accurate understanding of the divine. But how is this mundane piety compatible with philosophy and with the state?

Let us distinguish between two views about the relation between politics and religion. On one view, the two are continuous; politics expresses the religious ideal and is aimed at implementing that ideal. On the other, politics is independent of any particular religious conception of the good life; it seeks to facilitate individual self-expression and to minimize conflict while avoiding advocacy.[39] Both views are founded on the assumption that politics and religion are distinct domains, and in a sense Plato would not have accepted or even understood such a premise. But if he had, clearly he would have been attracted to the former of these conceptions. The problem is that he has more than one understanding of the religious life of the citizens in the ideal polis. How can a single polis encourage and indeed facilitate two ideals of the religious life?

The answer must be that the polis provides an institutional and cultural environment in which both philosophical piety and nonphilosophical polis religiosity flourish and function. A regimen of sacrifices, festivals, and celebrations for the ordinary citizens, filled with expressions of praise and gratitude, serves to enhance political life and to enable the good life to flourish *for all.* "Every man," Plato says, "must resolve to belong to those who follow in the company of the divine" (716b8–9). But what is it to "follow in the company of the divine"? For Plato, the polis citizen "follows in the company of the divine" in two ways, primarily by being a good person, moderate, wise, just, and so on, and secondarily through praise, gratitude, and offerings of all kinds. Both together constitute true polis piety. "If a good man sacrifices to the gods and keeps them constant company in his prayers and offerings and every kind of worship he can give them, this will be the best and noblest policy he can follow" (716d6–e1). The philosopher also "follows in the company of the divine," but he does so by living a life of rational aspiration and study and by serving the polis, thereby becoming like a god. In these ways, then, both philosophical and nonphilosophical piety coexist in the state, and each, in its own way, leads to a life with the gods.

I have tried to show how Plato's thinking is immersed in the very complex, variegated phenomenon of Greek religion. He takes its existence for granted, adopts features of it, adapts others, and rejects much of it. His relation to Greek piety, however, is deeper than an encounter with the world of Olympian deities, sacrifices, festivals, and so on; Plato also appropriates aspects of Greek ecstatic ritual as a framework for philosophical inquiry. It is this religious dimension that helps to show what makes philosophy so important to him.

NOTES

1 The best recent comprehensive account of Greek religion is Walter Burkert, *Greek Religion*, trans. John Raffan (Cambridge, Mass.: Harvard University Press, 1985). One might also consult Martin Nilsson, *Greek Folk Religion* (New York: Columbia University Press, 1940), *Greek Piety* (Oxford: Oxford University Press, 1948), and *A History of Greek Religion* (Oxford: Oxford University Press, 1952); Jon D. Mikalson, *Athenian Popular Religion* (Chapel Hill: University of North Carolina Press, 1983); and Robert Parker, "Greek Religion," in *The Oxford History of the Classical World*, ed. John Boardman, Jasper Griffin, and Oswyn Murray (Oxford: Oxford University Press, 1986), 254–74.

2 "Most excellent and just among gods" (*Euphr.* 5e). Cf. *Phdr.* 246e.

3 See *Laws* 843a, *Euthd.* 301b.

4 To see that not all Greeks revered Homer in the same way, one need only recall Xenophanes (D.K., B11), Heraclitus (D.K., B40), and Plato's critical account of the Homeric poems in the *Republic.*

5 One need only remember the almost superstitious fear that spread after the mutilation of the herms and the profanation of the Mysteries in 415 B.C. See C. Powell, "Religion and the Sicilian Expedition," *Historia* 28 (1979): 15–31; and Douglas M. MacDowell, *Andokides: On the Mysteries* (Oxford: Oxford University Press, 1962).

6 For discussion of Greek and Athenian festivals, see Burkert, *Greek Religion*; H. W. Parke, *Festivals of the Athenians* (Ithaca, N.Y.: Cornell University Press, 1977); L. Deubner, *Attische Feste* (Berlin: H. Keller, 1932).

7 See Parke, *Festivals*, 149–57.

8 Walter Burkert has a fascinating discussion of sacrifice and myth in *Homo Necans: The Anthropology of Ancient Greek Sacrificial Ritual and Myth* (Berkeley: University of California Press, 1983).

9 Burkert, *Greek Religion*, 55–75, and *Homo Necans.*

10 On oracles and divination, see H. W. Parke, *Greek Oracles* (London: Hutchinson, 1967) and *The Oracles of Zeus* (Cambridge: Harvard University Press, 1967); and Joseph Fontenrose, *The Delphic Oracle* (Berkeley: University of California Press, 1978).

11 Vincent Scully, *The Earth, the Temple, and the Gods: Greek Sacred Architecture* (New Haven: Yale University Press, 1979).

12 See G. Mylonas, *Eleusis and the Eleusinian Mysteries* (Princeton: Princeton University Press, 1961).

13 Corybantes were frenzied devotees of Kybele, the mother goddess from Asia Minor; they are often portrayed, in literature and vase painting, as dancing deliriously to Phrygian music of the flute (*aulos*).

14 Burkert, *Greek Religion*, 299. Burkert emphasizes that Pythagorean, Or-

phic, and Bacchic myths and rites, although distinct, do overlap: *Greek Religion,* 300; Walter Burkert, *Orphism and Bacchic Mysteries: New Evidence and Old Problems of Interpretation* (Berkeley: Center for Hermeneutical Studies in Hellenistic and Modern Culture, 1977) and *Ancient Mystery Cults* (Cambridge: Harvard University Press, 1987). See also Parker, "Greek Religion," 263–4.

15 See Michael L. Morgan, *Platonic Piety: Philosophy and Ritual in Fourth Century Athens* (New Haven: Yale University Press, 1990), 19, 199 nn. 51–3.

16 I shall say more about this belief in the soul's immortality when I discuss the *Meno.* Guthrie remarked that it was a very difficult idea for Greeks to accept, but there is evidence that the notion of an afterlife reaches far back in Greek literature and religious thought; see W. K. C. Guthrie, *The Greeks and Their Gods* (London: Methuen, 1950), 176, 180, 260–1.

17 Burkert, *Orphism and Bacchic Mysteries.*

18 The term is mine and is intended only as a helpful abbreviation. The themes of this polis tradition and this theology as articulated in tragic literature are explored by Hugh Lloyd-Jones, *The Justice of Zeus,* 2d ed. (Berkeley: University of California Press, 1983).

19 On Greek ecstatic religion and the Orphic-Bacchic-Pythagorean conglomerate, see E. R. Dodds, *The Greeks and the Irrational* (Berkeley: University of California Press, 1951); Burkert, *Ancient Mystery Cults;* Susan G. Cole, "New Evidence for the Mysteries of Dionysos," *Greek, Roman and Byzantine Studies* 21, no. 3 (1980): 223–38; Marcel Detienne, *Dionysus Slain* (Baltimore: Johns Hopkins University Press, 1979).

20 I believe that Plato wants us to treat Diotima as a prophetess associated with Dionysos and Pan. Pan was originally an Arkadian divinity, was brought to Athens shortly after Marathon (c. 490), and flourished in Athens as a divinity of fertility, love, beauty, and wealth. Pan is also associated with the panic of sudden threat and surprise. In Plato's mind, Pan, together with nymphs, sileni, and satyrs, are part of a Bacchic conglomerate. At the end of the *Phaedrus,* Plato has Socrates offer a prayer to Pan that eulogizes wisdom and the soul's well-being. Often Pan is viewed as an agent of religious possession and madness (*mania*). For a brilliant study of Pan, see Phillipe Borgeaud, *The Cult of Pan in Ancient Greece* (Chicago: University of Chicago Press, 1988).

21 See Powell, "Religion and the Sicilian Expedition"; MacDowell, *Andokides.*

22 Burkert, *Greek Religion,* 163.

23 Burkert, *Ancient Mystery Cults,* 97.

24 Burkert, *Greek Religion,* 290–5.

25 Jan Bremmer, *The Early Greek Concept of the Soul* (Princeton: Princeton University Press, 1983).
26 N. J. Richardson, "Early Greek Views about Life after Death," in *Greek Religion and Society*, ed. P. E. Easterling and J. V. Muir (Cambridge: Cambridge University Press, 1985), 65.
27 See Morgan, *Platonic Piety*, 47–54.
28 Burkert, *Greek Religion*, 297–8.
29 At *Phd.* 79d2 and 80d6, the Forms are called *katharon* ("pure"); at 80a3 and 80b1, they are called *theion* ("divine").
30 See Werner Jaeger, *The Theology of the Early Greek Philosophers* (Oxford: Oxford University Press, 1947); and Lloyd Gerson, *God and Greek Philosophy* (London: Routledge, 1991).
31 See Morgan, *Platonic Piety*, 115–16.
32 Plato's argument is also an early antecedent of the cosmological arguments of the Middle Ages; for example, see St. Thomas Aquinas, *Summa Theologica* I, 2, 3. See *Laws* 891e–899d; cf. *Sph.* 248.
33 *Laws* 898a3–6; see 897e11–898c8 in general.
34 Burkert, *Greek Religion*, 326–9, esp. 327.
35 *Laws* 899d–900b; cf. 885d.
36 *Laws* 900e; cf. *Rep.* 379a–c.
37 See *Rep.* 363a–366e and, for discussion, Morgan, *Platonic Piety*, 108–14.
38 Burkert, *Greek Religion*, 334; cf. *Laws* 738b–c, 759a–c, 848c–e; and *Rep.* 427b–c.
39 This distinction is adapted from Charles Larmore's distinction between the expressivist and modus vivendi approaches to the relation of politics and morality. See *Patterns of Moral Complexity* (Cambridge: Cambridge University Press, 1987), chaps. 3–5.

G. R. F. FERRARI

8 Platonic love

Plato does not have a comprehensive theory of love. Rather, he diverts certain received opinions about love[1] to his own peculiarly philosophic ends. He is not interested in telling us what it would be like to live with someone as a platonic lover. Or so I shall argue, from a reading of the *Symposium*[2] and the *Phaedrus*.[3] I shall ignore the social regulations for sexuality proposed in the *Republic* (III 402d–403c, V 459–461) and the *Laws* (VIII 835c–842a) as not directly relevant to what has most fascinated Plato's readers about his approach to love, and is the topic of this essay: namely, the bridge he constructs between love and philosophy. I shall also ignore the potentially relevant discussion of friendship (against the background of a love affair) in that subtle and complex dialogue, the *Lysis*,[4] in order to leave room to stretch myself to something worthwhile on the *Symposium* and *Phaedrus*. Of these two works, I shall focus on the former, for it alone among the dialogues is concerned exclusively with love.

I

The speechmaking of the *Symposium* is rooted in bad faith. The series of speeches in praise of love that makes up the bulk of the work is set in motion by a complaint attributed to Phaedrus (whom we shall meet again in the dialogue that bears his name). Is it not shocking, he is reported as saying, that, when it comes to eulogies, Eros, so ancient and so powerful a god, has been neglected in both

This essay is the better for discussion with Kate Toll and for the written comments of Richard Kraut and Anthony Price.

poetry and prose by authors who do not hesitate to laud other gods, or even, in one case, to sing the praises of salt (177a–c)? The complaint gains a certain plausibility from the piety of its terms (why stint any god of worship?), but loses it once we consider that erōs in Greek is not only the name of a god but a word that commonly means "love." When Anacreon writes, "With his huge hammer again Eros knocked me like a blacksmith and doused me in a wintry ditch" (fragment 413 in Denys L. Page, ed., *Poetae Melici Graeci* [Oxford, 1962]), he is not, or is not simply, narrating an exploit of the god, but is describing the hot and cold of love. With Aphrodite, now, it is different. Sex is her gift, but only figuratively can her name *mean* "sex" (just as the ordinary Greek for "wine" was *oinos,* and only figuratively *Dionysos*).[5] She is a goddess with a life and character of her own (see, e.g., the *Homeric Hymn to Aphrodite*). But there are no pre-Platonic narratives about the winged boy-god Eros; Eros is just love, however you spell him (and the Greeks lacked capital letters).[6] To praise Eros, then, is to praise love. But seen in this way, the task is not so obviously inviting as Phaedrus suggests. Phaedrus would know perfectly well that the poets, whom he can quote as well as anyone (witness 178b), had plenty to say about Eros, and that the foregoing snippet of Anacreon was a fair sample of much of it.[7] This force that falls like a blow, shivering the limbs, piercing the bones of its helpless victim, madding the mind – is this a candidate for praise? And yet, how not to welcome one of the greatest of human joys? The Greeks were thoroughly ambivalent about love; Eros, in Sappho's piquant formulation, is "bittersweet."[8] And so praise of Eros is rather more surprising than Phaedrus, his focus resolutely fixed on Love's godhead, seems prepared to admit. As surprising, perhaps, as praising salt (and remember, love is bitter as well as sweet).

This, then, is one element of bad faith in the instigation of the speeches we are about to examine. There is another. The round-robin of speeches might seem the epitome of moderation, for it ousts the enforced circulation of half-gallon toasts and the charms of the flute-girl (176e4–10). Eryximachus, the doctor, is happy to introduce moderation as a prescription for healthy living (176c5–d4). He gets his chance, however, only because the indulgence of the previous night has been so extreme as to leave even the heavy drinkers in the company reluctant for an encore (176a4–b8). This is an insalubrious motive for self-control. And it puts a sickly complexion on the fact that not one of the invited speakers – for the pattern will change with the incursion of Alcibiades – praises Eros for how he makes us feel when in love and excited.[9] (Instead his gifts will include moral growth, wholeness, social peace, graceful living, philosophic enlightenment). These men are hung over, after all (176d4); and that is a state in which excitement loses its allure. Socrates, however, is exempt from this aspersion, both because he was not present the night before, and because he never shows his drink (220a4–5). But we shall see that he takes advantage of Phaedrus's sanctimony and of the company's remarkable level of abstractedness. In order to consider more closely how he does this, let us begin by examining, briefly, the structure and development of the five encomia of love toward their climax in Socrates' report of the teachings of Diotima. (There are as many readings of this structure as there are readers of the *Symposium.*[10] I offer what follows not in order to add to their number but in the belief that the issue that I raise in its course is central to Plato's thoughts on love. I shall take it up again in discussing the *Phaedrus.*[11])

The chief structural marker in this series is Aristophanes' attack of hiccups (185d–e). Whatever they signify,[12] they serve the function of forcing the only change in the order of speakers (Eryximachus and Aristophanes are switched), and so compel the reader to notice that Plato, who plans all the coincidences in this work, felt that Eryximachus's speech properly belongs where he has arranged for it to be put, alongside the earlier speeches, while Aristophanes' speech is to be dissociated from them, and mark a fresh start.[13] In short, the hiccups seem to divide the speakers into two groups: Phaedrus, Pausanias, and Eryximachus, on the one hand; Aristophanes, Agathon, and Socrates, on the other. And the substantive issue that distinguishes them is this: The speakers of the first group draw a fundamental distinction (Phaedrus implicitly, the others explicitly) between a good and a bad variety of love, while those of the second group do not. This development comes to a head with Diotima's teaching that love in any of its manifestations is directed toward the good (205e7–206a1, 206a11–12).[14]

It may seem that Phaedrus does not belong with the first group so defined, since Pausanias takes him to task for having enjoined the company simply to praise Eros, without first specifying which Eros they were to praise; for there are two kinds of love, one good and praiseworthy, the other bad (179c–181a, 183d8–e2). But Pausanias is not contradicting Phaedrus, only setting his opinions off against the contrast that he has chosen to ignore. Both men agree to praise love only for the fillip it gives to virtuous conduct.[15] Phaedrus speaks of lovers stimulating one another to courage in battle and to self-sacrifice, Pausanias of lovers who fall for the good character of their sweethearts (183e5) and of sweethearts who will put themselves at the romantic disposal only of potential mentors (184c4–7). (In this emphasis the two men rely on the moral expectations deriving from the conventional asymmetry of love between Athenian males – the elder partner being expected to provide moral guidance and help with civic initiation in return for the sexual favors of the boy, who was to remain uninterested in the sex for its own sake.[16] They appeal to this connection with virtue even while mitigating its asymmetry.) Pausanias draws the obvious contrast with lovers who are more concerned for the body than the soul (181b3–4, 183d8–e1), and who therefore do not take virtue into account (181b5–6). Phaedrus does not; but the contrast is implicit in his claim to know of no greater good for a young boy than a "decent" or "worthy" (*khrēstos*) lover (178c3–5). Whatever Pausanias's claims (180c4–d3), he does not really alter the terms of Phaedrus's speech, nor does he rectify the bad faith at the root of things. He continues to sanitize love – this lover of the soul, who approves of those who pursue youths for their nobility of character even if they are uglier than some (182d7), but who, we are reminded, is himself the longtime lover of a noted beauty, Agathon.[17]

Next, Eryximachus the doctor, conveniently repositioned to follow Pausanias, announces that he will bring to completion Pausanias's contrast between good and bad, "heavenly" and "vulgar" love (185e6–186a3), and proceeds to inflate it into a cosmic principle of balance and imbalance in everything from medicine to music to meteorology, in an unconscious parody of pre-Socratic philosophers.

Aristophanes announces a break with Pausanias's and Eryximachus's scheme of things (189c2–3). He tells a tale that makes of love a search for primordial wholeness (192e10), each of us being as if a half-tally cut from a two-headed, eight-limbed ancestor, and longing to find our other half. The break, then, is to see love, not sundered into good and bad, but as a single aspiration, common to all, and directed (despite differences of sexual orientation) at the same generic object – wholeness. This emerges all the more clearly when we consider the list of fragmented descendants whose sexuality he chooses to trace – adulterers, Lesbians, eagerly passive homosexuals destined to a career in politics, but not, say, married couples or modest boys (191e–192a). By choosing his examples (at least the first and third)[18] from among social deviants, but betraying no hint of censure – indeed, going so far as to defend in this context the passive homosexuals whom he satirized in his plays[19] – he ostentatiously subordinates "good" and "bad" in love to the universal desire revealed by his allegorical depth psychology.

Agathon then returns to the importance of love's connection with the good, but within the new parameters that Aristophanes has set. Aristophanes had argued that all love is of the same generic object, wholeness; Agathon agrees with the structural claim, but contends that the single object of love is *kallos* – one word in Greek, but with a semantic range requiring many in English: the beautiful, the fine, the noble, the good (197b3–9).[20] The speakers of the first group had inferred the goodness and praiseworthiness of Eros largely from the goodness of his effects – masculine virtue, universal well-being. This left open the possibility, exploited by Pausanias and Eryximachus, that Eros could be blameworthy to the extent that his effects were bad. Agathon reverses this pattern – announcing the change in rhetorical strategy with a flourish (194e4–195a5). He first argues that Eros himself is entirely good, and only as a final matter notes that his effects are like him (197c1–3). Moreover, Eros for Agathon is beautiful and good, not because his effects are, but because he is love *of* the beautiful and good (he flees old age, resides in gentle souls, inspires artists of all sorts). Now, this is a most serious conclusion, and a crucial shift of interest, however frothy the arguments on which it rests (cf. 197e7–8). It is what enables Socrates, next to speak, to introduce Diotima's teaching that all love, ultimately, is love of the good, and for that reason commendable.[21]

He does so, however, by first correcting a misapprehension of Agathon's. That love is always *of* the beautiful and good does not imply that love *is* beautiful and good. Love, after all, is desire, and to desire is not yet to have (200a); so that if love is of beauty and goodness, love is without beauty and goodness. How then can love be beautiful and good (201a–c)? Whatever the merits of this argument,[22] it permits Socrates to move on, in his report of Diotima, to a doctrine that manages to subsume into itself important elements from the entire series of preceding speeches, while capping them with its special contribution.[23] For if love does not have beauty and goodness, this is not to say that love is ugly and bad (201e). Love is no god, but an intermediary, a "daemon" who communicates between gods and humans; not wise, but a lover of wisdom – a philosopher (202d–204c). Agathon failed to see that love's nature is to seek the good, rather than to possess it; but it turns out that he was not wrong to claim that love is praiseworthy in its very nature; for to seek the good is praiseworthy. And this is to reinstate the message of Aristophanes' tale: that love is above all a search for what has been lost. Aristophanes only misidentified the loss: It is not of our other half, but of our good (the point is made explicit at 205d10–206a1). And if love is an ongoing search for the good, then even the distinction between good and bad varieties of love developed by the first group of speakers, or something like it, can be accommodated; for a search is dynamic, and a search for the good will be better, the closer it comes to its goal. All love is one; all love is praiseworthy, insofar as it is love of the good; but some manifestations of it will be superior, others inferior. Thus, while all *love* is praiseworthy, not all *lovers* will be.[24]

II

If Diotima's teaching is large enough to embrace elements from all of the opinions heard so far, it may be thought to do so on pain of forgetting the topic. Love, it turns out, is a search for the good – but just as Eryximachus, crowning speaker of the first group, had bidden farewell to love between persons and taken us for a tour of the stratosphere, so Diotima, in the corresponding position within the second group, threatens with a description of great breadth to lose sight of the love that one human being conceives for another. Unlike Eryximachus, however, she recognizes the problem; indeed, it can be shown to govern the structure of her teaching.

Everyone wants the good, she gets Socrates to agree, because good things bring happiness, and everyone wants happiness. In this sense, everyone may be said to have "love" (*erōs*) for the good (205a). Indeed, the good is the only object of love, in that we love only what we consider good; for it makes no sense to say that we could love what we consider bad – that is, harmful – for us (205d10–206a1). (Here we see Socrates fictionally acquiring the philosophic position that he puts to extensive and notorious use in the early dialogues, e.g., *Meno* 77b–78b, *Grg.* 467c–468e.) Since, however, we differ in our conceptions of what will bring happiness, lovers of the good come in many varieties, and common parlance usually reserves the words "love" and "lover" (*erōs, eran, erastēs*) for those who seek that particular species of the good which is sexual love between persons (205d1–8).[25]

Thus Diotima distinguishes between a generic and a specific sense of *erōs.*[26] Clearly, only the latter is what Phaedrus intended in the complaint that sparked the evening's discourse. What is Diotima's warrant for enlarging the topic? In fact it is rather vague at this point. Before the discussion of generic love just summarized (205a–206a), she seizes upon Socrates' agreement that the lover seeks to possess the beautiful and asks him what the consequences of success would be for such a lover. Socrates is stumped. Diotima therefore proposed that they substitute "the good" for "the beautiful," correctly foreseeing that Socrates will find the question easier to answer in this form. Lovers of the good who manage to gain possession of good things, he responds, will be happy (204d–205a).[27] Before we know it, they are launched on the discussion of generic love. But what about the original question that stumps the young Socrates? We might have thought that Diotima's purpose in substituting the apparently easier question is to help him cope with the more difficult one. Yet she does not return to it – introducing instead a fresh question (206b1–4). Socrates, whom Diotima assumes to run after beautiful boys like all young men of his age (211d3–8), cannot say why he does so – cannot say what a person gains by possessing the beautiful. It turns out that he will not have the answer to Diotima's question until, after much preparatory teaching, she has spoken to him of the mysteries of the Beautiful itself (210a–212a). And it is here, we shall find, that her warrant for enlarging the topic to include generic love is finally made clear.

In order to prepare her initiate, Diotima returns to the topic of specific love ("[what] would be *called* love," 206b3)[28] and complicates its traffic with beauty. Specific love is in fact not, as Socrates (and Agathon) suppose, love of the beautiful, but rather "of begetting and giving birth in the beautiful" (206e5). Why so? Because it has been agreed that, speaking generically, love is not only love of the good but also the desire to possess the good always (206a); but the desire to possess the good *always* is really two desires, one for the good and one for immortality;[29] and "begetting" is the closest that a mortal creature can come to immortality (206e7–207a4).[30] In the specific case, beauty takes the role of midwife to generation (206d2–3), prompting those fertile in body, both animal and human, to engender offspring who can renew their line and (for humans) keep their name alive (206c1–5, 207a7–d3, 208e1–5), while those men who are more fertile in soul than body will be inspired by a boy who combines bodily beauty and beauty of character to give birth to fine discourse about civic virtue with a view to his education (209a5–c7).

Such lovers successfully establish a connection between the beautiful and the good. Beauty, whether of body or soul, is instrumental to their virtuous (that is, socially esteemed) conduct – procreation of loyal heirs, tutelage of the rising generation. Nevertheless, they cannot be said to have examined and understood that connection. Rather, it works its way through them; they are conduits for it. That is why Diotima relegates their love to the status of Lesser Mysteries (209e5–210a2).[31] What might have prompted them to a greater awareness is made clear for us, in the case of the lover fertile in soul, when Diotima describes his edifying discourse – his joint offspring with the beautiful boy – as itself "beautiful" (209c6–7). This is the first time that what issues from the act of "begetting in the beautiful" has itself been described as beautiful, and it reveals something that will be crucially important to love's Greater Mysteries: namely, that beauty can belong to the product as well as to the instrument of specific love. At the lesser level, however, the lover stimulated to "beautiful" conduct by beauty takes for granted what the beautiful is. His reason for preferring to beget fine discourse rather than fine children is that he appreciates the immortal name won through discourse by such poets as Homer and Hesiod, such lawgivers as Lycurgus and Solon. This is a pious roll call of cultural heroes. But Diotima is about to challenge such pieties. She will have harsh words, in the course of describing the Greater Mysteries, for those whose horizons are bounded by custom (210d1–2).[32] Similarly, at the level of the Lesser Mysteries she describes the ultimate good – the goal of generic love, toward which all human actions are directed

(208d8) – as "immortal virtue and the glorious fame that follows" (208d7–8). The "love of honor" (*philotimia*, 208c3) is the highest human aspiration here. But when introducing the topic of generic love, Diotima had prepared us to accept the "love of wisdom" (*philosophia*, 205d5) as one of its manifestations; and in the Greater Mysteries it will be philosophy that leads us to the ultimate goal (210d6). The transition from Lesser to Greater bears comparison, then, with the crucial shift of focus in the *Republic* from institutions grounded in the honor code (Books II–IV) to those derived from rule by philosopher-kings (Books V–VII).[33]

The final revelation in the Greater Mysteries of love – the vision of the Beautiful itself – will be disclosed only to those who follow a particular path of eroticism (210a2). The mark of the suitable initiate is that he does not take the nature of the beautiful for granted as would an honor lover, but is prone to become more deeply fascinated by the beauty that issues from his love than by the beauty that first attracted it. This displacement of attention is what motivates his climb to each new level of the upward path. Let us trace his progress. His point of departure is to be smitten with the bodily beauty of a particular person, which stimulates him to generate "beautiful discourse" (*logous kalous*, 210a8). Since the effect of this discourse is to prompt reflection on physical, but not also spiritual, beauty (210a8–b2), and since the production of edifying advice inspired by beauty of soul and body combined – comparable to the reaction of the spiritually fertile lover at the level of the Lesser Mysteries (209a8–c2) – is reserved for a later stage in the ascent (210b8–c3), it would seem that, whatever form the discourse takes, its content is limited to enthusiasm for the physical beauty and prowess of the beloved.[34] The philosophic initiate begins, then, at a level lower than that attained by the honor lover in the Lesser Mysteries (whom he will overtake in due course.)[35] His starting point is higher than the level of the fertile merely in body, however; for their love engenders human offspring (208e2–4), whereas his produces discourse. But what marks him out as having the potential to scale the philosophic heights is his further reaction to that discourse. His "beautiful" words have beauty as their topic[36] – not the beauty of *this* body alone, but also bodily beauty in general, because to praise something is to insert it in its comparison class. And now his thoughts turn toward the beauty to which the product of his love has drawn his gaze, at the expense of the beautiful individual who delivered him of that product. He reflects upon "beauty of [outward] form" in general, and sees that, since the beauty of any one beautiful body is akin to that of another, he would be "very foolish" not to think of bodily beauty as one and the same in all cases; which thought makes his feelings for the single beauty who inspired it seem to him now an overvaluation, and causes him to divide his enthusiasm among all exemplars of bodily beauty (210a8–b6). That all bodily beauty is "akin" is a thought likely to strike anyone who makes comparisons; that it is "one and the same" is a claim that perhaps only the Platonist would find it "very foolish" to deny. But that is surely the point: This lover is marked out for philosophy, the preserve of the few (cf. 209e5–210a2), by the peculiarity in his reaction.

We next find him having come to prize beauty of soul over beauty of body (210b6–7). We are not told how he made the transition, but only that these are stages along the way that he "must" visit (*dei,* 210a4) if he is to achieve the highest goal. Nevertheless, since a guide for the journey is only optional (211b7–c1), we are entitled to assume that he is not simply following authority, and to take this as an invitation to supply a reason for his development. (This may be Plato's way of testing his reader's own aptitude for the journey.) It is not far to seek. The lover who comes to be more occupied by thoughts and expressions of beauty than by the beauty of the body that prompted them, being marked thereby as a reflective and cultured type, will naturally be open to the attractions of the soul.[37] Again it is the beauty of an individual (a boy, as would be conventional in Athenian society for a love of this high-minded sort) that delivers him of his progeny, which again takes the form of discourse – this time of edifying speeches intended to bring out the beauty of the soul (that is, decency of character, 210b8)[38] entrusted to his care (210b8–c3). And again his focus shifts as a result from the beautiful target of his discourse to its beautiful topic. Compelled, in his role as mentor, to consider the beauty of activites and laws, he comes to a conclusion about it that is independent of his educative purpose (just as he spent more thought on bodily beauty in general than was necessary for the purpose of seduction): It too, like bodily beauty, is all of a kind (210c3–5).[39] (Here he goes beyond the fertile-souled pederast of the Lesser Mysteries, who merely produced his beautiful advice, but did not contemplate its beauty.) The result of the earlier conclusion had been to cut the physically beautiful individual down to size in the lover's estimation; the result now is to cut an individual *category* down to size:[40] The lover will think the beauty of bodies a thing of no importance (210c5–6). This is not a state of mind that he had already achieved when we found him prizing the beauty of soul over that of body (210b6–7).[41] That had been a natural accompaniment to his growing thoughtfulness, and a matter of what he found attractive in individuals (what is more, bodily beauty had continued to count, however marginally, as a condition of an individual's attractiveness to him – 210b8–c1); this is a considered judgment, which holds only categories in focus. The boy of beautiful soul has disappeared from view. We are not told what happens to him. While there is no reason to deny that the lover could continue to share with him the results of his later philosophic quest, the center of his emotional attention is no longer occupied by an individual person, or indeed by persons at all.[42] As an index of this development, it is when the beloved person falls from view that Diotima ceases to use the term "to love" (*eran*, 210a7, 210c1) and "lover" (*erastēs*, 210b5) to describe the initiate's relation to what he finds beautiful.[43] From now on, the fact that he continues to find the objects of his concern beautiful – indeed, increasingly beautiful (211d8–e3) – must do most of the work in convincing us that Diotima has not changed the subject.

At the next stage of his development, accordingly, he is not attached to an individual, but is attracted rather by the beauty of knowledge in its various forms, which causes him to give birth once again to beautiful discourse – now the discourse of philosophy (210b6–d6). While the upward move is, again, not explicitly justified, it is natural enough.[44] The lover has been contemplating the beauty of activities and laws – the principles by which we live. Any reader of the early Platonic dialogues can bear witness to the ease with which such contemplation gives rise to the question whether anyone has genuine knowledge of these matters – and so to the question of expertise in general. And now, as before, the initiate's concern is transferred from the beauty that enticed him to the beauty that he has generated. Since the range of knowledge is not limited in advance to a particular subject, but only to what can be known, the initiate has been led to contemplate "the great ocean of beauty" (210d4). He is looking back from the height he has scaled,[45] and sees beauty as a whole, but a whole of great multiplicity. Now he turns his face to the peak, and comes to see beauty as a unity. He catches sight of a single knowledge, which is knowledge of a single beauty – an individual, the Beautiful itself, which is described in the classic vocabulary of the Platonic Forms (210d6–b5). What has happened, then, is that, in a by-now familiar shift of focus, the initiate has turned from simply "doing" beautiful philosophy (considering what is beautiful in the varieties of knowledge – the beauty that attracted him, 210c7) to grasping the beauty *of* his philosophy (the beauty that he engendered, 210d5). He comes to understand what it is that makes possible the single knowledge of the beautiful toward which, as philosopher, he has been working: namely, the existence of the Beautiful itself.

Now, Plato has deliberately left as a mystery just what this claim amounts to (as he always does when introducing the Forms into his dialogues). Here I shall limit myself to the following: To say that the Beautiful itself exists is to claim that there *is* such a thing as beauty, independently of what we or any creature find beautiful (cf. 211b3–5); and that were there not, nothing at all would be beautiful (cf. *Phd.* 100d). But awareness of the truth of this claim, as Diotima describes it, is meant to hit like a hammer blow. It is not an academic decision to commit oneself to a variety of philosophic realism; it is more like an encounter with a beautiful individual, in whose presence one longs to stand (210e4–6, 211d8–212a2).[46] In short, it is more like love.

And so the initiate reaches the end of the line. The mechanism of shift in attention can lift him no further. It had worked by fastening on what rendered beautiful the discourse generated at each level; but at the summit, no discourse is generated. The Beautiful itself is beyond words (cf. 211a7). To attempt to describe it, as at 211a–b, is not to give birth to discourse in its presence; rather, it is to set out the prospect of standing in its presence as a goal, and as a spur to philosophic discourse, which is the means of achieving that goal (cf. Socrates' reaction at 212b1–4). What is generated at the summit is, for the first time, not described as a kind of discourse, but rather as "true virtue," which enables the initiate to become "beloved of the gods" and "immortal, if any human being can be" (212a). This is also the only offspring produced by the lover in his ascent that is not itself qualified as beautiful, and so far from there being any hint that he could transfer his concern from the Beautiful itself to the beauty of virtue, he is explicitly envisaged as spending his life in contemplation of the former (211e4–212a2). In marked contrast to the Lesser Mysteries, what virtue amounts to here is not clearly something other than the vision of the Beautiful that gives it birth. That is, it is unclear whether that vision is the cause of virtue or its occasion. At any rate, even if the two are to be distinguished, the emotional weight of the climax falls rather on the vision of the Beautiful (210e3–211b5, 211d1–212a2) than on its offspring (212a2–7).[47]

Let me draw together the threads of this account. I said that only after hearing of the Greater Mysteries would we understand Diotima's warrant for enlarging the topic from that of specific love (the love that people "fall in" with one another) to generic love (the love of the good which motivates all human action). Her warrant turns out to be this: In describing the initiate's progress, she has connected sexual passion to the life of true virtue (the pursuit of the good) by a series of plausible steps; and keeps touch throughout, by her appeal to the motive force of beauty, with how it is to be in love. The initiate falls in love with a fresh beauty at each stage. (This is what was missing from the Lesser Mysteries.) Moreover, he subsumes in his ascent the inferior forms of love, being led first by sexual desire, then by the ambition for honor, and finally by the love of learning (cf. 211c); so that his development seems a natural unfolding of the manner in which all would choose to realize the good, had they the ability (cf. *Republic* IX 580d–583b). Admittedly, what he communes with at the summit is the Beautiful itself, not the Good itself; and the relation between the beautiful and the good, here as elsewhere in Plato, is problematic. In view of such passages as 201c and *Phaedrus* 250c–d, let us say that the beautiful is thought of as the quality by which the good shines and shows itself to us. We can then claim that the ascent to the Beautiful itself is indeed also an ascent to the Good itself,[48] but described so as to bring out at every turn what it is about the good that captivates us.[49]

I also said that with Diotima's teaching Socrates would take advantage of the company's abstractedness and the whiff of bad faith that hangs about Phaedrus's and Eryximachus's challenge to the party. We can now see that Diotima's teaching exploits to the highest degree the conventional possibility of high-mindedness in the Athenian homosexual love affair – the idea that erotic energy should fuel the development of virtue. (This despite the fact that in the Greater

Mysteries Diotima, unlike the speakers of the first group, finds a place at the foot of the ascent for sexual desire by itself as a legitimate and essential species of love.) Socrates' speech is unabashedly an account of what love can do for philosophy, rather than an account of love for its own sake. Hence at the end he singles out as his reason for honoring Eros the fact that one could find no better "collaborator" (*synergon*) for the task of acquiring the ultimate possession (212b2–6) – that is, the vision of the Beautiful itself, together with true virtue and immortality. But this is only to say that his rhetorical strategy is all of a piece with the tone of the occasion and its effect on the five previous speakers. Phaedrus and Pausanias had described what love can do for manly virtue, Eryximachus what love can do for scientific investigation (e.g., 186b2–3, 187e6–8), Agathon what love can do for the appreciation of beauty (e.g., 196d6–e1, 197b8–9), and even Aristophanes, who has seemed to many modern readers to come closest to addressing what love is all about, offers his account (political conservative that he was) as a cautionary tale that shows what love can do for piety (193a3–d5).[50] Not that Plato means by this to present Socrates as failing to measure up to his promise to tell the truth about love (199b).[51] But it is a selective truth, reflecting only those facets of love that a philosopher would find most beautiful (cf. 198d5–6).

In order to emphasize what the occasion has caused us to miss so far, and why, Plato ends the *Symposium* with a seventh, unscheduled speech – the speech of Alcibiades. The new arrival restores the party to its proper level of alcoholic indulgence (213e7–214a1), and he alone speaks drunk (214c6–8), speaks from infatuation (cf. 222c1–3), and addresses love in its traditional bittersweetness (e.g., 216b5–c3). But this is to say that he alone betrays that he is *in* love, not that he alone understands love. Indeed, he does not even understand Socrates – that much is clear from his attempt to seduce him, and especially from his refusal to learn from its failure. Being in love, Alcibiades is the first speaker to praise his love object – Socrates, in his case – for how Socrates makes him, personally, feel (215e1–216c3, 219d3–e3). Moreover, of all the amazing exploits that he attributes to his hero (219e–221c), it seems that he regards as most amazing of all (for it is the emotional and structural core of his encomium) Socrates' success in making him feel as he does about Socrates – in captivating and shaming the beautiful

Alcibiades (see especially 216a8–b2). His is the version on a heroic scale of the danger that Apollodorus, hawking memberships to the Socratic fan club, had illustrated in the prologue on the level of farce: Instead of loving wisdom, he falls in love with the wisdom lover[52] – exactly the danger that Diotima attempts to exclude from her ladder of love by banishing individuals from the center of attention when the rung of philosophy has been reached. Socrates, good student of Diotima that he is, had attempted to tap the energy of Alcibiades' love and channel it away from himself and toward philosophy (218d6–b2).[53] But it is a volatile force to tap, and the saga of Alcibiades' disastrous political ambitions waits in the wings of this dialogue to testify to the difficulty of the task (cf. 216b5). (Perhaps also Plato thought the intellectual free-for-all at Athens a special obstacle to such a gradual doling out of wisdom as Diotima proposed; cf. *Rep.* VI 498a–c). And so we are reminded at the last that love is more awkward to praise than Phaedrus had initially made out.[54]

III

The atmosphere of the *Symposium,* until the incursion of Alcibiades (and with exception made for Aristophanes' sound effects), is formal, elegant, rule-bound, and restrained; that of the *Phaedrus* is intimate and improvisatory. Socrates gets away from it all. Alone with Phaedrus in a beautiful pastoral setting outside the city – unusual surroundings for him (*Phdr.* 230c6–e4)[55] – he is inspired by its influence and by Phaedrus's reading of a speech on love by the orator Lysias[56] to improvise a speech on the same topic, and then suddenly to repudiate it and improvise a further speech of recantation. These are speeches of uncharacteristic length, fluency, rhetorical grandeur, and poetic color (cf. 238c5–d3, 241e1–5, 257a1–6, c1–2). (We should not forget, however, that in the *Symposium* Socrates had been portrayed as equally at home with the drunk and the sober; *Smp.* 176c3–5, 220a1–5. It is typical of him to be capable of the untypical.) What the *Symposium* is only after Alcibiades has come on the scene, the *Phaedrus* is throughout. It should not surprise us, then, that love in the *Phaedrus* is presented in its traditional bittersweetness and with vivid emphasis on how the lover feels.[57]

To be bittersweet is to offer material for censure as well as praise.

(Alcibiades had both loved and hated Socrates for the feelings he aroused; *Smp.* 215e–216c.) Lysias's speech and the corresponding first speech of Socrates are critical of love. They marshal against love the traditional poetic complaint, as when Anacreon laments its hammer blow (cf. *Phdr.* 235c). The lover is knocked out of his senses (231d1–3, 241a2–4); how then can the boy he loves expect him to behave other than unreasonably? The lover is possessive (232c3–6, 239a7–b3), indiscreet (231e3–232a4), selfish – caring more for his own satisfaction than for the boy's development (232c–d, 239a, 239e–240a); above all he is fickle, and upon returning to his senses will cast the boy off without a thought (231a–d, 232e, 240e8–241b).[58] This is to see love-madness from the outside, from the viewpoint of the boy, who is not expected to share in its intensity and who can therefore be made to find it alien and off-putting.

After a violent change of heart, however (241e–243e), Socrates in his second and climactic speech finds the good in love-madness (244a6–8). Seeing the world now through the eyes of the lover, whose feelings he analyzes in depth (249d–254e), he derives the soul-shaking quality of the lover's experience from its origins in the vision that crowned Diotima's Greater Mysteries, the vision of the Beautiful itself – considered here not as a state of enlightenment attained only after long struggle, but as a memory of enlightenment stirred by the boy's beauty (254b), a memory that acts as a potential stimulant to that longer quest (256a7–b7). The fresher the memory, the less the lover will think indulgence of his bodily desire for the boy an appropriate response to it (250e–251a). Thus it is not only in his first speech that Socrates faults the sort of lover who allows his sexual hunger to dictate his behavior; so that in retrospect he reconciles the two speeches as containing, respectively, appropriate condemnation of an inferior type of love-madness and appropriate praise for a superior, "divine" type (265e–266a).

This contrast may remind us of nothing so much as Pausanias's sundering of "heavenly" from "vulgar" love in the *Symposium.* Does Socrates in the *Phaedrus,* then, contradict Diotima's teaching that all love is directed, ultimately, toward the good? He does not; but his account is psychologically more complex. Diotima discriminated among us according to the inferior and superior brands of eternal good for which each of our souls yearns; Socrates in the *Phaedrus* divides the soul itself into three parts, and assesses the superiority and inferiority of the individual lover according to the outcome of the power struggle among the yearnings represented by each part. None of these parts – allegorically portrayed as a charioteer with his team of two horses (246a) – is a yearning for the good as such.[59] Rather (and as in the similar tripartition developed in *Republic* IV and VIII–IX), that part of the soul which ought to dominate over the others, the charioteer, seeks wisdom, or truth (hence he alone can behold the realm of true being – the Forms – and feed on pure knowledge, 247c); the well-behaved white horse represents the love of honor and propriety (253d6; cf. the level of aspiration attained in the Lesser Mysteries); and the violent black horse (253e3), corresponding to what in the *Republic* is called, among other things, the "love of advantage" (e.g., at IX 581a7), represents the simple need to have one's way – limited in this context to sexual need. The charioteer and white horse tend naturally to pull in the opposite direction from the black horse, which will weigh them down in their ascent to the Forms (for this is a winged chariot) unless it receives proper training (247b2–5). Yet there is a unity to the parts also, for the entire soul, before its fall to earth, was feathered (251b7), and it is the nature of the feathers to be nourished by truth (248b5–c2).

Put without allegory: It is only at the level of the whole person, not the parts, that all love is directed, by its nature, toward the good. And to say that the whole person is naturally oriented toward the good is, more accurately, to say that, first, the charioteer of his soul is naturally oriented toward wisdom and truth; second, that the charioteer is natural ruler of his soul (although not necessarily the actual ruler of his soul) – as symbolized by his being in the driver's seat; and third (a corollary of the previous point), that it is when the charioteer is in charge that the entire soul is at its best, and the person lives the good life, the philosophic or "wisdom-loving" life (256b2–7). (Compare *Rep.* IX 586d: The other parts will attain their "truest" satisfactions when they follow the wisdom-loving part. This I take to be what Socrates means by describing the feathers of the entire soul as nourished by truth.)

There is, indeed, a simpler sense in which Plato believes that we are all naturally oriented toward the good: namely, that we all look to our ultimate benefit. (This, after all, was Diotima's teaching at *Smp.* 205d10–206a1; cf. *Rep.* VI 505d–e.) But the tripartite analysis – in particular, the fact that the wisdom-loving part is our *natural* ruler – reveals the deeper sense in which those in whom the charioteer lacks authority remain, as persons, lovers of the good, no less than those in whom it dominates. It is not just that they continue to seek what they (mistakenly) think will benefit them. Rather – as Plato argues most fully in the *Republic* – the natural authority of the wisdom-loving part continues to make itself felt, even in defeat, in the wretched emptiness of their lives. They live with the twistedness (though they could not acknowledge it is such) of those who deny their own nature – their nature as lovers of the good.[60]

The tripartite analysis of the soul in the *Phaedrus* also permits a more exact appreciation than in the *Symposium* of how it feels to fall in love, and why this feeling should awaken aspiration to the philosophic life. As in the *Symposium,* lovers are approved of who are not simply attracted to the beauty of their beloved's body but seek also to mold his character (*Phdr.* 250e–251a, 252c–253c); unlike in the *Symposium,* Socrates takes us behind the scene of such a lover's modest and respectful behavior toward his boy (254e8–255a1), and the spectacle he reveals to us within the lover's soul is a struggle of the utmost violence (253d–254e). The charioteer begins by trying to persuade the black horse, which if it had its way would lead the lover to do something "shocking and unlawful" (254b1; i.e., to attack the boy sexually),[61] but ends by dragging it to its haunches and drawing blood with the bit, not once but repeatedly. Let us look more closely at this development from inner persuasion to inner violence, for it is at the heart of what the *Phaedrus* has to say about love. It is crucial that the charioteer loses the struggle when he argues (for he agrees to do the horse's bidding and approaches the boy, 254b3–4), and wins it when he is violent (falling back on the reins in awe as the boy's flashing glance, seen close, recalls him to his primeval vision of Beauty; 254b5–c3). The difference in outcome is explained by a difference in motivation. While the parties in the soul are arguing, no distinction is made between the charioteer and the noble white horse, who share motivation and reaction: anger at the black horse for pushing them toward an unlawful deed (254a7–b3).[62] Yet we know from the earlier narrative of the fall of souls that only the charioteer saw anything of the Forms; neither horse (even in the best souls) managed to break the surface of the heavens to glimpse the place beyond (248a1–5). So it is that, although all three characters in the allegory catch the flashing glance of the boy, only in the charioteer does it spark a vision of the Forms.

What we witness at that moment is the charioteer coming into his own. When arguing, the charioteer's emotional attention had been focused on what we might call internal politics: establishing correct order in the team. But when he comes to recollect Beauty itself, his emotional attention is swept away by the object of this private memory, and he effectively forgets about his team. That is why his violence against them is not (as the attempt to persuade the black horse *is*) a purposeful act of control. Had it been, he might have thought to use main force only on the wayward black horse, not also on the obedient white (254c1–2). Rather, he falls back on the reins because compelled by awe at the sudden vision of the Forms (254b7–c1); his feelings as lover of the Forms leave him no gubernatorial option. In both cases, the charioteer's resistance to the demands of the black horse (at least for as long as that resistance holds up) corresponds to the same outward behavior of the lover: namely, self-control. The difference lies in motivation. The motivation of charioteer and white horse when together is the desire to do what the law enjoins; to remain within the bounds of social propriety. Even when the charioteer parts company with the noble horse, the sense of staying within bounds does not vanish from his thoughts, for he has a vision not of Beauty alone but of Beauty together with Moderation (254b6–7). But it is a different sense. He sees Beauty "on its holy seat" (254b7). The bounds that feature in this vision, then, are the bounds not of law but of the sacred. And the act of attacking the boy is avoided not as something socially forbidden but as something simply unbearable – a violation of all that really matters.[63] Nothing in the soul can resist the charioteer at that moment of realization. But when debating propriety with the black horse, he is untrue to the fullness of his motivation, and so fails to assert himself.

This development explains what might otherwise seem odd: that although the immediate effect of the charioteer's seizure is to prevent an outrage of convention and law, the behavior to which it will lead – as we know from the earlier description of the lover's antics in the social world – will be anything but conventional. The lover, we read, will for his beloved's sake "disdain the conventions and niceties of which he previously made a show" (252a4–5); he will give up family, friends, and wealth in order to be with his love. And this behavior makes good sense when seen as the outcome of the charioteer's shift of focus away from his team. In nonallegorical terms, this would represent someone inclining to act in an otherworldly fashion, as if not tied to a social and timebound existence; ready to throw all else to the winds for the sake of his love.[64] But this is an inclination common to the true lover and the true philosopher – notoriously so. Socrates here puts two clichés into a bottle – the temporary insanity of the infatuated lover, the hopeless impracticality of philosophers[65] – and shakes them into a cocktail of great strength and fizz. Simply put, his point is that love makes philosophers of us all.

But only for a while. It is not as if the lover's memory of the Beautiful itself somehow conveys him without effort to the peak of the initiate's ascent in Diotima's Greater Mysteries. The soul-shaking experience that Socrates describes, although it is not for all (being limited to those who had a full vision of the Forms when discarnate, and so do not rush to consummate their sexual desire but hold back in reverence; 250e–251a) is nevertheless for more than just philosophic types. The "inspired" lover (255b6), despite the fact that the initial vision of his charioteer transcends the motive of social repute, is just as likely to end up leading with his beloved a life that is merely honorable, rather than the philosophic life (256a–e). The inspiration of love opens a potential path but does not ensure that it will be followed; still less does it do the traveling.[66] Nor does Socrates tell us much about the subsequent journey for the philosophic types.[67] We learn that they, like other kinds of inspired lovers, will be encouraged in their own development by their concern to educate the beloved and bring out the character that they sense he shares with them (252e–253c). But it is the honor-loving couple who are described as pledged to one another and as regaining the wings of the soul together, and for the sake of their love (256d–e). The philosophic couple, who never consummate their sexual desire,[68] live a life "together in mind" (*homonoētikon,* 256b1), but a mind set on their remaining always in control of themselves and on regaining their wings for the sake of the good that awaits in the afterlife (the vision of the Forms) rather than for the sake of love (256b). Socrates, then, is not much more concerned in the *Phaedrus* than he was in the *Symposium* to answer our questions about the life of the philosophic couple as it develops.[69] For in the *Symposium,* the development we witnessed was of the philosophic lover alone; while in the *Phaedrus,* the focus is rather on the beginnings of love between philosophers than on its development.

For this reason, also, the place of Beauty in the two dialogues is different. Diotima's initiate comes to see Beauty just in itself; he comes to see, I suggested, that there *is* such a thing as Beauty, independent of what we find beautiful. The experience of the inspired lover in the *Phaedrus,* by contrast, is to shuttle in memory between the bodily beauty of the boy and the Beautiful itself. It is to be awoken by an exemplar of Beauty to the conviction that there is such a thing as Beauty. (The boy, too, comes to have this experience, seeing the lover's face transformed by love, made beautiful by the sight of beauty; 255b7–d3.)[70] This is a conviction available to all romantics, not just to philosophers. Hence Socrates' claim at 250d: The images of Beauty shine brightest of all images of the Forms in our world. And when that image of Beauty is human (contrast Socrates' reaction to the beauty of landscape, 230b2–c5 with disclaimer at d3–5), it is further possible to see in it an image of oneself – as both lover and boy do, in varying degrees of awareness (252d5–253c2, 255d3–d6). What happens next will depend on the kind of self that is seen. Only the philosopher, for whom self-inquiry is paramount (229e–230a), will glimpse in Beauty's image a self that not only reflects the Beautiful but is capable of reflecting upon it.

Bearing these contrasts between the two dialogues in mind, we should refrain from the attempt to situate the inspired lover of the *Phaedrus* at some precise point on the ascent undertaken by Diotima's initiate.[71] Diotima deals with honor lovers and wisdom lovers separately, in the Lesser and Greater Mysteries; Socrates in the *Phaedrus* melds them into the figure of the inspired lover. This is further evidence that Plato is not concerned to propound a comprehensive and unified theory of love – if any were needed in addition to the way in which we have seen love to be treated (that is, exploited) in the two dialogues. In both cases, Plato takes one of love's clichés and turns it to his metaphysical advantage. In the *Symposium,* the cliché is "love promotes virtue." In the *Phaedrus* it is "love is wild." From this source flow the differences between the two dialogues, their limitations, and their achievements.

NOTES

1 We need not fear to translate the Greek *erōs* as "love" (*pace* David Halperin, "Platonic Eros and What Men Call Love," *Ancient Philosophy* 5[1985]: 161–3). Admittedly, *erōs* is equivalent to our "love" only in contexts where sexual desire is appropriate (not, then, between family members; see K. J. Dover, *Greek Homosexuality* [Cambridge, Mass.: 1978], 42–54); but it is not – at least not in all contexts – simply equivalent to "sexual desire." The experiences of *erōs* described in the *Symposium* and *Phaedrus* are manifestly experiences of falling in, and being in, love.

2 Commentaries in English on the Greek text include Robert Gregg Bury, *The Symposium of Plato*, 2d ed. (Cambridge, 1932); and K. J. Dover, *Plato's Symposium* (Cambridge, 1980). Stanley Rosen, *Plato's Symposium*, 2d ed. (New Haven, 1987), is a book-length study of the dialogue in English.

3 Commentaries in English on the Greek text include W. H. Thompson, *The Phaedrus of Plato* (London, 1868); G. J. de Vries, *A Commentary on the Phaedrus of Plato* (Amsterdam, 1969); and C. J. Rowe, *Plato: Phaedrus* (Warminster, 1986) (includes translation). R. Hackforth, *Plato's Phaedrus* (Cambridge, 1952), is a translation with running commentary. Book-length studies of the dialogue in English include Ronna Burger, *Plato's Phaedrus: A Defense of a Philosophic Art of Writing* (University, Ala., 1980); Charles L. Griswold, Jr., *Self-Knowledge in Plato's Phaedrus* (New Haven, 1986); and G. R. F. Ferrari, *Listening to the Cicadas: A Study of Plato's Phaedrus* (Cambridge, 1987).

4 On this dialogue, see, e.g., David K. Glidden, "The *Lysis* on Loving One's Own," *Classical Quarterly* 31 (1981): 39–59; David B. Robinson, "Plato's *Lysis:* The Structural Problem," *Illinois Classical Studies* 11 (1986): 63–83; Anthony W. Price, *Love and Friendship in Plato and Aristotle* (Oxford, 1989), chap. 1; and, for a different approach, David Bolotin, *Plato's Dialogue on Friendship* (Ithaca, N.Y., 1979).

5 This is brought to our attention in the immediate context, at 177e: Aristophanes' plays are "all about Dionysus and Aphrodite" (that is, drinking and sex). The prosaic Greek for "sex" is not *Aphroditē* but *ta aphrodisia*, "the things of Aphrodite."

6 Cf. François Lasserre, *La figure d'Eros dans la poésie grecque* (Lausanne, 1946), 10–11.

7 Cf. Thomas Gould, *Platonic Love* (New York, 1963), 24; G. X. Santas, *Plato and Freud: Two Theories of Love* (Oxford, 1988), 16.

8 Fragment 130 in Edger Lobel and Denys Page, eds., *Poetarum Lesbiorum fragmenta* (Oxford, 1955). See, in general, Bruno Snell, *The Discovery of*

the Mind in Greek Philosophy and Literature (New York, 1982), 52–60; Lasserre, *La figure d'Eros;* and Anne Carson, *Eros the Bittersweet* (Princeton, 1986), esp. 3–9.

9 Agathon (at 196c4–7) mentions the common agreement that "no pleasure is stronger than Eros" only in order to prove that, since Eros is stronger than any pleasure, he must be self-controlled in the extreme!

10 For a sense of their variety consult Bury, *Symposium*, lii–iv.

11 See section III of this chapter.

12 For a compilation of suggestions, see Bury, *Symposium*, xxii–xxiii; Rosen, *Symposium*, 90–1. Note in this connection Aristophanes' quip at 189a.

13 Cf. Meyer W. Isenberg, *The Order of the Discourses in Plato's Symposium* (Chicago, 1940), 60; and Diskin Clay, "The Tragic and Comic Poet of the *Symposium*," in *Essays in Ancient Greek Philosophy*, ed. John P. Anton and Anthony Preus (Albany, 1983), 2: 188–9. To object (as do, e.g., G. K. Plochmann, "Hiccups and Hangovers in the *Symposium*," *Bucknell Review* 11 [1963]: 10; and W. K. C. Guthrie, *A History of Greek Phiposophy*, vol. 4 [Cambridge, 1975], 382) that had Plato attached significance to this order he could have so arranged the seating plan from the start, is to miss the point. It is because Plato attaches significance to this order that he has caused it to arrange and flag itself before our eyes.

14 "Is directed toward" rather than simply "is." It is not as if Diotima's doctrine would commit Plato to the belief that, say, the kind of "love" (*erōs*) manifested by the tyrant in *Republic* IX – namely, unrestrained lust – renders him praiseworthy. Diotima engages in depth psychology. The majority of lovers stand revealed by her as yearning for something more ultimate than the apparent object of their desire. Their apparent behavior can therefore be condemned, even while the object of their ultimate yearning is praised. (The depth psychology to which Plato actually appeals in his account of the tyrant's love, however, depends on a more elaborate theoretical framework than Diotima provides – that of the tripartite soul. This I shall discuss when we come to the *Phaedrus*, in section III.)

15 Phaedrus also briefly praises Eros, the god, for being among the oldest of divinities (178b). Here he scrambles to justify the implication of his initial complaint, that Eros's godhead is significant apart from his status as abstract force – a claim that the transparently allegorical quotes from Hesiod and Parmenides do little to support.

16 See in general Dover, *Greek Homosexuality*, esp. 202; Michel Foucault, *L'usage des plaisirs* (Paris, 1984); David Halperin, *One Hundred Years of Homosexuality* (New York, 1990); David Cohen, "Law, Society, and Homosexuality in Classical Athens," *Past and Present* 117 (1987): 3–21.

17 See 177d8–e1, 193b6–7; and for Agathon's beauty, 174a9, 212e8, *Prt.* 315d–e, and Aristophanes, *Thesmophoriazusae,* 191–2.

18 We know almost nothing about the classical Athenian attitude toward Lesbianism, beyond what we might infer from the fact that this is our only reference to it in the period, and from the treatment of women in general.

19 Dover, *Symposium, ad* 192a1.

20 Agathon plays with its range, distinguishing Eros's beauty from his virtue at 196b4–5, but dubbing *kallos* the undifferentiated object of such varied arts as poetry, medicine, and archery (197a6–b5). I will return to the relation between the beautiful (*kalon*) and the good (*agathon*) in Plato when considering the climax of Diotima's speech.

21 Michael C. Stokes, *Plato's Socratic Conversations* (Baltimore, 1986), 114–82, gives a detailed account of anticipations of Diotima in Agathon's speech.

22 For analysis of its logic, see R. E. Allen, "A Note on the Elenchus of Agathon: *Symposium* 199c–201c," *Monist* 50 (1966): 460–3; Martha C. Nussbaum, *The Fragility of Goodness: Luck and Ethics in Greek Tragedy and Philosophy* (Cambridge, 1986), 177–9; and Price, *Love and Friendship,* 18–20. They are perhaps taking the argument too seriously, given its shameless use of a trick against Agathon, namely, attributing the characteristic of lovers to a personified Love; this is a trick that governed Agathon's speech, but he plainly did not employ it in earnest. Cf. Michael J. O'Brien, " 'Becoming Immortal' in Plato's *Symposium,"* in *Greek Poetry and Philosophy,* ed. D. E. Gerber (Chico, Cal., 1984), 192 n. 23. (Price, however, denies that Socrates' use of this device is trickery.)

23 Cf. Isenberg, *Order of the Discourses,* 38, 59; R. A. Markus, "The Dialectic of Eros in Plato's *Symposium,"* in *Plato,* vol. 2, ed. Gregory Vlastos (Garden City, N.Y., 1971), 133.

24 Cf. note 14.

25 This we have seen to be the primary domain of these words. Like the English "love," however, the Greek terms can also be used with an inanimate object.

26 For discussion see Santas, *Plato and Freud,* 32–9.

27 This would be a truism, for the word translated as "happy" (*eudaimon*) commonly denotes an objective rather than subjective state of the person (see K. J. Dover, *Greek Popular Morality in the Time of Plato and Aristotle* [Oxford, 1974], 174).

28 Here I follow Bury, *Symposium, ad* 206b; Santas, *Plato and Freud,* 34.

29 For critical discussion of this inference see Santas, *Plato and Freud,* 35–6. The broader question, what relation Diotima's appeal to immortality bears to the treatment of immortality in other dialogues, is extremely

vexed. Those interested in pursuing it should begin with O'Brien, " 'Becoming Immortal.' "

30 Markus, "Dialectic of Eros," 138–40, compares this new emphasis on procreation to the abundant generosity of God in Christian theology. Yet Diotima introduces it as a mark of mortality (*hōs thnētōi*, 206e8). A. H. Armstrong, in "Platonic Eros and Christian Agape," *Downside Review* 79 (1961): 105–21, and "Platonic Love: A Reply to Professor Verdenius," *Downside Review* 82 (1964): 199–203, adopts toward the *Phaedrus* an approach similar to Markus's toward the *Symposium.*

31 For her use of the language of the Eleusinian Mysteries here, see Bury, *Symposium, ad* 210a; see also Thomas A. Szlezák, *Platon und die Schriftlichkeit der Philosophie* (Berlin, 1985), 259 n. 25. The ritual at Eleusis – the Greater Mysteries – was preceded, several months earlier, by a required ritual of preparation at Agrai – the Lesser Mysteries.

32 Cf. *Rep.* X 595b9–c3, *Phdr.* 278b7–e2.

33 Cf. Francis M. Cornford, *Principium Sapientiae* (Cambridge, 1952), 85. O'Brien (" 'Becoming immortal,' " 188–9) usefully compares other Platonic examples of the contrast between political and philosophical virtue. The choice of activities to exemplify types of generic love at 205d – money-making, love of sports, philosophy – seems parallel to the tripartite hierarchy of the ideal city in the *Republic,* with its productive class, its athletic soldier-guardians, and its philosopher-kings.

34 Here I follow Leon Robin, *Platon: Le Banquet,* in *Platon: Oeuvres complètes,* vol. 4, part 2 (Paris, 1966), xciii; and Price, *Love and Friendship,* 41.

35 *Pace* Terence Irwin, *Plato's Moral Theory* (Oxford, 1977), 167, who treats the philosophic initiate as equivalent to those fertile in soul in the Lesser Mysteries.

36 In view of 212a3–4 and *Ti.* 29b4–5, the underlying thought here may be that the beauty of the words *follows* from the beauty of the topic.

37 Cf. *Rep.* III 402c–e, where Glaucon – elsewhere in the work noted as an aficionado of the beautiful in body (474d–475a; cf. 468b) and a man of some culture (548d–e) – assents enthusiastically to the proposal that beautiful traits of character combined with outward beauty make the finest spectacle of all, and insists moreover that outer deficiency, unlike inner, does not disqualify a boy in the eyes of the cultured person (the *mousikos,* 402d8).

38 Cf. *Rep.* 538c and note 37.

39 The parallel between the two stages is marked in the Greek at 210c3 by the particle *au,* "correspondingly."

40 My English here reflects a correspondence between the vocabulary of the Greek text at 210b6 and at 210c5–6.

41 Cf. Price, *Love and Friendship,* 40.

42 The matter is controversial. For discussion see Gregory Vlastos, "The Individual as an Object of Love in Plato," in *Platonic Studies,* 2d ed. (Princeton, 1981), 33–5; Julius M. E. Moravcsik, "Reason and Eros in the 'Ascent'-passage of the *Symposium,*" in *Essays in Ancient Greek Philosophy,* ed. John P. Anton and G. L. Kustas (Albany, 1972), 1: 293; Irwin, *Plato's Moral Theory,* 169, 323 n. 58; Santas, *Plato and Freud,* 42; Price, *Love and Friendship,* 47–9.

43 Harry Neumann, "Diotima's Concept of Love," *American Journal of Philology* 86 (1965): 44. Diotima substitutes in this role verbs of seeing and contemplation (*passim*), recognizing (211c8), touching (212a4–5), and "being with" (211d8–212a2) (the last a sexual pun).

44 The text at 210c7 seems to say that the initiate is "led" to this new stage; but because of an awkwardness in the construction, some translate the term differently (e.g., Alexander Nehamas and Paul Woodruff, *Plato: Symposium* [Indianapolis, 1989], ad loc.), while some others emend. The transmitted text and the translation above is defended by Dover, *Symposium,* 155.

45 Bury, *Symposium, ad* 210d.

46 For an account of the Forms that emphasizes their status as individuals, see Richard D. Mohr, "Forms as Individuals: Unity, Being and Cognition in Plato's Ideal Theory," *Illinois Classical Studies* 11 (1986): 113–28.

47 Cf. Bury, *Symposium,* xlvi; and *pace* R. Hackforth, "Immortality in Plato's *Symposium,*" *Classical Review* 64 (1950): 44; Neumann, "Diotima's Concept," 42–3.

48 This is not to claim that its stages directly correspond to those of the ascent to the Good in Book VII of the *Republic.*

49 See further Leon Robin, *Théorie platonicienne de l'amour* (Paris, 1908), 220–4; Santas, *Plato and Freud,* 41; Price, *Love and Friendship,* 16; F. C. White, "Love and Beauty in Plato's *Symposium,*" *Journal of Hellenic Studies* 109 (1989): 149–57.

50 On Aristophanes cf. Isenberg, *Order of the Discourses,* 53.

51 *Pace,* Ulrich von Wilamowitz-Muellendorff, *Platon,* 2d ed. (Berlin, 1920), 169–76; Neumann, "Diotima's Concept," who argue that Plato wishes us to see Diotima as a suspect, sophistic figure. For an account that includes a full survey of scholarship on the figure of Diotima, see David Halperin, "Why Is Diotima a Woman?" in *One Hundred Years.*

52 Cf. Apollodorus's behavior in the *Phaedo* (117d). That the prologue emphasizes the telling and retelling of the long-ago conversation at Agathon's house – its being kept current – stands as a further illustration of this danger.

53 Cf. Bury, *Symposium,* lx–lxii; Szlezák, *Schriftlichkeit,* 262–70.

54 Some scholars understand Alcibiades' speech not just as a supplement to what has gone before but as a critique or subversion of it; see, e.g., H. G. Wolz, "Philosophy as Drama: An Approach to Plato's *Symposium*," *Philosophy and Phenomenological Research* 30 (1969–70): esp. 349–53; John P. Anton, "The Secret of Plato's *Symposium*," *Diotima* 2 (1974): 27–47; Michael Gagarin, "Socrates' Hybris and Alcibiades' Failure," *Phoenix* 31 (1977): 22–37; Nussbaum, *Fragility of Goodness*, 165–99; and the Lacanian analysis of John Brenkman, "The Other and the One: Psychoanalysis, Reading, the Symposium," in *Literature and Psychoanalysis*, ed. Shoshana Felman (Baltimore, 1982), 396–456, esp. 402, 430–2, 452. (For a literarily aware reading of Alcibiades' intervention that takes the more traditional stance, see Helen Bacon, "Socrates Crowned," *Virginia Quarterly Review* 35 [1959]: 415–30.) Nussbaum is especially impressed (as most readers have been to some extent) by the emphatic eccentricity of the figure of Socrates in this dialogue. But this impression needs to be tempered by taking into account the character and relation to Socrates of those who transmit the stories about him: Apollodorus, Aristodemus, Alcibiades.

55 For analysis of the setting consult, e.g. (in addition to the studies mentioned in note 3), Anne Lebeck, "The Central Myth of Plato's *Phaedrus*," *Greek, Roman and Byzantine Studies* 13 (1972): 280–3; A. Philip, Récurrences thématiques et topologie dans le *Phèdre* de Platon," *Revue de Metaphysique et de Morale* 86 (1981): 452–76; Kenneth Dorter, "Imagery and Philosophy in Plato's *Phaedrus*," *Journal of the History of Philosophy* 9 (1971):280–1.

56 Whether this is authentically by Lysias or a Platonic parody is disputed. See K. J. Dover, *Lysias and the Corpus Lysiacum* (Berkeley, 1968), 69–71.

57 It will become apparent that I read the *Phaedrus* rather as turning a different facet of love to the light of philosophy than as intended to provide a needed supplement to the *Symposium*, and still less to remedy a defect in it of which Plato had previously been unaware (*pace* Santas, *Plato and Freud*, 64; Price, *Love and Friendship*, 55, 85). This is not to deny that the *Phaedrus* may cast brighter illumination on certain points than the *Symposium* (as is provided, e.g., by its tripartite analysis of the soul, discussed below). But the claim could equally be justified vice versa. Since I deny that Plato is out to provide a comprehensive theory of love, I do not see the *Phaedrus* as written to fill the gaps.

58 Here I treat the two speeches as equivalent; more detailed analysis would reveal a development between them – see the studies cited in note 3.

59 Some scholars, however, argue that the wisdom-loving part of the soul is in itself the rational desire for what is good (Charles H. Kahn, "Plato's

Theory of Desire," *Review of Metaphysics* 41 [1987]: 80), or consists of rational desires for the overall good (Irwin, *Plato's Moral Theory,* 195).

60 Cf. note 14.

61 Dover, *Greek Homosexuality,* 44.

62 This point is reinforced in the Greek text by its use of the dual number to describe their reactions.

63 Cf. Price, *Love and Friendship,* 81.

64 I am indebted to Myles Burnyeat, "The Passion of Reason in Plato's *Phaedrus*" (unpublished manuscript), for the connection of thought here.

65 For the former, see, e.g., in the poets, Carson, *Eros the Bittersweet,* 7–8; elsewhere in Plato, *Smp.* 183a–b, *Rep.* I 329d1. For the latter, see *Phdr.* 269e3–270a8 (with Diogenes Laertius, II.6), *Rep.* 516e–517a, *Tht.* 173c–176a.

66 *Pace* Thompson, *Phaedrus,* ad 249e; and Griswold, *Self-Knowledge,* 124, who take Socrates to restrict inspired love to philosophic types. Hackforth vacillates (*Phaedrus,* 101). In Ferrari, *Listening to the Cicadas,* chap. 6, I myself confused the issue by using the term "philosophic lover" rather than "inspired lover."

67 Here I disagree with those scholars who believe that Socrates gives a further snapshot of their life together in his later description of the relationship between the dialectician and his pupil (e.g., Hackforth, *Phaedrus,* 164; Griswold, *Self-Knowledge,* 130; and cf. Elizabeth Asmis, "*Psychagogia* in Plato's *Phaedrus,*" *Illinois Classical Studies* 11 [1986]: 164). See Ferrari, *Listening to the Cicadas,* 230, and note 71 below.

68 Is their experience therefore comparable to a Freudian "sublimation" of sexual energy? Francis M. Cornford, "The Doctrine of Eros in Plato's Symposium," in *Plato,* ed. Gregory Vlastos (Garden City, N.Y.: 1971), 2:128–9, points out an important contrast: Whereas sublimation in Freud is the diversion of instincts originally sexual to a new, nonsexual aim, in Plato "the self-moving energy of the human soul resides properly in the highest part," so that "sublimation" in this case would be not simply a diversion of energy but a return of it to its source. See also Santas, *Plato and Freud,* 169–72; Anthony W. Price, "Plato and Freud," in *The Person and the Human Mind: Issues in Ancient and Modern Philosopy,* ed. Christopher Hill (Oxford, 1990), 244–52.

69 Vlastos's "Individual as Object" sparked considerable response on this topic, however. See, e.g., L. A. Kosman, "Platonic Love," in *Facets of Plato's Philosophy,* ed. W. H. Werkmeister (Assen, 1976), 53–64; Nussbaum, *Fragility of Goodness,* 166–7; Ferrari, *Listening to the Cicadas,* 182–4; Price, *Love and Friendship,* 10–12, 97–102. (For further bibliography see Halperin, "Platonic Eros," n. 13.)

70 On the mutuality of this love, see David Halperin, "Plato and Erotic Reciprocity," *Classical Antiquity* 5 (1986): 60–80.

71 I suggest, however (and here I supplement and modify my account of these matters in Ferrari, *Listening to the Cicadas,* chaps. 1 and 7), that the displacement of attention that we found to drive that ascent does indeed correspond to something in the *Phaedrus* – but to its overall structure as a dialogue, rather than to what Socrates says specifically about love. In effect, the action of the *Phaedrus* offers us an image of that mechanism of displacement (although not an exemplification, for Socrates and Phaedrus only play at being in love, e.g., 234d, 243e). An interest in Lysias's speech (an exercise in style) is overtaken in Socrates' second speech by an interest in its beautiful topic, love (257a3–4), via his intermediary first speech, in which he gives birth in the beautiful (the lovely location, 230b, 238d, and Lysias's speech as reflected in Phaedrus's shining face, 234d, 237a9) to a speech primarily intended as "seduction" of Phaedrus (237a10–b1). Having shifted his focus from speech prompted by beauty to the beauty of which it speaks, in the second part of the dialogue Socrates further displaces attention to the beauty in the speaking (258d), with his examination of the art of rhetoric. Compare the ascent, in the Greater Mysteries, from the level of moral practices and speeches aimed at individuals to that of types of knowledge, considered abstractly. (So here we move from a morally edifying speech, still ostensibly addressed, like the predecessor, to a beautiful boy – see 256e3–257a2 – to an inquiry into a branch of knowledge, the knowledge of speaking, conducted through the question-and-answer appropriate to philosophy.) And it will turn out that the engine of development for a true rhetorician is the same as that of the philosophic lover in the *Symposium:* namely, his being more concerned about his topic than about its seductive use (273e8–274a2, 278a5–b2). Perhaps, then, the ancient proposal was right: The *Phaedrus* is about "the beautiful in its manifold forms" (Iamblichus, cited and developed by Hermias, *Hermiae Alexandrini in Platonis Phaedrum Scholia,* ed. Paul Couvreur, [Hildesheim, 1971] 8–11). But the issue is highly controversial. In addition to the studies mentioned in note 3, consult, e.g., C. J. Rowe, "The Argument and Structure of Plato's *Phaedrus," Proceedings of the Cambridge Philological Society* 212 (1986): 106–25; Malcolm Heath, "The Unity of Plato's *Phaedrus," Oxford Studies in Ancient Philosophy* 7(1989): 151–74; and Asmis, *"Psychagogia."*

NICHOLAS P. WHITE

9 Plato's metaphysical epistemology

I

For some time philosophers have thought of epistemology and metaphysics as different branches of philosophy, investigating, respectively, what can be known and the basic properties and nature of what there is. It is hard, though, to see any genuine boundary here. The issues irresistibly overlap. Certainly in Plato there is no such divide. His views about what there is are largely controlled by ideas about how knowledge can be accounted for, and his thinking about what knowledge is takes its character from convictions about what there is that is knowable. As a result his doctrines have a different shape from characteristically modern ones.

Some earlier Platonic writings do have a somewhat modern look. Socrates was notorious for having questioned whether he knew much of anything, and for making people hesitant about their opinions (*Meno* 80c, 86b–c). Plato exploits this side of Socratic thought. The namesake of the *Euthyphro* judges that an action of his is pious. Socrates wonders whether Euthyphro ought to be confident about that judgment, and tries to make him less so. Elsewhere Socrates raises questions concerning his own judgments about which things are beautiful (*H. Ma.* 286c). Such questions seem to suggest a general policy of doubting, reminiscent to us of Descartes or of the various programs of ancient skepticism. In Socrates' efforts to overcome ignorance (*Meno* 86b–c) we might see a project of justifying beliefs like that of typical contemporary epistemologists.

Plato's thinking, though, moves in a different direction, and starts

I am greatly indebted to Richard Kraut for extremely helpful comments on an earlier draft of this paper.

from a different place, too. Questions concerning Euthyphro's judgments about what is pious and Socrates' judgments about what is beautiful arise from a very specific source, different from the sources of skepticism in its ancient and modern forms. It is emphasized that Euthyphro's judgment – that it is pious for him to prosecute his father for murder – is shocking to most people. But Plato does not infer simply that Euthyphro's capacities to judge such matters are fallible. He focuses on a particular question: whether Euthyphro knows *what piety is.* The unspoken suggestion is that the dispute between Euthyphro and his critics is due simply to a disagreement on that question, and that an incapacity correctly to resolve the disagreement must be due to a failure to answer the question rightly. At any rate Plato immediately turns to trying to solve the problem by giving a definition of piety.

A modern epistemologist would be concerned with the basis of our concept of piety, but he would also be worried about other sources of uncertainty and disagreement over which actions are pious. If he thought that piety was an objective property, as Plato evidently does (*Euphr.* 10d–11b), he might well think that even if we were all sure of what it was, we might still, through deficiencies in our powers of cognition, make mistakes and disagree about which things possess it. When Descartes doubted whether he was sitting by the fire, he did not focus on the question whether he understood what a fire was or what it was to sit by one.

Thus, although Plato raises questions that are similar to the ones that we now ask about the justification of beliefs, his questions cause him to search for definitions, not to combat any sort of general skepticism. The initial problem is whether or not something is *F*, but the question quickly becomes What is *F*-ness?

Questions of the form, What is *F*-ness? are precipitated by other issues besides those about which things are *F*. Notably there are causal or quasi-causal judgments about how a thing comes to be *F*. In the *Protagoras* and the *Meno,* it is how one comes to be virtuous, and in the *Laches* (189e–190c), how one becomes courageous. There are also judgments about what results from being *F*. In *Republic* I, it is whether being just is beneficial. Plato insists that to make these judgments we have to know what *F*-ness is (*Prt.* 360e–361c; *Meno* 71b, 100b–c; *La.* 189e–190c; *Rep.* 354a–b). So although his search for definitions (*logoi*) is stimulated partly by questions similar to modern epistemological ones, these other quasi-causal issues are at least as important in precipitating it.

Once the search for definitions has begun, problems about the entities that they deal with and our judgments involving them dominate Plato's thinking on metaphysics and epistemology together. The search for definitions itself becomes less important in his middle works than it was earlier. In the *Phaedo* it is hardly present, and indeed he perhaps announces there that it no longer occupies the same place in his method.[1] At the end of *Republic* I he says that in order to tell whether it is beneficial to its possessor we must know what justice is (354a–b). Subsequently he gives an account of justice in the city (433a–d) and in the soul (441d–442b), and uses these accounts to show that justice is indeed beneficial (see esp. 580b–c). On the other hand he refrains from stating a fully general definition of justice, and explicitly holds that the account of justice in an action is distinct from, though related to, the account of justice in a soul or city (443e–444a). Moreover his way of arriving at his description of psychic and civic justice is different from his procedure in the earlier dialogues, which was to present proposed definitions and to test them against counterexamples and other objections.

The story of Plato's metaphysics and epistemology in his middle works is thus no longer the story of his views about definitions. This is not to say that he had stopped believing in the possibility or desirability of establishing them. The *Republic* says that the philosopher and dialectician is the person who can produce the *logos* of the being of each thing (*ton logon hekastou . . . tēs ousias*, 534b). On the other hand the proposing and testing of definitions plainly does not have the same pivotal role in his method that it had before.

A central part, however, is played by his view that certain entities exist that have come standardly to be called Forms, *eidē* (and are also called Ideas, *ideai*, though they are not mental entities, contrary to the suggestion of the English word "idea"). These entities figure prominently in the *Phaedo, Symposium*, and *Republic*, which are the works I shall mainly treat here along with the *Hippias Major* and the *Timaeus* (I believe that these also defend essentially the same position).[2] I would maintain, in fact, that fundamentally the same views are defended in Plato's other works after the *Republic*, notably the *Theaetetus, Sophist, Parmenides*, and *Philebus*, though in them he does propose clarifications and some adjustments of his basic position. I do not believe that he gave to his views anything approaching a major overhaul.

The Forms are central to Plato's metaphysics and epistemology. So is the distinction between them and the objects of perception in the natural world around us. The contrast between these two sorts of entities is involved in his main theses about what there is and what can be known. Since this contrast is drawn in terms of both the metaphysical and the epistemological status of each kind of entity, his views about Forms and perceptible things fall simultaneously under both metaphysics and epistemology.

II

A good way to organize one's thinking about Plato's views is to begin from his only really explicit argument for the distinctness of Forms from perceptible objects, *Phaedo* 74b–c.[3] This argument contains two premises, one about equality and the other about perceptible things such as sticks and stones. Each premise formulates a crucial fact, as Plato sees matters, about Forms and perceptibles, respectively. By following out the lines of thought suggested by the two premises, we can gain a synoptic view of his ideas about Forms, perceptibles, and the differences between them.

The first premise concerns perceptible objects:

> (A) Equal sticks and stones sometimes, being the same, appear equal to one person and not to another.

As I understand him, Plato is alluding here to familiar facts about perceptual perspective, in particular the fact that a pair of equal objects will look equal to a person seeing them from one standpoint and unequal to someone looking at them from somewhere else.

The other premise concerns equality as we ordinarily think of it. This, Plato argues, turns out to be a Form distinct from perceptible objects:

> (B) The equals themselves (*auta ta isa*) have never appeared to you unequal, nor equality (*isotēs*) inequality.

Plato takes (A) and (B) together to show that equality is distinct from any perceptible equal things. If equality were simply perceptible things that are equal, he assumes, then to think of equality could only be to perceive them.[4] But by (A), perceptible equals can appear unequal. Now if equality were simply perceptible equals, then inequality would likewise be perceptible unequals. In that case equality would sometimes appear just as inequality does, since any equal perceptible objects must appear unequal in some circumstances. But by (B), equality never appears in such a way.

As we consider this argument a couple of points should be kept firmly in mind. The first is that the argument is expressly directed at someone who does not yet agree that equality is distinct from perceptibles, but who thinks instead that in some sense equality is, or "is nothing but," perceptible equal things.[5] Such a person is willing to assume, however, that equality does exist or "is something" (*Phd.* 64c, 65d), and that the word "equality" is the "name" of it (102a–b, c). A more hardbitten opponent, of course, would have said that there is no such thing as equality at all, but only perceptible equal things, and that the word "equality" itself does not designate anything whatsoever. Plato's actual opponent is milder than this. He allows Plato the word "equality" as a designation (in a broad sense) for something, and disputes with him only over whether "equality" designates some perceptible thing or things, or something distinct from them.

The second point to bear in mind is that because Plato's opponent starts out disbelieving that equality is a nonperceptible thing, his initial acceptance of (B) is supposed to reflect a naive judgment involving the term "equality" as ordinarily used, not a use of the term laden with elements of Plato's own metaphysical doctrine. The same is true of the other term that Plato uses here for this entity, "the equals themselves." Although Plato's use of "equality" and "the equals themselves" as interchangeable shows something about his doctrine, as we shall see (sections VII and XI), the argument is not intended by itself to commit the person accepting it to a sophisticated philosophical theory, but only to a relatively naive statement about equality, namely, that it is not any perceptible thing.

Consider premise (A), the easier one to understand and accept. Perceptible objects, Plato thinks, are invariably capable of presenting contrary appearances (cf. sections III and VI). They are necessarily embedded in a world that allows them to be perceived from different perspectives. Differences among these perspectives inevitably bring it about that a perceptible object can appear both one way and the contrary way, in some cases simultaneously (*Rep.* 523b–c, 524d–525a). Plato does not commit himself here to saying that this point holds for all predicates, but he does not exempt any predicates either.[6]

Premise (B) seems far more problematical. Plato takes it that when a person thinks of equality, it cannot appear to him that he is thinking of inequality. Plato believes, moreover, that this is a feature of the thing, equality, itself: that it is, when thought about, incapable of presenting a certain sort of appearance, the appearance of inequality.

The objection arises, however, that how such an object appears is not a feature of the object but of the way in which it is thought about, notably of the terms by which it is designated and brought, so to speak, into one's thinking. If equality can be referred to as "Plato's second-least favorite political concept," and if someone can use that phrase in the mistaken belief that Plato's second-least favorite political concept is inequality, then, it might be argued, such a person would be using the phrase to think about what is in fact equality while nevertheless taking it to be inequality. If what such an object "appears" to be is a function of the way in which it is thought of, and if such objects can be freely thought of by means of designations that reflect false identifications, like the one just given, then no object can be unmistakable in the way that Plato here claims that equality is.

We must accordingly suppose that for Plato not just any way of referring to a thing counts as relevant to (B). The case constructed in the previous paragraph would not count as equality's "appearing" to be inequality. Perhaps this is because in such a case equality is not felt to "appear" (*phainesthai*) at all to the person who is thinking about it. At any rate when equality does genuinely "appear" to a person, Plato thinks, it is incapable of presenting the appearance of inequality.

There is a reason why Plato was not deterred by the objection that how equality appears is dependent on the way in which it is brought into one's thinking. The reason is that the same does not seem to hold for perceptible objects. This fact, he thought, shows that perceptibles are by their nature deceptive in a way in which entities like equality are not.[7] Even when perceptible equal things are believed to be equal, and are introduced into one's judgment as, say, "those equal sticks over there," the tendency of the sticks to appear unequal from oblique perspectives is generally undiminished (see *Rep.* 602e–603a, where the same point is conveyed by a different example). In some cases, to be sure, the belief that they are equal will make a person adjust his thinking instantaneously to the oblique perspective and so regard them as equal, just as one takes a circular tabletop seen from an oblique angle to be in one sense circular-looking. On the other hand a person can easily ignore this adjustment, and realize that in another sense the sticks from many viewpoints do look unequal and the tabletop does look elliptical. Nothing like this, it would be argued, is true of equality or circularity. If one introduces an item into one's thought as equality, it seems impossible to think of any way in which it then appears as inequality.

Plato's opponent will be unimpressed. He will argue that something other than equality can still be introduced into one's thinking through a mistaken belief that it is inequality, so that in this way equality will be intrinsically no less potentially "deceptive" than perceptible equals are. And he will say that what makes it impossible to take something introduced into one's thoughts "as equality" to be inequality is not the nature of the object itself, but a feature of the term by which it has been introduced. I shall not try here to determine whether this reply leaves Plato any ground for maintaining that there is a difference between perceptible things and the entities putatively referred to by terms like "equality." I have said enough to show how his argument is motivated.

III

Taken in isolation, the argument at *Phaedo* 74b–c seems to deal with an epistemological matter, the difference between the kinds of appearances that can be presented by perceptibles and the things that Plato calls Forms. We saw the argument immediately lead, however, to a metaphysical claim about the natures of entities like equality, namely, that unlike perceptible things they are incapable of presenting certain sorts of appearances. Beyond this, however, there arises another metaphysical issue.

Immediately after this argument Plato says that perceptible equals are only "deficiently" equal, and in general that perceptible *F*'s are only "deficiently" *F* (*Phd.* 74d–75b). Some interpreters have taken this to mean that no sensible equals are exactly equal but are only approximately so. Plato never argues for such a contention, however, and it conflicts with much else of what he says.[8] We can make better sense of this claim of deficiency by taking it to follow directly from what he says in this argument itself. Perceptible equals are only deficiently equal precisely in that they inevitably present the appearance of being unequal.

This idea may seem like a crude conflation of epistemological and metaphysical theses. Why should something be the less *F* for appearing sometimes non-*F*?[9] But there is incontrovertible evidence that Plato espouses a view that he formulates in this way. When we see what he is up to, it will be clear that what seems like confusion is actually the result of a quite different notion of reality and objectivity from the one that we expect and are used to (cf. sections VI and VIII).

Republic 475c–480a is the only other passage in which Plato comes close to giving an explicit argument for saying that Forms are distinct from perceptibles. At 479a–c he maintains that every perceptible thing that appears beautiful appears ugly also, and analogously for "just," "double," "large," and "heavy."[10] As soon as he says this, however, he immediately infers that perceptibles "no more are than they are not what one calls them" (b9–10). That is, a perceptible thing no more is *F* than it is not *F*. This is a repetition of the contention in the *Phaedo* that perceptibles are only "deficiently" equal and the like.

Extending this line of thought, Plato goes on to say that since perceptible things no more "are than they are not," in that sense they are "between being and not-being" (479c7). On this basis he argues that perceptibles are not what "knowledge" (*epistēmē*) is concerned with; rather they are what "opinion" or "belief" (*doxa*) is about. Knowledge has to do with "being" or "what is," namely, Forms, which are implied to be distinct from perceptibles on the same ground as in *Phaedo* 74b–c, that is, by not presenting contrary appearances.[11]

There will be more to say about knowledge and belief later (section X). These passages show, however, that Plato interweaves a certain sort of epistemological consideration with what seems to us like a quite distinct ontological issue. By virtue of presenting contrary appearances, perceptible objects are said to possess properties "deficiently" and to be between being and not-being, and it is inferred that they are therefore the province of opinion rather than knowledge. From a modern point of view, it looks as though facts about what we can know and facts about the natures of certain sorts of objects are being curiously intermingled.

IV

To try to understand this state of affairs, it will be helpful to turn to a confusion that is often attributed to Plato, a confusion over relational notions. The grounds for this attribution can be illustrated from *Republic* 479a–b and 523e–524a. There Plato speaks of large and small, heavy and light, and hard and soft as "contraries," and says that it is characteristic of perceptibles to present contrary appearances, sometimes simultaneously (523b–c, 524d–525a). The objection is nowadays made that in fact these terms are not contrary but covertly relational, amounting respectively to "larger than," "smaller than," and so forth, and that if Plato had recognized this fact he would have realized that there is no contrariety involved, because being larger than one thing is not contrary to being smaller than another. Commentators have even carried the attribution of confusion to the point of supposing that at *Phaedo* 74b–c, Plato endorses the intelligibility of the idea of something's being equal but not equal to anything.[12]

That Plato was so fully confused about relations is made extremely unlikely by the fact that he plainly says that terms like "father," "brother," "master," "slave," and "knows" differ from others by being related to (*pros*) others (*Smp.* 199d–200a, *Prm.* 133e–134a). Moreover, there is an explanation available for the passages in the *Republic* that obviates the need to suppose any such confusion.

In the first place, as a philosophical matter it is a mistake to think that there is any easy way of paraphrasing ordinary uses of "large" or "heavy" or "hard" in relational terms. A number of recent discussions have shown that this is so even if we combine these words with sortal terms, as is often recommended, into phrases like "large flea" and "small elephant."[13] For example, the thought that "large flea" might be equivalent to "larger than most fleas," as is often thought, runs afoul of the fact that if the population of fleas contains, say, 100 fleas two millimeters long and 75 one millimeter long, then what is undeniably a large flea will be larger than less than one-half of the population. Somewhat similar considerations militate against the paraphrase "larger than the average flea." Conceivably there is some paraphrase that escapes this sort of problem, but if so it is not easy to discover, and Plato can hardly be accused of a blunder for having overlooked it.

Secondly, if we attend to what we consciously have in mind when we say that something is hard, for instance (*Rep.* 523e–524a), it seems plain that we do not intend to ascribe a relation to it, but rather a property that seems on reflection to be monadic. When we call a piece of Parmesan cheese hard, we are not thinking of some particular relatum and saying that the cheese is harder than it, nor are we even thinking of any definite reference class of things with which we are comparing it. Pieces of cheese, pieces of Parmesan cheese, things on the kitchen table, and so forth, all might be candidates, but it is artificial to say that a reference to any of them is actually part of the content of the judgment. Whether we are right to think of ourselves as making these nonrelational judgments, and whether this sort of introspection is ever or in principle a valid source of information about the content of our judgments, are not questions that I shall treat here. That Plato, like many philosophers, often uses such introspection is evident, and that is all that my interpretative aims require.

Though the alleged confusion over relations has often been proposed as an explanation of Plato's remarks about contraries at *Republic* 479a–b and 523e–524a, it never suited all of the examples that he uses there. These include "good," "just," and "holy," which do seem to have genuine contraries and do not much tempt us to paraphrase them in relational terms.[14] The best course is to recognize that Plato held that all of the notions expressed by these terms are (unlike those expressed by "brother," "master," etc.) nonrelational.

Plato's outlook is clearly exhibited at *Phaedo* 102b–c. He explicitly rejects an overtly relational sentence, "Simmias overtops (*hyperechei*) Socrates," because he says that it expresses the fact less well than "Simmias has tallness in relation to Socrates' shortness." He then goes on to speak casually of Simmias's tallness and Socrates' shortness (102d7, e2). He obviously recognizes something relational about attributions of tallness (note *pros*, "in regard, or relation, to," at 102b). Nevertheless he still thinks of what is attributed as a property, not itself a relation.[15]

A similar attitude is in evidence in the *Hippias Major.* Plato says, "The most beautiful pot is ugly, when grouped with girls" (289a4–5), and "If someone compares the class of girls with the class of gods, . . . won't the most beautiful girl appear ugly?" (a9–b3). What is being ascribed here is the property, ugliness, not the relation, being ugli*er than* something.

But however natural such attributions of nonrelational properties might have seemed to Plato, they certainly seem awkward in many cases. For example, although it is possible, introspectively, to think of heaviness or hardness as a property, it is more difficult to think of largeness in that way. Moreover, if largeness is to be a property, what property could it be? Finally there is the problem that explicitly worries Plato himself: If largeness is a property and smallness is its contrary, why do these properties seem to attach to one and the same thing simultaneously (*Rep.* 523b–c, 524d–525a)?

In spite of these difficulties, we need to understand that Plato did regard these terms as expressing genuinely nonrelational properties – as indeed they seem to introspection to be – and he worked out his position on that basis.[16] In so doing he was in effect working out a distinctive conception of reality (or, as we might put it, objectivity), that is, of what it is for something to be really (or objectively) *F.* Since this conception is unfamiliar to modern philosophy, we have to work carefully to discern its outlines (which will begin to appear more fully by section VI).

V

Plato sometimes uses the example of beauty (which in the *Symposium* he forcefully denies is a purely subjective matter) to express this conception. As we saw (in section IV), he thinks that when a pot is grouped with girls, we should say that it is ugly (*H. Ma.* 289a). Leaving aside other questions for the moment, we can see that the notion of ugliness here is the notion of a nonrelational property. To be ugly in this sense is just to be ugly – without reference to a particular context or a particular viewpoint or anything else. When we call something ugly, then even though we are in a particular situation and are comparing the thing to other things, we do not refer to the situation or the things *in our judgment itself,* and what we mean to say about the thing is just that it is ugly, period. The same idea emerges in *Symposium* 210d–211a. The notion of beauty described there is the notion of a thing's being beautiful nonrelatively to another part of the thing or to a time or place or relation or to whom it is beautiful or to what kind of thing it is or, indeed, to anything else.

Likewise at *Republic* 523e–524a. There Plato says that perception apprehends largeness and smallness and the like "deficiently" (e7). That is, the context in which a thing is viewed determines whether it will appear large or small (523e4–5). The same point is said to apply to thickness and thinness and hardness and softness. Plato is not denying that *whether or not something appears hard,* or the like, depends on the context. *The meaning or content of the judgment* that a thing is hard, on the other hand, seems to him to make no reference to that context. The implication is that the notions in question are notions of a thing's being, for example, hard, quite independently of the context. The contrast is drawn with a finger, which presents the appearance of being a finger quite apart from the context in which it is observed (523c11–d3). The notion of hardness in question is the notion of a thing's being hard in a sense into which mention of this or that circumstance does not enter.

Let us turn to Plato's remarks about time and tense, which show us another important way in which he thinks that the notions expressed by such terms are nonrelational. He frequently says that a thing that we now say is *F* will later cease to be so, and in general that perceptible things are subject to change (e.g., *Phd.* 78d–79a, 79c, 80b; *Rep.* 526e, 527b, 533b, 534a; *Ti.* 48e–49a, 51e–52a). He also says in the *Timaeus* that perceptibles, unlike Forms, involve "was" and "will be," whereas Forms involve only "is" (37c–38b). And a little later he says that if you have a piece of gold that is constantly being remolded into different shapes, it is "by far the best with regard to truth" to say that it is gold, rather than saying that it is a triangle or some other shape (50a–b).

Although it is often said that Plato's point is simply that if a thing is not permanently or essentially *F* it is a mistake to say that it really is *F*, this is an unsatisfactory explanation of his view. Why should we have wished to reserve "is" to be equivalent to "is essentially (or permanently)"? A philosopher could make such a terminological stipulation, but if it is not to seem arbitrary there needs to be some account of why he thinks that "is *F*" should not be attached to a thing if it is only temporarily *F*.

The explanation of his thinking is straightforward if we recur to the point that Plato derived from introspection of the meanings of our terms (section IV). If I say that a thing is a triangle, what I actually have in mind typically involves no reference to time at all. True, the thing that I refer to seemingly was previously and subsequently will be nontriangular. Nevertheless what I consciously think to say when I use the phrase "is triangular" is not "is triangular now" or "is triangular roundabout now" or "is triangular at 10:00 A.M. on such-and-such a date," or anything of that kind. Rather, the consciously entertained meaning of "is triangular" abstracts from and ignores all consideration of time. The point is not that it is felt to be false to say that a thing is triangular when one knows that it is only temporarily so. The point is that the introspectible notion expressed by the predicate incorporates no thought of time at all, so it is inappropriately applied to objects that are in time.[17]

The upshot is that the notions represented by predicates in general do not incorporate elements of time or tense. A person could understand these notions of being triangular and being equal even if he had no conception of temporality. That is Plato's picture. Thus he thinks of the demiurge in the *Timaeus* as comprehending all of the Forms before time has been created along with the cosmos and its ordered motion. The timelessness of the Forms is more than just a matter of their being the same through all time (though Plato often says that they are indeed always the same); it is that they lie "outside" of time in the "eternity" of which time is only an "imitation" (37d–e).

VI

Although it is plain in a general way that Plato's view of these notions involves abstracting from various sorts of relations to time, context, and perspective, it is not easy to see exactly how this is done. Here I shall try only to present some of the interpretative issues that must be taken into account, and to give an outline of how I think they should be handled.

Sometimes it looks as though the main thing that he is concerned with is relativity to the perspective of a person who is either perceiving a thing or thinking about it. For example, at *Republic* 479a–b, as I have said, Plato infers, from the fact that a perceptible thing can appear both beautiful and ugly, that it no more is than is not beautiful. Here it looks as though he is contrasting this way of being beautiful with something's somehow being beautiful independently of the perspective from which a person considers it.

In other places it seems that the pertinent relativity is to some feature of the circumstances in which the perceptible thing finds itself, not to the way in which it is observed. This seems to be so in the case of time. When a thing changes, it often has a characteristic at one time and a contrary characteristic at another time, regardless of whether anyone is observing or considering it.[18] This sort of change does not seem to arise simply from relativity to an observer.[19]

In other cases the situation is ambiguous, and the two types of relativity seem intertwined. At *Symposium* 210e–211a Plato describes the notion of something "not [1] beautiful in one way and ugly in another, nor [2] beautiful at one time but not in another, nor [3] beautiful in relation to (*pros*) one thing but ugly in relation to another, nor [4] beautiful here but ugly there, nor [5] beautiful to some but ugly to others." Of these, (5) seems to have to do with relativity to observer, and (1) might also, but (2)–(4) seem fairly plainly to involve the other sort of relativity, to the circumstances of the thing rather than to conditions of observation.

At *Phaedo* 97a–b, again, Plato seems to hold that sometimes when two things are far apart from each other, each "is one" and they are "not then two," but when they approach each other they "become two," though in other cases when something that "is one" is split, it "becomes two." It would seem in fact, however, that – if one is to talk in this way – things that are two are two regardless of their distance from each other. Perhaps what Plato has in mind is that their *appearing* two depends on its being possible to see them together.[20] Similarly at *Hippias Major* 289a–c, it is said that the most beautiful girl will appear ugly when compared with a god. Then Plato says that we should agree that the most beautiful girl *is* ugly when considered in relation to gods. It is not made explicit whether the girl's being ugly is supposed to be relative to the gods, relative to the observer comparing her with gods, or relative to both.

To take the case of beauty in the *Symposium* as an example again, the question is what notion of beauty Plato is referring to. Is it the notion of a thing's being beautiful somehow independently of the observer and the perspective that the observer occupies? Or is it the notion of a thing's being beautiful independently of its circumstances (apart from those of its being observed or considered)? For us nowadays it seems almost irresistible to think that it must be one or the other of these, but that it cannot be both.

In view of the evidence just cited, however, it seems to me clearly best to say that both kinds of independence are implicated in the notions that Plato is trying to express, and that (at least as far as present purposes are concerned) they are on a par with each other. The notion of beauty associated in the *Symposium* with the Form of the Beautiful, then, is the notion of a thing's being beautiful independently of both the perspective from which it is considered (whether by sense or through thought) and the circumstances in which it is located. Nothing in the passages cited indicates that either of these aspects of the matter should be omitted from the interpretation.

We can understand Plato's view as thus interpreted, and perhaps sympathize with it to some extent, if we continue to use introspection to think about what we mean when we ascribe such properties. When one says that a thing is beautiful, then – philosophical theories aside – one seems to mean that it has a certain property that does not involve either the thing's being examined from a certain standpoint or the circumstances surrounding it. That is, as far as what one has in one's consciousness is concerned, one seems to ascribe a property whose attaching to the thing is in a sense intrinsic, namely, in the sense that in the thought of the property there is contained no idea of either the fact that one is ascribing it from a certain perspective or the fact that the thing is placed in a certain situation. Of course, one *is* occupying a certain perspective as one is ascribing the property, and the thing *is* located in a certain situation. But the humdrum and yet – for the interpretation of Plato – crucial fact is that these two facts are not themselves *incorporated into the judgment* that one makes. (Of course, there are other judgments in which viewpoint and perspective are part of the content of what is judged, but they are another matter.) This is clearly true, for better or worse, of many of our ascriptions of beauty and justice and goodness, and also for many of our ascriptions of hardness, heaviness, and other such seeming properties. These facts enable us to have a clear sense of why Plato says the things that he says about such judgments and the notions that figure in them.

In outline, then, this is the conception of reality or objectivity that

Plato develops (cf. section IV). The notion of being really *F* is the notion of being *F* in a way that is independent of both the viewpoint of the judger and the circumstances of the object. It is thus the notion of being in a certain particular sense, as I have said, "intrinsically" *F*.[21] That term, though, has enough uses in philosophy to make its use here inadvisable and potentially misleading. The important thing to emphasize, for now, is not that it is the notion of a thing's being *F* "in and of itself," but what its being *F* thus is independent of – namely, viewpoint and circumstances.[22]

For us these days there seems to be something strange about Plato's combining into one idea these two kinds of independence. The combining becomes more readily intelligible when we notice the facts of introspection just described, which allow us a way of thinking of the two kinds of independence as on a par. The combining also illustrates Plato's disinclination to separate epistemological and metaphysical issues in the modern way. From an epistemological point of view the role of perspective in a judgment can seem paramount, whereas the role of the circumstances of the object seems like a different kind of consideration, involving the nature of the property that one is ascribing. But Plato does not divide the topic up in this way.

VII

Plato associates these notions with his special entities, the Forms. By "associate" I mean, for one thing, that he supposes that to understand the notion of an *F*, as explained above, is to stand in a certain cognitive relation to the Form of *F*. Saying what this cognitive relation might be is subject to numerous difficulties. Sometimes Plato portrays it as involving an ability to give a definition, as we saw (section I), which he seems to take as a specification or description or analysis of a Form. At other times he talks, to some degree metaphorically, as if it were a kind of intellectual "seeing" of the Form (*Rep.* 484c–d, 500c). Whatever the exact character and relationship of these two ideas may be, the relation of mind (and particularly reason) to Forms is the core of his view about what the understanding of our notions comes to.

Something similar to the latter idea arose earlier (section II) in the treatment of *Phaedo* 74b–c. If that argument is to make sense, we saw, not all ways of bringing equality into one's judgment can count as cases of equality's "appearing" one way or another. It seems that the kind of "appearing" that Plato has in mind takes place when one deliberately and consciously sets oneself to, as we might say, think about equality and consider what is true of it. Doing that presumably falls short of anything that anyone would call "intellectual seeing," but it is all that we need to discuss here of what might have led Plato to use that manner of speaking.[23]

Plato's association of the notions I have described with Forms is affected by another issue that arises in *Phaedo* 74b–c. Premise (B) receives two formulations, (1) "Equality has never appeared to you inequality", and (2) "The equals themselves have never appeared to you unequal," both seemingly presented as equivalent.

Formulation (1) seems to us relatively unproblematical, and so I have exploited it here so far. Formulation (2), though, raises difficulties connected with the matter of what is called "self-predication."[24] For (2) makes it sound as though equality can be described as itself "equals," that is, as if it were things that are equal. This difficulty has two aspects, one connected with the plural expression "equals themselves," and the other arising from the peculiarity of saying that equality is itself equal, regardless of how many things it might be. The former aspect I shall here treat as unimportant, since Plato soon switches to the singular "the equal itself" (74c4–5) and hardly ever uses the plural in speaking of Forms.

It is clear that Plato's argument for the distinctness of Forms does not itself require that the Form of *F* be in general *F*, and in view of the oddity of this idea it has understandably seemed to many interpreters better not to attribute it to him.[25] On the other hand there are numerous passages in which he seems to use language by which self-predication is very strongly suggested, including claims to the effect that perceptible objects are "imitations" or "copies" of Forms, which are "paradigms" for them (e.g., *Ti.* 28e, 49a; *Rep.* 540a). He also engages in later works (especially the *Parmenides* and the *Sophist*) in reasoning that might be taken, as it has been, as a criticism of his own earlier self-predicationist view. On the other hand the *Timaeus,* a late work, continues to treat Forms as paradigms and perceptibles as copies of them.[26]

Probably the best construal of this state of affairs is to affirm that Plato does believe that perceptible objects are in a sense imitations of Forms, but to deny that he intends this view in the way in which the self-predicationist interpretation takes it. Before we examine how this might be so (section XI), it will be helpful to look at some of his thinking about how the notions associated with Forms are in fact applied to perceptibles.

VIII

If Plato believes that we have the notion of a thing's being *F* – equal, beautiful, just, square, and so forth[27] – independently of its circumstances and the point of view from which it is regarded, and if he takes the understanding of such a notion to be the cognition of the Form of *F*, the question arises how he thinks such notions can be exemplified by perceptible objects. The best answer, I think, is to develop and clarify the line of thought pursued by those who say that according to him, perceptibles and Forms belong to different "types" or "categories" and that, more importantly, the way in which terms apply to perceptibles is different from the way in which they apply to Forms.[28]

The notion associated with the Form of *F* is the notion of a thing's being *F* in abstraction from or independently of viewpoint and circumstances. This emphatically does not mean that it is the notion of a thing's being *F* in *all* circumstances, at *all* times, and to *all* viewpoints. That would obviously be absurd. Rather, the idea is that conceiving of a thing's being *F* in this way does not involve bringing anything to mind about circumstances, times, or viewpoints at all. Such matters are simply not part of the notion and not part of the property that it expresses. For when we introspect the notion of what we ascribe when we say that an object is *F*, we can see that we have in mind the property of being *F* in a way that involves nothing about such things.[29] (When *F* is a relational term like "equal" or "brother" – cf. section IV – there is of course a reference to a correlate object, but not to any further viewpoint or circumstance with regard to which the relational property is thought of as attached to the thing.)

On the other hand difficulties arise when we apply such notions to perceptible things. Here it must be stressed that Plato thinks that we do, in our ordinary judgments, try to apply these notions to perceptibles. One's judgment that a perceptible thing is beautiful does not present itself to one's mind as the judgment that "This is beautiful as viewed by me from here when it is in such-and-such circumstances." Rather, it is normally the judgment that "This is beautiful," just like that with nothing added. Plato takes it as simply an undeniable fact that our perceptions stimulate us to make such judgments.[30] Never does he hint that we should reconstrue our judgments as really meaning "This thing is beautiful as viewed by me. . . ." If he had done that, the entire structure of his doctrine would have been different.[31] In particular, he would not have stuck so persistently as he does to terms like "beautiful," "equal," "hard," and so on. Instead he would have focused explicitly on complex, multirelational judgments. He would also have done the same if he had proposed a conceptual revision, leading us to replace "beautiful" and so forth with relational substitutes. But he suggests no such strategy.

Nor does he suggest another revision that his terminology might have allowed him. Along with the term "imitation" he uses the term "participation" for the relation of exemplification that a perceptible thing may bear to a Form. If we call a perceptible thing *F*, then we can say that it "participates" in *F*-ness. Plato never says, however, that "This is *F*," said of a perceptible thing, is *equivalent to* "This participates in *F*-ness" or could be replaced by it. As I have said, he thinks that the judgments that we actually try to make do express what we mean by the former sort of sentence. He does not entertain the prospect of a revamping of our way of thinking that would eliminate them. He only expects us to understand wherein they are inappropriate.

Plato thinks, then, that we unavoidably do try to apply to perceptibles the notions of being *F* viewpoint-independently and circumstance-independently (for brevity let me henceforth usually include time-independence under circumstance-independence). When we do, though, we face a problem. It strikes one in a certain situation as right to call a thing beautiful in such a sense. But in another situation or at another time it strikes one, or someone else, as right to call it ugly. Thus the viewpoint, time, or situation affects the seeming appropriateness of applying a term whose meaning, as we think about it, seems to involve no reference to such things. Our understanding of the terms that we apply, together with what our perceptions make us inclined to say about perceptible objects, turn out to be a misleading guide to what we shall be inclined to say about perceptible objects under other conditions. In this way Plato thinks of perceptibles as only "deficiently" fitting the notions that we try to use to describe them (cf. section III).

Plato's sense of the peculiarity of applying viewpoint- and circumstance-independent notions to perceptible objects is conveyed by his remarks in *Republic* 479b–c, where he tries to explain his contention that such objects are "between being and not-being" (479b6–7). Alluding to the fact that a perceptible thing that appears beautiful also appears ugly, he says that it is like things that "are ambivalent," which "it is impossible to think of . . . as being or as not being or as both or as neither" (479c3–5). Since he is using "being" here to represent the predicative notion of "being *F* (e.g., beautiful)" (cf. section III), his thought is that where a perceptible thing is concerned, there is something wrong with saying either that it is beautiful, that is not beautiful, that it both is beautiful and is not beautiful, and that it neither is beautiful nor is not beautiful. This proposition makes sense as an expression of the idea that the term is in a sense simply not applicable to the object at all.

IX

It still has to be explained, though, why Plato does not describe perceptibles in a different way, by finding a notion of a thing's being really *F* that could apply to them. After all, we do think that sticks can really be equal even though they often do not appear so. And when we think this, we apply a sense of "being equal" in which no notion of viewpoint seems to enter: The sticks simply are equal, quite apart from any consideration of how they appear. We also, for example, use a notion of being good under which a thing can be said to be good, quite regardless of its circumstances, consequences, or the like, and we sometimes apply this notion to perceptible things. We need to understand why Plato did not do the same thing.

Two factors are relevant here. First, his way of abstracting from circumstances is sweeping. In particular, his notion of being *F* involves no reference to time (section V). He rejects, in effect, the idea that most of what we say about perceptibles can be taken as relative to times – that "is *F*" can amount to "is *F* at time *t*." Conceiving simply of a thing's being *F*, he holds, does not involve thinking of its being in time at all. Second, his view that we do actually entertain and use these completely viewpoint- and circumstance-independent notions makes it seem implausible to him that any other notion of really being *F* could be legitimate. We might say that two sticks are equal independently of perspective and circumstances, but that would still leave us with their changeability. Plato would therefore say that we still are not operating with the notion that we really have in mind when we think of being equal, which is independent of all circumstances, including that of time and tense.[32] So because he believes that we have in mind such notions of being *F*, the kind of notion of objectivity or reality that satisfies us and allows us to apply it to physical objects would not seem to him to be a serious option.[33]

This is one important reason why Plato's epistemological enterprise is so different from modern theories. He has no interest, for instance, in the idea that a perceptible thing is *F* just in case it appears *F* to a standard observer in standard conditions. One problem is that picking out an observer as standard would be arbitrary.[34] At *Republic* 581e–583a, he says that the person who is familiar with all pleasures is the one who can tell which ones are most pleasant, but he never says that their being most pleasant simply consists in their being so designated by such an observer, and he goes on to give a metaphysical explanation of what being really pleasant does consist in (583b–586e). Similarly, in the *Theaetetus* he says that an expert is someone who can make judgments about how things are (170a–c), but he never hints that the expert could be specified by the conditions under which he forms his judgments.[35]

Plato's thinking is equally inhospitable to the idea that a perceptible thing is *F* just in case its being taken to be *F* causally explains its various appearances. This would be Russell's idea, for example, when he holds that what makes us say that the penny is really round is that its being round can be cited as the cause of its appearing round under some conditions and elliptical under many others.[36] Plato never broaches such an idea.[37] He would allow that a thing's being *F* can be part of what causes it to present various appearances,[38] but there is no reason to believe that he would accept the claim that *F*-ness just *is* the property of causing those appearances.

His rejection of such ideas as these fits with the fact that on his view, coming to conceive the notions that concern him is not, as empiricists regard it, a matter of constructing or deriving them from perceptual appearances. Although he says that perception stimulates us to bring certain notions to consciousness, they are notions that we already possess (*Phd.* 75a–d), through what he calls "recollection," without reliance on perceptual appearances.[39] There is therefore no paradox for him here in the idea that the notions do not properly fit perceptible things.

Plato's radical concept of reality – of things' really being *F*[40] – thus leads him away from any concept under which, in spite of conflicting appearances and on the basis of inferences from them, we could say that in the perceptible world things really are thus-and-so. Reality for him is indissolubly linked to objects of a different sort, the Forms.

X

In spite of his refusal to say that our notions properly apply to perceptible things, he nevertheless does not deny that we make judgments about them (cf. section VIII). We have a native propensity to make such judgments about perceptibles. Under certain conditions a perceptible object will strike us as having a certain character like that of a Form with which we already possess some sort of acquaintance (*Phd.* 75b–c), and we will call the object by the "name" (*epōnymia*) that we have associated with that Form (102a–d).[41] But Plato does not believe that these judgments are based on clear rational grounds. For at this stage we do not possess a clear knowledge of the Forms that we are in effect making use of, and we do not possess definitions of them (cf. section I). We simply have feelings for certain similarities between what we perceive and the notions that we already have in mind, and they incline us to make certain judgments. We simply make them, and many of them become customary (*nomima, Rep.* 479d3–4, 484d2). People who make these judgments uncritically do not even recognize the existence of Forms that represent their meanings (475b, 479a).

Plato allows a difference, though, between more and less defensible descriptions of perceptibles. The rulers in the *Republic,* for example, after they have gained full knowledge of the Forms of Goodness and Justice (540b, 534a–b), are better able to govern the city than they would otherwise be. The crucial reason is that they now know what it is for a city to be just (cf. section I). But they must also be supposed to realize which actions on their part would help lead the city in that direction. In *Republic* X the wise man whose son has died is able to determine, among other things, how he may best improve his condition (604c–d). In the *Phaedrus* Plato indicates that a person might learn to predict how certain sorts of speeches affect certain sorts of people (267*ff*, esp. 270b, 277a–b). In fact, the allegory of the cave at the beginning of *Republic* VII says that people can "divine" the future by remembering what sorts of events have occurred in sequence in the past (516c–d; cf. *Tht.* 171d–172b, 178a–179a, 186a–b).

On the other hand Plato believes that there are strict limits to the effectiveness of such efforts. The allegory of the cave strongly suggests that the regularities that can be observed are merely accidental ("which [shadows] have customarily [*eiōthei*] gone past earlier and later or at the same time," *Rep.* 516c10–d1), and indicates that using them as a basis of prediction is comparable to soothsaying (*apomanteuomenōi,* d2). Moreover, all the evidence seems to show that in Plato's view, the perceptible world is not deterministic or fully predictable.[42] He seems to believe that a priori investigation of Forms can yield general statements that roughly describe physical things. In their perceptible applications these general statements admit exceptions, but they are much more secure than statements derived simply from perceptual observation.[43] Taken in their pure application to Forms, however, they are exceptionless and certain.

At bottom, I think (though there is no space to explain the interpretation fully here) Plato rests this view on the idea that the properties that he associates with Forms are, in the way that we have seen, not properly exemplified by perceptible things. If "fire," for example, in a sense involving no relation to perspective or circumstances, could be applied to perceptibles, then he thinks that other features would attach to it by ironclad regularity.[44] But if the property of being fire seems attributable only in certain circumstances and from certain viewpoints, then the strict links to other features will be disrupted and become only probabilistic. The less relational the attachment of properties to a thing, so to speak, the more regular the linkage of the properties to each other.

As I briefly noted earlier (in section III), Plato maintained that we have knowledge (*epistēmē*) only of Forms, and only belief or opinion (*doxa*) about perceptibles (*Rep.* 475–480; *Ti.* 48e, 51d–52a). To explicate fully what he meant by saving this would require another essay. The foregoing observations, however, give some sense of what is involved. One element has to do with the possibility of well-founded predictions: Certain regularities hold securely for Forms but do not when one applies them to perceptibles.

The more fundamental element, however, has to do with the fact that whatever application of a term one is inclined to make to a perceptible object, it is guaranteed that other viewpoints and circumstances will yield a contrary inclination. If I am inclined to call something hard here and now, I will be inclined to call it soft at another point.[45] Nothing comparable is true of judgments about Forms. Moreover, the application of the notion of hardness to a perceptible is, as we have seen (in section VIII), a misapplication, in that it is an attempt to attribute a perspective- and circumstance-independent property to a thing that can be apprehended only from a perspective and within particular circumstances.

In the context of present-day epistemology Plato's view on this topic provokes puzzlement. He clearly is not concerned with whether or not judgments about particular perceptibles can be adequately justified. It is therefore difficult to interpret his views within an outlook that closely associates the concept of knowledge with a concept of the justification of belief. Rather, he is focused on the thought that perspective- and circumstance-independent notions that we have in mind are not applicable to perceptibles, and that judgments that try to apply those notions to sensibles are therefore never stable.

XI

The Form of *F*, Plato says, is the "paradigm" of which perceptible things that we call *F* are "imitations" or "copies," and this fact makes people ascribe a "self-predicationist" view to Plato (cf. section VII). For two reasons, however, his thought is not straightforwardly that the Form of *F* and perceptible things can all share the feature of being *F*.

For one thing, he is not willing to say that any perceptible objects are *F* in the way that the Form of *F* is. When we make judgments about them, as I have said, we do intend to say that they are, but our inclination to make any such judgments about them comes and goes, and that fact shows that something is wrong with them (section VIII). More importantly, however, his view is not that the Form of *F* is a thing that itself is, predicatively, *F* in a viewpoint- and circumstance-independent way. Rather, it is the notion, and also the property (cf. note 24), *of a thing's being F* in that way. The self-predicationist view would say that the Form of *F* is (predicatively) *F*. Plato's view is that the Form of *F* is what it is to be *F* apart from viewpoint and circumstances.

It is not surprising that he sometimes writes as though those features attach to the Form of *F* that instead properly would attach to a thing of which the Form is the notion, that is, a thing that is *F* independently of viewpoint and circumstances. After all, to conceive of the Form is precisely to conceive of a thing's being *F* in that way. I think, however, that this is not what he intends. When he exhibits difficulties with this idea (as he does in the so-called Third Man argument, of which two versions appear in *Parmenides,* at 131e–132b and 132d–133b), his aim, I think, is to make clear that he does not subscribe to it, and that although he may sometimes have failed to think and write clearly enough to avoid it completely, he regards such lapses on his part as deviations from his fundamental line of thought.

He often says that perceptible objects "partake" or "participate" in Forms. As he recognizes, the idea is obscure (*Phd.* 100d, *Prm.* 131–135), and his middle works do little to elucidate it. His later works try to explain it, especially the *Parmenides,* the *Sophist,* and the *Philebus* (though arguably they end up making matters more obscure). He faces more than just the now-traditional problem of the relation of particulars to universals. In addition, his notion of a thing's being perspective- and circumstance-independently *F,* and the relation of this notion to objects that can be apprehended only from a particular perspective and within particular circumstances, raise substantial difficulties of their own.

As I indicated earlier, Plato resists the idea that the circumstance- and viewpoint-independent notion of *F* might ever be definable in terms of a viewpoint- or circumstance-dependent notion – for example, that "hard" might be defined in terms of "harder than" or "hard compared to," or that "beautiful" might be explained in terms of "beautiful to so-and-so" or "beautiful in such-and-such circumstances." In fact it is clear that his sympathies lie with the reverse order of explanation. He thinks that our applications of terms to perceptible objects are developed in some way on the basis of our comprehension of the viewpoint- and circumstance-independent notions. This way of thinking might seem natural on grounds of introspection. After all, it seems intuitively easy to suppose that the notion expressed by "harder" is derived from the notion of "hard" plus some notion of greater or lesser degree, and that "beautiful to so-and-so" is built notionally from "beautiful" along with a notion of perspective. This might not be the logical order of explanation, but it has something to be said for it, notably a naive sort of naturalness. There are clear signs that Plato pursued this idea. The use that he is reported to have made of the notion of "the greater and the less" (or the "indefinite dyad") seems to me likely to have arisen from the aim of deriving some of our notions from a notion of comparison such as I have just alluded to.[46] Here again he may be said to have followed a course that introspection in some ways recommends.

Other problems about the relation between Forms and perceptibles are intensely troubling to him, but there is no space to deal with them here. One particularly severe one is his need, seemingly forced on him by a variety of considerations, to say that just like perceptible objects, Forms have features that we are inclined to ascribe to them only in certain circumstances.[47] Others arise from the need to explain why it is that although perceptibles have features only viewpoint-dependently, we nevertheless make the mistake of thinking otherwise. In the *Republic* he attempts such an explanation for the notion of pleasantness (which 583b–587b construes as fundamentally noncomparative). The *Timaeus* contains a number of such explanations for other notions.[48]

XII

Plato's metaphysical epistemology is too complex to be easily summed up. I have tried to show how thoroughly intertwined its metaphysical and epistemological elements are, and how much it differs from modern epistemological theories, while at the same time giving an outline of it that stands on its own apart from comparison to modern views. It seems to me that Plato's fundamental insight – that as they appear to introspection, many important notions are of things' having features in a way independent of one's own perspective and of the circumstances surrounding the objects about which the judgment is made – is correct as far as it goes. That is, Plato is correct about what our introspective capacities actually tell us about these notions and the properties that they purport to us to express. Whether Plato was right to develop this insight as he did, on the other hand, is far more doubtful, as is the question whether such introspection is a good philosophical guide. The falsity of the insight would necessarily call his whole metaphysics into question.

In spite of what introspection may indicate, it is highly questionable whether the properties that we ascribe to perceptible physical objects should be construed as actually viewpoint-, time-, and circumstance-independent in the way Plato takes them to be. Perhaps many of them, for example, should be taken as relations to times. Others of them are perhaps subjective, that is, are relations to observers or conditions of observation. Some may be comparatives, as those who criticize Plato have maintained, and others seem to be relational in other ways that he did not notice. Still others might be "syncategorematic" – for example, many uses of "good" may be equivalent to "good (as an) *F*."

These difficulties did not go unnoticed in antiquity. Aristotle maintained, for example, that Plato was wrong to think that we have a notion of goodness that abstracts from all circumstances and things to which it is applied, and took the same view about, for example, the notion of being (*Nichomachean Ethics* I.6). He also maintained that Plato was mistaken in thinking that certain relational notions can be understood in abstraction from their correlatives.[49]

A further problem arises for Plato from the fact that on certain plausible "holistic" views, the notions we employ, and perhaps also the properties they express, are each dependent for their identity on the others. As Plato's view about Forms begins to be expounded, it seems to tend toward a strict atomism.[50] Elsewhere, though, he seems to accept some sort of essential interrelation among Forms that has the epistemological consequence that knowledge of certain Forms, particularly the Good, is necessary for knowledge of the others (*Rep.* 510b, 511b, 517b–c, 519c–d, 526e). This idea is alluded to by Plato – though it is not clear to what conclusion – in later works, especially the *Theaetetus* and the *Sophist* (e.g., *Tht.* 206c–208b), and was perhaps developed by others in Plato's Academy into a thoroughgoing epistemological holism.[51]

An interesting historical question, which I shall not try to answer here, is whether Plato's distinctive approach to epistemological and metaphysical problems, differing as it does from so much modern epistemology and even from much ancient epistemology (notably the Skeptics and also the Stoics and Epicureans), is due to the idiosyncratic thinking of one philosopher, Plato, or whether it represents a general approach to these issues that was characteristic of the philosophical outlook of the period. I incline toward the former view, but it would be difficult to prove that it is correct.

NOTES

1 See Gareth B. Matthews and Thomas A. Blackson, "Causes in the *Phaedo*," *Synthèse* 79 (1989): 581–91.
2 I see no good reason not to regard the *Hippias Major* as genuine and as reflecting views of Plato's as of the time of the *Phaedo*. See Paul Woodruff, *Plato: Hippias Major* (Indianapolis, 1982), esp. 161–80. I also agree with the traditional dating of the *Timaeus* as a late work and with the view that it espouses essentially the same epistemological and metaphysical views as the middle works. For some considerations concerning its relative date see Ian Mueller, "Joan Kung's Reading of Plato's *Timaeus*," in *Nature, Knowledge and Virtue: Essays in Memory of Joan Kung*, ed. Terry Penner and Richard Kraut, *Apeiron* 22 (1989): 1–27; and William J. Prior, *Unity and Development in Plato's Metaphysics* (London, 1985), 168–93.
3 The interpretation of this argument to be given here is defended more fully in my "Forms and Sensibles: *Phaedo* 74B–C," *Philosophical Topics* 15 (1987): 197–214.
4 This presupposition raises difficult issues that cannot be fully treated here. In a nutshell, the problem is that Plato is tacitly ruling out the possibility that without there being such a nonperceptible entity as equality, "thinking of equality" might consist in something other than the mere perception of equal perceptible objects. For brief discussion see note 32.
5 For this way of characterizing the view of the opponents that Plato envisions see Terry Penner, *The Ascent From Nominalism* (Dordrecht, 1987), 54, 60, 95–121.
6 There are many problems about just which predicates Plato takes to correspond to Forms. For example, some interpreters think that, at least in his early–middle period, there are Forms corresponding only to cer-

tain predicates. For one main version of this interpretation see G. E. L. Owen, "A Proof in the *Peri Ideōn*," *Journal of Hellenic Studies* 77 (1957): 103–11. *Prm.* 130b–e is sometimes taken to be evidence for such an interpretation. I think that the passage should be explained in another way, and that it is weak evidence in the face of the fact that in earlier works Plato does not mention such a restriction. (A recurrent misreading of *Rep.* 523a–525 is sometimes used to support the contention that Plato does endorse the restriction there. Plato says there that some predicates appear to apply to the same perceptible object simultaneously, and that those predicates are the most apt to call forth the realization that Forms are distinct from perceptibles. Some interpreters, starting from Owen, mistake this for the quite different suggestion that only such predicates have Forms corresponding to them.)

7 See Gregory Vlastos, "Degrees of Reality in Plato," in *New Essays on Plato and Aristotle*, ed. Renford Bambrough (London, 1965), 1–19. Though the present interpretation is on this point much indebted to Vlastos's and to Owen's (in "A Proof") from which Vlastos's interpretation is substantially derived, there is much that surrounds Vlastos's account of this point that I would differ with, in particular the matters treated in sections IV–VIII of this chapter (cf. note 21).

8 See Owen, "A Proof"; Vlastos, "Degrees of Reality," 1–19; and Alexander Nehamas, "Plato on the Imperfection of the Sensible World," *American Philosophical Quarterly* 12 (1975): 105–17.

9 For further discussion of the role of this problem in Plato, see Myles Burnyeat, "Conflicting Appearances," *Proceedings of the British Academy* 65 (1979): 69–111.

10 Plato's treatment of "double" and "half" introduces special problems; cf. note 49.

11 There is no space here for an analysis of Plato's argument. The present interpretation of its conclusion is the traditional one. The conclusion as thus construed is treated later on as having been demonstrated (e.g., *Rep.* 507b, 484b, c–d, and 485b with 479a–b), and 475e–480a seems to me the only place where Plato could take the demonstration to be. It has been maintained, however, that this and related Platonic arguments are efforts to show, not that Forms are distinct from perceptible particulars, but that some important notions (particularly ethical ones) cannot be explained in terms of "observational" predicates. See esp. J. C. B. Gosling, "Republic V: *ta polla kala*," *Phronesis* 5 (1960): 116–28; Terence Irwin, *Plato's Moral Theory* (Oxford, 1977), 147–8, 151–2; Gail Fine, "Knowledge and Belief in *Republic* V," *Archiv für Geschichte der Philosophie* 60 (1978): 121–39; C. D. C. Reeve, *Philosopher-Kings: The Argument of Plato's Republic* (Princeton, 1988), 58–71.

12 See Owen, "A Proof," 110–11. For further criticism of the idea that Plato was confused about relations and more on the interpretation presented here, see my "Perceptual and Objective Properties in Plato," in *Nature, Knowledge and Virtue: Essays in Memors of Joan Kung*, ed. Terry Penner and Richard Kraut, *Apeiron* 22 (1989): 45–65, and references therein.

13 See John Wallace, "Positive, Comparative, Superlative," *Journal of Philosophy* 69 (1972): 773–82; Samuel Wheeler, "Attributives and their Modifiers," *Nous* 6 (1972): 310–34; and Philip Kitcher, "Positive Understatement: The Logic of Attributive Adjectives," *Journal of Philosophical Logic* 7 (1978): 1–17.

14 In "A Proof," G. E. L. Owen suggested that we classify all of the terms that Plato deals with here as "incomplete," requiring a filler to make their sense fully explicit. This might seem to work for "good," provided that it is taken to have to mean "good (as an) *F*," as some have claimed it should be. On the other hand Plato nowhere espouses that claim, and anyway there is no obvious way to apply it to "just" or "holy."

15 One way of thinking of the matter is to say that instead of thinking of relations as polyadic and instantiated by ordered sets of objects, he thinks of them as monadic properties that are each instantiated by a single object, but are nevertheless in some sense tied to each other in such a way that when one is instantiated by one thing, the other must be instantiated by another. See Hector-Neri Castaneda, "Plato's *Phaedo* Theory of Relations," *Journal of Philosophical Logic* 1 (1972): 467–80; with White, "Perceptual and Objective Properties," esp. 46–7. See also the treatment of "one" at *Prm.* 129c–d.

16 For us, though not for Plato, a natural way to explain these phenomena is to say that such terms function somewhat as demonstratives do. "That is the Acropolis" does not to introspection mean the same as "The freestanding object most salient in the scene ahead is the Acropolis," but nevertheless it is liable to the accepted as true just in cases where the freestanding object most salient in the scene ahead of the speaker and the hearer is the Acropolis. Very roughly, demonstratives do their job not simply by conveying a certain content directly (particularly not one that it consciously entertained), but by combining with the context to cause the hearer to fix on the object that the speaker means to say something about. A sentence with a term like "large" does its job, likewise, not by itself expressing as part of its meaning a particular sort of comparison to a particular reference class, but, again very roughly, by collaborating with the context to cause the hearer to fix on both a reference class and a place in it that suits what the speaker wishes to say about the object of which "large" is predicated. If different reference

classes are indicated simultaneously, sometimes the same thing can acceptably be called both large and small.

17 I would also argue that in Plato's view, concerning an object, action, or event in the past it can only be said that it was *F*, not that it *is F* (and analogously for the future). For this reason it is inappropriate to apply the term *F* to it in the particular time- and tense-independent sense that he thinks we have in mind for our terms. (This is part of the more complete story of why *Ti.* 37b–38c says that there is "was" and "will be" for perceptibles but not for Forms. It is also the reason why Plato usually emphasizes the *perishability* of perceptibles as much as their changeability: of anything that previously existed we have to say that it "was" *F*, even if it perhaps was *F* throughout its existence [cf. note 32]. Plato's point therefore does not require him to say – as he does not – that it is *false* that a thing is *F* if it no longer exists.)

18 Someone might think that change in an object could be thought of as generated merely out of a shift in the temporal perspective of an observer. For someone might claim "*X* is *F* at t_1 but not-*F* at t_2" just means "*X* is *F* as viewed from t_1 but not-*F* as viewed from t_2." Some passages in Plato suggest such an idea, but there is no space to investigate them here – and the claimed equivalence seems evidently false, since a thing viewed from one perspective can appear to have changed or to be going to change.

19 At *Tht.* 178–180, in arguing against the Protagorean relativist, Plato relies on the assumption that the passage of time cannot be supposed to take place only relative to the observer.

20 A related issue arises in connection with *Tht.* 154c–d.

21 Owen advanced the view that the Form of *F* is associated with the idea of something's being *F* "unqualifiedly" (*haplōs*) and *kath' hauto.* See "A Proof," esp. 107–11. Owen's view was a significant advance on previous interpretations, and the present way of understanding Plato is greatly indebted to it and to its development by Vlastos in "Degrees of Reality" (cf. note 7). However, Owen's view failed to recognize a number of important things. One is that Plato's notion of being *F* is perfectly compatible with a recognition that some terms are relational (cf. section IV and note 50). Another is that we must not confuse being *F* in this way with being *F* in all ways or at all times, and that (cf. "A Proof," 110–11) the point of Plato's notion is indeed to exclude relativity, not primarily contrariety. A third is that Plato's notion combines independence of the two kinds of "qualifications" highlighted here.

22 In other connections, though, a notion of a thing's being "intrinsically" *F* would be apt. For example, Aristotle uses the term *ousia* for something that is a "*kath' hauto,* or *per se,* being," in the sense of not depending (in

a certain sense) on anything else for its being. This idea is closely related to Plato's view that Forms are *ousiai*, and that the Form of *F* is the notion of a thing's being *F kath' hauto*, i.e., "intrinsically" in the sense described. (Note, though, that in this sense "intrinsically" is not equivalent to "essentially.")

23 See my *Plato on Knowledge and Reality* (Indianapolis, 1976), 91, on Plato's use of the metaphor of "seeing" Forms. For differing views on how seriously Plato takes the idea of some kind of "nondiscursive" cognition of Forms, see, e.g., ibid.; Gail Fine, "False Belief in the *Theaetetus*," *Phronesis* 24 (1979): 70–80; Richard Sorabji, "Myths about Non-Propositional Thought," in *Language and Logos*, ed. Malcolm Schofield and Martha Nussbaum (Cambridge, 1982), 295–314.

24 The term was coined by Gregory Vlastos, "The Third Man Argument in Plato's *Parmenides*," *Philosophical Review* 63 (1954): 319–49.

25 See esp. Penner, *Ascent from Nominalism*.

26 G. E. L. Owen, "The Place of the *Timaeus* in Plato's Dialogues," *Classical Quarterly* 3 (1953): 79–95. For some arguments against Owen's dating of the *Timaeus* in Plato's middle period, see the references in note 2 of this chapter.

27 Cf. note 6.

28 See, for example, Richard Patterson, *Image and Reality in Plato's Metaphysics* (Indianapolis, 1985).

29 The attentive reader will have noticed that I have often oscillated between speaking of "properties" and "notions" or "concepts." Plato's talk of Forms embraces both things, and for present purposes the differences between them can be left aside.

30 This is not to say that the making of such a judgment is itself the perception; cf. *Tht.* 184–186.

31 The closest he comes is his presentation of the "secret doctrine" of Protagoras in the *Theaetetus*, but even here he does not stick consistently to the linguistic revision (esp. at 171a–c, as is often pointed out).

32 Perhaps some features of perceptible objects are timeless and tenseless. For example it has been argued (for example by Irwin, *Plato's Moral Theory*, 319–20) that a particular action that is good is good independently of viewpoint, circumstances, and also time (because if it is good at one time, it is good at all times). This matter requires extended examination. I would argue that Plato thinks that we are inclined to call a particular action good, and the like, only by virtue of adopting a particular point of view. (I have also maintained that in his view, concerning an action in the past it can only be said that it *was* good, whereas the notion of being good is a tenseless notion; cf. note 17.)

33 In passing I earlier said that on Plato's view, if equality were perceptible

equals, then to think of equality could only be to perceive them (cf. note 4). We can now see, very sketchily, why this is so. For Plato to think that we could gain the idea of the equality of perceptible objects by something other than merely perception, he would need to have the idea of our somehow constructing, rather than merely apprehending by perception, the notion of a perceptible object's being really equal in spite of sometimes appearing unequal. But this is, as we can now see, not an idea that he has any interest in developing.

34 See Bertrand Russell, *The Problems of Philosophy* (London, 1912), chap. 2.

35 Indeed, he never even hints that such a strategy might be used against the Protagorean relativism that is there being discussed.

36 Russell, *Problems of Philosophy,* chap. 4.

37 *Sph.* 247d–e proposes that to be is to have the capacity (*dynamis*) of doing or suffering something. I do not think that Plato ever accepts an analysis of any property other than being in terms simply of its capacities or effects.

38 Such propositions are presupposed by the accounts of perception in *Ti.* 61*ff.*

39 For present purposes it does not matter whether Plato conceives of this process as genuinely one of recollection (see also *Meno* 80–86, 98–100). The important thing is only that the notions be already in the mind, and not put there by some process originating in perception.

40 This equivalence holds for present purposes (cf. section III). In a broader treatment one would discuss the *Sophist* and its role in developing Plato's notion of being.

41 The *Cratylus* discusses how this association is established. Cf. White, *Plato on Knowledge and Reality,* chap. 6; and Bernard Williams, "Cratylus' Theory of Names and its Refutation," in *Language and Logos,* ed. Malcolm Schofield and Martha Nussbaum (Cambridge, 1982), 83–93.

42 Gregory Vlastos, "The Disorderly Motion in the *Timaeus,*" *Classical Quarterly* 33 (1939): 71–83; Glenn R. Morrow, "Necessity and Persuasion in Plato's *Timaeus,*" *Philosophical Review* 59 (1950): 147–64; Harold Cherniss, "The Sources of Evil according to Plato," *Proceedings of the American Philosophical Society* 98 (1954): 23–30.

43 Cf. Alexander P. D. Mourelatos, "Plato's 'Real Astronomy': *Republic* 527d–531d," in *Science and the Sciences in Plato,* ed. John P. Anton (Delmar, N.Y., 1980), 33–73.

44 See my "The Classification of Goods in Plato's *Republic,*" *Journal of the History of Philosophy* 22 (1984): 393–421.

45 If one does not understand what Plato is doing, it becomes easy to think that he has confused two different kinds of problems that may affect a

tensed belief: (1) the fact that arguments may shake one's faith in it and cause the holder of it to give it up, and (2) the fact that the circumstances may change and cause the holder of it to give it up on that account. If I believe that Socrates is just, I may change my mind because someone convinces me that I have been mistaken; or Socrates may be corrupted and I may accordingly give up my belief that he is just. To Plato it does not matter that these two phenomena are different. They both illustrate equally the problem that he sees in applying "is just" to perceptibles, which is that one's inclination to apply a given predicate will in fact – for both sorts of reason – eventually somehow be countered by the inclination to apply the contrary.

46 See, for example, the passages collected by W. D. Ross as fr. 2 of the *De Bono* in *Aristotelis Fragmenta Selecta* (Oxford, 1955).

47 For example, I take it that according to the *Sophist,* being and not-being are such features, and that a particular problem arises because being itself can be said, in different relations, both to be and not to be.

48 For example, *Ti.* 61d–62b ("hot"), 62c–63e ("light" and "heavy").

49 See *De Sophisticis Elenchis* c. 31, 181b25–35, where Aristotle insists that "double" either means nothing when detached from the phrase "double of half" (26–28) or else means something different from what it means in the phrase (33–35). Owen, "A Proof," 110, mistakenly construes this as a general criticism of Plato for not understanding that some notions are relational. Recall that "double" is treated in a particularly problematical way at *Rep.* 479b (cf. note 10).

50 Note Plato's description of Forms as *monoeides, Phd.* 78d, 80b. I think that this description is to be connected with the fact that each Form is taken to be the Form of a single notion, *F*, detached from all others, as a comparison with *Smp.* 211a5–b1 seems to confirm.

51 See W. D. Ross, *Aristotle's Prior and Posterior Analytics,* corr. ed. (Oxford, 1957), 605, 659–660.

RICHARD KRAUT

10 The defense of justice in Plato's *Republic*

In this essay I will try to identify and explain the fundamental argument of Plato's *Republic* for the astonishing thesis that justice is so great a good that anyone who fully possesses it is better off, even in the midst of severe misfortune, than a consummately unjust person who enjoys the social rewards usually received by the just.[1] Plato's attempt to defend this remarkable claim is of course the unifying thread of the dialogue, but his argument ranges so widely over diverse topics that it is difficult to see how it all fits together, and anyone who attempts to state his argument must take a stand on interpretive issues about which there is considerable scholarly controversy.[2] The dialogue's difficulty is increased by Plato's failure to give any explicit justification for the complex moral equation he boldly announces: Justice discounted by pain and dishonor is more advantageous than injustice supplemented by the rewards of justice. Even if he manages to show that justice is the greatest single good, we are still left wondering whether its value is high enough to make this equation come out right. My main thesis is that the theory of Forms plays a crucial role in Plato's argument for that equation, but that the precise way in which that theory contributes to his defense of justice is difficult to recognize. It is hard to overcome a certain blindness we have to one of Plato's principal theses – a blindness we can find in one of Aristotle's criticisms of Plato's conception of the good. My goal is not to show that Plato's theory is defensible against

I am grateful to audiences at Clark University, Johns Hopkins University, Northwestern University, the University of Michigan, and Wayne State University for their comments on earlier drafts of this essay. In addition, I profited from the criticism of Christopher Bobonich, Sarah Broadie, Shelly Kagan, Ian Mueller, Constance Meinwald, and David Reeve.

all objections, once we correct for the mistake Aristotle makes. But I do think that there is something powerful in Plato's argument, and by criticizing Aristotle I hope to bring this feature to light.

I

I said that I will focus on Plato's "fundamental" argument that justice is in one's interest, but it might be wondered why any one argument should be singled out in this way and given special attention. For on the surface, the *Republic* seems to present four independent attempts to support the conclusion that justice pays apart from its consequences.[3] First, at the end of Book IV, we learn that justice is a certain harmonious arrangement of the parts of the soul. It is therefore related to the soul as health is related to the body, and since life is not worth living if one's health is ruined, it is all the more important to maintain the justice of one's soul (444c–445c). Second, in Book IX, Plato compares the five types of people he has been portraying in the middle books – the philosophical ruler, the timocrat, the oligarch, the democrat, and the tyrant – and declares that the happiest of them is the philosopher, since he exercises kingly rule over himself (580a–c). Third, Book IX immediately proceeds to argue that the philosophical life has more pleasure than any other, since the philosopher is in the best position to compare the various pleasures available to different types of people and prefers philosophical pleasures to all others (580c–583a). And fourth, the pleasures of the philosophical life are shown to be more real and therefore greater than the pleasures of any other sort of life (583b–588a).

Does Plato single out any one of these arguments as more fundamental than the others? It might be thought that his fourth argument – the second of the two that concern pleasure – is the one he thought most important, for he introduces it with the remark that "this will be the greatest and supreme fall [of injustice]" (*megiston te kai kuriōtatōn tōn ptōmatōn,* 583b6–7). This could be taken to mean that pleasure is the most important good in terms of which to make the decision between justice and injustice, and that the argument to come is the one that most fully reveals why justice is to be chosen over its opposite. But I think that such a reading would give this argument far more significance than it deserves, and that Plato's words can and should be given a different interpretation. As I read the *Republic,* its fundamental argument in defense of justice is the one that comes to a close in Book IX *before* anything is said about how the just and unjust lives compare in terms of pleasure. This is the argument that Plato develops at greatest length, and if it is correct it makes a decisive case in favor of the just life. It shows precisely what it is about justice that makes it so worthwhile. By contrast, the two arguments that connect justice and pleasure are merely meant to assure us that we do not have to sacrifice the latter good in order to get the former. They add to the attractiveness of the just life, but they are not by themselves sufficient to show that justice is to be chosen over injustice, as is the lengthier argument that precedes them.

Why should we read the *Republic* in this way, despite Plato's statement that "the greatest and supreme fall" of injustice comes with his final argument? The answer lies in the way he poses, in Book II, the fundamental question to which the rest of the dialogue is an answer. The thesis he there undertakes to prove is phrased in various ways: It is better (*ameinon*) to be just than unjust (357b1); justice must be welcomed for itself if one is to be blessed (*makarios,* 358a3); the common opinion that injustice is more profitable (*lusitelein*) must be refuted (360c8); we must decide whether the just man is happier (*eudaimonesteros*) than the unjust (361d3);[4] justice by itself benefits (*oninanai*) someone who possesses it whereas injustice harms (*blaptein*) him (367d3–4); we must determine the advantages (*ōpheliai*) of justice and injustice (368c6). Plato does not give any one of these phrases a special role to play in his argument, but moves back and forth freely among them. And he surely must be assuming that once the consummately just life has been shown to be more advantageous, even in the midst of misfortune, than the consummately unjust life, then he has given decisive reason for choosing the former over the latter.

Notice, however, that Plato never promises, in Book II, to show that justice provides greater pleasures than does injustice, and never even hints that he would have to defend this thesis in order to show that we should choose the just life. This suggests that the question whether the just or the unjust life has more pleasure will still be an open one, even after the greater advantages of the just life have been demonstrated. And of course, this suggestion is confirmed in Book IX: Having shown that the just person is happiest, Plato thinks it requires further argument to show that the just person also has the greatest pleasure. So, in order to accomplish the task Plato assigns himself in the *Republic* it is both necessary and sufficient that he show why justice is so much more advantageous than injustice. But he never says or implies that if he can show that justice brings greater pleasures, then that by itself will be a sufficient or a necessary defense of justice. By supporting justice in terms of pleasure, Plato is showing that there is even more reason to lead the just life than we may have supposed. But the fundamental case for justice has been made before the discussion of pleasure has begun.[5]

What then should we make of his statement that the "greatest and supreme fall" for injustice occurs in the battle over pleasure? A simple and plausible explanation of this phrase is provided by the fact that at the end of his last argument Plato claims that the philosopher's pleasure is 729 times greater than the tyrant's (587e). Whether Plato is serious about this precise figure or not – and I am inclined to think he is not – it provides an explanation of why he says that this last argument gives injustice its greatest defeat.[6] In no other argument had he tried to portray the gap between justice and injustice as so great in magnitude. Once we realize that Plato's remark admits of this interpretation, we can rest content with our earlier conclusion that pleasure has a modest role to play in the overall scheme of the *Republic*.

II

I will therefore set aside the two hedonic arguments Plato gives in Book IX and concentrate entirely on the single complex defense of justice that precedes them. But it might be thought that this material contains two separate arguments, for by the end of Book IV Plato already seems to have come to the conclusion that since justice is a harmony of the soul comparable to physical health, it is far superior to injustice.[7] We might therefore suppose that after Book IV Plato launches on a second and independent defense of justice, one that concludes in Book IX with the pronouncement that the life of the philosophical ruler is happiest. But Plato himself makes it clear that these two segments – Books II–IV on the one hand, Books V–IX on the other – cannot be isolated from each other in this way. For at the beginning of Book VIII we are told that the victorious pronouncement of Book IV – that the best person and city had been found – was premature (543c7–544b3). This means that the argument of Book IV is not complete after all, but is in some way strengthened by additional material presented somewhere between Books V and IX. For by admitting that Book IV did not yet discover who the best person is, Plato indicates that he had not at that point presented a full enough picture of the just life.[8] It would therefore be a mistake to examine the argument of Books II–IV in isolation from later material as though they were meant to provide a complete defense of justice.

Nonetheless, Plato clearly thinks that he has given at least a partial defense of justice by the end of Book IV; the fact that he goes on to strengthen the argument by giving a fuller picture of the just life does not mean that by the end of Book IV we have no reason at all to think that justice is superior to injustice. To understand the single argument that runs from Book II through Book IX, we must see why Plato arrives at a preliminary conclusion in Book IV and how the additional material that comes in later books strengthens that argument.[9]

To make progress on this interpretive question, let us begin with an observation with which all scholars would agree: One of the fundamental ideas that Plato puts forward in his defense of justice is that we should look for a *general* theory of goodness. His proposal is that when we say of a human body, or a human soul, or a political community, that they are in good condition, there is some common feature that we are referring to, and it is because they share this common feature that they are properly called good.[10] He expects his audience to agree with him that the goodness of a body – health – consists in a certain natural priority among various physical components; and he appeals to this point to support his claim that one's soul is in good condition if it too exhibits a certain order among its components (444c–e).[11] But the analogy between health and psychic well-being is by itself only of limited value, because it does not tell us anything about what sort of order we should try to achieve in the soul. What Plato needs, if he is to give a stronger argument from analogy, is a structure that has the same kind of components and can exhibit the same kind of balance as the soul. He thinks he can accomplish this by examining the question of what the best possible city is, for he believes he can show that the tripartite structure of the best political community corresponds to the structure of the human soul.[12] If he can convince us that these correspondences do exist, and if he can get us to agree that the city he describes is ideal, then he has some basis for reaching the conclusion that the ideal type of person is someone whose soul exhibits the same kind of order that is possessed by an ideal political community.[13]

But in Book IV Plato has not yet given us all of his arguments for taking the political community he is describing as ideal. For one of his main reasons for favoring the kind of city described in the *Republic* is that it alone is governed by individuals who have the wisdom needed to rule well; and that kind of political expertise is only presented in Books VI–VII. This is one reason for saying that the argument from analogy presented at the end of Book IV is incomplete. Furthermore, Plato has not yet said in Books II–IV everything he wants to say about the kind of order that should be established in the soul. He tells us that reason should rule and look after the well-being of the rest of the soul, that spirit should be its ally, and that the appetites should be kept in check (441e–442a). But what is it for reason to rule the soul? In what way can spirit help it? What would it be for appetite to grow too large? Of course, Plato has already given some content to these notions, for he has been describing the proper education of these elements of the soul since the end of Book II, and this gives us some sense of how they should be related to each other. But that education has not yet been fully described; the most important objects of study have still to be presented. When we find out more about what reason must occupy itself with, we will have a fuller idea of what it is for it to rule.[14]

III

We must now turn to Books V through VII to see how Plato's depiction of the philosophical life contributes to the argument that justice pays. We want to know what it is about this life that makes it so much more worthwhile than any other; and we must understand how this new material is connected to the argument from analogy that comes to a preliminary conclusion at the end of Book IV.

An answer to these questions must in some way or other appeal to Plato's belief in Forms – those eternal, changeless, imperceptible, and bodiless objects the understanding of which is the goal of the philosopher's education.[15] For the philosopher is defined as someone whose passion for learning grows into a love of such abstract objects as Beauty, Goodness, Justice, and so on (474c–476c). And as soon as Plato introduces this conception of who the philosopher is, he lets us know that it is precisely because of the philosopher's connection with these abstract objects that the philosophical life is superior to any other. Those who fail to recognize the existence of Forms have a dreamlike kind of life, because they fail to realize that the corporeal objects they perceive are only likenesses of other objects (476c–d).[16] In a dream, we confusedly take the images of objects to be those very objects. Plato's claim is that nonphilosophers make a similar mistake, because they think that the beautiful things they see are what beauty really is; more generally, they equate the many observable objects that are called by some general term, "*A*," with what *A* really is.[17] The philosophers are those who recognize that *A* is a completely different sort of object, and so they rid themselves of a systematic error that in some way disfigures the unphilosophical life. This is of course the picture Plato draws in the parable of the cave (514a–519d): Most of us are imprisoned in a dark underworld because we gaze only on the shadows manipulated by others; to free ourselves from this situation requires a change in our conception of what sorts of objects there are.

Plato's metaphysics is of course controversial, but our present problem is to understand how it contributes to the defense of justice. Suppose we accept for the sake of argument that at least these central tenets of his metaphysics are correct: There are such abstract objects as the Form of Justice, and to call acts or individuals or citizens just is to say that they bear a certain relationship to this Form. Calling an act just is comparable to calling an image in a painting a tree: The image is not what a tree is, and it is correct to speak of it as a tree only if this means that it bears a certain relation to living trees; similarly, just acts, persons, and cities are not what justice is, and it is correct to call them just only if this means that they participate in the Form of Justice.

If we accept this theory, we avoid the errors of non-Platonists; we recognize that a wider variety of objects exists than most people realize, and that our words constantly refer to these objects. Even so, we should still ask: Why would having this Platonic conception of the world make our lives so much better than the lives of non-Platonists? One possible answer Plato might give is that since knowledge of reality is a great intrinsic good, a life in which we know the truth about what exists is far superior to one in which we remain ignorant of the fundamental realities of the universe. But this strikes me as a disappointing answer, and I will soon argue that Plato has a better one. It is disappointing because it makes an assumption that would be challenged by anyone who has doubts about the merits of the philosophical life. To those who are not already philosophically inclined, it is not at all obvious that knowledge of reality is by itself a great intrinsic good. They can legitimately ask why it is worthwhile for us to add to our understanding of reality, if our failure to do so would not impede our pursuit of worthwhile goods. Plato cannot simply reply that knowledge is intrinsically worthwhile, apart from any contribution it may make to the pursuit of other goals. That would beg the question in favor of the philosophical life.

It might be thought that for Plato knowledge of the Forms is valuable precisely because it is a means to some further goal. For example, he might claim that unless we study the Form of Justice, we are likely at some point to make errors in our judgment of which acts, persons, or institutions are just; and when we make errors of this sort, we will also make bad decisions about how to act. But if this is Plato's argument, then he again begs the question. For we can ask why it is so important to discover how to act justly in all situations. Of course, if acting justly is good for the agent, and knowledge of the Forms is an indispensable means to this end, then one must acquire that knowledge. But this argument merely assumes the thesis that Plato sets out to prove: that acting justly is a good for the agent.

Perhaps he assumes that knowing the Forms is worthwhile not merely as a means to action but because in coming to understand the Forms we develop our capacity to reason.[18] Human beings are not just appetitive and emotional creatures; we also have an innate interest in learning, and if this aspect of our nature is not developed our lives become narrow and impoverished. One problem with this answer is that people differ widely in the degree of intellectual curiosity they possess, and the kinds of objects that satisfy their curiosity also differ widely. Those who have little or no bent for abstract studies can satisfy their curiosity in simple ways, and again Plato would be begging the question if he simply assumed that having an easily satisfied appetite in matters of reasoning disqualifies one from leading a good life. Furthermore, as Plato is aware, it is possible to spend a great deal of one's time on intellectual matters without ever arriving at the realization that the Forms exist. Those who study the universe and seek to explain all phenomena without appealing to Forms surely develop the reasoning side of their nature; it is not sheer emotion and appetite that leads them to their theories. Even so, they are not leading the philosophical life, according to Plato's narrow conception of philosophy, and so they don't have the best kind of life. If he thinks that intellectuals who deny the existence of Forms fail to develop their capacities and therefore fall short of happiness, he owes his reader some argument for this thesis.

IV

I believe that Plato's answer to this question is staring us in the face, but that we fail to recognize it because initially it strikes us as doubtful or even unintelligible. My suggestion is that for Plato the Forms are a good – in fact they are the greatest good there is.[19] In order to live well we must break away from the confining assumption that the ordinary objects of pursuit – the pleasures, powers, honors, and material goods that we ordinarily compete for – are the only sorts of goods there are.[20] We must transform our lives by recognizing a radically different kind of good – the Forms – and we must try to incorporate these objects into our lives by understanding, loving, and imitating them, for they are incomparably superior to any other kind of good we can have. This is why Plato thinks that the philosopher is so much better off for having escaped the confines of the dreamlike existence of the ordinary person: The objects with which the philosopher is acquainted are far more worthy objects of love than the typical objects of human passion. So Plato is not claiming that it is intrinsically good to have a complete inventory of what exists or that developing and satisfying our intellectual curiosity is inherently worthwhile, regardless of the sorts of objects to which our curiosity leads us. Rather, he takes the discovery of the Forms to be momentous because they are the preeminent good we must possess in order to be happy, and he takes reason to be the most worthwhile capacity of our soul because it is only through reason that we can possess the Forms. If there were nothing worthwhile outside of ourselves for reason to discover, then a life devoted to reasoning would lose its claim to superiority over other kinds of life.[21]

The interpretation I am proposing has some resemblance to the way Aristotle treats Plato's moral philosophy. According to Aristotle, we can discover what kind of life we should lead only by determining which good or goods we should ultimately pursue. He considers competing conceptions of this highest good and takes the Platonist's answer to be that it is not some humdrum object of pursuit like pleasure or virtue but is rather the Form of the Good. Aristotle of course rejects this answer, but it is significant that he takes the Platonist to be saying that a certain Form is the highest good and should therefore play the role non-Platonists assign to pleasure, honor, or virtue. So interpreted, the Platonist is not simply saying that the Form of the Good is an indispensable means for determining which among other objects are good; it itself is the chief good.[22] My interpretation is similar in that I take Plato to treat the Forms in general as a preeminent good; the special role of the Form of the Good will be discussed later.

At this point it might be asked whether the theory I am attributing to Plato is intelligible. For perhaps a Form is simply not the sort of thing that a person can have or possess. Of course, a Form can be studied and known, but studying something does not by itself confer ownership. The moon, for example, might be a beautiful object worthy of our study, but no one in his right mind would say that the moon is a good he possesses by virtue of studying it. Similarly, the claim that the Form of the Good is not the sort of thing that can be possessed is one of Aristotle's many objections to the Platonist conception of the good (*N.E.* 1096b35). Aristotle takes Plato to be saying that the ultimate end is the Form of the Good, and objects that it is disqualified from playing this role because it is not an object of the right type. It might be thought that this objection is so powerful that out of charity we should look for a different interpretation from the one I am proposing.[23]

But I think Aristotle's objection is weak. Of course it is true that if we take the possession of a thing to be a matter of having property rights to it, then studying the Form of the Good does not confer such rights, and it is hard to understand what it would be to possess a Form. But we can speak of having things even though we have no property rights in them; for example, one can have friends without possessing them. And we can easily understand someone who says that in order to live a good life one must have friends. What it is to *have* a friend is quite a different matter from what it is to possess a physical object; it involves an emotional bond and activities characteristic of friendship. What it is to have a certain good varies according to the kind of good it is; different types of goods do not enter our lives in the same way. And so the mere fact that a Form cannot be possessed (that is, owned) gives us no reason to reject Plato's idea that if one bears a certain relationship to Forms – a relationship that involves both emotional attachment and intellectual understanding – then one's life becomes more worthwhile precisely because one is connected in this way with such valuable objects.

In fact, there are similarities between the way in which persons can enter our lives and improve them and the way in which Plato thinks we should be related to the Forms. We can easily understand someone who says that one of the great privileges of his life is to have known a certain eminent and inspiring person. Even if one is not a close friend of such a person, one may have great love and admiration for him, and one may take pleasure in studying his life. That is the sort of relationship Plato thinks we should have with the Forms – not on the grounds that loving and studying are good activities, whatever their objects, but on the grounds that the Forms are the preeminent good and therefore our lives are vastly improved when we come to know, love, and imitate them.

Suppose it is conceded that if the Forms are a good, then they are the sorts of things that can improve our lives when we are properly related to them. Nonetheless, it might still be asked whether we can make sense of the idea that they are good. If someone says that water is a good thing, we might be puzzled about what he has in mind, and we might even be skeptical about whether water is the sort of thing that can be good in itself (as opposed to a mere means).[24] Similarly, we might have doubts about Plato's Forms: How can such objects, which are so different in kind from such mundane goods as health and pleasure, be counted as good? And if he cannot convince us that they are good, then of course he has no hope of persuading us that they are vastly better than such ordinary goods as pleasure, health, wealth, power, and so on.

For Plato's answer to our question, What is it to say of something that it is a good thing? we might turn for help to his discussion of the Form of the Good. But although he insists on the preeminence of this Form, he does not say precisely what he takes goodness to be; he simply says that it is not pleasure or knowledge (505b–506e). There is a marked contrast here between the fullness of his account of what justice is and the thinness of his discussion of goodness. We learn what it is to call a person, act, or city just, and we see the feature that they all have in common, but Plato points to no common feature of all good things. So he does not take up the project of showing that Forms are preeminent by stating what property goodness consists in and arguing that they exhibit that property more fully than anything else.

Perhaps we can discover why Plato thinks of Forms as goods if we focus on their distinguishing characteristics and ask which of them Plato might put forward as points of superiority over other objects. For example, he thinks that Forms are more real than corporeal objects, and presumably he counts this as evidence of their superiority in value.[25] But this point will not take us as far as we need to go, because he thinks that objects that are equally real can nonetheless differ greatly in value. Consider two bodies, one of them healthy, the other diseased: One is in better condition than the other, but Plato never suggests that one of them must therefore be more real than the other. Though Forms are more real than other types of objects, we cannot treat differing degrees of reality as what in general constitute differences in value.

But our example of the healthy and diseased bodies suggests another line of reasoning: Plato equates health, the good condition of the body, with a certain harmony among its elements; and he argues that justice, the good condition of the soul, is also a certain kind of harmony among its parts; and so the thought suggests itself that he takes the goodness of anything of a certain kind to be the harmony or proportion that is appropriate for things of that kind. According to this suggestion, the goodness of Forms consists in the fact that they possess a kind of harmony, balance, or proportion; and their superiority to all other things consists in the fact that the kind of order they possess gives them a higher degree of harmony than any other type of object.[26]

Clearly Plato does think that the Forms exhibit the highest kind of orderly arrangement. He says that the philosopher looks away from the conflict-ridden affairs of human beings to things that are unchanging and ordered (*tetagmena,* 500c2); by studying the divine order (*kosmos,* c4) her soul becomes as orderly and divine as it is possible for a human soul to be (c9–d1). Even the beautiful patterns exhibited in the night sky fall short of the harmonies present in true shapes and numbers, since the corporeality of the stars makes deviation inevitable, whereas the incorporeality of the Forms ensures that the orderly patterns they exhibit will never deteriorate (529c7–530b4). But he does not say precisely what the orderliness of the Forms consists in; bodies, souls, and political communities exhibit order (and therefore goodness) when their parts or components are related to each other in suitable ways, but we are not told whether the Forms have parts or whether they achieve their order in some other way. Perhaps this explains Plato's refusal to say what the Form of the Good is (506d–e); though goodness simply is some kind of harmony, he had not yet reached a firm grasp of what this harmony is in the case of Forms, and so he could not put forward a general characterization of harmony that would apply equally to the various kinds of harmony exhibited by living bodies, souls, stars, and Forms. But in any case, we can now see how Plato would try to address doubts about whether Forms are the sorts of objects that can intelligibly be called good. He would reply by appealing to his discussion of politics, the soul, and health: In all of these cases, the goodness of a thing consists in a kind of order; and so if the Forms can be shown to have the kind of order that is appropriate for things of that kind, they too will be good. And if they necessarily have a higher degree of order than anything else, then they are the best goods there can be.[27]

V

It may now be asked how any of this provides Plato with a defense of the virtue of justice. Even if we see why he thinks that the philosophical life is best, we still can ask why this should be regarded as a defense of *justice.* Why is the philosopher the paradigm of the just person? Part of Plato's reply, as I understand it, is as follows:[28] When the ideal state properly educates individuals to become philosophers, their emotions and appetites are transformed in a way that serves the philosophical life, and these affective states no longer provide a strong impetus toward antisocial behavior, as they do when they are left undisciplined (499e–500e). Someone who has been fully prepared to love the orderly pattern of the Forms will be free of the urge to seek worldly advantages over other human beings or to engage in the sort of illicit sexual activity to which people are led by unchecked appetites. Furthermore, such a person is in the best possible position to make wise political decisions; having understood the Forms, she can see more clearly than others what needs to be done in particular circumstances (500d–501a). One of the things we look for, when we seek a paradigm of the just person, is someone who has these intellectual and affective skills.[29]

It is tempting to protest at this point that Plato is being extremely naive. After all, we all know people who have impressive intellectual abilities but who are hardly models of justice. And of course there is nothing to prevent such individuals from recognizing the existence of abstract objects, and even loving the contemplation of the orderly pattern among such objects. Consider a Platonist mathematician who occasionally gets drunk and indulges in other behavior that conflicts with Plato's description of the just individual. Aren't such individuals living refutations of Plato?

I believe not, for I don't take him to be making the implausibly strong claim that the love of abstract objects by itself guarantees just behavior or the emotional discipline that characterizes the just person. Rather, his weaker and more plausible claim is that one will be in the best position to lead a life dominated by the love of Forms if one trains the nonrational components of one's soul to serve one's love of philosophy. It is this weaker claim that lies behind his portrayal of the philosopher as the paradigm of human justice. By putting oneself into the best position to lead the philosophical life, one develops the intellectual and emotional skills that we look for in a completely just person. The mere existence of unjust lovers of abstract objects does not by itself refute Plato, for the issue is not whether they exist but whether the psychological condition that underlies their injustice makes them less able to profit from their recognition of abstract objects. It might be argued, against Plato, that sensuality, greed, and large appetites for food and drink make one all the more able to understand and love the orderly realm of the Forms, but it is far from obvious that this is so. He is not being unreasonable in assuming that these emotional states are on the contrary obstacles to the philosophical life.

We should recall, however, that Plato promises to do more than merely show that justice is a great good. He has to show that it is a greater good than injustice, so much so that even if the normal consequences of justice and injustice are reversed it will nonetheless be better to be just than unjust. The paradigm of justice must be punished because he is thought to be unjust; and the paradigm of injustice is to receive the honors and rewards because he appears to be just. How can Plato show that even in this situation it is better to be just?

The answer lies partly in the way he describes the situation of the completely unjust person, that is, the tyrant. Such a person is allowed to live out his fantasies of power and eroticism without restraint, and Plato's case against such a life is that this lack of restraint will inevitably exact a devastating psychological toll. When erotic desires are allowed to grow to full strength, they become impossible to satisfy; rather than leading to a life of peace and fulfillment, they leave one with a chronic feeling of frustration (579d–e). Similarly, tyrannical power inevitably gives rise to continual fear of reprisals and an absence of trust in one's associates (576a, 579a–c). The failure to impose any order on one's appetites makes one the victim of frequent and disorganized internal demands (573d). So, in order to achieve great power and intense sexual pleasure, the tyrant must lead a chaotic life filled with anguish, fear, and frustration. No one who reads this account of the tyrannical life could seriously hold it up as a model of how human beings should live. When the immoralist praises the life ruled by unrestrained desires for power and pleasure, he simply fails to think through the consequences of giving these desires free rein. He responds to something in human nature, for Plato agrees that no one is completely free of the impulses that the immoralist champions (571b–572b). The presence of these illicit urges seems to lend some credibility to the immoralist's doubts about whether justice is a virtue, for the praise of immorality answers to something within us. Plato's response to the immoralist is that when we seriously consider the psychological consequences of magnifying the power of our illicit urges, the life of maximal injustice loses its appeal. This is something he thinks we will be able to see without having the benefit of the theory of Forms; he invokes the Forms because they are the objects around which the best kind of human life must be built, but he makes no appeal to these objects when he tries to convince us that the tyrannical life is miserable.

Again, it is possible to protest that Plato's argument is naive. It seems to rest on the empirical assumption that anyone who possesses tyrannical power will also have sexual obsessions, and this makes it easier for him to make such a life look unattractive. But in fact such an empirical assumption is unwarranted: It is certainly possible to tyrannize a community and hold all other passions in check.[30] Here too, however, I think Plato is less vulnerable to criticism than we might have thought. His portrait of the tyrant is not meant to be an exceptionless empirical generalization about what such individuals are like. Rather, he is developing the portrait of the unjust life that is presented in Book II when Glaucon and Adeimantus try to make such a life look attractive. According to their portrait, the unjust man can seduce any woman who appeals to him; he can kill anyone he wants (360a–c). Plato's idea is that if these features of injustice capture its subrational appeal, then it is fair to describe the paradigm of injustice as someone whose sexual appetites and murderous tendencies are extreme. If that is how he is proceeding, then it is irrelevant that in fact tyrants need not be dominated by sexual appetite.

Plato's portrait of the tyrant makes it clear that his argument for justice does not rest solely on the metaphysics of the middle books and the political theory of the early books but also relies on various assumptions about human psychology. Certain desires, if unchecked, lead to the sorts of consequences – frustration, fear, pain – that everyone tries to avoid and that no one regards as compatible with a fully happy human life. What Plato is assuming is that the life of the completely just person is not marred by these same features. Fear, frustration, and chaos are not the price philosophers must inevitably pay for having a love of the Forms and for giving this passion a dominant role in their lives. On the contrary, those who are in the best position for studying the Forms will have modest and therefore easily satisfied appetites, and will be free of the competitive desire for power that typically sets people at odds and destroys their tranquillity. So the philosophical life will include the felt harmony of soul that everyone can recognize and value, as well as the more complex kind of harmony that one can understand only through a philosophical investigation of the parts of the soul and of the metaphysical objects that enter one's life when reason rules.

We can now see why Plato is confident that he can prove that justice pays even when he allows the just person and the unjust person to reverse their roles in Book II. Even if the just person is mistakenly dishonored and punished, she will still be at peace with herself; she will be free of the chaos and frustration that make the life of the tyrant so repellent. In place of the great physical pain imagined for the just person, the tyrant must endure great psychological pain. Neither is in an enviable condition, but there is a major difference that Plato thinks counts decisively in favor of the just person: her understanding and emotions gain her entrance into a world of completely harmonious objects, and so she possesses the greatest good there is. We have finally answered the question with which we began: The consummately unjust person has troubles that counterbalance the pain and dishonor imagined for the just person, and if these were the only factors involved in their comparison, it might be difficult to decide whose situation is worse; but once the possession of the Forms is added to the just person's side of the equation, the advantage lies with her, overwhelmingly so because of the great worth of that nonsensible realm.[31]

VI

One important feature of Plato's theory has not yet been discussed, and it is best brought to light by considering a well-known internal difficulty in his argument. He says that the philosophers of the ideal city must not be allowed to study the Forms without interruption, but must instead return to the darkness of the cave and help administer the political community (519d–521b, 540a–b). Why won't the philosophers be tempted to resist this requirement, however just it may be, since it seems to conflict with their self-interest?[32] After all, life in the open air illuminated by the Form of the Good must be better than life in the subterranean atmosphere in which one must rule the state. Won't the philosophers be strongly tempted to think of ways in which they can escape such service? If so, they cannot be held up as paragons of justice. Furthermore, this example seems to show that justice does not always pay: If one could unjustly escape service to the community and continue contemplating the Forms, one would do what is best for oneself, but one would not act justly.

Plato is completely confident that the individuals he has trained for the philosophical life will accept this requirement. After all, he says, they are just, and the requirement is just (520e1). But why doesn't he see any problem for his theory here? Why doesn't it leap to his eye that ruling is contrary to the philosopher's interests, so that this feature of his ideal state presents a clear counterexample to his thesis that justice pays? One possible answer to this question is simply that Plato is willing to make exceptions to this generalization.[33] But it is unlikely that he would restrict himself to the weak claim that justice is *usually* in one's interests. It is more fruitful, I think, to look at the problem in the reverse manner: Plato thinks that ruling the state is a just requirement, and since he believes that justice is always in one's interest, he must think that somehow it does pay to rule the city. The question is how he could believe this.

He tells us at one point that when philosophers look to the harmonious arrangement of the Forms, they develop a desire to imitate that harmony in some way or other (500c). And then he adds that if it becomes necessary for the philosophers to imitate the Forms by molding human character in their likeness, they will be in an excellent position to do this job well. So it is clear that when the philosophers rule, they do not stop looking to or imitating the Forms. Rather, their imitative activity is no longer merely contemplative; instead, they start acting in a way that produces a harmony in the city that is a likeness of the harmony of the Forms. Furthermore, were they to refuse to rule, they would be allowing the disorder in the city to increase. Were any single philosopher to shirk her responsibilities, and let others do more than their fair share, then she would be undermining a fair system of dividing responsibilities. The order that would be appropriate to their situation would be undermined. And so failure to rule, whether in an individual philosopher or in a group of them, would create a certain disharmony in the world: Relationships that are appropriate among people would be violated. And in creating this disharmony, the philosopher would in one respect cease to imitate the Forms. She would gaze at the order that is appropriate among Forms but would thereby upset an order that is appropriate among human beings.

What this suggests is that Plato has the resources for showing that justice is in one's interests even when it requires forgoing some purely philosophical activity. What he must hold is that one's highest good is not always served by purely contemplating the Forms;[34] rather, one's highest good is to establish and maintain a certain imitative relationship with the Forms, a relationship that is strained or ruptured when one fails to do one's fair share in a just community. The person who is willing to do her part in a just social order, and whose willingness arises out of a full understanding of what justice is, will see the community of which she is a part as an ordered whole, a worldly counterpart to the otherworldly realm of abstract objects she loves. When she acts justly and does her fair share, she sees herself as participating in a social pattern that approximates the harmony of the Forms, and she therefore takes her good to be served by acting justly. In making this connection between social harmony and the harmony of abstract objects, Plato offers an account of the positive appeal that justice in human relationships should have for us. We are – or should be – attracted to justice in human relationships; when we act justly, we should do so not merely because of the absence of such motives as greed, sensuality, and the desire to dominate others. Rather, we should see something attractive about communities and relationships in which each person does his or her appropriate part, and we should be loathe to violate these relationships because of our love of justice. If I have understood Plato correctly, he recognizes that justice as a relationship among human beings can have this positive appeal.[35]

VII

I said at the beginning of this chapter that there is something powerful in Plato's argument that justice pays. What I have in mind is his thesis that the goodness of human life depends heavily on our having a close connection with something eminently worthwhile that lies outside of ourselves. To live well one must be in the right psychological condition, and that condition consists in a receptivity to the valuable objects that exist independently of oneself. If one is oblivious to these objects and devotes oneself above all to the acquisition of power, or the accumulation of wealth, or the satisfaction of erotic appetites, then one will not only become a danger to others but one will fail to achieve one's own good. Psychological forces that lead to injustice when they become powerful are forces that should in any case be moderated for one's own good, for when they are too strong they interfere with our ability to possess the most valuable objects.

Even if we reject Plato's belief in Forms or his thesis that goodness consists in harmony, we should recognize that there are many different ways of trying to sustain his attempt to connect the goodness of human life with some goodness external to one's soul. Christianity provides an obvious example, for it holds that the external good is God and that no human life is worth leading unless God is somehow present in it. Another example can be found in Romantic conceptions of nature, according to which a person who is cut off from the beauty of the natural order has been excluded from his home and must lead an alienated existence. We can even see some similarity between Plato's theory and the idea that great works of art so enrich human lives that the inability to respond to their beauty is a serious impoverishment.

In this last case, the valuable objects are created by human beings, but nonetheless it could be held that one's good consists in learning how to understand and love these objects. Someone can reasonably say that her life has been made better because she has come to love one of the cultural products of her society – a great novel, for example. This does not have to mean that the novel has taught her lessons that have instrumental value or that it has brought forth psychological capacities that would otherwise have lain dormant. It is intelligible to say that a relationship to a certain object – something beautiful in nature, or some work of art, or a divinity – by itself makes one's life better. And that seems to represent the way many people view their lives, for it is difficult to sustain the belief that one's life is worthwhile if one sees and feels no connection between oneself and some greater object.

Plato would of course reject these alternatives to his theory: He claims that the natural world for all its beauty is no model of perfection and that the works of poets are of lesser value still. Perhaps then we should distinguish a weak from a strong form of Platonism: Weak Platonism holds that the human good consists in having the proper relationship to some valuable object external to oneself, whether that object be a work of art, one's family or political community, the natural world, or a divinity. Strong Platonism goes further and holds that the valuable object in question must be some eternal and unchanging realm. What is distinctive of Plato's own view, of course, is that the objects in question are the Forms. But even if his particular version of Platonism is rejected, it should be recognized that some form of this doctrine, strong or weak, is deeply appealing to many. Plato might be pleased and not at all surprised that watered-down forms of Platonism have had such a long history.

NOTES

1 See *Rep.* 360e–362c for the contrast between the just and unjust lives. (All future page references will be to this dialogue, unless otherwise noted.) It should be emphasized that Plato is not trying to show that it is advantageous to *act justly* regardless of one's psychological condition. His claim is that it is advantageous to be a *just person.*

2 I have learned most from these studies: Julia Annas, *An Introduction to Plato's Republic* (Oxford, 1981); Terence Irwin, *Plato's Moral Theory* (Oxford, 1977); C. D. C. Reeve, *Philosopher-Kings: The Argument of Plato's Republic* (Princeton, 1988); Nicholas P. White, *A Companion to Plato's Republic* (Indianapolis, 1979). Among older treatments still worth consulting are R. C. Cross and A. D. Woozley, *Plato's Republic: A Philosophical Commentary* (London, 1964); Horace W. B. Joseph, *Essays in Ancient and Modern Philosophy* (Freeport, N.Y., 1971); N. R. Murphy, *The Interpretation of Plato's Republic* (Oxford, 1951); Richard Nettleship, *Lectures on the Republic of Plato,* 2d ed. (London, 1962).

3 Here I am setting aside the arguments of Book I of the dialogue and concentrating entirely on the issue as it is reintroduced at the beginning of Book II. Plato must have believed that the arguments of Book I were in some way deficient; otherwise there would be no need to reopen the question in Book II. Perhaps their deficiency lies principally in their schematic nature: They need to be buttressed by political theory, metaphysics, and psychology. An alternative reading is that in Book II Plato thinks that the earlier arguments are entirely of the wrong sort. For this interpretation, see Irwin, *Plato's Moral Theory,* 177–84; Reeve, *Philosopher-Kings,* 3–24. I also set aside the further considerations Plato mentions in Book X at 612b*ff:* These are the worldly and otherworldly rewards the just can expect to receive. It is precisely these rewards that Plato agrees to overlook when he promises in Book II to show that justice is in our interest, apart from its consequences. It should be emphasized that Plato thinks these rewards make the just life even more desirable. He agrees that the just person who suffers the torments described at 361e–362a suffers a loss of well-being and is no paradigm of happiness. When he refers to wealth and other "so-called goods" at 495a7, his refusal to call them goods outright should be taken to mean that these ordinary objects of pursuit are not in all circumstances good; he cannot hold the stronger thesis that they are never good, for then the social rewards of justice would be a matter of indifference. There has been considerable discussion

of what Plato means by saying that justice is good *in itself.* See Annas, *Introduction,* chap. 3; Cross and Woozley, *Plato's Republic,* 66–9; M. B. Foster, "A Mistake of Plato's in the *Republic,*" *Mind* 46 (1937): 386–93; Irwin, *Plato's Moral Theory,* 184–91, 325–6; C. A. Kirwan, "Glaucon's Challenge," *Phronesis* 10 (1965): 162–73; J. D. Mabbott, "Is Plato's *Republic* Utilitarian?" *Mind* 46 (1937): 468–74; David Sachs, "A Fallacy in Plato's *Republic,*" *Philosophical Review* 72 (1963): 141–58; Reeve, *Philosopher-Kings,* 24–33; Nicholas P. White, "The Classification of Goods in Plato's *Republic,*" *Journal of the History of Philosophy* 22 (1984): 393–421.

4 Readers of the *Republic* should bear in mind that Plato does not use *eudaimonia* (often translated "happiness") and its cognates to refer to the feeling of pleasure. For Plato, to seek one's own happiness is simply to seek one's own advantage, and so to discover what happiness is one must determine where a human being's true interests lie.

5 At 589c1–4 Plato distinguishes between praising justice for its advantages and praising it for its pleasures (cf. 581e7–582a2, 588a7–10). This implies that the two arguments from pleasure in Book IX are not addressed to the issue of whether justice or injustice is more advantageous. For an alternative reading, see J. C. B. Gosling and C. C. W. Taylor, *The Greeks on Pleasure* (Oxford, 1982), 98–101; their interpretation is endorsed by Reeve, *Philosopher-Kings,* 307 n. 33. For further discussion of this alternative, see my review of Reeve's *Philosopher-Kings* in *Political Theory* 18 (1990): 492–6.

6 For discussion of Plato's calculation, see Reeve, *Philosopher-Kings,* 150–1. He argues that the correct figure should be 125.

7 Or, following Annas, *Introduction,* 168–9, we might think that Plato is arguing for two different conclusions: The earlier material is designed to show that justice is good in itself, apart from happiness; whereas the later material does try to link justice and happiness. But we should reject her statement that "the notion of happiness has not occurred" in Book IV. When Plato asks at 444e7–445a4 whether justice is more profitable (*lusitelei*) than injustice, he is in effect asking whether the just person is happier. As Book II shows, the thesis Plato is trying to prove can be formulated in several terms that are treated equivalently. Annas's interpretation was proposed earlier by Mabbott, "Is Plato's *Republic* Utilitarian?," 62.

8 Other passages show that Plato does not take himself to have fully revealed in Book IV what justice is: See 472b7 and 484a7–8.

9 For the contrary view – that Plato does not attempt to give *any* argument in Books II–IV for the thesis that justice is advantageous – see Nicholos P. White, "The Ruler's Choice," *Archiv für Geschichte der*

Philosophie 68 (1986): 34–41. But I think 444e7–445b7 rules this out: The interlocutors here agree that justice is advantageous and that injustice is not; and surely they think that they have some reason for this conclusion. I take 445b5–7 to mean that the conclusion has not been supported as fully as possible, and that the fuller argument is now to come. Despite this difference, White and I agree that Books II–IX should be read as a single continuous argument in defense of justice.

10 This is of course a consequence of Plato's general principle that whenever we call a group of things by the same name there is something they all have in common. See, for example, *Meno* 72b–c and *Rep.* 596a. Plato's assumption that goodness is a single thing is attacked by Aristotle in the *Nicomachean Ethics* I.6.

11 More fully, the argument is this: (1) Health is the preeminent good of the body, in the sense that life is not worth living when one's body is completely lacking health. (2) What makes health so worthwhile is that it involves a natural balance of elements – certain elements appropriately dominate certain others. (3) Justice involves an analogous balance in the soul. (4) Since justice has the same good-making characteristic as health, it must be equally true that life is not worth living if one is greatly deficient in justice. The crucial premise is (3), and to support it Plato appeals to the analogy between city and soul. But even if Plato had completely left aside the idea that health involves a balance, the main argument from analogy of Books II–IV would still remain: What is best for the polis is an internal balance, and so we should expect the same to hold true of the individual. The appeal to health is an attempt to strengthen the argument by adding one more case in which advantage can be equated with proper balance.

12 For discussion of Plato's argument for the tripartition of the soul, see John M. Cooper, "Plato's Theory of Human Motivation," *History of Philosophy Quarterly* (1984): 3–21; Irwin, *Plato's Moral Theory,* 191–5; Terry Penner, "Thought and Desire in Plato," in *Plato,* vol. 2, ed. Gregory Vlastos (Garden City, N.Y., 1971), 96–118; Reeve, *Philosopher-Kings,* 118–40.

13 Plato's strategy would fail if it were impossible to say anything about what a good city is without first knowing what a good person is or what human happiness is. Books II–IV try to convince us that we can discover a good deal about how a political community should be organized, even before we address the question of human virtue and happiness. For the view that the argument of II–IV begs the question against Thrasymachus by simply assuming at 427e–428a and 433a–435a that justice is a virtue, see Michael C. Stokes, "Adeimantus in the *Republic,*" in *Law, Justice and Method in Plato and Aristotle,* ed. Spiro Panagiotou (Edmon-

ton, 1985). Stokes thinks that Plato is not really addressing his argument to a radical critic of justice like Thrasymachus; rather, he is speaking to Glaucon and Adeimantus, who are already half-convinced when the argument begins. A similar view is defended by Reeve, *Philosopher-Kings*, 33–42; contrast Martha C. Nussbaum, *The Fragility of Goodness* (Cambridge, 1986), 155–6. I believe that Plato is trying to persuade Thrasymachus (see 498d) and that he does not take his argument to beg the question against him, but the issue requires more discussion than I can give it here.

14 The limitations of Plato's argument as it develops from Book II to Book IV are emphasized by John M. Cooper, "The Psychology of Justice in Plato," *American Philosophical Quarterly* 14(1977): 152–3; Irwin, *Plato's Moral Theory*, 216–17; and White, "Ruler's Choice," 39.

15 Among the most important passages characterizing the Forms are *Phd.* 65d–66a, 74b–c, 78c–80b; *Phdr.* 247c; *Rep.* 477a–480e; *Smp.* 210e–211e; *Ti.* 27d–28a, 38a, 52a–b; *Phil.* 59c. For a thorough examination of Plato's reasons for postulating the existence of Forms, see Terry Penner, *The Ascent from Nominalism* (Dordrecht, 1987).

16 For a lucid interpretation of this aspect of Plato's theory, see Richard Patterson, *Image and Reality in Plato's Metaphysics* (Indianapolis, 1985).

17 See Penner, *Ascent from Nominalism*, 57–140.

18 See Irwin, *Plato's Moral Theory*, 236, for the claim that Plato's defense of justice depends on the idea that we must develop all of our capacities.

19 The principal textual support for this reading derives from the many passages in which Plato describes the Forms as the proper objects of love: 476b, 480a, 484b, 490a–b, 500c, 501d. They could not be such unless they are good (*Smp.* 204d–206a). I am not claiming that according to Plato each Form counts as a separate good; rather, it is the ordered whole constituted by the Forms that is a good, although some of the individual Forms (Goodness, Beauty, etc.) may by themselves be goods. Of course, if my interpretation is to be an improvement over the ones just considered, then Plato cannot simply *assume* that the Forms are a great good. His argument for this claim will be discussed later. It might be asked how the Forms can be the greatest good, since that distinction is reserved for justice (366e9). But there is no real conflict here. When Plato says that justice is the greatest good, he does not mean that the universe has no better object to show than a just human being; the Forms are superior to this. He means rather that possessing justice is better for us than possessing any other type of good; and this is compatible with the claim that the Forms are the supreme objects. For on my reading, being fully just and fully possessing the Forms are the same

psychological state, and so there is no issue about which state it is better to be in.

20 It is widely recognized that according to Plato happiness consists in possessing good things – a point he takes to need no argument. See *Smp.* 204e–205a. What is distinctive of my interpretation is the suggestion that Plato defends the philosophical life (and therefore the life of consummate justice) by adding to the conventional list of goods.

21 The pattern of argument in the *Philebus* is similar: Reason is declared to be a more important component of the good human life than pleasure because it is more akin than pleasure to the good. Here, as in the *Republic,* something outside of human life is taken to be ideal, and those elements of human life that most fully approach this ideal are to receive priority.

22 This is why his discussion in *N. E.* I.6 of the Platonic conception of the Good is not out of place. Aristotle also considers the possibility that for the Platonist the Good is not itself a desirable object but is instead a tool for gaining the knowledge we need to make practical decisions. See 1096b35–1097a6. But this is an alternative to the main conception of the Good that he considers in I.6.

23 Thus G. X. Santas, "Aristotle's Criticism of Plato's Form of the Good: Ethics without Metaphysics?" *Philosophical Papers* 18 (1989): 154. He takes Aristotle to be obviously right that a Platonic Form is not the sort of thing that can be possessed, and defends Plato by denying that his theory makes any such claim. Instead, he takes Plato merely to be saying that the Form of the Good must be known, the better to possess other goods. A related view seems to be presupposed by Nussbaum, who takes Plato to believe that "the bearers of value are activities." See *Fragility of Goodness,* 148. On this view, the Forms themselves cannot be "bearers of value," since they are not activities. Rather, they have value because they are the objects of pure, stable, truth-discovering activity. See pp. 145–8.

24 See Paul Ziff, *Semantic Analysis* (Ithaca, N.Y., 1960), 210, 216. His view is that when we call something "good" we are saying that it "answers to certain interests" (p. 117). Unless we are provided with further information, it is not clear how water can meet this condition. Of course, on my reading, Plato is not merely saying that the Forms answer to certain interests. They are good quite apart from our interests, and because of their great goodness it is in our interest to possess them.

25 The analogy of the cave (514a–517c) and the critique of artistic imitation in Book X (see esp. 596a–597d) bring out this aspect of the theory most fully. See too 477a, 478d, 479d. For discussion, see Gregory Vlastos, "Degrees of Reality in Plato," in *Platonic Studies,* 2d ed. (Princeton,

1981), 58–75. Vlastos holds that the Forms are fully real in two senses: they have the highest degree of cognitive reliability, and they have a kind of value that "transcends the usual specifications of value" (p. 64). Of course, Plato cannot simply lay it down without argument that Forms have this transcendent value, nor can he infer that they have it merely because of their greater cognitive reliability.

26 So read, the arguments of Books II–IV and of V–IX are mutually supporting: The later material adds content and support to the thesis that justice is a psychological harmony, and that thesis in turn supports the identification of being in good condition with being harmoniously arranged.

27 Some support for this interpretation comes from the *Philebus,* since Plato there appeals to measure and proportion to explain the nature of goodness (*Phil.* 64d–e). Throughout the cosmos, and not merely in human affairs, wherever limit is imposed on the disorder inherent in the unlimited, a harmonious unification is achieved, and this harmony is what makes things good. See *Phil.* 23c–26d. I take Plato to be saying that a thing of one type is better than something of the *same* type if it has a greater degree of the harmony appropriate for things of that type; and a thing of one type is better than something of a *different* type if things of the first type can achieve a higher degree of harmony than things of the second. Harmony is for Plato a form of unification, and so on my view he connects goodness and unity. Note his emphasis on unity as the greatest civic good: 462a–b; cf. 422e–423c. On the role of unity in Plato's argument, see White, *Companion,* 31, 38–40. For further discussion of the Form of the Good, see Cooper, "Psychology of Justice," 154–5; Irwin, *Plato's Moral Theory,* 224–6; G. X. Santas, "The Form of the Good in Plato's *Republic,*" in *Essays in Ancient Greek Philosophy,* ed. John P. Anton and Anthony Preus (Albany, 1983), 2:232–63; and Reeve, *Philosopher-Kings,* 81–95.

28 In section VI, I will discuss another part of Plato's answer: Some acts of justice imitate the Forms.

29 For further discussion of the ways in which Plato's novel understanding of justice is related to the ordinary Greek conception, see Gregory Vlastos, "Justice and Happiness in the *Republic,*" in *Platonic Studies,* 2d ed. (Princeton, 1981), 111–39. This is a response to Sachs, "A Fallacy in Plato's *Republic,*" which argues that these two conceptions are unconnected. Some other responses to Sachs are Annas, *Introduction,* chap. 6; Raphael Demos, "A Fallacy in Plato's *Republic?*" *Philosophical Review* 73 (1984): 395–8; Irwin, *Plato's Moral Theory,* 208–12; Richard Kraut, "Reason and Justice in Plato's *Republic,*" in *Exegesis and Argument,* ed. E. N. Lee, Alexander P. D. Mourelatos, and R. M. Rorty (Assen, 1973), 207–24; and Reeve, *Philosopher-Kings,* chap. 5.

30 For this criticism of Plato, see Annas, *Introduction,* 304.

31 Here my reading differs from that of Nicholas P. White, "Happiness and External Contingencies in Plato's *Republic*," in *Moral Philosophy*, ed. William C. Starr and Richard C. Taylor (Milwaukee, 1989), 1–21. He denies that Plato tries to defend the thesis (one that White labels "absurd") that "every just person is at every moment better off than every unjust person," regardless of differences in their good or bad fortune (p. 16). Rather, he takes Plato to hold the weaker view that justice "is the best strategy" over the long run, and he thinks Plato's defense of this thesis is not completed until Book X. On this reading, when the just person is on the rack, he is at that point worse off then an unjust person basking in undeserved glory. This commits Plato to the view that if the just person *dies* on the rack, and so has no long run, then despite the fact that he chose the best strategy, his life is worse than the lives of some who are unjust.

32 The philosophers' motivation for ruling has received much discussion but no consensus has emerged. For some of the conflicting views, see Annas, *Introduction*, 266–71; Cooper, "Psychology of Justice," 155–7; Irwin, *Plato's Moral Theory*, 242–3, 337–8; Richard Kraut, "Egoism, Love and Political Office in Plato," *Philosophical Review* 82 (1973): 330–44; Reeve, *Philosopher-King*, 95, 197–204; White, *Companion*, 44–8, 189–96; White, "Ruler's Choice."

33 For the view that Plato makes an exception in this one case, see White, "Ruler's Choice."

34 I do not believe that Plato ever claims or commits himself to the thesis that the best human life is the one that has the greatest amount of purely contemplative activity. What he does clearly hold is that such activity is better than political activity (520e–521a); but this does not entail that pure contemplation that creates injustice is more advantageous than political activity that is justly required.

35 For a fuller presentation of the interpretation I have given in this section, see my "Return to the Cave: *Republic* 519–521," in *Proceedings of the Boston Area Colloquium in Ancient Philosophy*, vol. 7, ed. John J. Cleary (forthcoming).

ELIZABETH ASMIS

11 Plato on poetic creativity

In Book X of the *Republic,* Plato expels the poetry of Homer and his followers – "the poetry of pleasure," as he calls it – from his ideal state by observing that there is an ancient quarrel between philosophy and poetry. At the same time, he expresses a willingness to put aside the quarrel. His spokesman, Socrates, throws out a challenge: If the poetry of pleasure or its defenders can show that it is "not only pleasant, but also useful for cities and human life," they would gladly receive it back (607a–e). Plato returns to this challenge in his last work, the *Laws.* The tragic poets approach the lawmakers and ask, May we bring our poetry to your city? The lawmakers reply that they, the lawmakers, are "poets" too, rivals and competitors in making the "most beautiful drama." Their drama is the state, an "imitation of the most beautfiul and best life." If the tragedians can show them dramas that agree with theirs, they will be allowed to perform; otherwise not (817a–d).

In the *Laws,* Plato takes the more conciliatory stance of one who admits rather than expels, but the quarrel persists. Only the type of poetry that is politically correct is permitted; the rest is banished. The reason is that poets and lawmakers are rivals in fashioning human life. Both are at once "makers" (the etymological meaning of *poiētai,* "poets") and "imitators" of moral values; and in a well-ordered society they must speak with one voice. This subordination of poetry to politics has offended many readers of Plato from antiquity to the present. Plato sees the poet primarily as a maker of ethics, and this concern appears strangely one-sided. What makes his posi-

I am very grateful to Richard Kraut for his helpful suggestions on this paper.

tion especially jarring is that, like another famous literary moralist, Tolstoy, he was himself a consummate literary artist. Yet Plato has a much more complex view of poetry than his strict morality suggests. Along with his censorship goes a far-ranging exploration of poetic creativity. Trying out various approaches in different dialogues, Plato enters into a dialogue with himself; and the tensions and variations in his own thinking illuminate many aspects of the aesthetics of poetry. Plato's discussions are worth taking seriously, even though some of his conclusions are repugnant – to himself in part, as well as to his readers.

Plato's quarrel with poetry takes its start in the fact that Greek poets had a crucial role in the creation and transmission of social values.[1] It was traditionally believed that poets, like prophets, were inspired directly by the gods with wisdom about the human and divine condition. It was the prerogative of poets to make known the past, present, and future to their contemporaries and future generations by oral performances of their poems. Prose writings and books did not become common until the fifth century B.C., and even then the primary method of publishing a work was oral performance. The poems were chanted or sung, usually to instrumental accompaniment, at gatherings that ranged from private affairs to celebrations held by an entire community or region, such as the dramatic festivals in honor of Dionysos. Most occasions had a religious setting, and many poetic performances were a form of religious worship. The audiovisual role of television in modern technological society provides a partial analogy to Greek oral culture. It differs in that it usually lacks the immediate impact of an event that engages one's most deeply held beliefs. To grasp the role of poetry in ancient Greece, one might think of Hindu religious drama – in which gods confront the audience directly in terrifying struggles between good and evil – and gospel meetings, along with rock concerts, opera, and television.

The values transmitted in poetry evolved continuously. While many poems – most prominently those of Homer – were passed on with little or no change from one generation to the next, poets and performers were continually reinterpreting their past. Poets not only preserved values, but also questioned and subverted the traditions they inherited, and long before Plato's attack on poetry, there were poets who condemned poets. The first known critical attack on poetry was by the poet Xenophanes in the sixth century B.C. In the same epic meter used by Homer and Hesiod, Xenophanes denounced these poets for "attributing to the gods everything that is a shame and reproach among humans – to steal, commit adultery, and deceive one another."[2] The quarrel continued with Heraclitus's stern verdict that Homer and Archilochus "deserve to be thrown out of the contests and beaten with the rod."[3] Heraclitus used prose, but his attack belongs to the same tradition of criticism as that of Xenophanes. About the same time, Parmenides laid the foundations of metaphysics and logic in a poem modeled in part on Homeric epic. The dramatists of the fifth century quarreled with their poetic predecessors no less vehemently than earlier poets did.

Plato's view of the quarrel between poetry and philosophy involves a third group, the sophists. Their name, "wise men" (*sophistai*), which soon became a term of derision, shows that they considered themselves heirs and rivals to the poets. In Plato's *Protagoras*, Protagoras (fl. c. 450 B.C.), leader of the first generation of sophists, proclaims that he was the first person to claim a place openly within the tradition of Greek educators (316–317c). As heir to the poets, he considers the most important part of education to be the criticism of poetry (338e–339a), and he illustrates his contention by attacking a well-known poem by Simonides. In their challenge to the poetic tradition, the sophists used a new weapon, prose. Partly, they discovered new possibilities of language in prose; partly, they attempted to capture the power of poetry by modeling their prose on poetic usage. One new use of prose was to engage the listener in an exchange of questions and answers, with the aim of scoring a victory by forcing the respondent to agree with whatever is proposed. Socrates' dialectical method is a development of this invention. The sophists were also the first to teach methods of argument. Unlike the poets, they claimed no authority for their teachings except their own "wisdom." They emphasized the practical utility of their teaching, which they regarded as the culmination of a series of inventions devised by humans for their own advancement.

Along with their new use of language, the sophists developed theories of language. We are fortunate that one of the few extant writings of the sophists contains a brief theory of language – the first in the Western tradition. In the *Encomium of Helen*, Gorgias (fl. c. 430 B.C.)

personifies language, *logos*, as a "great potentate, who with the tiniest and least visible body achieves the most divine works."[4] The "works" created by language are, remarkably, its effects on others. When *logos* is accompanied by persuasion, it "shapes the soul as it wishes." Just as drugs can drive various humors from the body and end either illness or life, so language can set up various emotions in the soul, and "drug and bewitch with an evil persuasion."[5] As evidence, Gorgias cites poetry and magical incantations as well as scientific, forensic, and philosophical prose. Defining poetry as "language with meter," he points out that by implanting intense fear, pity, or yearning in the listener, it makes the soul "suffer an affection of its own" at the fortunes and misfortunes of others.[6] Elsewhere, Gorgias singles out tragedy as a kind of deceit. In this case, the speaker is justified in practicing the deceit, as the listener is wise for being deceived.[7] In the *Encomium*, Gorgias explains that *logos* would not have the power it does if there were not such a wide field of ignorance. As it was, we have only partial knowledge of the past, present, and future; language fills this gap by supplying fallible beliefs to the soul.[8]

In this theory of language Gorgias classifies poetry as a subdivision of language, while extending its power to all of language. He adopts a simple scheme of cause and effect: A message is sent from speaker to a recipient who accepts it passively by a change in his soul. The listener is momentarily put in the power of another, as demonstrated most vividly by the effect of poetry and magical spells.[9] The speaker controls the listener not by any insights that he has, but by the language that bears his message. In general, what language creates is neither knowledge nor proposals by themselves, but beliefs and emotions imprinted in the souls of others. It is not an instrument of learning, but of persuasion. This theory of language fits within a general theory of the effect of the perceptible environment on a person. Just as language shapes the soul by being heard, so objects of sight shape the soul by being seen. Examples adduced by Gorgias are the terror produced by the sight of enemy soldiers as well as the delight caused by paintings and statues.[10] Artistically fashioned objects, whether heard or seen, have the same kind of impact on the soul as other objects of experience.

In his response to the poets and sophists, Plato sought to change language into an instrument of investigation and moral reform. He aimed in short to replace the *logos* of the poets and sophists with the *logos* of the philosophers – those who love wisdom, rather than those who pretend to it. He generally draws a distinction between the disinterested creativity of the poets and the sophists' self-interested manipulation of language; but at times his criticism of the poets and the sophists merge. In the *Apology* and *Meno* very briefly, and in the *Ion* at length, Plato takes the additional view of the poet as a divinely inspired individual and finds a flaw in it: Poets speak by divine inspiration without knowing what they say. In the *Apology,* Socrates tells that when he went to the poets to test the Delphic oracle, he found that, although they said "many beautiful things," they were utterly incapable of explaining what they said. Thereupon he concluded that they composed "not by wisdom, but by some natural talent and inspiration," like prophets.[11] He suggests in the *Meno* that poets are inspired with correct beliefs by a god.[12] Having such beliefs, he maintains, is not sufficient for having knowledge or being a teacher. In the *Ion* Socrates extends the poet's inspiration to the performer and the listener: All hang in a chain from an original divinity – poet first, then performer, then listener – like successive iron rings from a magnet. None of these human links has a "craft" (*technē*) because none has any knowledge of what he is doing.[13]

This is a picture of innocence as well as ignorance. In both the *Apology* and the *Ion,* however, ignorance is accompanied by delusion. In the *Apology,* Socrates points out that poets think they are wise about matters in which they are not. In the *Ion,* Plato exemplifies this delusion by the rhapsode Ion, who starts by claiming that he knows everything that Homer does and ends with the ridiculous assertion that he knows at least how to be a general. Ion is a false teacher, Plato implies, because he claims to be able to explain what Homer said, when he cannot.[14] The link with deity, moreover, does not preclude a poet's words from being false, as Socrates insinuates when he requires that the correctness of poems be judged by an expert. Nothing indeed prevents the poet, or any other inspired creature, from being as fatuously ill-informed as Ion. Although Ion bears the brunt of Socrates' attack, Plato indicates that divine possession is a bad reason to regard anyone – even "the best and most divine of poets," Homer (530b10) – as an authority.

The traditional link with deity appears very precarious, then, so much so that what is commonly revered as divine inspiration threatens to dissolve into an all-too-human talent.[15] In the *Ion* Plato already suggests that the rhapsode does not wholly hang from a divine source: Ion acknowledges that he pays great attention to the crowd, to see whether they hang on his words; for otherwise he will lose money (535e). In his concern for money and reputation as well as his practice of poetic exegesis, Ion has much in common with the sophists. It is not surprising, then, that in another early diaglogue, *Gorgias,* Socrates associates poetry with the rhetoric of the sophists. The whole dialogue is an attack on Gorgias's theory that language is a great power; and incidentally Socrates brings poetry into the attack. Socrates does not indeed dispute Gorgias's contention that language has great power over the listener; his whole attack rests on a tacit acceptance of this view. Instead, he argues that those who use language unjustly have no power; for they lack the power to accomplish what they really want – justice in their own souls. The rhetoric of the sophists, Socrates charges, is a pseudo-craft, a mere "semblance" (*eidōlon*) of the political craft of justice. It is a flattery of the soul, just as cookery is a flattery of the body. Instead of seeking what is best, it only seeks to gratify the crowd by taking their likes and dislikes as a standard.[16] Rhetoric shares this aim with poetry. For when stripped of melody, meter, and rhythm, poetry is a form of "public speaking" (*dēmēgoria,* a term whose meaning verges into "demagoguery") – a "rhetoric" of the theater – that aims to flatter the populace.[17]

In the *Gorgias,* Socrates subverts the claim of the sophists to have a craft that improves human life. Correcting the sophistic theory of language, he claims that poets, too, are adept only at pandering to the crowd. This is an abrupt change from the qualified respect that Socrates shows the poets in the other early dialogues. Socrates builds up to his conclusion by an inductive chain in which he argues that public musical performances, from flute playing and lyre playing to choral productions, dithyrambic poetry, tragedy, and finally all poetry, aim only to gratify the audience. In constructing this sequence, Socrates has the respondent agree that the "revered and wondrous" poetry of tragedy (502b1) also aims at the pleasure rather than the improvement of the spectators. The respondent's ready assent is surprising in view of the traditional respect bestowed on poets as divinely inspired teachers. But the response is not at all implausible as a complaint against contemporary tragedy, as practiced, for example, by Euripides.[18] By a bold inductive leap, Socrates extends the complaint against musical and dramatic performances to all of poetry. As in the *Ion,* he does not attack the most respected of all poets, Homer, directly. Instead, he attacks theatrical productions and infers that all poetry plays to the crowd.

Having broken the link with deity, Socrates suggests a different reason why poetry, in common with rhetoric, has such great power over the listener: The poet's *logos* shapes the soul by indulging the listener's craving for pleasure. This *logos* has no autonomous power; it is parasitic upon the desires of the listener, and the author's creativity is nothing but an adaptation of words to the beliefs of the listener. Plato therefore undermines Gorgias's theory of language in another way. While admitting that language has power over another's soul, he proposes that this power is dependent on the condition of the listener's soul. If the listener is morally feeble, the ostensible power of the *logos* consists, paradoxically, in strengthening this weakness; in short, it is utterly frail. With an allusion to Socrates' trial, Plato has Socrates suggest that he may be the only person to practice the true craft of politics (521d). His *logos* cannot but offend the crowd since it aims at moral improvement.

The *Symposium* marks an important change from the early dialogues. Plato now uses his new theory of Forms to present poetry more favorably than in any other dialogue. He subsumes poetic activity under the Form of beauty and makes love its motive force. Poetry becomes a private concern – an act of communication between a lover and his beloved. The whole theory is attributed to Diotima, the prophetess who acts as Socrates' teacher. She begins her analysis with a complex definition of love, *erōs,* as an intermediary between gods and human beings, and as a desire for the creation of an immortal good in something beautiful.[19] Drawing a distinction between those who are creative in body and those who are creative in soul, Diotima exemplifies the latter by poets and "inventor" craftsmen, along with lawgivers. They are all creators of "prudence" (*phronēsis*) and other forms of "goodness" (*aretē*). Being "divine" in soul, they are pregnant with their offspring from an early age and give birth to them when they come upon a beautiful soul joined to a beautiful body. The act of procreation consists in an abundance of words about goodness, spoken to the beloved with the aim of "educating" him to be a good person and to "practice" (*epitēdeuein*) the right way of life.

Lover and beloved then join in a close and stable union to rear what has been created. Examples of such offspring are the poems of Homer and Hesiod and the laws of Lycurgus and Solon.[20]

From this explanation of intellectual creativity, Diotima proceeds to what she calls the "perfect" mysteries (210a). She reveals an ascent from an attraction to beautiful bodies, to an appreciation of beautiful souls and practices (*epitēdeumata*), to a contemplation of knowledge, and finally to a vision of beauty itself. The second main stage consists in valuing beauty of soul much more highly than beauty of body. Although Diotima does not assign a place to the poets in this ascent, there are sufficient similarities in her account to suggest that their endeavors may be mapped onto it. By valuing psychic beauty jointly with bodily beauty and concerning themselves with correct practices, the poets appear to be ascending from the first to the second main stage. Diotima's description of those who have attained the second stage as "giving birth to and seeking words that will make the young better" (210c) echoes her previous description of the poets and others. The next main stage is the creation of philosophical discourse, as stimulated by the beauty of the various kinds of knowledge. Finally, the philosophically strengthened person has a vision of beauty itself and produces no longer "semblances (*eidōla*) of goodness," but true goodness, constituting a godlike immortality (212a). The poets therefore appear to occupy an honorable position between the masses and the philosophers. Creators of "semblances of goodness," they are nonetheless advancing along a path that leads to philosophy and true goodness.

Diotima offers a new interpretation of divine inspiration as the stirring of moral insight in the soul. Teeming with these insights from youth, the poet shapes and improves them in response to the moral beauty of another. Poetic creation thus becomes a joint enterprise, nurtured by the sympathetic response of a privileged listener. This is the opposite of the theatrical poetry denounced in the *Gorgias*. Very strikingly, Diotima does not draw a distinction between the creation of a poem and the creation of moral goodness. In her account, the poet is a creator of moral goodness and the poem serves only as a means of conveying this goodness. This poetic ontology is fundamental to Plato's whole conception of poetry: A poem is a linguistic reflection, or image, or a psychic disposition. It is essentially a moral rather than a linguistic construct; formulated in language, it is realized by being imprinted in the soul of another. This subordination of linguistic to moral form explains another oddity in Diotima's story. We might expect her to associate beauty directly with the poem; instead she associates it with the soul of the beloved. The reason is that a poem's beauty is a response to the moral beauty of the listener. The goodness of a poem is judged by reference to an ideal beauty that is identical with moral goodness.

Plato is often thought to have lacked a notion of poetry as an expression of personal feelings and beliefs.[21] Between his theory of imitation, as developed in the *Republic*, and the traditional assumption of divine inspiration, he seems to leave no place for self-expression in poetry, as proposed so vigorously by the Romantics. Yet in the *Symposium* Diotima comes close to formulating a version of the notion of art as self-expression. She views poetic creativity as an inner spring that wells forth from the poet's soul and is continually replenished by communion with another. Although Diotima explains this creativity as a semidivine force, love, striving to attain a transcendental beauty, it is an intensely personal endeavor, strengthened by an interpersonal bond. As a search for moral goodness, poetic activity is inseparable from self-searching and self-awareness. Like the other "inventors" and lawgivers, the poet gives voice to his own aspirations as he attempts to transcend his own mortal existence by union with another.

Whereas in the *Gorgias* Socrates took theatrical poetry as the paradigm of all poetry, Diotima implicitly takes love poetry as her paradigm. This is an unusual view, which goes against both ancient and modern conceptions of the poet as a self-sufficient genius. Yet it serves to explain another commonly recognized element in poetry, the universality of its values. In Diotima's account, the poet's concern with human values, like that of the legislator and others, takes the form of a devotion to another human being, serving as an alter ego; and from this basis it extends to the rest of humankind. This approach to immortality allows Diotima to give approval to traditional poetry, beginning with Homer and Hesiod, and by implication to such poets as the comic playwright Aristophanes and the tragedian Agathon, whose eulogies of love in the *Symposium* provide vivid confirmation that their poetic creativity is inspired by love.

Love poetry, indeed, becomes the model of all intellectual creativity. All the discourses spoken at the banquet exemplify Diotima's analysis of intellectual creativity and all may be mapped along

Diotima's ascent. Alcibiades fills in details about the highest form of creativity, the philosopher's, in the crowning speech of the *Symposium*, his tribute to Socrates. He compares Socrates' words to carved sileni – uncouth on the outside, but "most divine" on the inside, "having very many representations of goodness in them" (222a). These words have the power to bewitch and possess the listener, like the music of Marsyas or the Sirens. As Alcibiades testifies about himself, Socrates' words reduced him to a tearful frenzy of self-recrimination; they filled him with a sense that his life was not worth living as it was (215d–216c). Alcibiades transfers to Socrates the power of enchantment traditionally assigned to poets, with the important difference that Socrates' words incite his listener to look into himself. Socrates practices in a much-heightened form what Diotima's poets attempt to do.

It is easy to overlook Diotima's remarks on poetry in the *Symposium* in view of the much more extended treatment in the *Republic.* In this dialogue, Plato considers poetry in the first place as a means of educating children to be Guardians in his ideal state. Since Plato believes that children's souls are especially malleable, he is especially concerned with the impact of poetry on them; but he soon extends his concern to adults.[22] The public returns to replace the privileged listener. The whole discussion consists of two parts, whose relationship has been much debated. Plato purges poetry in Books II and III; then he returns to this purge in Book X by explaining in detail what is wrong with the poetry that he eliminated. In the two parts, Plato builds a powerful new theory of poetry as "imitation," *mimēsis.*

In Books II and III, Socrates argues, first, that poets must present the truth about the gods and heroes, who are to serve as models of goodness. Second, poets must "imitate" only good individuals or individuals engaged in good action, so that their listeners may in turn imitate only good.[23] By "imitation" (*mimēsis*), Socrates means "impersonation" (392d–394c). The poet "imitates" another whenever he speaks the words of a character in direct speech, as though he were that character. By contrast, the poet "narrates" whenever he reports in his own person what a character is doing or saying. As moral educator, the poet must imitate only morally good speech, and he must narrate all the rest. For the poet's experience becomes the listener's, by a similar transfer of experience as is assumed in the *Ion*'s image of the iron rings. If the listener persists in imitating the same kinds of characters from childhood, he ends up by having the same moral configuration (395d).

Earlier in Book II, Socrates' healthy city, the "city of pigs," had become isolated and feverish by the admission of imitators, such as painters, poets, rhapsodes, actors, dancers, and others (373b). Subsequently Socrates purges this city; and his first and main concern is poetry. Like a physician, he reconstitutes poetry as a health-giving drug. Plato agrees with Gorgias that poetry has the power both to heal and to poison the soul, and that it is especially effective because it can make a person assume the identity of another. In his analysis, which has the dry detachment of a clinical dissection, Socrates associates this special power with a particular type of diction, "imitation." It poses a special danger because it removes the distance of personal judgment. The right kind of poetry, therefore, will have only a small amount of imitation, consisting only in the imitation of the good, and it will have much narration (396e). This requirement automatically eliminates traditional tragedy and comedy, as Socrates' interlocutor recognizes. As Socrates hints, it also eliminates Homeric epic (394d). After determining the right proportion of imitation and narration, Socrates completes his pharmaceutical activity by prescribing melodies and rhythms that suit the content. Just as the language must mark the difference between good and bad, so the melodies and rhythms must reinforce this difference by resembling the simplicity and restraint of morally good habits. With its kernel of imitation, the new poetry is carefully designed to confer a maximum of moral benefit by providing an experience that simulates that of a good person as closely as possible.

Just as the physician of so many of his examples does not hesitate to drive out corruption by the most violent and painful means, Socrates purifies the city by expelling the offending poets, who also give the most pleasure, and forcing the rest to comply with the laws. The poets, he decrees, "must be directed and forced to implant the image (*eikona*) of a good moral habit in their poems, or not compose poems in our midst" (401b). Socrates' violence reaches a shocking climax in his banishment of the poet who can imitate anyone and anything. He proclaims the expulsion in a resounding sentence: If "a man who is able to become every kind of individual (*pantodapos*) because of his wisdom and to imitate all things" were to come to our city, wishing to perform his poems, we would honor him as "sacred (*hieron*), marvelous, and giving pleasure," but say that "there is no such man in our city nor is it lawful that he should come to be, and we would send him off to another city, pouring myrrh on his head and crowning him with a chaplet" (398a). There is no such man in the new city because none is allowed to assume more than one role, especially not a combination of virtue and vice. Reverentially, Socrates does not name the man; but everything points to Homer. The "sacred" poet, though revered, is a blight upon the city; and he is sent off, consecrated to a god like a scapegoat.[24]

From the purge of poetry, Socrates moves to a general cleansing of the city and a general theory of the arts (401a–d). Not only must poets be forced to create images of goodness, but all artists and craftsmen must do likewise. Paintings, weavings, embroideries, houses, and all equipment whatsoever must express beauty and seemliness, so that the young will receive this seemliness into their souls. Still showing the concerns of a physician, Socrates compares this aesthetic environment to a healthy place, in which the inhabitants are caressed by gentle breezes from their surroundings. He assumes that sounds, shapes, and indeed all sensory objects – both natural and artificial – have qualities that resemble moral qualities, and that these qualities have a direct influence on the moral habits of the perceiver. Not only the beliefs conveyed by language, but also sensory stimuli that do not engage one's cognitive faculties at all, shape the moral habits of the soul. Like Gorgias, Plato assumes that sensory objects, like language, shape the soul directly. But his association of moral character with sensory objects is new; and it is highly questionable. It is a far step from demanding that the language, music, and rhythms of poems must suit the content to claiming that sounds and other sensory objects express or resemble moral character. In Plato's general aesthetics, the whole sensory environment is an image, or "iconic" symbol, of moral goodness or badness.[25] Unsatisfactory as this claim is in its context, it anticipates the metaphysical system that will be proposed subsequently in the *Republic*, according to which the sensible world is ultimately an image of the Form of the Good. The sensible world contains images of goodness; and the human craftman must emulate the divine craftsman by creating images of goodness of his own.

In the *Republic* Book X this true aesthetics fades from sight, so much so that Plato has been thought to abandon it altogether. This book, which contains Plato's most searching analysis of what poetry is, raises serious problems of interpretation. The first problem is: What and how much poetry does Plato expel? In particular, what is the meaning of Socrates' introductory statement that they were right, in founding the city, "not to admit in any way any [part of poetry] that is mimetic (*mimētikē*)."[26] This announcement is clearly a reference to the purge of poetry in Book III. But in Book III Plato certainly did not ban all poetic *mimēsis*. Is there a discrepancy then? Some scholars have argued that there is no clash, whereas many others have argued that Plato has shifted position. The decisive point in favor of the first interpretation, it seems to me, is that "mimetic" can mean not only "imitating," but also "imitative" in the strong sense of "given to imitation," with the connotation of "indiscriminately imitative" or "all-mimetic." As others have pointed out, this strong sense has already been prepared in Book III.[27] There is, then, neither a terminological nor a substantive clash with the earlier discussion. For "mimetic" poetry is not *just* poetry that imitates, it is poetry that imitates anything at all. In Book III Socrates expelled the poet who is indiscriminately mimetic – in short, the "mimetic" poet; and in Book X he defends this expulsion.

This is not to deny that in Book X Plato shifts away from the earlier discussion both in his terminology and in his proposals. He returns to the problem of poetry because the metaphysics and psychology that he developed in the meantime provide a new justification for the expulsion of mimetic poetry; and this new investigation is accompanied by a new use of terms. In keeping with his use of "mimetic" to imply "indiscriminately imitative," Plato now uses the terms "imitation" (*mimēsis*) and "imitator" (*mimētēs*) in the new senses of "indiscriminate imitation" and "indiscriminate imitator." At the same time he adds a new dimension to the meaning of there terms: "mimetic" poetry, like all "imitation," is not only indiscriminately imitative, but also thoroughly imitative – imitative to the core – because it is at two removes from genuine creation. As an "imitation" of the manifold world of human action, it is at the farthest distance from the creation of genuine goodness. Although it might be argued that this definition applies to all poetry, Plato carefully restricts his analysis to the indiscriminately imitative poetry that he banished in Book III. The first restriction occurs in the introductory phrase "any [part of poetry] that is mimetic" (595a), with the implication that some is not "mimetic." Subsequently, Socrates repeatedly singles out tragedy, with its leading practitioner Homer, as exemplifying mimetic poetry. When he reiterates his order of banishment in Book X, he describes the poetry that he expels as the "poetry of pleasure and *mimēsis*."[28] Along with this expulsion, Socrates proposes to keep "hymns to gods and praises of the good" (607a4). Just as he argued in Book III, the poetry that he permits is a celebration of divine and human goodness; and nothing contradicts the conclusion of Book III that this poetry requires a correct mixture of impersonation – *mimēsis* in the earlier, narrower sense – and narration.

The second main problem is: What precisely is the new sense of "imitation"? Plato develops his answer in three stages, in which he successively reduces mimetic poetry into an object of detestation. First, he defines "imitation" in general; second, he shows that the poetry of Homer and his successors fits this definition; and third, as the climax of the entire argument, he shows that Homer and all other imitative poets corrupt the listener with their poems and therefore deserve to be banished.[29] In all three stages, Plato bases his conclusions on an analogy between the painter and the poet; and a major challenge to interpretation is to determine the relevance of this comparison. Since the analogy works differently in different stages of the argument, it is useful to consider each stage in turn, while keeping in mind the overall structure of the argument.

Plato builds his new definition of "imitation" directly on the conclusions of Book III. There he banished the poet who "is able to become every sort of individual because of his wisdom and to imitate all things." Plato now explains this "wisdom" (*sophia*). It is no wisdom really, but fakery, because it is just like taking a mirror and reflecting all things in it. The person who looks as though he can make all things is a "marvelous sophist" (*sophistēs*, 596d1), but he only seems "all-wise" (*passophos*) to the ignorant (598d3–4). He looks like a "maker" (*poiētēs*); in fact, he is an "imitator," not a real maker or craftsman, but a pseudo-maker of pseudo-creations. Plato brings in his metaphysics of Forms, together with the painter, the carpenter, and God himself, in order to reduce this amazingly prolific "maker" into a mere shadow of a maker.[30]

Apart from one reference to the "maker of tragedy" (597e6), the "poet" (*poiētēs*) is present in this first stage of the argument only implicitly – though very emphatically – as "maker." The "imitator" is represented by the painter, who makes all things by making appearances of them, just like the person with the mirror. He imitates objects made by human craftsmen, such as the bed made by the carpenter. Above the carpenter is God, maker of the Form of the bed, on which the carpenter models his creations. The painter's imitations are at two removes from real being, the Forms; and the painter is at two removes from the one truly genuine maker and craftman, God. To this basic scheme Plato adds a refinement that will be of crucial importance later (597e–598d). The painter does not imitate the objects of human craftsmanship as they are, but as they appear. For example, he imitates the bed as it appears from the side or the front, not as it is. His imitation, therefore, and all imitation in general, is the imitation of an appearance, not of things as they are in this world. In short, an imitation is a "semblance (*eidōlon*) that is far from the truth," and the imitator knows nothing about any of the crafts that he imitates.

Plato's mirror simile has had an overwhelming influence on the interpretation of his aesthetics and on aesthetic theory in general. It stands as a compelling symbol of the view that it is the job of the artist to copy nature. But Plato's use of the simile needs to be interpreted with some care. In the first place, Plato thinks that copying things of the sensible world is a perversion of the poet's function; it is what the mimetic poet does. In the second place, the mimetic poet does not aim to give faithful representations of the sensible world: he gives impressions of it. The commonplace dichotomy between mirroring and self-expression in the acts does not really fit Plato's use of the mirror simile. As some of the Romantic spokesmen for an expressive theory of art themselves pointed out, there is no incompatibility between imitation and self-expression. In the *Republic* Plato combines the two approaches by requiring both external models and a personal response. Just as the painter renders aspects of reality as they appear to him, so the poet renders his own impressions of reality. These appearances prompt the ignorant to take them for the real thing; but they are nonetheless distortions produced by the imitator's own view of the world. Even though the brief account of poetry in the *Symposium* comes much closer to the Romantic notion of self-expression, the artist in the *Republic* also draws on his own inner resources – in particular, as will become clearer, his emotional inclinations – to give an interpretation of the external world.

Plato fills in gradually in the course of the discussion how the poet's impressions correspond to those of the painter; and this elaboration shows that the analogy between painting and poetry is not as ill-conceived as has sometimes been thought. If we wish to keep the simile of the mirror, it turns out that the mirror is the poet's own soul: The external world is refracted by the poet's soul, not cast back as a faithful reproduction.

Plato's hierarchy of being has also proved misleading. It might seem that the poet can escape the shadowy unreality of his pseudo-craft by moving higher on the scale, either to an imitation of the Forms themselves or, at least, to a faithful replica of sensible reality. The first alternative is barred by the argument, which is presented later, that if the poet did model his creations on the Forms, then he would be a maker of human conduct in this world, taking his place among the craftsmen of this world; he would not devote himself to making "semblances" of goodness (599a–600e). This argument has been perceived as a serious difficulty for the view that in Book X Plato leaves open the possiblity of a morally beneficial craft of poetry, as proposed in Books II and III; and we shall return to this problem. The second alternative is also barred. As Collingwood has argued, since imitations and sensible things are distinct categories of being, there is no way in which the imitator can attain the truthfulness of his model.[31] Just as the carpenter cannot recreate a Form, neither can the imitator recreate a sensible object. To suppose otherwise would be, let us say, like supposing that Picasso can recreate a woman by combining various aspects of her face and body in a single picture. It might be objected that painters can make more or less realistic copies. But a photographic type of realism is what Plato most decries, as the most perfect illusionism. Although Plato indicates in the third stage of his argument that a poet would err less if he did approximate sensible reality more closely, he nowhere proposes that a poet should model his work more closely on the actual world. His reason is that hanging on sensible reality, without independent guidelines, can only produce further distortions of reality.[32]

In the second stage of his argument, Plato launches his direct attack against poetry by reducing Homer and his followers from the position of educators of the Greeks to the level of ignorant imitators. There are those, he mentions, who assign a knowledge of all crafts to Homer (598d–e); he will not address this claim. What he will investigate is whether Homer had any knowledge of "the greatest and most beautiful things" about which he attempts to speak, that is, "about wars, generalship and the administration of cities, and about the education of a human being" (599c–d). His first reference is an allusion to the *Ion*.[33] The second part of his statement is an allusion to Diotima's claim in the *Symposium* that Homer and other poets are among those who "educate" men and lead them to right "practices." Diotima proposed that "by far the greatest and most beautiful part of prudence concerns the administration of cities and households" (209a5–7); and she associated the poets, as exemplified by Homer and Hesiod, with the lawgivers, in particular Lycurgus and Solon, and with inventive craftsmen in general, as creators of prudence and other forms of goodness. Plato now expels Homer and the poets from this group.

With a point-by-point refutation of Diotima's account in the *Symposium*, Socrates argues that Homer did not know what "practices" (*epitēdeumata*) make humans better either as a community or as private individuals.[34] Homer was not a good lawgiver like Solon or Lycurgus, or an innovator in the crafts such as Thales; and he was not a private educator. In particular, his "companion" Creophylus would provide a laughable example of an educated disciple (600b6–9). This obscure reference to Creophylus fills in a gap in Diotima's account by supplying an example of someone allegedly loved and educated by Homer. Socrates also brings Hesiod into his attack by suggesting that Homer's and Hesiod's contemporaries would hardly have let them roam around singing if they really had been able to help others become good. His conclusion that all "poetic persons starting with Homer" are "imitators of semblances of goodness" (600e4–5) assigns a new meaning to an expression used in the *Symposium*. There all except those who had reached the very pinnacle of enlightenment were destined to create only "semblances of goodness." Now Homer and the other poets are singled out as creating "semblances" that are fakes.

In this part of the argument, then, Plato corrects the positive view of poetry that he presented in the *Symposium*. He now drives a wedge between Diotima's view of poetic creativity and the "perfect" mystery of the upward ascent. Instead of progressing toward knowledge, poets are exposed as cultivating ignorance. Poetic education is a fraud because poets don't know what they are talking about. This is a further development of a view sketched in the *Apology* and *Ion.* But Plato also keeps in mind the possibility that he canvassed in the *Meno,* that correct belief may be just as good a guide as knowledge. "So as not to leave things half said," Socrates goes on, mimetic poets also lack the right belief that comes from taking instructions from a user (601c–602a). Socrates resorts once again to the analogy of the painter and now pairs him with a different type of craftsman, the maker of reins and bridles. Although the latter lacks knowledge, he makes a good product by acquiring correct belief from a user who has knowledge. By contrast, the painter of reins and bridles neither has knowledge himself nor acquires correct belief by associating with a user who knows. Similarly, the mimetic poet has neither knowledge nor correct belief. In his ignorance, he imitates what appears beautiful to the ignorant masses (602b), as suggested previously in the *Gorgias.*

The first two stages of the argument prepare the third, which culminates in the reiteration of the expulsion order, now addressed explicitly against Homer and his successors.[35] So far, Socrates has shown that Homer and the others have nothing but a semblance of wisdom. Now he shows that this semblance is a corruption of the soul. By revealing the moral ugliness of traditional poetry and its power to corrupt even the best citizens, he reduces it to the lowest level of abomination, so that it must surely be purged. For the last time, Socrates takes the painter as an analogue of the poet. Just as the painter creates impressions that are accepted uncritically by the beholder without any attempt at calculation, so all imitation appeals to the nonrational, worthless part of our soul (602c–603b). This use of the painter analogy is perhaps the weakest part of Plato's entire argument. But it has the merit of signaling that the response to a work of art differs fundamentally from the response to a real-life situation. The beholder of a painting does not measure the impressions before him against reality; he is seduced by appearances to accept them as they are, without bothering to calculate how close they are to the real thing. Plato touches on the notion that a work of art is valued for its own sake, insulated from real-life concerns by a suspension of disbelief. He spurns this outlook on art because he thinks that make-believe is harmful unless it agrees with a transcendent reality.

After depreciating the painter, Socrates goes on to show what the reader has been waiting for all along, an explanation of what sort of appearances are produced by the mimetic poet. The mimetic poet imitates humans engaged in action and thinking, with attendant pain or pleasure, that they are faring well or badly (603c). Moreover, he tends to imitate the release of emotions, such as grief, laughter, lust, and anger, instead of the control of the emotions by reason. He has a "natural" propensity to the emotional part of the soul, for it is easy to imitate. This part is also easy to appreciate, especially by the crowd in the theater. Therefore, in order to win fame among the many, the imitative poet directs all his efforts to it (604e–605a).

In case the mirror simile, along with the examples of the painter, carpenter, and bridle maker, misled the reader into thinking that the poet creates word pictures, as it were, of objects such as couches and bridles, he is now set straight. The poet imitates moral goodness and badness, as shown in human actions, beliefs, and feelings. The depiction of Achilles driving a chariot or running around the plain of Troy, for example, is incidental to the imitation of his moral character. Corresponding, therefore, to the Form of the couch or table are the Forms of the virtues – justice, moderation, courage, and wisdom.[36] The mimetic poet creates nothing but distortions of these qualities, since he looks only to what humans actually do and is drawn, moreover, to the opposite of virtuous behavior – the disorderly rule of the emotions. It would be bad enough if he merely imitated human conduct as it is; instead, he imitates it as it appears to the worthless part of his and everyone else's soul. Instead of showing us Oedipus, let us say, bringing order to the city by his wisdom, he dwells on the agony of his downfall. Oedipus's success would be too boring to most people. As in the *Gorgias,* Plato condemns poetry as theatrical demagoguery, aiming to please the crowd by indulging its ignoble desires. He also takes back the view of poetic creativity that Diotima sponsored in the *Symposium.* Substituting base terms for Diotima's language of love and goodness, Socrates claims that all imitation "consorts with and is a companion (*hetaira*) and friend (*philē*) to something far from prudence in us for the purpose of nothing healthy or true"; in short, "being worthless, it associates with something worthless and creates worthless things."[37] In contrast with Diotima's poet, who is united by love to a beautiful soul and creates prudence, the mimetic poet prostitutes himself in the service of the worthless part of the human soul and creates nothing but worthlessness.

In many respects, Plato's mimetic poet stands for what many of us value most in poetry. He creates his poems in response to the spectacle of human action about him. Immersed in this world, he derives all his inspiration from it, ranging over it with a full engagement of his emotions, entrancing others as he is entranced by life. Plato casts out this poet on the ground that his emotional intensity "feeds" (606b–d) and strengthens the emotional part of the listener's soul, like a malignant cancer, while weakening the rational part. In conflict with the good lawgiver, the mimetic poet "implies a bad constitution privately within the soul of each person" (605b). Worst of all, this poetry is so powerful that it corrupts not only the many, but the better sort (with very few exceptions) who ordinarily try to control their emotions by reason (605c–606d). For they are seduced into gaining pleasure by letting go of their emotions, with the excuse that it is not disgraceful to share the emotions of someone else.

There are many ways of resisting Plato's diagnosis of the effects of mimetic poetry while accepting much of his analysis of what the poet does. Aristotle takes the view that the emotionality of poetry cleanses instead of corrupts. Without denying the power of poetry to shape moral habits, we might look for an escape in Plato's analogy of the painter. In creating his illusions, one might argue, the painter does in fact carefully measure appearance against reality. In foregrounding one aspect of the table or couch, for example, he calculates how this aspect is related to the whole and indicates this relationship to the beholder. This sort of measuring is wholly intrinsic to the work of art; there is no reality apart from that of the artistic object itself. Similarly the poet, even though he may emphasize the emotions, sets them in the wider context of a moral order. Oedipus's suffering is the more acute because of his search for wisdom; and when the theatergoer suffers with him, his suffering is a measure of his recognition of the nobility of Oedipus's character. By opposing the emotions to rational insight, Plato closes off this way of defending poetry as a genuinely creative endeavor.

In Plato's view, how can the poet escape degradation? This question takes us back to our first problem. What room is left for the type of poet who implants "the image of a good moral habit" in his poems, as proposed in Book III? It makes little difference whether Plato exempts a part of poetry from his attack in Book X if his analysis precludes there being such a part. Plato, I suggest, has worked an answer into his attack. The politically correct poet does not indeed look to the Forms; for if he did, he would be a creator of actual goodness in human beings – a lawgiver in fact. But it is open to him to take correct beliefs from the lawgiver, the user of his poems. Nor need one look for such instruction. Socrates' entire analysis of poetry in Books II and III is nothing other than an elaborate rule book, devised by the founders of the city for the instruction of poets. Having correct beliefs, the poet is raised to the level of a craftsman, like the carpenter, the bridle maker, and all the other nonphilosophical craftsmen in the new city. Like the rest, the poet has the position of serving the lawgiver. Instead of imitating humans as they are or appear to be, he creates images of humans as they should be, by taking directions from the lawgiver, who looks toward the Forms. It is very doubtful whether this type of poet, coerced and working according to rule, could have any appeal except to the lawgiver's educational zeal. Plato's own analysis of the mimetic poet as exuberantly – even though morbidly – creative highlights this difficulty. In the *Republic,* Plato presents just two possibilities: the poet follows his own inclinations and corrupts, or he is coerced into improving others. Nor does the painter or any other artist fare any better. Like all the other craftsmen in the new city, they must create a moral environment for the citizens; and they cannot achieve this by being enamored of the sights and sounds of this world.

Plato reconsiders the place of poetry in human life in the *Phaedrus.* As though dissatisfied with his coercion of poetry in the *Republic,* Socrates proclaims that no one can become a good poet unless inspired with divine madness. In a brief, traditional definition of poetry that is reminiscent of the *Symposium,* Socrates explains that possession by the Muses gets hold of a "tender" soul and "educates" later generations (*Phdr.* 245a). Poetic possession is one of four types of divine madness, along with prophecy, ritual, and love (*erōs*); love is the best madness of all. Since divine madness is responsible for the "greatest goods" to humans (244a), we might expect poetry to have some role in the soul's return to heaven. But Socrates explains this ascent as motivated entirely by love. Moreover, he places the "poetic person" surprisingly low in his ranking of lives. The best life is that of the "philosopher or lover of beauty or a musical and erotic person (*philosophou ē philokalou ē mousikou tinos kai erōtikou*)." There follow the lawful king or military commander, the politician or businessman, and the trainer or physician. Fifth is the life of the prophet or conductor of rites; sixth is the "poetic person (*poiētikos*)" or anyone else concerned with *mimēsis'*; seventh is the craftsman or farmer; eighth is the sophist or demagogue; and ninth and last is the tryant (248d–e). The "poetic person" is lowest of the four types of divinely inspired persons, with the prophet and conductor of rites just above him. Divine inspiration is no more a guarantee of enlightenment than it is in the *Apology* or *Ion.*

Whereas in the *Symposium* Plato included poetry among the works of love, he now demotes it by distinguishing it from love as a separate kind of madness. As suggested by the conjunction of poetry with *mimēsis,* this demotion appears indebted to the *Republic.* At the same time, Plato softens the position of the *Republic* by ranking the mimetic poet one step above the manual worker. Divine inspiration, it seems, assures the mimetic poet a place above ordinary craftsmen and two ranks above the sophist by infusing some educational value into his poems. But it is not nearly sufficient to raise him to the level of the "erotic" person, the truly "musical" person who is inspired by the Muses with the only genuine beautiful discourse, that of the philosopher.

In the *Phaedrus,* then, Plato drives another wedge between traditional poetry and philosophy. At the same time, he proposes a transformation of all types of discourse – in particular, poetry, political rhetoric, and legal language – into philosophical discourse. The main topic of the *Phaedrus,* like that of the *Gorgias,* is rhetoric. But "rhetoric" is now taken explicitly in the broad, etymological sense of "art of speaking" in general, so as to subsume public speaking. Defining "rhetoric" as a "leading of the soul (*psychagōgia*) by words" in both private and public (261a), Socrates gradually transforms the basic meaning of *psychagōgia,* "conjuring" and "enchantment," which fits the sophistic view of language, into the sense of "leading the soul" to the truth, which fits philosophical discourse. In the course of Socrates' examination, rhetoric becomes the art of dialectic or "discussion." It requires, first of all, the ability to define and divide the subject matter correctly, and, further, a knowledge of the types of souls and their occurrences, together with a knowledge of the kinds of language, so that the speaker may adapt his language to the soul of each listener. Socrates exemplifies this genuine art of rhetoric throughout the *Phaedrus.* Using various kinds of language, including a "mythic hymn" adorned with "poetic" words, he leads his companion, Phaedrus, to an understanding of the proper use of language.[38] Genuine rhetoric may include prose speeches and poetry, but it is essentially an act of communication between two individuals. The main reason that Plato rejects writing as serious use of language is that he thinks it precludes this communication.

Plato's new, comprehensive theory of language is accompanied by a new theory of love. Revising Diotima's view of intellectual creativity in the *Symposium,* Plato now proposes that only the philosophical use of language is genuinely an act of love, aimed at enlightening the beloved as well as oneself. Poetry without philosophy is without love or insight; but it can be transformed into genuinely creative discourse. At the end of the *Phaedrus,* Socrates asks Phaedrus to relay a message from the Muses: Their message to Lysias and any other speechmaker, as well as to Homer and any other poet and to Solon and any other writer of laws, is that if they know the truth about what they composed, and can defend what they wrote by speaking about it, while showing that what they wrote is worthless, then they deserve the name of "philosopher" rather than the name that corresponds to their compositions – that is, "speechwriter," "poet," or "lawgiver" (278b–e). Plato's own dialogues may be regarded as attempts to exemplify this use of language. We may call them poetry as a tribute to Plato's literary skill.[39] But from Plato's point of view it would be more accurate to regard them as adumbrations or "semblances" of how all sorts of language – poetic, political, legal, and the rest – may be transformed into philosophical discourse.

In the *Phaedrus* Plato adds to his range of portraits of the poet the limiting case of the composer of poetry who is truly inspired. This is no longer a poet, but a philosopher. His compositions are but moments of thought, frozen in language and worthless in themselves. The serious part of his endeavors consists in the discussion that supports and supplements his compositions. Like islands in a sea of reflection, the compositions are merely stages on the way to a distant goal. Although Plato withholds from this type of composer the title of "poet," he presents a highly appealing model of a poet's goal. For this creator of poetry is neither fettered by laws nor blinded by appearances. What makes this model of poetry particularly attractive is that although Plato considers the linguistic construct worthless in itself, he assigns to it a special merit of its own – organic unity. Like any composition, a poem must have its parts fitted into a harmonious whole, with middles and extremities, like the body of an animal (264c, 268c–d). This organization is determined not only by the subject matter, but also by the needs of the listener. While organic unity may be regarded as an aesthetic property – and Aristotle would later treat it as such by making it the focus of his analysis of poetry – Plato subordinates it to a moral purpose. The unity of the composition reflects both the truth of what is said and the moral aspirations of the listener and speaker. The completeness of the text contrasts with the incompleteness of the striving that inspires it, and so signals its own incompleteness. In emphasizing the worthlessness of the composition, Plato warns the reader not to be seduced by its merit as an artistic creation into accepting it as a definitive statement. The cult of texts, oral or written, is alien to Plato.

One does not want to leave the last word on poetry to the *Laws,* where Plato reduces the poet once more to a servant of the lawmaker. The old Athenian who has replaced Socrates as Plato's chief spokesman suggests that the discussion that he and his companions have had about the laws is a kind of "poetry": It is, indeed, the most suitable of all poems and prose works for children to hear and teachers to approve (811c–e). In this rivalry with the poets, the lawmakers will surely lose if we appoint as judge the Socrates of the *Phaedrus.*

NOTES

1 In his pioneering study *Preface to Plato* (Cambridge, Mass.: Harvard University Press, 1963), Eric Havelock emphasizes the importance of oral poetic teaching in Greek society.
2 D.K., 21 B 11.
3 D.K., 22 B 42.
4 D.K., 82 B 11, 8.
5 D.K., 82 B 11, 13–14.
6 D.K., 82 B 11, 9.
7 D.K., 82 B 23.
8 D.K., 82 B 11, 11.
9 Gorgias sought to recreate the enchantment of poetry in his own prose by using balanced clauses and sound pattern to emulate the rhythms of poetry. See Jacqueline de Romilly, *Magic and Rhetoric in Ancient Greece* (Cambridge, Mass.: Harvard University Press, 1975), 8–11.
10 D.K., 82 B 11, 15–19.

11 *Ap.* 22a–c.
12 *Meno* 99c–d.
13 *Ion* 533d–534d, 535e–536d.
14 Ion prides himself not only on being able to recite Homer's poems, but also on being able to explain his meaning better than anyone else (*Ion* 530b–d).
15 See further Paul Woodruff, "What Could Go Wrong with Inspiration? Why Plato's Poets Fail," in *Plato on Beauty, Wisdom, and the Arts*, ed. Julius Moravcsik and Philip Temko (Totowa, N.J.: Rowman & Littlefield, 1982), 137–50.
16 *Grg.* 464b–465d, 500e–501c; the term *eidōlon* occurs at 463d2 and e4.
17 *Grg.* 501d–503b, with the term *dēmēgoria* at 502c12 and d2.
18 In the *Frogs* (1009–10), Aristophanes has Euripides say that poets are admired because they make the citizens better. Aristophanes here convicts Euripides with his own words: Euripides subverts traditional morality, even though, like the sophists, he claims to make the citizens better. Iris Murdoch points out that "like all puritans Plato hates the theatre" (in *The Fire and the Sun* [Oxford: Clarendon Press, 1977], 13).
19 See esp. *Smp.* 206e–207a.
20 *Smp.* 209a1–e4. There is no need to emend *theios* ("divine," 209b1), which occurs in all the manuscripts. This entire section deals with what A. W. Price calls "educative pederasty" in *Love and Friendship in Plato and Aristotle* (Oxford: Clarendon Press, 1989), 27–9. *Toutōn* at 209a9 refers to *hōn* at 209a4, that is, to the entire group of psychically creative individuals. The problems raised by Price and K. J. Dover (ed., *Plato's Symposium* [Cambridge: Cambridge University Press, 1980], 151–2) about poetry and legislation dissolve when these are taken as the two main examples of psychic, that is, educational, creativity.
21 M. H. Abrams discusses the distinction between imitative and expressive theories of art in his highly influential book *The Mirror and the Lamp* (New York: Oxford University Press, 1953).
22 *Rep.* 377a–b, 378d–e, 380c1, 387b4.
23 At 396c5–e2, Socrates specifies that the poet must imitate good characters most of all when they act prudently and less when they err, and that the poet will imitate unworthy characters only briefly when they do something worthwhile. Socrates does allow that "for fun" (*paidias charin*, 396e2) a poet may occasionally imitate someone unworthy.
24 On the purification (*katharmos*) of a city by the expulsion of a human scapegoat (*pharmakos*), see Walter Burkert, *Greek Religion*, tr. John Faffan (Cambridge, Mass.: Harvard University Press, 1985), 82–4. In one text, the scapegoat is "decked in boughs and sacred vestments" before being chased away. Socrates uses *diakathairein* and *kathairein* at *Rep.*

399e5 and 8. In his far-ranging study "Plato's Pharmacy," in *Dissemination,* tr. Barbara Johnson (Chicago: University of Chicago Press 1981), esp. 134, Jacques Derrida suggests that Socrates is a scapegoat, *pharmakos,* as well as *pharmakeus* ("sorcerer," see esp. *Smp.* 203d8), expelled from Athens by poison. Homer's banishment may be viewed as an ironical counterpart of Socrates' execution.

25 See further Bernard Bosanquet, *A History of Aesthetic* (London: Swan Sonnenschein, 1892), esp. 49.

26 *Rep.* 595a5: τὸ μηδαμῇ παραδέχεσθαι αὐτῆς ὅση μιμητιΚή.

27 Elizabeth Belfiore, in "A Theory of Imitation in Plato's *Republic,*" *Transactions of the American Philological Association* 114 (1984): 126–7, argues for this meaning, which was first proposed by V. Menza in "Poetry and the *Technē* Theory," Ph.D. dissertation Johns Hopkins University, 1972), 161–3. Menza (132, 161–2) reasonably takes the occurrence of μιμητικός at 395a2 as an implicit definition of the term. Following Menza, Belfiore translates μιμητική as "versatile imitation." G. R. F. Ferrari also adopts this interpretation in his chapter "Plato and Poetry" in *The Cambridge History of Literary Criticism,* ed. George A. Kennedy (Cambridge: Cambridge University Press, 1989), 124–5.

28 *Rep.* 607c5. At 607a5, he calls this poetry the "sweetened Muse" (ἡδυσμένην Μοῦσαν). At 600e4–6, Socrates claims that "all poetic persons (*poiētikous*), starting with Homer, are imitators of semblances of goodness" and the rest; cf. 601a4. This has often been interpreted as a general claim about "poets." But it can be taken only as a claim about the poets of Greek tradition. Moreover, although *poiētikos* may be used as a synonym of *poiētēs,* "poet," Plato appears to use the term (in the *Republic* at least) in the same way as "mimetic," with the special connotation of "given to poetry," that is, "given to imitations"; see esp. 607a2, where Homer is described as "most poetic" (*poiētikōtaton*).

29 The three stages are 595c7–598d6, 598d7–602b11, and 602c1–608b2.

30 As Harold Cherniss, "On Plato's *Republic* X 597B," *American Journal of Philology* 53 (1932): 233–42, has argued, Plato is not here revising his theory of Forms by making God their creator, but brings in God merely for the sake of the analogy. Socrates himself qualifies this stratagem by the tentative "we might say" at 597b6.

31 R. G. Collingwood, "Plato's Philosophy of Art," *Mind* 34 (1925): esp. 157–9. For a different view, see Alexander Nehamas, "Plato on Imitation and Poetry in *Republic* 10," in *Plato on Beauty, Wisdom, and the Arts,* ed. Moravcsik and Temko (Totowa, N.J.: Rowman & Littlefield, 1982), esp. 60–3.

32 In the *Sophist,* Plato develops his ideas on imitation further by dividing *mimētikē* into (a) the making of images (*eikastikē*), which consists in

preserving the proportions of the "paradigm," and (b) the making of appearances (*phantastikē*), which changes the proportions of the paradigm so as to make it appear beautiful (235b–36c). In the *Republic, mimētikē* does not include (a), which may be taken as a philosophical descendant of the craft of making an "image" (*eikona*) of goodness, as proposed in Book III of the *Republic.* In the *Sophist* Plato explores the connection between poetry and sophistry by casting the sophist in turn as an imitator of appearances. The poet does not appear explicitly, but fits the category of the simpleminded imitator who wrongly thinks she knows; by contrast, the sophist is a dissembling imitator (268a).

33 See esp. *Ion* 536e1–3, where Ion claims that Homer speaks well about "everything whatsoever."

34 The *Symposium* is generally thought to be close in date of composition to the *Republic.* It seems to me that the much more elaborate account of the Forms and of the ascent to knowledge in the *Republic* is subsequent to the account in the *Symposium,* and that Socrates' criticism of Homer and all traditional poetry in Book X is additional evidence for dating the *Symposium* before the completion of the *Republic.*

35 Julia Annas, "Plato on the Triviality of Literature," in *Plato on Beauty, Wisdom, and the Arts,* ed. Moravcsik and Temko (Totowa, N.J.: Rowman & Littlefield, 1982), 1–28, argues that there is a serious discontinuity in the argument; for Plato regards poetry as trivial in everything except the very last part of the argument (605c–608b), where it suddenly appears as a danger to mankind.

36 See further M. Pabst Battin, "Plato on True and False Poetry," *Journal of Aesthetics and Art Criticism* 36 (1977): 163–74.

37 *Rep.* 603a12–b4: πόρρω δ' αὖ φρονήσεως ὄντι τῷ ἐν ἡμῖν προσομιλεῖ τε καὶ ἑταίρα καὶ φίλη ἐστὶν ἔπ' οὐδενὶ ὑγιεῖ οὐδ' ἀληθεῖ. . . . φαύλη ἄρα φαύλῳ συγγιγνομένη φαῦλα γεννᾷ ἡ μιμητική. Cf. 605a9–b2.

38 *Phdr.* 265c1 and 257a5; cf. 241e1–3. See further Elizabeth Asmis, "*Psychagogia* in Plato's *Phaedrus,*" *Illinois Studies in Classical Philology* 11 (1986): 153–72.

39 Martha Nussbaum suggests in *The Fragility of Goodness* (Cambridge: Cambridge University Press, 1986), 227, that the *Phaedrus* may be the first example of the "philosophical poetry" now proposed by Plato.

CONSTANCE C. MEINWALD

12 Good-bye to the Third Man

Plato's commitment to what has been called "self-predication," that is, to sentences of the form

Bravery is brave

The Large is large

is one of the most evident and characteristic features of his work. This commitment figures in dialogues of all three periods, and is so far from optional as to be at the foundation of Platonism.[1] Yet these sentences immediately produce negative reactions in us.[2] The first one displayed above, for example, seems clearly false. It seems to be attributing a feature to Bravery that it could not have – we can hardly imagine it performing deeds of valor or bearing up under adversity. The characteristic claim that the Large is large without qualification seems ludicrously to take its subject as another thing like an elephant, only bigger. The presence of claims of this type in Plato's text can make us feel that his way of thinking is not merely foreign to us, but seriously confused as well. Aristotle's rude and dismissive outburst "So good-bye to the Forms. For they are nonsense"[3] seems about right.

Our background suspicion that the Platonic Forms may not really be respectable makes the *Parmenides* especially intriguing to us. For

This paper explores some applications of the main innovation that emerged from the *Parmenides* on the interpretation I developed in my book *Plato's Parmenides* (New York, 1991). Thanks to Richard Kraut for giving me this opportunity to address readers who may not wish to concern themselves with all the issues treated in this book. I am extremely grateful to Charles Chastain, Dorothy Grover, Wolfgang-Rainer Mann, Pamela Meinwald, and Marya Schechtman for being "test readers" of drafts of this essay.

that dialogue owes its fame to the presence, in its first part, of an exchange between a young Socrates and a venerable Parmenides. The utterances of Socrates are reminiscent of statements that are widely regarded as constituting Plato's theory of Forms, as presented in the *Republic* and the *Phaedo.* Yet here, when questioned by Parmenides, Socrates fails repeatedly to uphold his views, and falls into perplexity. This passage has seemed to generations of readers to show a sensitivity to the kinds of problems they themselves associated with Platonism (including but not confined to confusion over self-predication). Did Plato come to hold the view that Platonism was misguided, or was he able to react in some positive way?

The natural starting point for answering this question is to study the rest of the dialogue to see whether it addresses the problems raised in the first part. Plato himself indicates that this approach is correct: He makes Parmenides tell Socrates that the reason he has gotten into trouble is that he has posited his Forms too early, before having "exercised"; the second part of the dialogue then consists of a demonstration of the exercise recommended.[4] Since Plato meant the second part of the dialogue to bear on the problems of the first, we must understand the new exercise it contains if we wish to assess Plato's response to the famous problems.

Yet this approach is not generally taken. The common types of approach that are taken are two. At one extreme we find a large body of work seeking to discover Plato's response to selected problems from the first part of the dialogue by careful study of that part alone. (I will discuss this approach and give references for it in the next section, in the context of considering the function of the passage.) And at the other extreme we find an approach that jumps out of the *Parmenides* entirely, trying to project Plato's reactions to its problems from what he says in other works. Harold Cherniss is perhaps the most famous representative of this group.[5] But the claims Cherniss made in connection with what is sometimes called the Third Bed Argument in the *Republic* (alternatively the "Third Couch") have not convinced many philosophers. The conjectures Cherniss based on the appearance of the language of model and copy in the *Timaeus* seem now to be receiving renewed expression.[6] But we should note that this type of reasoning leaves itself open to reservations of three kinds. First, even if Plato continued to make characteristic claims, this does not by itself show that he had in hand definite and adequate solutions for the problems associated with them.[7] Second, we can only be confident that Plato went forward with a positive response to the problems if we see him building the theory of Forms *after* he articulated the problems. Thus attempts to reason from passages in the *Timaeus* become involved in the controversy (given unfortunate animus by the magisterial sarcasms of Owen and Cherniss)[8] over the dating of the *Timaeus.* Third, passages from other dialogues do not contain evidence that Plato thought they had anything to do with the problems of the *Parmenides.*[9]

For these reasons then, it is clearly undesirable to have to rely solely on projections from other works in forming one's view of Plato's response to the problems of the *Parmenides.* This brings us back to the second part of the dialogue – the natural place to which Plato himself indicates we should look. There is in fact a very good reason why scholars have not been applying its lessons to the famous problems: there has been no agreement about what its lessons are.[10] Thus J. L. Ackrill in 1984 called the second part of the *Parmenides* "Plato's most intractable text," and David Bostock in his 1988 book on the *Theaetetus* writes, "Now of course one can never tell, with any argument in the second part of the Parmenides, what Plato himself thought of it."[11] Indeed, the surface strangeness of this text can make it look unlikely to yield results that could be useful: Many of its arguments are seemingly so bad as to be embarrassing, and they are arranged so as systematically to produce apparently contradictory conclusions. Yet as the longest stretch (almost thirty Stephanus pages) of uninterrupted argument in the Platonic corpus it ought to be of considerable philosophical importance. In fact, it does deserve our attention. Its superficial eccentricity has delayed recognition of what is really a sound and congenial character. Having approached the arguments systematically and read them in light of Parmenides' methodological remarks, I believe that the second part of the *Parmenides* is intelligible after all. A positive and crucial innovation – a distinction between two kinds of predication – emerges, with whose help we can recognize the exercise to consist of good arguments to conclusions not contradictory after all.

The recognition of this innovation provides us with new apparatus for dealing with the problems of the first part of the dialogue, now with improved prospects of recovering Plato's response. For the present essay I have selected two important problems: the notorious

Third Man and the one Plato himself called the "greatest difficulty." I will start with an initial treatment of the problems, turn to an exposition of what I take to be the main innovation of the second part of the dialogue, and finally apply this innovation to the selected problems. It will turn out that Plato continues to uphold self-predication sentences. But he develops a use for them on which their truth conditions are entirely different from the ones we have been giving them.[12]

I. THE PROBLEMS INTRODUCED

It will be useful to start with some general consideration of the first part of the dialogue and its function. This text (if we break off before the description of the new exercise, perhaps in 135d3, just after Parmenides has congratulated Socrates on his efforts) has the appearance of a work complete in itself; in particular it resembles the canonical Socratic dialogue (that is, it resembles Plato's own early productions). For there is a general pattern there. Some philosophically interesting subject comes up. One of the persons present can be expected to be an expert on this subject. This person enters into conversation with Socrates about the subject matter of his supposed expertise, answering a series of questions. By dialogue's end, the interlocutor has revealed that he is not in a position to uphold his views: His confusion is such that he has not managed to avoid contradicting himself.

The twist in our dialogue is that Socrates (here a youth) is the interlocutor, while the venerable Parmenides is the questioner. Socrates presents himself as an expert on Forms by his aggressive criticism of Parmenides' Eleatic comrade, Zeno. For Socrates' criticisms are made from the standpoint of a view relying crucially on assertions about Forms. Yet these Forms are not things that everyone knows about, but are rather special theoretical entities. Someone who uses controversial assertions about special theoretical entities as a basis for attacks on others ought to be an expert on the relevant theory, so Socrates ought to understand Forms. But notoriously, when Parmenides questions him further about his views on Forms, Socrates falls repeatedly into difficulties, and admits his perplexity.

The resemblance of the first part of the *Parmenides* to an early dialogue taken in its entirety perhaps gives it the air of something to be studied by itself. And certainly the obscurity of the rest of the dialogue adds to the attraction of concentrating one's attention on this more accessible portion of the text. In fact, a great deal of very careful work has been done to analyze particular arguments from this passage.[13] My purpose is not to offer detailed discussion of any such work. But I think that consideration of certain presuppositions shared by many of these interpretations will help to organize preliminary discussion of the passage. For this purpose I will start by identifying what I take the characteristic pattern of these interpretations to be. That pattern combines concentration on the first part of the dialogue with the beliefs that each argument in the passage should be treated as a *reductio ad absurdum*, and that study of these arguments will allow us to determine whether Plato knew what to reject (and, if he did know, what it was).[14]

Despite the attractions of this approach, recognition has been growing recently that it is inappropriate.[15] First of all, one cannot take this approach without ignoring the explicit indication of the transitional passage (135c8–137c3) that the exercise forming the second part of the dialogue is relevant to handling the problems of the first part. As I mentioned earlier, Parmenides there tells Socrates that he won't be able to get things right until he has done a certain exercise, and is prevailed upon to demonstrate that exercise. The second part of the dialogue is just this demonstration. We can spell out the implications of this connection between the two parts of the dialogue in terms either of our approach to the passage or of our understanding of Plato's development. In terms of our approach to the passage, the connection indicates that we should not, after all, treat the first part of the dialogue in isolation; despite its resemblance to an early dialogue it cannot be regarded as self-contained. In terms of Plato's development, the connection between the two parts of the dialogue means that we should not derive our account of Plato's development from analysis of the first part's problems only; since he presents the dialectical exercise as relevant to handling those problems, it is only fair to try to understand that exercise.[16]

A second consideration involves what one might call the logical import of the passage. As already noted, we have here, as in many a Socratic elenchus, a person who tries repeatedly to sustain conversation on some favorite subject matter but ends each time in admitting that he has contradicted himself. This result shows, at a minimum, that the person does not have knowledge of the subject in question – if he did (given Plato's strong conception of knowledge) he would be able to avoid contradiction. Yet while it is clear, if the interlocutor admits that he contradicts himself, that something has gone wrong, this by itself does not tell us what the source of the problem is. For, as we would put it, any one of the premises the interlocutor has been willing to accept may have been false, or he may, starting from true premises, have made some illicit inference from them.

There is controversy between scholars of the Socratic elenchus concerning whether, when repeated over time, that procedure might not have positive results, and concerning what the status of those results would be.[17] However, a difference between our exchange and those making up Socrates' program of moral inquiry renders the difficult question of so-called elenctic confirmation irrelevant for our purposes. This difference is that the program of moral inquiry consisted in a large number of conversations with a variety of interlocutors taking place over a long period, while the present exchange is clearly a unique occasion, and meant to have its effect as such.

Let us return, then, to consideration of the case in which someone fails the elenchus on a single occasion. We have noted that the fact that the interlocutor contradicts himself does not automatically prove, of any specific premise, that *it* is false. However, sometimes we are faced with an argument that has this purpose, and so it is worthwhile to consider what facts can be used in deciding when to take an argument in this way. It seems that the paradigmatic *reductio* works as follows: It makes explicit all of its premises, so that we can see that all but one are already known to be true, while that one is marked out as vulnerable. It then proceeds by explicit and irreproachable reasoning to derive an unacceptable conclusion. This clearly indicates that we should reject the targeted premise. Of course, many actual examples of *reductio* arguments are more casual than the paradigmatic *reductio* as I have described it. But, while they may neglect to make all their premises and all the reasoning from them explicit, their basic strategy requires that they make it possible for us to identify which premise is supposed to be rejected, and that they also make possible sufficient identification of what else is involved so that the target premise can be seen to be the most vulnerable element.

If we now consider our passage with this description of the effective *reductio* in hand, we can see how far the passage is from matching the description. (The claims of this paragraph will be confirmed when we turn to discussion of the individual arguments.) For one thing, often the very premises that *reductio*-oriented readers wish to reject are unexpressed. A premise that does not appear in the text can *a fortiori* not be marked as the target of the exercise. And more importantly, the arguments are underspecified in a strong sense: Not only does the text often not set out enough premises for the announced conclusion to follow, but there is just not enough information from which to determine exactly what we are supposed to understand as completing the arguments. And different ways of completing the arguments are not just trivially different. (The variety of formulations of the Third Man Argument that have been produced by careful interpreters is a sign of the extent to which that argument is underspecified, while the heat of their disagreement with each other indicates that the different formulations differ importantly.)

In short, all too often in our passage, the text does not effectively target a determinate premise for destruction, nor does it give us a sufficient sense of what else is involved to ensure that some putative target premise is indeed the most vulnerable element. Yet an author providing a *reductio* must do both these things. Plato is so far from having produced arguments here that follow the *reductio* strategy effectively that we must doubt whether he can have intended the passage to function in that way.

Let us now draw together the two general observations we have made on Socrates' falling into difficulties. (1) Our final response to the issues raised here is to be determined by our understanding of the second part of the dialogue. (2) The arguments that appear in this passage are extremely underspecified. It seems to me that (1) indicates that the purpose of the first part of the dialogue is introductory: It motivates us to work at the difficult developments of the second part of the dialogue, given that we have some interest in the concerns of the first part. (One might compare Book I of the *Republic*, which clearly has a purpose of this kind.) Given this purpose, (2) no longer appears to be a weakness in composition, rendering the arguments strangely ineffective in their task of proving certain claims to be false. It rather serves to help in the characterization of Socrates. His getting into trouble on the basis of sketchy arguments indicates something important about his personal level of expertise: that he is inexpert. This is of course compatible with the harsh evaluation that he holds determinate beliefs that are provably false. But it is equally compatible with the milder evaluation that he is not yet able to bring to bear the doctrines or specifications that would allow him to avoid trouble. According to this milder evaluation, his notions simply require further explication and understanding. Since Plato has refrained from writing the sort of passage that would force on us the harsh evaluation of Socrates, there is some hope that the milder one is what he intended. And this hope is nourished by the remarks Parmenides makes at 133b6–9, 135a7–b2, 135b5–c3, 135c8–d3, and 135d8–e4. In these remarks, Parmenides commends Socrates for his interest in Forms and his eager impulse toward arguments, says that an able person could deal even with the "greatest difficulty" that arises for Form theory, and announces that Forms are necessary if one is not to destroy thought. That is, even Parmenides, the poser of the problems, endorses Socrates' program.

What this passage shows about Socrates is therefore that he is *not yet* an adequate exponent of the theory of Forms. Because of the unmistakable resemblance of Socrates' views here to those expressed by the Socrates of the middle dialogues, this passage has traditionally been regarded as a comment by Plato on the status of the so-called middle theory, but considerable disagreement has centered on the content of Plato's comment. My study of this portrait of Socrates suggests that we ought to regard Plato as telling us that his middle-period works do not contain a fully and adequately developed theory of Forms.

Thus, as I see it, his care in being guided by Plato's text has led Gregory Vlastos rightly to coin his famous phrase that our passage is a "record of honest perplexity."[18] But while Vlastos's concentration on the first part of the dialogue led him to attribute the perplexity to Plato as he wrote the *Parmenides*, I believe the second part of the dialogue shows Plato himself to hold more adequate views than does the character Socrates. The immaturity of Socrates (at around twenty, he is significantly younger than he was in the preceding works) indicates that the Platonism he offers is itself somewhat immature.[19]

I believe, then, that the overall purpose of the passage we have been discussing is to prepare interest for the hard work that lies ahead by showing that Plato's famous middle-period presentation of Forms is insufficiently developed. (I do not wish to take a stand on what Plato's private views were during the middle period; I attribute insufficient development only to the views *as they appear* in the dialogues of that time. I do not know how to decide between the positions [*a*] that Plato's own views were not more developed, and [*b*] that Plato had adequate views whose exposition he considered out of place given the subject matter and purpose of the works in question.) To find out whether further development will involve rejection of any of the basic tenets, or will simply require handling them in a more sophisticated way, we must come to understand the second part of the dialogue. But before doing that, let us look at our two selected passages so as to get some feelings for the issues that are in play.

* * * * *

The argument that appears at 131e8*ff* has had a career quite independently of the rest of the *Parmenides*; it has been a subject of enormous interest to Plato's rivals and admirers alike since antiquity, when Aristotle popularized the Third Man as a crucial problem for Platonism.[20] Nevertheless Plato's presentation is brief and without fanfare, bringing foward only the following consideration:

> Large things must have some one thing in common [the Large].
>
> The Large and the other large things now require to have something new in common, by which all of them will appear large.

This gives rise not only to a "Third Large," but is supposed to be reiterated to yield an unending series of Forms; Socrates regards such a result as unacceptable.

Clearly, what we have in the text is not enough fully to specify the argument in question. But we can see that some version of the claim that the Large is large must play a role here. And as soon as this becomes apparent, the idea that Socrates' basic views may be viable might appear quixotic; the claim in quesion here seems simply false. By the end of this essay we will see that Plato believed with justification that the situation was more complicated than that. At this stage

Socrates glimpses (rightly) that the self-predication sentence must express an important truth, but in his immaturity he misinterprets the sentence, and so gets into trouble. (As we could put it, he acquiesces in illicit inference as a result of a mistake in semantics.) It is crucial for the understanding of Plato's philosophy to come to understand that the form of words guarantees that each such sentence expresses *some* truth, and that Plato is the heir of a program that gave a central explanatory role to sentences of this type.

To take the first of these points first, we must start from the circumstance that expressions of the form "the Large," "the Beautiful," "the Just," can be used in Greek to refer to two very different kinds of things. "The Just," for example, can refer on the one hand to something that happens to be just (or to whatever does), and on the other, to what it is about these things that is just. Similarly, "the Beautiful" could be used of vases or of Helen, but could also be used to refer to what is beautiful about these things. Abstract nouns like "justice" and "beauty" come to be used increasingly in Plato's time as a way of being unambiguous in one's reference to the second kind of thing; Plato himself uses both forms of words extensively.

What is relevant for present purposes comes from thinking about the fact that in describing the second kind of use we employed phrases like "what is just about just things," "what it is about Helen that is beautiful."[21] In these phrases "just" and "beautiful" are *already being predicated.* This suffices to guarantee that

> The Just is just [or: Justice is just]

and

> The Beautiful is beautiful [or: Beauty is beautiful]

must hold. They do no more than repeat the predications we accepted within the relative clauses glossing our subject terms. To interpret these sentences may be nontrivial, but the point is that even without making up one's mind about how they are to be understood, one can see that they must express some truths. (It is the fact that a competent speaker of Greek automatically knows that sentences so framed must express truths that accounts for Protagoras's acceptance of "Justice is just" and "Peity is pious" at *Protagoras* 330c2–e2. He certainly does not have a Platonist metaphysics and is not accepting these sentences as an expression of his devotion to Form theory.)

The other background we need to fill in now is the work of the pre-Socratic natural philosopher Anaxagoras.[22] Anaxagoras developed a theory to account for the phenomena of generation, destruction, and change in face of the Eleatic proscription against attributing any change or not-being to what is. (In what follows I will use "change" in a wider sense to cover generation and destruction as well.) He was one of a generation of pluralists who explained what we ordinarily think of as change in terms of rearrangement of elements that are eternal and unchanging, except in position. Such a strategy involves seeing what we ordinarily think of as individuals – the trees and horses, the fish and lakes of our daily world – as composites. For Anaxagoras, these familiar objects are composed of shares or portions of certain basic stuffs, such things as the Hot, the Cold, the Bright, the Dark, Gold, Bark, Wood, Blood, Bone, and so on for a very long list. These shares stand to the composite objects in a simple relation: We can think of them as physical ingredients. Thus if the lake becomes warm we are to think of it as getting an increased share of the Hot; its continuing wetness is due to its having a long-standing and large portion of the Wet. Anaxagoras thought of the basic constituents as having the very qualities they contributed to composites. Thus the Hot – the totality of heat in the world – was itself hot. This gave a very easy explanation of how the basic constituents accounted for the features of the observable world: Since they had the relevant qualities themselves, so did the shares of them that composites got; that is, the basic stuffs were in a position to endow participants with portions of their own qualities. To resume our example, when the lake warms up it gets an additional share of the Hot; the share is itself hot and this accounts satisfactorily for the change in the lake.

It will by now have become evident in what way Anaxagoras's work prefigured Plato's. Both undertake to explain everything about the derived entities in terms of their getting shares of, that is, participating in, the fundamental ones. (While Anaxagoras uses the same language of participation as Plato does, notice that for the pre-Socratic there is no mystery about what is: It is having a portion of some stuff as an ingredient or physical constituent of onself.)

Readers may already have recognized (as Plato did before us) that while this approach works well in some cases, it cannot just be generalized straightforwardly. One can hardly claim that when someone becomes beautiful this is because of the mere physical addition of a share of some elemental stuff, the Beautiful, qualitatively identical with what the Manhattan skyline loses as it becomes overbuilt. Similarly, something's largeness is not adequately conceived of as a transferable physical ingredient. While one might respond to this recognition simply by throwing up one's hands, Plato more optimistically sought to retain the basic explanatory scheme. That is, he retained the central tenets of the Anaxagorean theory:

> Things are *X* because they participate in the *X*
>
> The *X* is itself *X*

despite recognition that in general (and in particular for many of the qualities that interested him) an interpretation in terms of material transfer of portions of ingredients themselves having the properties in question will not work. What Plato had to do was to find a model for participation other than getting a physical share of a thing, and find the interpretation (guaranteed as we have seen by their linguistic form to exist) on which the self-predication sentences are true.

* * * * *

Though the Third Man is often seen as *the* argument against Socrates, Plato clearly did not see it as the only serious difficulty, since he made Parmenides refer to another one as the "greatest" and placed this greatest difficulty prominently, at the end of the series.[23] What we see here is that Socrates does not have fine enough control of his belief in the special status of Forms to prevent that belief's committing him ultimately to the irrelevance of his Forms to the world around us.

The difficulty takes its starting point from the conjunction of the claim that since Forms are *kath' heauta* (literally, "by or in relation to themselves") they cannot be in us, with the observation that Forms associated with relations have their being in relation to other Forms, and not in relation to the things around us, while the things around us are related to other things around us, and not to the Forms. To take an example more congenial to our sensibilities than the ones that appear in the text, we are the siblings of each other, not of the Forms; nor do the Forms have us as their relatives, for they are relatives only to each other.

To see how the difficulty develops, we can follow the sample argument given in the text in terms of Knowledge and its special branches (not identified more particularly), and see how the argument would go in the case of Arithmetic. In that case, the claim about the patterns of relations yields:

> Arithmetic knows the Numbers[24] (and presumably not anything around us).
>
> The knowledge of this world knows numerous collections of objects around us (and presumably not the Numbers).

Now since the knowledge of this world (which we might have) does not know the Numbers, and since we are obviously not Arithmetic itself, nor do we have it among or in us (by the claim that the status of Forms prevents their being in us).

> We do not know the Numbers.

A fortiori we are not in a position to apply knowledge of the Numbers in order to derive our knowledge of numerous collections of objects around us. Moreover, there is no such application of Arithmetic to the sensible world. For, by the claim about the pattern of relations, only *we and the things around us,* and not Arithmetic, are related to sensible objects. Given the explicitly made point that the particular branches of knowledge know the particular Forms, we can see that the availability of this type of argument will prevent us from knowing any of the "things that are," and will also prevent any of the Forms from explaining our world at all.

The stress in setting up this problem on the claim that Forms are what they are only in relation to Forms, while we are what we are only in relation to other sensibles, indicates that it will bear on this problem if we come to see that there *is* a way in which sensible particulars have their being in relation to Forms. Socrates now thinks he cannot posit such a relation without thereby making Forms degenerate into just more mundane things around us.

We can conclude our initial treatment of the problems with a summary. Socrates, starting from well-motivated claims, somehow gets into difficulty, showing that he is unable competently to deal with the entities he is so eager to introduce. Plato meant this to indicate the limitations of his earlier presentation of his own theory of Forms. But he suggested the second part of the *Parmenides* would help with further successful development of the theory, and we have seen no reason to consider this impossible.

II. PLATO'S INNOVATION

It is now time to turn to the second part of the dialogue. I believe that Plato so composed that exercise as to lead us to recognize a distinction between two kinds of predication, marked in the *Parmenides* by the phrases "in relation to itself" (*pros heauto*) and "in relation to the others" (*pros ta alla*). These phrases belong to the kind of use of the Greek preposition *pros* ("in relation to") in which a sentence of the form

A is *B* in relation to (*pros*) *C*

indicates that some relation unnamed in the sentence is relevant to *A*'s being *B*. In cases of this kind, the context provides information that allows identification of the relation in question. In the *Parmenides,* the in-relation-to qualifications indicate the relations that ground each of two kinds of predication.[25] In this way, they mark a difference in the way in which *B* can be predicated of *A*. Thus, the difference between what holds of a subject in relation to itself and what holds of the same subject in relation to the other is not simply due to the distinction between the others and the subject. It derives more fundamentally from the fact that a different relation is involved in each kind of case. A predication of a subject in relation to itself holds in virtue of a relation internal to the subject's own nature, and can so be employed to reveal the structure of that nature. A predication in relation to the others by contrast concerns its subject's display of some feature, which Plato takes to be conformable in general to something other – namely the nature associated with that feature.

To prepare now for a precise specification of the first of these two kinds of predication, let us consider the sort of genus-species tree familiar from the Linnaean classification system. To illustrate the idea, we might imagine a tree showing the Animals. We can imagine dividing Animal into Vertebrate and Invertebrate, dividing Vertebrate in turn into Mammal and so on, and continuing with such divisions through Feline and Cat, to produce at last such *infimae species* as Persian Cat.[26] In the *Sophist, Statesman,* and *Philebus* Plato devotes a great deal of attention to such trees, discussing explicitly the methodology of constructing them, as well as providing numerous examples. In such a tree, a kind *A* appears either directly below or far below another kind *B* if what it is to be an *A* is to be a *B* with a certain differentia (or series of differentiae) added.[27] That is, the natures of *A*'s and *B*'s are so related that being a *B* is part of what it is to be an *A*.

In any such case, *B* can be truly predicated of *A* (or of the *A*) in relation to itself, and so can *A*, and so can any of the differentiae *D*. The idea here is that this kind of predication is grounded in the structure of the nature in question: *A*'s nature is what it is to be (an) *A* – that is, (a) *B* with . . . with *D*, and it is in virtue of this that the predications hold. (I will sometimes use the phrase "tree predication" for this type.)

It may be helpful at this point to take some examples of true tree predications. We will get sentences like:

The Just is virtuous.

Triangularity is three-sided.

Dancing moves.

The Just is just.

It is clear that such sentences come out true in Plato's work, as well as fitting our characterization of predication of a subject in relation to itself.

The Just is virtuous

holds because of the relationship between the natures associated with its subject and predicate terms: Being virtuous is part of what it is to be just. Or we can describe the predication as holding because Justice is a kind of Virtue. If we assume that to be a triangle is to be a three-sided plane figure (i.e., that Triangle is the species of the genus Plane Figure that has the differentia Three-Sided), then

Triangularity is three-sided

holds too. We can also see that

Dancing moves

is a true tree predication, since Motion figures in the account of what Dancing is. Finally,

The Just is just

turns out to exemplify the limit case of predication of a subject in relation to itself: It is uninformative but safe. Thus self-predication sentences can be used to make true tree predications, though not all tree predications are of the form: The *A* is *A*.[28]

Predication of a subject in relation to itself takes some explaining because we ourselves are not in the habit of making such predications. Predication in relation to the others is much easier to understand, because this is the category into which Plato would put our own common or garden predications. (Thus I will sometimes call these "ordinary" or "everyday" predications.). For example:

Aristides is just

Northern Dancer is a horse

The Triangle is intelligible

and in general all sentences which we could describe nontechnically as concerning the displays of features by individuals count in our present terminology as predications in relation to the others. This is because Plato characteristically holds that Justice, Horsehood, and Intelligibility have crucial roles to play in the states of affairs in question here: Nothing can be just without Justice having something to do with it, and so on. Fuller formulations accordingly would run:

Aristides is just in relation to Justice.

Northern Dancer is a horse in relation to Horsehood.

The Triangle is intelligible in relation to Intelligibility.

These formulations make explicit the bearing of a relation to something that is in general other than the subject of the sentence, and this makes apposite the name "in relation to the others." Thus whenever a sentence:

A is *B*

concerns the display of features by an individual, we classify it as a predication in relation to the others.

* * * * *

The crucial distinction of the *Parmenides,* which I have just explicated, coincides with the distinction between the *kath' hauto* and *pros allo* uses of "is" in the *Sophist.* These were described in Michael Frede's *Prädikation und Existenzaussage.*[29] His contribution to the present volume (Chapter 13) provides a shorter exposition in English. Section III summarizes his interpretation of what he there calls the "first" and "second" uses of "is" in the *Sophist.* These correspond respectively to the *Parmenides'* predication in relation to itself ("tree" predication) and predication in relation to the others ("ordinary" predication). Perhaps it will be helpful to mention now a minor point where our accounts differ: Frede's account of the *Sophist* associates only the second use of "is" with participation, while the *Parmenides* seems to me to speak of participation in connection with both kinds of predication.

While my original purpose was simply to understand the *Parmenides* itself, part of the interest of the interpretation that I have developed lies in its strengthening of the evidence we now have that Plato made such a distinction and considered it of wide import. Extended discussion of the *Sophist* would take us out of the bounds set for this essay; nevertheless, it may be useful to make four points very briefly. First and most obviously, the basic fact that we can make independent cases from two different dialogues for Plato's use of this distinction is significant. Second, the circumstance that Plato uses slightly different language for the distinction in the two texts is typical of his compositional style, which generally relies on use of ordinary language in such a way as to make technical points (rather than introducing and adhering rigidly to special technical terms). I believe we should regard the occurrence of a unique pair of phrases as neither necessary nor sufficient for the operation of any one distinction. Thus we should not feel any worry over the circumstance that the Academy sometimes in other contexts uses phrases superficially similar to those of the *Sophist* to mark the familiar (and different) distinction between relational and nonrelational terms.[30] Third, the starring role of the distinction in the *Parmenides* can explain why Plato relied on the distinction at *Sophist* 255c12–13 not only without explaining it, but without even drawing our attention to its importance: there was no need to do these things, because of the fanfare he had already given the distinction when he introduced it in the *Parmenides.* Fourth, if, as now appears, the distinction is introduced as being of great systematic importance in the *Parmenides,* it would naturally be ready to be used as needed subsequently, so that there is no reason to require its later application to be limited to *Sophist* 255.[31]

* * * * *

We can now make some observations about Plato's distinction that will be useful later. First, we can note briefly that the implicit bearing of one member of the pair "in relation to itself"/"in relation to the others" on any form of words

A is *B*

is independent of whether *B* is a relational predicate. Because our examples have not yet explored how this works, it may be helpful to consider a relational case now. For example,

Lady Lufton is kind

can be expanded to show to whom she stands in the kindness relation, thus:

Lady Lufton is kind to Fanny.

From Plato's point of view, this assertion, telling us as it does about Lady Lufton's display of a feature, is a predication in relation to the others; more specifically, it is a predication in relation to Kindness. Thus we can write most fully:

Lady Lufton is kind to Fanny in relation to Kindness.

The relation to Kindness is of course not the kindness relation but the relation (unnamed in the sentence) of conforming to, which was introduced above.

To conclude our exploration of Plato's innovation before going on to apply it, I will show that certain sentences can be used to make predications *of either of the two types.* The force these assertions have on particular occasions of use, and hence their truth conditions and sometimes their truth-values as well, depend on the kind of use.

Sentences whose subject terms name Forms can be used to make predications of either kind. That is, one can employ the form of words:

The *A* is *B*

on some occasions to make tree predications, and on different occasions to make ordinary ones. The force of the tree predication is: Being *B* is part of what it is to be *A*. By contrast, the ordinary predication has the force: The Form *A* displays the feature associated with the word "*B*." These need not have the same truth value, and they always have different truth conditions. This will be easy to see if we take some examples. The tree predication

Cathood has vertebrae

is true: Having vertebrae is part of what it is to be a cat. But the ordinary predication that could be made by the same form of words is ludicrous. That is, as an ordinary predication

Cathood has vertebrae

is plainly false; only sensible animals that inhabit the world around us display the feature in question.

The difference between the two uses of the sentences is especially obvious in this case because they have different truth-values. Let us now consider a case that will show the more subtle difference that still obtains even when the truth-values are the same.

The Just is not curved

could be used to make a true predication of either kind, but these would still not be the *same* assertion; they would not have the same force. As a tree predication the sentence holds in virtue of the fact that being curved is not part of what it is to be just. As an ordinary predication the sentence holds in virtue of the distinct fact that the Form, the Just, is not a curved object, that is, does not display curvature.

Now that we have seen that a form of words

The *A* is *B*

can be used to make predications of each of our two kinds, we will have an important interpretative choice whenever we come across a sentence of this form. We will have to be guided by our sense of the argumentative context in determining the force on a given occasion of any such sentence.

III. THE INNOVATION APPLIED

We are now ready to return to the problems of the first part of the dialogue. But before considering them individually, let us consider the situation in a more general way. The views of the Socrates of the first part of the dialogue have always reminded readers of certain passages from the great middle-period masterpieces, perhaps especially the *Republic* and the *Phaedo.* For convenience, I will call the position produced by concretizing the suggestions of those passages in the most simpleminded way " 'Platonism.' " The purpose of the scare quotes is of course to mark the fact that I question whether Plato himself had any enduring commitment to this position. There is, however, no doubt that many people have thought that he did.

Intuitively, the most bizarre feature of "Platonism" was that it thought of Beauty as the single most beautiful thing, of Largeness as doing its job by outclassing all other objects in size, and so on. That is, "Platonism" was supposed to be a view that believed in entities that managed feats of superinstantiation that ought to be impossible.[32] And it cast these entities in the functional role of properties. Beauty, for example (the single most beautiful thing), was supposed to be somehow the common thing among a group of sensible beautiful individuals. (This is of course why the Forms have a series of names of the form "Beauty," "Justice," "Largeness," as well as "the Beautiful," "the Just," and "the Large.") Thus, as an anachronistic reader might put it, "Platonism" makes the ridiculous mistake of thinking that properties do their job by having the very properties they are. The superexemplification theory of Forms seems obviously to be a mistake.

Let us see how our investigation of the vital innovation of the *Parmenides* is connected with all this. Clearly, the superexemplification view results naturally in taking sentences of the form

Bravery is brave

to be doing the same kind of thing, or describing the same kind of state of affairs, as those like

Achilles is brave.

That is, the superexemplification view assimilates the crucial self-predication sentences to everyday true predications in relation to the others.

Earlier, when discussing the situation of the immature Socrates, I developed the thought that while self-predication sentences may be trivially false on one reading, Plato had good reason for wanting to find another reading on which they are true. The distinction between kinds of predication can now be seen to be the distinction between these two readings. That is, for example, the ordinary predication

> Bravery is brave

may well be false. If being brave is a matter of behaving in a certain way in fearsome circumstances (or indeed is any condition on people or their behavior), then Bravery does not seem to be the kind of thing that could be brave in relation to the others (i.e., that could display the feature in question). Nevertheless,

> Bravery is brave

can still be true when it is made as a tree predication. As we have seen, a single form of words can change its truth-value, depending on which kind of predication it is being used to make. Self-predication sentences will always be true when they are used to make tree predications. It was the failure of the immature Socrates to recognize that this reading was the one to go for that led him as I put it to misinterpret his own theory.

* * * * *

Let us now consider the application of Plato's innovation to our selected problems. It applies straightforwardly to the Third Man Argument.

> Large things must have some one thing in common [the Large]

is in itself not problematic; Plato can continue to analyze this in terms of the large things being related to a single Form, the Large. We noted before that, while the argument is seriously underspecified, it relies on some version of the crucial claim

> The Large is large

in order to reach the threatening conclusion

> The Large and the other large things now require to have something new in common, by which all of them will appear large.

Indeed, the production of new Larges depends crucially not just on the claim being made that the Large itself is large, but on that claim's being treated in the same way that

> Mont Blanc is large

would be. To begin with, the Large itself and the original group of visible large things are treated as being large *in the same way.* This induces the notion that we have a new group of large things whose display of a common feature must now be analyzed in the same way the display of the common feature of the original group was. If this is taken to require the introduction of a new Form, a regress is started. And the regress will be vicious given the purpose of Forms. Each Form purports to be the single thing that grounds and explains the predications it is invoked in connection with and should therefore not yield to an unending series of further Forms.

But now that we have exercised, we can see immediately that there are two different predications the single form of words

> The Large is large

could be used to make. It is important to Plato to maintain the tree predication. But we are now clear that that predication does not claim that the Large itself is large in the same way that the original groups of large things is. It therefore does not force on us a new group of large things whose display of a common feature requires us to crank up our machinery again and produce a new Form.

It may be helpful to consider also the example of Man.

> Man is man

and

> Man has vertebrae

are ridiculous if we read them as being the same sort of assertion as

> Socrates has vertebrae.

However,

> Man has vertebrae

does express a truth that conveys part of the structure of the world, namely that having vertebrae is part of what it is to be a man. Since he takes them to express the real structure of the world, it will always be important to Plato to maintain the tree predications. But the crucial point is to realize that he has an interpretation of these important sentences on which they make no claims about the Forms' exhibiting features. The *Parmenides* has emerged as showing conclusively that Plato does not suppose each property to do its job by having the property that it is. Since his support of the self-predication sentence does not require him to take Man itself as an additional member of the group that displays the feature common to men, and as requiring a new Form to explain the display of this new group, there will be no regress. Plato's metaphysics can say good-bye to the Third Man.

* * * * *

The "greatest difficulty" will now appear to be no difficulty at all; it too admits a straightforward application of our distinction. The easiest way into the difficulty will be to return to the particular version of it I developed using the case of Arithmetic. In this case, the claim about the pattern of relations yielded

> Arithmetic knows the Numbers (and presumably not anything around us)

and

> The knowledge of this world knows numerous collections of objects around us (and presumably not the Numbers).

Then since this world's knowledge did not know the Numbers, and since we were obviously not Arithmetic itself, nor could we have it in us, it followed that

> We do not know the Numbers.

A fortiori we could not be in a position to apply knowledge of the Numbers in order to derive our knowledge of numerous collections of objects around us. And moreover, by the claim about the pattern of relations, there could in principle be no such application of Arithmetic. For by that claim, only we and the things around us, not Arithmetic, could be related to sensible objects.

Let us proceed by collecting the responses that we are now able to make to some of the statements that play a crucial role in generating this result. As noted above,

> Arithmetic knows the Numbers

formerly had always a strange ring; we felt a little unsure what it meant, perhaps even embarrassed by it, and were accustomed to peoples' hurrying it by with the thought that it is the sort of thing Plato presumably did believe. Now we have an interpretation on which it can be asserted unproblematically, for we can make the following tree predications without embarrassment:

> Arithmetic knows the Numbers[33]

and

> It is not the case that Arithmetic knows the things around us.

Further, we can certainly say

> It is not the case that knowing the Numbers can be predicated of our knowledge in relation to itself

and

> It is not the case that knowing the Numbers can be predicated of us in relation to ourselves.

Plato would regard the first two of these four statements as being true in virtue of the fact that the correct account of Arithmetic is that it is knowledge of the Numbers and not anything in terms of things around us (in this sense Plato is indeed a Platonist). And the last pair of assertions also holds: We and our knowledge are not the kind of things that figure in the structures represented by tree predications.

We now come to the crucial point. None of this gives us grounds for rejecting the ordinary truth

> We know the Numbers.

This is of course true as a predication in relation to the others, and the claims we have just accepted are not at all incompatible with it.

Thus the crucial inference that the difficulty needs to make at this point (to: We do not know the Numbers) cannot now be made.

Earlier I pointed out the emphasis in this problem on the claim that Forms have their being only in relation to other Forms, while we are what we are only in relation to other sensibles. The fact that sensible particulars are indeed what they are in relation to the Forms is thus relevant to this problem. Forms do have their being in relation to forms – the nature of Siblinghood is not given in terms of us. And we are of course the siblings of each other and not the Sibling itself. But let us now consider this claim that we are siblings of each other more closely. Because it concerns our display of features, Plato will regard it as a predication in relation to the others. (This is the basic Platonist move of regarding sensibles as dependent on the Forms.) That means the most fully specified way of putting it is

We are siblings of each other in relation to the Sibling.

Of course here, the relation to the Form is not the sibling relation. Thus, it can be true both that we are siblings of each other and not of the Form, and that we are what we are (namely, siblings) in relation to the Form. This is ultimately why the Form is not competing with our blood relatives.

The basic innovation of the second part of the *Parmenides* has applied directly to these two problems (and indeed, as I have argued elsewhere, enables an aspiring Platonist to handle all the problems of the first part of the dialogue). This gives us good grounds for an answer to the question concerning Plato's state of mind. He was able after all to respond to the problems, avoiding difficulty and finding satisfactory interpretations for the claims characteristic of his program. In conclusion, let us step back to get a broader view.

IV. THREE STORIES OF PLATO'S DEVELOPMENT

A very unhappy story of Plato's career has been increasingly out of fashion in the last half-century. (Though, as is often the case with old fashions, it continued to be followed by people out of the circle of the trendsetters.) In this most unhappy story, Plato started writing with a gracious compliment to his master. The high literary achievement of the middle-period works coincided with a philosophical high point: a heady and confident time of glorious dogmatism. Then, after a major crisis in which he attacked and actually destroyed the theory that was his masterpiece, Plato spent his last years in extensive critical activity. His now-failing literary powers produced the late dialogues as a record of this barren final period.

A second and completely opposite story has been in vogue more recently. (R. E. Allen, writing in 1965, said of this view that it "[had] grown increasingly prominent in recent years, and [was] liable to become still more prominent in future."[34] By now the heyday of this view has passed, and we find Malcolm Schofield in 1990 announcing that "the paradigm . . . is becoming frayed at the edges . . . and the search for alternative paradigms is under way.")[35] This second kind of interpretation, which received perhaps its greatest impetus from Gilbert Ryle, regards the theory of Forms of the middle period as a hopelessly flawed creation, whose hopelessness was realized by Plato himself in the *Parmenides.* He was then in a position to do some good philosophy in the late period. This story is in a way happier, but the attribution to Plato of a middle theory that can only be nonsense is a problem. Moreover, it seems to me unsatisfying in its separation of the passages expressive of the greatest motivation and excitement from the program of the dialogues it regards as containing Plato's enduring philosophical contributions. There is something in Allen's complaint that this is "the portrait of a man who abandoned a voyage of discovery for essays in county cartography."[36]

Opposite as they are, these stories have something crucial in common: that the *Parmenides* records Plato's realization of the unviability of a determinate theory of Forms contained in the middle dialogues, and so ushers in a late period whose program would have to be entirely different from that of the middle works. My study of the *Parmenides* indicates that we need not accept this. We can rather see our dialogue as indicating where the underdetermined middle-period view of Forms required further development, and as contributing toward that development a key innovation that should allow unimpeded natural growth of the theory in the late period. This makes available a story of Plato's career that could avoid attributing total nonsense to him at any period, would tell of a fruitful late period instead of a barren one, and would not cut the final investigations off from the exciting motivating passages of the middle period.

I offer the following as a third story. In the early dialogues Plato showed, following Socrates, that people who might have been expected to have knowledge on various matters turned out not to. They were revealed in this condition in a series of elenctic confrontations, by being unable to sustain discussion on the subjects of their supposed expertise without falling into contradiction. The middle works then presented Plato's own theories of these matters, including justice, love, the soul, and rhetoric. These theories were associated with some metaphysical remarks, and in effect Plato claimed that the failures of others resulted from their ignorance of metaphysics.

But the extreme brevity of the passages devoted to metaphysics in the middle dialogues indicates that laying down dogmatically the tenets of a mature theory is not their main task.[37] Thus I regard these passages as indicating the motivations and outlines of views that it is not their purpose fully to develop. Indeed, I believe these passages underdetermine the "theory" to be attributed to their author. It can come as a surprise on rereading these passages to see how much more specific are the doctrines on sensibles to which Plato commits himself than are those on Forms. The language of the middle dialogues has some tendency to suggest – but is not sufficient to demonstrate – that Plato was a "Platonist."

I believe that Plato composed the first part of the *Parmenides* in order to exhibit where his middle-period description of Forms needed development. Our view of Plato's ability to sustain that development need no longer derive from scrutiny of this passage alone. Nor need we rely solely on complicated conjectures involving the evidence of other dialogues. The *Parmenides* as a whole gives the best possible evidence for Plato's response to the problems it introduces. If I am right or even on the right track, the dialogue shows that his response was successful. As the late period began, the theory of Forms was in new leaf.

NOTES

1 The term "self-predication" is used in slightly different ways by different scholars. I use it to pick out sentences *of the form* I gave, with no stipulation about their interpretation. We can see examples of Plato's commitment at *Prt.* 330c2–e2 (early), *Phd.* 100c4–6 (middle), and *Sph.* 258b9–c3 (late).

2 Negative opinions about self-predication have been frequently expressed; I here offer a sampling. Sir David Ross pointed out the self-predications at

330c2–e2 in the *Protagoras* as an example where a "mistake occurs in its crudest form" (*Plato's Theory of Ideas* [Oxford, 1951], 88). C. C. W. Taylor in his commentary on the same passage reports that "the confusion amounts to a failure to distinguish between being an attribute and having it" (*Plato's Protagoras* [Oxford, 1976], 112). And Gregory Vlastos, in his editor's Introduction to *Plato: A Collection of Critical Essays,* vol. 1, *Metaphysics and Epistemology* (Garden City, N.Y., 1970), tells us that "had Plato known the Russellian paradox, he would have seen instantly the absurd consequences of "The *F* is *F*' for most values of *F*" (p. 2).

3 *Posterior Analytics* 83a32–33.

4 By "the second part of the dialogue" I understand from 137e4 to the end.

5 Cherniss discusses whether Plato thought the Third Man Argument fatal to his theory in *Aristotle's Criticism of Plato and the Academy* (Baltimore, 1944), 293–300. The broader context is his treatment of Aristotle's use of the argument, starting on p. 289.

6 To take two examples from the present volume, in section III of editor Richard Kraut's Chapter 1 and section VII of Nicholas P. White's Chapter 9.

7 So A. Wedberg, "The Theory of Ideas," in *Plato,* ed. Vlastos, 1: 44 n. 20.

8 G. E. L. Owen, "The Place of the *Timaeus* in Plato's Dialogues," *Classical Quarterly* 3 (1953): 79–95; H. F. Cherniss, "The Relation of the *Timaeus* to Plato's Later Dialogues," *American Journal of Philology* 78 (1957): 225–66.

9 The single exception to Plato's silence in later dialogues about problems from the first part of the *Parmenides* is the reprise of the one-many problem in the *Philebus* (14c1*ff*). But this is only one from a long list of problems, and exactly how and even where the *Philebus* might solve it is inexplicit.

10 Of course, individuals have worked on the second part of the *Parmenides* over the centuries. We have treatments of the dialogue as a whole as well as papers on the second part alone. From antiquity a large portion still survives of the neo-Platonist commentary of Proclus (now translated into English by Glenn R. Morrow and John M. Dillon as *Proclus' Commentary on Plato's Parmenides* [Princeton, 1987]). Contributions made in our century include the Budé edition of Auguste Diès (*Platon: Oeuvres complètes,* vol. 8 [Paris, 1923]); Max Wundt, *Platons Parmenides* (Stuttgart, 1935); Francis M. Cornford, *Plato and Parmenides* (London: 1939); Gilbert Ryle, "Plato's *Parmenides,*" *Mind* 48 (1939): 129–51, 302–25; G. E. L. Owen, "Notes on Ryle's Plato," in *Ryle: A Collection of Critical Essays,* ed. Oscar P. Wood and George Pitcher (Garden City, N.Y., 1970), 341–72; R. E. Allen, *Plato's Parmenides* (Minneapolis, 1983); Mitchell Miller, Jr., *Plato's Parmenides* (Princeton,

1986); and Kenneth M. Sayre, *Plato's Late Ontology* (Princeton, 1983). But the approaches of these authors, and their results, vary enormously, and their combined efforts led to no consensus among philosophers and classicists generally.

11 Ackrill's assessment appears in his memorial piece "Gwilym Ellis Lane Owen," *Proceedings of the British Academy* 70 (1984): 493. The Bostock remark is at *Plato's Theaetetus* (Oxford, 1988), 214.

12 As Stephen Menn has pointed out to me, it is certainly no novelty to say that for Plato the Form *F* is *F* of itself while particulars are *F* in some other way, and to claim that this bears on the Third Man. In this sense my treatment is of a familiar kind. What makes it fresh is that it goes on, guided by the text of the *Parmenides,* to spell out the force of this type of locution.

13 An enormous vogue for this sort of thing was established by Gregory Vlastos, "The Third Man Argument in Plato's *Parmenides,*" *Philosophical Review* 63 (1954): 319–49. Other notable contributions are those of Wilfred Sellars, "Vlastos and the Third Man," *Philosophical Review* 64 (1955): 405–37; P. T. Geach, "The Third Man Again," *Philosophical Reivew* 65 (1956): 72–82; Colin Strang, "Plato and the Third Man," *Proceedings of the Aristotelian Society,* supp. vol. 37 (1963): 147–64; Gregory Vlastos, "Plato's 'Third Man' Argument (*Parm.* 132A1–B2): Text and Logic," *Philosophical Quarterly* 19 (1969): 289–301, which has a useful bibliography of articles published on its subject; S. Marc Cohen, "The Logic of the Third Man," *Philosophical Review* 80 (1971): 448–75; and Sandra Peterson, "A Reasonable Self-Predication Premise for the Third Man Argument," *Philosophical Review* 82 (1973): 451–70. While the Third Man has received the lion's share of the attention, one author who has recognized that the "greatest difficulty" deserves sustained work is Sandra Peterson, in "The Greatest Difficulty for Plato's Theory of Forms: the Unknowability Argument of *Parmenides* 133c–134c," *Archiv für Geschichte der Philosophie* 63 (1981): 1–16.

14 Although authors I group together here as following a single pattern all agree that the arguments they discuss are, so to speak, trying to follow the *reductio* strategy, there is important disagreement among them on the question whether Plato knew what the trouble was, or whether he remained unable to see this and even unable to formulate his argument correctly. But I group them together because Gregory Vlastos (the leading exponent of the latter opinion) takes for granted that we should approach (an argument from) the passage by making an explicit and formal reconstruction of the argument, and by diagnosing the trouble.

15 Kenneth Sayre (from whose treatment in *Plato's Late Ontology* I have learned the most), R. E. Allen in his *Plato's Parmenides,* and M. Miller

in his book of the same name have recognized this point. But because of the prestige of the authors who followed the pattern described above and the inclusion of their papers in influential collections, I suspect that the pattern is still dominant. Partly for this reason and partly because my detailed views are different from those of the other authors, I will go on to offer my own discussion.

16 It has been pointed out to me that those who have worked on the first part of the dialogue in isolation might not endorse the claim that it can be fully understood without reference to the second part of the dialogue. They may have been proceeding on the sensible plan of starting by getting clear about a manageable chunk of text. But this still seems to me to leave their work open to the charge that its approach is inappropriate. Moreover, whether or not the authors of these papers believed that approaching these arguments in isolation was the ideal way to handle Plato's text, their articles have had the effect of leading many readers to suppose that it is – since it is the procedure of so much influential work.

17 Terence Irwin's discussion in *Plato's Moral Theory* (Oxford, 1977) has played a major role in the controversy. (But perhaps unfortunately for present purposes, it is scattered throughout the book.) An important recent pair of contributions is the exchange between Gregory Vlastos and Richard Kraut in *Oxford Studies in Ancient Philosophy* 1 (1983): 27–58, 59–70.

18 Vlastos, "The Third Man Argument in the *Parmenides*," as reprinted in *Studies in Plato's Metaphysics*, ed. R. E. Allen (London, 1965), 254.

19 127b1–c5 tells us that at the time of their meeting, Parmenides was about sixty-five, Zeno nearly forty, and Socrates very young.

20 See the commentary of Alexander of Aphrodisias, *in Metaphysica* 84.21*ff.* I follow the established practice of calling Plato's argument the Third Man Argument even though that name does not match his formulation. No differences between the Man and the Large are relevant for our purposes. For an interesting discussion of the difference between the two for Aristotle and the significance of his formulating the argument in terms of Man, see Alan Code, "On the Origins of Some Aristotelian Theses about Predication," in *How Things Are: Studies in Predication and the History of Philosophy*, ed. J. Bogen and J. E. McGuire (Dordrecht, 1985), 104–10.

21 I take the content of this paragraph from a seminar of Michael Frede's at Princeton.

22 On Anaxagoras's physical theory in connection with Plato, see David J. Furley, *The Greek Cosmologists* (Cambridge, 1987), 1: 45–8, 61–3, 65–70, 171–3; J. Brentlinger, "Incomplete Predicates and the Two-World Theory of the *Phaedo*," *Phronesis* 17 (1972): 61–79; and David J. Furley,

"Anaxagoras in Response to Parmenides," *Canadian Journal of Philosophy,* supp. vol. 2 (1976): 61–85.

23 Perhaps a comment on the sense in which this difficulty can be the greatest is also in order here. It certainly does not strike many now as harder to deal with than the Third Man. Plato may mean not that this problem is the hardest to handle, but rather that this difficulty, if not handled, involves the worst result. (K. Sayre suggests this, *Plato's Late Ontology,* 34–6.) For the difficulty, while it initially seems to be concerned only with Forms associated with relations (as Mastership is associated with the mastery relation), ultimately leads to the consequence that no Forms can do their basic job of explaining the sensible world and grounding our knowledge of it.

24 Perhaps even more than "The Large is large," this type of claim strikes us as foreign. On the only interpretation that we find natural, it is grotesquely false: so much so that puzzlement should arise about why Plato represents it as acceptable. As with "The Large is large," it will turn out that Plato distinguishes two interpretations of this sentence: On one (our natural reading) he can join us in rejecting it, but on the other we can join him in finding it acceptable.

25 The development of this interpretation of the qualifications is the central chap. 3 of my *Plato's Parmenides,* to which I refer readers interested in more than the bare assertions of the present essay.

26 I base this example on the discussion in J. C. B. Gosling's commentary, *Plato: Philebus* (Oxford, 1975), 156*ff.* Obviously it sketches the tree in question only partially. Note that this sketch assumes, as is generally done, that the trees do not go down as far as sensible individuals or features unique to them.

27 The"kinds" of late dialogues are Forms. The circumstance that we respond to Plato's late treatment of *eidē* by abandoning the translation "Forms" and preferring "kinds" or "species" should not mislead us into thinking that Plato has changed the subject.

28 Sometimes in what follows, I will remind readers of how tree predications function by speaking somewhat loosely of one nature's being part of another, and so on. I of course do not mean to exclude the limit case in which the natures are identical, but it is too cumbersome always to be mentioning it.

29 *Prüdikation und Existenzaussage, Hypomnemata* 18 (Göttingen, 1967). Frede's interpretation is often assimilated to the one advanced by G. E. L. Owen in "Plato," in *Plato,* ed. Vlastos, 1:223–67; and elsewhere. While both authors have encouraged this through footnotes expressing agreement, it is of great importance to recognize that the agreement is primarily a matter of their both rejecting the view that the *Sophist*

distinguishes between *existence* and a two-place notion. It is a mistake to assume that all the details of their positive interpretations will agree. In fact Owen constantly puts his view in terms of a distinction between identity and predication, which (while he does not explicate it fully) does not seem to coincide with Frede's distinction. It is telling that Owen illustrates his distinction in "Aristotle on the Snares of Ontology," in *New Essays on Plato and Aristotle,* ed. Renford Bambrough (London, 1965), 71, with the sentences "Arrowby is mayor of Margate" (identity) and "Arrowby is idle" (predication). In Frede's terms *neither* of these sentence illustrates the *kath'hauto* use of "is."

30 Vlastos regards the latter as "the" distinction associated with this language, in "An Ambiguity in the *Sophist,*" in *Platonic Studies,* 2d ed. (Princeton, 1981), 288–90 n. 44.

31 Thus we can answer the objection of Vlastos ("Ambiguity in the *Sophist,*" n. 44) that even if Frede's characterization of the 255 distinction were correct we would have no right to use it outside 255, even at 256.

32 At least in many cases, Largeness seems problematic. And examples can be multiplied. For example, this "theory" seems committed to taking Manyness as the single (!) most multitudinous thing.

33 This is equivalent to: Arithmetic is knowledge of the Numbers. We can imagine characterizing branches of knowledge according to their objects, so that we give accounts like: Grammar is knowledge of language. On this scheme, Arithmetic is the Form of knowledge that deals with numbers. (Cf. Peterson, "The Greatest Difficulty for Plato's Theory of Forms," 4–6).

34 R. E. Allen, "Introduction," in *Studies in Plato's Metaphysics,* ed. R. E. Allen (London, 1965), ix–x.

35 Malcolm Schofield, "Editor's Notes," *Phronesis* 35 (1990): 327.

36 Allen, "Introduction," xi.

37 Here I am gratified to find myself in agreement with Jowett, whose assessment seems to me to apply today as well as it did in the nineteenth century when he wrote: "Plato's doctrine of ideas has attained an imaginary clearness and definiteness which is not to be found in his own writings. The popular account of them is partly derived from one or two passages in his Dialogues interpreted without regard to their poetical environment" (*The Dialogues of Plato,* 4th ed. [Oxford, 1953], 2: 13).

13 Plato's *Sophist* on false statements[1]

In Plato's dialogue the *Sophist,* the main interlocutors, the Eleatic Stranger and Theaetetus, are trying to determine the nature of the sophist. Given that the phenomenon of the sophistic movement is so many-faceted and somewhat amorphous, it is not surprising that the first attempts in the dialogue to get a grip on the elusive reality underlying this phenomenon turn out to be not particularly successful, since they at best capture some superficial feature of the sophist. These features are recapitulated at 231c8–e7.[2] Then, in 232a1*ff,* a renewed attempt is made to capture the sophist; this attempt seems to go more to the heart of the matter, but runs into difficulties whose resolution occupies the remainder of the dialogue. The suggestion is that the sophist has a remarkable ability to represent things in a way that makes this representation, the sophist's statement about things, appear and seem to be true, though, in fact, it is not. This raises a series of difficulties, first alluded to in 235d2, then again in 236c9*ff,* and spelled out in considerable detail in 236d9*ff.* These problems the sophist will exploit to the fullest to reject the characterization suggested and thus again to elude capture (cf. 239c9*ff.*, 241a3). The difficulties, in brief, amount to this: There are problems about the very possibility of false statements. For a statement, in order to be a statement at all, has to manage to say something, that is, there has to be something that gets said by it. But both in ordinary Greek and in the language of Greek philosophers a false statement is one that says what is not (or: what is not being).[3] Yet what is not being does not seem to be something that is there to get said. Hence it would seem that there is nothing that gets said by a false statement. But in this case it fails to be a statement. So it seems that there can be no false statements. But, if there is a problem about the possibility of false statements, there is – *a fortiori* – also a problem about the possibility of false beliefs (of false *doxa*), about something's seeming (*dokein*) to somebody, but not being a certain way. And if there is a problem about the possibility of false beliefs, there also is a question concerning the possibility of false appearances. Indeed, there is a problem about appearances as such; given that they are not the real, the true thing itself, but just an appearance of it, they in some way do lack reality and, in some special sense, which is difficult to pin down, truth (cf. 236e1–2, 239c9–240c6).

In the *Sophist* Plato tries to deal with most of these problems. But he does focus on the central problem of false statements. Here he primarily tries to show that and how there can be such a thing as a false statement, and in the course of this he tries to clear up the confusions that give rise to doubts about the very possibility of false statements. His view seems to be that these confusions have at least two sources. First, they rest on a misunderstanding of the negative particle "not" in "not being"; because of this misunderstanding one tends to think that what is not, or what is not being, is nothing whatsoever and hence not something that, for example, could get said in a statement. Secondly, there is considerable confusion about what a statement is. Hence one fails to realize that the truth or falsehood of a statement is a matter of what gets said in the sense of what gets said about, or predicated of, a subject. Once we realize this, and once we understand how the expression "not being" is to be construed, Plato thinks, we also see that it is entirely unproblematic to say that what gets said by a false statement is something that is not. It is something that is perfectly real, it just happens to be something that is not (true) in the case of the particular subject in question that it gets said of.

Given this diagnosis of the problem, Plato proceeds in two stages. He first (241c7–259c4) tries to show that it is unproblematic to say that there is something that is not. He then (259c5*ff*) turns to statements to show in which way it is unproblematic to say of a statement that it asserts something that is not. In this way he tries to accomplish the task he had set himself at the outset when he said (236e4–237a1): "For how one should put the matter when one says or thinks that there really are falsehoods and, in uttering this, not to get involved in contradiction, that, Theaetetus, is altogether difficult." We should note that the aim Plato sets himself in a way is a rather modest one; it is not to solve all difficulties one might want, or be able, to raise concerning false statements, but to find a coherent way of thinking about them such that, thought of in this way, they no longer seem to pose a problem.

The discussion of what it is to be something that is not, that is, to be something that is not being, takes up a much larger space, though, than the discussion of what it is to be a false statement. At least in part this is so because Plato thinks that the notion of something that is, of a being, is no less puzzling than the notion of something that is not, and that the two puzzles are related. So the problems about not being, on Plato's view, are not just due to problems about the proper understanding of the function of "not" in ". . . is not being," they are also due to problems about the proper understanding of being. What is more, the problems about being stand in the way of properly understanding what a statement is. Hence when Plato finally at 242b6*ff* actually sets out to refute Parmenides and to show that there is something that is not, he does so by first calling into question our understanding of "being" (cf. 243c2–5, 250e5*ff*), which turns out to be as problematic as "not being." He then (251a5*ff*) turns to at least a partial resolution of the problems about being before he returns to the problem of not being. Hence the considerable overall length of the discussion of how we should understand the phrase "not being" or "what is not."

Instead of discussing all this, though, I want in what follows to focus on the discussion of false statements. Hence I will, only very briefly, comment on the remarks about being, and, in somewhat more detail, consider the remarks about what it is to be not being, to the extent that this seems necessary to understand Plato's resolution of the difficulty concerning false statements.

I. THE PROBLEM OF BEING

The problem about being, in a nutshell, seems to be this. Suppose we follow the philosophers in their attempt to determine and identify what is to count as a being (cf. 242c5–6); and suppose we decide in the end that we have to recognize as being whatever is in motion and whatever is at rest, and that these two classes exhaust what there is (cf. 249c10–d4). There still is a problem about what being is (249d6*ff*). Though it is true that whatever is is in motion or is at rest, being itself is neither in motion nor at rest. Neither to be in motion nor to be at rest is what it is to be; and hence what is, as such, in itself, by itself, is neither in motion nor at rest. It is by itself just what it is to be. But if it is neither in motion nor at rest, it does not seem to be a being (250c1–d5).

To see the solution to this problem, we have to see how each thing can be said to be lots of things, not just what it is by, or in, itself (if it is the kind of thing that is something by itself), but also other things that it is not by itself, but by standing in the appropriate relation to something else. Thus being, of itself, is just whatever it is that it is to be. But this does not prevent it from being at rest, or from being in motion, by standing in the appropriate relation to rest, or to motion. What makes it difficult to see this is that this problem is entangled with a problem about statements. There is the view of some of Plato's contemporaries (perhaps, e.g., of Antisthenes) that it does not make sense to say of something that it is something else, to say of something that it is something that it is not. It is fine, they seem to argue, to call a man "man" and what is good "good"; but how can one say of a man that he is good, if a man is not what is good, but something else (cf. 251a5*ff*)?. This involves a misunderstanding of what statements are. To make a statement is not just a matter of calling a thing by its own specific name. It is rather a matter, as Plato will point out later (262d2–6), of naming something so as then to go on to say something about it. But this failure to understand what statements are, to understand how something can be said to be lots of things and can be called by many different names (cf. 251a5–6), gets aggravated by, as it in turn aggravates, a failure to understand being.

The crucial point to understand here is a point Plato makes in a much-debated passage in 255c12*ff.* The being that we attribute to things is of two kinds (cf. 255d4–5). Some of the things we say something is, it is by itself; other things we say something is, it just is with reference to something else, it is by standing in the appropriate relation to something else. Thus Socrates is or is a being, for instance, in being white. But white is not something Socrates is by himself; it is something he only is by being appropriately related to something else, namely the color white. He only is a being in this particular way, or respect, namely in being white, by standing in a certain relation to something else, namely color. He is white, not by being this feature, but by having this feature. He is white, as we may say, by "participation" in something else. The color, on the other hand, is said to be white, not by participating in, by having, this feature, but by being it. Similarly the color is a color, not by having this sort of feature, but by being this sort of feature. Hence it is not just white, but also a color, by itself. On the other hand, it is different from the color pink. And though there is a sense in which it is different from the color pink by being the color white, this is not the relevant sense here. It is not part of being the color white not to be the color pink. So the color white is different from pink by being appropriately related to something else, namely to difference. And so, quite generally, the color white is a being in two quite different ways. It is a being by being whatever it is by itself, for example, white and a color; it also is a being by being appropriately related to other things, such as difference, so as to be, for example, different from pink. Once we understand that being takes these two forms, we also understand how it is possible that we can tell a thing not only by its specific name, but by many names, how, for instance, we can say of the color white not only that it is white, but also that it is a being, that it is different from pink, and that it is identical with itself. Moreover, we can explain how being itself can be in motion or at rest, though of itself it is neither.[4]

But, what is more, we begin to see how the solution of the problem concerning being sheds light on the problem concerning not being. It lies in the very nature of being that whatever is, is many things that it is not, namely whatever it is with reference to something else.

This interpretation crucially rests on the assumption that Plato in 255c12–13 distinguishes two uses of ". . . is . . . ."[5] Since I want to assume that Plato in what follows continues to rely on this distinction, but since this interpretation of 255c12–13 has been challenged, I want to make a few remarks in its defense. It has been attacked, for instance, by David Bostock in his "Plato on 'is not,' " *Oxford Studies in Ancient Philosophy* 2 (1984): 89. To begin with, it should be noted that the distinction is not supposed to be the distinction of two senses of the incomplete use of ". . . is . . . ," let alone the distinction between the "is" of identity and the "ordinary" copulative, predicative "is." What speaks decisively against this is that Plato recognizes just one idea of being and that he talks throughout the dialogue as if this one idea was involved both in saying that not being is, namely not being (258b11–c4), and in saying that something is, namely different from something (263b11). It is one and the same being (255d5) that we are attributing to something in both cases. Moreover, the two uses are such that ". . . is . . ." in its first use could not be replaced by "is identical with" without changing the meaning. To say that man is a rational animal is not to say that man is identical with a rational animal. To say that man is a vertebrate or that white is a color clearly is not to make an identity statement, though it is a case of saying what man is of himself or what white is of itself.

It also would be a mistake to think, as Bostock seems to suppose, that the distinction of the two uses is supposed to be a grammatical or logical distinction, if by this we mean a distinction that can be made independently of the metaphysics we rely on. Thus, contrary to what Bostock (p. 92) seems to think, "Socrates is a man" and "Socrates is the man in the corner" for Plato clearly are cases, not of the first, but of the second use of ". . . is . . . ," given that Socrates, on Plato's view, is not a human being in himself, but only by participation in something else, namely the form of a man. But though Socrates and man, on this view, are two different items of which the first participates in the second, we are not even tempted to think that "Socrates is a man" means that Socrates is different from man, or that Socrates participates in man. Hence we also should not be tempted to think that "not being is not being" means that not being is identical with not being. Indeed, it is not the case that the identity of *X* and *Y* constitutes either a necessary or a sufficient condition for the truth of "*X* is *Y*" in the first use of ". . . is . . . ." It does not constitute a necessary condition since white of itself is a color. And it does not constitute a sufficient condition, given that, for example, "The same is the same (i.e., with itself)" should be a case of the second use of ". . . is . . . ," as "The different is the same (i.e., with itself)" clearly is. This also allows us to distinguish different kinds of self-predication and to claim that the kind of self-predication Plato had been interested in all along, and continues to hold on to, is the one that innocuously involves the first use of ". . . is . . . ."

With this unfortunately rather brief and sketchy account of the resolution of the problem about being, let us turn to how Plato tries to deal with the problem of not being.

II. THE PROBLEM OF NOT BEING

The resolution of the difficulties concerning what is not begins at 255e8. It clearly falls into four parts:

1. 255e8–257a12: Plato shows that things, indeed the form of being itself, can be said to be not being.
2. 257b1–257c3: Plato tries to show that the difficulties concerning what is not have their source in misconstrual of the word "not" in the phrase "not being."
3. 257c4–258c5: Plato tries to show not only that there are things that are not, but what the nature of not being is.
4. 258c6–259c4: Plato gives a summary that leads to the discussion of statements.

Let us first consider 255e8–257a12. In the preceding section Plato had shown that there are five distinct genera or forms of particular importance: being, motion, rest, the same, and the different. In 255e8*ff* he singles out motion and argues that motion, being different from rest, the same, the different, and being, is not rest, is not the same, is not different,[6] and hence also, *pari ratione*, is not being (cf. 256c10–d10). For this he relies on the single fact that if *X* is different from *Y* we can say that *X* is not *Y*. From this, in 256d11–12, he draws the following inference: "Hence, of necessity, not being is in the case of motion and all other forms." The following lines (256d12–e4) make it clear how this inference is to be understood. Given that not only motion, but all other forms (except, of course, being itself) are different from being, it will be true of all of them that they are not being. So "something that is not being," far from being a phrase that cannot possibly be applied to anything correctly, does at least characterize all forms other than being. We should also note in passing the language of the conclusion; Plato seems to be using an expression like "*F* (or: *F*-ness) is in the case of *a*" if it is true that *a* is *F*. Underlying this language there seems to be the notion that one way for *F* to be is for there to be some *a* that is *F*.

In 256e6–7 Plato draws a further conclusion from the argument that begins with 255e8: "Hence, with reference to each form there is much which is being, but an immense amount which is not being." Here we seem to have the same manner of speaking that we noted in the preceding conclusion, except that we now not only talk about something that is, or is being, with reference to a given subject, but also about items that are not, or are not being, with reference to a given subject. It seems that this language is to be understood in the following way: just as *F*-ness is said to be in the case of *a* if *a* is *F*, so *F*-ness is said not to be, to be something that is not, or to be not being, with reference to *a*, if *a* is not *F*. At least on this assumption we can see how the conclusion would follow from the preceding argument. There are lots of things that motion is not, for example all the other forms. And what is true of motion is, of course, true of all other forms. So it is true with reference to each form, that there is an immense number of things that it is not, or is not being. So here is a second apparently quite problematic way in which even forms can be said to be not being. It is not only that each particular form is not the form of being, it also is the case that any other form is not this particular form and that, in that sense, it is not being with reference to any form other than it.

Finally, at 257a1*ff*, Plato shows that even the form of being itself can be said not to be or to be something that is not, namely all the things that are different from it. From the way Plato talks here it is also clear that he regards something's not being *F* as a further way in which something is not, that is to say as something that is not being. For he says (257a4–5) "Being, hence, is not in as many ways as there are other things." If, with this in mind, we return to 255e8*ff*, we notice that Plato already there, when he argued that motion is not rest, the same, the different, or being, apparently had taken these as ways in which motion is not or is not being. For in each case he had paired off the negative statement about motion with a positive statement that was supposed to show that motion is, as by being different, or the same, or being. Thus there is yet a further way in which things are not, or are not being, namely just by not being this, that, or other.

Let us summarize the results of this section. There are various ways in which we can say of something that it is not being that seem entirely innocuous. It is generally accepted that if *X* and *Y* are different, we can say "*X* is not *Y*." Hence, since all other things are different from the form of being, each of them can be said to be not being. This seems to be unproblematic. But there are more interesting ways in which something can be said to be not being. For *X* not to be

Y is for *X* in a way not to be, namely *Y*; at the same time this also is for *Y* in a way not to be, namely with reference to, or in the case of, *X*. But that *X* is something that in this way is not, obviously does not mean that *X* is nothing. It is something, for example different from *Y*. Indeed, it would not have this way of being something that is not, namely *Y*, unless it was being, namely different from *Y*. Similarly, that *Y* is something that is not in this way obviously does not mean that *Y* is nothing. *Y*, as we have shown, is lots of things, for example different from *X*. So there are here two further ways in which something can be said to be not being: (i) the way an *X* can be said not to be insofar as it is not some *Y*, and (ii) the way a *Y* can be said not to be insofar as it is not with reference to some *X*. Obviously, the second way is just the converse of the first. In any case, it is clear that there is an entirely unmysterious way in which there are things that are not being.

With this we can turn to the next section, 257b1–257c3, in which Plato tries to explain where people got confused when they came to think that there is no such thing as what is not. The claim is that they came to think "what is not" or "not being" must refer to the contrary of what is. What is, is something of which it is true that it is in some respect. Instead of realizing that what is not, by contrast, is something of which it is not true that it is in this respect, they assumed that it is something of which it is not true that it is in any respect. But this understanding is not justified by the use of expressions of the form "not *X*." What is meant by expressions of this form is not something that somehow is contrary to *X*.

This much, perhaps, is rather uncontroversial. But interpreters have had great difficulty with Plato's own positive characterization of the use of expressions of the form "not *X*" and in particular his elucidation of the expression "not being." To understand Plato's remarks, we have to keep in mind the close connection between these remarks and the preceding passage. Plato begins with a remark about "not being" (257b3–4). He says, "Whenever we talk of what is not being, we do not, it seems, talk of something contrary to being, but only of something different." The qualification "it seems" indicates that the remark is to be understood in light of what precedes. But what is meant also becomes clearer when we look at the next sentence (257b6–7): "When, e.g., we speak of something as 'not big,' do we then seem to you to indicate by this phrase the small rather than the equal?" As is clear from the fact that this is presented as an elucidation of the preceding sentence (cf. Theaetetus's question in 257b5 to which this is a response), but also from the "e.g." (*hoion*), talking of something as not big is supposed to be a case of talking of something as not being. It seems immediately obvious in which way it is a case of talking about something as not being: It is a case of talking about something as not being in a certain way, namely as not being big. And that this is the correct way to understand the text is supported by the following considerations. In light of 255e8–257a12, we should assume that the not being we talk about in 257b3 is either (i) the not being of something which is not the form of being, or (ii), more generally, the not being of something that is not something or other, or (iii), finally, the converse of (ii), the not being of something that is not with reference to something or other. Now it is quite true that something that is not being insofar as it is not the form of being, is not the contrary of being, but just different from it. But what is not big is not an example of what is not being by not being the form of being. Nor is the not big a straightforward example of what is not being with reference to something or other. Plato here does not seem to think of a case in which it would be false to say of something that it is not big, but rather of a case in which it would be true to say of something that it is not big, and he seems to be saying about this case that to say of something that it is not big is not to say that it is small. Hence it seems that the not being Plato is talking about here in 257b3 is the not being of something that fails to be something or other, for example to be big. And this fits the fact that this was the kind of not being Plato had last talked of in the preceding passage, when he had said that even the form of being itself in many ways is not being, namely in not being all the things that differ from it. Moreover, it is true that what is not being in that way, for example by being not big, is not the contrary of what is being in this way, but simply different. For what is not big is not contrary to what is big, but merely different from what is big. This is clear because, though one way of being different from what is big (relative to something) is being small (relatively), another way of being different from what is big is to be of equal size. Quite generally, then, "not *X*" applies to something that merely differs from what is *X*.

Now the crucial difficulty is how Plato can assume, as I have just taken for granted, that the kind of not being that is involved in something's not being big, or in something's being not big (Plato does not seem to distinguish the two) is the same as the kind of not being that is involved in motion's not being rest, the same, the different, being, or any other form. Interpreters are agreed that Plato in 257b3 or in 257b6 shifts to a different kind of case. Up to this point he has been talking about cases in which something straightforwardly is different from something else, more specifically about cases in which a form is different from some other form. The feature smallness, for instance, is different from the feature bigness. And thus smallness, we can say, is not bigness, or, if we grant Plato his language, the small is not the big, or even smallness is not big. But at 257b3 Plato begins to talk of what is not being, for example about what is not big, as if this at least covered the case of what fails to be big, not by being different from the feature bigness, but by failing to have it. And this seems to be a radically different kind of case. That Plato moves, without warning, from one kind of case to the other, might make us suspect that he is just confused. This is what Bostock is arguing. Less charitably we might think that Plato is cheating. But most interpreters have tried to be charitable and, moreover, to find some way to free Plato of the charge of confusion. Yet it is difficult to see how we can avoid attributing some confusion to Plato.

The problem cannot be solved by claiming that Plato in 257b3*ff* is *just* making a point about the use of "not" in expressions like "not big," quite generally in expressions of the form "not *F*," and hence also in the expression "not being," namely the point that "not" does not signify contrariety. It is true enough that he does make a point about the use of "not" in expressions of the form "not *F*," but it also seems to be true that, in making this point, he believes he has made a point about what is not something or other. It is misleading to say, as Owen does ("Plato on Not-Being," 232, 237, 238), that Plato here offers an analysis of expressions like "not big" and tries to explain "not being" in analogy to them. Talking of something as not big is, at the same time, treated as a case of talking of something as not being rather than as a mere analogue of it.

The difficulty precisely is that Plato moves from talking about motion's not being rest to something's not being big, as if the not being in both cases were the same kind of not being. And this does, indeed, seem to be his considered view. For when in 257c4*ff* he moves on to explain what the nature of not being is, he specifies

(258a11*ff*) *one* nature that supposedly is involved in all cases of not being we have been considering, that is to say, on anybody's interpretation, both in cases of simple nonidentity and in cases of what we would regard as ordinary negative predication. It is also clear from this that Plato cannot mean to solve the problem by distinguishing two senses of ". . . is not . . ." or "not being." He must assume that there is one sense of ". . . is not . . ." involved both in "motion is not rest" and in "Theaetetus is not flying." The problem obviously is how he can assume this.

We make this a hopeless task if we think of Plato as moving from negations of identity to considering falsehood in predicative statements, as Owen does (p. 237). To begin with, the move in question here is not the move to falsehood in predicative statements, but rather the intermediate move to, as it seems to us, negative predicative statements, a move Owen tellingly glosses rather too quickly (pp. 237–8). But, more importantly, it is a mistake to assume that Plato thinks of the earlier statements simply as negations of identity. If he did, the task would be hopeless. He rather must think that if *X* and *Y* are not identical and we thus say that *X* is not *Y*, we are not, in saying this, denying the identity of *X* and *Y*, but are attributing not being to *X*. And he must equally assume that to say of a small thing that it is not big is to attribute the very same not being to it; it is to say of it that it is not, namely big.

Nevertheless it seems that Plato must want to make some distinction here. For consider the following. The small is different from the big. Hence the small is not the big. Plato allows himself to move from this to "The small is not big" (presumably relying on the fact that this is the denial of "The small is big" in the use of ". . . is . . ." in which this is true if "The small by itself is big" or "The small by its very nature is big" is true). So we have both "The small is not big" and "This (a small thing) is not big." There seems to be a clear difference between the two statements. The first seems to deny that something is a certain feature, the second that something has a certain feature. What means does Plato have to locate this difference?

Even without getting into the details of the subsequent section 257c4*ff*, we can note already here that Plato does not identify not being with difference, but with a particular form or kind of difference, with "a part of the different." Hence he cannot assume that "The small is not the big" or "The small is not big" means, or should be analyzed as, "Smallness is different from bigness." I take it that he thinks it should be analyzed as "The small is different from what is big." And I also take it that he thinks that "This (a small thing) is not big" should similarly be analyzed as "This is different from what is big." This explains why he thinks that there is just one account for the use of "not," that there is no ambiguity in "big" or "the big," that there is no ambiguity in "difference" or in ". . . is not . . . ." But we can also readily see how Plato can, if he wants to, distinguish the two kinds of cases we want him to distinguish. He can do so by distinguishing the two uses of ". . . is . . ." in ". . . is big."

In a third section (257c4*ff*), then, Plato tries to show that what is not or is not being, far from being nothing at all and unthinkable, far from being an impossible and illegitimate subject of discourse, constitutes a definite, specifiable kind. At the same time we are supposed to see that, given the way this kind is constituted, what is not is as real as what is. Take what is not beautiful. It is constituted, to begin with, by difference. Difference is something that is. But difference always is difference from something, just as knowledge is knowledge of something. Thus there is difference from the beautiful, that is, from what is beautiful. It sets off a class of things, namely all those things that are not beautiful, over against another class of things, namely all those things that are beautiful. Since difference is perfectly real and the beautiful is perfectly real, difference from the beautiful, and hence being not beautiful, is perfectly real and unproblematic, as real as the beautiful. So in this sense the not beautiful constitutes an unproblematic class of things, no less real than the beautiful. Similarly with not being. It involves a difference, and, more specifically, a difference from what is or is being in a certain way. There is nothing mysterious about this. And this specific difference sets off a class of things, namely all those things that are not in the same way, over against another class of things, namely all those things that are in this way. To be not being just is to be something that is set off from what is in a certain way, something that is different from what is being in this way. In this sense not being is as real as being and hence a nature of its own.

One may be worried here about the phrase "in a certain way" which I have introduced into the account. It reflects the fact that being for Plato always is a matter of being something or other. And correspondingly not being always is a matter of not being in a certain regard, respect, or way. There is no such thing as unqualified not being. This seems to be captured by Plato in the summary that follows, where he talks of not being as the part of the different that is set over against a particular kind of being (*pros to on hekaston*, 258e1).[7] So to be not being is to be something that is different from something that is in a certain way, in a certain regard.

What is clear now, as a result of the discussion of this section, is something that was not clear in the previous section about the use of "not," and that we, at best, could have gotten out of that section by a prejudicial interpretation of the words that " 'not' put in front signifies one of the things which are other than the name which follows it, or rather, which are other than the things which are designated by the name which is applied to them and which follows the negation" (257b10–c2). What is clear now is that Plato understands "not being" and ". . . is not . . ." in such a way that it covers the case in which something fails to be something in that it fails to have a certain feature. It is clear now that "not being" is intended to cover the case of what we would call ordinary negative predication. Given all this, we have no difficulty in understanding what Plato has to say when we turn to the next section, 258c7*ff*, the recapitulation of the argument. But this recapitulation also is puzzling and, indeed, must be confusing, if one has not been able to see how Plato takes the cases discussed in the first section to be cases of not being precisely in the sense at issue here, that is to say at issue in statements like "Theaetetus is not flying." For in 259a5*ff* Plato explains again how unproblematic it is to say of something that it is not or that it is not being. Take the form of the different; it is different from being; hence it is not being (259a6–b1). The form of being is different from all other forms; hence it, too, is not, namely all these other forms (259b1–5). Similarly each of the other forms is different from the rest; hence each of the other forms in many ways is not (259b5–6). Now it is true that this shows that there is a use of ". . . is not" or ". . . is not being" that is innocuous, but the question is whether this is going to help us much if we want to understand how statements can be false. All along, down to the end of the summary, Plato is relying on the fact that if *X* and *Y* are different we can say that *X* is not *Y*. And on the basis of this he has thought that we are justified in saying that *X* is not or that *X* is not being, namely *Y*. He also has relied on the fact that in the case in which *Y* is the form of being itself, it will be true immediately of anything other than being that it is not being.

Now if one believes that the negative statements in the first section (255e8–257a12) are non–identity statements, that they have to be analyzed as stating of some form *X* that it is different from some form *Y*, then this summary must be very confusing. For the sense of "*X* is not *Y*" that we need in order to understand false statements clearly is not the sense of "*X* is different from *Y*." For if it is false that some particular object *a* is beautiful, we want to say something to the effect that "*a* is beautiful" is false because *a*, in fact, is not beautiful. And *a*'s not being beautiful is not a matter of *a*'s being different from beauty or the beautiful. It would be different from beauty even if it were beautiful by participation in beauty. So the account of not being that we need for false statements has to be more complex than an account according to which to say that *X* is not *Y* is just to say that *X* is different from *Y*. So, if the summary is supposed to give us the result that we will need to explain false statements, it seems that it does not even come near to giving us what we need, as along as we hold on to the assumption that Plato regarded the negative statements in the first section as non–identity statements.

What this, I take it, shows is that it was wrong all along to assume that Plato takes statements like "The different is not the same" to be non–identity statements to be understood in the sense of "The different is different from the same." He takes them to be attributing not being to the subject in the same sense in which he takes "*a* is not beautiful" to attribute not being to *a*. But even if one sees this, it has to be granted that it is puzzling that Plato in the summary returns to the cases of not being that do not seem worrisome and that, in any case, we are not worried about if we are worried about false statements. Perhaps the explanation is that Plato in the summary wants to emphasize again how unproblematic it is to talk of something as not being, and that to talk of something that is not is not to talk of something that is nothing at all.

For our purposes we may sum up the result of the discussion so far in the following way. Plato thinks that there is a use of ". . . is not . . ." in which *X* can be said to be not *Y* if *X* is different from what is *Y*, where both the form *Y*-ness and whatever participates in this form count as something that is *Y*. Correspondingly he finds it unproblematic to claim that *X* is something that is not, for instance in not being *Y*. He, correspondingly, introduces (256e6–7) a converse use of ". . . is not . . . ." If *X* is not *Y*, *Y*-ness can be said to be not with reference to *X*. And this, correspondingly, is to say that *Y*-ness is different from what is with reference to *X*. And this again is to be understood in such a way that both difference and difference from the same count as what is with reference to difference, though in different ways. This, Plato thinks, suffices to understand the not being involved in false statements. But to understand the way in which false statements involve not being we have to have a better understanding of statements. And so this is the topic he turns to next.

III. FALSE STATEMENTS

Now the crucial move Plato makes to arrive at a more adequate understanding of statements is to point out that to make a statement we have to do two things: (1) identify an item we mean to say something about, and (2) specify something we mean to say about it. Hence a statement will minimally consist of two parts, a part identifying a subject of discourse and a part by means of which something gets said about the subject. That a statement manages to single out a subject is a condition for having a statement in the first place. Hence its truth or falsehood is a matter of what then gets said about this subject; that is, the locus of truth or falsehood, as it were, is not the statement as a whole, but the predicative or stating part of it. To put the matter differently: To make a true statement is to say something about something that is true of that something; correspondingly, to make a false statement is to say something about something that is false about, that is not true of, that something. So the problem about a false statement is not that it is about nothing. It is about whatever the subject expression names as the subject of the statement. Now the fact that something is true of a given subject, of course, does not mean that it is true of any subject. It will, at least as a rule, be false of some subjects. Conversely, what is false of a given subject will not, at least as a rule, be false of all subjects, but be true of something. So there is no problem about what gets attributed in a false statement as such, either. If there is a problem at all, it must be a problem about attributing it to a subject it is not true of. But this now does not seem to be problematic anymore, either. For to say something false about something, that is, to say something about something that is not true of it, now just seems to be a matter of saying something that is a perfectly good thing to say about something, except that it happens to be different from what is true about this particular subject. So if we know what it is for a statement to be about something, if we know what it is to be true of or about something, and if we know what it is to be different from what is something, we should have no problem understanding how there can be false statements. Or we can put the matter thus: Once we have seen that to be what is not is just a certain way of being different, and if we know what it is to be a statement and what it is to be what is not, we should have no problem seeing the possibility of false statements. This, in a nutshell, seems to be Plato's solution.

But let us look at the details of Plato's discussion concerning statements more closely. Central to it is the claim that a statement minimally has two parts, a name (*onoma*) and a verb (*rhēma*), as Plato identifies the two kinds of parts (262c4*ff*). The function of the name is to name, to refer to, something. But it is only by adding a verb that we "get somewhere," as Plato puts it rather vaguely (262d4), that we can be said to say (*legein*) something (262d5), whence also the resulting complex expression is called a *logos* (262d5–6). Obviously there are all sorts of problems here about the identification and characterization of the two kinds of expressions that minimally constitute a statement. Thus, if, as seems likely, "name" (in the sense of the ancient grammarians) and "verb" here are supposed to refer to the respective word-classes, we, strictly speaking, only get a characterization of an irrelevant subclass of statements, whereas it seems that Plato is aiming at a characterization of simple (i.e., nonmolecular) statements quite generally and really is looking for syntactical categories. The semantic characterization of the two kinds of expressions seems inadequate (cf. 262a3–7), however we interpret their classification, whether by word-class or by syntactical category. But whatever the difficulties and the problems may be, this much seems to be right – and noting it seems to constitute a major advance – that simple statements are constituted by two parts with radically different functions, one part whose function is to name, refer to, to identify a subject, and another part by means of which we say something, state something, predicate something of or about the subject.

Having clarified this, Plato turns to two features of statements of which he obviously supposes that they need to be kept strictly apart: (1) they are statements about something, and (2) they have, as he puts it, a certain quality, that is, they are true or false (262e4*ff*). A surprising amount of attention is given to the first feature (cf. 262e11–263a10, 263c5–12). It is made clear that these not only are two different features, but that the first is independent of the second. In order to have a statement that is true or false we first of all have to have a part of the statement that manages to specify a subject, and which subject it does specify, at least in principle, is settled independently of what gets said about this subject and, *a fortiori,* of its truth or falsehood. Plato quite pointedly lets the Eleatic Stranger settle the question of reference for the sample statements discussed before he lets him go on to consider their truth or falsehood.

Some of the relevance of the care and detail with which this is discussed becomes apparent, if we turn to the historical background. As we noted above there were some unclarity and confusion about the object of the verb "to say" (*legein*). This could lead to the view that what a statement said was what a statement was about. Thus, for example, Euthydemus, in the dialogue of his name (*Euthd.* 283e9–284a1), asks Ctesippus: If one says something false, "does one do so in saying the thing the statement is about?" And Ctesippus answers in the affirmative. From this Euthydemus infers that there cannot be such a thing as making a false statement. For the statement must be about something that is, whereas what gets said by a false statement is something that is not. To clear up this puzzle we need to be clear that what a statement is about is something independent of its being true or false, and that what gets said about this subject is another thing, and that it is this latter thing that is true or false.

There is another historical puzzle, or perhaps rather set of puzzles, that Plato seems to have in mind here. There was the view, which Aristotle repeatedly attributes to Antisthenes, that there is no such thing as statements contradicting each other (*Met.* 1024b26*ff; Top.* 104b20*ff*). In fact, in the *Metaphysics* Aristotle links this view to the view that there can be no false statements. Antisthenes' view, according to Aristotle's testimony in the *Metaphysics* (1024b32–4), was that each thing has its unique *logos* or statement, which identifies or spells it out. This has always reminded scholars of the view expounded at the beginning of the last section of the *Theaetetus,* according to which, if a statement can be made about something at all, it must be its own statement, a statement proper and peculiar to it (cf., e.g., *Tht.* 202a6–8). And it also reminds one of the view attacked in the *Sophist* itself (251a5*ff*), according to which each thing should be addressed only by its own name, and not by the name of something else, so that we should not call, for example, an object "white," since "white" is the name of a color and an object is not a color. But, however this may be, we can see how, if each thing has its own statement and all statements have to be the statement of some one thing, contradiction will be impossible. For, of two apparently contradictory or even just contrary statements only one can be the statement of the thing in question. In this case the other statement will fail to be a statement of the thing in question, and thus will be a true statement about something else or will fail to be a statement of anything, and hence will also fail to be false.

In the *Euthydemus,* 285d7*ff,* we get a somewhat different version of this *antilogia* argument, which here is said to be quite common and attributed to associates of Protagoras or even earlier dialecticians (286c2–3). Here it is argued that for two persons to contradict each other they could not be producing the statement of the same thing, which would be the same statement and hence not yield any disagreement (286a4–7). Nor would there be any disagreement if neither of them produced the statement of the thing in question (286a7–b3). So if there is to be even the appearance of a disagreement, it must be the case that one person is producing the statement of the thing in question, whereas the other produces a statement that disagrees, that is in conflict with the first statement. But in that case the second person must be producing a statement of something else, in which case there is no contradiction. Or he fails to produce the statement of anything, in which case he does not manage to say anything, let alone to contradict the first speaker (286b3–6). In what follows Socrates takes this, too, to be an argument concerning the possibility of false statements. It may be noted in passing that this and similar arguments somewhat gain in plausibility if they are associated with certain metaphysical views, for example the denial of nonsubstantial change.

Now one reason why one may suspect that Plato here, too, is thinking of a version of this argument is, apart from its relevance and appropriateness, a striking linguistic detail in the passage we are considering: Instead of just using the language of "The statement is about *X* (*peri*)," for example, "about you," it also talks of "the statement of *X*" and "*X*'s statement," e.g., "the statement of you" and "your statement" (cf. 262e6, e14; 263a4, a5, a9, c7), sometimes combining both ways of talking (cf. 263a4, a5, a9–10), without in these cases maintaining a definite order that would allow us to say that one way of speaking was supposed to elucidate the other (cf. "about me and mine" in 263a5 and "mine and about me" in 263a9–10). Given this, given that the language of "about" is perfectly clear, and given that the language in terms of possessive pronouns is neither ordinary nor natural, it is difficult not to see it in an allusion to the way of thinking about statements underlying the *antilogia* argument and, indeed, to the *antilogia* argument itself. The point, then, would be that what a statement is about and what gets said about it in the statement are two things to be distinguished, which in fact may be, and normally are, different even if the statement is true. Thus there may be conflicting statements about the same thing, and one of them may be true and the other false. Nor does it follow from the fact that what gets said by the false statement is false, and something that is not, that what the statement is about is something that is not, let alone that it is about nothing.

It also becomes clear what we have to say about a view that is related to Antisthenes' position or to the one reflected in the *Euthydemus*, but that in one regard significantly differs from them. Antisthenes' view was that each thing at best has one statement. At this point in the *Sophist* we have already argued that "Each thing has many statements," to stay with the language of Antisthenes and the sophists (cf. Aristotle, *Met.* 1024b32*ff*). But somebody might still want to hold on to the view that there are no conflicting or false statements, that an apparently conflicting or false statement in reality is a true statement about a different subject. Thus, if Socrates is healthy, somebody might take the view that this was a statement about Socrates, but more precisely about a healthy Socrates, and that the statement "Socrates is ill" was not in conflict with it, let alone false, since it was about a different Socrates, namely one who was ill. Note that in 263c7 the Eleatic Stranger assures himself that Theaetetus is going to grant that the statement "Theaetetus is flying" is about himself who actually is sitting (cf. 263a2), rather than about somebody else. To take such a view, again, among other things, is to fail to see that it is one thing for a statement to be about a certain subject and quite another thing for this subject to have something said about it that is true or false of it; it is a failure to realize that what the statement is about in theory is settled independently of what then gets said about it, whether it is true or not.

So, to conclude our review of Plato's discussion of this feature of statements, Plato is quite willing to grant that a statement cannot be a statement about nothing, that a statement has to be about something (263c9–11). But he resists, as relying on some confusion about statements, any move to argue that false statements as such are about what is not and hence about nothing. Having a better understanding of statements and having a better grasp of what it is to be something that is not, we now are in a position to understand precisely in what sense a false statement is a statement that states something that is not, and this in such a way that we can see that this is entirely unproblematic.

We can thus, finally, turn to the discussion of the crucial feature, the quality of statements, their being true or false (cf. 263a11–d5). To begin with, though, a brief comment on the term "quality" here (cf. 262e5, e9; 263a11, e2). The mere language, relying on the familiar contrast between the what it is, or essence, of a something (cf. 260e4–5, 263c2) and the what it is like, suggests that a statement is a statement independently of its being true or its being false. A statement is a statement by (1) managing to specify a subject and (2) saying something about this subject. Once these two conditions are satisfied we have a statement, and the question whether the statement is true or false only arises, Plato, in using this language, is claiming, once both conditions are satisfied. Moreover, he is claiming that to understand truth and falsehood we have to focus on what gets said in the sense of what gets said about the subject, that is to say we have to focus on the predicate.

Plato first turns to the (*ex hypothesi*) true statement that Theaetetus is sitting, but considers it quite generally as a true statement about Theaetetus. What he seems to aim at is a general characterization of true statements. In any case, he characterizes the statement about Theaetetus in the following way (263b4–5): *legei . . . ta onta hōs estin peri sou.* This, taken by itself, is ambiguous in various ways. Given the ambiguity of *hōs,* it might mean that a true statement says things that are *as* they are, or that a true statement says of things that are *that* they are. The parallel uses of *hōs* in 263b9, 263d1, and 263d2 suggest that the latter is meant. There is a further ambiguity, depending on whether *onta* refers to predicates that are affirmatively true of the subject or whether the claim is supposed to cover all predications, whether affirmative or negative. Given that this seems to be intended as a characterization of at least simple true statements in general, we should assume that *onta* is to be taken in the latter sense. There is yet a further question, namely whether *peri sou* goes with *onta* or *estin.* A comparison with 263b11 shows that it certainly goes with *onta,* though possibly with both. Given this disambiguation, the claim seems to be that a true statement says of what in fact is, namely about, or with reference to, the subject, that it is. The phrase "what is about, or with reference to, *X*" obviously is a bit of quasi-technical language that needs some elucidation. We readily recognize something like the converse use of ". . . is . . ." which we discussed earlier in connection with 256e6, a passage Plato himself seems to be referring to a few lines further down (263b11–12) to explain his language here. I say "something like," though, because there seems to be a slight difference. If we assume that Plato is trying to explain here the truth of true statements in general, and not just the truth of affirmative statements, we have to assume that he now allows "*F*" in "*F* is something that is with reference to *a*" to be itself of the form "not *G.*" Plato's view about true statements, then, seems to be this. Corresponding to the set of true simple statements about *a,* there will be a set of *F*'s that are with reference to *a.* And a true statement will be one that says of such an *F* that is with reference to *a* that it is, or that it is with reference to *a.*

Consider "Theaetetus is sitting." For this to be a statement in the first place it has to be about something, it has to manage to refer to, to name something, which then we can go on to say something about. It does so in referring to Theaetetus. For Theaetetus is something that is there to be talked about. So there is no problem in this regard. There also is no problem about sitting. There is such a thing as sitting. One can give a coherent account of what it is, and (let us assume) a complete account of the world would be impossible without some reference to sitting. Moreover it is clear that there is such a thing as sitting insofar as there are things that are sitting, and so also in this regard sitting is something that is, namely with reference to them. So there is no problem, as far as sitting is concerned. The only question is whether sitting is something that is with reference to Theaetetus, or – to put the matter the other way around – whether Theaetetus is sitting. And the claim is that "Theaetetus is sitting" is true precisely if sitting is something that is with reference to Theaetetus.

But if all this is clear, we should have no problems with false statements, either. Take "Theaetetus is flying." There is no problem about what the statement is about. It is about Theaetetus, and he is something that is. There is no problem, either, about what gets said about the subject, that is, about flying. There is such a thing as flying. One can give a coherent account of it. A complete description of the world will have to make some reference to it. There surely is such a thing as flying, insofar as there are plenty of things that are flying. The only question is whether flying is something that is with reference to Theaetetus. If it is not, then the claim is false. But this now is not a problem, either, given what we have said earlier about not being, or what it is to be not. That flying is not with reference to Theaetetus just means that flying happens to be different from what is with reference to Theaetetus, that is, flying is not one of the *F*'s that are with reference to Theaetetus. But this does not mean that flying is nothing at all. We have already seen that it is something that is, and this in more than one way. Indeed, its not being in the case of Theaetetus itself is just another regard in which it is something that is, namely different from whatever is with reference to Theaetetus.

But, given that this is the point that Plato has been working up to so carefully from 236e onward, let us consider in detail how he himself now resolves the question of false statements and how he deals with this particular example. He turns to the false statement in 263b7. This is what he says: *ho de dē pseudēs hetera tōn ontōn.* It is clear that this sentence is elliptical and has to be understood as parallel to the corresponding "men" clause about the true statement "Theaetetus is sitting" in 263b4–5. Thus understood, it will be rendered in the following way: The false statement then speaks of (*legei*) things other than those that are. For the claim about true statements had been that they say of those things that are that they are. There is a slight difficulty here: It holds of true statements in general that they say of those things that are that they are; but when we are talking about a particular statement, as we are here, it, strictly speaking, only says of one of the things that are that it is, and not, as Plato puts it, of the things that are that they are. But this should not particularly worry us. Plato could have said in 263b3–4 that the true statement says of something that is that it is (*on ti hōs esti*). But he wants to get a reference to the whole class of things that are, relative to a given subject, into the characterization of the true statement, as this will be needed to get an adequate characterization of the false statement. This corresponds to the need for a universal quantifier in a proper characterization, first, of the use of ". . . is not . . ." along Plato's lines, and then of falsehood, a need several commentators rightly have insisted on.[8] Only thus can Plato say that the false statement says, speaks of, something other than *any* of the things that are, that is, something other than any of the things that are in relation to the given subject. For it is clear that it will not do simply to say of a false statement that it speaks of something other than something that is. To be false it has to speak of something other than any of the things that are, namely with reference to the given subject. Moreover, it is clear, given the parallel to 263b4–5, that 263b7 has to be understood in this sense: The false statement says of something other than whatever is in relation to a given subject that it is, namely in relation to that subject. Hence Plato can move on to claim in 263b9: "Hence it says of what is not that it is." Obviously, all he does here is (a) to supply the "that it is" that had to be understood with 263b7 from 263b3–4, and (b) to move from "other than whatever is" to "what is not." That latter move is covered by our earlier explanation of how, for example, what is not beautiful or big is just what is other than whatever is beautiful or big. Correspondingly what is other than whatever is being is not being.

We now have allowed ourselves for the first time in the dialogue since the problem arose to say that a false statement states, says, speaks of (*legei*) what is not. But we also know in what sense this has to be understood, and why, thus understood, it does not pose any problems. To say what is not is to say of something other than whatever is in relation to a given subject that it is. To do away with any residual qualms we may have, Plato in 263b11–12 goes on to explain the phrase "what is not" as it is used in 263b7. There is a minor textual problem here that hardly affects what Plato means to say. The first word in 263b11 is given by the manuscripts as *ontōs*. If we follow the transmitted reading, Plato would be explaining that, though a false statement says, or talks of, what is not, what it is talking of is something that really (*ontōs*) is, namely different. To be more precise, he would be explaining that the false statement says about the given subject something that really is, namely different. We would have to understand this in the following sense: The false statement says about the given subject something that really is, namely different from whatever is with reference to this subject. But we could have Plato say something that comes much closer to this, if, instead of the received text, we followed Cornarius's conjecture, adopted by all modern editors, and read *ontōn* for *ontōs*. We would get closer still, if we conjectured *tōn ontōn*.[9] But whichever text we adopt, the point Plato is trying to make is clear enough. To say what is not is to say something that is not altogether nothing, but something that is; in fact, it can only be called "not being" insofar as it is, namely different from what is with reference to the given subject. And at this point (263b11–12) Plato reminds us of our earlier finding that with reference to everything there is much that is and much that is not. Given the language he must be referring back to 256e6–7. But this has constituted a major problem for scholars that we need to look at in some detail.

Plato's thought here in 263b seems to be the following. Take the false statement that Theaetetus is flying. It says of Theaetetus something that is not with regard to him, namely flying. It presents, talks of, something that is not, namely flying, as if it were in relation to Theaetetus. This is supposed to be unproblematic, because we have already seen earlier that in relation to anything there are lots of things that are not. And so flying is just one of those things that are not with reference to Theaetetus. And this is what makes the statement that Theaetetus is flying false; it presents flying as something that is with reference to Theaetetus, when, in fact, it is not, when, in fact, flying is different from whatever is with reference to Theaetetus (cf. 263d1–2), or, to put the matter yet differently, when, in fact, Theaetetus is not flying.

But if we look back at the claim in 256e6–7, to which Plato seems to be referring in 263b11–12, it was arrived at by considering cases in which *X* and *Y* are different, in which we hence can say that *X* is not *Y*, and, moreover, hence can say that *Y* is not being with reference to *X*. And, given that for any *X* there are lots of things *X* is different from and that hence *X* is not, we were able to say that with reference to everything there are lots of things that are not being with reference to it. But this, it is thought, does not help here, since, though it is true enough that Theaetetus and flying are not the same thing, that Theaetetus is different from flying and hence that Theaetetus is not flying, this is not the sense we need to explain why it is false to say that Theaetetus is flying. For even if it were true that Theaetetus is flying, it still would be the case that Theaetetus and flying are not the same thing and that hence in that sense Theaetetus is not flying. So this cannot be what explains the falsehood of "Theaetetus is flying."

Given their understanding of 256e6–7 and of the preceding section, given in particular their assumption that in this section statements of the form "*X* is not *Y*" express non–identity statements, commentators also are rightly puzzled why Plato here in 263b does not refer to the later part of the discussion of not being, where – on anybody's interpretation – Plato tries to come to terms with what we would regard as ordinary negative predication (cf. McDowell, "Falsehood and Not-being," 122*ff;* cf. Bostock, "Plato on 'Is not,' " 111). It should be clear by now that Plato's reference back to 256e6–7 only makes sense, because Plato all along did not understand the statements of the form "*X* is not *Y*" in that section as non–identity statements, not as statements of difference, but as statements of not being, that is to say as statements of a particular way of being different. And Plato even there must have thought that this way of being different was exhibited not only in those cases in which two forms are different from each other, but also in those cases in which something fails to have a certain feature. So already 256e6–7 has to be understood as involving the use of ". . . is not . . ." that Plato needs to rely on in 263b. What the subsequent discussion, 257b1*ff,* added was an understanding of this use that allowed one to see that it also covered the case of negative predication. It took the subsequent discussion to determine the nature of the very not being whose being we had ascertained by 256e6–7. This is what allows Plato in 263b to refer back to 256e6–7, rather than to, say, 258b. So, though there are details of the text that require further clarification, and though it seems that even with further clarification we would wish Plato to have been clearer and more precise on certain points, the outline of his argument and his general position are reasonably clear and do not seem to be vitiated by confusion.

IV. CONCLUSION

In fact one thing that is striking about the *Sophist,* in comparison to the earlier dialogues, is its "dogmatic" and systematic character. It sets out carefully constructing a series of puzzles, *aporiai.* In this respect its first half resembles the early dialogues or even its immediate predecessor, the *Theaetetus.* But then it turns toward a resolution of these *aporiai.* In this regard the procedure of the dialogue reminds one of the methodological principle Aristotle sometimes refers to and follows, the principle that on a given subject matter we first of all have to see clearly the *aporiai* involved before we can proceed to an adequate account of the matter, which proves its adequacy in part by its ability both to account for and to resolve the *aporiai* (cf. *De An.* I, 2, 403b20–21; *Met.* B1, 995a27*ff*). And the *Sophist* proceeds to resolve these difficulties in a very systematic and almost technical way. By careful analysis it tries to isolate and to settle an issue definitively. In this regard it does stand out among all of Plato's dialogues. And because of this it also is more readily accessible to interpretation. If, nevertheless, we do have difficulties with this text, it is in good part because in his day Plato was dealing with almost entirely unexplored issues for whose discussion even the most rudimentary concepts were missing. Seen in this light, Plato's solution of the difficulty presented by false statements is a singular achievement.

NOTES

1 I am particularly indebted to the following papers: G. E. L. Owen, "Plato on Not-Being," in *Plato,* edited by Gregory Vlastos (Garden City, N.Y., 1970), 1: 223–67; John McDowell, "Falsehood and Not-being in Plato's *Sophist,*" in *Language and Logos,* ed. Malcolm Schofield and Martha Nussbaum (Cambridge, 1983), 123; David Bostock, "Plato on 'Is not,' " *Oxford Studies in Ancient Philosophy* 2 (1984): 89–119.

2 I quote the text in Dies's edition in the Budé series; its line-numbers at times differ from those of Burnet's text.

3 In Greek: *mē on;* in what follows, I will render this and *ouk on* indiscriminately by "what is not" or "what is not being" or even just "not being."

4 For a different interpretation of the problem, see Jean Roberts, "The Problem about Being in the *Sophist,*" *History of Philosophy Quarterly* 3 (1988): 229–43.

5 I developed and argued for this interpretation at great length in *Prädikation und Existenzaussage, Hypomnemata* 18 (Göttingen, 1967), 12–36. It was then, following a suggestion by R. Albritton, adopted by Owen in "Plato on Not-being"; Owen had originally taken a different view of the passage (cf. *Journal of Hellenic Studies* 20 (1957): 107 n. 25). Cf. Owen's first footnote to the reprint of "Plato on Not-being" in Owen, *Logic, Science and Dialectic,* ed. Martha Nussbaum (Ithaca, N.Y., 1986), 104.

6 There are technical reasons why Plato here moves back and forth between "different" and "the different." As I noted earlier, there is, according to Plato, a (self-predicational) way of being different, and generally of being *F,* such that difference or the different is different in this way (and generally *F*-ness or the *F* is *F*); thus not to be different in this way is not to be the different, just as being different in this way is to be the different.

7 Translators tend to construe *hekaston* with *morion;* wrongly, as the preceding part of the sentence shows. Difference is distributed among all things that are with reference to each other, i.e., it is distributed among things that are not beautiful with reference to things that are beautiful, among things that are not big with reference to the things that are big, etc.; the *pros to on hekaston* clearly picks up the *pros allēla.*

8 Cf. David Wiggins, "Sentence Meaning, Negation, and Plato's Problem of Not-being," in *Plato,* ed. Gregory Vlastos (Garden City, N.Y., 1970), 1: 299; McDowell, "Falsehood and Not-being," 123; Bostock, "Plato on 'Is not,' " 113.

9 There are yet other possibilities, e.g., *ontōs de ge onta hetera tōn ontōn peri sou.*

DOROTHEA FREDE

14 Disintegration and restoration: Pleasure and pain in Plato's *Philebus*

> Each of us will be trying to prove some condition or state of the soul to be the one that can render life happy for all human beings. – *You* that it is pleasure, *we* that it is knowledge.
>
> (*Phil.* 11d)

Although the main topic of the *Philebus,* the rivalry between pleasure and knowledge as candidates for the dignity of the highest good in human life, is a familiar one from the early Socratic dialogues on, for the wider congregation of Plato's admirers the *Philebus* to this very day remains largely *terra incognita.* It is regarded as one of the late and difficult dialogues, an area for the specialist who has mastered the intricacies of the late Platonic doctrine that we find more alluded to than explained in the *Parmenides,* the *Theaetetus,* and the *Sophist.* What frightens the student of Plato's ethics off the territory is most of all the long "dialectico-metaphysical preface" of the *Philebus* (14c–31b). For the first quarter of the dialogue is filled with a rather complex discussion of dialectical procedure, dealing with "the one and many," and with a new kind of ontological classification that is, at least at first sight, more bewildering than enlightening and may exhaust the reader's patience before he has even penetrated to the lengthy discussion of different sorts of pleasures that starts at 31b and fills most of the rest of the dialogue.

The specialist, on the other hand, usually confines herself to the first part of the *Philebus,* which contains the discussion of the "dialectical procedure" and the suggested new ontological classification;

I am grateful to Richard Kraut for his help, which far exceeded an editor's concerns. His penetrating questions forced me to clarify the argument at various crucial points, and his correction of my English saved me from many awkward phrases.

she is not amused by the subsequent long-winded discussion of pleasure and pain and of their shortcomings, since it seems not to contribute anything to our understanding of the metaphysical first part. The suspicion has sometimes been entertained that, Plato's claims to the contrary notwithstanding, the dialectical-metaphysical part is only loosely connected with the discussion of hedonism vs. intellectualism and that it may have been used as a preface because Plato saw the need to put his thoughts on paper somewhere, without caring too much about its integration into the text.[1]

Our situation with respect to the dialogue is therefore rather paradoxical: The "general" reader cannot and the specialist will not deal with it as a whole. As a consequence the *Philebus* has remained largely excluded from the discussion of Plato's philosophy, even though it is acknowledged that it may contribute significantly to our understanding of the possible revisions in the philosopher's later thinking. This omission is all the more paradoxical, since at least a bird's-eye view of the dialogue (one that avoids the nitty-gritty of the detailed analysis) will show that Plato himself never loses sight of his aim. The arbitration between knowledge and pleasure is the express motive throughout, not only in the long discussion of different kinds of pleasure and knowledge and in their final ranking (31b–67b), but also in the "metaphysical preface." An overview of the dialogue as a whole and of this metaphysical preface in particular will therefore have to serve as an introduction to the central topic of this essay, the nature of pleasure and pain. As will gradually emerge, the long preface is in fact quite indispensable for a proper understanding of the determination of the nature of pleasure and pain, as well as of their evaluation on the scale of goods.

For economy's sake this essay will be mostly expository, and omit a critical discussion of Plato's position on the nature of pleasure, its drawbacks and advantages. It will also have to refrain from an engagement with many of the important textual and philosophical problems raised in the extensive secondary literature.[2]

I. THE STRUCTURE AND CONTENT OF THE DIALOGUE AS A WHOLE

The set-up of the discussion is quite straightforward. We find Socrates engaged in the defense of the superiority of knowledge against a group of uncompromising hedonists who regard only a life of pleasure as worth living (11a–12b). At the outset Philebus, the lazy beauty of the day, hands over the discussion to his follower and admirer Protarchus, who remains Socrates' partner for the rest of the dialogue. Through a comparison of the nature and benefits of pleasure and knowledge respectively (31b–66d), Socrates finally wins his case and convinces Protarchus. For it turns out that in the final ranking of goods only certain kinds of pleasures, the true and pure ones, are accepted as good at all, and even they end on the fifth and last place on the scale of goods, clearly outstripped by reason and knowledge (65a–67b).

This conversion of the hedonist proceeds in stages. At first Socrates has to insist, against his opponent's resistance, on the need for a differentiation between the various kinds of pleasures and knowledge that can only be achieved through an orderly treatment of their unity and plurality. This claim allows Socrates to elaborate on the appropriate method of dialectic. He enjoins that any science has to start out with a proper "collection" of the genus; it must then provide a complete and numerically exact division into subgenera and species, before it can finally admit the unlimited multitude of individual instantiations. The procedure thus incorporates both limit (*peras*) and the unlimited (*apeiron*): without such a methodological procedure no satisfactory knowledge in any discipline can be reached.[3] If the specialist's appetite is whetted by this introduction to the method of dialectic, which is nowhere as elaborate as in this passage of the *Philebus*, it is soon frustrated, however. For Plato lets Socrates dismiss the dialectical method ("the gift of the gods to mankind," 16c) almost as soon as he has introduced it, because it turns out not to be necessary for the pursuit of their particular topic. Instead, a "sudden memory" has belatedly come to Socrates that allows him to dispense with the dialectical treatment of all kinds of pleasure and knowledge respectively (20b). According to Socrates, neither pleasure nor knowledge taken by themselves can fill the bill of what makes a human life good by procuring our happiness, since the good must be "perfect, sufficient and worthy of choice." Neither pleasure nor knowledge passes this test. For nobody could want a life of pleasure without any kind of reason, nor a life of reason without a morsel of pleasure. Only a *mixed life* that contains both pleasure and reason is sufficient in that respect and must therefore be superior to the life of the hedonists as well as that of the "intellectualists." So the partner's task now turns on the question whether either pleasure or reason is more closely related to what is responsible for the goodness of the "combined life," and therefore deserves at least the second prize on the scale of goods (21d–23b).

This investigation of whether pleasure or knowledge is more akin to the good forces Socrates to start with a new distinction or division of "all there is now in the universe" into four kinds (23c–27c): the unlimited, limit, their mixture, and the cause of the mixture (23c–d). This new ontology is exemplified by a few cases that make clear what he has in mind. In nature there are countless things that are "unlimited" in the sense that they in themselves have no definite degree (as we would say). These are entities that shift on a continuous scale, such as what is hotter and colder, faster and slower, and so forth; they possess no definite nature until a definite and stable "limit" or measure is imposed on them. Such a limit is attained, according to Plato, when they reach a stable or harmonious state, which therefore represents a mixture of the unlimited and the limit. As instances of such stable mixtures he refers to good weather, health, strength, and beauty (24b, 25e, 26b). It seems that for Plato not just *any* degree in the continuum of opposites will do, but that only harmonious and stable combinations deserve the title of a "mixture of limit and the unlimited." For only such mixtures display the appropriate measure. The fourth class that is added is that of the causes of the generation of such "measured" (*emmetron*) mixtures (26e).

This ontological distinction at first sight seems to relate directly to the dialectical method. For it presupposes, as Socrates asserts, partly new devices, but partly the "same ones as they used before" (23b). But if the specialist in Platonic metaphysics now hopes that the ontological division of "all there is" with the help of the concepts of limit, the unlimited, their mixture, and the cause of such mixtures will shed further light on the nature of Plato's late dialectic and metaphysics, this hope will at best be partially fulfilled. The "same devices," unfortunately, seem to be the same only in name. For in the dialectical method "limit" had referred to the unity of the genus and to the number of its subgenera and of the species contained in it, while the "unlimited" comprised the innumerably many different instances. Now, by contrast, the "unlimited" are continua of opposite qualities, the hotter and colder, while "limit" is the proportion that is necessary to turn the continua into harmonious mixtures of these opposites. Why does Plato even pretend that the function of "limit" and "unlimited" in the two passages is the same (23b–c)? This question has not only considerably hampered the interpretation of the *Philebus* itself,[4] but also vexed scholars, who see in this passage the missing link between Plato's late dialectic and metaphysics, as we have it in the dialogues, and the report on Plato in Aristotle's *Metaphysics*, in which "limit" and "unlimited" are crucial concepts.[5] No attempt will be made here to settle the issue how, precisely, these two passages are related to each other, because this would require an extensive discussion of the text and of the ample literature; it would prevent progress on our own topic. We will rather have to focus on the question of what the two passages contribute to what follows in the dialogue itself, to the clarification of the nature of pleasure and knowledge.

What made at least a brief summary of this fourfold division necessary here is the fact that Plato actually uses it in the subsequent discussion, and that he comes back to it explicitly in his final settlement of the arbitration between pleasure and knowledge. As to its immediate purpose, the fourfold division allows Socrates to determine the genera that contain pleasure and reason: Pleasure belongs to the unlimited (the "more and less"), while reason – as Socrates establishes by an elaborate argument that depicts human reason as a descendant of the cosmic divine reason – belongs to the fourth class of "all there is," to the class of the causes of successful mixtures (27e–31b).

The subsumption of pleasure under the class of unlimited, the more and less, turns out to be the first step toward its "degradation." It allows Socrates to urge the view that pleasures by themselves are in need of moderation and harmonization. If they are good, their goodness does not come from their own generic nature but is conditional on something besides pleasure itself. "So we have to search for something besides its unlimited character that would bestow on pleasure a share of the good" (28a). What that condition is will gradually become apparent once different kinds of pleasures and pains have been defined and their origin explained: Pleasures arise in living beings that are in a state of harmony, the *mixed* class. When such a harmonious state is disrupted, the creature experiences pain; when it is restored, pleasure ensues. So the goodness of the different kinds of pleasures clearly depends on the kinds of restorations they are; and this is indeed the topic that Socrates pursues in the long middle part of the dialogue, which is designed to sort out "true and false" pleasures (31b–55c). We will have to turn to Socrates' critique of hedonism in detail later to see what justifies the claim that pleasure and pain can be "true or false."

Evenhandedness in the comparison of pleasure and knowledge in their kinship to the good demands also a critique of reason and knowledge. It gets rather short shrift (55c–59b), but Socrates manages to come up with a constructive critique: Some of the intellectual disciplines are "truer," that is, purer, than others; pure and exact sciences are better than applied sciences, and dialectic is the purest of all. This critique of both pleasure and knowledge allows Socrates to return to his original set of questions: What is the happy mixed life, what is responsible for its goodness, and how are pleasure and reason related to what makes the good life good (59b)? The final answer that crowns Protarchus's conversion from hedonism to a mitigated "intellectualism" brings no surprises: Only a mixed life that compromises both pleasure and knowledge can be regarded as the happy life. But while this life must comprise all intellectual disciplines, even the less pure and exact ones, because they are necessary for a successful life under earthly circumstances, only a very restricted set of pleasures is acceptable for the good life. Besides the true and pure pleasures Socrates includes "the pleasures of health and of temperance and all those that commit themselves to virtue" (63e), that is, those that lead to health and harmony of soul and body.

In the final ranking of goods Plato seems to be even more restrictive. A comparison of reason and pleasure with the threefold good, the combination of truth, beauty, and proportion, yields the following scale (66a–c): First come measure and proportion (limit), second the harmonious mixtures (the limited), third rank goes to reason and intelligence (its cause), fourth place to "the soul's own properties, to knowledge, the arts and true judgment" (the limited in a less pure condition), and fifth and last place is assigned to true and pure pleasures (the unlimited sanctioned by limitation).[6]

The justification of this final ranking of goods should not exercise us here. It is important to note, however, that Plato has completed his project with the help of the fourfold division of "all things that are now in the universe." If one wonders why reason does not obtain first place (especially in view of the repeated exaltation of the divine reason [*nous*] throughout the dialogue), it should be kept in mind that this scale of goods is tailored toward the explanation of the good *human life.* Plato is here not talking about the good as such, but about the factors responsible for making our life good. This is not to say that the human good can be or is treated in the *Philebus* in isolation from the overall cosmic good; the ranking on the scale of human goods leaves open, however, what relationship and ranking Plato would envisage for proportion and the divine reason themselves. The focus on the human good also explains the separation of reason and intelligence from the other kinds of human intellectual capacities, as well as the admission of right judgment (*doxa*) and pure pleasures.[7] To describe the rationale for the final scale more concretely: First comes the ingredient (proportion) that makes the good life good, second comes the harmonious life itself, third comes the cause in us that allows us to aim for proportion and harmony, fourth the sciences and arts we have to acquire for the successful guidance of a "measured" life, and finally come the pure pleasures that enrich the imperfect human life without detriment to truth, proportion, and beauty. With this final ranking Socrates has fulfilled the promise he made at the beginning of the discussion, to arbitrate in the contest between pleasure and intelligence. As this brief overview has shown, Plato has never lost sight of his own project, but carried out as promised and made use of the dialectical and ontological distinctions where appropriate.

Before we can take a closer look at the details of the discussion of the nature of pleasure and pain, the different kinds of disintegrations and restorations themselves, and the critique that emerges in this discussion, we have to raise a problem that affects our evaluation of the dialogue as a whole. Why does Plato here return to a question that he had left largely untouched after the *Republic,* the question of the good life and the rivalry between reason and pleasure? And why does he see the necessity to go into a long-winded ontological explanation of the nature of pleasure again, after he seems to have come to a satisfactory conclusion about it in Book IX of the *Republic*?

Connected with this last question is also our irritation with the form of the dialogue. What is disturbing is the fact that we seem to have a normal Socratic discussion in front of us, in what seems to be one of Plato's latest works.[8] Prima facie the *Philebus* does not seem to display any of the dramatic features of the other late dialogues. Socrates himself is guiding the discussion. There is no man from Elea, as there is in the *Parmenides*, the *Sophist*, and the *Statesman*. Nor is there a Pythagorean taking over from Socrates, as there is in the *Timaeus*. And we do not find ourselves removed from Athens to Crete, under the guidance of an unnamed Stranger from Athens, as we do in the *Laws*. Nor do we find any such elaborate introduction as presented in some of the middle or earlier late dialogues, such as the *Symposium*, the *Parmenides*, and the *Theaetetus*. We are instead back in Athens, plunged right into the middle of a lively dispute between a Socrates and interlocutors not much different from the ones we are used to in the "Socratic" dialogues.

There are, to be sure, some differences, apart form doctrinal innovations. Socrates does not plead ignorance anywhere, elenchus is confined to the first part where Protarchus confesses his reduction to speechlessness (21d), and the discussion ends with positive results. But the *Philebus* shares such traits, after all, with other middle dialogues, like the *Phaedo* and the *Republic*. It also shares with them the liveliness of the discussion, a concern for drama not found in the other late works. Protarchus, Socrates' main interlocutor, is not at all reduced to the ayes and nays of the respondents in the second part of the *Parmenides*, the *Sophist*, and the *Statesman*; he plays an active role to the very end of the discussion. There is true antagonism, wit – including sexual innuendoes – and a gradual conversion.[9] If one looks at the dramatic form, it is almost as if Plato wanted to prove to the world that even in his ripe old age he was quite capable of composing lively dialogues, and also that Socrates had by no means been forgotten!

Since such speculations on Plato's personal motives for his reversion to the form of his Socratic dialogues must remain idle, a more promising explanation would seem to lie in the topic, the discussion of the nature of pleasure as a competitor with reason for the honor of the highest good. Plato would have found it difficult to summon either an Eleatic or a Pythagorean as the leader of such a discussion and there were good reasons to let Socrates take up the challenge. Plato, it seems, reverted to the earlier form of Socratic dialogues because he wanted to reopen a question that had been a major concern of the earlier Platonic Socrates, the debate on the nature and evaluation of pleasure. As a closer analysis of the long discussion of pleasure in the *Philebus* will show, there is indeed an abundance of doubtlessly intentional allusions to these earlier discussions of pleasure, as we find them in the *Protagoras,* the *Gorgias,* the *Phaedo,* and the *Republic.* The *Philebus,* then, reverts to the earlier form of Socratic dialogues because Plato regarded the question of the concept of pleasure and its role as a good in human life as unfinished business. This will remain the working hypothesis for the rest of this essay. But what, precisely, prompted this reversion, especially in view of the fact that some of Socrates' claims in the middle part of the *Philebus* seem mere repetitions of what is contained in those earlier works? It remains to be seen whether they are in fact repetitions and not rather improvements on these earlier attempts. To see what improvements may have seemed necessary we have to take a look at Plato's earlier treatment of pleasure. At the same time, this will help us to clarify why Plato subjects pleasure to such protracted scrutiny in the *Philebus,* and thereby also shed some light on the need for the dialectical preface.[10]

II. REVIEW OF PLATO'S EARLIER THEORIES OF PLEASURE

The first extensive treatment of hedonism is found in the *Protagoras,* and by general consent this treatment is at the same time the most puzzling one (351b–358a).[11] For Socrates proposes without comment the hedonistic position that pleasure is "the good" and confines himself to an "intellectualization" of hedonism, with the simple argument that even the hedonist needs reasoning because there must be an "art of measuring" pleasures and pains when a decision is necessary (356d). Socrates argues that persons who claim that they have been "overwhelmed by passion" when they give in to the temptation of an imminent pleasure at the cost of a later pain are wrong in their account. What really happens is that they "mismeasure" the pleasures: They deem the present pleasure (e.g., of eating a lavish dinner) as much larger than the later ensuing pain (whether stomachache or anguish over weight gain). So there is no such thing as "reason being overcome by passion." Reason remains the master throughout; it merely makes a mistake: It falls prey to an optical illusion concerning the relative size of the present pleasure and the later pain.

Plato very likely never accepted such an intellectual hedonism for himself. He could have used any other standard of the good and adduced the same measuring argument to show that reason must always be the supreme arbiter. It may be one of the ironical points aimed at in the *Protagoras* that the sophist, who nobly refuses to accept unmitigated hedonism, does not manage to extract himself from Socrates' argument. The very fact that the definition of virtue as the art of measuring pleasure and pain is not exploited any further and that the dialogue ends in perplexity should warn us not to take it as Plato's own definition or as his intended solution. But whatever may be the point of the argument in the *Protagoras,* Plato cannot have been satisfied with it as a sufficient critique of hedonism that even here reason remains supreme. Nevertheless, that goods of any kind must (among other things) be measurable and therefore open to rational control is a point Plato kept in mind over years, as is clear from the fact that the question of measuring pleasure reappears in the *Philebus.* The possibility of mismeasurement turns up as constituting one of the many "falsities of pleasures" that Socrates discusses at great length. Plato, it seems, never forgot the "art of measuring pleasure and pain" introduced in the *Protagoras.*

The *Gorgias* takes quite a different road of attack. Callicles is an unmitigated hedonist (as Protagoras was not) who professes not to be open to Socratic intimidation (cf. his great speech in 482c–486c). He will not be cajoled into admitting any difference among pleasures that would import anything like the need for the rule of reason over them. He wants them all! Even the threat of moral turpitude is at first not effective, nor is the demonstration that he will be condemned to the Sisyphean labors of an eternal hunt for satisfaction (493a–b). But Socrates catches Callicles in the end. Such unseemly pleasures as that of scratching when itching, especially when one thinks of a catamite's degenerate pleasures, or the pleasure of the coward who runs away in battle, are too much for this aristocrat. His defeat is sealed when he concedes that there must be better and worse pleasures and thus a rational "master art of life" that discriminates between them (501a).

Interestingly, no such appeal to moral taste is made in the *Philebus* at all, although the example of the pleasure of scratching is taken up again and supplemented with even more vivid descriptions ("leaping, kicking, color changes, distortion of features, shouting around like a madman," 45d–47a). The critique in the *Philebus*, however, does not exploit our aesthetic revulsion or moral scruples; there is no *ad hominem* argument here. Instead, such pleasures are judged from a scientific, almost medical point of view: They are really mixtures of pleasure and pain, and constitute unwholesome excitements.[12] Once again we see that Plato has not forgotten his earlier treatment of pleasure; he echoes his old examples but transforms the doctrine.

In no dialogue does Socrates show himself as much of an antihedonist as he does in the *Phaedo* (64d–69e). Pleasure here seems to be entirely confined to the body. It is depicted as one of the encumbrances and disturbances that the body imposes on the soul as long as the soul is confined to that prison. The philosopher is gladly preparing for death because this means release from the shackles of the body and from the distractions of the mundane pleasures, which allow at best for vulgar prudence in the hunt for more pleasures (68e). Although it is not impossible that Plato meant to leave room for separate pleasures of the mind, since he calls the philosopher the "lover of wisdom" (*erastēs*, 66e), nothing is made here of any higher pleasures for the philosopher.

The *Republic* represents quite a change of mind by introducing a systematic differentiation among pleasures, in the sense that there are true and pure and good pleasures of the rational part of the soul, and at least relatively good ones in the other two parts, provided that they follow the rule of reason and do not submit to tyrannical and licentious pleasures (580d–588a). The idea of assigning different kinds of pleasures to each of the three parts of the soul may well have been an afterthought of Plato's, for it is not introduced until Book IX, where he adds it as one more point in his proof of the enormous superiority of the life of the paragon of justice, the philosopher.[13] Free from all tyrannical fetters and fears, the philosopher enjoys not only superior pleasures, but also *more* pleasures than all others (in fact he lives 729 times more pleasantly than the tyrant! 587e).

The passage constitutes quite an advance on Plato's side because it permits him to justify a systematic differentiation among pleasures and to formulate general criteria for their evaluation. Pleasures are called (a) "motions of the soul" (*kinēsis*, 583e) and (b) "fillings of a lack" (*plērōsis*, 585b). These two accounts are not in rivalry, as witnessed by the fact that Plato moves freely from the one to the other, but they are obviously supposed to complement each other. What Plato tries to capture by the two terms seems to be the following. The conception of pleasure as a "motion" allows him to distinguish between the kinds of pleasures that are mere liberations from pain ("motions from below") and the *true* pleasures that proceed from a neutral or middle state "upward" to sheer pleasure (584b–e). The conception of "filling" or "fulfillment" focuses on the content of the pleasures and justifies the discrimination among things the person is filled with: The pleasure of learning is a filling with true, reliable, and good things, while other fillings have neither true nor clear nor fully real objects (585a–586b).

The combination of the two accounts permits Plato to demonstrate the great superiority of the philosopher's pleasures over everyone else's. They involve no liberation from pain but are motions toward the true "above"; they are fillings with real and true being. So the account serves the purpose it is supposed to serve in *Republic* IX. It is, however, an account that relies on a metaphorical use of the crucial terms ("filling," "moving truly upward") and on a mixture of the metaphors that does not bear too close a scrutiny. It remains unclear, for instance, whether the liberations from pain are pleasures at all, or whether (as the epithet "illusory" suggests) they are only semblances of pleasures.[14] This would work for the motion metaphor with its distinction between three levels (the above, middle, and below) and do away with the mistake of treating the middle state of rest as a pleasure (583c–584a); but it would have the consequence that liberations from pain are not pleasures at all. The filling metaphor does not allow such a distinction of three levels, since there is no middle state discernible in this case, nor does it explain why such fillings are actually "mixed with pain" and do not merely have pain as their precondition. Plato could of course try to claim that assuagements of pain, as in hunger and thirst, are not real fillings, but he clearly does not want to go this far. Instead, he only draws the conclusion that such pleasures are fillings with what is *less* real, true, and pure, and winds himself through a long series of constructions that exploit the comparative (585b–e) so as to avoid a clear pronouncement about the exact status of such pleasures. So he ends up with the contrast between one genuine and two bastard pleasures for the three parts of the soul (587c), and leaves the reader with the puzzle of how, precisely, this bastard state is to be interpreted.

A total discrediting of all but a few pure true and unmixed pleasures would not really serve Plato's purpose in the *Republic,* which is to demonstrate the superiority of the philosopher's pleasures over all others. The denial of the existence of real pleasures for the lower two parts of the soul would be rather an overkill; not only would it be a self-defeating denial of the phenomena, it would make nonsense of the calculation of the superiority of the philosopher's pleasures (587d–e); one can compare and multiply only what exists and is, in principle, comparable. So Plato must have regarded the "bastardization" of the common pleasures as a proper compromise. But he could not have regarded this as a final and satisfactory treatment of the concepts of pleasure and pain themselves because it clearly leaves us with the uncertainty whether liberations from pains are pleasures or not. Whether Plato did regard it as satisfactory when he wrote the *Republic* and reversed himself only much later must remain a moot point. He may well have realized then and there that more needed to be said about the problem.

The *Philebus,* I propose, brings order into this diffuse picture presented by *Republic* IX and takes up suggestions from earlier dialogues as well, and this task explains the reappearance of Socrates and the return to the Socratic method of inquiry.[15] The whole problematic is an eminently Socratic concern. But the *Philebus* does not only discuss pleasure in a more orderly fashion. It does so on the basis of a new ontology of pleasure and pain. And therefore Plato prefaces the resumption of his old problem with the exposition of the dialectic method and the new division of all beings. Although the dialectical procedure is not officially pursued after its introduction, the new systematic procedure does in the end lead to a satisfactory definition of pleasure and pain and to equally satisfactory criteria for a distinction between different kinds of pleasures and knowledge.

III. PLEASURE AND PAIN IN THE *PHILEBUS*

This much should be uncontroversial: The dialectic approach, as sketched in 16c–17a, would demand a definition of pleasure as a unitary phenomenon, a complete subdivision of the different kinds of pleasures, and it would also have to include an explanation of how many species of pleasures there are, and how they differ. The same procedure would have to be applied to pleasure's rival, knowledge.

That Socrates, thanks to a sudden "inspiration," comes across an easier way to decide the question whether pleasure or reason is the highest good, should increase rather than settle our curiosity about why he can dispense with the dialectical method after he had asserted so emphatically that without this work "you will count for nothing and amount to nothing" (17e). "Divine assistance" allows him to omit this strenuous enterprise, but this explanation must leave us less than satisfied.

The student of the divisions (*dihairesis*) in the *Sophist* (219a–232a; 264b–268d) and in the *Statesman* (258b–268d; 274e–end) will probably regard this shortcut in the *Philebus* with unmitigated relief, in view of those long and still far-from-complete (!) exercises devoted to the divisions of all arts. But it is not just the shudder provoked by the thought of the ordeal of a complete division of all pleasures and all kinds of knowledge that justifies our gratitude for Socrates' parsimony in the *Philebus.* There are good reasons to doubt that a completion of dialectical divisions, ending with two Porphyrean "Christmas trees" of all pleasures on one side and all intellectual disciplines on the other, would be of any real use. What could Socrates' next step be? A comparison of the two trees, branch by branch, to see which one is better, or a quantitative analysis as to which of the two has a larger number of better branches? But what could be the criteria for such a piecemeal comparison or an overall reckoning?[16]

If a complete division would be unmanageable and of no use anyway, we are back with our old problem, to explain the purpose of the introduction of dialectic in the first place. Did Plato have a negative end in view, namely to prevent the possible misunderstanding that the long discussion of pleasures and pains and of the different kinds of knowledge respectively are meant to represent a proper *dihairesis*? There may, of course, be something to this suggestion. A better explanation emerges, however, if we take note of the fact that Socrates does make use of the method of dialectic at least in part, even though he does not come up with a neat tree of divisions, nor with a numerically exact account of the species of pleasures or knowledge that could claim completeness of *dihairesis.*

If Socrates suggests that his new ontological distinction uses at least "in part" the "arms" provided by the dialectical method because he makes use of the terms "limit" and "unlimited," although in a quite different sense, this is rather a (consciously) misleading depiction (23c). It is not the equivocal use of these two terms that justifies the claim that he uses "some of the old armament," but the fact that he actually follows some of the prescriptions of dialectic! In establishing the "four kinds of things that exist now in the universe," he proceeds quite in agreement with the dialectical method, as far as he goes. For he establishes the unity of the genus with care (25a: "for whatever is dispersed and split up into a multitude we must try to work out its unifying nature as far as we can see, if you remember"). Collection and a certain amount of division (even if not divisions into all subgenera and ultimate species) are the tasks Socrates pursues in his discussion of the four kinds of beings (25d5; 26d).

The immediate advantage of this metaphysical approach is obvious: at least pleasure can now find its unmistakable place on the ontological map. It belongs to one of the four types of *onta* ("beings"). We are told what its genus is, what constitutes the unity of the genus, and also how pleasure differs from other kinds of *apeira*. All unlimited entities consist in a continued flux (24d), so they are motions. These motions terminate when order is imposed; this imposition of a limit leads to the establishment of a definite being, the successful mixture (*genesis eis ousian*, 26d). Pleasures are motions of "filling" that are terminated by such an imposed order. At first sight the achievement of this preliminary determination of pleasure as a kind of boundless motion or filling may seem small. But in fact it is quite a step forward. All perceived restorative processes are now real pleasures; there can no longer be any concern with semblances of pleasures or bastard pleasures. Furthermore, things in motion are now included among the *onta*, they are no longer of such dubious status that one cannot even refer to them in any definite way, as we find it, for instance, in the *Theaetetus*, where objects in motion cannot be grasped by any firm notion at all and cannot even be called "somethings."[17]

If the introduction of a special genus for things in flux represents a change of mind on Plato's side, so that change and changeable things can now be included among the things that are, and can be subjects of knowledge, this change was, of course, prepared by the inclusion of motion on the list of the Forms in *Parmenides* (129d–e) and on the list of the "most important kinds" in the *Sophist* (254c–d). The *Philebus* is, then, not unique in giving generation and change a definite place among the things that are. But only in the *Philebus* does Plato give a specific explanation of what constitutes the unity of their genus, how they differ from the other genera that there are – that is, what constitutes the unity of the genus of the unlimited and the more and less, and what particular subgenus of all *apeira* it is that contains pleasure and pain. For this division allows Socrates to proceed to a more precise definition of pleasure and pain. "When the natural combination of limit and unlimitedness that forms a live organism is destroyed, this destruction is pain, while the return towards its own nature, this general restoration, is pleasure" (32b).

This definition, as we will see, is sufficient to explain the nature of all pleasures of both soul and body, and it forms the basis of the critique of pleasure that is to follow. Further reflection on this definition will show why pleasure cannot be the good as such but can at best be a conditional good. Properly understood, all pleasures presuppose a disintegration, a disturbance of the harmonious integrity (the good mixture). Welcome as such a restoration must be, freedom from such disruptions would clearly be a much better option. This is indeed the conclusion Plato draws immediately: there is a third condition, besides pleasure and pain, and "perhaps there would be nothing absurd if this life turns out to be the most godlike" (33b).[18]

The third state of *integrity* replaces the state of rest that Plato in the *Republic* had placed "in between" the "truly upward" motion of "genuine" pleasure and the "bastard" pleasure of liberation from pain. This third state is here no longer a second-best, nor is it placed between pleasure and pain; it is now the end point of all restorations and therefore above both pleasure and pain. It turns out to be the best of all states to attain. If it is not here declared to be the winner in the competition for the good in human life, that is because it is not possible for us to remain permanently in a state of harmony. "We necessarily are always experiencing one or the other [i.e., pleasure or pain], as the wise men say. For everything is in an eternal flux, upward, and downward" (43a). The reason for Socrates' pliability earlier in the *Philebus* in favor of a life that contains some pleasure becomes apparent now: It is humankind's constantly shifting state that makes pleasures desirable, if not all pleasures, then at least some of them. Pleasure is clearly a *remedial* good; as a motion toward fulfillment it is desirable for all those who suffer from a deficiency, and we all are always in fact subject to some deficiency or other!

Plato has thus discarded the *Republic*'s troublesome distinction between motions that are pleasures but "not quite real ones": All motions that are restorations are real pleasures. The "trick argument" of the *Republic* that pleasure may be mere liberation from pain, and pain loss of pleasure, does not work anymore; it had prompted Plato there to distinguish between real pleasures, bastard pleasures, and the state of rest between them (584a–b). In the *Philebus* pleasure and pain each have their own reality. How, precisely, they are related to each other, and how they are sometimes confused with each other (as well as with the third, the pleasure- and pain-free state of integrity) will be discussed later when we look at different points of criticism in Plato's evaluation of pleasures and pains.

The general definition of pleasure as restoration of natural integrity is soon modified in the *Philebus* by an important qualification that appears necessary when Socrates tries to introduce the further subdivision between pleasures of the soul and pleasures of the body. Strictly speaking, pleasures and pains are never a matter of the body alone, because only those disturbances in the body are pains and those restorations pleasures that are perceived by the soul (33c–d; 35b).[19] This leads to the definition of the so-called pleasures of the body as perceptions. They are to be distinguished from the pleasures that the soul can experience all by itself. These are specified, at least at first, as the pleasures that the soul has originally experienced *with* the body and can then reexperience all by itself through memory. Only incidentally does Plato indicate that such recollections may include other kinds of experiences, like those of learning (cf. 34b, *mathēmatos*).

Plato then adds a further significant feature of the mechanism that is in place even in the case of the most simple pleasures and pains. That there is the "perception of a disintegration" is not enough to explain what goes on when we experience hunger or thirst. In each case the soul does not merely notice the emphasis of the body, but it desires at the same time the respective "filling" and thus employs memory. Desire is therefore not a matter of the body at all; it is a pain of the soul that brings it in touch with the appropriate filling. And such pains and pleasures turn out to be necessary for the preservation of every animal (35c–d). The fact that the soul can anticipate pleasures that it has experienced before with the body explains then why it can, in particular situations, experience a rather complex "syndrome" of pleasures and pains. Being in pain because of some loss, it can anticipate the coming restoration and enjoy it in the certainty of this expectation.[20] Alternatively, it may realize the hopelessness of its situation and therefore be in "twofold pain" (35e–36c).

Plato's careful analysis of the physiological and psychological mechanism that underlies even the most simple-looking pleasure or pain and that allows for combinations of pleasures and pains is not an end in itself. It prepares the ground for the extensive critique of pleasure that is based on the result of this preliminary analysis (36c: "let us apply the results of our investigation of these affections. . . ."). The critique fastens on the content of pleasures and turns first to pleasures that are free from disturbances by the body, the pleasures of expectation or anticipation. To argue that pleasures can involve expectations is to pave the way to their evaluation; for these pleasures of anticipating future goods are the means by which Socrates introduces the possibility of attributing truth and falsehood to pleasures and pains. An expectation can obviously be mistaken, he suggests; therefore pleasures of anticipation can be false.

In spite of his careful step-by-step preparation of the troublesome subject, Socrates encounters tenacious resistance from Protarchus, who has been a cooperative partner until now: "How could there be false pleasures and pains?" (36c). This dramatic change shows that Plato does not want to smuggle in his controversial conception of false pleasures by exploiting the malleability of the half-converted hedonist. When he introduces it he does so by drawing our full attention to its controversial nature: Protarchus keeps up his resistance and forces Socrates to give a detailed defense (36c–41a).

IV. THE FALSITY OF PLEASURES AND PAINS

Protarchus is not the only one to give vent to skepticism in the face of Socrates' contention that there can be truth and falsity in pleasures and pains. Many scholars nowadays agree with Protarchus.[21] One of the main difficulties is that Plato uses "truth" and "falsity" in different senses in the long ensuing discussion. As Gosling put it in his commentary, "it seems impossible to acquit Plato of the charge of rank equivocation."[22] That there is equivocation seems indeed undeniable. In the different parts of the long critique of the pleasures, "truth" and "falsity" are obviously used in different senses. But a close look will show that this equivocation is not anything Plato wants to deny or be acquitted of. It seems to be a quite conscious and explicit move on his part to use truth and falsehood in a loose way whose precise meaning depends on the different specifications under discussion. His overall intention in the ensuing discussion of false pleasures is to show that there are many different ways in which there can be something wrong with them, so as to make good on his claim that pleasures are only a "sometime-good." There are, roughly, four different ways in which pleasures and pains can be "false" in this loose, commonsense meaning of "falsity." We will follow Plato through the text and see what kinds of falsity he has in mind, and whether his critique is valid or not. He discusses the following different cases, which we will evaluate by looking at a prototype:

1. Falsity of pleasures and pains as propositional attitudes (36c–41b) – the Dairymaid's pleasures.
2. Falsity of overrated pleasures and pains (41b–42c) – Esau's pleasures.
3. Falsity in the identification of pleasure with freedom from pain (42c–44d) – the Ascetic's pleasures.
4. Falsity of pleasures intrinisically mixed with pains (44d–50e) – Calliclean pleasures.

The definition of pleasure as restoration of a natural state of harmony allows Socrates to proceed with a critique of pleasure that fastens on several possible shortcomings intrinsic to such restorations – with the exception of (3), where pleasure is not a restoration at all but is confused with the state of harmony itself. The basic idea in this critique is a very simple one: If all pleasures are restorations or "fillings of a lack," then our evaluations must turn on the object and the conditions of different restorations, as well as on the question whether there is in fact a restoration. To express the same point in the more picturesque language of "filling," the question is whether there is a filling, what the filling is a filling with, and how the filling is achieved. There is a wide range of possible disturbances of soul and body in the sense suggested by Socrates. Any kind of perceived lack or deficiency can be the source of pleasures as the replenishments of such lacks.[23] In order to provide some basis for a critical evaluation of the goodness of the different kinds of pleasures, Socrates has to show what different types of shortcomings there can be. This explains the length of the middle part of the *Philebus,* the (to many readers tedious) exposition of the pleasures of soul and body.

Plato's definition of pleasure as a perceived filling or restoration is designed to cover all kinds of pleasures; it precludes the identification of pleasure with a simple indistinct feeling that merely accompanies these processes or results from them. Pleasure is for him not an epiphenomenon in the sense that it is an unspecific kind of "glow" that supervenes on experiences and could arise from any source. A supervenient state of excitement or elation would not, as such, be open to any further evaluation: In that case it does not matter where the pleasure comes from (push-pin or poetry); all that matters is that we are pleased. Such an epiphenomenal view, it seems, was initially presupposed by Protarchus when he tried to reject any kind of differentiation among pleasures ("the pleasures come from different sources; but they are not at all opposed to each other," 12d). If Protarchus is later still restive at some points of Socrates' critique of pleasure, this shows that he is not quite ready to give in to Socrates' new conception of the nature of pleasure or that he has not quite realized the full extent of the implications of this new conception. His main objections are ventured against the first kind of falsity of pleasures; it is also the one that has received the most flak from contemporary critics. We will therefore turn to the "Dairymaid's pleasures" first.

(1) The question why Plato thinks that there are false pleasures in the literal or "propositional" sense of falsity has been much debated in recent years.[24] How could pleasures be false, except in a rather metaphorical sense of "false" that signifies no more than that there is something wrong with them? As the elaborate analysis at the beginning of the discussion of false pleasures and pains shows, Plato's conception presupposes that not all pleasures are simple conditions of the body or the mere awareness of the soul of what is going on in the body. Of course I cannot be wrong about my pain of "feeling emptied out" nor about my actual pleasure of "feeling filled." But these simple kinds of "fillings" are not what interests Plato for the most part. He is much rather concerned with the role that the mind plays in many of our experiences. The first step in the ascription of propositional content to pleasure is his claim that the soul

can, thanks to memory, experience the same kinds of things all by itself that it has once experienced with the body; so it can anticipate future pleasures as real (36c–42c). Such pleasures are not mere feelings, nor are they daydreams. They are hopeful (or fearful) states that anticipate future states of affairs as facts; they are therefore what contemporary philosophers call "propositional attitudes" and can be true or false in the same sense as other such states.[25]

Although Plato has, of course, no such terminology at his disposal, his elaborate explanations designed to show that some pleasures and pains are mental processes like beliefs, allow us to attribute such a theory to him. Our experiences are *logoi* (statements) "written into the soul as into a book," often supplemented by pictures (*eikones*), which can be actualized by the soul itself (38e–39b). If the soul entertains pleasant expectations or visions about the future as accurate depictions of the future, then these *logoi* or images are true or false, as happens in the case of the Dairymaid. She anticipates the pleasures of a golden future that will come from selling her milk at a good price and further prudent investments. The hapless Dairymaid's pleasures turn out to have been false anticipations: One wrong step makes all her pleasant calculations null and void.

To make Plato's theory of true or false pleasures acceptable, we have to agree to two conditions: that there are expectations of future states of affairs (as in the case of the Dairymaid's depiction of a golden future) and that such states of affairs are experienced as fillings of a lack. It is the Dairymaid's poverty that makes her entertain and enjoy such high hopes. If she was only daydreaming, enjoying the mere thought or the picturing without putting any trust in the anticipated state of affairs, or if she were in no need of such riches, there would be no disappointment, no painful farewell to chicken, piglet, calf, and cow.

Is it plausible to assume that the soul can "fill itself" with pleasant *logoi* or pictures? There is no reason to reject such "fillings," once we accept Plato's story of how the soul builds up its stock of interpretations of the world in a silent dialogue (38c). The existence of such a stock of experiences in the soul makes it possible to project a similar experience into the future, an experience that is quite independent of actual physical pleasures and pains. If such mental actualizations are pleasant anticipations of the future, and the future turns out to be the way it was envisaged, then the pleasures have been true; if it does not turn out in the way envisaged, then the pleasures have been false.[26] So the gist of the argument is that some pleasures are actually *logoi* or pictures; they do not merely follow or accompany them. Hopes, that is, pleasant expectations, are *logoi* (40a6–7), and so are the corresponding pictures; some of them are clearly false, and such seems to be the case in Socrates' example of the man who often "sees himself as rich" and envisages all the pleasures that result from it. These pleasures often turn out to be empty hopes, as Plato indicates when he adds the qualification that only persons who are beloved by the gods are usually right in their anticipations (39e–40b). Had the gods been favorable to our poor Dairymaid, her pleasures of anticipation would have been true. As it was, she entertained vain hopes, that is, false pleasures.[27]

That Plato focuses on true or false anticipations does not mean that only future pleasures (or pains, when the anticipations are of future ills) can be true or false. If they stand in the center of his discussion, that is because in their case it is most obvious that we enjoy the propositional content and not the "thing" in question. If Plato had concentrated on examples in the present or the past, it would have been much more difficult to point out that a *logos* plays an important role in our pleasures. That there are such false propositional pleasures in the present or the past becomes obvious if we look at some examples: Sophocles' Electra "falsely" grieves over her brother's death; Clytemnestra "falsely" enjoys her relief. Both grieve over or enjoy a *logos,* not the actual state of affairs, or more precisely, they grieve over or enjoy a state of affairs under a given false *description.* What is crucial here is that we often enjoy what we enjoy only under one description and not under another. Some persons can only enjoy a present if they know that it was expensive; some of our friends will not enjoy our company if they know that we are visiting them only because other plans have fallen through; the spectators enjoy an exciting move in a game only if their own team accomplished it, and so on. The *logoi* and pictures we carry in our souls thus play a powerful role in determining whether we enjoy what we experience, how we enjoy it, and whether it is a thing that ought to be enjoyed.[28]

(2) That pleasures can have propositional content makes it possible to evaluate, even morally evaluate, the pleasures we enjoy; it also makes it possible to compare, to measure, and to experience pleasures as having a certain size or worth. This seems to be the

rationale for introducing the "false," that is, disproportionate, pleasures that we may here call Esau's pleasures.

If pleasures can be *logoi,* then it makes sense to revive Socrates' old idea in the *Protagoras* of measuring pleasures and pains against each other. Driven by hunger (the pain of emptiness and the desire for filling), Esau was induced to overrate the worthwhileness of filling himself with a dish of lentils to the point where he thought the pleasure was worth the price of his primogeniture, that is, the future pain of its loss. Plato compares this situation to an optical distortion. Just as we may misjudge the size of what we see from far away in comparison to what we see close up, so we may be misled in our appreciation of the "size" of pleasures and pains (41d). The size of the hunger seen from nearby creates enormous desire for replenishment with food, so that Esau takes inordinate pleasure in his repast, falsely enjoying the experience as well worth the future pain of his loss.

If the pleasure itself is experienced as something quantifiable, then this pleasure as enjoyed can be false, and Plato is right that "more is enjoyed" than is actually warranted. So enjoying something as an "enormous pleasure" would then be false, while enjoying it as a medium-size or as a small pleasure would have been true. If indeed we are willing to grant Plato that we sometimes make it part of our pleasure that it is of a certain magnitude (enjoying an A+ or a B− pleasure), we will also agree with him that to the degree to which our estimate of the pleasure was not justified we enjoyed a wrong "portion" of it, that is, more than is actually "there." Such a hedonic calculus makes sense if we can experience pleasures and pains as having a certain quantum or worth. Experiences need not be as remote as Esau's case may look to us. We often do not enjoy a $25 dinner that we might well have enjoyed if we had eaten it as a $7.50 dinner. So not only does pleasure have its price, we enjoy it as having a price. And just as one may pay a "false" (i.e., inflated) price for some good, so one may enjoy a false or inflated pleasure, that is, enjoy it as if it were worth more than it actually is.

Plato himself gives only a short treatment to the problem, and we may surmise that the reason for mentioning it at all is not only that such cases occur in everyday life, when we ask ourselves whether some pleasures are "worth the pain," but because he wants to give the old argument of the *Protagoras* its place in his final and definitive discussion of pleasure. So the "art of measuring pain and pleasure" is vindicated as one of the means to sort out worthwhile pleasures and pains.

(3) After the overinflated pleasures, Plato takes up "even falser pleasures" (42c–44d) – pleasures so false that they are not pleasures at all. It is at first sight surprising that Plato mentions the neutral state and its distinction from pleasure and pain here once again, in spite of the fact that he had made it clear before how rest differs from both pleasure and pain (32d–33c). There is, of course, a colloquial use of "false" that Plato can exploit here: A false Rembrandt is no Rembrandt, and false friends are not friends. But there are more serious reasons than the existence of this *façon de parler* to include a discussion of what is not a false pleasure but a false conception of pleasure (44a). First of all, Socrates had agreed earlier, at least tentatively, that it is impossible for us to believe that we are pleased when we are not (36e). This is now corrected: It is indeed possible to mistake a state of undisturbedness for a state of pleasure.[29] Secondly, Plato seems to answer an unnamed Ascetic who proposed such a conception of pleasure. This is not the place to speculate who the "difficult person" might have been whose harshness made him, as Plato claims in a rare ascription of psychological motivation, "refuse to acknowledge anything healthy in pleasure, even to the point that he regarded its very attractiveness itself as witchcraft rather than true pleasure" (44c–d).[30]

The temptation to confuse the state of rest with pleasure or pain had been one of Plato's concerns in the passage in the *Republic* discussed earlier. If he wants to straighten out these difficulties in the *Philebus* he has to give precise reasons why contentment cannot be a pleasure, even though he himself regards it as the best possible state. It cannot be regarded as a pleasure because it is not the restoration of a lack. To stress this point is of great importance for Plato's attempt to refute philosophical hedonism, and this must be the reason why he returns to the difference several times in the dialogue. Socrates therefore does not agree with this anonymous curmudgeon. At the same time the Ascetic's complaints against the "unsound" character of pleasure as such serve Socrates as a welcome occasion to sort out what makes certain pleasures unsound, so he uses the Ascetic as a "guide." The pursuit of this question will eventually lead to the correct determination of true, in the sense of unblemished, pleasures.

(4) Unsound as a whole are what I call the Calliclean pleasures, made famous by Callicles' fervent plea for a life of unimpeded pursuit of ever-new excitement. These are here called the pleasures of excess (44e–50e). According to Socrates the Ascetic's denial that there is anything sound in what ordinary people call pleasure is the result of his focus on pleasures in their most intense form, when our bodies are in a diseased state. For such a diseased state intensifies our awareness of all physiological changes, and release from a state of distress is therefore felt most keenly. "Do they not feel greater deprivations, and also greater pleasures after their replenishment" (45b). Such pleasures result not only from a diseased body, but equally result from a diseased soul ("a vicious state of soul and body," 45e). Plato's own diagnosis of such "overheated" pleasures differs from that of the Ascetic, who denies them the status as pleasures at all and recognizes only freedom from pain as pleasurable. For Plato such experiences remain pleasures, but they are not true pleasures because they are inextricably mixed with pain: "the bittersweet condition that first causes irritation and later on turns into wild excitement" (46d). So they are false in the sense in which we colloquially call impure gold false gold.

Depending on the kind of diseased state, the pain involved may be small or large, and the release may be felt more or less strongly. If grave irritation is the preponderant state and the release insignificant, we call the whole state "pain"; if there is only a mild irritation that is totally outweighed by wild excitement of release, we call the overall phenomenon "pleasure." The funny description of this inflamed state leaves no doubt that these are the Aphrodisian pleasures without which neither Callicles nor Philebus find life worth living (47a). Neither of the two conditions is a true, unmixed pleasure or pain.

If Plato's description of these incensed pleasures of excess reminds us strongly of the discussion of Callicles' pleasures of the superior man in the *Gorgias*, there is a major difference in Plato's critique in the *Philebus*. We are not asked to reject the pleasures because there is something unseemly about them, in the way Socrates forced Callicles to scorn the catamite's pleasures, because even ruthless Callicles was not unscrupulous enough to claim that such a life was really the good life, worthy of a gentleman. In the *Philebus* it is regarded as a sufficient critique of pleasure that such frolickings are necessarily mixed with pain, and that this is in fact so in a "vast number of cases." Plato, as stated earlier, seems to have exchanged his earlier aesthetic-moral criteria of evaluation for scientific-medical ones.[31] He does not have to shock a recalcitrant opponent into submission: The unsoundness of soul and body alone is a sufficient criterion for the judgment of such pleasures. The drastic depiction of the mad pleasures of excess is here only dramatic by-work. If Socrates does not refrain from a well-aimed stab at Philebus's morality (46b), this does not serve any purpose in the argument itself; it seems rather designed to show how far Protarchus has moved away from his previous unconditional hedonistic stance ("Your description fits exactly the preconceptions of the common run of people, Socrates," 47b).

The analysis of the mixed pains and pleasures of the body, amusing as it is to read, is not the end of Plato's critique. The ensuing introduction of the mixed pleasures of the soul by itself seems to be the real focus of his discussion of mixed pleasures, the discussion of the emotions and their conditions (47d–50c). Here Plato is truly innovative: All our passionate affections turn out to be mixtures of pleasures and pains, and we call them one or the other because there is a preponderance of one or the other, just as there was in the conditions of the body. He insists that all our painful emotions, such as rage, longing, lamentation, love, jealousy, and envy, are deprivations of some sort or other that contain a portion of pleasure. That Plato should come to such a negative evaluation of the emotions is no surprise: They are all motions of the soul, disturbances or restorations of the harmony of contentment.

Unfortunately, Plato does not give a more detailed elucidation of the kinds of pleasures that he sees contained in all of these affections, with the exception of rage; here he refers to Homer as his witness that rage contains a certain sweetness, "sweeter than soft-flowing honey." The sweetness in rage is most likely the sweetness of anticipated revenge; and anticipation of the opposite state (47c) is probably also the explanation for the mixed nature of all other emotions. As disturbances or deficiencies, they contain a desire for the opposite state, and the *logoi* or images we possess will make us envisage their fulfillment. All longing will contain an element of anticipated assuagement, lamentation of consolation, love of success with the loved, jealousy and envy of satisfaction in seeing oneself triumphant over the other. Plato clearly sees the same emotional ambiguity at work in drama, both in tragedy, where there is "laughter mixed with weeping" (48a), and in comedy, where our laughter is conditioned by ill will against those we laugh at.[32]

Plato's claim that there is a fundamental ambiguity at work in the emotions concerned with comedy and tragedy seems to refer both to the personae in the drama and to the audience. He confines himself, once again, to an all-too-short summary of his views, but it is well worth speculating what his reasons are. Comic amusement is often regarded as one of the most innocent pleasures. By working out that it is in fact based on envy or malice, Plato may intend to show that there are no innocent emotions. Laughter in comedy, so he points out, is a kind of rejoicing at our neighbor's misfortune;[33] it is laughter at his ignorance, when he prides himself falsely on his beauty, wealth, or smartness. Plato's underlying assumption is that without an inherent resentment against our neighbor we would not find such a display of his folly amusing. So even the innocent-looking comic amusement presupposes a kind of moral lack or disintegration: without the ill will (a negative feeling or need) no such "filling" as the spectacle of the other's foolishness would give us any pleasure. That *Schadenfreude* is not the purest pleasure, contrary to what a German proverb claims, everyone will know who has ever analyzed the edge that is contained in such feelings.

Plato is certainly the first to put the double-sidedness of our emotions into full relief. If he is right, all our emotions involve a kind of moral lack and are the sign of an unsound state of our soul. It must be a lack or disturbance, because otherwise we would be at peace with others and ourselves. It must be moral, because such enjoyments are pleasures with a propositional content: We enjoy the spectacle of our neighbor making a fool of himself, so long as he is weak (because he cannot revenge himself on us), while such a display of ignorance in a powerful neighbor causes fear in us, because she is capable of taking revenge. Having such content, our emotions are subject to moral judgment: There is unjust envy, as there is just rejoicing (49c–d). More importantly for Plato's theory, in none of these cases can the simple fact that we are enjoying ourselves prove that such pleasures are good, or that they are true, that is, pure, pleasures. If he is right, the pursuit of the excitement of cultural pleasures or pains in drama or comedy is to be regarded with distrust, because they may further incense our already disharmonious souls.[34]

It would have been interesting to see Plato spin out these rather fascinating remarks about the ambiguity of the emotions into a full-fledged new critique of the educational influence of tragedy and comedy. No mention is made of any positive influence of the arts on our emotions, or of a profitable employment of their "restorative powers": It is quite conceivable that Aristotle's much-debated theory about the "purification" of our affections was influenced by the discussion of the impurity of our emotions in the *Philebus*.[35]

V. TRUE PLEASURES

After the long discussion of the manifold shortcomings of pleasures there is a relatively short treatment of the *true* pleasures (51b–55). The "truth" of these pleasures is as equivocal as their "falsity" had been. If pleasures are to attain truth they must be unmixed with pain and have the appropriate size, and there must not be any falsehood involved in the object of the pleasure. True to the definition that all pleasure is the filling of a lack or the restoration of a deficiency, only such fillings can be regarded as true pleasures that are based on an "unfelt lack" ("imperceptible and painless," 51b), while the restoration is perceptible and pleasant. Of the sensory pleasures only very few fulfill these conditions, such as the pleasures of smell or of beautiful sights and sounds. Even among these Plato imposes further rigid limitations concerning their content: Only those are acceptable as pure pleasures whose beauty is not relative to anything else and does not depend on particular conditions. Such are the pure colors or the pure lines of geometry; but not the colors or shapes of any particular objects, for their beauty is determined by the purpose the object serves or by the connection it stands in, like the beautiful sounds in a melody that may be out of place or in the wrong mode and thus ugly. Therefore it is not surprising to see that, of the many necessary pleasures of restoration, in the end only a few have any chance to get into the exalted rank of things that deserve to be put on the scale of goods. Especially among the sensory pleasures, the purity conditions (given the fact that there are so few patches of pure white and so few instances of unblemished Anaturals) ensure that only those instances of pleasures that are small in amount, great in purity, and unmixed with pain possess the right "moderation" (52c).

This stricture applies even to the pleasures of learning. They hold a much more modest place here than the intellectual pleasures had obtained in *Republic* IX; for they seem to have lost a lot of the luster assigned there to the philosopher's glorified pleasures. There is no trace now of a calculation that makes them come out exponentially superior to all others. The reason for the much more subdued role of intellectual pleasures in the *Philebus* cannot lie only in the point that Plato does not here maintain a privileged position for the "first part" of the soul;[36] it must also be a consequence of the fact that among all intellectual activities only learning can be a pleasure at all. Being true to his definition of pleasure as the filling of a lack, Plato can no longer accept any other pleasures of the mind, such as pleasures of "contemplating reality" (*Rep.* 581e). The wise man does not need any filling but lives, as far as humanly possible, in a state of self-sufficiency and contentment. Plato is not very explicit about this new limitation of the pleasures of the mind, but learning is the only intellectual pleasure he mentions, and he takes pains to assure us that this pleasure is based on a painless lack (51e). That he has no use for pleasure in philosophical contemplation itself is due to the fact that he does not make the distinction between process and activity that allowed Aristotle to grant pleasure to all of our successful activities, especially to the philosopher's.[37]

It may look at first sight rather peculiar that Plato treats anything that we do not "have" as a lack, so that there is a "painless lack" of beautiful sounds, sights, or smells when we happen not to see, hear, or smell anything. The peculiarity vanishes if we realize that this is his ultimate explanation of why human beings would and could not choose a life without pleasure, even though a life of total imperturbability would, in principle, be "more divine." Such a life is simply not open to human beings: There are lots of things we do not have, know, hear, feel, or see, and that will enrich our existence even if we do not have any perceived need for them. We are born as needy creatures, and as Plato's reference to the possibility of a "painless loss" of knowledge (52a–b) reminds us, a state of completion once attained need not remain such; everything that is not strictly eternal needs constant maintenance and restoration, even knowledge. Human beings never live in permanent possession of the good, in a state of continued perfect self-sufficiency (60c).[38]

But if pleasure is a restoration that is necessary for a fulfilled life and enriches it, why, so one may feel prompted to ask, is it not regarded as a good *per se*? This is the question Socrates turns to in his conclusion of the long critique of hedonism. The point is a purely ontological one. Even the true and pure pleasures remain processes that lead to the restoration of being (*ousia*), but they never have being in themselves nor a permanent immutable nature.[39] As processes they will always be inferior to the end that terminates them, that "for the sake of which" they happen. Even the best kind of generation is only good relative to the being that is its end, but it is not desirable in and for itself. Good pleasures are good because of the harmonious state they lead to; this end imposes limit on the pleasures and justifies their place on the lowest rung of the final scale of goods. But though such pleasures of generation or restoration are necessary and even good for us, it would be foolish to claim that it is the pursuit of fillings that makes our life worth living rather than the state of fulfillment itself. It would be a confusion of means and ends (54e).

We have to refrain here from a critical analysis of Plato's treatment of the different disciplines of knowledge, their relative purity and truth, which fulfills Socrates' promise (22c) to subject knowledge to the same critical scrutiny as pleasure. The distinction between pure sciences and applied sciences (55c–59b) would deserve an essay of its own, one that would also have to deal with the difficult question of Plato's conception of dialectic as the "insight into true reality" (59d), which is more hinted at than discussed in the *Philebus*. The existence of these hints seems to speak against a "revisionist" interpretation,[40] and for the assumption that Plato still holds in the main the same metaphysical doctrine that we find in dialogues of the earlier late period. There is no support for the claim that separate Forms have been given up, especially in view of the fact that he refers to the eternally selfsame as the object of real knowledge, in contradistinction to the changeable objects of belief (59a–e). Plato's silence as to the precise nature and origin of the harmonious limit – the truth, proportion, and beauty that make all things good – does not permit us to go beyond these hints and to import any further-reaching new metaphysical doctrine. In can be no accident that he remains uncommitted in the passage where he sums up the difficulties of the theory of the Forms (15a–c).[41]

Leaving these problems open for future scholarly debate, we should in concluding return again to the initial question of why Plato lets Socrates conduct this investigation. As our discussion has shown, Plato has arrived at a conception of pleasure that differs significantly from his earlier one, in spite of undeniable continuities. The fourfold ontological distinction seems tailored for his development of this new conception. So why did he resurrect Socrates as the protagonist in a discussion that turns out to be quite remote from the earlier treament of pleasure, both in its means and in its ends?

It had been suggested above that it must be the topic, the concern with pleasure, that prompted Plato to let Socrates conduct the discussion once again. But this cannot be the whole story. There is indeed more of a continuity than the new ontological framework lets one suspect. If pleasure is now defined as a "coming into being" and as something that is as such neither good nor bad, then this constitutes the development of ideas that have been advocated by an earlier Socrates, even if he himself did not extend this earlier doctrine to give pleasure its proper ontological niche. It was the Socrates of the *Symposium* who had described the philosopher as the "mighty *daimon,*" the son of Poverty and Plentiful, whose needy state and love for wisdom urges him on in search of perfection (*Smp.* 202e*ff*). The best kind of pleasure, one may supply from the perspective of the *Philebus,* is the kind that consists in the process of the eternal hunt for knowledge envisaged in the *Symposium.* It is this need for fulfillment that drives the soul in the *Phaedrus* up and around in pursuit of its deity, and the Socrates of that dialogue is no longer averse to seeing something divine in such a "manic" endeavor of the soul (*Phdr.* 244*ff*).

To deal with such processes is not the dialectician's business, for he is the perfectly wise man whose concern is "being, true reality and the eternally self-same" (58a); it is the the concern of the seeker for completion, whose representative is the poor, unshod, but relentless and indefatigable Socrates portrayed in the *Symposium,* or the concern of the rueful singer of a palinode in favor of love in the *Phaedrus.* The progress toward perfection is what the best kind of pleasure in human life represents, and that is why a human life would not be desirable without pleasure: Insofar as it is human it is incomplete and needs the constant tending and completion that the Socratic philo-sopher (although not the Platonic dialectician) craves for.

This is not the only Socratic element in the *Philebus*, however. The "medical" character of the treatment of pleasure and pain has been stressed before. It is hardly an accident that so much emphasis is put on the conception of pleasure as the restoration of a naturally harmonious state. Health and harmony of soul and body had been the hallmarks of the conception of goodness advocated by the Socrates of the earlier dialogues, such as the *Gorgias* and the *Republic*. In the *Philebus* pleasure (in its best form) finally finds its place in this ontological scheme as the restoration of the natural harmony of soul and body. This shows that the medical analogy that justified Socrates' criticism of his contemporaries' morality has never been given up; it has been redescribed in new terms that tie together being and becoming, the imposing of limits on the unlimited. Socrates' doctors, his horse and dog trainers who strive for excellence in their subjects, have not been forgotten.[42]

Critics of the coldness of Plato's conception of love, which seems to take so little notice of the essence of our passionate commitments, will probably not see any great improvement in the revision of the conception of pleasure in the *Philebus*.[43] Does the new "medical" treatment of pleasure as restoration and the question of the soundness of our emotions in general not display the same kind of disrespect toward what we regard as essential about ourselves as human beings? Plato, the philosopher whose striving for perfection constituted the basis of his lifelong attachment to Socrates, would not deny that love and pleasure make us human; he came to see that and why they cannot and should not be eradicated but even deserve to be cultivated. This is just what the *Philebus* was designed to confirm; our needy state is precisely what makes us human, but it is also what makes us all too human. It is a necessary ingredient of our mortal condition.

NOTES

1 For a discussion of the problems of coherence, cf. esp. the commentary by J. C. B. Gosling, *Plato: Philebus* (Oxford, 1975), ix–xxi, notes ad loc., and Epilogue, 226–8.

2 No more than a few references to the literature can be given here: Helpful are the introduction and notes in R. G. Bury, *The Philebus of Plato* (Cambridge, 1897); R. Hackforth, *Plato's Examination of Pleasure (The Philebus)* (Cambridge, 1945); and the commentary in Gosling, *Plato: Philebus.* For further discussion see Hans-Georg Gadamer, *Platos Dialektische Ethik – Phänomenologische Interpretation zum Philebus* (Leipzig, 1931); W. D. Ross, *Plato's Theory of Ideas,* 2d ed. (Oxford, 1953); I. M. Crombie, *An Examination of Plato's Doctrines,* 2 vols. (London, 1962, 1963); R. Shiner, *Knowledge and Reality in Plato's Philebus* (Assen, 1974); J. C. B. Gosling and C. C. W. Taylor, *The Greeks on Pleasure* (Oxford, 1982); and most recently, C. Hampton, *Pleasure, Knowledge, and Being: An Analysis of Plato's Philebus* (Albany, 1990). All of these works contain extensive bibliographies and discussions of the relevant literature. For a discussion of the dialectical-metaphysical part, see esp. G. Striker, *Peras und Apeiron: Das Problem der Formen in Platons Philebus, Hypomnemata* 30 (Göttingen, 1970); K. Sayre, *Plato's Late Ontology: A Riddle Resolved* (Princeton, 1983); and R. M. Dancy, "The One, The Many, and the Forms: *Philebus* 15b1–8," *Ancient Philosophy* 4 (1984):160–93.

3 The model of such a division is that of the art of writing: You cannot claim mastery until you not only know that "letter" is the *genus* that unifies all sounds, but also know all the subgenera (vowels and consonants) and the sub-subgenera of semiconsonants, consonants, and mutes. Further division renders the *species* of the letters; it ends with the unlimited multitude of actual instantiations of letters. Music is the other example Plato discusses. Because of the complexity of the systems of Greek scales (classical Western music contains nothing that is comparable) we have to omit the discussion of music here. Cf. Gosling, *Plato: Philebus,* 155–81.

4 Cf. esp. Striker, *Peras und Apeiron;* and Gosling, *Plato: Philebus,* 185–206. The unity of the *Philebus* is discussed by O. Letwin, "Interpreting the *Philebus,*" *Phronesis* 26 (1981):187–206. It is also the main concern of Hampton, *Pleasure, Knowledge, and Being.*

5 The debate about the connection between the *Philebus* and Aristotle has not come to rest since Henry Jackson first tried to establish it; see H. Jackson, "Plato's Later Theory of Ideas," *Journal of Philology* 10 (1882): 253–98. The most recent contributions have been made by Sayre, *Plato's Late Ontology,* 84*ff,* 133*ff;* and Hampton, *Pleasure, Knowledge, and Being,* 1–7, 95–101. Since the terminology of *peras* and *apeiron* is not used elsewhere in Plato, the *Philebus* must be the work where this doctrine manifests itself, if Aristotle is not either missing the mark or referring to the arcane source of Plato's oral teaching, the "unwritten doctrine." So far attempts to use these passages to solve the riddle of Plato's late ontology have not led to satisfactory results.

6 The formulation in the text (66c–d) does not definitely settle the question whether Plato regards this list of goods as closed or whether there is a possible sixth class of less pure and true pleasures, as Hackforth suggests in his commentary (*Plato's Examination,* 140 n. 3). If Plato is as restrictive as he seems, the pleasures admitted as necessary to the good life would only be *remedial* goods (63e, e.g., gymnastic and the painful exercises to acquire virtue). If this is the solution to the problem, then not all acceptable ingredients of the good human life are on the list of goods because they do not satisfy the "truth, beauty, proportion" test.

7 The question why reason and intelligence (*nous* and *phronēsis*) form a class separate from science, art, and true judgment (*epistēmē, technē,* and *doxa orthē,* 66b–c) can only be touched here: The latter are acquired skills that allow for different degrees of purity, while the former are the capacities that make such acquisitions possible in the first place. For the importance of the focus on the human good, see Gosling, *Plato: Philebus,* 132–3, 224–6.

8 A late date for the *Philebus* is supported by stylometry as well as reasons of doctrine. See H. Thesleff, *Studies in Platonic Chronology* (Helsinki, 1982), esp. 198–200. For a relatively earlier date, cf. R. A. H. Waterfield, "The Place of the *Philebus* in Plato's Dialogue," *Phronesis* 25 (1980): 270–305; and the introduction to his translation, *Plato: Philebus* (Harmondsworth, 1982).

9 Protarchus is at first a convinced hedonist. He is obviously a friend and admirer of Philebus, doing his best to please him. After a tense and almost hostile beginning (see 13b–d), Protarchus, son of Callias (19b), disciple of Gorgias (58a), turns into an attentive and cooperative interlocutor, a reformable version of Callicles (with true knowledge, good will, and frankness; see *Grg.* 487a). He changes his allegiance without coercion or obsequiousness and ends up a Socratic rather than a hedonist.

10 This can only be a very brief summary. For further discussion and references see Gosling and Taylor, *Greeks on Pleasure,* chaps. 3–6; and my "Rumpelstiltskin's Pleasures: True and False Pleasures in Plato's *Philebus,*" *Phronesis* 30 (1985):151–80, esp. 151–61.

11 Whether the *Protagoras* in fact temporally precedes the *Gorgias* is not of any great importance here. It is assumed here because the antihedonist stance of the *Gorgias* is in line with the position in the *Phaedo* and the *Republic.* But since I take it that the position of the *Protagoras* is merely the exploration of a hypothesis anyway, which Plato did not adopt for himself (as his contempt for such "vulgar" calculations in *Phd.* 69a shows), it is immaterial at what point of time he made it. For differing possible interpretations see G. Vlastos, "Introduction," in *Plato: Protagoras* (Indianapolis, 1956); T. Irwin, *Plato: Gorgias* (Oxford, 1979), 121*ff;*

D. Zeyl, "Socrates and Hedonism – *Protagoras* 351b–358d," *Phronesis* 25 (1980):250–69; and, for the most recent discussion of the question, R. Weiss, "Hedonism in the *Protagoras* and the Sophist's Guarantee," *Ancient Philosophy* 10 (1990):17–39.

12 The reason for calling this a "medical" point of view will be discussed more extensively later. By refraining from mixing the question of moral standards with that of the ontology of pleasure, Socrates can avoid the battle at two fronts he had to fight against Callicles, by forcing him to grant that "leaks" are never desirable while at the same time conceding that some are especially bad.

13 In *Rep.* VI 505b–c pleasure and knowledge are both rejected as definitions of the good; pressed for specification the champions of knowledge will have to beg the question and resort to "knowledge of the good," while the hedonist will have to admit the existence of bad pleasures. No other differentiations of pleasures, such as the possibility of pleasures of knowledge, are mentioned here.

14 The term *eskiagraphēmenē* (583b) means literally "a thing painted with its shadow" in order to produce the illusion of a three-dimensional physical object. For a survey of "unsatisfactory points in the *Republic* account," see also Gosling and Taylor, *Greeks on Pleasure,* 126–8.

15 That it is the need for orderliness that dictates the setup in the discussion of the *Philebus* is indicated by this: Plato mentions the postponement of the discussion of certain shortcomings of pleasures because he did not want to run different points of criticism together (see 47c–d:"I did not mention earlier . . .").

16 The same objection has been raised by Donald Davidson, "Plato's Philosopher," *The London Review of Books* 7, no. 14 (1985):15–17. He draws the conclusion that the *Philebus* represents a renunciation of Plato's preoccupation with dialectic as the philosopher's concern. It is difficult to say whether this is really a final renunciation on Plato's part rather than an ad hoc solution for the comparison of pleasure and knowledge. In what follows it will be argued that it is the nature of pleasure as the filling of a lack itself that makes a complete division undesirable, if not outright impossible.

17 Cf. *Tht.* 156*ff.* Whether Plato ever agreed with such a Heraclitean stance cannot be discussed here; his earlier theory of the Forms seems to have provided for a definite nature of changeable objects only insofar as they participated in the Forms. On Plato and the flux see T. Irwin, "Plato's Heracliteanism," *Philosophical Quarterly* 27 (1977):1–13.

18 That the restoration of being (*ousia*) can at best be the means (as generation) to the good is indeed the conclusion of the long discussion of pleasures in 53c–55a: "But if pleasure really is a kind of generation, then

we will rightly place it in a class different from that of the good." This only rules out that pleasure is good by definition, it does not preclude that some pleasures are good; the fact that true and pure pleasures are on the final list of goods even though they presuppose an unfelt lack shows that processes are not *eo ipso* excluded from the realm of the good.

19 Later (43c) a further specification will be added: only *significant* changes are pleasures and pains, while moderate ones have no such effect.

20 Such a suspension between a present pain and a future pleasure is the new "in-between" situation (35e) that replaces the *Republic*'s "rest" as a state between true pleasure and liberation from pain.

21 Among the skeptics are J. C. B. Gosling, "False Pleasures: *Philebus* 35c–41b," *Phronesis* 4 (1959):44–54; to which there is a reply by A. Kenny, "False Pleasures in the *Philebus*," *Phronesis* 5 (1960):45–92; and brief rejoinder by Gosling, "Father Kenny on False Pleasures," *Phronesis* 5 (1960):41–5. See further J. C. Dybikowski, "False Pleasures in the *Philebus*," *Phronesis* 15 (1970):147–65; Gosling, *Plato: Philebus*, 214–20; Gosling and Taylor, *Greeks on Pleasure*, Appendix A, 429–53.

22 *Plato: Philebus*, 212.

23 The immense range of possible disturbances and their restorations in soul and body may be one of the main reasons for Socrates' reluctance to engage in *dihairesis* proper.

24 Most of the literature (see note 21) focuses on the "propositional" sense of "false."

25 Cf. Bernard Williams, "Pleasure and Belief," *Proceedings of the Aristotelian Society* (1959):57–72. Williams's articles started the long debate on the justifiability of Plato's theory in the *Philebus*. For a defense of Plato's conception of false pleasures, see T. Penner, "False Anticipatory, Pleasures," *Phronesis* 15 (1970):166–78; and my "Rumpelstiltskin's Pleasures," 165–79. Hampton's ("Pleasure, Truth and Being in Plato's *Philebus*," *Phronesis* 32 [1987]:253–62) objecting to my defense of "propositional truth" – that this does not do justice to Plato's conception of truth as a whole – misses my (explicitly limited) point; no more than an explanation of the *possibility* of such "false pleasures" was intended.

26 "If we notice that a pain or pleasure is mistaken in what it is pleased or pained about" (37e). Protarchus finds it as hard to accept the view that pleasures are not merely *accompanying* our judgments as do some of the modern critics of "propositional pleasures." Socrates for the moment retreats to accept the point that pleasures and pains "accompany" judgments. But the subsequent elaboration makes it clear that the whole enjoyment provided by the soul's inner dialogue or the painter's work consists in nothing but the *logoi* or pictures in the soul. So Socrates' momentary retreat is not an admission of defeat.

27 ". . . it follows that there are false pleasures in the human soul that are quite ridiculous imitations of true ones, and also such pains" (40c).

28 Plato's seeming reserve, when he lets Protarchus continue with his lingering doubts about false pleasures does not weaken the case. For Socrates is quite in the affirmative: "There certainly are, I at least am convinced" (41b). That Plato often refrains from driving a point home with vigor must be seen against the background of *Phdr.* 273–6: He does not hand out truths that can be learned by rote, but leaves it to the intelligent reader to draw his own conclusions.

29 This (in Plato's eyes false) conception of pleasure as peace of mind was later developed by Epicurus, who ranked the stationary (katastematic) pleasures above the dynamic (kinetic) pleasures. Cf. Diogenes Laertius, X, 136–138. Plato would, of course, agree with Epicurus that imperturbability is best; he would disagree about calling it pleasure. On Epicurus see Gosling and Taylor, *Greeks on Pleasure,* 365–74; Philip Mitsis, *Epicurus' Ethical Theory* (Ithaca, N.Y., 1988), chap. 1.

30 For this question see M. Schofield, "Who Were οἱ δυσχερεῖς in Plato, *Philebus* 44*a* ff.?" *Museum Helveticum* 28 (1971):2–20. He argues for Plato's nephew Speusippus and assumes that the "difficulties" are logical ones. My own suspicion is that Plato here humorously characterizes his own attitude of an earlier stage (in his "scientific" phase). Not only is the "unsoundness" of pleasures discussed in *Rep.* IX, but the same phrase is used in the passage in the *Phaedo,* where Plato has nothing good to say about pleasure at all (*ouden hygies oud'alēthes echēi*). On Speusippus in the *Philebus* see also Gosling and Taylor, *Greeks on Pleasure,* 231–40.

31 This does not rule out that moral evaluation of the propositional content of the relevant pleasures is important for Plato. If he does not here appeal to our moral intuitions to rule out certain pleasures as wrong, it is because his purpose is to show first on purely ontological, i.e., nonmoral, grounds that and why pleasures can be false. So the *Philebus* contains, in Kantian terms, the groundwork of any future morality of the emotions.

32 On pleasure in tragedy and comedy cf. also *Rep.* X 606b–c.

33 This is true even for the "unquenchable laughter" of the immortal gods in their amusement at limping Hephaistos's peace-making efforts, *Iliad* I, 599–600.

34 It is difficult to say, *ex silentio,* whether Plato has given up other points of criticism against fiction, or whether he refrains from it because its distortion of reality is less relevant for the critique of pleasure than the unsoundness of the emotions themselves.

35 *Poetics* 6, 1449b28. The basic idea would be that our emotions can be freed of unjust "edges," as well of all unhealthy inflation.

36 This need not constitute any revision in Plato's psychology; it may rather be connected with Plato's concern to maintain the generic unity of all pleasures.

37 Plato seems to have conceived of thought as "motionless," so that knowledge itself, like its objects, is always in the same state (cf. *Phil.* 55a, 59c). For Aristotle's theory of pleasure (see *N. E.* X) see Gosling and Taylor, *Greeks on Pleasure,* 301–14; cf. also J. Urmson, "Aristotle on Pleasure," in *Aristotle,* ed. Julius Moravcsik (Garden City, N.Y., 1967), 323–33; J. Annas, "Aristotle on Pleasure and Goodness," in *Essays on Aristotle's Ethics,* ed. A. O. Rorty (Berkeley, 1980), 285–99.

38 This question has been further pursued in my paper "The Impossibility of Perfection," *Review of Metaphysics* 39 (1986):729–53.

39 For a further discussion of the dimension between being and becoming, see M. Frede, "Being and Becoming in Plato," *Oxford Studies in Ancient Philosophy,* supp. vol. (1988):37–52.

40 "Revisionists" go on the assumption that the difficulties for the theory of the Forms raised by Plato in the first part of the *Parmenides* led to a revision of the theory in the late dialogues. The "unitarians" deny any significant change. Among the revisionists for the *Philebus* are Gosling, *Plato: Philebus;* Shiner, *Knowledge and Reality;* Shiner, "Must *Philebus* 59a–c Refer to Transcendent Forms?" *Journal of the History of Philosophy* 17 (1979): 71–7; Henry Teloh, *The Development of Plato's Metaphysics* (University Park, Pa., 1981). A unitarian interpretation is argued for by R. Hackforth, *Plato's Examination of Pleasure (The Philebus)* (Cambridge, 1945); R. Mohr, "*Philebus* 55c–62a and Revisionism," in *New Essays on Plato,* ed. F. J. Pelletier and J. King-Farlow (Guelph, 1983), 165–70, with a response by Shiner at 171–80; Waterfield, "Place of the Philebus"; and Hampton, *Pleasure, Knowledge, and Being.* For a careful review of the history of the controversy see W. Prior, *Unity and Development in Plato's Metaphysics* (London, 1985).

41 The insistence on the continuity in doctrine of the *Philebus* with the earlier dialogues is a major virtue of Hampton's book. It is to blame also for its main shortcomings, however. In battling against all "revisionist" tendencies by interpreters who want to see major changes in the theory of Forms of Plato's late dialogues she overlooks important changes, especially changes concerning the conception of pleasure itself between *Rep.* IX and the *Philebus.*

42 The allusion is to the Socratic notion that human beings need tending that ought to be in the hands of experts, analogous to the doctor's solicitude for the body and the trainer's for the "virtues" of his horses or dogs. See *Ap.* 25b, *Grg.* 464a*ff;* Callicles even loses patience with Socrates' analogies (*Grg.* 491a).

43 For a constructive criticism of the shortcomings of Plato's conception of love, see G. Vlastos, *The Philosophy of Socrates* (Garden City, N.Y., 1971) 3–42. The issue is further discussed in M. Nussbaum, *The Fragility of Goodness* (Cambridge, 1986), chaps. 6 and 7.

TREVOR J. SAUNDERS

15 Plato's later political thought

Does Plato have a "later" political theory, as distinct from an earlier? It is certainly easy to suppose so. Read the *Republic* and you confront the most radical political system ever devised. Plato's key argument is that ruling a state is or should be a skill, based on precise knowledge of certain suprasensible, eternal, and unchanging realities called Forms (*ideai*), notably those of the social and political virtues, but also those of the rest of reality. On the strength of such insight, the rulers of Callipolis ("Splendid City"), a highly trained cadre of Guardians, or Philosopher-Kings, exercise direct and total political control; and lawmaking is accordingly treated by Plato in a decidedly offhand manner, as a humdrum business on which the Guardians will spend little time.[1]

If you are by now gasping with astonishment or even indignation at the audacity of these proposals, you have every justification; for at first sight Plato's thought seems almost unintelligible. For what are Forms, and why ought they to have such a drastic effect on practical politics? The explanation, though full of philosophical problems that cannot be explored here, can be stated quite briefly. A Form, say of virtue, is the essence of virtue, what it really is, as distinct from the individual things or actions or people that instantiate it in this world; for they only share in the Form of Virtue in varying degrees; they are not Virtue Itself. Now the Greek word usually translated "virtue" is in fact better rendered by "excellence" – excellence for *something*. The kind of excellence that interests Plato is human excellence, that set of qualities thanks to which we are excellently equipped to perform human functions excellently, and so achieve human *eudaimonia*, "happiness," "success," "fulfillment." The Philosopher-Kings, equipped as they are with precise knowledge of the Form of *aretē*,[2] will naturally embrace it and be supremely virtuous themselves; and they will also be able to discern infallibly whether and how far a given action or institution is a virtuous one. Further, they will take care, by various means, to transmit their knowledge, or rather an approximate version of it called "right opinion," to the rest of the state,[3] which will in proportion to its limited understanding practice "ordinary" or "demotic" virtue, and so enjoy a limited measure of *eudaimonia*.

The central proposition of Plato's political thought in the *Republic* is therefore that human *eudaimonia* depends on possessing *aretē*; that fully to possess *aretē* requires an understanding of its Form; and understanding the Form is a philosophical activity. The dependence of morality and politics on philosophy is the distinctive mark of the *Republic*.

Turn now to the *Laws*, the last and longest of Plato's dialogues, and prepare for a shock. With the possible exception of a few final pages, it is wholly devoid of the theory of Forms. After three preliminary "books" on moral and educational theory, the entire work is devoted to a discursive and painstaking account of the formation and administration of a "practical utopia," Magnesia. The Philosopher-Kings have vanished without trace; the only vestige of rule based on metaphysical or theoretical insight of a more than ordinary kind is the supremacy of the Nocturnal Council, which is composed of gentlemen-farmers – intelligent and educated indeed, but hardly philosophers. The state is administered under an extensive and detailed corpus of constitutional, civil, and criminal law, some of it of vertiginous complexity. It is very hard not to feel that one has entered a different world, in which the cutting edge of Plato's political thought, metaphysics, has been lost.

The simplest explanations of this startling state of affairs are methodological. One could straightforwardly infer that Plato has now abandoned the theory of Forms. Or one could argue that the mere absence of its metaphysical underpinning from a description of a political structure does not in itself show that that underpinning does not exist. The political structures both of the *Republic* and of the *Laws* are, in the most general terms, hierarchical and authoritarian; that of the *Republic* purports to depend on the theory of Forms; so it is natural to suppose that the same is true of that of the *Laws*. The *Laws* would then take the shape it does because Plato chooses to present the results of that dependency, in a practical work intended for consumption by nonphilosophers,[4] without dwelling on the metaphysics, which he presupposes but either suppresses or at any rate keeps in the background. Therefore, one might conclude, Plato does not have a "later" political philosophy; the *Republic* and the *Laws* are simply different sides of the same cloth.

Fortunately, however, we are in a position to do rather more than conjecture. There is a limited amount of evidence to suggest that in his later years Plato was still trying to root politics in the *terra firma* of philosophy.[5]

The *Politicus* ("Statesman," i.e., one who engages in *politika*, the affairs of the state, *polis*) is ostensibly a search for the definition of the Statesman, that is to say the person who possesses *politikē epistēmē*, political knowledge. Such a person, it is argued, would be entitled to rule even without laws, and even without the consent of his subjects; for after all, by definition, he *knows* what is best for them.[6] So far, this view is very much in the spirit of the *Republic*, which distinguished sharply between the sure "knowledge" of the Guardians and the mere "right opinion" of the rest of the state. So too is the firm distinction between the overarching and all-controlling function of the Statesman on the one hand, and the essentially ancillary functions of all other occupations, both of peace and of war.[7] But it is the method, apparently a difficult one,[8] by which the Statesman is separated off from all these, that is important: *dihairesis*, "division," of things according to their real kinds; for we are explicitly told that the purpose of the search for the Statesman is not for its own sake, but in order to make us *dialektikōteroi*, "more dialectical," "better at philosophical discussion," on all subjects.[9] Evidently an ability to perform division, to establish an accurate taxonomy of things, is a philosophical ability; and it is by implication part of the Statesman's intellectual equipment, of his political knowledge and skill.[10] And the "kinds" into which he "divides" things have apparently suprasensible counterparts, which it is his ultimate aspiration to understand. Though Plato's language in describing these counterparts is ambiguous and allusive, it strongly suggests Forms.[11]

The ideal ruler would in that case be one with *politikē epistēmē* somehow based on a knowledge of relevant Forms. He would be qualified to prescribe what ought to be done in every detailed situation and by every person without being constrained by any law, even his own. Such a paragon is, at best, rare.[12] The second-best form of government, therefore, is a good code of laws, "imitations of truth" in that they incorporate as far as possible the insights of a Statesman with genuine *politikē epistēmē*.[13] And the most important task of such political skill is to weave together by a variety of social contrivances the active and aggressive members of the *polis* with the inactive and compliant, so that the social structure achieves a firm texture, neither too hard nor too soft.[14] With this aim of a harmony of belief and action in the *polis* the dialogue closes.

So it looks as if Plato still maintains, as a theoretical ideal, the ruler with insight into Forms. Politics is, or should be, still anchored in metaphysics. Plato may have believed that proposition fervently; but for the purposes of the *Politicus* he keeps it in a shadowy background. The ideal, perfectly knowledgeable, godlike Statesman retreats to the wings; and into the limelight comes the wise, benevolent Statesman with practical experience, a human being legislating for human beings.[15] The emphasis shifts from the rule of philosophers to the reign of good law, tempered in its flexibility by the prudent practical judgment with which it is applied.[16]

The *Laws* exhibits a similar but a more interesting pattern of evidence. In all its 327 Stephanus pages there is not a single passage that indisputably refers to the Forms; but there are several that give hints. The most explicit passage is the one that describes the program of higher study to be carried out by the Nocturnal Council, a body that Plato intends to be the supreme intellectual force in Magnesia, its "anchor."[17] Its membership will be the state's wisest and most distinguished officials.[18] Its curriculum includes mathematics, astronomy, theology, law, and moral theory.[19] Its members are expected to study the problem of the one and the many; they must attempt to look beyond the many dissimilar instances of something *pros mian idean*, "to a single shape/form"; and they must concentrate on the way in which the virtues are individually distinct, and yet "one."[20]

This and other features of the Council's curriculum are strongly reminiscent of Plato's discussions of Forms in earlier dialogues. To anyone disposed to believe that Plato never abandoned the Forms, such passages will seem to bring them very near indeed. But his words are both brief and vague. Attenuated interpretations of them are available; and in particular it is impossible to know whether the full hierarchy of Forms elaborated in the *Republic,* culminating in the Form of the Good, is implied. Certainly much of the rest of the Council's curriculum seems more physical than metaphysical: for example, the rational movements of the heavenly bodies as evidence of design in the cosmos; the priority of soul over matter; and the nature and functions of the gods.[21] However, none of these topics can be shown to preclude a continued belief in Forms; indeed, such a belief may be implied by a number of passages that betray a keen interest in division.[22] The most reasonable conclusion is surely that Plato did still hold to at least some version of the theory of Forms, and for the purposes of the *Laws* was careful, right at the end of that work, where philosophy is presented as the savior of the state, to direct the studies of the members of the Nocturnal Council in that direction, so as still to do what he could to ground practical politics in philosophy.[23]

But there lies the rub. We may speak airily of "grounding" or "rooting" politics in philosophy, or of "basing" it on metaphysics, or of "linking" to the Forms; but what does such language mean? Suppose you are a Guardian or a member of the Nocturnal Council, and after much strenuous study and contemplation you arrive at the vision or knowledge of the Form of a particular virtue (e.g., courage) or of Virtue in general. Just how are you better off? What sort of tool have you for the conduct of politics, the framing of a constitution, or the drafting of moral rules? If the Form of Virtue can be expressed in the form of a definition of Virtue, could one simply describe some action that is a candidate for the title "virtuous," put it against the yardstick of the definition, and see if it matches? These matters are highly uncertain: Plato is very clear that there is a connection, but never tell us what it is.[24] He seems simply to assume that knowledge of the higher reality constitutes some sort of control on that of the lower, such that the knower always knows what is virtuous in this world, and acts accordingly. As for division, even in his relatively realistic mood in the *Politicus,* his keen awareness of its difficulty and complexity never leads him to conclude that divisions of things might be arbitrary or conventional; the divisions always have to be genuine, reflecting the real suprasensible structure that somehow lies behind them.[25]

It is therefore worth underscoring what a remarkable phenomenon the *Laws* is.[26] The longest work of the philosopher who is commonly thought of as the arch-idealist among idealists is stuffed with a mass of constitutional, administrative, legal, religious, and social detail; and nowhere does it tell us, except in the foggiest terms, how that detail is supposed to be related to metaphysical realities. We ought therefore to wonder about the status of what we read. Plato may have felt he had attained full metaphysical understanding, and may therefore have framed the institutions of the *Laws* in the perfect confidence that they reflected metaphysical realities at a level of approximation appropriate to the circumstances he envisaged in Magnesia. But this seems improbable, on simple a priori grounds. It is much more likely that in the *Laws* Plato formulates a set of proposals in such a manner as he feels sure, from a combination of experience and philosophical reflection, he would have to formulate them, if only he did in fact have a full understanding of the Forms. The *Laws*, on this view, is a work written on the basis of an incomplete understanding. Hence, though Plato is emphatic on some matters (on the tight connection between *aretē* and *eudaimonia*, for instance),[27] on others he can be quite tentative.[28] The *Laws* is not a work that suggests its author is confident about everything.[29]

That means, if we wish to understand what Plato is doing in the *Laws*, to analyze his proposals as he himself would, and to judge why he prescribed institutions, *a*, *b*, *c*, and not institutions *x*, *y*, *z*, we have to do some work of our own; and that, of course, is what Plato's dialogues always do require of us. Where may we start?

Observe first the very strongly marked hierarchical structure of the state. The fiction of the *Laws* is that an Athenian Stranger (clearly Plato himself), Cleinias (a Cretan), and Megillus (a Spartan) fall to discussing plans for a colony (Magnesia) to be founded in the South of Crete. In the course of Book IV[30] the Stranger invites his companions to suppose that the colonists have arrived and are waiting to be addressed. What they hear is an edifying protreptic on their forthcoming religious duties. Here is another speech, which the Athenian could have delivered but did not:

"Future members of Magnesia: This new state of yours is intended to be a very good one. It will be administered not in the spirit of any current ideology, but in accordance with the truth about the world. After all, you would not wish to conduct your lives in any manner that is not based on the truth, would you? Now you may not be aware that philosophy has shown us that the truth is expressed by

Forms – abstract ideas of things, very difficult to understand except by intelligent people who have put much effort into the job. However, that effort has been made; and you will find that the state you are about to join is run largely by people who have attained some insight into these things, and to a lesser degree by those who have lesser insight, but who have accepted the doctrines taught them by the others. It is all a question of reason: The more rational you are, the more you can understand the truth, and the more you will have authority in the state you are about to found."

Hence as one works one's way through the detail of Magnesia's structure and administration, one becomes aware of an elaborate hierarchy of knowledge, control, and influence. To speak very compendiously, gods rule (or in some sense oversee) human beings, officials rule nonofficials, free human beings rule slaves, citizens rule foreigners, the old rule the young; and the title of the rulers to rule is some form of superior knowledge.[31]

Some peculiarly Platonic features apart (e.g., the Nocturnal Council and the ability of women to hold office), this is very much the sort of pecking order that might appeal to a wide range of political and social allegiances. Plato is in this instance working with the grain: He finds it possible to use common Greek assumptions and common Greek institutions for his own purposes, namely, to ensure that reason and knowledge of the Forms, however dimly grasped by the Nocturnal Council, and however imperfectly transmitted by them to the rest of the state, have the maximum possible diffusion in Magnesia.[32] In this sense, what dictates the structure and administration of Magnesia is, however remotely, the Forms.

But Plato clearly feels that his success in constructing a philosophically based state will vary. Like the divine Demiurge ("craftsman") of the *Timaeus*, who in constructing the world has to make the best of the material that lies to hand, Plato has to do what he can with the whole array of contemporary institutions and laws, and with his new colonists, who have a wide variety of assumptions, expectations, and political, social, and religious beliefs.[33] His job, therefore, as a craftsman-lawgiver, becomes complex: It calls for selection, judgment, and indeed ingenuity.

His first job is to select his human "material." Only those persons who seem suitable will be admitted to the new state.[34] Even then, Plato wants to know as much about their habits and opinions as he can: He has great mistrust of the secrecy inseparable from private family life, and fears that all sorts of undesirable practices may go on undetected. There is some evidence that he would have extended the research, presumably legal and philosophical, for which he pleaded (in terms that remind us of Socrates) in the *Politicus*,[35] to sociological investigation of the Magnesians' characters, practices, and opinions. Before the craftsman can fashion, he must know his materials.[36]

As a result of such investigation, Plato will be able, in all realism, to achieve some things but not others. He will aim as high as he can, but will be careful to retain a fall-back position. This is the principle of the sliding scale. It emerges in many contexts,[37] but perhaps at its most explicit in the matter of property. The ideal would be a total community of possessions, which would discourage the evils associated with the institution of private ownership and foster the community of sentiment that Plato wishes to achieve. But he knows it is impractical; so the Magnesians will be permitted, within certain limits, to own their own property. And he acknowledges that in certain circumstances he may have to relax standards even further.[38]

But the obvious way to avoid having to relax standards is to ensure that no member of the state should even desire it; and Plato accordingly provides for a comprehensive program of persuasion and education to make as sure as he can that the Magnesians' likes and dislikes and reasoned convictions become what he wishes them to be. Mere vocational training exists in the system, but the chief emphasis is moral; and the Minister of Education provides a direct doctrinal/philosophical link with the Nocturnal Council. The whole of Book VII is devoted to education, but the topic recurs constantly throughout the work; and the *Laws* itself is in effect claimed to be Magnesia's best educational text.[39]

It is hardly necessary to give a résumé of all Plato's educational measures, for good accounts exist elsewhere.[40] But it is worth dwelling on one central point. Magnesia's program of education is Plato's bid for the hearts and minds of the Magnesians; and he is not prepared to brook rivals. His intention is that Platonic tastes, Platonic values, and Platonic ideology should be fully accepted by the Magnesians at large, not merely in conscious preference to other values, but because other values are simply not there to compete; for the notion that the world might be other than it is constitutes a danger.

To be sure, he wants the Magnesians to understand their laws *gnomēi,* "by reason, judgment"; but only when a man has shown himself to be beyond likely corruption is he allowed to travel abroad and make principled comparisons with foreign institutions; the Nocturnal Council has oversight of such excursions, and is encouraged to have wider mental horizons.[41] But the general run of Magnesians are to be totally immersed in Platonic values. Plato's pressures on them are intense and relentless.

Let us glance at a few of his techniques. The most obvious is the strict censorship of doctrinally undesirable artistic productions.[42] The most insidious is perhaps the use of the pleasure to be had from the arts to recommend doctrinally correct tenets to the feelings.[43] The best-known is the provision of dignified and edifying "preambles" to the legal code in general and to the constituent parts of it, designed, by a combined appeal to sensibility and reason, to persuade the bearer that the laws are to be obeyed.[44] And the most elaborate is the full-dress refutation, occupying almost the whole of Book X, of the three heresies that in Plato's view encourage us to break the link between virtue and *eudaimonia,* a cardinal doctrine.[45] All these and similar techniques amount to a most determined attempt to ensure that the Magnesians think as he wishes. He is in a sense cultivating the "consent of the governed" to his political structures; but it is perhaps truer to say that by exerting pressure he forces this consent into existence.

Another excursus, less long but even more radical, concerns penology.[46] It is addressed to the Magnesian citizens in their capacity as jurors. Athenian courts followed a partly retributive and partly deterrent policy. Plato, however, is wholly utilitarian. He separates off recompense to the injured party (which must be paid in every case) as a nonpenal measure, designed to restore the two sides to friendship. The purpose of punishment proper is not primarily to deter the offender by the prospect of further suffering, but to cure him of his psychic injustice, a "disease" that like medical disease he cannot have chosen to contract. For bad moral states, like bad physical states, are disadvantageous to their possessors; therefore, "no one is evil voluntarily."[47] Offenses are involuntary, and thus retributive punishment is misdirected. The purpose of punishment ought to be the "cure" of mistaken opinions and bad moral states. To achieve that, *any* measure, whether painful or not, may be used. In order to give effect to this policy, Plato writes a model penal code, based on Athenian law but freely modified both in large matters and in countless significant details.[48]

Here again there is a vigorous attempt to persuade the Magnesians to think Platonically.[49] A modern law school tries to teach its students not just the law but to think like lawyers; it inculcates a cast of mind, not just a body of knowledge. Plato approaches his task in the same way. The Magnesians jurors have to act in accordance with special assumptions and policies. Instead of asking, What does this convicted offender deserve to suffer retributively, in the light of the damage or injury he has caused?, they must ask, What does that damage or injury tell us about the state of his soul, and what penalty does he deserve to undergo to cure it? "Deserve," *axios,* takes on a different meaning. So too do *timōria,* "vengeance," "punishment," and *dikē,* justice," "punishment." *Timōria* acquires a disreputable connotation: "backward-looking retributive suffering that does the offender no good"; *dikē* comes to mean "punishment systematically calculated to reform him for the future."[50] Familiar vocabulary is used, but it acquires a new content. No wonder the penological excursus is prefaced by a long apologia for philosophical legislation.

But it is time to turn from philosophical and educational theory to more concrete matters. One enters Magnesia (visitors are not excluded)[51]; one strolls around; what does one see?

One sees a state whose wealth comes from agriculture, not commerce. The land is divided into 5,040 inalienable "portions" or "lots" (*klēroi*), one for each of the 5,040 adult male citizens;[52] 420 such lots constitute the territory of each of the twelve "tribes." On the way to the central city, one notices that each tribal division has a village. Dotted around are the dwellings of the citizen-farmers; and there are various other buildings for administrative, legal, religious, educational, and social purposes. One finds that the people one meets fall into four social categories: the free citizens and their wives and children; their slaves; resident aliens; and visiting aliens of diverse kinds. After a while, two features of Magnesian life become conspicuous: There is no undue poverty or wealth, and the range of economic activity permitted to those of citizen rank is strictly limited, since slaves do much of the manual work and trading and handicrafts are in the hands of resident aliens (metics).[53]

All these provisions are the practical expressions of well-known Platonic preoccupations. Wealth, poverty, trade, and handicrafts tend to diminish a man's virtue and to unfit him for a civilized life; they lead him to value the interests of the body over those of the soul.[54] The relationship of Plato's economic regulations to historical practice is a fascinating topic, but too extensive for consideration here.[55] Suffice it to note that Plato manipulates: He grants with one hand and claws back with the other. His central concern is to control private life.[56] He grants private property – but wealth over a certain level is subject to a tax of 100 percent.[57] He allows private families (they are indeed the bedrock institution of the entire state)[58] – but he wants all citizens and their wives to attend communal meals organized on the Spartan/Cretan model.[59]

How is the state governed and administered? The Stranger describes its constitution as "midway" between monarchy and democracy.[60] Summarized and slightly expanded, his explanation is as follows. Ideally, a state should be run by a single person of supreme virtue and political wisdom. Such a person rarely or never exists; and in any case we shall always be faced with the democratic demand for purely arithmetical[61] equality of political power (one man, one vote, in the modern expression). But the many are always less capable of political wisdom;[62] so the best way of framing a constitution is to combine two modes of distributing power: *election*, which (if we are lucky) will enable the state at large to appoint to office the (moderately numerous) persons best qualified by character and intelligence to hold it, and *the lot*, which guarantees some political influence to the common man, however rudimentary his political virtue. Political power will thus be diffused throughout the state; but the use of the lot should be confined to the smallest possible compass.

Hence the Stranger's task is to inject into the constitutional structure various means of maximizing the influence of those Magnesians who are more rational and virtuous than others. But does not Magnesia have the same array of constitutional features as is commonly found in Greek states at large, and conspicuously in democratic Athens – an Assembly of adult male citizens, a Council, and an Apparat of officials, not to speak of courts with large juries ensuring popular participation in the administration of the law? Can the Stranger manipulate such institutions in a Platonic direction? Indeed he can; and his methods are full of interest. I instance four only; close inspection of the fine print could well reveal others.

1. The Nocturnal Council, which is obviously intended to mediate philosophy to the state in the course of its strong influence on the state's day-to-day administration, is composed of persons who have attained membership on the basis of personal qualities only. As far as I can see, the lot plays no part whatever in the sequence of events leading to their appointment; they are members either by virtue of some conspicuous attainment or ability or by virtue of some office to which they have at some time been elected, not chosen by lot to any degree at all.[63] Here then, in such supreme governance as Magnesia has, election holds the field and the lot is nowhere. The Nocturnal Council is in effect an intellectual and moral aristocracy. As far as constitutional machinery goes, it has only a slender connection with the rest of the state; it does not have to seek approval for its decisions; and much of its activity and influence is no doubt intended to be informal, and perhaps covert.[64]
2. In the election of the most powerful officials, the Guardians of the Laws,[65] the ten most senior of whom are members of the Nocturnal Council, the number of candidates is whittled down first to 300, then to 100, and finally to 37. Electors who wish to vote in the final stage are obliged to confer solemnity on their vote by walking between the victims of a sacrifice. The effect will be to exclude from the final and decisive vote a number of the poorer citizens, who cannot afford the expense.[66]
3. The Assembly, to which all adult male citizens belong simply by having that status, and the Council, a select executive body of 360 members, seem to have on the whole a more restricted range of powers than in Athens.[67] Two details are to be noticed:
   a. In the elections to the Council,[68] all members of all four property classes vote for ninety members from each class. Voting is compulsory, on pain of a fine. But members of the fourth (poorest) class need not take part in the election of Councillors from the third class, and mem-

bers of the fourth and third classes need not take part in the election of the Councillors from the fourth class. In both these elections there will thus be a preponderance of "wealthy votes" over poor ones; for the well-off will vote because of the fine, and the poorly off will tend not to (no doubt they will be glad to get on with their work). On the standard assumptions[69] that there are fewer rich than poor, or even if they are equal in numbers, there will in this method of voting be a pronounced oligarchic influence in the election of Councillors from among the poor.

b. Similarly, members of the two wealthier classes are fined if they fail to attend meetings of the Assembly, whereas no such obligation is normally imposed on members of the two poorest classes.[70]

The upshot of (2) and (3) is a slightly curious one. To wisdom and virtue as qualifications for political power we are to add wealth. Plato perhaps feels that membership in one of the two higher property classes is a sign of industry, thrift, and modest desires. These are no small virtues; and since there is a strict upper limit on wealth in Magnesia, they are unlikely to degenerate into greed. At any rate, possession of wealth in Magnesia confers some modest political clout. The concession to demotic virtue is a shrewd one, and goes some way to meeting the oligarchic sentiment that some Magnesians may have, namely that wealth deserves power.[71]

Although Plato talks in rather static terms of the Magnesian constitution as "midway" between monarchy and democracy, what he in effect does is to allow contrary pressures or tensions to conflict dynamically. A certain shifting balance is struck not only between the two conceptions of equality represented by the use of election and the lot, and so between rich and poor,[72] but (i) between an official's freedom and discretion on the one hand, and on the other the risk of prosecution for misconduct during his tenure[73] and the necessity to undergo "scrutiny" at the end of it;[74] and (ii) between the authority of boards of officials to take binding decisions on their own, and their obligation to act in concert with other officials or pass cases on to a superior authority.[75] But we must not suppose that this attempt to hold opposing tensions in equilibrium is either (a) the modern doctrine of the separation of powers, legislature, executive, and judiciary each checking the other, or (b) a way of running harmoniously a "mixed society," in which various ideologies or ethnic groups are accorded esteem in their own right, but have to coexist indefinitely. Plato's playing off of one pressure against another takes place within, and should serve to reinforce, what is intended in time to be a single ideology, in which the ends of society will not be in dispute. If that is the mark of a totalitarian society, then Plato is a totalitarian.[76]

Another balance he strikes is between fidelity to the letter of the law and discretion in its application. Magnesia is a "law state," and laws as instruments of government are imperfect: They cannot meet the peculiar circumstances of every case, and need interpretation and application by persons acting according to their spirit rather than their bare wording.[77] Hence although Plato is emphatic that the Magnesians should give the laws unconditional obedience,[78] he is well aware that they will have to exercise enlightened flexibility in their day-to-day enforcement.[79] In fact, one of the reasons why certain selected Magnesians are encouraged to travel abroad is that no state that obeys its laws merely by habit without grasping them by "understanding," "judgment," "reason" (*gnomēi*) will in the end be able to preserve them intact.[80] The "observers," "ranging over land and sea," are therefore to consult foreign experts and inquire into the laws and jurisprudence of other countries, with a view to strengthening the legal system of Magnesia. Insofar as this is a philosophical activity (questions of intent, responsibility, penology, and psychology could presumably arise), Plato is trying to ensure that Magnesia is founded on philosophical insight: The observers report to a full meeting of the Nocturnal Council,[81] which no doubt attempts to feed into the legal code any new ideas and practices of which they approve.[82]

Plato adopts a good deal of contemporary Athenian law and legal practice, but in a decidedly critical spirit, and the list of modifications he makes is long and various. Apart from his radical new penology, which we have already described, perhaps his most significant innovations are (i) the institution of a less confrontational and more interventionist and inquisitorial legal procedure than prevailed in Athens,[83] and (ii) appeal, not allowed in Athens, from the verdicts of the "tribal" courts (the Magnesian counterparts of the regular Athenian courts, *dikastēria*) to a higher tribunal.[84] As for his other measures, I venture to quote again Morrow's splendid tribute:

> The pattern he lays down is in the main the procedure of Athenian law, with its freedom of prosecution and its rich variety of actions and remedies; but it is Athenian law modified at many points in directions, we may say, that are suggested by that law itself. In giving to the presiding magistrates power to control the pleading and prevent the introduction of irrelevant and misleading matter, in introducing something like inquisition of witnesses and principals, in excluding the opportunities for rhetorical jousting afforded by the archaic challenge to the oath and the challenge to the torture, in enlarging the range of competent witnesses and enforcing a litigant's right to compel their assistance, in eliminating the oath of witnesses and principals, in relying at all stages upon written documents, and in invoking the power of the state to assist a litigant in enforcing a judgment obtained in court – in all these provisions Plato's law, while still essentially Attic in character, embodies a conception of the judicial process broader and more enlightened than ever characterized Athenian practice at its best.[85]

If we ask what specifically *philosophical* principles, or in particular what connections with the Forms, lie behind this impressive collection of measures, it is once again hard to give an answer. For they are reforms such as could perfectly well be arrived at empirically by anyone concerned with the most efficient ways to ensure justice in the courts. But perhaps it is this very notion of justice that gives us a clue. As we have seen, Plato redefines it. The purpose of his legal code is not to make a criminal suffer "justly," that is, reciprocally, but to treat him in such a way that he will become "more just." Now the various unjust states of offenders are hard to diagnose with precision, and there is a constant risk that misdiagnosis will result in prescription of the wrong cure. Hence Plato's close attention to calm, prolonged, impartial, and scrupulously accurate legal procedure.[86] For only if the criminal is made "just," that is, virtuous, by "cure," will he have correct moral belief or disposition and thus attain some measure of human *eudaimonia*. Legal provisions are in the service of a penology that depends on a certain philosophical position. So if we wish to describe them as "philosophically grounded," it will be in some end-related sense: they are the most efficient means by which a man whose moral beliefs are (involuntarily) erroneous or whose desires are (involuntarily) wrongly directed may have his psychic state diagnosed and then cured. Bad court procedure would be concerned with something other than that diagnosis, and hence ultimately with something other than human *eudaimonia;* hence the very severe view Plato takes of the kind of pleading that perverts the work of the courts[87] – for it impedes human "happiness."

The same end-related view should be taken of the entire constitutional and economic structure of Magnesia. Insofar as the Nocturnal Council attains knowledge of the Forms, or the "genuine" divisions of reality, and mediates it by a variety of methods to its fellow citizens at large, its task can only be hindered by excessive poverty and excessive wealth,[88] or by indulgence in retail trade, or by the temptations put in a man's way by (say) unlimited tenure of office or the lack of scrutiny at its expiration. Economics and constitutional law dance to the tune of moral theory.[89]

So too do theology and religion, though at a higher intellectual level. Most of Book X is an elaborate theodicy designed to persuade Magnesians of the following propositions:

1. That the world is in some sense a rational construction, in which thought, design, and calculation are "prior" to nature, matter, and chance.
2. That the heavenly bodies, which move in regular and rational patterns, are gods.
3. That the gods are not indifferent to mankind; they have a warm regard for the virtuous and a detestation of the wicked. They reward the former and punish the latter; they are virtuous themselves, and cannot be begged off by sacrifices and prayers.

Strict laws are laid down for the repression of both impious actions and heretical opinions.[90] The Magnesians are to take part in a regular series of religious ceremonies and the accompanying social celebrations; worship at private shrines is forbidden,[91] for it can all too easily reinforce the belief that the gods can be bribed to overlook misdeeds. The reason why Plato pays extraordinary attention to religious belief and practice is his firm conviction that no one persuaded of propositions (1)–(3) above, and in particular (3), will go to the bad morally[92] in the belief that *eudaimonia* is independent of *aretē.*[93] Hence he presses theology and religion into the service of the moral, legal, and constitutional orthodoxies of Magnesia. Book X is in fact his most sustained attempt to mold the minds of the Magnesians into the shape he requires. It does of course contain much passionate protreptic; but its ratiocination is more than elementary: There is an analysis of the various kinds of motion, some discussion of how the heavenly bodies propel themselves, and an important attempt to present eschatology in terms of cosmic physics.[94] Plato is only too aware that the Magnesians, and particularly potential heretics among them, have brains as well as feelings.[95]

Plato's radicalism in confronting and manipulating historical institutions is by now, I hope, apparent. But his most radical step has yet to emerge: It is to require that the legislator and statesman, in exercising *politikē epistēmē,* concern himself with the *aretē* and hence *eudaimonia* not merely of the adult male citizen, but of all other parts of the population, namely, women, slaves, and foreigners. Even in these days of women's liberation, it is still not generally known that in the *Laws* Plato allows and indeed encourages women to take a large share in public life. Not only are they to join in the program of athletic and military training; not only are they to dine communally, like their husbands, and be educated precisely as the men are in political virtue;[96] they are actually to hold public office. True, they have to wait until the age of forty to do so, presumably in consideration of their careers as childbearers, whereas a male may hold office from the age of thirty.[97] But Plato is simply acting consistently with the principles of the *Republic:* In the crucial respects, a woman's potential ability is not inferior to a man's, and to refuse to use them is to waste half the state's human resources.[98] In the *Republic* there were accordingly Philosopher-Queens as well as Philosopher-Kings.[99] In the *Laws,* the principle has been universalized: *All* citizen women, however unlike Philosopher-Queens they may be, are to take part in public affairs. One may wonder how often they would in fact be elected, given the likelihood of male prejudice; perhaps Plato was covertly relying on the results of the use of the lot to familiarize the practice. At all events, it is important to realize that Plato is not actuated by any special admiration for the female sex as such,[100] nor by any sympathy with the idea that women are or should be equal to men in every social and legal particular, or with any such thing as "women's liberation"; he regards the matter purely as one of efficient use of available abilities.

Plato treats the handling of slaves as something of a problem.[101] He admits that some slaves are sterling characters who do their owners great good; but he is sharply conscious of the possibility of insubordination or even revolt. He recommends that masters should refrain from arrogantly ill-treating their slaves, but that they should be decidedly firm with them, chastising them justly; one should never be familiar with them, and everything said to them should be an order. In the legal code, slaves are accorded less protection against harm than free men, and some of the penalties visited on them for serious offenses are of horrible savagery.[102] In general, Plato thinks of a slave as a creature with a low level of reason and moral virtue, and hence of little capacity to live that rational and civilized life which constitutes human *eudaimonia.* But he does not believe they have no capacity for *eudaimonia* at all: One almost incidental remark seems to indicate that although bringing up slaves properly is primarily in their masters' interests, it is also in the interests of the slaves themselves, that is, their *eudaimonia.*[103] In a hard-nosed and calculating way, Plato brings the happiness of slaves within the benevolent concern of political science.[104] And to an even more attenuated degree he is concerned with the virtue of foreigners too, both resident and itinerant: The former should possess *sophrosunē,* "moderation," "restraint"; and both, like the slaves, are capable of moral improvement as a result of punishment for offenses.[105]

This care for the admittedly limited *aretē* and *eudaimonia* of the subordinate sections of the population raises interesting questions of theory. Is it simply instrumental, and intended merely to subserve the *eudaimonia* of adult male citizens? Or is there the germ of the notion that the legislator ought to have some universal concern for all human beings, regardless of political status? Whatever its motivation and purpose, Plato's concern for the *eudaimonia* of the entire state at least exists; and it is pregnant with possibilities for future philosophies, notably Stoicism and Christianity.

After these heady speculations, it is time to tug ourselves back to the central problem: Is the *Laws* a work of philosophy or not? We may consider general principles first, then specific constitutional and social detail; and essentially the same problem arises in both cases.

(1) Obviously Magnesia is constructed on certain principles – for example, moderation, compromise, the rule of law. But that does not make the *Laws* a work of philosophy in any strong sense. For these principles are pragmatic: One does not have to be a philosopher to

excogitate them. They are of course open to philosophical analysis; but they do not *have* to be based on any metaphysical belief in suprasensible realities such as Forms. Admittedly, one possible way of connecting moderation, compromise, and so on, to such realities would be to treat them as examples of "due" or "appropriate" measure, which in the *Politicus*[106] is "divided" from "relative" measure; for as we have seen, Plato seems to think that "divisions" reflect some higher structure of reality. But the nature of this relationship remains obscure: The difficulty is that achieving "due" measure looks like an entirely empirical exercise.

(2) So what relationship could there be between the detail of Plato's concrete practical proposals and his metaphysics? Consider the concept of the sliding scale. There is in the *Laws* a clear tension between what Plato would *like* to prescribe and what he feels he can achieve in practical terms – in a word, a tension between ideal and real. Now our immediate temptation is to suppose that the ideal must be Forms: Plato brings each institution of Magnesia as near as possible to its perfect exemplar. That is, he has his eye constantly on the Forms of (say) Court, Office, or Property Class, and seeks to perform accurate "divisions" of such things for deployment in Magnesia.[107] But if that is what he thinks he is doing, he keeps his *modus operandi* veiled.

(1) and (2) sketch possibilities only. What is possible to say with safety is that, if his concern is with Forms at all, it appears to be with the Forms of moral virtues. In that case, the sliding scale of preferred and less preferred institutions in Magnesia simply reflects a pragmatic judgment about *conditions facilitating* an intellectual grasp of those virtues, and hence the invariable practice of them.[108]

If we were to tax Plato on the point and ask him why this or that institution of the *Laws* subserves this purpose, while some other does not, he would make, I think, a twofold reply. "First, you are quite right in supposing I am working on a purely pragmatic level, in this sense: No man who is excessively poor or rich or money-loving or mean or ambitious or belligerent can acquire virtue, even on the humdrum level of 'demotic' virtue; for that he needs security, order, rational cooperation with his fellow men, and leisure (not idleness on the one hand nor luxury on the other). These are the sort of criteria on which I have constructed Magnesia. But second, if my intentions are fulfilled, and the Magnesians succeed under the guidance of the Nocturnal

Council in obtainiong some intellectual grasp of Virtue, it is surely improbable that the kind of life they will then lead will be wholly different from the one they have led so far – rather, their lives will gradually improve in moral quality, as a result of their improved understanding. After all, there must be *some* relationship between 'ordinary' or customary virtue based on imperfect understanding induced by myth and so forth, on the level of 'right opinion,' and a perfect grasp of what Virtue Itself is, based on reason. The life you led when you were in the process of improving your understanding of virtue is thus an excellent preparation and foundation for the life you will lead when you have obtained it.[109] In that sense, the *Laws is* a work of philosophy – in spite of some people who fondly think I have abandoned metaphysical idealism. This work is my final attempt to mark out for mankind the path to *eudaimonia;* for as I say in it clearly and often enough,[110] no man without virtue can be happy. That is the philosophy on which my *Laws* is based."

We are now in a position to face the question, What is the relationship between the state Magnesia and the state Callipolis?[111] Expressed in its sharpest form, my answer would be: There is no relationship. They are the same Platonic state – but placed at two points on a single sliding scale of political maturity. Now a politically mature Platonic state is, essentially, one governed by persons with metaphysical insights; and the hypothesis of Callipolis is that that kind of rule is achievable. The hypothesis of Magnesia is that it has not yet been achieved, and may indeed never be; nevertheless, Magnesia contains as an integral part of itself machinery embodying a continuing aspiration to it. It is crucial to this aspiration that the demotic virtues possessed by the second and third classes of Callipolis be fostered and stabilized in Magnesia as far as circumstances and the character of the inhabitants permit: hence the elaborate social and educational provisions that occupy so many pages of the *Laws.* In this carefully prepared soil, the rule of philosophy may take root and gradually grow. But even if the philosophical aspiration were to come to nothing, at least a superior "law state" will have been constructed.

Plato's political theory, so often thought of as "top-down," is in this important sense "bottom-up." Even in the *Republic,* it was a worry that the conditions for the building of Callipolis would never be ripe;[112] and it seems that when Plato came to select states to which he would be prepared to send political advisers from the Academy, he rejected those where he felt conditions were unpropitious.[113] The whole purpose of the *Laws* is to produce a state in which conditions would be very propitious indeed.

It is, I believe, in this positive, forward-looking, and aspirational way that the *Laws* is interpreted best; and like Plato himself at the end of many of his works, I will now tell a likely story. When he wrote the *Laws*, he was well into his seventies. He knew he could not live much longer. The search for the nature of virtue was in his view still unfinished business. He therefore set out, in fine, vigorous detail, a blueprint for a second-best ideal state, which would foster the demotic virtues to the greatest extent he deemed practical; and he directed the members of the Nocturnal Council toward further philosophical inquiry, both by themselves and in consultation with the Academy (there is a strong hint of help from that quarter).[114] Of course, Plato could hardly have expected a body such as the Nocturnal Council to succeed on its own in a philosophical inquiry in which the Academy had so far failed. But the final paragraph of the *Laws* keeps the lines of communication open from the Academy to the Council,[115] and so ultimately from the Academy to the world of even plainer men. There is no dimming of his zeal for the *aretē* and *eudaimonia* of mankind; for that, after all, is what philosophy is *for.*

If this admittedly unprovable reconstruction is correct, then the *Laws* has a good claim to be the most ambitious of all Plato's writings: It supplies a program of combined practical work and theoretical inquiry for the years after his death.

NOTES

1 *Rep.* 425a–427a; but laws of some kind there will certainly be: 458c, 502b–c.

2 In the *Republic* Plato is especially concerned with justice, that virtue specifically relevant to social and political relationships; but that does not affect this very compendious account of his fundamental position.

3 I.e., Assistant Guardians (less highly trained philosophically), and the so-called third class (without philosophical education).

4 The "popular" character of the *Laws* is the subject of Herwig Görgemanns, *Beiträge zur Interpretation von Platons Nomoi* (Munich, 1960).

5 Dates: *Republic,* probably 380s and/or 370s; *Politicus,* probably middle or late 360s; the *Laws,* a jumbo-dialogue, presumably occupied Plato at least intermittently for some years before his death in 347.

6 *Pol.* 292b–293c; cf. 296a*ff.*

7 *Pol.* 287bff. W. K. C. Guthrie, *A History of Greek Philosophy,* vol. 5 (Cambridge, 1978), 188–9, provides a handy list of them. Plato would have agreed with Talleyrand: "War is much too serious a thing to be left to military men."

8 *Phil.* 16b–c.

9 *Pol.* 285d.

10 I cannot find that this point is made in so many words; but it is hard to see how the Statesman can carry out his task of "weaving" (*Pol.* 302b) without performing many "divisions," notably of characters of men and the offices they are to fill (311a). Cf. the final sentence of Julius M. E. Moravcsik, "The Anatomy of Plato's Divisions," in *Exegesis and Argument,* ed. E. N. Lee, Alexander P. D. Mourelatos, and R. M. Rorty (Assen, 1973), 324–48: "Within the context of Plato's thought, the Method of Division should be viewed as yet one more attempt to link the theoretical and the practical, and to insist that the latter can be solved successfully only if such solutions are based on an adequate conception of the former."

11 Guthrie, *History of Greek Philosophy,* 5:168, 172–3, 175–80. Constraints of space forbid a rehearsal of the crucial passages, which are *Pol.* 262a–b, 285d–286b (on which see G. E. L. Owen, "Plato on the Undepictable," in *Exegesis and Argument,* ed. Lee, Mourelatos, and Rorty [Assen, 1973]: and J. B. Skemp, *Plato's Statesman,* 2d ed. [Bristol, 1987], 241*ff*), 286d8–9, 300c–e. The problem is bound up with the wider and controversial issue of what role, if any, the Forms play in Plato's later thought in general, not merely in political theory; see G. E. L. Owen, "The Place of the *Timaeus* in Plato's Later Dialogues," *Classical Quarterly* 3(1953): 79–95; and the huge later literature, summarized by Guthrie, *History of Greek Philosophy,* 5: 243. On the ontological status of the Forms assumed in "division," see Moravcsik, "Anatomy of Plato's Divisions."

12 *Pol.* 293a, 297b–c; cf. *Laws* 875c–d.

13 *Pol.* 300c. Six constitutions are then distinguished, apart from rule by a statesman with *politikē epistēmē:* (i–iii) *with law,* democracy (least good), aristocracy (middlingly good), monarchy (best); (iv–vi) *without law,* tyranny (worst), oligarchy (middlingly bad), democracy (least bad). The key to the gradings is that democracy is least powerful for good or ill (303a), because of the fragmentation of power among many people (presumably agreement and concerted action are hard to achieve); contrariwise, single rule is most powerful (708e–712a, in the course of a different grading of constitutions, makes explicit the point about the relationship between numbers and power).

14 Cf. *Laws* 734e–735a.

15 The point of the myth of the *Politicus* (268d–274d) is that in the current cosmic era mankind is on its own: Men, not gods, administer men's lives (274d*ff*; cf. *Laws* 732e, 853c*ff*). The value of practical experience is recognized at *Pol.* 300b.

16 *Pol.* 294a*ff*, 300c–d.

17 *Laws* 961c.

18 The various categories of members are set out, with slight discrepancies, at 951d*ff* and 961a–b.

19 961c–968e describes the Council's functions and course of study. There are adumbrations of it at 632c and 817e–818a.

20 965c2*ff*. Presumably a preliminary answer is that the virtues are all "one" in that they are all *knowledge*.

21 966c–968b; cf. 817e–818a, and indeed the whole of Book X.

22 See, e.g., the passages cited in note 28, and cf. R. F. Stalley, *An Introduction to Plato's Laws* (Oxford, 1983) 136, on 630e–631a.

23 Useful discussions of the Forms in the *Laws* are V. Brochard, "Les Lois de Platon et la théorie des Idées," in *Etudes de philosophie ancienne et de philosophie moderne*, ed. V. Delbos (Paris, 1926), 151–68; Guthrie, *History of Greek Philosophy*, 5:378–81 (both asserting their presence); and Stalley, *Introduction to Plato's Laws*, 133–6 (skeptical). 967e seems to refer to the use to be made of philosophy (if that is what "the Muse" means: see Saunders, "Notes on the *Laws* of Plato," *Bulletin of the Institute of Classical Studies*, supp. 28 [London, 1972], n. 10) to "arrive at practices of moral character and at rules consistently." He who can do this has more than "the demotic virtues" (968a2).

24 *Phil.* 62a*ff* even toys with the notion that a man could know the Forms but have an inadequate grasp of their instantiations in this world. Nor does *Laws* 967e tell us *how* philosophy is used to arrive at moral rules (cf. note 23).

25 *Pol.* 262a*ff*, 285a–b; cf. *Phdr.* 265e and note 28.

26 I cannot go into its literary merits and demerits. All human life is in it, and one can perhaps catch something of Plato himself: the benevolent testiness of 761c5–d3 (did he enjoy a hot bath, and had he suffered from incompetent doctors?) and the almost comic outrage of 918e–919b (had he been stung by innkeepers?).

27 *Laws* 660d–663d, 732e–734e, 743c; cf. the unyielding assertiveness of 860d*ff*, on "no one is evil voluntarily" (on which more later in this chapter).

28 For instance, there is hesitation reminiscent of the *Politicus* in the difficulties over division into precise categories at 866d7*ff*. The division he eventually adopts is "closest to the *truth*" (not just "most convenient" or the like, 867b3). Contrast 861b, where Plato is certain that existing

legislators have divided wrongly. On the other hand, he is not at all sure how to distinguish magic from medicine, 932e*ff.*

29 859b: "We are turning into legislators, but are not so yet" – a remark that is (perhaps) a disclaimer of the status of a "true" legislator.

30 715e*ff.*

31 I forbear to list the dozens of passages in the *Laws* necessary for setting out the hierarchy in its full complexity: They would amount to a large proportion of the text. As to knowledge, see esp. 690b and 875c–d, in addition to the description of the Nocturnal Council, 951c*ff,* 960*ff.*

32 964a*ff.*

33 858a–c, 707e–708e; see Glenn R. Morrow, "The Demiurge in Politics: the *Timaeus* and the *Laws,*" *Proceedings of the American Philosophical Association* 27 (1953–4): 5–23; André Laks, "Raison et plaisir: pour une charactérisation des *Lois* de Platon," in *La naissance de la raison en Grèce,* ed. J. F. Mattéi (Paris, 1990), 291–303; and Laks, "Legislation and Demiurgy: On the Relationship between Plato's *Republic* and *Laws,*" *Classical Antiquity* 9 (1990): 209–29.

34 736a–c.

35 *Pol.* 299b–e; cf. *Phaedrus* on the orator's need to "know souls" (269c*ff*) and *Laws* 738e. See Saunders, " 'The RAND Corporation of Antiquity'? Plato's Academy and Greek Politics," in *Studies in Honour of T. B. L. Webster,* ed. J. H. Betts, J. T. Hooker, and J. R. Green (Bristol, 1986), 1:207–8 and refs. Reporting on opinion and practice in the state is presumably one of the functions of the promising young men who are the "eyes" of the Nocturnal Council (964e–965a). We have to realize, of course, that information gathering is, for Plato, not simply an exercise of academic sociology, much less undertaken in order to respond to whatever "public opinion" wants; his clipboard is in the service of political control.

36 Cf. the Stranger's topographical inquiries about Magnesia at the start of Book IV.

37 See, e.g., 841a–842a, on high and less high sexual standards, and cf. 858a.

38 739a–e; but the whole sequence from 736c to 746d should be read.

39 811c–812a.

40 Glenn R. Morrow, *Plato's Cretan City: A Historical Interpretation of the Laws* (Princeton, 1900), 297–398; Stalley, *Introduction to Plato's Laws,* 123–36.

41 951a*ff;* cf. later in this chapter.

42 802a*ff,* 817a–e, 858c–e.

43 653b, and Book II in general.

44 718a–723d. The language of the preambles is somewhat heightened, and there is frequent use of colorful myth.

45 See further discussion near the end of this chapter.

46 856e–864c, a difficult text, elucidated in Saunders, *Plato: The Laws* (Harmondsworth, 1970), 361, 367–9; cf. 933e*ff.*

47 860d; cf. 734b. The formulation is a version of the "Socratic" paradox, "no one does wrong voluntarily." For early formulations of this paradox, see *Prt.* 345d–e and *Grg.* 509e.

48 This is the subject of my *Plato's Penal Code* (Oxford, 1991). Plato's modifications are rarely evident from a mere reading of the *Laws* in isolation from the sources for Greek law.

49 Note how they are encouraged to attend trials: 855d. Good law *educates:* it is an expression of reason (957c; cf. 714a1–2, 857c–e).

50 728c, as elucidated by Saunders, "Notes on the *Laws,* n. 23; and Saunders, "On Plato, *Laws* 728bc," *Liverpool Classical Monthly* 9 (1984): 23–4. Cf. Mary Margaret Mackenzie, *Plato on Punishment* (Berkeley, 1981), 196.

51 952d*ff.*

52 A number convenient for administrative purposes: 737e–738a.

53 This paragraph extracts salient points from 736c–738a, 739e–741a, 744a–745e, 778a–779d, 794a, 842b–850d, 919d–920c, which should be read *in extenso.* As to trade, though Magnesia is not a commercial state, it recognizes the necessity of a certain minimum of trade internal to itself; see the stringent regulations at 915c–922a. The lot is not only inalienable, but must always retain a certain minimum of property (744d–e); poverty below this level is not permitted.

54 631b–d, 661a–e, 726e*ff,* 741e.

55 On family law, see Morrow, *Plato's Cretan City;* Josef Bisinger, *Der Agrarstaat in Platons Gesetzen* (Wiesbaden, 1925); E. Klingenberg, *Platons νομοὶ γεωργικοί und das positive griechische Recht* (Berlin, 1976); and Walter G. Becker, *Platons Gesetze und das griechische Familienrecht* (Munich, 1932).

56 Cf. 779d–780a, 788a–c, 909d–910.

57 744e–745b. There are also strict rules of bequest and inheritance, 923a*ff.*

58 See, e.g., 717b–718a, 729c, 771a–776b, 783b–785b, 841c–842a.

59 779d–781d. See Morrow, *Plato's Cretan City,* 393–8 for the interpretation of this section. The inclusion of women is, as the Stranger indicates, a sensational innovation; see in general E. David. "The Spartan Sussitia and Plato's *Laws,* " *American Journal of Philology* 99 (1978): 486–95,

60 756e*ff;* cf. *Pol.* 300e*ff* and note 13; he means in effect an aristocracy. On 708e*ff,* where for the founding of the state Plato prefers a good single ruler, see Stalley, *Introduction to Plato's Laws,* 90–2; cf. also 691b*ff* on "middle" or "mixed" constitutions in history.

61 On "arithmetical" as opposed to "geometrical" equality (*in*equality

granted to *un*equals) see also Aristotle, *Politics* III ix, xii; V i, and the illuminating article by F. David Harvey, "Two Kinds of Equality," *Classica et Mediaevalia* 26 (1965): 101–46.

62 *Pol.* 292e–293a, 297b; cf. *Rep.* 494a.

63 Admittedly, the lot may enter into the appointment of priests (759b–c) and certain priests are indeed members of the Nocturnal Council (951d8). But priesthood is not in itself a qualification for membership: awards of merit are necessary. This requirement may point to the high officials known as Scrutineers (of other officials at the end of their term, 946b), who may in exceptional circumstances be elected by lot (946a*ff*); but it is not clear that Scrutineers are priests, nor whether, if so, they automatically count as having won merit awards. Cf. Morrow, *Plato's Cretan City*, 503.

64 964e–965a; cf. 758c5–d2. I therefore find it hard to accept Charles L. Griswold, Jr.'s recent conclusion, which in any case conflicts with 756e, that "*politike episteme* and the virtues will best flourish in the context of a *democracy* [italics added] ruled by law." See Griswold, "*politike episteme* in Plato's *Statesman*," in *Essays in Ancient Greek Philosophy*, vol. 3, ed. John P. Anton and Anthony Preus (Albany, 1989), 162.

65 753a*ff.* No doubt this title is intended to be reminiscent of the Guardians of the *Republic.*

66 Cf. *Rep.* 378a.

67 Morrow, *Plato's Cretan City*, 157–78.

68 756b–e.

69 Aristotle, *Politics* 1281a11–28, 1318a26. Even if all members of all classes elect from all classes compulsorily, a small first (rich) class still has ninety Councillors, just as many as a large fourth (poor) class.

70 764a.

71 744a*ff*; cf. Aristotle, *Politics* 1283a16*ff*, 1301a25*ff*; cf. 1280a22–5.

72 Compare the mixing of social classes in the arrangement of marriages, 773a–e.

73 761e*ff*, 928b, 941a, 946d–e, 947e–948b, 955c–d.

74 Office holding in Magnesia, as in Athens, is generally limited to a set number of years. On the scrutiny, *euthuna*, an Athenian practice that Plato adopts enthusiastically, see 945b*ff.*

75 E.g., 761d–e, 847b.

76 The world's experience of Nazism, fascism, and Communism prompted from the 1930s onward a series of attacks on Plato's political thought on grounds of totalitarianism. The most vigorous assault was by K. R. Popper, *The Open Society and its Enemies*, vol. 1 (New York, 1963); the fullest defense was by Ronald B. Levinson, *In Defense of Plato* (Cambridge, Mass., 1953).

77 875d; cf. earlier in this chapter.

78 700a, 715b–d, "servants of the laws"; cf. 957b. Law is after all "the distribution of reason" (714a2).

79 925d*ff*, and cf. their discretion in the fixing of punishments, discussed earlier in the chapter. The discretion is, of course, not unfettered, but subject to firm guidelines.

80 951a–c, and note the description of virtue as the harmony of emotion and reason (653a–c; cf. 688b).

81 952b.

82 Just how they are to do so is, however, not clear. Plato is reluctant to countenance frequent changes to Magnesian law, since it is already very good (and probably also because such changes suggest a state unsure of its moral aims). But he allows refinement of them, especially in the early years of the state, at least in some areas (769b*ff*, 722a–d, 957a–b). No doubt principled adjustments suggested by the Nocturnal Council would be more acceptable to him than ad hoc tinkering. See Morrow's discussion, *Plato's Cretan City*, 500–3; cf. *Pol.* 299b*ff* on excessive fidelity to existing laws, and the need for *zētein*, "inquiry," "research."

83 766d, 768a, 875e–876b, 855c–856a; cf. Auguste Diès and Louis Gernet, "Introduction," *Platon: Oeuvres complètes*, vol. 2, part 1, *Les Lois* (Paris, 1951), cxl–cxliv.

84 768b–c, 956c.

85 See Saunders, *Plato: The Laws*, 31–2; Morrow, *Plato's Cretan City*, 295–6.

86 766d–768a, 855c–856a, 875e–876e, 936e–938c, 949a–b, 956d–958a.

87 937d–938c.

88 Cf. 679b–c. Note how the discussion of these states at 742c*ff* is related to the "starting-point" and wish" of the legislator (on which see also 770c*ff*). There is no asceticism here, no belief that poverty ennobles the soul. Cf. Benjamin Franklin: "[I inserted in my *Almanac*] proverbial sentences, chiefly such as inculcated industry and frugality as the means of procuring wealth, and thereby securing virtue; it being more difficult for a man in want to act always honestly, as, to use here one of those proverbs, *it is hard for an empty sack to stand upright*" (*The Autobiography of Benjamin Franklin*, chap. 7; his italics).

89 See in particular 742c–744a and 770b–771a, and cf. 802c2–4 on the control of dancing, etc.

90 907b–910d.

91 716d*ff*, 803e1–2, 816c–d, 828a–d, 909d*ff*.

92 885b.

93 905b.

94 903b*ff*.

95 See 885c*ff*, esp. 886d *sophoi*, "clever," and 908e. His description of the *euētheia*, "naiveté," of early men, who believed what they were told, is a real *cri de coeur* (679c).

96 770c–d, 780a*ff*, 796c, 804d*ff*, 833c–d.

97 785b. It is slightly curious that we hear directly of the provision only this once. No song-and-dance is made about it (contrast the cases of the communal meals, education, and the army). But David Cohen's review of the indirect evidence ("The Legal Status and Political Role of Women in Plato's *Laws*," *Revue Internationale des Droits de l'Antiquité* 34 [1987]: 27–40) convinces me that this passage is to be taken seriously. Yet what voting rights they have is rather less clear. I add one more indication that Plato regarded female virtue as not essentially inferior to male: In his penal code, penalties are frequently graded in severity on the basis of the social class (free, slave; citizen, alien) of the offenders, and therefore the presumed level of their virtue, but *never* by reference to their sex (except the one special case at 932b–c, on the basis of the same age distinction as at 805e). For a full review of the evidence for Plato's treatment of women in the *Laws*, and a less favorable assessment than mine, see Susan Moller Okin, *Women in Western Political Thought* (Princeton, 1979).

98 *Laws* 805a, 806c.

99 *Rep.* 451b*ff* may well imply that in Callipolis women of the second and third classes will be doctors, soldiers, etc., on an equality with men.

100 See *Laws* 781a–b, *Rep.* 455d–e.

101 The main discussion is at *Laws* 776b–778a.

102 On slaves in the *Laws*, the classic investigation is Glenn R. Morrow, *Plato's Law of Slavery in its Relation to Greek Law* (Urbana, Ill., 1939).

103 777d: "[Masters should] train them properly, according them respect not only for their (i.e., the slaves') sakes but even more for their own." Good training of slaves conduces to masters' *eudaimonia*, which is diminished if their slaves do not enjoy such *eudaimonia* as they are capable of; for then they become rebellious. Refraining from ill-treatment of slaves will "sow the seeds of virtue" (777e1) – in slaves? or in their masters, who thereby avoid sullying their own souls?

104 Cf. Morrow, *Plato's Law of Slavery*, 43–4.

105 850a–d, 941e.

106 *Pol.* 283b–287b.

107 See note 10.

108 This position is in many ways Aristotle's too: The good *polis* provides the material environment, and social and political structure, in which human *aretē*, and hence human *eudaimonia*, can flourish.

109 At 967e–968a the members of the Nocturnal Council are required to

have certain attainments "in addition to the demotic virtues": Some sort of progress from a lower level of virtue to a higher seems to be envisaged.

110 He means, e.g., 660d–663d.

111 For further discussion of this important question, see Laks, "Raison et plaisir," and Laks, "Legislation and Demiurgy."

112 *Rep.* 471c–474b; cf. 540d–541b.

113 E. g., Diogenes Laertius, III 23, and in general Saunders, "The RAND Corporation of Antiquity?," 1:202–3 and refs. The evidence for the Academy's interventions in Greek politics is, however, of uncertain reliability. Some of it comes from the *Letters* that pass under Plato's name; but some of them are, and all of them may be, spurious. Even so, one should read at least the *Seventh* and *Eighth Letters;* there are several points of contact with the *Laws* (see Glenn R. Morrow, *Plato's Epistles,* 2nd ed. [Indianapolis, 1962]). On the relevance to his political theory of Plato's own attempts at political reform in Sicily, see my translation, *Plato: The Laws,* 27–8, 545–7.

114 *Laws* 968b.

115 969d.

BIBLIOGRAPHY

All works cited in this volume, together with some additional material, are listed below under one or more headings. Editions of the Greek texts of individual works of Plato are classified with the secondary literature on those texts, as are translations of individual works with commentary. The following headings are used:

- I. Plato
  - A. Comprehensive Greek texts
  - B. Comprehensive translations
  - C. Background to Plato: History and culture
  - D. Background to Plato: Philosophy and science
  - E. General discussions of Plato's thought
  - F. Methods of interpretation
  - G. Chronological and linguistic studies
  - H. Socrates and the early dialogues
  - I. Metaphysics and epistemology
  - J. Ethics, political philosophy, and moral psychology
  - K. Art and poetry
  - L. Eros
  - M. Mathematics
  - N. Studies of single works
    1. *Meno*
    2. *Phaedo*
    3. *Symposium*
    4. *Republic*
    5. *Phaedrus*
    6. *Parmenides*
    7. *Theaetetus*
    8. *Timaeus*
    9. *Sophist*

I. PLATO

A. COMPREHENSIVE GREEK TEXTS

A commonly used edition of the entire corpus is:

Burnet, John. *Platonis Opera.* 5 vols. Oxford: Clarendon Press, 1900–7. (Often called the Oxford Classical Text [O.C.T.].)

There is also a twelve volume edition of Plato's works (called the Loeb Classical Library) with Greek text and English translation (by various hands) on facing pages published in Cambridge, Mass., by Harvard University Press and in London by William Heinemann (reprinted 1961–84). Similarly, there is a fourteen-volume Greek–French edition by various hands (published "sous le patronage de l'Association Guillaume Budé" and hence referred to as the Budé edition) published in Paris by Société d'Edition, Les Belles Lettres, 1951–64.

B. COMPREHENSIVE TRANSLATIONS

New translations into English, many of them accompanied by commentary, emerge nearly every year. In addition, one can generally rely on (1) translations of Plato's works by various hands published by Penguin Books (Harmondsworth, England) and by Hackett Publishing Company (Indianapolis). The translations in the Loeb Classical Library and the Budé edition mentioned above are also worth consulting in many cases. Careful study of particular passages is often aided by consulting different translations. A widely used and convenient one-volume translation by various hands of all of the dialogues (except those of questionable authenticity) and letters can be found in:

Hamilton, Edith, and Cairns, Huntington, editors. *The Collected Dialogues of Plato.* New York: Pantheon, 1961. Princeton: Princeton University Press, 1971.

A multivolume translation, widely used for nearly a century and still worth consulting, is:

Jowett, Benjamin. *The Dialogues of Plato.* 3d ed. 5 vols. Oxford: Clarendon Press, 1892. 4th ed. 4 vols. Oxford: Clarendon Press, 1953.

An excellent translation of the entire corpus by a single hand is under way, beginning with:

Allen, R. E. *The Dialogues of Plato.* Vol. 1. New Haven: Yale University Press, 1984. (Contains *Euthyphro, Apology, Crito, Meno, Gorgias,* and *Menexenus.*)

C. BACKGROUND TO PLATO: HISTORY AND CULTURE

Adkins, Arthur W. H. *Merit and Responsibility: A Study in Greek Values.* Oxford: Clarendon Press, 1960.
"Homeric Values and Homeric Society." *Journal of Hellenic Studies* 91 (1971): 1–14.
"Merit, Responsibility, and Thucydides." *Classical Quarterly* 25 (1975): 209–20.
"Problems in Greek Popular Morality." *Classical Philology* 73 (1978): 143–58.
Borgeaud, Phillipe. *The Cult of Pan in Ancient Greece.* Chicago: University of Chicago Press, 1988.
Bremmer, Jan. *The Early Greek Concept of the Soul.* Princeton: Princeton University Press, 1983.
Burkert, Walter. *Orphism and Bacchic Mysteries: New Evidence and Old Problems of Interpretation.* Berkeley: Center for Hermeneutical Studies in Hellenistic and Modern Culture, 1977.
Homo Necans: The Anthropology of Ancient Greek Sacrificial Ritual and Myth. Berkeley: University of California Press, 1983.
Greek Religion. Translated by John Raffan. Cambridge, Mass.: Harvard University Press, 1985.
Ancient Mystery Cults. Cambridge, Mass.: Harvard University Press, 1987.
Cohen, David. "Law, Society, and Homosexuality in Classical Athens." *Past and Present* 117 (1987): 3–21.
Cole, Susan Guettel. "New Evidence for the Mysteries of Dionysos." *Greek, Roman and Byzantine Studies* 21 (1980): 223–38.
Creed, J. L. "Moral Values in the Age of Thucydides." *Classical Quarterly* 23 (1973): 213–31.
de Romilly, Jacqueline. *Magic and Rhetoric in Ancient Greece.* Cambridge, Mass.: Harvard University Press, 1975.

de Ste. Croix, G. E. M. *The Class Struggle in the Ancient Greek World from the Archaic Age to the Arab Conquests.* Ithaca, N.Y.: Cornell University Press, 1981.

Detienne, Marcel. *Dionysos Slain.* Baltimore: Johns Hopkins University Press, 1979.

Deubner, L. *Attische Feste.* Berlin: H. Keller, 1932.

Dodds, E. R. *The Greeks and the Irrational.* Berkeley: University of California Press, 1951.

"The Religion of the Ordinary Man in Classical Greece." In *The Ancient Concept of Progress and Other Essays on Greek Literature and Belief,* edited by E. R. Dodds, 140–55. Oxford: Clarendon Press, 1973.

Dover, K. J. *Greek Popular Morality in the Time of Plato and Aristotle.* Oxford: Basil Blackwell, 1974.

Greek Homosexuality. Cambridge, Mass.: Harvard University Press, 1978.

Easterling, P. E., and Muir, J. V., editors. *Greek Religion and Society.* Cambridge: Cambridge University Press, 1985.

Ehrenberg, Victor. *From Solon to Socrates: Greek History and Civilization during the Sixth and Fifth Century B.C.* 2d ed. London: Methuen, 1973.

Finley, M. I., editor. *The Legacy of Greece: A New Appraisal.* Oxford: Clarendon Press, 1981.

Fontenrose, Joseph. *The Delphic Oracle.* Berkeley: University of California Press, 1978.

Foucault, Michel. *L'usage des plaisirs.* Paris: Gallimard, 1984.

Graf, Fritz. *Eleusis und die orphische Dichtung Athens in vorhellenistischer Zeit.* Berlin: Walter de Gruyter, 1974.

Grote, George. *A History of Greece.* 6th ed. 10 vols. London: Dent, 1888.

Guthrie, W. K. C. *The Greeks and their Gods.* London: Methuen, 1950.

Havelock, Eric. *Preface to Plato.* Cambridge, Mass.: Harvard University Press, 1963.

Heinrichs, Albert. "Changing Dionysiac Identities." In *Jewish and Christian Self Definition,* edited by Ben F. Meyer and E. P. Sanders. Vol. 3. London: SCM Press, 1982.

Hornblower, Simon. *The Greek World 479–322 BC.* London: Methuen, 1983.

Hussey, E. L. "Thucydidean History and Democritean Theory." In *Crux* (*Essays Presented to G.E.M. de Ste Croix*), edited by Paul Cartledge and F. D. Harvey, 118–38. London: Duckworth, 1985.

Jones, A. H. M. *Athenian Democracy.* Oxford: Basil Blackwell, 1957.

Kidd, Ian. "The Case of Homicide in Plato's *Euthyphro.*" In *Owls to Athens: Essays on Classical Subjects presented to Sir Kenneth Dover,* edited by E. M. Craik, 213–22. Oxford: Clarendon Press, 1990.

Kitzinger, Rachel. "Alphabets and Writing." In *Civilization of the Ancient*

Mediterranean, edited by Michael Grant and Rachel Kitzinger, 1: 397–420. New York: Scribner's, 1988.

Lasserre, François. *La figure d'Eros dans la poésie Grecque.* Lausanne: Imprimeries Réunies, 1946.

Lewis, David. "The Political Background of Democritus." In *Owls to Athens: Essays on Classical Subjects presented to Sir Kenneth Dover,* edited by E. M. Craik, 151–4. Oxford: Clarendon Press, 1990.

Lloyd-Jones, Hugh. *The Justice of Zeus.* 2d ed. Berkeley: University of California Press, 1983.

Long, A. A. "Morals and Values in Homer." *Journal of Hellenic Studies* 90 (1970): 121–39.

MacDowell, Douglas M. *Andokides: On the Mysteries.* Oxford: Oxford University Press, 1962.

The Law in Classical Athens. London: Thames and Hudson, 1978.

Mikalson, Jon D., *Athenian Popular Religion.* Chapel Hill: University of North Carolina Press, 1983.

Mossé, Claude. *Athens in Decline 404–86 B.C.* Translated from the French by Jean Stewart. London: Routledge & Kegan Paul, 1973.

Mylonas, G. *Eleusis and the Eleusinian Mysteries.* Princeton: Princeton University Press, 1961.

Nilsson, Martin. *Greek Folk Religion.* New York: Columbia University Press, 1940.

Greek Piety. Oxford: Oxford University Press, 1948.

A History of Greek Religion. Oxford: Oxford University Press, 1952.

Ober, Josiah. *Mass and Elite in Democratic Athens: Rhetoric, Ideology, and the Power of the People.* Princeton: Princeton University Press, 1989.

Parke, H. W. *Greek Oracles.* London: Hutchinson, 1967.

The Oracles of Zeus. Cambridge: Harvard University Press, 1967.

Parke, H. W. *Festivals of the Athenians.* Ithaca, N.Y.: Cornell University Press, 1977.

Parker, Robert. "Greek Religion." In *The Oxford History of the Classical World,* edited by John Boardman, Jaspar Griffin, and Oswyn Murray, 254–74. Oxford: Oxford University Press, 1986.

Miasma: Pollution and Purification in Early Greek Religion. Oxford: Clarendon Press, 1983.

Powell, C. "Religion and the Sicilian Expedition." *Historia* 28 (1979): 15–31.

Richardson, N. J. "Early Greek Views about Life after Death." In *Greek Religion and Society,* edited by P. E. Easterling and J. V. Muir. Cambridge: Cambridge University Press, 1985.

Roberts, J. W. *City of Sokrates: An Introduction to Classical Athens.* London: Routledge & Kegan Paul, 1984.

Samuel, Alan E. "Calendars and Time-Telling." In *Civilization of the An-*

cient Mediterranean, edited by Michael Grant and Rachel Kitzinger, 1:389–95. New York: Scribner's, 1988.

Scully, Vincent. *The Earth, the Temple, and the Gods: Greek Sacred Architecture.* New Haven: Yale University Press, 1979.

Snell, Bruno. *The Discovery of the Mind in Greek Philosophy and Literature.* New York: Dover, 1982.

Solmsen, Friedrich. *Intellectual Experiments of the Greek Enlightenment.* Princeton: Princeton University Press, 1975.

Stephens, Susan A. "Book Production." In *Civilization of the Ancient Mediterranean,* edited by Michael Grant and Rachel Kitzinger, 1:421–36. New York: Scribner's, 1988.

Taylor, C. C. W. "Popular Morality and Unpopular Philosophy." In *Owls to Athens: Essays on Classical Subjects presented to Sir Kenneth Dover,* edited by E. M. Craik, 233–43. Oxford: Clarendon Press, 1990.

Walbank, F. W. "The Problem of Greek Nationality." In *Selected Papers: Studies in Greek and Roman History and Historiography,* chap. 1. New York: Cambridge University Press, 1985.

D. BACKGROUND TO PLATO: PHILOSOPHY AND SCIENCE

Barnes, Jonathan. *The Presocratic Philosophers.* 2 vols. London: Routledge & Kegan Paul, 1979.

Cope, E. M. "The Sophists." *Journal of Philology* 1 (1854): 145–88.

Cornford, Francis MacDonald. *Principium Sapientiae.* Cambridge: Cambridge University Press, 1952.

Dicks, D. R. *Early Greek Astronomy to Aristotle.* Ithaca, N.Y.: Cornell University Press, 1970.

Diels, Hermann, and Kranz, Walther, editors. *Die Fragmente der Vorsokratiker,* 6th ed. Berlin: Weidmann, 1952.

Furley, David J. "Anaxagoras in Response to Parmenides." In *New Essays on Plato and the Pre-Socratics,* edited by R. A. Shiner and J. King-Farlow. *Canadian Journal of Philosophy,* supplementary vol. 2 (1976): 61–85.

The Greek Cosmologists. Vol. 1, *The Formation of the Atomic Theory and its Earliest Critics.* Cambridge: Cambridge University Press, 1987.

Furth, Montgomery. "Elements of Eleatic Ontology," *Journal of the History of Philosophy* 6 (1968): 111–32. Reprinted in *The Pre-Socratics: A Collection of Critical Essays,* edited by Alexander P. D. Mourelatos, 241–70. Garden City, N.Y.: Anchor Books, Doubleday, 1974.

Gerson, Lloyd. *God and Greek Philosophy.* London: Routledge, 1991.

Gillispie, Charles Coulston, editor. *Dictionary of Scientific Biography.* 16 vols. New York: Scribner's, 1970–80.

Heath, Thomas. *A History of Greek Mathematics.* Vol. 1. Oxford: Clarendon Press, 1921.

Irwin, Terence. *Classical Thought.* Oxford: Oxford University Press, 1989.

Jaeger, Werner. *The Theology of the Early Greek Philosophers.* Oxford: Oxford University Press, 1947.

Kahn, Charles H. "Pythagorean Philosophy Before Plato." In *The Pre-Socratics: A Collection of Critical Essays,* edited by Alexander P. D. Mourelatos, 161–85. Garden City, N.Y.: Anchor Books, Doubleday, 1974.

The Art and Thought of Heraclitus. Cambridge: Cambridge University Press, 1979.

Kerferd, G. B. *The Sophistic Movement.* London: Cambridge University Press, 1981.

Kirk, G. S., Raven, J. E., and Schofield, M. *The Presocratic Philosophers.* 2d ed. Cambridge: Cambridge University Press, 1983.

Lloyd, G. E. R. *The Revolutions of Wisdom: Studies in the Claims and Practice of Ancient Greek Science.* Berkeley: University of California Press, 1987.

Morrison, J. S. "Antiphon." In *The Older Sophists: A Complete Translation by Several Hands of the Fragments in Die Fragmente der Vorsokratiker, edited by Diels-Kranz,* edited by Rosamund Kent Sprague. Columbia: University of South Carolina Press, 1972.

Owen, G. E. L. "Eleatic Questions." *Classical Quarterly* 10 (1960): 84–102. Reprinted in G. E. L. Owen, *Logic, Science, and Dialectic: Collected Papers in Greek Philosophy,* edited by Martha Nussbaum, 3–26. Ithaca: N.Y.: Cornell University Press, 1986.

Sidgwick, Henry. "The Sophists." In *Lectures on the Philosophy of Kant and Other Philosophical Lectures and Essays.* London: Macmillan, 1905.

Taylor, C. C. W. "Pleasure, Knowledge, and Sensation in Democritus." *Phronesis* 12 (1967): 6–27.

van der Waerden, B. L. *Science Awakening.* New York: Oxford University Press, 1963.

Vlastos, Gregory. "On Heracleitus." *American Journal of Philology* 76 (1955): 337–68.

"Ethics and Physics in Democritus." In *Studies in Presocratic Philosophy,* edited by David J. Furley and R. E. Allen, 2:381–408. London: Routledge & Kegan Paul, 1975.

E. GENERAL DISCUSSIONS OF PLATO'S THOUGHT

Cherniss, Harold. "The Philosophical Economy of the Theory of Ideas." *American Journal of Philology* 57 (1936): 445–56. Reprinted in *Studies in Plato's Metaphysics,* edited by R. E. Allen, 1–12. London: Routledge & Kegan Paul, 1965. Also reprinted in Harold Cherniss, *Selected Papers,* edited by Leonardo Taran, 121–32. Leiden: E.J. Brill, 1977.

"Some War-Time Publications Concerning Plato." *American Journal of Philology* 68 (1947): 113–46, 225–65. Reprinted in Harold Cherniss, *Selected Papers,* edited by Leonardo Taran, 142–216. Leiden: E.J. Brill, 1977.

"Review of G. C. Field, *Plato and his Contemporaries.*" *American Journal of Philology* 54 (1978): 79–83. Reprinted in Harold Cherniss, *Selected Papers,* edited by Leonardo Taran, 133–7. Leiden: E.J. Brill, 1977.

Crombie, I. M. *An Examination of Plato's Doctrines.* 2 vols. London: Routledge & Kegan Paul. New York: Humanities Press, 1962, 1963.

Field, G. C. *Plato and his Contemporaries: A Study in Fourth Century Life and Thought.* London: Methuen, 1930. 3d ed., 1967.

Findlay, J. N. *Plato: The Written and Unwritten Doctrines.* New York: Humanities Press, 1974.

Friedländer, Paul. *Plato.* Translated by Hans Meyerhoff. 3 vols. New York: Pantheon, 1958–69.

Gosling, J. C. B. *Plato.* London: Routledge & Kegan Paul, 1973.

Grote, George. *Plato and the Other Companions of Sokrates.* 2d ed. 3 vols. London: J. Murray, 1867.

Grube, G. M. A. *Plato's Thought.* 2d ed. Indianapolis: Hackett, 1980.

Guthrie, W. K. C. *A History of Greek Philosophy.* Vols. 1–5. Cambridge: Cambridge University Press, 1962, 1965, 1969, 1975, 1978.

Reale, Giovanni. *A History of Ancient Philosophy.* Vol. 2, *Plato and Aristotle,* edited and translated from the 5th Italian edition by John R. Caton. Albany: State University of New York Press, 1990.

Ritter, Constantin. *Platon: Sein Lebens, seine Schriften, seine Lehre.* 2 vols. Munich: C.H. Beck, 1910.

Robinson, R., and Denniston, J. D. "Plato." In *Oxford Classical Dictionary,* 2d ed., edited by N. G. L. Hammond and H. H. Scullard, 839–42. Oxford: Clarendon Press, 1970.

Ryle, Gilbert. "Plato." In *The Encyclopedia of Philosophy,* edited by Paul Edwards, 6:314–33. New York: Macmillan and Free Press, 1967.

Shorey, Paul. *What Plato Said.* Chicago: University of Chicago Press, 1933.

The Unity of Plato's Thought. Chicago: University of Chicago Press, 1960.

Taylor, A. E. *Plato the Man and his Work.* 5th ed. London: Methuen, 1948.

Vlastos, Gregory. *Platonic Studies.* 2d ed. Princeton: Princeton University Press, 1981.

Wilamowitz-Moellendorff, Ulrich von. *Platon.* 2d ed. 2 vols. Berlin: Weidmann, 1920.

F. METHODS OF INTERPRETATION

Burnyeat, Myles. "Sphinx Without a Secret," *New York Review of Books* 32 (May 30, 1985): 30–6.

Coventry, Lucinda. "The Role of the Interlocutor in Plato's Dialogues." In *Characterization and Individuality in Greek Literature,* edited by Christopher Pelling, 174–96. Oxford: Clarendon Press, 1990.

Derrida, Jacques. "Plato's Pharmacy." In *Dissemination,* translated, with an introduction and additional notes by Barbara Johnson, 61–171. Chicago: University of Chicago Press, 1981.

Griswold, Charles L., Jr., editor. *Platonic Writings, Platonic Readings.* New York: Routledge, 1988.

Shorey, Paul. *The Unity of Plato's Thought.* Chicago: University of Chicago Press, 1960.

Stokes, Michael C. *Plato's Socratic Conversations: Drama and Dialectic in Three Dialogues.* Baltimore: Johns Hopkins University Press, 1986.

Strauss, Leo. *Persecution and the Art of Writing.* Glencoe, Ill.: Free Press, 1952.

Tigerstedt, E. N. *Interpreting Plato.* Uppsala: Almquist & Wiksell International, 1977.

Weingartner, Rudolf H. *The Unity of the Platonic Dialogue.* Indianapolis: Bobbs-Merrill, 1973.

G. CHRONOLOGICAL AND LINGUISTIC STUDIES

Arnim, H. von. "Sprachliche Forschungen zur Chronologie der platonischen Dialoge." *Sitzungsberichte der Kaiserlichen Akademie der Wissenschaften in Wien: Philos. Hist. Klasse* 169.1 (1912): 1–210.

Baron, C. "Contributions à la chronologie des dialogues de Platon." *Revue des Etudes grecques* 10 (1897): 264–78.

Billig. L. "Clausulae and Platonic Chronology." *Journal of Philology* 35 (1920): 225–56.

Blass, Friedrich W. *Die attische Beredsamkeit.* Leipzig: Teubner, 1874.

Brandwood, Leonard. "The Dating of Plato's Works by the Stylistic Method: A Historical and Critical Survey." Ph.D. thesis, University of London, 1958.

A Word Index to Plato. Leeds: Maney & Son, 1976.

The Chronology of Plato's Dialogues. Cambridge: Cambridge University Press, 1990.

Díaz, Tejera A. "Ensayo de un metodo lingüístico para cronología de Platón." *Emerita* 29 (1961): 241–86.

Dittenberger, W. "Sprachliche Kriterien für die Chronologie der platonischen *Dialoge.*" *Hermes* 16 (1881): 321–45.

Janell, G. "Quaestiones Platonicae." *Jahrbücher für classische Philologie,* Supp. 26 (1901): 263–336.

Kaluscha, W. "Zur Chronologie der platonischen Dialoge." *Wiener Studien* 26 (1904): 190–204.

Ledger, Gerard R. *Re-counting Plato: A Computer Analysis of Plato's Style.* Oxford: Clarendon Press, 1989.

Lutoslawski, Wincenty. *The Origin and Growth of Plato's Logic With an Account of Plato's Style and of the Chronology of his Writings.* London: Longmans, Green, 1897.

Mueller, Ian. "Joan Kung's Reading of Plato's *Timaeus.*" In *Nature, Knowledge and Virtue: Essays in Memory of Joan Kung,* edited by Terry Penner and Richard Kraut. Edmonton, Alberta: Academic Printing and Publishing. *Apeiron* 22 (1989): 1–27.

Ritter, Constantin. *Untersuchungen über Platon: Die Echtheit and Chronologie der Platonischer Schriften.* Stuttgart: Kohlhammer, 1888.

"Unterabteilungen innerhalb der zeitlich ersten Gruppe platonischer Schriften." *Hermes* 70 (1935): 1–30.

Ross, W. D. *Plato's Theory of Ideas.* Oxford: Clarendon Press, 1951. 2d ed. 1953.

Ryle, Gilbert. *Plato's Progress.* Cambridge: Cambridge University Press, 1966.

Schanz, M. "Zur Entwicklung des platonischen Stils." *Hermes* 21(1886): 439–59.

Siebeck, Hermann. *Untersuchungen zur Philosophie der Griechen.* Halle: J.C.B. Mohr, 1888.

Thesleff, Holger. *Studies in Platonic Chronology.* In *Commentationes Humanarum Litterarum* 70 (1982). Helsinki: Societas Scientarum Fennica, 1982.

Wishart, D., and Leach, S. V. "A Multivariate Analysis of Platonic Prose Rhythm." *Computer Studies in the Humanities and Verbal Behavior* 3 (1970): 90–9.

H. SOCRATES AND THE EARLY DIALOGUES

Allen, R. E. *Plato's "Euthyphro" and the Earlier Theory of Forms.* London: Routledge & Kegan Paul, 1970.

Beversluis, John. "Socratic Definition." *American Philosophical Quarterly* 11 (1974): 331–6.

Bolotin, David. *Plato's Dialogue on Friendship.* Ithaca, N.Y.: Cornell University Press, 1979.

Brickhouse, Thomas C., and Smith, Nicholas D. *Socrates on Trial.* Princeton: Princeton University Press, 1989.

Dodds, E. R. *Plato: Gorgias.* A Revised text with introduction and commentary. Oxford: Clarendon Press, 1959.

Frede, Dorothea. "The Impossibility of Perfection: Socrates' Criticism of Simonides' Poem in the *Protagoras.*" *Review of Metaphysics* 39 (1986): 729–53.

Geach, P. T. "Plato's *Euthyphro:* An Analysis and Commentary." *Monist* 50 (1966): 369–82.

Gentzler, Jyl. "Knowledge and Method in Plato's Early through Middle Dialogues." Ph.D. thesis, Cornell University, 1991.

Gifford, Edwin Hamilton. *The Euthydemus of Plato.* With revised text, introduction, notes and indices. Oxford: Clarendon Press, 1905. Reprint. New York: Arno Press, 1973.

Glidden, David K. "The *Lysis* on Loving One's Own." *Classical Quarterly* 31 (1981): 39–59.

Heidel, W. A. *Plato's Euthyphro.* With introduction and notes. Greek Series for Colleges and Schools. New York: American Book Company, 1902.

Irwin, Terence. *Plato's Moral Theory: The Early and Middle Dialogues.* Oxford: Clarendon Press, 1977.

Plato: Gorgias. Translated with notes. Oxford: Clarendon Press, 1979.

"Coercion and Objectivity in Plato's Dialectic." *Revue Internationale de Philosophie* 40 (1986): 49–74.

"Socrates and the Tragic Hero." In *Language and the Tragic Hero,* edited by Pietro Pucci, 55–83. Atlanta: Scholars Press, 1988.

"Socrates and Athenian Democracy." *Philosophy and Public Affairs* 18 (1989): 184–205.

Kahn, Charles H. "Did Plato Write Socratic Dialogues?" *Classical Quarterly* 31 (1981): 305–20.

"The Beautiful and the Genuine: A discussion of Paul Woodruff, *Plato, Hippias Major.*" *Oxford Studies in Ancient Philosophy* 3 (1985): 261–88.

Kidd, Ian. "The Case of Homicide in Plato's *Euthyphro.*" In *Owls to Athens: Essays on Classical Subjects Presented to Sir Kenneth Dover,* edited by E. M. Craik, 213–22. Oxford: Clarendon Press, 1990.

Kraut, Richard. "Comments on Gregory Vlastos, 'The Socratic Elenchus.' " *Oxford Studies in Ancient Philosophy* 1 (1983): 59–70.

Socrates and the State. Princeton: Princeton University Press, 1984.

Nehamas, Alexander. "Socratic Intellectualism." In *Proceedings of the Boston Area Colloquium in Ancient Philosophy,* edited by John J. Cleary. Vol. 2. Lanham, Md.: University Press of America, 1987.

Patzer, Andreas, editor. *Der Historische Sokrates.* Darmstadt: Wissenschaftliche Buchgesellschaft, 1987.

Penner, Terry. "Socrates on Virtue and Motivation." In *Exegesis and Argument: Studies in Greek Philosophy Presented to Gregory Vlastos,* edited by E. N. Lee, Alexander P. D. Mourelatos, and R. M. Rorty, 133–51. Assen, Netherlands: van Gorcum & Comp., 1973.

"The Unity of Virtue." *Philosophical Review* 82 (1973): 35–68.

"Socrates on the Impossibility of Belief-Relative Sciences." In *Proceedings of the Boston Area Colloquium in Ancient Philosophy,* edited by John J. Cleary, 3:263–325. Lanham, Md.: University Press of America, 1988.

"Power and Desire in Socrates: The Argument of *Gorgias* 466a–468e that Orators and Tyrants have no Power in the City." *Apeiron* 24 (1991): 147–202.

Reeve, C. D. C. *Socrates in the Apology.* Indianapolis: Hackett, 1989.

Robinson, David B. "Plato's *Lysis:* The Structural Problem." *Illinois Classical Studies* 11 (1986): 63–83.

Robinson, Richard. *Plato's Earlier Dialectic.* Oxford: Clarendon Press, 1953.

Ross, W. D. "The Problem of Socrates." *Proceedings of the Classical Association* 30 (1933): 7–24. Reprinted in *Der historische Sokrates,* edited by Andreas Patzer, 225–39. Darmstadt: Wissenschaftliche Buchgesellschaft, 1987.

Santas, Gerasimos Xenophon. *Socrates: Philosophy in Plato's Early Dialogues.* London: Routledge & Kegan Paul, 1979.

Stokes, Michael C. *Plato's Socratic Conversations: Drama and Dialectic in Three Dialogues.* Baltimore: Johns Hopkins University Press, 1986.

Stone, I. F. *The Trial of Socrates.* Boston: Little, Brown, 1988.

Taylor, A. E. *Varia Socratica: First Series.* Oxford: James Parker, 1911. Reprint. New York: Garland Press, 1987.

Taylor, C. C. W. *Plato's Protagoras.* Translated with notes. Oxford: Clarendon Press, 1976.

Vlastos, Gregory. *Plato: Protagoras.* Edited with an introduction. Indianapolis: Bobbs-Merrill, 1956.

"Introduction: The Paradox of Socrates." In *The Philosophy of Socrates: A Collection of Critical Essays,* ed. Gregory Vlastos. Garden City, N.Y.: Anchor Books, Doubleday, 1971.

Platonic Studies. 2d ed. Princeton: Princeton University Press, 1981.

"Socrates on the 'Parts of Virtue.' " In *Platonic Studies,* 418–23. 2d ed. Princeton: Princeton University Press, 1981.

"The Unity of the Virtues in the *Protagoras.*" In *Platonic Studies,* 221–69. 2d ed. Princeton: Princeton University Press, 1981.

"What did Socrates Understand by his 'What is *F*' Question?" In *Platonic Studies,* 410–17. 2d ed. Princeton: Princeton University Press, 1981.

"The Socratic Elenchus." *Oxford Studies in Ancient Philosophy* 1 (1983): 27–58.

"Socrates' Disavowal of Knowledge." *Philosophical Quarterly* 35 (1985): 1–31.

"Elenchus and Mathematics." *American Journal of Philology* 109 (1988): 362–96.

"Socrates." *Proceedings of the British Academy* 74 (1988): 89–111.

Socrates: Ironist and Moral Philosopher. Cambridge: Cambridge University Press, 1991.

Vlastos, Gregory, editor. *The Philosophy of Socrates: A Collection of Critical Essays.* Garden City, N.Y.: Anchor Books, Doubleday 1971.

Weiss, Roslyn. "Hedonism in the *Protagoras* and the Sophist's Guarantee." *Ancient Philosophy* 10 (1990): 17–39.

Woodruff, Paul. *Plato: Hippias Major.* Translated, with commentary and essay. Indianapolis: Hackett, 1982.

"Plato's Early Theory of Knowledge." In *Companions to Ancient Thought 1: Epistemology,* edited by Stephen Everson, 60–84. Cambridge: Cambridge University Press, 1990.

Zeyl, Donald. "Socrates and Hedonism – *Protagoras* 351b–358d." *Phronesis* 25 (1980): 250–69.

I. METAPHYSICS AND EPISTEMOLOGY

Ackrill, John. "In Defense of Platonic Division." In *Ryle: A Collection of Critical Essays,* edited by Oscar P. Wood and George Pitcher, 373–92. Garden City, N.Y.: Anchor Books, Doubleday, 1970.

"Gwilym Ellis Lane Owen." *Proceedings of the British Academy* 70 (1984): 481–99.

Allen, R. E. "Participation and Predication in Plato's Middle Dialogues." *Philosophical Review* 69 (1960): 147–64. Reprinted in *Plato: A Collection of Critical Essays.* Vol. 1, *Metaphysics and Epistemology,* edited by Gregory Vlastos, 167–83. Garden City, N.Y.: Anchor Books, Doubleday, 1970.

Allen, R. E., editor. *Studies in Plato's Metaphysics.* London: Routledge & Kegan Paul, 1965.

Burnyeat, Myles. "Conflicting Appearances." *Proceedings of the British Academy* 65 (1979): 69–111.

Cherniss, Harold. *Aristotle's Criticism of Plato and the Academy.* Baltimore: Johns Hopkins University Press, 1944.

Fine, Gail. "The One Over Many." *Philosophical Review* 89 (1980): 197–240.

"Separation." *Oxford Studies in Ancient Philosophy* 2 (1984): 31–87.

"The Object of Thought Argument." *Apeiron* 21 (1988): 137–42.

"Plato on Perception." *Oxford Studies in Ancient Philosophy,* supplementary vol. (1988): 15–28.

Frede, Michael. "Being and Becoming in Plato." *Oxford Studies in Ancient Philosophy,* supplementary vol. (1988): 37–52.

Gentzler, Jyl. "Knowledge and Method in Plato's Early through Middle Dialogues." Ph.D. thesis, Cornell University, 1991.

Irwin, Terence. "Plato's Heracliteanism." *Philosophical Quarterly* 27 (1977): 1–13.

Krämer, Hans Joachim. *Plato and the Foundations of Metaphysics.* Edited and translated by John R. Caton. Albany: State University of New York Press, 1990.

Lloyd, A. C. "Non-Discursive Thought – An Enigma of Greek Philosophy." *Proceedings of the Aristotelian Society* 70 (1969–70): 261–74.

Mohr, Richard D. "Forms as Individuals: Unity, Being and Cognition in Plato's Ideal Theory." *Illinois Classical Studies* 11 (1986): 113–28.

Moravcsik, Julius M. E. "The Anatomy of Plato's Divisions." In *Exegesis and Argument: Studies in Greek Philosophy Presented to Gregory Vlastos,* edited by E. N. Lee, Alexander P. D. Mourelatos, and R. M. Rorty, 324–48. Assem, Netherlands: van Gorcum & Comp., 1973.

"Understanding and Knowledge in Plato's Philosophy." *Neue Hefte für Philosophie* 15/16 (1979): 53–69.

Morgan, Michael L. *Platonic Piety: Philosophy and Ritual in Fourth-Century Athens.* New Haven: Yale University Press, 1990.

Owen, G. E. L. "A Proof in the *Peri Ideōn.*" *Journal of Hellenic Studies* 77 (1857): 103–11. Reprinted in *Studies in Plato's Metaphysics,* edited by R. E. Allen, 293–312. London: Routledge & Kegan Paul, 1965. Also reprinted in G. E. L. Owen, *Logic, Science, and Dialectic: Collected Papers in Greek Philosophy,* edited by Martha Nussbaum, 165–79. Ithaca, N.Y.: Cornell University Press, 1986.

Patterson, Richard. "The Eternality of Platonic Forms." *Archiv für Geschichte der Philosophie* 67 (1985): 27–46.

Image and Reality in Plato's Metaphysics. Indianapolis: Hackett, 1985.

Penner, Terry. *The Ascent from Nominalism: Some Existence Arguments in Plato's Middle Dialogues.* Dordrecht: D. Reidel, 1987.

Peterson, Sandra. "The Greatest Difficulty for Plato's Theory of Forms: the Unknowability Argument of *Parmenides* 133c–134e." *Archiv für Geschicte der Philosophie* 63 (1981): 1–16.

Prior, William J. *Unity and Development in Plato's Metaphysics.* London: Croom Helm, 1985.

Robinson, Richard. *Plato's Earlier Dialectic.* Oxford: Clarendon Press, 1953.

Ross, W. D. *Plato's Theory of Ideas.* Oxford: Clarendon Press, 1951. 2d ed. 1953.

Sayre, Kenneth M. *Plato's Late Ontology: A Riddle Resolved.* Princeton: Princeton University Press, 1983.

Schofield, Malcolm. "The Dénouement of the *Cratylus*." In *Language and Logos: Studies in Ancient Greek Philosophy Presented to G.E.L. Owen*, edited by Malcolm Schofield and Martha Nussbaum, 61–81. Cambridge: Cambridge University Press, 1982.

"Editor's Notes." *Phronesis* 35 (1990): 327–34.

Scott, Dominic. "Platonic Anamnesis Revisited." *Classical Quarterly* 37 (1987): 346–66.

Teloh, Henry. *The Development of Plato's Metaphysics*. University Park: Pennsylvania State University Press, 1981.

Vlastos, Gregory. "Degrees of Reality in Plato." In *New Essays on Plato and Aristotle*, edited by Renford Bambrough. London: Routledge & Kegan Paul, 1965. Reprinted in Gregory Vlastos, *Platonic Studies*, 58–75. 2d ed. Princeton: Princeton University Press, 1981.

Vlastos, Gregory, editor. *Plato: A Collection of Critical Essays*. Vol. 1, *Metaphysics and Epistemology*. Garden City, N.Y.: Anchor Books, Doubleday, 1970.

Wedberg, A. "The Theory of Ideas." In *Plato: A Collection of Critical Essays*. Vol. 1, *Metaphysics and Epistemology*, edited by Gregory Vlastos, 28–52. Garden City, N.Y.: Anchor Books, Doubleday, 1970.

White, Nicholas P. *Plato on Knowledge and Reality*. Indianapolis: Hackett, 1976.

"Perceptual and Objective Properties in Plato." In *Nature, Knowledge and Virtue: Essays in Memory of Joan Kung*, edited by Terry Penner and Richard Kraut. Edmonton, Alberta: Academic Printing and Publishing. *Apeiron* 22 (1989): 45–66.

Williams, Bernard. "Cratylus' Theory of Names and its Refutation." In *Language and Logos: Studies in Ancient Greek Philosophy Presented to G.E.L. Owen*, edited by Malcolm Schofield and Martha Nussbaum, 83–94. Cambridge: Cambridge University Press, 1982.

Woodruff, Paul. "Plato's Early Theory of Knowledge." In *Companions to Ancient Thought 1: Epistemology*, edited by Stephen Everson, 60–84. Cambridge: Cambridge University Press, 1990.

J. ETHICS, POLITICAL PHILOSOPHY, AND MORAL PSYCHOLOGY

Bambrough, Renford, editor. *Plato, Popper, and Politics*. Cambridge: Cambridge University Press, 1967.

Barker, Ernest. *Greek Political Theory: Plato and His Predecessors*. London: Methuen, 1918.

Gosling, J. C. B., and Taylor, C. C. W. *The Greeks on Pleasure*. Oxford: Clarendon Press, 1982.

Griswold, Charles L., Jr. "*Politike episteme* in Plato's *Statesman.*" In *Essays in Ancient Greek Philosophy,* vol. 3, edited by John P. Anton and Anthony Preus. Albany: State University of New York Press, 1989.

Harvey, F. David. "Two Kinds of Equality." *Classica et Mediaevalia* 26 (1965): 101–46. Emended in "Corrigenda." *Classica et Mediaevalia* 27 (1966): 99–100.

Irwin, Terence. *Plato's Moral Theory: The Early and Middle Dialogues.* Oxford: Clarendon Press, 1977.

"Socrates and Athenian Democracy." *Philosophy and Public Affairs* 18 (1989): 184–205.

Kahn, Charles H. "Plato's Theory of Desire." *Review of Metaphysics* 41 (1987): 77–103.

Klosko, George. *The Development of Plato's Political Theory.* New York: Methuen, 1986.

Kraut, Richard. "Review of *Plato's Moral Theory,* by Terence Irwin." *Philosophical Review* 88 (1979): 633–9.

Levinson, Ronald B. *In Defense of Plato.* Cambridge, Mass.: Harvard University Press, 1953.

Mackenzie, Mary Margaret. *Plato on Punishment.* Berkeley: University of California Press, 1981.

Nussbaum, Martha C. *The Fragility of Goodness: Luck and Ethics in Greek Tragedy and Philosophy.* Cambridge: Cambridge University Press, 1986.

Penner, Terry. "Thought and Desire in Plato." In *Plato.* Vol. 2, *Ethics, Politics, and Philosophy of Art and Religion,* edited by Gregory Vlastos, 96–118. Garden City, N.Y.: Anchor Books, Doubleday, 1971.

"Plato and Davidson: Parts of the Soul and Weakness of Will." In *Canadian Philosophers. Canadian Journal of Philosophy,* supplementary vol. 16 (1990): 35–74.

Popper, K. R. *The Open Society and its Enemies.* Vol. 1, *The Spell of Plato.* 4th ed. New York: Harper & Row, 1963. 5th ed. 1966.

Price, Anthony W. *Love and Friendship in Plato and Aristotle.* Oxford: Clarendon Press, 1989.

"Plato and Freud." In *The Person and the Human Mind: Issues in Ancient and Modern Philosophy,* edited by Christopher Hill, 247–70. Oxford: Oxford University Press, 1990.

Sabine, George Holland. *A History of Political Theory.* 4th ed. Hinsdale, Ill.: Dryden Press, 1973.

Saunders, T. J., " 'The RAND Corporation of Antiquity'? Plato's Academy and Greek Politics." In *Studies in Honour of T.B.L. Webster,* edited by J. H. Betts, J. T. Hooker, and J. R. Green, 1:200–10. Bristol: Classical Press, 1986.

Smith, Nicholas D. "Plato and Aristotle on the Nature of Women." *Journal of the History of Philosophy* 21 (1983): 467–78.

Strauss, Leo. *The City and Man.* Chicago: University of Chicago Press, 1964.

Vlastos, Gregory. "Socratic Knowledge and Platonic 'Pessimism.' " Review of *The Development of Plato's Ethics,* by John Gould. *Philosophical Review* 66 (1957): 226–38. Reprinted in Gregory Vlastos, *Platonic Studies,* 204–17. 2d ed. Princeton: Princeton University Press, 1981.

Wender, Dorothea. "Plato: Misogynist, Paedophile and Feminist." *Arethusa* 6 (1973): 75–80.

K. ART AND POETRY

Annas, Julia. "Plato on the Triviality of Literature." In *Plato on Beauty, Wisdom, and the Arts,* edited by Julius Moravcsik and Philip Temko, 1–28. Totowa, N.J.: Rowman & Littlefield, 1982.

Battin, M. Pabst. "Plato on True and False Poetry." *Journal of Aesthetics and Art Criticism* 36 (1977): 163–74.

Belfiore, Elizabeth. "A Theory of Imitation in Plato's *Republic.*" *Transactions of the American Philological Association* 114 (1984): 121–46.

Bosanquet, Bernard. *A History of Aesthetic.* London: Swan Sonnenschein, 1892.

Brock, Roger. "Plato and Comedy." In *Owls to Athens: Essays on Classical Subjects Presented to Sir Kenneth Dover,* edited by E. M. Craik, 39–51. Oxford: Clarendon Press, 1990.

Clay, Diskin. "The Tragic and Comic Poet of the *Symposium.*" In *Essays in Ancient Greek Philosophy,* edited by John P. Auton and Anthony Press, 2: 186–202. Albany: State University of New York Press, 1983.

Collingwood, R. G. "Plato's Philosophy of Art." *Mind* 34 (1925): 154–72.

Ferrari, G. R. F. "Plato and Poetry." In *The Cambridge History of Literary Criticism,* edited by George A. Kennedy, 92–148. Cambridge: Cambridge University Press, 1989.

Greene, W. C. "The Spirit of Comedy in Plato." *Harvard Studies in Classical Philology* 31 (1920): 63–123.

Menza, V. "Poetry and the *Technē* Theory." Ph.D. dissertation, Johns Hopkins University, 1972.

Moravcsik, Julius, and Temko, Philip, editors. *Plato on Beauty, Wisdom, and the Arts.* Totowa, N.J.: Rowman & Littlefield, 1982.

Murdoch, Iris. *The Fire and the Sun: Why Plato Banished the Artists.* Oxford: Clarendon Press, 1977.

Woodruff, Paul. "What Could Go Wrong with Inspiration? Why Plato's Poets Fail." In *Plato on Beauty, Wisdom, and the Arts,* edited by Julius

Moravcsik and Philip Temko, 137–50. Totowa, N.J.: Rowman & Littlefield, 1982.

L. EROS

Armstrong, A. H. "Platonic Eros and Christian Agape." *Downside Review* 79 (1961): 105–21.

"Platonic Love: A Reply to Professor Verdenius." *Downside Review* 82 (1964): 199–208.

Carson, Anne. *Eros the Bittersweet.* Princeton: Princeton University Press, 1986.

Cornford, Francis MacDonald. "The Doctrine of Eros in Plato's *Symposium.*" In *Plato: A Collection of Critical Essays.* Vol. 2, *Ethics, Politics, and Philosophy of Art and Religion,* edited by Gregory Vlastos. Garden City, N.Y.: Anchor Books, Doubleday, 1971.

Gagarin, Michael. "Socrates' Hybris and Alcibiades' Failure." *Phoenix* 31 (1977): 22–37.

Gould, Thomas. *Platonic Love.* New York: Free Press of Glencoe, 1963.

Halperin, David. "Platonic Eros and What Men Call Love." *Ancient Philosophy* 5 (1985): 161–204.

"Plato and Erotic Reciprocity." *Classical Antiquity* 5 (1986): 60–80.

Kosman, L. A. "Platonic Love." In *Facets of Plato's Philosophy,* edited by W. H. Werkmeister, 53–69. Assen, Netherlands: van Gorcum & Comp., 1976.

Price, Anthony W. *Love and Friendship in Plato and Aristotle.* Oxford: Clarendon Press, 1989.

Robin, Leon. *Théorie platonicienne de l'amour.* Paris: Alcan, 1908.

Santas, Gerasimos Xenophon. *Plato and Freud: Two Theories of Love.* Oxford: Basil Blackwell, 1988.

Vlastos, Gregory. "The Individual as an Object of Love in Plato." In Gregory Vlastos, *Platonic Studies,* 3–37. 2d ed. Princeton: Princeton University Press, 1981.

M. MATHEMATICS

Burnyeat, Myles. "Platonism and Mathematics: A Prelude to Discussion." In *Mathematics and Metaphysics in Aristotle,* edited by Andreas Graeser, 213–40. Bern and Stuttgart: P. Haupt, 1987.

Cherniss, Harold. "Plato as Mathematician." *Review of Metaphysics* 4 (1951): 395–425. Reprinted in Harold Cherniss, *Selected Papers,* edited by Leonardo Taran, 222–52. Leiden: E. J. Brill, 1977.

Cornford, Francis MacDonald. "Mathematics and Dialectic in the *Republic* VI–VII." *Mind* 41 (1932): 37–52, 173–90. Reprinted in *Studies in Plato's Metaphysics,* edited by R. E. Allen, 61–96. London: Routledge & Kegan Paul, 1965.

Frajese, Attilio. *Platone e la matematica nel mondo antico.* Rome: Editrice Studium, 1963.

Gillispie, Charles Coulston, editor. *Dictionary of Scientific Biography.* 16 vols. New York: Scribner's, 1970–80.

Gulley, Norman. "Greek Geometrical Analysis." *Phronesis* 3 (1958): 1–14.

Heath, Thomas. *A History of Greek Mathematics.* Vol. 1. Oxford: Clarendon Press, 1921.

Lasserre, François. *Die Fragmente des Eudoxos von Knidos.* Edited and translated, with commentary. Berlin: de Gruyter, 1966.

De Léodamas de Thasos à Philippe d'Oponte. Vol. 2, *La scuola di Platone.* Naples: Bibliopolis, 1987.

Morrow, Glenn R., translator. *Proclus: A Commentary on the First Book of Euclid's Elements.* Princeton: Princeton University Press, 1970.

Morrow, Glenn R., and Dillon, John M., translators. *Proclus' Commentary on Plato's Parmenides.* With introduction and notes by John M. Dillon. Princeton: Princeton University Press, 1987.

Mueller, Ian. "On the Notion of a Mathematical Starting Point in Plato, Aristotle, and Euclid." In *Science and Philosophy in Classical Greece,* edited by Alan Bowen, 59–97. London and New York: Garland, 1991.

N. STUDIES OF SINGLE WORKS

1. *Meno*

Bluck, R. S. *Plato's Meno.* Edited with an introduction and commentary. Cambridge: Cambridge University Press, 1961.

Heitsch, Ernst. "Platons hypothetisches Verfahren im *Menon.*" *Hermes* 105 (1977): 257–68.

Moravcsik, Julius M. E. "Learning as Recollection." In *Plato: A Collection of Critical Essays.* Vol. 1, *Metaphysics and Epistemology,* edited by Gregory Vlastos, 53–69. Garden City, N.Y.: Anchor Books, Doubleday, 1970.

Nehamas, Alexander. "Meno's Paradox and Socrates as a Teacher." *Oxford Studies in Ancient Philosophy* 3 (1985): 1–30.

Sharples, R. W. *Plato, Meno.* Edited with translation and notes. Warminster, Wiltshire: Aris & Phillips, 1985. Chicago: Bolchazy-Carducci, 1985.

Thompson, E. Seymer. *The Meno of Plato.* With introduction, notes and excurses. London: Macmillan, 1901.

Vlastos, Gregory. "*Anamnesis* in the *Meno.*" *Dialogue* 4 (1965): 143–67.
White, Nicholas P. "Inquiry." *Review of Metaphysics* 28 (1974): 289–310.

2. *Phaedo*

Bostock, David. *Plato's Phaedo.* Oxford: Clarendon Press, 1986.
Brentlinger, J. "Incomplete Predicates and the Two-World Theory of the *Phaedo. Phronesis* 17 (1972): 61–79.
Castaneda, Hector-Neri. "Plato's *Phaedo* Theory of Relations." *Journal of Philosophical Logic* 1 (1972): 467–80.
Gallop, David. *Plato, Phaedo.* Translated with notes. Oxford: Clarendon Press, 1975.
Hackforth, R. *Plato's Phaedo.* Translated, with introduction and commentary. Indianapolis: Bobbs-Merrill, 1955.
Kung, Joan. "Plato's Criticism of Anaxagoras on Mind and Morality in Nature." *Proceedings of the Tenth University of Dayton Philosophy Colloquium, University of Dayton Review* 16 (1982): 65–76.
Matthews, Gareth B., and Blackson, Thomas A. "Causes in the *Phaedo.*" *Synthèse* 79 (1989): 581–91.
Nehamas, Alexander. "Plato on the Imperfection of the Sensible World." *American Philosophical Quarterly* 12 (1975): 105–17.
Plass, Paul. "Socrates' Method of Hypothesis in the *Phaedo.*" *Phronesis* 5 (1960): 103–15.
Vlastos, Gregory. "Reasons and Causes in the *Phaedo.*" *Philosophical Review* 78 (1969): 291–325. Reprinted in *Plato: A Collection of Critical Essays.* Vol. 1, *Metaphysics and Epistemology,* edited by Gregory Vlastos, 132–66. Garden City, N.Y.: Anchor Books, Doubleday, 1970.
White, Nicholas P. "Forms and Sensibles: *Phaedo* 74B–C." *Philosophical Topics* 15 (1987): 197–214.

3. *Symposium*

Allen R. E. "A Note on the Elenchus of Agathon: *Symposium* 199c–201c." *Monist* 50 (1966): 460–3.
Anton, John P. "The Secret of Plato's *Symposium.*" *Diotima* 2 (1974): 27–47.
Bacon, Helen. "Socrates Crowned." *The Virginia Quarterly Review* 35 (1959): 415–30.
Brenkman, John. "The Other and the One: Psychoanalysis, Reading, the

Symposium." In *Literature and Psychoanalysis*, edited by Shoshana Felman, 396–456. Baltimore: Johns Hopkins University Press, 1982.

Bury, Robert Gregg. *The Symposium of Plato*. 2d ed. Cambridge: Cambridge University Press, 1932.

Dover, K. J. "The Date of Plato's *Symposium*." *Phronesis* 10 (1965): 2–20.

Plato's Symposium. Cambridge: Cambridge University Press, 1980.

Hackforth, R. "Immortality in Plato's *Symposium*." *Classical Review* 64 (1950): 43–5.

Halperin, David. "Why Is Diotima a Woman?" In *One Hundred Years of Homosexuality*, 113–51. New York: Routledge, 1990.

Isenberg, Meyer W. *The Order of the Discourses in Plato's Symposium*. Private Edition. Chicago: University of Chicago Libraries, 1940.

Markus, R. A. "The Dialectic of Eros in Plato's *Symposium*." In *Plato: A Collection of Critical Essays*. Vol. 2, *Ethics, Politics, and Philosophy of Art and Religion*, edited by Gregory Vlastos. Garden City, N.Y.: Anchor Books, Doubleday, 1971.

Moravcsik, Julius M. E. "Reason and Eros in the 'Ascent'-passage of the *Symposium*." In *Essays in Ancient Greek Philosophy*, edited by John P. Anton and G. L. Kustas, 1:285–302. Albany: State University of New York Press, 1972.

Nehamas, Alexander, and Woodruff, Paul. *Plato: Symposium*. Translated with introduction and notes. Indianapolis: Hackett, 1989.

Neumann, Harry. "Diotima's Concept of Love." *American Journal of Philology* 86 (1965): 33–59.

O'Brien, Michael J. " 'Becoming Immortal' in Plato's *Symposium*." In *Greek Poetry and Philosophy*, edited by Douglas E. Gerber, 185–206. Chico, Cal.: Scholars Press, 1984.

Plochmann, G. K. "Hiccups and Hangovers in the *Symposium*." *Bucknell Review* 11 (1963): 1–18.

Robin, Leon. *Platon: Le Banquet*. In *Platon: Oeuvres complètes*, edited and translated. Vol. 4, Part 2. Paris: Société d'Edition, Les Belles Lettres, 1966.

Rosen, Stanley. *Plato's Symposium*. 2d ed. New Haven: Yale University Press, 1987.

Stokes, Michael C. *Plato's Socratic Conversations: Drama and Dialectic in Three Dialogues*. Baltimore: Johns Hopkins University Press, 1986.

Szlezák, Thomas A. *Platon und die Schriftlichkeit der Philosophie*. Berlin: de Gruyter, 1985.

White, F. C. "Love and Beauty in Plato's *Symposium*." *Journal of Hellenic Studies* 109 (1989): 149–57.

Wolz, H. G. "Philosophy as Drama: An Approach to Plato's *Symposium*." *Philosophy and Phenomenological Research* 30 (1969–70): 323–53.

4. *Republic*

Adam, James. *The Republic of Plato.* Edited with critical notes and an introduction. 2 vols. Cambridge: Cambridge University Press, 1902.

Annas, Julia. "Plato's *Republic* and Feminism." *Philosophy* 51 (1976): 307–21.

An Introduction to Plato's Republic. Oxford: Clarendon Press, 1981.

Bloom, Allan. *The Republic of Plato.* Translated with notes and an interpretive essay. New York: Basic Books, 1968.

Cherniss, Harold. "On Plato's *Republic* X 597B." *American Journal of Philology* 53 (1932): 233–42. Reprinted in Harold Cherniss, *Selected Papers,* edited by Leonardo Taran, 271–80. Leiden: E.J. Brill, 1977.

Cooper, John M. "The Psychology of Justice in Plato." *American Philosophical Quarterly* 14 (1977): 151–7.

"Plato's Theory of Human Motivation." *History of Philosophy Quarterly* 1 (1984): 3–21.

Cross, R. C., and Woozley, A. D. *Plato's Republic: A Philosophical Commentary.* London: Macmillan, 1964.

Demos, Raphael. "A Fallacy in Plato's *Republic?*" *The Philosophical Review* 73 (1964): 395–8. Reprinted in *Plato: A Collection of Critical Essays.* Vol. 2, *Ethics, Politics, and Philosophy of Art and Religion,* edited by Gregory Vlastos, 52–6. Garden City, N.Y.: Anchor Books, Doubleday, 1971.

Fine, Gail. "Knowledge and Belief in *Republic* V." *Archiv für Geschichte der Philosophie* 60 (1978): 121–39.

"Knowledge and Belief in *Republic* V–VII." In *Companions to Ancient Thought: Epistemology,* edited by Stephen Everson. Cambridge: Cambridge University Press, 1990.

Foster, M. B. "A Mistake of Plato's in the *Republic.*" *Mind* 46 (1937): 386–93.

Gosling, J. C. B. "Republic V: *ta polla kala.*" *Phronesis* 5 (1960): 116–28.

Joseph, Horace W. B. *Essays in Ancient and Modern Philosophy.* Freeport, N.Y.: Books for Libraries Press, 1971.

Kirwan, C. A. "Glaucon's Challenge." *Phronesis* 10 (1965): 162–73.

Kraut, Richard. "Egoism, Love and Political Office in Plato." *Philosophical Review* 82 (1973): 330–44.

"Reason and Justice in Plato's *Republic.* In *Exegesis and Argument: Studies in Greek Philosophy Presented to Gregory Vlastos,* edited by E. N. Lee, Alexander P. D. Mourelatos, and R. M. Rorty, 207–24. Assen, Netherlands: van Gorcum & Comp., 1973.

Review of *Philosopher-Kings,* by C. D. C. Reeve. *Political Theory* 18 (1990): 492–6.

"Return to the Cave: *Republic* 519–521." In *Proceedings of the Boston Area Colloquium in Ancient Philosophy,* edited by John J. Cleary. Vol. 7. Forthcoming.

Laks, André. "Legislation and Demiurgy: On the Relationship between Plato's *Republic* and *Laws.*" *Classical Antiquity* 9 (1990): 209–29.

Mabbott, J. D. "Is Plato's *Republic* Utilitarian?" *Mind* 46 (1937): 468–74. Reprinted in *Plato.* Vol. 2, *Ethics, Politics, and Philosophy of Art and Religion,* edited by Gregory Vlastos, 57–66. Garden City, N.Y.: Anchor Books, Doubleday, 1971.

Mourelatos, Alexander P. D. "Plato's 'Real Astronomy': *Republic* 527d–531d." In *Science and the Sciences in Plato,* edited by John P. Anton, 33–73. Delmar, N.Y.: Caravan Books, 1980.

Mueller, Ian. "Ascending to Problems: Astronomy and Harmonics in *Republic* VII." In *Science and the Sciences in Plato,* edited by John P. Anton, 103–21. Delmar, N.Y.: Caravan Books, 1980.

Murphy, N. R. *The Interpretation of Plato's Republic.* Oxford: Clarendon Press, 1951.

Nehamas, Alexander. "Plato on Imitation and Poetry in *Republic* 10." In *Plato on Beauty, Wisdom, and the Arts,* edited by Julius Moravcsik and Philip Temko, 47–78. Totowa, N.J.: Rowman & Littlefield, 1982.

Nettleship, Richard. *Lectures on the Republic of Plato.* 2d ed. London: Macmillan, 1962.

Okin, Susan Moller. "Philosopher Queens and Private Wives: Plato on Women and the Family." *Philosophy & Public Affairs* 6 (1977): 345–69.

Women in Western Political Thought. Princeton: Princeton University Press, 1979.

Reeve, C. D. C. *Philosopher-Kings: The Argument of Plato's Republic.* Princeton: Princeton University Press, 1988.

Sachs, David. "A Fallacy in Plato's *Republic.*" *Philosophical Review* 72 (1963): 141–58. Reprinted in *Plato: A Collection of Critical Essays.* Vol. 2, *Ethics, Politics, and Philosophy of Art and Religion,* edited by Gregory Vlastos, 35–51. Garden City, N.Y.: Anchor Books, Doubleday, 1971.

Santas, Gerasimos Xenophon. "The Form of the Good in Plato's *Republic.* In *Essays in Ancient Greek Philosophy,* edited by John P. Anton and Anthony Preus, 2: 232–63. Albany: State University of New York Press, 1983.

"Aristotle's Criticism of Plato's Form of the Good: Ethics without Metaphysics?" *Philosophical Papers* 18 (1989): 137–60.

Smith, J. A. "General Relative Clauses in Greek." *Classical Review* 31 (1917): 69–71.

Sorabji, Richard. "Myths about Non-Propositional Thought." In *Language and Logos: Studies in Ancient Greek Philosophy Presented to G.E.L. Owen,* edited by Malcolm Schofield and Martha Nussbaum, 295–314. Cambridge: Cambridge University Press, 1982.

Stokes, Michael C. "Adeimantus in the *Republic.*" In *Law, Justice and Method in Plato and Aristotle,* edited by Spiro Panagiotou, 67–96. Edmonton: Academic Printing & Publishing, 1985.

Vlastos, Gregory. "Justice and Happiness in the *Republic.*" In *Plato.* Vol. 2, *Ethics, Politics, and Philosophy of Art and Religion,* edited by Gregory Vlastos, 66–95. Garden City, N.Y.: Anchor Books, Doubleday, 1971. Reprinted in Gregory Vlastos, *Platonic Studies,* 111–39. 2d ed. Princeton: Princeton University Press, 1981.

"Was Plato a Feminist?" *Times Literary Supplement,* March 17–23, 1989: 276, 288–9.

White, Nicholas P. *A Companion to Plato's Republic.* Indianapolis: Hackett, 1979.

"The Classification of Goods in Plato's *Republic.*" *Journal of the History of Philosophy* 22 (1984): 393–421.

"The Ruler's Choice." *Archiv für Geschichte der Philosophie* 68 (1986): 22–46.

"Happiness and External Contingencies in Plato's *Republic.*" In *Moral Philosophy,* edited by William C. Starr and Richard C. Taylor, 1–21. Milwaukee: Marquette University Press, 1989.

Williams, Bernard. "The Analogy of City and Soul in Plato's *Republic.*" In *Exegesis and Argument: Studies in Greek Philosophy Presented to Gregory Vlastos,* edited by E. N. Lee, Alexander P. D. Mourelatos, and R. M. Rorty, 196–206. Assen, Netherlands: van Gorcum & Comp., 1973.

5. *Phaedrus*

Asmis, Elizabeth. "*Psychagogia* in Plato's *Phaedrus.*" *Illinois Classical Studies* 11 (1986): 113–28, 153–72.

Burger, Ronna. *Plato's Phaedrus: A Defense of a Philosophic Art of Writing.* University, Ala.: University of Alabama Press, 1980.

Burnyeat, Myles F. "The Passion of Reason in Plato's *Phaedrus.*" Unpublished manuscript.

Derrida, Jacques. "Plato's Pharmacy." In *Dissemination,* translated with an introduction and additional notes by Barbara Johnson, 61–171. Chicago: University of Chicago Press, 1981.

de Vries, G. J. *A Commentary on the Phaedrus of Plato.* Amsterdam: Hakkert, 1969.

Dorter, Kenneth. "Imagery and Philosophy in Plato's *Phaedrus.*" *Journal of the History of Philosophy* 9 (1971): 279–88.

Ferrari, G. R. F. *Listening to the Cicadas: A Study of Plato's Phaedrus.* Cambridge: Cambridge University Press, 1987.

Griswold, Charles L., Jr. *Self-Knowledge in Plato's Phaedrus.* New Haven: Yale University Press, 1986.

Hackforth, R. *Plato's Phaedrus.* Cambridge: Cambridge University Press, 1952.

Heath, Malcolm. "The Unity of Plato's *Phaedrus.*" *Oxford Studies in Ancient Philosophy* 7 (1989): 151–74.

Howland, R. L. "The Attack on Isocrates in the *Phaedrus.*" *Classical Quarterly* 31 (1937): 151–9.

Lebeck, Anne. "The Central Myth of Plato's *Phaedrus.*" *Greek, Roman and Byzantine Studies* 13 (1972): 267–90.

Philip, A. "Récurrences thématiques et topologie dans le *Phèdre* de Platon." *Revue de Metaphysique et de Morale* 86 (1981): 452–76.

Rowe, C. J. "The Argument and Structure of Plato's *Phaedrus.*" *Proceedings of the Cambridge Philological Society* 212 (1986): 106–25.

Plato: Phaedrus. With translation and commentary. Warminster: Aris & Phillips, 1986.

Thompson, W. H. *The Phaedrus of Plato.* With English notes and dissertations. London: Bell & Whittaker, 1868.

6. *Parmenides*

Allen, R. E. "Participation and Predication in Plato's Middle Dialogues." *Philosophical Review* 69 (1960): 147–64. Reprinted in *Plato: A Collection of Critical Essays.* Vol. 1, *Metaphysics and Epistemology,* edited by Gregory Vlastos, 167–83. Garden City, N.Y.: Anchor Books, Doubleday, 1970.

Plato's Parmenides. Minneapolis: University of Minnesota Press, 1983.

Code, Alan. "On the Origins of Some Aristotelian Theses about Predication." In *How Things Are: Studies in Predication and the History of Philosophy,* edited by J. Bogen and J. E. McGuire, 101–31, 323–6. Dordrecht: D. Reidel, 1985.

Cohen, S. Marc. "The Logic of the Third Man." *Philosophical Review* 80 (1971): 448–75.

Cornford, Francis MacDonald. *Plato and Parmenides.* Translated with an introduction and running commentary. London: Routledge & Kegan Paul, 1939. Reprint. Indianapolis: Bobbs-Merrill, no date.

Diès, Auguste, editor. *Platon: Oeuvres complètes.* Vol. 8. Paris: Société d'Edition, Les Belles Lettres, 1923.

Dodds, E. R. "The *Parmenides* of Plato and the Origin of the Neoplatonic One." *Classical Quarterly* 22 (1928): 129–42.

Geach, P. T. "The Third Man Again." *Philosophical Review* 65 (1956): 72–82.

Meinwald, Constance C. *Plato's Parmenides.* New York: Oxford University Press, 1991.

Miller, Mitchell, Jr. *Plato's Parmenides.* Princeton: Princeton University Press, 1986.

Morrow, Glenn R., and Dillon, John M., translators. *Proclus' Commentary on Plato's Parmenides.* With introduction and notes by John M. Dillon. Princeton: Princeton University Press, 1987.

Owen, G. E. L. "Notes on Ryle's Plato." In *Ryle: A Collection of Critical Essays,* edited by Oscar P. Wood and George Pitcher, 341–72. Garden City, N.Y.: Anchor Books, Doubleday, 1970. Reprinted in G. E. L. Owen, *Logic, Science, and Dialectic: Collected Papers in Greek Philosophy,* edited by Martha Nussbaum, 85–103. Ithaca, N.Y.: Cornell University Press, 1986.

Peterson, Sandra. "A Reasonable Self-Predication Premise for the Third Man Argument." *Philosophical Review* 82 (1973): 451–70. Emended in "A Correction." *Philosophical Review* 84 (1975): 96.

Proclus. *Commentarium in Platonis Parmenidem.* In *Procli Philosophi Platonici Opera Inedita,* edited by Victor Cousin. Paris: Minerva, 1864.

Ryle, Gilbert. "Plato's *Parmenides.*" *Mind* 48 (1939): 129–51, 302–25. Reprinted in *Studies in Plato's Metaphysics,* edited by R. E. Allen, 97–147. London: Routledge & Kegan Paul, 1965.

Sayre, Kenneth M. *Plato's Late Ontology: A Riddle Resolved.* Princeton: Princeton University Press, 1983.

Sellars, Wilfred. "Vlastos and the Third Man." *Philosophical Review* 64 (1955): 405–37.

Strang, Colin. "Plato and the Third Man." *Proceedings of the Aristotelian Society,* supplementary vol. 37 (1963): 147–64. Reprinted in *Plato: A Collection of Critical Essays.* Vol. 1, *Metaphysics and Epistemology,* edited by Gregory Vlastos, 184–200. Garden City, N.Y.: Anchor Books, Doubleday, 1970.

Vlastos, Gregory. "The Third Man Argument in Plato's *Parmenides.*" *Philosophical Review* 63 (1954): 319–49. Reprinted in *Studies in Plato's Metaphysics,* edited by R. E. Allen, 231–63. London: Routledge & Kegan Paul, 1965.

"Plato's 'Third Man' Argument (*Parm.* 131A1–B2): Text and Logic." *Philosophical Quarterly* 19 (1969): 289–301. Reprinted with appendices in Gregory Vlastos, *Platonic Studies,* 342–65. 2d ed. Princeton: Princeton University Press, 1981.

Wundt, Max. *Platons Parmenides.* Stuttgart: Verlag W. Kohlhammer, 1935.

7. *Theaetetus*

Annas, Julia. "Knowledge and language: the *Theaetetus* and the *Cratylus*." In *Language and Logos: Studies in Ancient Greek Philosophy Presented to G.E.L. Owen*, edited by Malcolm Schofield and Martha Nussbaum, 95–114. Cambridge: Cambridge University Press, 1982.

Bostock, David. *Plato's Theaetetus*. Oxford: Clarendon Press, 1988.

Burnyeat, Myles. "Socrates and the Jury: Paradoxes in Plato's Distinction between Knowledge and True Belief." *Proceedings of the Aristotelian Society*, supplementary vol. 54 (1980): 173–92.

The Theaetetus of Plato. With a translation by M. J. Levett, revised by Myles Burnyeat. Indianapolis: Hackett, 1990.

Fine, Gail. "False Belief in the *Theaetetus*." *Phronesis* 24 (1979): 70–80.

McDowell, John. *Plato: Theaetetus*. Translated with notes. Oxford: Clarendon Press, 1973.

8. *Timaeus*

Cherniss, Harold. "The Sources of Evil According to Plato." *Proceedings of the American Philosophical Society* 98 (1954): 23–30. Reprinted in *Plato*. Vol. 2, *Ethics, Politics, and Philosophy of Art and Religion*, edited by Gregory Vlastos, 244–58. Garden City, N.Y.: Anchor Books, Doubleday, 1971. Also reprinted in Harold Cherniss, *Selected Papers*, edited by Leonardo Taran, 253–60. Leiden: E.J. Brill, 1977.

"The Relation of the *Timaeus* to Plato's Later Dialogues." *American Journal of Philology* 78 (1957): 225–66. Reprinted in *Studies in Plato's Metaphysics*, edited by R. E. Allen, 339–78. London: Routledge & Kegan Paul, 1965. Also reprinted in Harold Cherniss, *Selected Papers*, edited by Leonardo Taran, 298–339. Leiden: E.J. Brill, 1977.

Cornford, Francis MacDonald. *Plato's Cosmology: The Timaeus of Plato*. Translated with a running commentary. London: Kegan Paul, 1937.

Kung, Joan. "Tetrahedra, Motion, and Virtue." *Nous* 19 (1985): 17–27.

"Why the receptacle is not a mirror." *Archiv für Geschichte der Philosophie* 70 (1988): 167–78.

"Mathematics and Virtue in Plato's *Timaeus*." In *Essays in Ancient Greek Philosophy*, edited by John Anton and Anthony Preus, 3: 309–39. Albany: State University of New York Press, 1989.

Morrow, Glenn R. "Necessity and Persuasion in Plato's *Timaeus*." *Philosophical Review* 59 (1950): 147–64. Reprinted in *Studies in Plato's Metaphysics*, edited by R. E. Allen, 421–37. London: Routledge & Kegan Paul, 1965.

"The Demiurge in Politics: The *Timaeus* and the *Laws*." *Proceedings of the American Philosophical Association* 27 (1953–4): 5–23.

Mueller, Ian. "Joan Kung's Reading of Plato's *Timaeus*." In *Nature, Knowledge and Virtue: Essays in Memory of Joan Kung*, edited by Terry Penner and Richard Kraut. Edmonton, Alberta: Academic Printing and Publishing. *Apeiron* 22 (1989): 1–27.

Owen, G. E. L. "The Place of the *Timaeus* in Plato's Dialogues." *Classical Quarterly* 3 (1953): 79–95. Reprinted in *Studies in Plato's Metaphysics*, edited by R. E. Allen, 313–38. London: Routledge & Kegan Paul, 1965. Also reprinted in G. E. L. Owen, *Logic, Science, and Dialectic: Collected Papers in Greek Philosophy*, edited by Martha Nussbaum, 65–84. Ithaca, N.Y.: Cornell University Press, 1986.

Sorabji, Richard. *Time, Creation and the Continuum*. Ithaca, N.Y.: Cornell University Press, 1983.

Taylor, A. E. *A Commentary on Plato's Timaeus*. Oxford: Clarendon Press, 1928.

Vlastos, Gregory. "The Disorderly Motion in the *Timaeus*." *Classical Quarterly* 33 (1939): 71–83. Reprinted in *Studies in Plato's Metaphysics*, edited by R. E. Allen, 379–420. London: Routledge & Kegan Paul, 1965.

Plato's Universe. Seattle: University of Washington Press, 1975.

"The Role of Observation in Plato's Conception of Astronomy." In *Science and the Sciences in Plato*, edited by John Anton, 1–31. Albany: Eidos Press, 1980.

9. *Sophist*

Ackrill, J. L. "ΣΥΜΠΛΟΚΗ ΕΙΔΩΝ." *Bulletin of the Institute of Classical Studies* 2 (1955): 31–5. Reprinted in *Plato: A Collection of Critical Essays*. Vol. 1, *Metaphysics and Epistemology*, edited by Gregory Vlastos, 201–9. Garden City, N.Y.: Anchor Books, Doubleday, 1970.

"Plato and the Copula: *Sophist* 251–59." *Journal of Hellenic Studies* 77 (1957): 1–6. Reprinted in *Plato: A Collection of Critical Essays*. Vol. 1, *Metaphysics and Epistemology*, edited by Gregory Vlastos, 210–22. Garden City, N.Y.: Anchor Books, Doubleday, 1971.

Bostock, David. "Plato on 'Is Not.' " *Oxford Studies in Ancient Philosophy* 2 (1984): 89–119.

Cambell, Lewis. *The Sophistes and Politicus of Plato*. With a revised text and English notes. Oxford: Clarendon Press, 1867.

Frede, Michael. *Prädikation und Existenzaussage. Hypomnemata* 18. Göttingen: Vandenhoeck & Ruprect, 1967.

McDowell, John. "Falsehood and Not-being in Plato's *Sophist*." In *Language and Logos: Studies in Ancient Greek Philosophy Presented to G.E.L.*

Owen, edited by Malcolm Schofield and Martha Nussbaum, 115–34. Cambridge: Cambridge University Press, 1982.

Moravcsik, Julius M. E. "Being and Meaning in the *Sophist." Acta Philosophica Fennica,* Fasc. 14. Helsinki, 1962.

Owen, G. E. L. "Plato on Not-Being." In *Plato: A Collection of Critical Essays.* Vol. 1, *Metaphysics and Epistemology,* edited by Gregory Vlastos, 223–67. Garden City, N.Y.: Anchor Books, Doubleday, 1970. Reprinted in G. E. L. Owen, *Logic, Science and Dialectic: Collected Papers in Greek Philosophy,* edited by Martha Nussbaum, 104–37. Ithaca, N.Y.: Cornell University Press, 1986.

Roberts, Jean. "The Problem About Being in the *Sophist." History of Philosophy Quarterly* 3 (1986): 229–43.

Vlastos, Gregory. "An Ambiguity in the *Sophist."* In *Platonic Studies,* 270–322. 2d ed. Princeton: Princeton University Press, 1981.

Wiggins, David. "Sentence Meaning, Negation, and Plato's Problem of Non-Being." In *Plato: A Collection of Critical Essays.* Vol. 1, *Metaphysics and Epistemology,* edited by Gregory Vlastos, 268–303. Garden City, N.Y.: Anchor Books, Doubleday, 1970.

10. *Statesman*

Ackrill, John. "In Defense of Platonic Division." In *Ryle: A Collection of Critical Essays,* edited by Oscar P. Wood and George Pitcher, 373–92. Garden City, N.Y.: Anchor Books, Doubleday, 1970.

Cambell, Lewis. *The Sophistes and Politicus of Plato.* With a revised text and English notes. Oxford: Clarendon Press, 1867.

Dorter, Kenneth. "Justice and Method in the *Statesman."* In *Law, Justice and Method in Plato and Aristotle,* edited by Spiro Panagiotou, 105–22. Edmonton: Academic Printing & Publishing, 1985.

Griswold, Charles L., Jr. "*Politike episteme* in Plato's *Statesman."* In *Essays in Ancient Greek Philosophy,* edited by John P. Anton and Anthony Preus. Vol. 3. Albany: State University of New York Press, 1989.

Miller, Mitchell H., Jr. *The Philosopher in Plato's Statesman.* The Hague: Martinus Nijhoff, 1980.

Moravcsik, Julius M. E. "The Anatomy of Plato's Divisions." In *Exegesis and Argument: Studies in Greek Philosophy Presented to Gregory Vlastos,* edited by E. N. Lee, Alexander P. D. Mourelatos, and R. M. Rorty, 324–48. Assen, Netherlands: van Gorcum & Comp., 1973.

Owen, G. E. L. "Plato on the Undepictable." In *Exegesis and Argument: Studies in Greek Philosophy Presented to Gregory Vlastos,* edited by E. N. Lee, Alexander P. D. Mourelatos, and R. M. Rorty, 349–61. Assen, Netherlands: van Gorcum & Comp., 1973. Reprinted in G.E.L. Owen,

Logic, Science, and Dialectic: Collected Papers in Greek Philosophy, edited by Martha Nussbaum, 138–47. Ithaca, N.Y.: Cornell University Press, 1986.

Skemp, J. B. *Plato's Statesman.* A translation of the *Politicus* of Plato, with introductory essays and footnotes. London: Routledge & Kegan Paul, 1952. 2d ed. Bristol: Bristol Classical Press, 1987.

11. *Philebus*

Bury, Robert Gregg. *The Philebus of Plato.* Edited with introduction, notes and appendices. Cambridge: Cambridge University Press, 1897. Reprint. New York: Arno Press, 1973.

Dancy, R. M. "The One, The Many, and the Forms: *Philebus* 15b1–8." *Ancient Philosophy* 4 (1984): 160–93.

Davidson, Donald. "Plato's Philosopher." *The London Review of Books* 7, no. 14 (1985): 15–17.

Dybikowski, J. "False Pleasure and the *Philebus.*" *Phronesis* 15 (1970): 147–65.

Frede, Dorothea. "Rumpelstiltskin's Pleasures: True and False Pleasures in Plato's *Philebus.*" *Phronesis* 30 (1985): 151–80.

Gadamer, Hans-Georg. *Platos Dialektische Ethik – Phänomenologishe Interpretation zum Philebus.* Leipzig: Felix Meiner, 1931. Reprinted in *Platos Dialektische Ethik und andere Studien zur platonishen Philosophie.* Hamburg: Felix Meiner, 1968.

Gosling, J. C. B. "False Pleasures: *Philebus* 35c–41b." *Phronesis* 4 (1959): 44–54.

"Father Kenny on False Pleasures." *Phronesis* 5 (1960): 41–5.

Plato: Philebus. Translated with notes and commentary. Oxford: Clarendon Press, 1975.

Hackforth, R. *Plato's Examination of Pleasure (The Philebus).* Cambridge: Cambridge University Press, 1945. Reprint. Indianapolis: Bobbs-Merrill, no date.

Hampton, Cynthia. "Pleasure, Truth and Being in Plato's *Philebus:* A Reply to Professor Frede." *Phronesis* 32 (1987): 253–62.

Pleasure, Knowledge, and Being: An Analysis of Plato's Philebus. Albany: State University of New York Press, 1990.

Jackson, H. "Plato's Later Theory of Ideas: The *Philebus* and Aristotle's *Metaphysics* 1.6." *Journal of Philosophy* 10 (1882): 253–98.

Kenny, A. "False Pleasures in the *Philebus:* A Reply to Mr. Gosling." *Phronesis* 5 (1960): 45–92.

Letwin, Oliver. "Interpreting the *Philebus.*" *Phronesis* 26 (1981): 187–206.

Mohr, Richard D. "*Philebus* 55c–62a and Revisionism." In *New Essays on*

Plato, edited by F. J. Pelletier and J. King-Farlow, 165–70. Guelph: Canadian Association for Publishing in Philosophy, 1983. *Canadian Journal of Philosophy,* supplementary vol.

Penner, Terry. "False Anticipatory Pleasures: *Philebus* 36a3–41a6." *Phronesis* 15 (1970): 166–78.

Ross, W. D. *Plato's Theory of Ideas.* Oxford: Clarendon Press, 1951. 2d ed. 1953

Schofield, Malcolm. "Who Were οἱ δυσχερεῖς in Plato, *Philebus* 44a ff.?" *Museum Helveticum* 28 (1971): 2–20.

Shiner, Roger. *Knowledge and Reality in Plato's Philebus.* Assen, Netherlands: van Gorcum & Comp., 1974.

"Must *Philebus* 59a–c Refer to Transcendent Forms?" *Journal of the History of Philosophy* 17 (1979): 71–7.

Striker, Gisela. *Peras und Apeiron: Das Problem der Formen in Platons Philebus. Hypomnemata* 30. Göttingen: Vandenhoeck & Ruprecht, 1970.

Waterfield, Robin A. H. "The Place of the *Philebus* in Plato's Dialogues." *Phronesis* 25 (1980): 270–305.

Plato: Philebus. Translation with introduction and notes. Harmondsworth: Penguin Books, 1982.

12. *Laws*

Becker, Walter G. *Platons Gesetze und das griechische Familienrecht.* Munich: C.H. Beck, 1932.

Bisinger, Josef. *Der Agrarstaat in Platons Gesetzen.* Wiesbaden: Dieterich, 1925.

Brochard, V. "Les *Lois* de Platon et la théorie des Idées." *Etudes de philosophie ancienne et de philosophie moderne,* edited by V. Delbos, 151–68. New ed. Paris: J. Vrin, 1926.

Cohen, David. "The Legal Status and Political Role of Women in Plato's *Laws.*" *Revue Internationale des Droits de l'Antiquité* 34 (1987): 27–40.

David, E. "The Spartan Sussitia and Plato's *Laws.*" *American Journal of Philology* 99 (1978): 486–95.

Diès, Auguste, and Gernet, Louis. "Introduction." In *Platon: Oeuvres complètes.* Vol. 2, Part 1, *Les Lois,* edited and translated by Edouard des Places. Paris: Société d'Edition, Les Belles Lettres, 1951.

Görgemanns, Herwig. *Beiträge zur Interpretation von Platons Nomoi.* Munich: C.H. Beck, 1960.

Klingenberg, E. *Platons* νομοὶ γεωργικοί *und das positive griechische Recht.* Berlin: Schweitzer, 1976.

Laks, André. "Raison et plaisir: pour une caractérisation des *Lois* de Platon." In *La naissance de la raison en Grèce. Actes du Congrès de*

Nice, mai 1987, edited by J. F. Mattéi, 291–303. Paris: Presses Universitaires de France, 1990.

Morrow, Glenn R. *Plato's Law of Slavery in its Relation to Greek Law.* Urbana, Ill. University of Illnois Press, 1939.

"The Demiurge in Politics: the *Timaeus* and the *Laws.*" *Proceedings of the American Philosophical Association* 27 (1953–4): 5–23.

Plato's Cretan City: A Historical Interpretation of the Laws. Princeton: Princeton University Press, 1960.

Pangle, Thomas L. *The Laws of Plato.* Translated, with notes and an interpretive essay. New York: Basic Books, 1980.

Saunders, T. J. *Plato: The Laws.* Translated with an introduction. Harmondsworth: Penguin Books, 1970.

"Notes on the *Laws* of Plato." *Bulletin of the Institute of Classical Studies,* Supplement 28. London: University of London, 1972.

"Penology and Eschatology in Plato's *Timaeus* and *Laws.*" *Classical Quarterly* 23 (1973): 232–44.

Bibliography on Plato's Laws. 1920–76, with additional citations through March 1979. 2d ed. New York: Arno Press, 1979.

"On Plato, *Laws* 728bc." *Liverpool Classical Monthly* 9 (1984): 23–4.

Plato's Penal Code. Oxford: Clarendon Press, 1991.

Stalley, R. F. *An Introduction to Plato's Laws.* Oxford: Basil Blackwell, 1983.

13. *Letters*

Edelstein, Ludwig. *Plato's Seventh Letter.* Leiden: E.J. Brill, 1966.

Gulley, Norman. "The Authenticity of Plato's Epistles." In *Pseudepigrapha I,* chap. 5 Fondation Hardt: Geneva, 1972.

Levison, M., Morton, A. Q., and Winspear, A. D. "The Seventh Letter of Plato." *Mind* 77 (1968): 309–25.

Morrow, Glenn R. *Plato's Epistles.* A translation with critical essays and notes. 2d ed. Indianapolis: Bobbs-Merrill, 1962.

von Fritz, Kurt. "The Philosophical Passage in the Seventh Platonic Letter." In *Essays on Ancient Greek Philosophy,* edited by John P. Anton and George L. Kustas, 1:408–47. Albany: State University of New York Press, 1971.

White, Nicholas P. *Plato on Knowledge and Reality.* Indianapolis: Hackett, 1976.

O. ORAL DOCTRINES

Cherniss, Harold. *The Riddle of the Early Academy.* Berkeley: University of California Press, 1945.

Findlay, J. N. *Plato: The Written and Unwritten Doctrines.* New York: Humanities Press, 1974.
Gaiser, Konrad. "Plato's Enigmatic Lecture *On the Good.*" *Phronesis* 25 (1980): 5–37.
Krämer, Hans Joachim. *Plato and the Foundations of Metaphysics.* Edited and translated by John R. Caton. Albany: State University of New York Press, 1990.
Sayre, Kenneth M. *Plato's Late Ontology: A Riddle Resolved,* Princeton: Princeton University Press, 1983.
Vlastos, Gregory. Review of *Arete bei Platon und Aristoteles,* by H. J. Krämer. *Gnomon* 41 (1963): 641–55. Reprinted as "On Plato's Oral Doctrine." In Gregory Vlastos, *Platonic Studies,* 379–403. 2d ed. Princeton: Princeton University Press, 1981.

II. ARISTOTLE AND LATER CLASSICAL THOUGHT

Ackrill, J. L. "Aristotle on *Eudaimonia.*" *Proceedings of the British Academy* 60 (1974): 339–59. Reprinted in *Essays on Aristotle's Ethics,* edited by Amélie Oksenberg Rorty, 15–33. Berkeley: University of California Press, 1980.
Annas, Julia. "Aristotle on Pleasure and Goodness." In *Essays on Aristotle's Ethics,* edited by Amélie Oksenberg Rorty, 285–99. Berkeley: University of California Press, 1980.
Barnes, Jonathan, editor. *The Complete Works of Aristotle.* 2 vols. Princeton: Princeton University Press, 1984.
Irwin, Terence. *Aristotle's First Principles.* Oxford: Clarendon Press, 1988.
Kung, Joan. "Aristotle on Thises, Suches, and the Third Man Argument." *Phronesis* 26 (1981): 207–47.
Lynch, John Patrick. *Aristotle's School: A Study of a Greek Educational Institution.* Berkeley: University of California Press, 1972.
Mitsis, Philip. *Epicurus' Ethical Theory: The Pleasures of Invulnerability.* Ithaca, N.Y.: Cornell University Press, 1988.
Owen, G. E. L. "Aristotle on the Snares of Ontology." In *New Essays on Plato and Aristotle,* edited by Renford Bambrough, 69–95. London: Routledge & Kegan Paul, 1965. Reprinted in G.E.L. Owen, *Logic, Science, and Dialectic: Collected Papers in Greek Philosophy,* edited by Martha Nussbaum, 259–78. Ithaca, N.Y.: Cornell University Press, 1986.
Urmson, J. "Aristotle on Pleasure." In *Aristotle: A Collection of Critical Essays,* edited by Julius M. E. Moravcsik, 323–33. Garden City, N.Y.: Anchor Books, Doubleday, 1967.

von Fritz, Kurt. *The Theory of the Mixed Constitution in Antiquity: A Critical Analysis of Polybius' Political Ideas.* New York: Columbia University Press, 1954.

Walsh, James J. *Aristotle's Conception of Moral Weakness.* New York: Columbia University Press, 1963.

III. PLATONISM AFTER PLATO

Armstrong, A. H., editor. *The Cambridge History of Later Greek and Early Medieval Philosophy.* Cambridge: Cambridge University Press, 1967.

Blumenthal, H. J., and Markus, R. A., editors. *Neoplatonism and Early Christian Thought: Essays in Honour of A.H. Armstrong.* London: Variorum, 1981.

Cassirer, Ernst. *The Platonic Renaissance in England.* Edinburgh: Nelson, 1953.

Chadwick, Henry. *Early Christian Thought and the Classical Tradition.* Oxford: Clarendon Press, 1966.

Dillon, John M. *The Middle Platonists, 80 B.C. to A.D. 220.* Ithaca, N.Y.: Cornell University Press, 1977.

Dodds, E. R. "The *Parmenides* of Plato and the Origin of the Neoplatonic One." *Classical Quarterly* 22 (1928): 129–42.

Findlay, J. N. "Appraisal of Platonism and its Influence." In *Plato: The Written and Unwritten Doctrines,* 350–412. New York: Humanities Press, 1974.

Gersh, Stephen. *Middle Platonism and Neoplatonism: the Latin Tradition.* 2 vols. Notre Dame, Ind.: University of Notre Dame Press, 1986.

Hankins, James. *Plato in the Italian Renaissance.* 2 vols. Leiden: E.J. Brill, 1991.

Klibansky, Raymond. *The Continuity of the Platonic Tradition During the Middle Ages: Outlines of a Corpus Platonicum Medii Aevi.* London: Warburg Institute, 1939.

Lloyd, A. C. *The Anatomy of Neoplatonism.* Oxford: Clarendon Press, 1990.

Merlan, Philip. *From Platonism to Neoplatonism.* 3d ed. The Hague: Martinus Nijhoff, 1969.

Pater, Walter. *Plato and Platonism: A Series of Lectures.* Oxford: Basil Blackwell, 1973.

Patrides, C. A., editor. *The Cambridge Platonists.* Cambridge: Cambridge University Press, 1969.

Reale, Giovanni. *A History of Ancient Philosophy.* Vol. 4, *The Schools of the Imperial Age,* edited and translated from the 5th Italian edition by John R. Catan, 165–449. Albany: State University of New York Press, 1990.

Rees, D. A. "Platonism and the Platonic Tradition." In *The Encyclopedia of Philosophy*, edited by Paul Edwards, 6: 333–41. New York: Macmillan and Free Press, 1967.

Rist, J. M. *Plotinus: The Road to Reality.* Cambridge: Cambridge University Press, 1967.

Schmitt, Charles B., editor. *The Cambridge History of Renaissance Philosophy.* Cambridge: Cambridge University Press, 1988.

Sorabji, Richard. "Myths about Non-Propositional Thought." In *Language and Logos: Studies in Ancient Greek Philosophy Presented to G.E.L. Owen*, edited by Malcolm Schofield and Martha Nussbaum, 295–314. Cambridge: Cambridge University Press, 1982.

Turner, Frank M. *The Greek Heritage in Victorian Britain.* New Haven: Yale University Press, 1980.

Wallis, R. T. *Neoplatonism* London: Duckworth, 1972.

IV. MISCELLANEOUS

A. EDITIONS, TRANSMISSION, AND STUDY OF ANCIENT TEXTS

Badawi, Abdurrahman. *La transmission de la philosophie grecque au monde arabe.* 2d ed. Paris: Libraire Philosophique, J. Vrin, 1978.

Bond, Godfrey W. *Euripides: Heracles.* Oxford: Clarendon Press, 1981.

Cousin, Victor. *Proclus: Commentarium in Platonis Parmenidem.* In *Procli Philosophi Platonici: Opera Inedita.* Paris: Minerva, 1864.

Couvreur, Paul, editor. *Hermiae Alexandrini in Platonis Phaedrum Scholia.* Hildesheim: Olms, 1971.

Creutzer, F. *Olympiodorus: In Platonis Alcibiadem Commentarii.* Frankfurt: Officina Broenneriana, 1821.

Diels, Hermann, and Kranz, Walther, editors. *Die Fragmente der Vorsokratiker.* 6th ed. Berlin: Weidmann, 1952.

Dover, K. J. *Aristophanes' Clouds.* Edited with an introduction and commentary. Oxford: Clarendon Press, 1968.

Lysias and the Corpus Lysiacum. Berkeley: University of California Press, 1968.

Friedlein, G. *Proclus: In Primum Euclidis Elementorum Librum Comentaria.* Leipzig: Teubner, 1873. (English translation by Glenn Morrow. Princeton: Princeton University Press, 1970.)

Gaiser, Konrad. *Philodemus: Academica.* Supplementum Platonicum, I. Stuttgart–Bad Cannstatt: Fromann-Holzboog, 1988.

Griffith, Mark. *Aeschylus: Prometheus Bound.* Cambridge: Cambridge University Press, 1983.

Heyduck, Michael. *Commentaria in Aristotelem Graeca.* Vol. 1: Alexander of Aphrodisias. *In Aristotelis Metaphysica Commentaria.* Berlin: Georgius Reimerus, 1891.

Jebb, R. C. *The Attic Orators from Antiphon to Isaeos.* 2 vols. London: Macmillan, 1893.

Kock, Theodorus, editor. *Comicorum Atticorum Fregmenta.* 3 vols. Leipzig: Teubner, 1880–8.

Lasserre, François. *Die Fragmente des Eudoxos von Knidos.* Edited and translated, with commentary. Berlin: de Gruyter, 1966.

De Léodamas de Thasos à Philippe d'Oponte. Naples: Bibliopolis, 1987.

Lobel, Edgar, and Page, Denys, editors. *Poetarum Lesbiorum fragmenta.* Oxford: Clarendon Press, 1955.

Long, H. S. *Diogenes Laertius: Vitae Philosophicorum.* 2 vols. Oxford: Clarendon Press, 1964. (Translated into English by R. D. Hicks. *Diogenes Laertius: Lives of Eminent Philosophers.* 2 vols. Cambridge, Mass., and London: Harvard University Press and William Heinemann, 1925.)

Page, Denys L. editor. *Poetae Melici Graeci.* Oxford: Clarendon Press, 1962.

Ross, W. D. *Aristotle's Metaphysics.* A revised text with introduction and commentary. 2 vols. Oxford: Clarendon Press, 1924.

Aristotelis Fragmenta Selecta. Oxford: Clarendon Press, 1955.

Aristotle's Prior and Posterior Analytics. With introduction and commentary. Oxford: Clarendon Press, 1957.

Reynolds, L. D., and Wilson, N. G. *Scribes and Scholars: A Guide to the Transmission of Greek and Latin Literature.* 3d ed. Oxford: Clarendon press, 1991.

Sandys, John Edwin. *A History of Classical Scholarship.* 3 vols. New York: Hafner, 1958.

Westerink, L. G. *Olympiodorus: Commentary on the First Alcibiades of Plato.* Amsterdam: North Holland, 1956.

Anonymous Prolegomena to the Philosophy of Plato. Amsterdam: North Holland, 1962.

B. MODERN AND CONTEMPORARY WORKS

Abrams, M. H. *The Mirror and the Lamp: Romantic Theory and the Critical Tradition.* New York: Oxford University Press, 1953.

Burnyeat, Myles. "Wittgenstein and *De Magistro.*" *Proceedings of the Aristotelian Society,* supplementary vol. 61 (1988): 1–24.

Frege, Gottlob. "On Sense and Reference." In *Translations from the Philosophical Writings of Gottlob Frege,* edited by Peter Geach and Max Black. 2d ed. Oxford: Basil Blackwell, 1960.

Geach, P. T. "Good and Evil." *Analysis* 17 (1956): 33–42. Reprinted in *Theories of Ethics,* edited by Phillipa Foot, 64–73. London: Oxford University Press, 1967.
Goldman, Alvin. *Epistemology and Cognition.* Cambridge, Mass.: Harvard University Press, 1987.
Hampshire, Stuart. *Thought and Action.* London: Chatto & Windus, 1959.
Harman, Gilbert. *Change in View.* Cambridge, Mass.: Bradford Books, 1986.
Kitcher, Philip. "Positive Understatement: The Logic of Attributive Adjectives." *Journal of Philosophical Logic* 7 (1978): 1–17.
Kripke, Saul. *Naming and Necessity.* Cambridge, Mass.: Harvard University Press, 1980.
Larmore, Charles. *Patterns of Moral Complexity.* Cambridge: Cambridge University Press, 1987.
Leibniz, G. W. *New Essays on Human Understanding.* Translated and edited by Peter Remnant and Jonathan Bennett. Cambridge: Cambridge University Press, 1981.
Philosophical Essays. Translated by Roger Ariew and Daniel Garber. Indianapolis: Hackett, 1989.
Locke, John. *An Essay Concerning Human Understanding.* Edited with an introduction by Peter H. Nidditch. Oxford: Clarendon Press, 1975.
Putnam, Hilary. "The Meaning of 'Meaning.' " In *Philosophical Papers,* 2: 215–71. Cambridge: Cambridge University Press, 1975.
Russell, Bertrand. *The Problems of Philosophy.* London: H. Holt, 1912.
Smyth, Herbert Weir. *Greek Grammar.* Cambridge, Mass.: Harvard University Press, 1963.
Stich, Stephen, editor. *Innate Ideas.* Berkeley: University of California Press, 1975.
Wallace, John. "Positive, Comparative, Superlative." *Journal of Philosophy* 69 (1972): 773–82.
Wheeler, Samuel. "Attributives and Their Modifiers." *Nous* 6 (1972): 310–34.
Whitehead, Alfred North. *Process and Reality: An Essay in Cosmology.* Edited by D. R. Griffin and D. W. Sherburne. Corrected edition. New York: Free Press, 1978.
Williams, Bernard. "Pleasure and Belief." *Proceedings of the Aristotelian Society* (1959): 57–72.
Ziff, Paul. *Semantic Analysis.* Ithaca, N.Y.: Cornell University Press, 1960.

INDEX OF NAMES AND SUBJECTS

INDEX OF PASSAGES